The Originary Structure

The Works of Emanuele Severino

Series editors: Giulio Goggi, Damiano Sacco and Ines Testoni

This book series presents for the first time in the English language the translation of the most important works written by the major twentieth-century Italian philosopher Emanuele Severino. The volumes are translated and edited by scholars and philosophers with an extended knowledge of Severino's theoretical apparatus who provide critical contributions, introductions and explanatory glosses.

The series publishes Severino's theoretical volumes as well as his more interdisciplinary books, and will be of interest not only to philosophers but also to readers of cultural and critical theory, the philosophy of religion and the philosophy of science.

Series Editors
Giulio Goggi, Editor of the *Journal of Fundamental Ontology*, and vice-president of ASES (Society for Emanuele Severino Studies)

Damiano Sacco, ICI Berlin, Germany

Ines Testoni, University of Padova, Italy

Other Titles in the Series
Beyond Language, Emanuele Severino
Law and Chance, Emanuele Severino

The Originary Structure

Emanuele Severino

Edited and Translated by
Damiano Sacco

BLOOMSBURY ACADEMIC
LONDON • NEW YORK • OXFORD • NEW DELHI • SYDNEY

BLOOMSBURY ACADEMIC
Bloomsbury Publishing Plc, 50 Bedford Square, London, WC1B 3DP, UK
Bloomsbury Publishing Inc, 1359 Broadway, New York, NY 10018, USA
Bloomsbury Publishing Ireland, 29 Earlsfort Terrace, Dublin 2, D02 AY28, Ireland

BLOOMSBURY, BLOOMSBURY ACADEMIC and the Diana logo are trademarks of Bloomsbury Publishing Plc

First published in 1981 in Italy as *La struttura originaria* by Adelphi Edizioni © Adelphi Edizioni s.p.a. Milano, 1981

This book has been translated thanks to a translation grant awarded by the Italian Ministry of Foreign Affairs and International Cooperation.

Questo libro è stato tradotto grazie a un contributo per la traduzione assegnato dal Ministero degli Affari Esteri e della Cooperazione Internazionale italiano.

First published in Great Britain 2026
English language translation © Damiano Sacco 2026

The translation of this book has been realised thanks to a grant awarded by
SEPS – SEGRETARIATO EUROPEO PER LE PUBBLICAZIONI SCIENTIFICHE.

Via Val d'Aposa 7 - 40123 Bologna
seps@seps.it - www.seps.it

Damiano Sacco has asserted his right under the Copyright, Designs and Patents Act, 1988, to be identified as Translator of this work.

Series design: Ben Anslow
Cover image: Emanuele Severino (Photo by Leonardo Cendamo/Getty Images)

All rights reserved. No part of this publication may be: i) reproduced or transmitted in any form, electronic or mechanical, including photocopying, recording or by means of any information storage or retrieval system without prior permission in writing from the publishers; or ii) used or reproduced in any way for the training, development or operation of artificial intelligence (AI) technologies, including generative AI technologies. The rights holders expressly reserve this publication from the text and data mining exception as per Article 4(3) of the Digital Single Market Directive (EU) 2019/790.

Bloomsbury Publishing Plc does not have any control over, or responsibility for, any third-party websites referred to or in this book. All internet addresses given in this book were correct at the time of going to press. The author and publisher regret any inconvenience caused if addresses have changed or sites have ceased to exist, but can accept no responsibility for any such changes.

A catalogue record for this book is available from the British Library.

A catalogue record for this book is available from the Library of Congress.

ISBN: HB: 978-1-3504-9878-5
PB: 978-1-3504-9877-8
ePDF: 978-1-3504-9880-8
eBook: 978-1-3504-9879-2

Series: The Works of Emanuele Severino

Typeset by Newgen KnowledgeWorks Pvt. Ltd., Chennai, India
Printed and bound in Great Britain

For product safety related questions contact productsafety@bloomsbury.com.

To find out more about our authors and books visit www.bloomsbury.com and sign up for our newsletters.

Contents

Foreword, Damiano Sacco		vi
Introduction		1
1.	The exposition of the originary structure	71
2.	The immediacy of being	99
3.	The immediacy of the non-contradictoriness of being	123
4.	The aporia of nothingness and its resolution	153
5.	The structure of the totality of the Ph-immediate	173
6.	The analysis of the originary meaning: Semantic simplicities and semantic complexities	195
7.	Logical immediacy and logical mediation	211
8.	The ground *qua* contradiction	251
9.	Dialectic	275
10.	The manifestation of the whole	307
11.	The abstract (Γ_a) (and concrete) concept of the originary as the originary problem and contradiction	343
12.	The inherent contradictoriness of the negation of the presence of being	375
13.	Originary metaphysics	385
Notes		417
Index		447

Foreword

Damiano Sacco

The Ground

I. The enquiry that appears here for the first time in English translation consists of an exposition of the structure of the ground – *the* ground: the ground of everything that is and appears. Since every being is and appears to the extent that its being and its appearing conform to the structure of that ground, this (structured) ground is nothing but the concreteness of being itself: the self-grounding of being in its self-structuring. Immediately, this enquiry appears to repeat the original guiding question of traditional metaphysics: namely, the determination of the principle or ground of everything that is, the ἀρχὴ τοῦ παντὸς. The present enquiry, however, aims to repeat that question in order to determine the structure in accordance with which that question is originarily answered: in that the appearing of the answer to the guiding question of metaphysics ('what are beings?', 'what is being?') coincides with the ground that affords the very being and appearing as much of that answer as of that question. That is to say, that question is and appears insofar as it is *originarily* answered; originarily: namely, insofar as the very being and appearing of that question has already determined the answer that the question appears to have separated from itself. There is therefore one answer that originarily answers the question – an answer that therefore contains all those other answers that are not co-originary with the question itself. That is to say: if these latter answers are the original answers of metaphysics and of its history – which are 'original' and not 'originary' precisely insofar as they locate an origin (an ἀρχή) that is separated from the question itself – that originary answer is the originary and concrete ground that includes within itself all the original (abstract) grounds of metaphysics and of its history: the ἀρχὴ τῶν ἀρχῶν. The originary ground is therefore the ground of itself and of all other appearing grounds – which only *appear* to be other than the one, unique and self-grounding ground. The originary ground is thus the one ground as part of which ground and ground of ground (ground and self-ground, ground and grounding) coincide.

Equivalently: 'The originary structure is the originary meaning itself; it is the originary opening of meaning':[1]

> If one wishes to disregard the originary structure, one places oneself in the domain of meaninglessness. It is therefore only insofar as *one already is* within the originary opening of meaning that the very *question* concerning meaning acquires a meaning;

by acquiring it, however, that question is superseded, *qua question*, by the originary answer. That is to say, the question is authenticated (= made meaningful) as soon as it is answered. This very 'answering' consists in the very conferring of a meaning on that question. Accordingly, the originary answering does not answer anything, or, equivalently, it does not presuppose anything that it has not itself posited.[2]

The Heideggerian question of being, *qua* originary question of the ground, is thus originarily answered.[3]

II. In concrete detail, then, the originary structure is the structure of the concrete immediacy or self-grounding of being (i.e. of everything that, in being grounded, is). The latter, i.e. immediate being, is precisely being that is structured according to the concrete structure of immediacy; that is to say: 'Being that is immediately present – the "immediate", as that which comes to constitute the subject of the originary judgement, or, more precisely, as element of that structuring of the meanings of immediacy that precisely constitutes the subject of the originary judgement – is what, in order to be affirmed, does not require or presuppose anything other than its own presence, or does not presuppose anything other than itself *qua* present: τὸ δι' αὐτὸ γνώριμον; the *per se notum*'[4] (or, equivalently: 'Originary truth is immediacy itself – i.e., a saying that is mediated by no other saying and that is therefore the ground of every saying'[5]). Immediate being, however, is concretely immediate only to the extent that it includes its very immediacy: namely, to the extent that its immediacy is not something that immediate being has to include at an additional or later moment relative to the moment of its positing, but something that is *originarily* posited with the very positing of immediate being: 'The concrete [is] the co-originarity of the positing of being and of the positing of the immediacy of that positing.'[6] Equivalently, immediate being is concretely immediate to the extent that its immediacy is originarily predicated of it, rather than being *presupposed* to this predication: 'What is posited as ground is what is posited – vis-à-vis the determinations that pertain to its content – *in the very act* with which it is posited as ground: or, more precisely, what is posited as ground is not a content that is presupposed to or separated from its being posited as ground.'[7] If immediate being were presupposed to the predication of its immediacy, this very predication would be something impossible: precisely to the extent that it would affirm of being (which, prior to the predication of its immediacy, is not immediate) that it is something immediate (and it would affirm of that immediacy, which prior to that predication is not the immediacy of being, that it is the immediacy of being). The originary structure is instead the structure of the originary saying, i.e. the structure of that saying that coincides with its immediate self-being: 'The saying of Necessity is the appearing of the identity between that of which something is said and that which is said of it.'[8] In other words, it is of being-that-is-immediate that immediacy is predicated (it is being-that-is-immediate that is immediate) – and this immediacy is itself not something presupposed to the acquiring of its content, but it is the very immediacy-of-being. The originary positing of being ('the originary judgement') thus constitutes the concrete meaning of identity or tautology: the concrete meaning of the self-being of being.

Insofar as the ground is concretely and originarily posited together with the determinations that originarily pertain to it, the ground is *incontrovertible*: it is that away from which it is not possible to turn (*contra-vertere*), for every turning must take place as part of the originary place or back-ground constituted by the incontrovertible ground itself. Equivalently, the incontrovertible is *that the negation of which is self-negating*. Every negation that attempts to negate the incontrovertible negates in fact its very own ground, and it therefore fails to negate the incontrovertible in that it has always already failed to constitute itself as such a negation:

> The negation is not superseded insofar as it is formally attested to be contradictory – the negation is superseded insofar as it is attested that it fails to posit itself as a negation, unless by grounding itself in what it negates, and thus only if it negates itself. The negation, failing to free itself from that which it negates, bears it within itself; not only does it fail to shake what it negates off its back, in order to hold it at arm's length and pass sentence on it, but what it thinks it has before itself as something sentenced actually stands behind it and directs all its thoughts, including the thought that passes the sentence. The law of being is the destiny of thinking, and thinking is always a testimony of this law: namely, it always affirms it, even when it is not aware of it, or when it negates it.[9]

The originary refutation (ἔλεγχος) of every negation of the incontrovertible constitutes its incontrovertibility: 'The ἔλεγχος is precisely the verification of this self-supersession of the negation; i.e. it is the verification that the negation does not exist as a *pure* negation – as a negation that, in order to constitute itself, has no need to affirm that which it negates.'[10] The originary ἔλεγχος, however, does not only pertain to the principle of non-contradiction, as in the case of the Aristotelian ἔλεγχος (*Metaphysics*, Γ, 4), but to the totality of concrete being: i.e. to the totality of everything that is and appears. Being (everything that is) *is* to the extent that it is what is originarily grounded: i.e. what cannot be negated – the incontrovertible. Once again, however, the incontrovertibility of the incontrovertible is not something that is externally predicated of the incontrovertible, but the incontrovertible is incontrovertible precisely to the extent that its incontrovertibility is originarily posited with it. In other words, the ἔλεγχος of the self-being of beings (of the incontrovertible) is not something separated from the abstract or universal self-being of beings, but it is one of its individuations:

> To the Aristotelian observation that there can be no demonstration of the first principle, it is necessary to add that it is in fact the ἔλεγχος that is 'grounded' in the self-being of beings. For, indeed, the ἔλεγχος is an *individuation* of the universality of the self-being of beings; that is to say, this individuation is incontrovertible *because* the universal self-being of beings is incontrovertible, and that individuation is therefore 'grounded' in this universality – and not vice-versa. The universality of the self-being of beings, *however*, cannot be independent of and isolated from that individuation constituted by the ἔλεγχος: precisely because the ἔλεγχος is the appearing of the incontrovertibility (or irrefutability) of that self-being. This self-being is incontrovertible – i.e. it appears in its incontrovertibility – *only* because

the ἔλεγχος *appears*. Once again, the authentic ground therefore consists in the *synthesis* between the self-being of beings and the ἔλεγχος (the synthesis between the universality of that self-being and its individuation constituted by the ἔλεγχος), and it is this synthesis that grounds its elements (which, in turn, are something authentically grounded only insofar as they are distinct and not separated from that synthesis – for, to the extent that they are separated, they are not something grounded, but negations of the ground).[11]

The originary structure is therefore the self-structuring structure of the incontrovertible determinations of the one incontrovertible and self-grounding ground. Each of these determinations is once again not something that is abstractly separated from that ground (i.e. something abstractly 'grounded'), but it is concretely part of the structure of the ground. (Abstracted from its ground, instead, each of these determinations – and, in fact, each meaning – is an abstract meaning; the aporias of abstract set theory, *qua* abstract theory of abstractly complex meanings, and first of all Russell's aporia or paradox, are traced as part of the originary structure to the abstraction of a meaning from its meaningfulness or ground).[12] Accordingly, of each of these determinations it must be repeated what has been affirmed in relation to the ἔλεγχος. Quoting at length:

> The 'ground' of the affirmation of each of these determinations is the formal essence of destiny [the originary structure] (i.e. that 'ground' is the synthesis between that essence and another determination or other determinations that are grounded in this way in that essence), and not vice-versa. *And yet*, each of these determinations is necessarily implied by that essence, which cannot be what it is – i.e. it cannot be the incontrovertible – and it cannot appear without the being and the appearing of these determinations. If the 'ground' is something that, in order to be such, does not need what is 'grounded', and is therefore isolated from the latter (which instead needs to be supported by that 'ground'), the formal essence of destiny [the originary structure] cannot be the 'ground' of those determinations, because it is the incontrovertible only to the extent that it is in a synthesis with them. Beyond this contradictory meaning of ground, the *ground* of the incontrovertibility of both the appearing of each of those determinations and the very appearing of the self-being of beings is constituted by that synthesis (that is to say, the ground of the fact that the elements of the synthesis are incontrovertible determinations is that very synthesis) – accordingly, however, the ground is not a dimension independent of and isolated from that which it grounds, but it is the ground in the sense that it is the synthesis in which it consists that is the ground of the incontrovertibility of the elements of the synthesis, as distinct from the latter, and not these elements, as thus distinct, that are the ground of the incontrovertibility of that synthesis. The authentic *ground* therefore consists in the totality of its determinations, i.e. it consists in the very set d', d'', ..., d^n, insofar as the latter also includes the formal essence of destiny [the originary structure], as well as the determinations that are 'grounded' in that essence. The ground is the unity of the ground and that which is grounded (i.e. the unity of the ground, as distinct from that which is grounded, and that which is grounded, as distinct from the ground).[13]

Any other ground – i.e. any other saying that is not the originary saying – *qua* negation of the originary ground, is grounded in the originary structure, and, abstracted from the latter, it is originarily self-refuting. This includes every other abstract ground, every absolutely Other ground, as well as every absolute groundlessness, abyss or lack of ground.[14]

III. In the Preface to the *Science of Logic*, Hegel refers to 'the strange spectacle of a cultured nation without metaphysics'.[15] This claim appears to have retained its significance to this day – except that this strange spectacle appears to have now extended to the entirety of one global civilization. And it is indeed a strange and uncanny spectacle, in that the civilization that appears to dominate the entirety of the earth – and to hold the greatest power for transforming, altering and destroying the world (both the 'material' world of nature and the 'ideal' one of knowledge) – appears to do so without any ground for either being able to do so or for being certain of having done so. Indeed, that civilization is able (but in fact: appears to be able) to now transform, alter and destroy the totality of the world precisely to the extent that it has now destroyed every form of ground: the self-coherence of idealism precisely constituting the most definitive destruction of every ground. Hegel writes: 'The principle of the dialectic corresponds to the notion of God's *might*. We say that all things (i.e. everything finite as such) come to judgment, and in that saying we catch sight of the dialectic as the universal, irresistible might before which nothing can subsist, however firm and secure it may deem itself to be.'[16] That is to say: it is possible for the world – once again understanding this 'world' as the totality of the appearing content, be it natural, cultural, material, linguistic, etc. – to be available for an unlimited transformation precisely to the extent that every ground has been disposed of. For every ground – precisely – grounds the relation between beings (either between the totality of beings, or at least between the ground and that part of beings that are grounded by the ground) in a necessary way, and the necessity of these relations constitutes a constraint and a limit to the possibility of transforming and altering the world. Accordingly, the spectacle of the utter transformability of the world (*qua* unconstrained possibility of creating and destroying appearing contents) appears to be precisely grounded in that 'strange spectacle' of a civilization without metaphysics. Or, in other words: the condition of possibility of the appearing of the spectacle of the civilization that claims to hold sway over the entirety of the earth is precisely the destruction of every ground that would limit and constrain the transformation of the world.

Everything appears to be able to be transformed, and to be other than what it (presently) is, for the impossibility of that transformation would precisely constitute a necessary ground to be destructed. Every necessary ground and every sufficient reason thus appears to enforce a form of violence by constraining the original possibilities (the freedom) of entities. The destruction of every necessary ground therefore appears as the destruction of the violence of every ground (and of the ground of every violence). Except that, having posited the impossibility of every ground, the domain that opens up appears to be precisely that of an unconstrained *violence*: everything that is and appears appears to be able to be created and destroyed, appropriated and expropriated, to be part of a battlefield in which the most powerful force (the most powerful form of violence) is able to have the last say about its truth (this truth now precisely appearing as a *value* determined by the very force that has been victorious – i.e. most powerful – in the struggle to determine the value and the truth of that entity). There thus appears a dialectical overturning in the presence of violence in the world: once every form of violence has been disposed of (once the violence of every ground and the ground of every violence have been destructed), every being finally appears to be free – *free* to be part of the domain of unconstrained violence.

Both forms of violence, however – namely, both the violence of every abstract ground that appears to appropriate the meaning of truth and the violence of that groundlessness that appears to expropriate the truth of every meaning – are in fact originarily *grounded* in the abstraction from the originary ground: namely, in 'that extreme violence that constitutes the utterly unexplored underground, the ultimate and essentially hidden origin of all the forms of violence from which the revolutions of the West attempt to free themselves.'[17] This violence constitutes the originary violence as part of which *both* the violence of every abstract ground and the violence of every abstract destruction of the ground appear (or, in fact: *appear* to appear). For, indeed: 'The repudiation of violence expresses a different form of violence. Violence is the transcendental determination of the "world". [...] One seeks an alternative to the devastation of things, without realising that from the outset in Western civilisation the "thing" has been precisely understood as that which must be subjected to the most extreme violence, *qua* absolute availability for annihilation and for the impact that projects it into existence and into the modifications of existence. As part of the "world", this destructive productivity is the "truth" of things, and violence is not an "injustice".'[18]

Once again, however, even the most advanced form of the apparatus of science and technics – understanding with this term every praxis, *poíesis, téchne,* thinking, art, politics, *philosophy* that appears to be successful in transforming a part of the world (a part of something that is and appears) – does not know (and *cannot* know) the ground for being able to do so: it *cannot* know this ground, precisely because it is abstracted from the *originary* meaning of what it believes to accomplish (this abstraction constituting the originary alienation): namely, from the originary meaning of the transformation of the world that it believes to accomplish (the originary meaning of the becoming of what is and appears). 'The transformation of the world that it believes to accomplish' means: the apparatus of science *believes* to accomplish its ends through a set of means at its disposal, but it *convinces* itself (it *believes* in its belief) of having done so precisely by establishing the very conditions of its apparent success: 'It is not because science "objectively" succeeds in dominating the earth that there is a universal consensus concerning the existence of this domination; on the contrary, it is because there is such a consensus that it is possible to affirm that, "objectively", science dominates the earth. This "objective domination" is constituted in the last instance by the social recognition of that domination. [...] It is science itself that "decides" that certain events constitute the social recognition of its domination, and that therefore decides that its domination consists in them.'[19]

Contemporary philosophy, *qua* abstract destruction and deconstruction of every ground, and scientific thinking, the guiding principle of which appears to find one of its most coherent expressions in the impossibility of metaphysics first asserted by neo-positivism, thus share the same soul: which, in the last instance, rests on the positing of the impossibility of any ground. (Or, equivalently: philosophy and science appear to constitute two sides of the same endeavour, the former ensuring the theoretical conditions of the praxis of the latter). The 'cunning of reason' thus appears to take its last and most ingenious form by letting individuals believe that an accomplished destruction of every ground and every reason (*Grund*) will entail their liberation from the violence of the necessary and unalterable constraints entailed by those grounds; having been freed from every necessary ground and every necessary reason (and, therefore, from every cunning of reason, too), individuals will be able to let everything be what it is, and themselves be what they are. The liberation from one kind of violence thus appears to be the condition of possibility of another kind of violence, which consists in the creation and destruction of everything that is, as realized by that civilization of Technics that appears to hold sway over the earth.

IV. The lack or impossibility of every ground is, however, as stable and reliable a ground as any other abstract ground. Stable means: abstract – that is to say, the absence of every ground categorically and necessarily does not signify the non-absence (i.e. the presence) of any ground. Or, equivalently, the absence of every ground is an abstract de-finition, de-cision or positing: i.e. one that is abstractly abstracted from what it is not. As such, it is necessarily grounded in that structure of all possible grounds that in this book is referred to as the 'originary' [*originaria*] structure (translated as 'originary' precisely in order to distinguish it from every original ground or origin).[20] This ground – i.e. precisely the ground of the absence of every ground – is the ground that 'in this place and age' grounds everything that is and appears. It takes the form of the freedom of science and philosophy, in their unified attempt to further the development of the civilization of technics and technology, *qua* realization of the limitless transformability of everything that is and appears; it takes the form of absolute chance, *qua* essence of every physical, symbolic, societal, cultural and linguistic event (for any restriction to that absolute chance would constitute a law and the absolute relation imposed by a ground; cf. *Law and Chance*), i.e. the form of the very necessity of contingency, which opens the very domain of the eventuality of the event; it takes the form of the absolute free play of signifiers, words and languages, the absolute transformability of every meaning and the disappearance of every fixed referent, the absolute interpretability of every appearing content, the disappearing of every irrefutable fact, and the establishing of a generalized (self-)hermeneutics of the real (Hegel writes: 'From the mistaken view that the inadequacy of finite categories to express truth entails the impossibility of objective cognition, we derive a justification for pronouncing and denouncing according to our feelings and subjective opinions. Assurances present themselves in place of proofs, along with stories about all the "facts" that are to be found in "consciousness"; and the more uncritical they are, the more they count as "pure" '[21]); it takes the form of a globally self-regulating autarchic anarchy and anarchic autarchy (or 'democracy'), which aims to dispose of any non-procedural principles, rights and laws that could limit its self-advancement: this advancement precisely consisting in its liberation from those principles, rights and laws (while always being grounded in the non-procedural principle of the impossibility of every non-procedural principle); it takes the form of the limitless expansion of the emancipation of the human, i.e. the emancipation from all those grounds and origins that appear to constrain the domain of human possibilities (these grounds and origins being determinations that originally limit an individual by assigning a certain determination or set of determinations that, in one way or another, are original to the extent that they are assigned at or before birth); it takes the form of the freedom to will and desire ever new dimensions of willing and desiring, or the form of the will to increase the possibility of what can be willed (i.e. the will to increase the power of the will, *qua* will-power, and, therefore, will to power – the power of the will constituting the very being of the will) and the will to decrease and eliminate what the will does not will, i.e. the will to increase the pleasures of the will (*qua* self-increase of the power of the will) and to eliminate the dimension of pain present within the will (*qua* decrease of that power) (and, ultimately, to eliminate that ultimate form of pain and impossibility constituted by the very death of the will – the necessity of which would constitute an abstract ground for which there can be no sufficient reason); it takes the form of everything that is and appears 'in this place and age', to the very extent that this 'place' and 'age' are originally opened by that very ground, *qua* place that can have no boundaries and *qua* age that can have no fixed temporal coordinates – an infinite universe of ever new material, ideal, semantic and imaginary universes, the infinite possibility of infinite possibilities.

This, the extent to which today, as ever, an enquiry into the ground is as timely (and what is most timely) as it is untimely (and what is most untimely).

V. Emanuele Severino (1929–2020) appears as the author of this work. As Severino recalls on the very first page of the Introduction to the 1981 edition of this work, however: 'The originary structure of the truth of being is not the "theoretical product" of any human (as a single individual or as a social group), and nor is it "God" or something produced by a god. It is rather the always already open site of Necessity and of the originary meaning of Necessity.'[22] That is to say, the originary structure, as the ground of everything that is and appears, is also the ground of that set of convictions, beliefs, thoughts and feelings that appear to have historically claimed to be the author of the present book. The relation between that author and the structure that he wishes to present in this book appears, however, to be a *unicum* in the history of the relations between authors and 'their' texts. For this text, which is the first in a lifelong enquiry that comprises almost a hundred volumes, sets the very parameters as part of which any belief of ownership (of texts, ideas, thoughts, meanings, etc.) can first appear, and delineates the extent to which any such belief must first of all appear *as* a belief, or an interpretation: i.e. the interpretation that believes that a certain set of appearing contents may be gathered together and referred to as the empirical person 'Emanuele Severino', and that another set of appearing contents may be interpreted to be the text written by that author. Immediately, then, this line of considerations appears to insert this reflection into that most distinctive thread of questioning that, in the second part of the last century, has enquired into the 'death' of the author, the question of the ownership or signature of a text, and so forth. The latter set of reflections, however, is once again to be traced to that abstract positing of the absence of every ground that, above, has been claimed to constitute *the* very ground of the present age (which is once again, the very age as part of which something like a 'present' comes to lose its temporal coordinates). As part of the ungrounding of this ground, every necessary relation that could hold together the appearing contents of either the author or the text comes to disappear, and, therefore, so does every connection between the two poles of the author–text relation (thus leaving them floating in an infinite play of hermeneutical relations, the by-product of which is the mere semblance of something like texts, contexts, authors, etc.).

Once again, however, one thing is to indicate a specific content (*including* the very dissolution of the abstract concepts of the author, the text, their relation, etc.), and another is to indicate the structure that must ground everything that is and appears (*including* the very being and appearing of the dissolution of the author–text relation). The relation between this structure and the author that indicates it is therefore a *unicum* that cannot be subsumed under any of the concepts of (the lack of) authorship that appear in the history of authors and texts: neither in the authorship of a philosophical text, nor in the recounting of a myth, nor in the exposition of a sacred text – and yet, in a certain sense, that *unicum* presents the authentic (or 'originary') traits of these three types of 'authorship'. For the originary logos is precisely that ever-present content, which does not and can never belong to an author, but to which every author belongs, as the finite belongs to the infinite, and untruth to truth, and which the author tries to present, thus having first of all to present the way in which the author participates in it while trying and believing to abstract from that content in order to testify to it. The relation between the 'author' and the 'content' at stake here is then that of a *testimony*, in which the witness must, to a certain extent, be part of the matter of the testimony in order to be able to witness it, while also having to some extent to be removed from it in order to be able to bear witness or testify to it (this antinomic relation between the witness and the matter of the testimony being precisely that condition of possibility of the testimony, which is at the same time a condition of its impossibility – whence that testimony remains a belief or a faith in having testified to what it wanted to testify to). Starting with the the author's later works, and once the object of this testimony comes to be referred to as 'the destiny of necessity' (above: 'the always already open site of Necessity and of the originary meaning of Necessity'), that testimony begins to refer to itself as 'the language that testifies to destiny' [*il linguaggio che testimonia il destino*]. The Italian '*testimoniare*' includes both the meaning of witnessing and of testifying to something; that is to say, that language (that testimony) testifies to the ever present content that is always witnessed and borne witnessed to by every witness, appearing site and testimony. For that language testifies to both that site (the destiny of necessity) that is immediately its own witness (the gaze of destiny [*lo sguardo del destino*] being precisely the site in which event and witness originarily coincide) and to that site (the language that testifies to the destiny of necessity) that testifies to the former site, and that, precisely because it attempts to testify to it, fails to do so (and yet it can fail only because it must share a segment with that site – *this* shared segment being the content of the originary testimony). That testimony therefore consists of 'a heeding of truth – a heeding that, precisely insofar as it is a faith, is *destined* to fail to heed that truth. Insofar as it is heeded "by me", i.e. by the faith in which "I" consist as a mortal individual, truth cannot be truth, and I am destined to remain only the desire, *in indefinitum*, for that truth – i.e. precisely, and to the letter, a philo-sopher."[23] Equivalently:

> The Necessity that is always already open outside of the isolation of the earth and the history of the West is not a doctrine that may be handed over by one person to another, and nor is it something that may be 'understood' by one person or by many. Insofar as it is 'understood' by one person or by many, Necessity simply becomes a 'perspective' of the one or of the many, i.e. something that cannot be Necessity. The testimony of Necessity may be 'heeded' – if, however, as part of that heeding, Necessity appears as such, the heeding one may not be 'one of us', a mortal or a god; it may not be 'my neighbour'. If Necessity may not be what 'one' uncovers, which is thus confined within the limits of the gaze of that one, neither can Necessity be what is heeded by an 'other', or by 'others'. If, as part of this heeding, Necessity appears as Necessity, the heeding one cannot but be Necessity itself, and that heeding constitutes once again its appearing.[24]

VI. *La struttura originaria* (1st edition, 1958) is the first volume in a six-decade long enquiry into the determinations of the structure of truth (i.e. the truth of being). This means that while that structure constitutes the ever present background of the appearing of everything that is, the *extent* to which that structure may be testified to as part of language can vary (whereas, once again, that structure itself is the invariable background as part of which every variation appears). This entails that the language that testifies to that structure may testify to certain elements that, from the standpoint of a later stage of the testimony of that structure, can appear to be untenable. This is above all the case in relation to a specific theoretical nexus of *The Originary Structure* (as detailed in Severino's extensive Introduction to the 1981 edition of the book – the present translation being a translation of this latter edition). Concisely: the first edition of *The Originary Structure* still struggles to reconcile the appearing of the becoming of beings (the appearing of the arising from nothingness and annihilation of beings) with the originary truth of the self-being of being (the impossibility for being not to be). To this extent, in *The Originary Structure*, Severino still attempts to hold firm both poles of this aporia: that of the self-differentiation of being and that of its originary self-identity. The most significant development in the testimony of the originary structure takes place a few years after the publication of *The Originary Structure*, with the appearing of the essays 'Returning to Parmenides' (1964) and its 'Postscript' (1965) (later collected in *The Essence of Nihilism*). In these two essays, Severino is able to show that the manifest becoming of beings conforms to the originary structure of the truth of being only if *every being is eternal*, and if the becoming of beings *consists in the appearing and disappearing of these eternals* (i.e. their entering and leaving the eternal 'circle of appearing'). (The eternity of every being is a – primary – individuation of the universal opposition between every being and its other, i.e. an individuation of the self-being of beings.) That is to say, with *The Essence of Nihilism*, Severino comes to the conclusion that *The Originary Structure* still remains under the sway of nihilism precisely to the extent that, in that former study, beings' arising from nothingness and returning to it is held firm as a manifest content of appearing. With *The Essence of Nihilism*, Severino's testimony is now able to conclude that what appears does *not* and *cannot* manifest this creation and annihilation ('the φαίνεσθαι is silent about being that does not appear'[25]), and that any belief to the contrary must entail some *nihilistic* residue: precisely to the extent that every becoming entails, and is made possible by, a thinking that conceives of every being as a nothingness (*nihil*). The faith in the existence and self-evidence of becoming, *qua* annihilation and creation of being, constitutes the original belief that underlies the entirety of the history of nihilism. It is however only insofar as a being (every being) is abstractly separated from its being that it can be claimed to arise from or turn into nothingness, and it is precisely because of this abstract separation of a being from its being (and, therefore, from its eternity) that this being (every being) is a nothingness: 'The fundamental thought of metaphysics is that beings, *as such*, are nothing'[26]; 'The structure of the West consists in the will for beings to be time (and, therefore, nothing)'[27]. (This essence, however – the essence of nihilism – remains in an essential way in the unconscious of the 'West' or 'metaphysics': 'Metaphysics conceals – i.e. it keeps unsaid – what it says: namely, it conceals what its explicit saying means, or it denies that its explicit saying says the nothingness of beings. It does not directly say that beings are nothing, but it says something – the ἐπαμφοτερίζειν of beings – that necessarily implies the nothingness of beings.'[28])

All of this is included in the 1981 Introduction, which is part of the present translation. What that Introduction does not include, instead, are the further determinations that are introduced by Severino's testimony after that edition of *The Originary Structure*. While those further developments cannot be presented here (and they above all include the determination of the necessity with which the eternals appear as part of the circle of appearing, as well as the determination of the necessary occurrence of the completion of the series of eternals that constitute the history of the essential alienation of nihilism),[29] it should, however, be noted that, as Severino famously states at the very beginning of the 1981 Introduction to the present enquiry, '*The Originary Structure* remains to this day the ground as part of which all my writings receive the meaning that pertains to them'.[30] That is to say, on the one hand, all of Severino's writings – like every other being – receive their own meaning as part of their appearing in and through the originary structure of the truth of being; on the other hand, all those writings are part of the one project, inaugurated in *The Originary Structure*, which consists in the gradual unfolding of the testimony of the determinations of that structure. This unfolding may certainly have to halt before certain obstacles, and, at other times, it may have to retrace its steps: that is to say, that unfolding may err (and, to the extent that this unfolding is abstracted from what it testifies to, this unfolding *must* err), but always while testifying to the unerring truth of being, as it structures itself according to the originary structure of its truth.

VII. The meaning of translation that follows from the theoretical apparatus of the language that testifies to destiny has already appeared in the translator's prefaces of *Law and Chance* and *Beyond Language*.[31] This meaning of translation is not 'one' of the possible meanings or concepts of translation, but, once again, it constitutes the 'originary' meaning of translation: 'originary', in this instance, because it is grounded in the originary meaning of abstraction – which is to say, in the abstraction of the originary meaning. That is to say, every translation (and therefore: every becoming, every individuation or subsumption of a concept, every application of a form, every inclusion of a matter, etc.) may *appear* to take place only insofar as a meaning (a being) is abstracted from its meaning (from its being): and therefore, and primarily, only insofar as the totality of meaning is abstracted from the meaning of this totality (i.e. insofar as the totality of being is abstracted from its being). The original translation is therefore the original abstraction: which is to say, the very abstraction of the abstract meaning of abstraction. Every other abstraction or translation may only take place as part of the background of the meaning of abstraction or translation that is obtained through the abstraction of meaning from the meaning of meaning, or of ground from the ground of ground. (As part of the language that testifies to destiny, this original abstraction is referred to as the 'isolation of the earth': 'The isolation of the earth is the abstract concept of the abstract as part of which every abstract conception of the abstract is possible.')[32]

The history of the translations of being is the history of the abstract concepts of being (the history of metaphysics): namely, the history of the abstractions, negations or translations of the one concrete self-grounding ground. To the extent that each of these negations or abstractions of the ground (or, according to the lexicon of the present enquiry, every 'abstract concept of the abstract') can in fact only *appear* to appear – for the concrete ground is the unabstractable itself, the inalienable, that which determines the concrete meaning of impossibility *qua* impossibility of any expropriation or appropriation of the ground – every negation of the ground is originarily negated, i.e. it only *appears* to negate the ground: this appearance being instead concretely included in the ground itself. The *apparent* translations or abstractions of the ground thus constitute the abstract history of the ground, which itself concretely appears as part of the concrete (time-less) presence of the present (Hegel writes: 'While the Idea itself is this passing-over or rather self-translation into the *abstract understanding*, it is also eternally *reason*; it is the dialectic that makes this product of the understanding, this diversity, understand its own finite nature once more, makes it see that the independence of its productions is a false semblance, and leads it all back to unity.')[33] In this sense, the originary structure constitutes the untranslatable structure of the concrete impossibility of translating or abstracting the concreteness of the ground.

(Concerning the structuring of abstract presence – *qua* abstract structuring of the present content and of the presence, form or time of that present content – which emerges from the abstraction of the concrete appearing of concrete presence, or the concrete presence of concrete appearing, i.e. of *this* appearing, which appears here and now, *prior* to the abstraction of any here from any now, and of any being from any time, cf. my forthcoming *Meta-Physika. Volume I: The Appearing of Presence.*)

The translator's prefaces of *Law and Chance* and *Beyond Language* do not directly address the matter of responsibility concerning the question of translation. For, in expressing my gratitude to Giulio Goggi and Ines Testoni for their support in settling several editorial questions, as my co-editors in the series of *The Works of Emanuele Severino*, I must add, as it is customary, that the responsibility for any error lies in any case solely with me. This responsibility, together with the affection for our collaboration, remains, however, an abstract meaning: that is to say, an abstract translation through which 'I' – *qua* empirical 'I', i.e. *qua* original translation of the concreteness of appearing into the appearing of an abstract content to an abstract form (precisely, this 'I') – believe to create, express and convey meanings: which, one way or another, are all aimed at sustaining in existence, accruing and reinforcing that meaning that 'I' believe to be. Translating *The Originary Structure*, however, does precisely not mean translating the originary structure (the untranslatable), and a text is a translation of *The Originary Structure* only and precisely to the extent that it testifies – as in the case of the language that testifies to destiny – to its very own failure to testify to or translate that untestifiable and untranslatable semantic complex. That is to say (cf. 'Beyond Translation' in *Beyond Language*), this text is a translation of *The Originary Structure* to the extent that this translation, too, testifies to the untranslatability and incontrovertibility of the originary structure, and to the extent that, in so doing, this testimony *does* nevertheless, in one way or another, translate or modify that concreteness ('it says the unsayable'), while at the same time constituting a *unicum* among all the translations of the concreteness of appearing precisely to the extent that it testifies to the untranslatability of that concreteness; to this extent, this translation and the language that testifies to destiny appear together in their sharing a concrete and concretely present meaning both with one another and with that untranslatable concreteness. Insofar as this translation includes this concrete meaning, 'I' am not *responsible* for it – in the same way in which the language that testifies to destiny is not 'responsible' for the concrete meaning that it shares with the meaning to which it testifies. 'I' do not *respond* for it to the extent that there is and there can be nothing of that meaning that I can will, appropriate or expropriate, but 'I' – every abstract 'I' – is part of the concrete self-will, self-appropriation and self-expropriation of that concreteness: in such a way that there can be a response to the testimony of that concreteness only if the one that responds is the one that gives the call ('if there exists a heeding of the testimony of destiny, that heeding is the *self*-heeding of destiny'[34]), and only if that responsibility coincides with the concrete self-response of its immediate self-appearing.

Introduction

Emanuele Severino

1. Nihilism and *The Originary Structure*

The Originary Structure (1958) remains to this day the ground as part of which all my writings receive the meaning that pertains to them. *The Essence of Nihilism* states that in 'Returning to Parmenides' – which occupies a privileged position among those writings:

> An attempt is made at tracing and bringing to light the fundamental thought that guides and gathers the endless multitude of categories and events that comprise the civilisation of the West: the thought as part of which everything is by now thought and experienced, a thought whose authentic meaning may not be thought before having successfully moved outside of it, along a path that is yet untrodden. This dominant thought of the West is nihilism: the standpoint from which beings *qua* beings are thought and experienced as a nothingness. The nihilistic ground of our civilisation may be grasped only by embarking on and keeping to the testimony of the truth of being. The latter is recalled in 'Returning to Parmenides' as to its essential traits, but that mention constantly refers to a previous enquiry into *The Originary Structure* of the truth of being, an enquiry that attempts to express that testimony in the most determinate and concrete way.[1]

The originary structure of the truth of being is not the 'theoretical product' of any human (as a single individual or as a social group), and nor is it 'God' or something produced by a god. It is rather the always already open site of Necessity and of the originary meaning of Necessity. The necessity that the essence of the West should be nihilism may only appear as part of that site. It is only as part of the originary structure of Necessity that the structure of the essential alienation of the West may appear. The incipit of *Gli abitatori del tempo*,[2] too, states that the aim is to

> further extend the attempt at leading the structure of Western civilisation into language. That structure encloses every particular and specific element of our history, and it is therefore ever present; and yet, its authentic meaning may only be grasped in an underground that lies far deeper beneath the one explored by

Hegel, Marxism, psychoanalysis, structuralism and Nietzschean-Heideggerian hermeneutics. That underground may only be reached by not embarking on a path in the company of the historical constructs advanced to different extents by our culture; in fact, that underground may be reached only by altogether not embarking 'on a path', but rather allowing the site of Necessity (that is, the originary structure of Necessity), which is always already open *outside of* the structure of the West, to be testified to by language – and to be testified to as something that is separated by an abyss from that other site, which consists precisely in the structure within which the history of the West unfolds. If this latter structure remains the essential unconscious of our civilisation, that former structure – the site of Necessity – is the unconscious of that unconscious, the underground of that underground, the enclosure of that which encloses.

For the first time, but in the most determinate and concrete way, *The Originary Structure* precisely attempts to express the unconscious that lies behind the very unconscious structure of the West: the underground that lies deeper beneath the very underground constituted by the fundamental thought as part of which everything is by now thought and experienced by the civilization of the West. This means that among the endless multitude of languages that participate in the language of the West – this being by now the only language spoken on earth, as well as the most rigorous and expressive form reached by the language of mortals – a language begins to speak in *The Originary Structure*, which speaks a different tongue: that of the testimony of Necessity.

Upon starting to speak a new language, one remains for a long time under the sway of one's mother tongue: this is the language into which mortals are born. Mortals are the strife between the site of Necessity and the conviction, i.e. the will – which arises in that site – that the earth is a secure region.[3] The earth: that is to say, the totality of things, be they human or divine, as they come and as they go – as they enter the circle of the appearing of Necessity and as they leave it. The conviction that the earth is a secure region isolates the earth from Necessity; it separates the earth from destiny. The mother tongue of mortals devotes all its words to the testimony of this isolated earth. Isolated from Necessity (Necessity being also what must necessarily pertain to the earth – i.e. the destiny of the earth), however, the earth appears as a nothingness. It is on the grounds of this appearing of the nothingness of the earth that nihilism is able to step forth as the dominant thought of the West. It is by being grounded in the alienation that separates the earth from destiny – an alienation that constitutes the very being-mortal of mortals – that the alienation of nihilism is able to step forth. This alienation, in turn, does not simply ground all thoughts, theories and intellectual processes but, by now, also the entirety of the works and historical actions of the West.

At its surface – namely, as to what the West believes to know, and to which it thus testifies in its language – the West wills for the things of the earth, *qua* things, *not* to be a nothingness. Even when the West abandons things to their extreme impermanence, and sees how they are traversed and consumed by nothingness, at its surface, the West rejects the idea that – however, restricted and exposed the space may be in which things succeed in not being a nothingness – in that very space, things, *qua* things, should be a nothingness. Starting with Greek thought, however, and once and for all, the West consists *at the same time* in a will for things, *qua* things, to be something that issues from nothingness and returns to it – i.e. to be something that is, but that could have also not been. This will does not realize what it truly wills (namely, what necessarily pertains to what it believes to will). That will does not simply will for things to turn into nothingness and issue from it; that will wills the extreme form of the folly: that being-a-thing should, as such, coincide with and mean being-a-nothingness; that a thing, precisely insofar as it is not a nothingness, should be a nothingness. This is the nihilism that the 'consciousness' of the West pushes back into its unconscious, without letting it surface in its own language.

That nothingness of the earth, however, appears – within the deepest and untestified region of the unconscious of the West – precisely as a result of the isolation of the earth from Necessity. That nothingness of the earth is precisely what the will of the West truly wills, as soon as – in willing for the earth to be a secure region – it wills for the things of the earth to consist of an issuing from nothingness and a returning to it. The mother tongue of mortals testifies to the solitude of the earth: not in the sense that it asserts the nothingness of the things of the earth, but in the sense that this nothingness comes to the surface, and therefore conceals itself, precisely in and through the way in which the language of the West asserts the non-nothingness of things. It is, however, only insofar as that language appears in the appearing of Necessity that what comes to the surface in it may be recognized as an absolute negation of what is concealed in what it says, and that very language may be thus recognized as a testimony of the solitude – i.e. the nothingness – of the earth.

And yet, precisely because it *starts* to speak the language of the testimony of Necessity, *The Originary Structure* remains under the sway of the language that testifies to the isolation of the earth from Necessity.

Not only: while admittedly starting to speak an essentially different language, this book makes no attempt at leaving behind the philosophical idioms of the West. For, indeed, one does not speak a language that differs from the one of mortals by devising new linguistic forms, but insofar as language itself is exposed to the shine of Necessity, and the light of a new meaning is cast on its words. In and through this light, even the matter and the rhythm of words are different. And yet, this difference is impenetrable, hidden by the obtrusiveness of the essential persistence of the fundamental linguistic forms. Left to itself, the language of *The Originary Structure* thus fosters a misunderstanding – which is even greater the more that language appears to particularly care about its own rigour and formal transparency.

Let us consider this question in more detail.

The originary structure of Necessity is, in the first place, the (concretely determined) opening of meaning itself, which may not be negated by humans or gods at any time, under any circumstances or in any universe. It *may not* be negated in that the negation of that opening (i.e. of the meaning that opens up in it) supersedes itself: that is, it places itself before its own negative force and is overturned by it. The originary structure is altogether *free* from its own negation – and, for this reason, it is the structure of Necessity – insofar as it is essentially *connected* to the self-negation of its negation. Necessity is such insofar as the negation of Necessity is necessarily self-negating.

Necessity, precisely insofar as it is a *structure*, is not a semantic point but a relation of semantic domains. In *The Originary Structure*, these domains are named 'logical immediacy' ('L-immediacy') and 'phenomenological immediacy' ('Ph-immediacy').[4] The 'immediate' has nothing to do with 'common consciousness' or the 'natural' appearing of things independently of, or beyond, any theoretical understanding or interpretation of the 'datum' of experience. The 'immediate' is what appears in and of itself as Necessity, *without being mediated* by anything else. The 'originarity' of the originary structure precisely consists in the 'immediacy' of that structure. In *The Originary Structure*, the immediacy *of the connection* between meanings (= signifying things = signifying of things = beings) is posited as 'logical' immediacy (the logical character, i.e. the logos, being precisely the connection between meanings), and the immediacy of this logical character is referred to as the 'principle of non-contradiction'. The immediacy *of the disclosure*, i.e. of the appearing of the different forms of connections that link meanings, is named 'phenomenological' immediacy.

The 'principle of non-contradiction' and the 'phenomenology' referred to in this book, however, differ in an essential way from the principle of non-contradiction and the phenomenology that are fundamental elements of nihilism, which is to say, of the alienation of the West. The principle of non-contradiction precisely constitutes the specific way in which, at the surface of the West, the non-contradictory character of beings is established – these very beings being themselves understood, in the unconscious of that principle, as a nothingness. In thinking the non-contradictoriness of a being, the principle of non-contradiction does indeed think this being as something that is a being and not a non-being, as long as it is (i.e. as long as it is a being), but that principle also thinks that being as something that can also not be; thought as to this non-being, a being is therefore thought as something that, *qua* being, is nothing. Phenomenology itself, since the Greek φαίνεσθαι and up to Husserl's phenomenology, consists, on the one hand, in an acknowledgement of the possibility that beings, leaving or not having yet entered appearing, should turn into or still be a nothingness, and, on the other hand, it consists in the conviction of 'seeing' the becoming of beings, namely, their issuing from nothingness and their returning to it; this is the becoming that necessarily entails the nothingness of beings *qua* beings, and that is, however, not seen by phenomenology as to this implication. Phenomenology, *qua* fundamental element of Western thought, conceals in its own unconscious the conviction that beings are nothing – as it happens with the principle of non-contradiction – while letting that conviction come to language in the disguised form of the conviction that the becoming of beings (i.e. their issuing from nothingness and returning to it) appears (i.e. is a phenomenological content), or in the form of the conviction that, outside of the dimension of appearing, beings can be nothing.

The Originary Structure, on the contrary, states:

> Even when realising that the principle of non-contradiction is not only a rule of thought, but it concerns being itself [= beings], if one then regards being (what is non-contradictory) as in itself indifferent as to its own being or non-being – in such a way that through the principle of non-contradiction one states nothing but that being is, when it is, and that being is not, when it is not – one still

regards non-contradictoriness itself in a formal way, and, exactly for this reason, one negates it: precisely because the supposition of a moment in which being is not is allowed to persist. It is part of the very meaning of being that being must be – accordingly, the principle of non-contradiction does not simply express the self-identity of an essence (or its difference from the other essences), but the identity of essence and existence (or the otherness of essence from non-existence) (Chapter 13, §6).

The 'formal' conception of the non-contradictoriness of beings, however – which is in truth a negation of the non-contradictoriness of beings – dominates the entirety of the historical existence of the principle of non-contradiction; accordingly, this book persists in naming 'principle of non-contradiction' something that remains not only beyond the historical meaning of that principle but also beyond its very essence. This is due to the fact that this book emphasizes the *explicit* intent of that principle – namely, its will for beings to be non-contradictory – rather than its *implicit* and unconscious one: namely, the will for beings to be nothing. Or, equivalently, this book lays emphasis, within language, on the abstract element that is seemingly shared by the truth of being and by the alienation from that very truth: the non-contradictory character of being. This abstract element, however, is only *seemingly* shared by the two, because it does not consist of a universal that is individuated in different ways (as part of truth and as part of the alienation from truth), while nevertheless persisting *as such* in both of these individuations; on the contrary, it consists in a 'universal' that, as part of its individuation in the alienation of truth, simultaneously *negates itself* (i.e. constitutes itself as an unconscious will for beings to be nothing). Accordingly, it is only by abstractly separating the individuation of this element from its self-negation as part of that same individuation that it is possible to regard it as an element that is shared by the truth of being and by the alienation of that truth.

In *The Originary Structure*, however, the testimony of the impossibility for beings not to be also moves the meaning of 'phenomenology' – i.e. the concept of the appearing of beings – towards the truth of being. The truth of being, *qua* Necessity of the connection that links *every* being to its being (i.e. to its not being a nothingness), is at the same time the truth of the appearing of being: namely, the Necessity for the becoming of beings to not appear as an issuing from nothingness and a returning to it, but as an appearing and disappearing of something that, insofar as it is a being, is necessarily connected to its being – and is thus eternal.[5] However, it is precisely in the way in which it establishes the meaning of 'phenomenology' that this book, while starting to speak the language of the testimony of Necessity, remains under the sway of the language that testifies to the isolation of the earth from Necessity. It is precisely for this reason that, above, it was stated that in *The Originary Structure* the testimony of the impossibility for beings not to be *moves* the meaning of 'phenomenology' *towards* the truth of being; that is to say, an element of the truth of being (the L-immediacy) moves the other element (the Ph-immediacy, i.e. 'phenomenology') towards the meaning that pertains to it as part of the concrete unity of the two elements – without yet reaching it, for this latter element is still only moved towards that unity (while admittedly reaching its extreme vicinity).

Nevertheless, precisely due to its being moved towards the truth of being, 'phenomenology' presents in this book a meaning that differs in an essential way from the one that pertains to the historical existence of that concept. Section 26 of Chapter 13, titled 'Becoming as the Appearing of the Immutable', begins with this passage:

> The totality of Ph-immediate being, as the horizon in which the birth and the annulment of being come to be manifested, must therefore [namely, once it has been affirmed that *everything*, i.e. *every* being, is immutable, §8] be determined as the horizon in which the appearing and disappearing of being is manifest; that is to say, that which, from a standpoint that remains at a simple consideration of the totality of Ph-immediate being (or, equivalently: that which from the standpoint of the concept Γ_a), manifests itself as an *arising* and an *annulment* is revealed, as part of the concrete structuring of the originary, as an *appearing* and a *disappearing*.

The 'standpoint that remains at a simple consideration of the totality of Ph-immediate being' is the standpoint that *abstractly separates* the appearing of beings from the impossibility for beings not to be (i.e. that abstractly separates the Ph-immediacy from the authentic and concrete meaning of the L-immediacy, as part of which the opposition of a being to its other is *at the same time* the opposition of that being to its being-nothing). The 'concept Γ_a' (considered in a determinate way in Chapter 11) precisely consists in the appearing of beings in their being thus abstractly separated. The passage quoted above therefore states that if the appearing of beings is abstractly separated from the impossibility for beings not to be, then the becoming of beings is manifest in the form of their issuing from nothingness and their returning to it; on the contrary, 'as part of the concrete structuring of the originary' (i.e. as part of the concrete relation between Ph-immediacy and L-immediacy, which is a negation of their abstract separation), the becoming of beings is manifest as the appearing and disappearing of the immutable. 'Phenomenology' is in this way inscribed into the originary structure of Necessity, which confers upon it an essentially different meaning – since, as part of the historical existence of phenomenology, the explicit will to acknowledge what appears, to the extent to which it appears, conceals an unconscious will to conceal the appearing beings with the nihilistic form of their issuing from nothingness and returning to it. Since this form is posited as the content of appearing, phenomenalism thus belongs to the essence of phenomenology, and the unconscious will to conceal the content of appearing with that form is protected by the will for beings, *qua* beings, to be nothing – namely, by the will that constitutes the essential (and itself hidden) meaning of that form.

And yet, in the passage quoted above (and as part of the very general stance of the book), if the will that wills that beings be nothing no longer directly protects the will to conceal the content of appearing with the form of nihilism, this will to conceal nevertheless continues to be operative, and the will for beings to be nothing thus continues to be implicitly operative within it. For, indeed, as part of the originary structure of Necessity, beings' issuing from nothingness and returning to it is *not* something that, while being posited as part of the concrete structuring of the originary as an appearing and disappearing of the immutable, *nevertheless* continues to *appear* as an issuing from nothingness and a returning to it. The impossibility for beings not to be does *not* step in as an interpretative model that leads what nevertheless continues to be the *actual* appearing of an issuing from nothingness and a returning to it towards another meaning (i.e. towards the meaning of appearing and disappearing). This means that *the impossibility* for beings not to be *is such* precisely insofar as it originarily structures itself together with the necessity that *the authentic and actual content of appearing* should not consist of beings' issuing from nothingness and returning to it, but of their appearing and disappearing. In *The Originary Structure*, on the contrary, Ph-immediacy is the 'horizon in which the birth and the annulment of being come to be manifested' – *not only* insofar as that immediacy is *abstractly separated* from the impossibility for being not to be (i.e. from the concrete meaning of L-immediacy) *but also* insofar as it is regarded as being simply *distinct* from this impossibility: in such a way that this impossibility does not at the same time coincide with the *impossibility* of the appearing of any issuing from nothingness and returning to it, but it only comes to *integrate* the meaning of becoming, *qua* issuing from nothingness and returning to it, with the meaning of becoming *qua* appearing and disappearing of the immutable. This integration marks the farthest point to which the domination of nihilism extends in *The Originary Structure*, and it also marks the farthest point to which the testimony of the truth of being may extend as part of a language in which there still persists the conviction that the issuing from nothingness and returning to it of beings appear (that is to say, as part of a language that still remains under the sway of the language that testifies to the isolation of the earth from Necessity). As part of this language, the testimony of the truth of being is so radical that it goes so far as affirming, in that very language, an element that negates one of the essential traits of that very language (i.e. the element that consists in the positing of manifest becoming as the appearing and disappearing of the immutable).

The configuration of Chapter 13 is precisely determined by the contrast between the language of the testimony of Necessity and the language that testifies to the isolation of the earth from Necessity itself. (It is only insofar as the earth is thus isolated that the becoming of the things of the earth may be understood – and it must necessarily be understood – as an issuing from nothingness and a returning to it, and that, understood in this way, it may be accepted as part of the content of appearing). For, while, on the one hand, that chapter asserts the eternity of every being, on the other hand, the assertion that becoming consists of the appearing of the eternal does not rule out but overlaps with and complements the assertion that this issuing from nothingness and returning to it appears. The unity of these two sides is thus expressed in the assertion that the whole, *qua* immutable, is *other* than the totality of appearing beings (i.e. other than the totality of the Ph-immediate) – this otherness being an otherness between two positive elements, one of which is nevertheless necessarily posited as the totality of the positive, while the other one, *qua* positive element that adds nothing to the totality of the positive, is posited as something that might not have been or that might not be. This outcome of Chapter 13 is thus directly linked to the persistence of nihilism as part of a language in which Necessity – which always already abides outside of nihilism – starts to be testified to. Once again, however, Chapter 13 – on which, as stated in the

1957 'Note', the *entirety* of the enquiry of *The Originary Structure* converges – is also the place where all the voices that in this book testify to the originary structure of Necessity outside of the nihilism and isolation of the earth come together and gain prominence.

Precisely as a result of the convergence of the entirety of the enquiry on Chapter 13, however, *all* the linguistic forms that in this book appear to sound as a direct expression of the presence of nihilism ('annulment', 'still being nothing', ' no longer or not yet existing', 'being able to turn into nothing', 'being something that could have remained a nothingness', etc.) *must* be understood in light of the meaning conferred upon them by the testimony (converging on Chapter 13) of the impossibility for beings *qua* beings not to be. *Throughout* the unfolding of this book, the language that speaks of an issuing from nothingness and a returning to it therefore 'interprets' this occurrence as the appearing and disappearing of the immutable Whole. This is an 'interpretation' that does not appear as a hermeneutical hypothesis, problem, decision or faith but as the necessary truth of what appears (while nevertheless being an 'interpretation', in that it integrates the content that is believed to be appearing – i.e. that issuing from nothingness and returning to it – with a meaning that is not regarded as an appearing content: i.e. the appearing and disappearing of the eternal Whole). Nihilism consists in holding that this 'interpretation' interprets a 'datum' of experience as part of which beings appear as issuing from nothingness and returning to it. A non-nihilistic comprehension of the language of *The Originary Structure* – which rescues it from a nihilism to which, as a matter of fact, it is nevertheless still exposed – perceives instead that this 'datum' or 'given' [*dato*] is altogether not such, but it is the content of a *nihilistic* interpretation of what is authentically given (i.e. it is the content of the interpretation – opposed to the 'interpretation' that constitutes the necessary truth of beings – which expresses the will to power in its originarily willing the nothingness of beings). At the same time, that comprehension also perceives that this other 'interpretation', which posits the Necessity for 'becoming' to consist in the appearing and disappearing of the immutable, does not contradict the datum that it interprets. This means that if the linguistic forms that in this book appear to express a direct presence of nihilism are understood – in addition to their being inscribed in that necessary 'interpretation' – *not as the expression of a content that is regarded as being given* but as the expression *of a nihilistic faith that believes this content to be given*, then the *entirety* of the language of *The Originary Structure* speaks the language of Necessity, and *entirely* frees itself from the sway of the language of the West and of the isolation of the earth.

At the same time, however, even the title of Chapter 13, 'Originary Metaphysics', lends itself to a misunderstanding, since – as it is also the case throughout the entire development of the enquiry – it names 'metaphysics' the language that starts to express and negate the essence of nihilism beyond the history of the West, i.e. it refers to that language with the name of the fundamental protagonist of the history of nihilism. Nevertheless, if 'metaphysics' is the language that expresses both the relation of beings with the *totality* of being and the fundamental meaning of this relation, then this book (together with all my other writings) is 'metaphysics'. That is to say, metaphysics may take both the form of nihilism (this being the historical form of metaphysics) and the form of the negation of nihilism. It is precisely insofar as *The Originary Structure* does not focus on the historical meaning of the word 'metaphysics' (i.e. on the meaning of this word that holds sway throughout history) but on the meaning that is *shared* by metaphysics *qua* historical event and *qua* negation of nihilism that this book may qualify as 'metaphysics'. The language of *The Essence of Nihilism*, on the contrary, instead of laying emphasis on the semantic forms shared by nihilism and by its negation – such as, precisely, the reference to the totality of beings – emphasizes the nihilistic component that is shared by both historical metaphysics and by the anti-metaphysical stance of contemporary culture, and it therefore refrains from calling 'metaphysics' the appearing of the totality of beings in accordance with which Necessity is originarily structured.

In an analogous fashion, while in *The Essence of Nihilism* the word ἐπιστήμη indicates the very Necessity of the originary structure (i.e. the *standing* of De-stiny, which does not *stand* because it tames the insurgence of the becoming of things, but because, outside of the conviction that becoming exists, i.e. outside of the alienation, *things themselves* appear as a *standing*), the later writings retain instead the historical meaning of the word ἐπιστήμη. Accordingly, this word is taken to express the will to control the issuing from nothingness and returning to it (a will to domination that, precisely as such, constitutes the most radical acknowledgement of the existence of what it aims to dominate), thus opening a dimension that asserts itself and 'stands' (ἴσταται) 'over' (ἐπί) everything – and, therefore, also over everything that, issuing from nothingness, threatens the existent or tries to elude it by taking refuge in nothingness. (This same remark should be repeated for what concerns the words 'God' and 'Sacred': in *The Essence of Nihilism*, these words are still uttered with the intention of naming those elements of the originary structure of Necessity that consist, respectively, of the Totality of beings and of that which, relative to that structure, succeeds in constituting itself as *the problem*; in the later writings, instead, they are returned to their historical meaning, i.e. to the meaning as part of which they appear as decisive determinations of the essential alienation of the will to power).

All of this, however, does not mean that the segment that is shared by metaphysics, *qua* historical event, and by *The Originary Structure* (this segment consisting precisely in the reference to the totality of beings) has the same extension as the segment shared by Western metaphysics and by that anti-metaphysical stance (this segment being instead nihilism itself). This is the case even though there in fact exists an analogy between these two shared segments. For, indeed, as part of the historical reference to the totality of beings, the nihilistic meaning of beings inevitably leads (throughout the history of the West) towards the twilight of the notion of totality – for, as the ultimate epistemic form, the totality anticipates every novelty of becoming, and renders the arising of beings from nothingness impossible. This arising is the very becoming of which that anticipation constitutes the most radical form of acknowledgement, in such a way that the reference to the totality is destined to be replaced by the reference to the part, characteristic of the specialized knowledge of science.[6] In an analogous way, as part of that historical reference to the totality of beings, the very meaning of the totality of beings as such inevitably leads to the twilight of the nihilistic meaning of beings – despite the fact that the twilight of the notion of totality manifests itself in the form of that boundless grandness of events constituted by the civilization of technics, whereas, up to now, the twilight of nihilism does not manifest itself in anything but in the language that begins to testify to the truth of being. This analogy, however, does not entail that what is united by the nihilistic meaning of beings has the same extension as what is united by the reference to the totality of beings: nihilism is shared by the entire history of the West, while the reference to the totality of being is only shared by *The Originary Structure* and one instance of that history – i.e. the one consisting of metaphysics *qua* historical reference to the totality of being.

This book testifies to the site that is always already open outside of the history of the West and outside of the isolation of the earth – thus exceeding the entirety of the dimension (the history of the West) that includes metaphysics as a historical event. It is precisely for this reason that if this book may qualify as 'metaphysics' for the reasons indicated above, it nevertheless stands in an essentially more radical remove from metaphysics *qua* historical event than the remove that is believed to be secured by the various anti-metaphysical stances and scientific specializations: for that is the same remove that separates it from every anti-metaphysical stance and every form of scientific-technological knowledge and praxis.

2. The structure of saying

Analogously, the meaning assigned by this book to 'analytic', 'synthetic *a priori*' and 'synthetic *a posteriori*' propositions is essentially different from the one that pertains to these expressions in traditional philosophical language. What is essentially different is first of all the very meaning of *being a proposition*.

The originary structure is a *structure* in that it is a *predication*: i.e. a relation in which something is said of something else precisely insofar as this other is what it is. As such, what is said is dedicated (*prae-dicatum*) to this other. This *saying* is not an action of a mortal (or of a god – it is not an action in any way). In order to express it, the uncommon Latin form *dix*, formed from *dico* in the same way in which *lex* is formed from *lego*, might be appropriate. Saying consists in the appearing of the relations between things; therefore, it also consists in the appearing of the relation between things and those other things that consist of the signs of things and of their relations.

Saying, however, *qua* originary structure, is the *identity* between what is said and that of which this is said; that is, it is the appearing of *the identity* of the things that are related. That relation is an *identity*. If, of something, something *other* is said than what that something is, this saying says that something is other than itself – that it is not itself: namely, this saying is a contradiction. A contradiction, however, is not that the negation of which is self-negating; on the contrary, contradicting oneself (a saying that negates itself) is such a negation. The fact that saying, *qua* originary structure, is the appearing of an *identity* means that it is only insofar as saying is an appearing *identity* that it is that the negation of which is self-negating.

A proposition – of any kind ('analytic', 'synthetic *a priori*', 'synthetic *a posteriori*') – may constitute a saying that is part of the originary structure of Necessity only insofar as it consists in the first place of this identity. The distinction between the different kinds of proposition is *internal* to the single meaning that propositions, *qua* predications, may take insofar as they constitute themselves as the originary structure itself (or as one of its elements). A 'synthetic proposition', such as 'this lamp is lit', too – if it belongs to the originary structure (that is, if it is one of the predications that are structured as the originary structure) – must necessarily constitute itself as an identity: i.e. as a saying that does not say that something is *other* than itself, or identifies that something with its other, but says this something in its self-identity.

This identity has nothing to share with the first of the three hypotheses considered in chapter 37 of the *Sophist*: namely, that there exists no κοινωνία (i.e. predication) among different determinations, in such a way that the only admissible saying (λέγειν, 251b) would be given by 'tautological' propositions, such as 'man is man' or 'good is good', rather than by synthetic propositions such as 'man is good' (or 'this lamp is lit'). For, indeed, we are not claiming that a synthetic proposition such as 'this lamp is lit' is *simpliciter* a contradiction, but that it is a contradiction insofar as it is uttered by the language of the West. Insofar as that proposition belongs to the originary structure (i.e. insofar as it is a necessary saying) it is not a contradiction, since it necessarily constitutes itself as an identity – an identity, *however*, as part of which that proposition does not lose the different determinations that comprise it, transforming itself in a proposition such as 'this lamp is this lamp'.

At the same time, the irony that Plato shows in considering the proponents of that first hypotheses betrays an essential weakness, for while it is true that their theory of the falsity of every non-tautological proposition is itself a non-tautological proposition, it is also true that every non-tautological proposition consists in an identification of two non-identical elements – i.e. in the affirmation that something is something other than that first something (the affirmation that A is non-A) – and it is therefore a contradiction. While Plato leaves the problem unsolved, it is precisely on the grounds of the logic of that first hypothesis that, according to Hegel, *every* proposition is a contradiction ('propositions' constituting for Hegel expressions of the finite). This is the case not only for synthetic propositions but also for tautologies themselves, for if in '$A = A$' ('A is A') the other of A 'appears only as illusory being, as an immediate vanishing', and 'the movement' that goes beyond A 'returns into itself', i.e. falls back onto A (*Science of Logic*, II, chapter 2, 'Identity', Remark 2), at the same time, this appearing of the other is not as null as being unable to entail a contradiction between the fact that 'identity [$A = A$] says nothing' – i.e. it does not result in anything in its moving beyond A – and the fact that, however, in order to be able to 'return into itself', this movement must have moved beyond A: i.e. it must have moved A to an identification with something different from A itself (albeit something different that vanishes as soon as it is reached by A).

Except that, in *The Originary Structure* (Chap. 3, §§10–14; Chap. 6, §§9–18), it is shown that, in a proposition of the kind $A = A$, the contradiction does not simply obtain between the 'nullness' and the '*illusory being*' of the other of A, as claimed by Hegel, but between the nullness and the *existence* of the other of A. For, indeed, the A that appears as predicate is necessarily different from the A that appears as subject: otherwise, the identity between A and A would not be able to arise; that is, one would not be dealing with $A = A$, but simply with A. Accordingly, since not only 'synthetic' propositions ($A = B$) are contradictory but also 'tautological' ones

($A = A$), no proposition may, *qua* contradiction, belong to the originary structure of Necessity. This book precisely indicates (cf. the chapters cited above) the way in which the different kinds of propositions – insofar as they belong to the structure of Necessity, i.e. insofar as they are a necessary saying – all constitute themselves as an identical saying.

This means that *The Originary Structure* testifies to – says – a meaning of *saying* that lies in the most extreme remove from the meaning in accordance with which the West says. That remove is extreme because the saying of the West is dominated by nihilism not only with respect to what this saying says but also – and this is the aspect that we are now considering – insofar as this saying is a saying. The isolation of the earth from Necessity is the ground of the occurrence of nihilism, and nihilism is the form of isolation that dominates the history of the West. This is the isolation of beings from their being, which enables their being regarded as a nothingness. The isolation of the earth from Necessity, however, is at the same time the ground of the meaning within which the West says. The saying of the West is rooted in the same ground of nihilism – i.e. the isolation of the earth from Necessity – not only *by virtue of what* it says (what it says being, precisely, nihilism itself) but also *insofar as it is a saying*. The nihilism of the West and the sense in which the West is a saying are linked to one another in and through the isolation of the earth. In the history of the West, saying, *qua* saying, is a form of isolation even when, with Hegel, Western thinking intends to posit itself as the most radical negation of that isolation.

In its most elementary form, the κοινωνία of determinations is a unified duality – the duality of thing (πρᾶγμα) and action (πρᾶξις) – which is expressed by a saying (λόγος) in uniting thing and action 'by means of a noun and a verb' (συνθεὶς πρᾶγμα πράξει δι' ὀνόματος καὶ ῥήματος, *Sophist*, 262e). In going beyond the noun, the saying does not encounter anything but the verb, i.e. what is other than the noun. Aristotle takes up this concept at the beginning of the *De Interpretatione*: if a verb (and the verb par excellence for Aristotle is the verb being) is not *added* to the noun – ἐὰν μὴ τὸ εἶναι … προστεθῇ, 16a 17–18 – then there is no saying. This adding indicates the *otherness* of what is added with respect to that to which it is added. In the *De Interpretatione*, Aristotle specifies that this saying (λόγος), *qua* apophantic saying, is a whole, each part of which, 'separated' (κεχωρισμένον), signifies as a φάσις ('word'): namely, as a noun that does not consist of a synthesis or diairesis, i.e. a κατάφασις ('affirmation', synthesis) (16b 26–8). According to Plato and Aristotle, true saying expresses what is. Having realized that saying is, as such, contradictory (what saying as such is for Hegel being indeed the saying of the West), Hegel asserts that the contradiction of saying is attested by experience. (This, however, does not mean that Hegel rejects the principle of non-contradiction but that, according to him, reality consists of thought in its leaving the contradiction behind – 'experience' belonging precisely to the moment in which thought contradicts itself.)

The saying of the West is, in its essence, a *saying that is a contradiction*, i.e. it is understood as a moving beyond: a moving beyond as part of which that from which the moving beyond begins comes to simply encounter something that, in not being that beginning, is its *other* (and is therefore an otherness, which thus determines a contradiction even if it is not recognized as such an otherness). For what concerns this essence, modern logic does not deviate from the Platonic-Aristotelian meaning of saying. According to Boole (who, in turn, in an Aristotelian way, traces all verbs to the verb 'being', regarded as having both an existential and a copulative meaning), a proposition is explicitly posited as an equation, in which the symbol '=' expresses the form of the verb 'being', and the two terms of the equation (which are different even if expressed by the same variable) come to be identified. The notion of 'propositional function', introduced by Frege and Russell, does not constitute a negation of the attributive propositions of classical logic but regards them as a limiting case of propositional functions: i.e. the case in which a function is saturated by the introduction of only one argument. At the same time, if attributive propositions may be regarded as a limiting case of propositional functions, the latter are presented as propositions that, in turn, lend themselves to being regarded as instances of attributive propositions: i.e. precisely as those instances in which the predicate does not express a relatively simple state but a relatively complex action (such that it involves a plurality of individuals as active and passive elements). If a judgement of the kind 'Caesar conquered the Gauls' (which, in *The Laws of Thought*, is used by Boole to prove that all verbs may be reduced to the verb 'being', and which, in *Funktion und Begriff*, is used by Frege to introduce the notion of propositional function) is associated to the scheme xRy, or $f(x,y)$, one believes to thus be highlighting the *relation* between two concrete individuals, which would be left unexpressed in the traditional scheme 'S is P'. In fact, the very meaning of that being-in-relation is left completely undetermined, and this precisely takes place because that being-in-relation continues to be implicitly understood as a predicate in the traditional sense: i.e. as that simple *other* that is encountered by what is part of the relation. Being-in-relation means *being* in relation: saying that Caesar conquered the Gauls means (precisely as remarked by Boole) that Caesar *is* in a certain relation with the Gauls. 'In a certain relation with the Gauls' is precisely the *other* of Caesar with which Caesar is identified.

Authentic saying, however – the saying of the originary structure of Necessity – is not a contradiction attested by 'experience'. The contradiction of saying does not belong to the essence of saying – and nor is it therefore a content of appearing – but it is the outcome of the mutual *separation*, i.e. *isolation*, that comes to enclose the elements of saying.

This lamp is lit. (A is B; $A = B$). This lamp, however, to which the being-lit pertains, is not a lamp to which that being-lit does not pertain: that is to say, it is not a being-a-lamp that is separated from its being-lit and whose meaning is meaningful separately from the meaning of its being-lit. If the meaning of this lamp is meaningful separately from the meaning of its being-lit, then this lamp, insofar as it is thus separately meaningful, is a not-being-lit; as a result, saying that this lamp is lit entails that this being-lit is made to pertain to a lamp that is not a being-lit. If this lamp, to which the being-lit pertains, is meaningful *simply qua* being-this-lamp, i.e. if it is not *at the same time* meaningful as something to which the being-lit pertains – if it is meaningful in its simply being closed within its meaning, rather than in its being open to its predicate – then the predicate comes to pertain to something to which that predicate does not pertain; and, in and through this pertaining, the subject is *simpliciter* something (i.e. the predicate) that it is not.

Saying that this lamp is lit therefore means that the being-lit does not simply pertain to this lamp but to this-lamp-that-is-lit. The predicate pertains to a subject that is open to the predicate and in relation with it. Analogously, it is the predicate *of* the subject that pertains to the subject (that is to say, the being-lit that pertains to this lamp is not simply meaningful as a being-lit that is not the being-lit of this lamp – it is not meaningful separately from the meaning of this lamp – but it is the being-lit-of-this-lamp). It is this-lamp-that-is-lit that is lit – i.e. that is the being-lit-of-this-lamp. Saying is not a synthesis of subject and predicate (namely, the synthesis that continues to play a fundamental role in Western logic even after the integration of attributive logic through the modern logic of relations), but it is the identity between the relation of the 'subject' to the 'predicate' and the relation of the 'predicate' to the 'subject'.

If the semantic element 'this lamp is lit' coincides with the relation between 'subject' and 'predicate' that constitutes itself in the identity between this lamp that is lit and the being-lit of this lamp, and if this semantic element is indicated by the equation $A = B$, the semantic element 'the being lit is of this lamp', *qua* relation between 'predicate' and 'subject' that obtains as part of that identity must be indicated by the equation $B = A$. The language of the West, which is already no longer at ease with the semanteme 'the being lit is of this lamp', then certainly refuses to trace 'the being lit is *of* this lamp' to 'the being lit *is* this lamp', and rejects this latter expression as meaningless. And yet, saying that this lamp is lit means that the brightness in which that being-lit consists is not a generic brightness that is isolated from its specific context, and nor is it a star, an earthly fire, or a lightning, but it is precisely this lamp, this specific visible form that emanates this light. That being-lit is this being-a-lamp (for this lamp is this being-a-lamp), and the predicate 'lit' that pertains to the lamp is a being-lit. Therefore, if it is this-lamp-that-is-lit that is lit – namely, that is the being-lit-of-this-lamp, i.e. that is the being-lit-that-this-lamp-is – this identity between the relation of the 'subject' to the 'predicate' and the relation of the 'predicate' to the 'subject' is expressed by the equation

$$A (= B) = B (= A),$$

which can also be expressed in the form $(A = B) = (B = A)$.

In this expression, the 'equals' sign that links the two equations in parentheses has a different meaning compared to the 'equals' signs that form the two equations. That first 'equals' sign is the originary identity, separately from which the identification of A with B ($A = B$) and of B with A ($B = A$) is a contradictory affirmation of the identity of non-identical elements (A, B). *Isolated* from the originary identity $(A = B) = (B = A)$, the two equations that constitute that identity are contradictions. The identity is *originary* because, if it were the result of a 'movement', it would itself be contradictory. As the result of a 'movement' – which would first lead A to be identified with B, and then to the identification of that first identification with the identification of B with A (this latter identification, insofar as it begins from B, differing from the one that begins from A) – the identity $(A = B) = (B = A)$ would be a contradictory identification of two different contradictions.

What, in traditional philosophical language, is referred to as a 'synthetic proposition' $(A = B)$ is therefore one of the forms of the alienation of truth. When, in the language of the West, one simply says that this lamp is lit, one is not faced with a linguistic simplification that strips the equation down to what is strictly indispensable; one is on the contrary faced with the isolation of $A = B$ from the originary identity $(A = B) = (B = A)$, and, through this isolation, $A = B$ becomes an independent semantic atom that ends up appearing as a contradiction even as part of the very alienation of truth. Moreover, it is not only 'synthetic propositions' that are contradictions but every propositional form ('identical', 'analytic', 'synthetic *a priori*') of the language of the West. Even in stating that this lamp is this lamp ($A = A$) one posits an irreducible difference between the subject and the predicate: precisely because one posits *their* identity (i.e. the identity between *A and* itself) – thus positing, once again, two different elements as being identical.

Once again, however, in the originary structure of Necessity, A, which is A, is not an A that remains separated from A, and that, in its being thus separated, posits itself as that to which being-A pertains: on the contrary, it is to A-that-is-A that being-A pertains, and this latter A is in turn the very being-A of A (i.e. of that first A-that-is-A). Accordingly, the equation $A = A$ is not a contradiction only insofar as it is structured according to the originary identity

$$(A = A) = (A = A),$$

i.e. only insofar as it is not isolated from this identity. The isolation of the subject from its predicate (i.e. the isolation due to which the predicate, in pertaining to that isolated subject, is *in any case* something different that is identified with that from which it differs) is the same isolation of the subject-predicate relation from the originary identity between the subject-predicate relation and the predicate-subject one.

The identity of $A = B$ and $B = A$ has nothing to do with a kind of reversal of the traditional theory of the 'conversion' of propositions. In the originary structure, saying – for instance – that all stars are bright is not equivalent to saying that all instances of bright [*tutti i luminosi*] (all bright things) are stars, but that the bright is all the stars. The bright [*Il luminoso*] (being bright, brightness) is the essence of all bright things insofar as they are bright. Saying that all stars are bright means saying that all stars are the bright, in that they are some of the things that are the bright, and not in that they are all the bright things; i.e. it means saying that all stars are the bright insofar as that bright is their bright, and not insofar as it is the bright of all bright things. Accordingly, saying that the bright is all the stars does not mean saying that the bright is all the stars insofar as it is the essence of all bright things, but insofar as it is the essence of some bright things: i.e. of those that are stars. The bright is the essence of all bright things, but the bright is not all the stars insofar as it is the essence of all bright things, but insofar as it is the essence of some of them. Saying is therefore part of the originary structure insofar as it says that all the stars that are bright are the bright that is all the stars – the expression 'all the stars that are bright' pointing to the opposition between the totality of stars *qua* not isolated from its brightness and the totality of stars *qua* isolated from that brightness, and not to the opposition between bright and non-bright stars.

The isolation of the subject from the predicate of saying is grounded, like every other isolation, in the isolation of the earth from Necessity. The originary isolation of the earth grounds every other isolation as part of the isolated earth. The isolation that constitutes the saying of the West thus finds, as part of its own ground, the isolation that constitutes the nihilism of the West. It is therefore only if a being is isolated from its being and is thus posited as a nothingness that the saying of the West isolates the subject from the predicate: and, therefore, the subject-predicate relation from the originary identity of saying. And it is only if the saying of the West consists of this isolation that beings are isolated from their being and are regarded as a nothingness. This is the case for every saying of the West. Considering, then, that saying of the West that says that *a being is* (= a being exists), in this saying, the isolation of that being from its being (existing) is, on the one hand, the contradictory identification of those different elements that consist of that being and of its 'is' (its existing) (these being different in the same way in which, in 'A is A', A is different from A, or, in 'A is not non-A', A is different from 'not being non-A'); on the other hand, this identification is something that arises, which links elements (a being and its being) that are assumed to be originarily isolated, in such a way that that being, isolated from its being, is a nothingness (i.e. the nothingness that is inadvertently posited as a being by the arising identification), and the being of that being, isolated from the latter, is the being of nothing.

In *The Originary Structure*, it is entirely explicit that the different kinds of propositions, as they appear to the eye of Western thought, are self-contradictory connections – that is, alienations of truth – and that the saying of Necessity has a meaning that differs in an essential way from the one established by the logical thinking of the West. And yet, this book continues to refer to the different ways in which the originary identity of the saying of Necessity structures itself as 'analytic', 'synthetic' and 'synthetic *a priori*' propositions – the difference of these ways being given by the different types of equations that are identified as part of the originary identity (cf. Chapter 3, §§9–14; Chapter 6, §§9–13; Chapter 9, §§15–22; Chapter 13, §§1–7). That is to say, that difference is given by the fact that those equations, *as concretely distinct* from the originary identity of saying, entail that their own negation is, respectively, immediately self-contradictory, not immediately self-contradictory or self-contradictory in a mediated way. *As concretely distinct*, that is to say, *not* as isolated and separated from the originary identity, but regarded in their simple differing from the latter; this is the simple differing, i.e. the concrete distinguishing, by virtue of which, in $(x = y) = (y = x)$, $x = y$ is not $(x = y) = (y = x)$. It is precisely in their being thus concretely distinct that they may be regarded as something whose negation is not immediately self-contradictory. For, if those equations are not considered as to their being concretely distinct, but as to their isolation from the originary identity of saying, then they are immediately self-contradictory regardless of their content. As concretely distinct from the originary identity of saying, these equations do not therefore coincide with that κατάφασις that, according to Aristotle, cannot constitute itself as a part of a λόγος ἀποφαντικός: precisely because that κατάφασις is the equation $x = y$ as separated from the originary identity (i.e. such that in that equation the subject is isolated from the predicate).

The saying of the originary structure, however, is not a self-contradiction not only insofar as the subject of the predication is not isolated from its predicate – and, therefore,

$x = y$ is not isolated from $(x = y) = (y = x)$ – but also insofar as the predications that form the originary structure are not mutually isolated. Their mutual isolation is indeed a saying that once again constitutes itself as an identification of each predication with that *other* of itself that consists in the coexistence of all the other predications of the originary: in such a way that the originary structuring of those predications would constitute the utmost form of identification of the non-identical.

Since the saying of Necessity is the appearing of the identity between that of which something is said and that which is said of it, *being* coincides with this identity. This lamp (which is lit) *is* its being-lit: that is, it *identifies itself* (it has always already and forever identified itself) with its being-lit. The saying of Necessity is the appearing of the *self-being* of what is said. That saying says this self-being also when *being* appears in its 'existential' meaning, 'This lamp *is*'. This latter assertion means 'This lamp is (a) being', namely, 'This lamp is (a) *self-being*'. The self-being of this lamp means the identity between this lamp and its self-identity (in the sense that it is this-lamp-that-is-a-self-being that *is* – i.e. that identifies itself with – its self-being).

Being coincides with self-being; but this self-being coincides with *not being a nothingness*. Saying that this lamp is (i.e. is a self-being) means saying at the same time that this lamp is not a nothingness; that is, *being* is a synthesis of a self-being and of a not being a nothingness. A *being* is the synthesis of *that*, of which it is said that it is, and of its *being*.

As part of the saying of Necessity, the meaning of 'is' (i.e. of self-being) is at the same time copulative and existential. The copulative 'is' is existential, and vice-versa (cf. Chapter 6, §13). The meaning of 'existing' coincides with that of self-being, i.e. with something's staying by itself while always already standing outside of nothingness.

These remarks show the mistake of the theorem formulated in §5 of Chapter 6, according to which 'is' is a *simple* meaning, i.e. a meaning that is not amenable to analysis. It is beyond question that, already in *The Originary Structure*, the 'is' that appears in saying that something is does not only mean the *being* of that something, but also its *not being a nothingness* (= *its being a non-nothingness*); that is, the 'is' is a synthesis of being and of not being a nothingness. The 'being' that appears in this synthesis, however (i.e. the 'is' *qua* element of this synthesis) is precisely regarded as a simple meaning – as that '*absolutely simple*' discussed by Hegel at the beginning of the *Logic*, which is precisely Parmenides' 'being' as understood from Plato to Hegel. In *The Originary Structure* (Chap. 2, §2), that simple is regarded as the 'is' that is said to pertain to every determination, and that is referred to as 'formal being'. As part of that understanding, Parmenides' 'being' can be regarded neither as a subject nor as a predicate. With his 'parricide', Plato posits this 'being' as the predicate of all determinations.

However, precisely insofar as Plato, in the *Sophist*, leaves the enquiry into the meaning of 'being' open, it follows that 'being' itself, in becoming the predicate of all determinations, preserves, as a matter of fact, that character of semantic simplicity that pertains to it when, with Parmenides, it is neither a subject nor a predicate. In thinking 'being' (i.e. the 'is' *qua* 'formal being') as the simple, one remains under the sway of the way in which Plato carries out the parricide. If the parricide is effectively the single step forward taken by Western thinking relative to Parmenides (cf. *The Essence of*

Nihilism), 'being', however, in becoming the predicate of every determination – that is, in becoming, within the testimony of language, what it has always been as part of the structure of Necessity – cannot remain the simple, but it must be the semantic complexity constituted by the *self-being* of identity (which is already a semantic complexity in its distinguishing itself from the meaning of *not being a nothingness*).

It is therefore inevitable that the proof – appearing at the beginning of §5 of Chapter 6 – of the semantic simplicity of this formal being should turn out to be false. It is effectively the case that if 'being' were a complex meaning, the moments of this meaning would themselves have to *be* (for something complex may not consist of something that is not); from this, however, it does not follow that 'the moment would already include what should result from the synthesis with the other moments'. Stating that, of a moment, one must predicate its *being* is not equivalent to stating that the meaning of the predicate should come to be included in the meaning of the moment of which that predicate is predicated.

3. The immediacy of the structure of saying

In *The Originary Structure*, however, the meaning of the expressions 'analytic propositions', 'synthetic propositions' and the like also diverges from that of the philosophical tradition in another respect.

Logical immediacy is the immediacy of the identity/non-contradictoriness of beings *qua beings*; that is to say, of every being: of the totality of beings. Phenomenological immediacy is the immediacy of the appearing of appearing beings *qua appearing beings*; that is to say, of every appearing being: of the totality of appearing beings. The identity/non-contradictoriness *of a specific* being is not therefore necessary insofar as this being is *this* being, but insofar as this being, like every other being, is *a being*. For, otherwise, the identity/non-contradictoriness of another specific being would fail to be necessary. Concerning the appearing of the pertaining of a specific determination (i.e. being) to a certain other one – for instance, concerning the appearing of the pertaining of this being-lit to this lamp – this pertaining is not necessary insofar as this appearing determination is *this* appearing determination, but insofar as this appearing determination, like every other appearing determination, is *an appearing determination*. For, otherwise, the pertaining of a determination to another specific appearing determination would once again fail to be necessary.

This means that what is logically immediate is the identity/non-contradictoriness *of the totality* of beings, and that what is phenomenologically immediate is the appearing *of the totality* of the appearing connections (a connection being precisely the pertaining of a determination to another one). The predications $(A = A) = (A = A)$ and $(A = B) = (B = A)$ – where A and B each indicate a particular being – insofar as they are concretely *distinct* from what is, respectively, logically and phenomenologically immediate (i.e. from the totality of logos and from the totality of appearing), are not something immediate, but something *mediated*: namely, something that is mediated by its belonging to the totality of the immediate (i.e. the totality constituted by the immediate). As distinct from the logically immediate, the predications that, like $(A = A)$

$= (A = A)$, affirm the identity/non-contradictoriness of a specific being do not form a multiplicity of analytic propositions but belong to the set of mediated propositions ('synthetic *a priori* propositions') – the *only* analytic proposition being the one that expresses the logically immediate. In turn, the predications that, like $(A = B) = (B = A)$, as concretely *distinct* from the phenomenological immediate, affirm an appearing connection (among determinations) do not form a multiplicity of synthetic *a posteriori* propositions, but belong (*qua* synthetic *a priori* propositions of a specific kind) to the set of mediated propositions – the *only* synthetic *a posteriori* proposition being the one that expresses the phenomenological immediate. (The logical immediate, *qua* identity/non-contradictoriness of the totality of beings, and the phenomenological immediate – *qua* totality of appearing beings – constitute the ground of all immediate predications by *including* in themselves those predications, for something mediated is part of the totality in that it is distinct from the totality of which it is a part).

Nevertheless, if the predication $(A = A) = (A = A)$ is not regarded as to its being concretely *distinct* from the logical immediate but as to its *being in relation* to the latter – i.e. *as* an individuation of the concrete universality constituted by the logical immediate – then, the very relation of $(A = A) = (A = A)$ to the immediate, which includes both this predication and that immediate, coincides with the immediate itself.[7] In this sense, there exists a multiplicity of analytic propositions: in the sense that the identity/non-contradictoriness of every being, *in its being in relation to the immediate*, coincides with the immediate itself. The inclusion of the identity of A in and by the immediate does not coincide with the latter's inclusion of the identity of B, C ...; it is in this sense that it is possible to talk about a multiplicity of analytic propositions (namely, the identity of A, B, C ...). And yet, in its including the identity of A, the immediate includes the identity of B and of every other being; in its including the identity of B, the immediate includes the identity of A and of every other being; accordingly, the content that is posited in and through this multiplicity of inclusions is *the same*, and it is this same content that constitutes itself as the one analytic proposition.

The same remarks must be extended concerning the predication $(A = B) = (B = A)$, regarded not in its being concretely distinct from the phenomenological immediate, but in its *being in relation* with the latter (that is to say, once again, regarded *as* an individuation of the concrete universality constituted by the totality of the phenomenological immediate). *As part of this relation,* $(A = B) = (B = A)$ coincides with that very immediate, and so does every appearing connection (among determinations). That is to say, as part of its relation with the totality of appearing, every particular appearing connection is that very totality. The relation between an appearing connection and the totality of appearing is distinct from the relation between the other connections and that same totality – and it is in this sense that there exists a multiplicity of synthetic *a posteriori* propositions; and yet, the content that is posited in and through each of these relations is always *the same*, and it is this same content that constitutes itself as the one synthetic *a posteriori* proposition.

If, instead, the predications of the type $(A = A) = (A = A)$ and of the type $(A = B) = (B = A)$ are regarded as to their being isolated from, respectively, the logical and the phenomenological immediate, then, on the one hand, the immediate consists of a totality that is not a totality in that it does not include that part that has been isolated from it, and, on the other hand, the isolated part (i.e. the isolated predication) is a negation of the originary structure of Necessity. Concerning the isolated predications of the type $(A = A) = (A = A)$, this latter assertion is the case because the identity of a particular being (A) may not be posited insofar as every being is identical (for, through this reference to the totality of beings, the condition of the isolation of the identity of A from the totality of the identical would not obtain); therefore, the identity of A must be posited insofar as A is this particular being A, in such a way that the identity of B, C and of every being from which A is isolated is thus ruled out. Analogously, concerning the isolated predications of the type $(A = B) = (B = A)$, the connection between two appearing beings (A, B) may not be posited insofar as it is necessary to posit the totality of the appearing determinations, to the extent that this totality appears (for, once again, the reference to the totality of appearing would rule out the isolation of the connection between A and B); therefore, the connection between A and B must be posited insofar as this appearing connection is this particular connection, in such a way that all other appearing connections – from which the connection between A and B is isolated – are thus negated.

Lastly, if the isolation obtains between logical immediacy and phenomenological immediacy – that is, between the identity/non-contradictoriness of beings and their appearing – then, on the one hand, that isolated identity is the identity of a being whose existence may be negated, for the immediacy of the appearing (Ph-immediacy) of an identical being may not appear within the horizon of an isolated identity (and, since the very identity of a being is a being, the identity of this being may be negated, for the immediacy of the appearing of the being constituted by the very isolated identity of a being does not appear within the isolation of that identity); on the other hand, the isolated appearing of a being is the appearing of a being that may be posited as being different from itself and as being identical to its other, since the immediacy of the identity (L-immediacy) of an appearing being may not appear as part of the isolated appearing of that being (and, since the very appearing of a being is a self-identity, the appearing of a being, *qua* isolated from the identity of that being, may be posited as the non-appearing of that being).

The predication that expresses the concrete relation between logical immediacy and phenomenological immediacy is therefore an expression of the same structuring of the originary as such. This predication is expressed by the following identity, which is in turn structured according to the scheme $(x = y) = (y = x)$:

The L-immediacy of beings (namely, beings in their being immediately self-identical and non-contradictory – this first term corresponding to the first x in the scheme), *which is immediately present (i.e. Ph-immediate)* (this second term corresponding to the first y of the scheme) coincides with *the immediate presence (i.e. the Ph-immediacy)* (this third term corresponding to the second y of the scheme) *of the L-immediacy of beings* (this fourth term corresponding to the second x of the scheme).

Insofar as the relation between L-immediacy and Ph-immediacy obtains in the form of the *identity* between, on the one hand, the synthesis of L-immediacy and Ph-immediacy, and, on the other hand, the synthesis of Ph-immediacy and L-immediacy, L-immediacy, as the immediacy of the identity of beings, is the unity of itself and of Ph-immediacy. (And, in the same way in which, in the originary structure, saying that this lamp is lit means saying that the being-lit is this lamp, saying that identity is present means saying that presence is an identity.) And yet, this unity is the originary structure of Necessity only insofar as it, too, in belonging to the L-immediacy of beings (and in being, in fact, the most concrete expression of that immediacy) *appears*, i.e. it is Ph-immediate: in such a way that the synthesis between L-immediacy and Ph-immediacy does not only exist in the form of an L-immediacy but also in that of an Pḥ-immediacy – these two forms being part of a synthesis, rather than being isolated from one another. That is to say, the synthesis of L-immediacy and Ph-immediacy obtains in the form of the synthesis between L-immediacy and Ph-immediacy. The very equation $(x = y) = (y = x)$ belongs to, and is in fact a concrete expression of, its own element x (the L-immediacy) that, in being y (Ph-immediate), is y (the being Ph-immediate) of x – where the appearing of this equation belongs to the y that is predicated of x.

Or: identity is present; the identity between identity and presence (the identity constituted by the equation $(x = y) = (y = x)$) belongs to an identity that is present, and the presence of the identity between identity and presence belongs to the presence of identity. The synthesis between L-immediacy and Ph-immediacy precisely consists, *qua* originary structure of Necessity, in that whose negation is self-negating – a self-negation whose meaning is explicitly determined in *The Originary Structure*, but which finds its most concrete expression in *The Essence of Nihilism* ('Returning to Parmenides', §6). The equation $(x = y) = (y = x)$ (interpreting again the variables as indicated above) entails that not only is it contradictory that $y = x$ should not pertain to $x = y$, but it is also contradictory that y should not pertain to x (or x to y). It has already been stated that the existence of an identity that is not present may be negated. That is to say, by negating that identity is present it is possible to affirm that there exist no identical beings. Let us then add that, through this negation, one still allows the positing of the nothingness of something that, however, *qua* identical being, is not a nothingness. By negating that the presence of a being coincides with the presence of the identity of that being, the being that is present is precisely posited in its being non-identical: i.e. in its being contradictory. That is to say, in the language of *The Originary Structure*, the identity of L-immediacy and Ph-immediacy is an analytic proposition – and, in fact, *the* analytic proposition in its concreteness.

This is the case even if, in *The Originary Structure*, the nihilism of the conviction that being's issuing from nothingness and returning to it is a content of appearing extends to the very distinction between analytic and synthetic *a posteriori* propositions, i.e. extends to the remove in which this distinction lies relative to the language of the philosophical tradition.

If *every* proposition that belongs to the structure of Necessity is an identity, there is nevertheless a difference between a proposition of the type $(A = A) = (A = A)$ and one of the type $(A = B) = (B = A)$. In *The Originary Structure*, this difference is expressed by stating that while in the first kind of propositions it is not only the non-pertaining of $A = A$ to $A = A$ that is self-contradictory, but also the non-pertaining of A to A, in the second kind of propositions it is only the non-pertaining of $B = A$ to $A = B$ that is self-contradictory, but not the non-pertaining of B to A (or of A to B) (cf. Chapter 6, §11). This means, for instance, that if it is self-contradictory for this-lamp-that-is-lit *not* to be the being-lit-of-this-lamp, it is instead not self-contradictory for this lamp not to be lit – i.e. for A not to be B. A 'synthetic *a posteriori* proposition' is then $(A = B) = (B = A)$ in its being related to the totality of appearing (i.e. in its not being separated from that totality); an 'analytic proposition' is then $(A = A) = (A = A)$ in its being related to the totality-universality of the identity of beings.

Asserting, however, that the negation of $A = B$ is not self-contradictory means asserting that it is not self-contradictory for that non-nothingness constituted by $A = B$ to turn into nothing. *The Originary Structure* explicitly realizes (cf. Chapter 12, §7) that this way of understanding synthetic *a posteriori* propositions indicates a sanctioning of the nothingness of beings – and yet, the outcome of this aporetic situation is determined, in this book, by a redoubling of the meaning of *a posteriori* synthesis, due to which, *on the one hand*, every *a posteriori* synthesis is an eternal, and it is therefore impossible for B not to pertain to A, while, *on the other hand*, it is believed that the annulment of beings appears, and therefore that so does the non-pertaining of B to A (namely, it is believed that, when this lamp is switched off, the no longer existing, i.e. the nothingness, of this-lit-lamp is something that appears).

If the testimony of the originary structure of Necessity frees itself from the nihilism of the conviction of the self-evidence of the nullification of beings, the difference between $(A = A) = (A = A)$ and $(A = B) = (B = A)$ appears according to a different meaning. The synthesis constituted by this lamp that is lit (the synthesis of A and B) is, like every being, an eternal. Not only: the fact that *this* lamp (which is lit) should not (or no longer) be lit is something that already in this book appears as being immediately self-contradictory; that is to say, the being-lit of this lamp necessarily and essentially belongs to the this-ness of this lamp. Therefore, asserting that *this* lamp is lit is an analytic assertion. In this book, the synthesis that is not regarded as being immediately self-contradictory (even though it is considered to be contradicting what appears, to the extent that this lit lamp appears) does not consist in the fact that *this* lamp is not (= is non-)lit, but that *a persistence* of this lamp is not lit: i.e. that what is not lit is *not* this lamp insofar as it is *this* lamp, but insofar as it also *persists* after the situation in which 'it' is lit. This 'it' indicates what is *shared* by this lamp that is lit and by what of that lit lamp persists when that lamp is no longer lit: i.e. what is shared by these two different forms of this-ness. While, in *The Originary Structure*, persistence itself is still one of the categories of nihilism (insofar as, despite holding firmly that every being is eternal, that persistence is at the same time conceived of as the residue of an annihilation of beings), outside of nihilism, persistence consists in the gradual appearing of the different forms of this-ness that are united by a shared element – each of these forms of this-ness being itself an eternal. Persisting does not mean continuing to be part of being through a process of annihilation of what does not persist; persisting means continuing to be part of appearing through the process of the arising, as part of appearing, of what does not persist (i.e. the arising of the forms of this-ness that gradually appear).

This meaning of persistence, however, is not contradictory only if the synthesis beyond which what persists persists is not of the type $(A = A) = (A = A)$ but of the type $(A = B) = (B = A)$. The concept of a being that, while persisting, should no longer be identical to itself or no longer other than its other is immediately self-contradictory; on the contrary, the concept of a persistence of A (call this A') beyond the synthesis

$(A = B) = (B = A)$ – a concept of persistence as part of which the synthesis $(A'=$ non-$B) = ($non-$B = A')$ should come to appear – is not immediately self-contradictory (A', in this example, being this lamp insofar as it is not lit, i.e. insofar as it is non-B). In other words, this lamp that is lit – namely, $(A = B) = (B = A)$ – is an eternal being; however, the existence of that other eternal being that consists of this lamp that is not lit – i.e. which is $(A'=$ non-$B) = ($non-$B = A')$ – is not immediately self-contradictory; and, in fact, not only is the existence of that other eternal being not immediately self-contradictory, but it has itself come to be part of the appearing content, following the appearing of $(A = B) = (B = A)$.

4. Dialectic

The meaning of 'dialectic', too, and of the relation between the 'concrete' and the 'abstract', is expressed in *The Originary Structure* through a language that, starting to speak the language of the testimony of Necessity, moves that meaning towards an overcoming of the dominant thinking of the West. The possibility of a misconception, however, is here all the greater since the way in which the meaning of dialectic and of the relation between the concrete and the abstract appears in this book is strictly connected to the interpretation that this book gives of Hegel's dialectical method – an interpretation that, more generally, is an aspect of the overall stance taken by *The Originary Structure* towards Western philosophical thought. The language of this book begins to testify to what can in no way be traced back to Western thought – that is, Necessity, in the gaze of which the alienation of the West comes to appear – and yet, despite this, that thought continues to be regarded, as a whole, as something that can successfully be reconciled with the authentic meaning of the originary structure. That is to say, that thought continues to be regarded as a content that foreshadows, even if in an inadequate way, the fundamental elements of that structure, and the inadequacy of this foreshadowing, despite its depth, is nevertheless not regarded as a symptom of the erring that belongs to the alienated essence of Western thought, but only as the symptom of an inability to coherently and rigorously unfold the positive character and truth of that thought.

In its essential meaning, the 'concrete' is the very structuring of the originary: namely, that unification of the elements of the originary by virtue of which the negation of the originary is self-negating; the 'abstract' is a particular component or element of that structure (for instance, a particular predication or a non-predicative content such as this lamp). Necessity is precisely the originary structure *qua* structure of a content whose negation is originarily self-negating. As part of nihilism and the isolation of the earth, 'necessity' is instead (in its different historical forms) that form of will to power that wills to dominate the becoming (i.e. the issuing from nothingness and returning to it) of beings – a form of will to power that is destined to be overthrown by the faith in the unpredictable novelty of becoming.

The originary structure is the originarily necessary connection that links the determinations of the originary. This connection is an organism of predications that is unified by the predication that affirms the identity of L-immediacy and Ph-immediacy.

In the language of this book, the 'concrete concept of the abstract' is the appearing of a particular determination (i.e. a particular element) of the originary as a determination that, while being distinct from the other determinations of the originary, is nevertheless necessarily linked to them. The concrete concept of the abstract is therefore the very originary structure in its being determinately related to its constituting elements. The 'abstract concept of the abstract' is the appearing of a particular determination of the originary as a determination that is not only distinct from the other determinations of the originary but that is also separated from them. Every negation of the originary is an abstract concept of the abstract, since every negation is a particular determination of the originary that is separated from the necessary relation that links it, *qua* negated, to the originary structure. Every abstract concept of the abstract is a negation of the originary precisely insofar as it is – explicitly or implicitly – a negation of the necessary connection in which the originary structure consists. Since the originary structure is the structure of Necessity only insofar as it is a negation of its own negation, the originary structure is the concrete concept in its negating the abstract concept of the abstract – and, therefore, the present and possible totality of the abstract concepts of the abstract.

However, precisely insofar as the abstract concept of the abstract is a negation of the originary structure – in that it is a negation of the necessary connection between the abstract and the originary concrete – that concept is for that very reason a negation of L-immediacy: i.e. it is a self-contradictory affirmation, a contradiction. The necessary connection between the abstract and the originary concrete *constitutes* the meaning of the abstract as such – i.e. of the abstract *qua* distinct determination. The abstract (every abstract) is the meaning that it is – it consists in the meaning in which it consists – precisely insofar as it is necessarily connected to the originary concrete. It is precisely the *necessity* of this connection that constitutes the meaning of the abstract. If that connection were accidental, the meaning of the abstract would be indifferent to it. This means that the meaning of the abstract, in its being part of that necessary connection, *differs* from the meaning of the abstract, in its not being part of that connection. If A is the meaning of an abstract determination in its concrete appearing as a determination that is distinct from and at the same necessarily connected to the originary, outside of this connection A is not A, and it is not meaningful as A: that is to say, what is A as part of the connection is non-A – it is meaningful as non-A – outside of the connection.

A's standing outside of that connection, however – precisely because that connection is necessary – constitutes the meaning of impossibility. What is impossible is precisely a content that is affirmed in and through an abstract concept of the abstract. This concept does not affirm that what is A as part of the necessary connection is non-A outside of that connection (this affirmation being not a negation of the originary structure, but the concrete concept itself, the truth of what it means for what is part of that necessary connection to stand outside of that very connection); nor does that concept assert that this being necessarily connected to the originary – which, instead, in its specificity, pertains to A – does not pertain to non-A (this affirmation, too, belonging to the concrete concept of this non-A, for the latter is what is effectively posited as part of the concept that aims to posit A as independent of any of its connections with its other;

therefore, that specific being necessarily connected to the originary, which instead pertains to A, may not pertain to non-A).

The abstract concept of the abstract is a negation of L-immediacy insofar as it affirms that A is A – i.e. that A is meaningful as A – independently of any connection between A and its other (i.e. insofar as, in that concept, A appears as not being thus necessarily connected – the positing of A's semantic dependence on that connection precisely consisting in the positing of the necessity of that connection). The abstract concept of the abstract refers indeed to the abstract – i.e. to a delimited determination of the originary – in its appearing as a determination that is what it is *insofar as it is necessarily connected to the originary*. The abstract, referred to by the abstract concept of the abstract (the abstract A in the example), is an abstract that is meaningful as part of a *concrete* concept of the abstract: that is, it is an abstract that appears as being necessarily connected to the originary. The abstract that is enclosed by the isolating mesh of the abstract concept of the abstract is a segment of the originary insofar as the latter is concretely structured in its originarity. This segment (A) may therefore appear as part of the abstract concept of the abstract only insofar as that structuring appears – that is, only to the extent that the concrete concept of the abstract appears: namely, only insofar as the originary structure appears. *It is of this segment (A)* that the abstract concept affirms that its being meaningful in the way it is meaningful (i.e. its being meaningful as A) is independent of any connections to its other.

What is *in truth* affirmed in affirming that A is A independently of the connection of A to its other is therefore that A is non-A: precisely because what is meaningful as A as part of that necessary connection is meaningful as non-A outside of that connection, in such a way that what the abstract concept in truth predicates of A is not A, but non-A. What appears *in truth* as part of the abstract concept of the abstract is the being non-A of A, even though the abstract concept posits this as the being A of A. The contradictory character of the abstract concept appears *as such* only as part of the concrete concept of the abstract (for, within the abstract concept, this contradictory character appears, but not as such, but precisely in the form of the self-identity of A). The abstract concept of the abstract identifies A (*qua* determination that is necessarily connected to the originary) to an 'A' that, regarded as being independent of its connection to the originary, is in truth a non-A; the abstract concept thus identifies this non-A (which consists of what is in truth posited if A is regarded as being independent of its originary connection with the originary) with A (*qua* determination that is concretely connected to the originary). This identification is possible – that is, the abstract concept is possible – only if within the abstract concept *both* of the identified terms appear: that is, only if as part of that concept there appears the very originary structure from which the abstract concept isolates the abstract (i.e. the originary structuring of A that constitutes the necessary connection of A to the originary).

Were the abstract A that is considered by the *abstract* concept not the abstract A as a *concretely* conceived determination, that abstract would be an 'A' that differs from A (i.e. from A *qua* determination thus concretely conceived): that is to say, it would be an 'A' that constitutes itself outside of the necessary connection to the originary that makes A into a concretely conceived determination – and, therefore, it would be a non-A. Accordingly, the identification of this 'A' with that non-A would not be a contradictory affirmation, but an identification of non-A with non-A; that is to say, that identification would not constitute the abstract concept of the abstract, but the necessary affirmation of the self-identity of what is in truth posited when A is separated from the originary.

As part of the abstract concept of the abstract, the non-A that is identified with A does not appear *as* a non-A, of which it is affirmed that it is A, but *as* an A, of which it is affirmed that it is A. As separated from every relation, A is necessarily (i.e. within the concrete concept of the abstract) non-A. This does not mean that, in and through the separation of A, something like A effectively succeeds in constituting itself, and that this A, having thus constituted itself, is then recognized as a non-A. Through the separation of A from every relation, something like A does not effectively succeed in constituting itself; that is to say, the concept of such a separation is self-contradictory – and it precisely consists in the abstract concept of the abstract, which attributes to A a predicate (its being separated from every relation) whose pertaining to A is impossible (it is impossible that this predicate should pertain to A because A is A only as part of the necessary relation of A to the originary totality of the concrete).

The abstract concept of A, however, precisely because it attributes that predicate to A necessarily constitutes the appearing of A: i.e. it constitutes the appearing of that concrete meaning of A relative to which that predicate is an impossible predicate. The separation of A is the impossible, the non-existent, but the abstract concept of this separation necessarily implies that concrete concept of A – i.e. the appearing of that necessary relation between A and the originary concrete – from which the abstract concept of A separates A itself (i.e. within which the abstract concept conceives of A as being thus separated). The separation of A is the impossible: within the abstract concept of A, however, the appearing of this separation consists, on the one hand, in the appearing of the concrete meaning of A (i.e. the appearing of the meaning relative to which that separation is an impossible predicate), and, on the other hand, precisely in the appearing of A in its being thus separated – whereby, thus separated, A is not A: it is non-A. As part of that abstract concept, a predicate (i.e. that separation) comes to be attributed to A (which appears in its being A, i.e. in its concrete meaning); relative to that predicate, however, the subject of the predication is not, in truth, A, but non-A. A is thus identified with non-A.

On the one hand, however, this abstract concept – while still necessarily implying the appearing of the concrete meaning of A, i.e. while still implying the appearing of the originary structure of Necessity – regards the originary structure as a nothingness (i.e. insofar as it affirms the independence of A from every relation, it regards as a nothingness the originary structure as such – namely, the originary structure *qua* ground of which A may not be independent); as a result, the concrete meaning of A appears in that abstract concept, but not *as* a concrete meaning. On the other hand, the abstract concept of A – insofar as it constitutes the appearing of A in its being separated, i.e. insofar as it necessarily constitutes the appearing of a non-A – is an appearing as part of which non-A does not appear *as* non-A, but *as* A: precisely as the A of which the abstract concept predicates a separation. (For, indeed, non-A appears as non-A as part of the concrete concept of the abstract concept of A: i.e. as part of the concrete concept in which there appears the necessity for A, as separated, to be non-*A*. 'As separated' means exactly 'as non-*A*': precisely because the necessity of the connection of which *A* is part necessarily entails that *A* is *A* only as part of that connection, and that, if separated from it, *A* is in truth non-*A* – namely, it entails that the separation is in truth a contradiction.)

And yet, if affirming that *A* is separated – if the abstract concept of *A*, in which *A* appears as being separated – necessarily entails that what the separation is predicated of is not *A*, but a non-*A* (i.e. if the fact that *A*, as separated, is a non-*A* belongs to the originary structure of Necessity), for that structure it still remains a *problem* what the *determinate meaning* of the non-*A* that effectively appears is. This determinate meaning of non-*A* effectively appears in the abstract concept of *A*, but the originary structure is not yet able to identify it. (*To the eye* of that abstract concept, the non-*A* that effectively appears appears as *A*; however, the non-*A* that effectively or necessarily appears *as part of* that abstract concept cannot even appear *as* non-*A*, for the appearing of non-*A* as such entails the appearing of *A* – i.e. the appearing of *A* as a concrete meaning – and *A*, as a concrete meaning, only appears in and through its necessary connection to the originary concrete, and not insofar as a separation is predicated of it: i.e. insofar as it is a non-*A*. For this reason, too, the non-*A* that is effectively posited in and through the abstract concept of *A* appears as a non-*A* – whose determination remains, however, a problem – only as part of the concrete concept of the abstract concept of *A*.) This problematic character of non-*A* is expressed in *The Originary Structure* in stating that the 'outcome' of the abstract concept of the abstract (the 'outcome': i.e. what is in truth posited in and through that concept) is a 'contradictory' of that abstract – but, precisely, it remains undetermined if that contradictory is a 'contrary' of *A*, or simply something that differs from *A*, or, even, nothing (in this last case, the abstract concept of the abstract coming to constitute itself as the identification of the abstract and nothingness).

In *The Originary Structure*, 'dialectic' is, in its central meaning, the relation between the concrete concept of the abstract and the abstract concept of the abstract – the relation by virtue of which the originarity of that concrete concept is a negation of the contradictory character of the abstract concept of the abstract. The necessary connection in accordance with which the originary is structured is necessary precisely insofar as it is a negation of the contradiction (i.e. of the negation of the L-immediacy) determined by the isolation in which the abstract concept confines the elements of the originary. In the language of *The Originary Structure*, 'dialectic' is the negation of this contradiction, and this contradiction (namely, the identification of the abstract and its contradictory, i.e. the identification of *A* and non-*A*) is a 'dialectical contradiction'.

5. *The Originary Structure* and the Hegelian dialectic

The Originary Structure strives to trace back to a 'dialectic' understood in this way what it regards as the essence of the Hegelian dialectical method: i.e. of the dialectical method as a semantic theory – as the most radical attempt in the history of Western thought to ground the inseparability of the opposites. The 'limits of Hegel's contribution' are certainly explicitly identified (cf. Chapter 9, §§10–11) – and in an analytic context that has been barely touched upon in this Introduction; moreover, Hegel's text is of interest essentially for theoretical purposes, rather than for a historical investigation. In its essence, even if not explicitly, *The Originary Structure* (cf. Chapter 9, §10, a) also anticipates the fundamental critical remark that in *Essenza del Nichilismo* ('Risposta alla Chiesa', VI)[8] and in *Gli abitatori del tempo* ('Tramonto del marxismo', 3) is addressed to the dialectical method *qua* semantic theory: namely, that it implicitly *presupposes* that necessary connection between the opposites, which instead appears in the concept of that method as a *result* – i.e. as the unity of the opposites in which the dialectical contradiction results. Accordingly, that unity of opposites, which *in actu signato* results from the superseding of the contradiction – and which, therefore, does *not* coincide with the originary – serves instead *in actu exercito* as the very originary whose violation by the abstract understanding determines the dialectical contradiction. Therefore, if the fundamental aim of the Hegelian dialectical method, *qua* semantic theory, is to ground the necessary connection between determinations – namely, the necessary connection that constitutes the essence of the ἐπιστήμη – this grounding is reduced to a *petitio principii*: precisely in that the necessary connection that appears as a superseding of the dialectical contradiction, and that is therefore a result, is at the same time the originary whose violation by the isolating and separating understanding causes that contradiction, in such a way that the constitution of the latter remains groundless. As part of the Hegelian attempt at grounding the necessary connection of the opposites, the ἐπιστήμη, *qua* fundamental immutable – *qua* god of the gods of the West – makes the greatest attempt at dominating becoming and not being overthrown by it. These consequences are not yet unfolded in *The Originary Structure*, but it is completely explicit, on the one hand, that the separation of the determinations from the originary (i.e. that the abstract concept of the abstract) is contradictory only if the necessary connection coincides with the originary itself, and, on the other hand, that in the Hegelian dialectical method this necessary connection does not coincide with the originary, but it is a result: it is something mediated.

And yet, what remains altogether unsaid within the language of *The Originary Structure* is that the meaning of 'dialectic' in this book aims at something that is radically different from the essence of the Hegelian dialectical method. This latter method is certainly a semantic theory, but it is a theory of meaning conceived of as *becoming* (i.e. as an issuing from nothingness and a returning to it); in *The Originary Structure*, 'dialectic' is indeed accompanied by the nihilism of the faith in the self-evidence of becoming, but this conviction accompanies it externally: it does not determine its constitution. That is to say, in its essence, 'dialectic' is the structure that pertains to meaning *qua* being that is and for which it is impossible not to be.

The Hegelian dialectical method aims to constitute the essential determination of beings *qua* beings: i.e. of meaning *qua* meaning. It is 'the absolutely infinite force [*die schlechthin unendliche Kraft*], to which no object [*kein Objekt*], presenting itself as something external, remote from and independent of reason, could offer resistance or be of a particular nature in opposition to it, or could not be penetrated by it'. This 'absolutely infinite force' is 'the movement of the Concept', granted that Hegelian idealism thinks that 'the Concept is everything [*der Begriff alles*], and its movement is the universal absolute activity [*die allgemeine absolute Tätigkeit*], the self-determining and self-realizing movement [*die selbst bestimmende und selbst realisierende Bewegung*]' (*Science of Logic*, III, Section Three, Chapter 3). The 'movement of the Concept' is the essence of beings *qua* beings. The claim that movement should be the essence of beings is not an assertion that Western thought (above all as part of the self-transparency that obtains with Hegel's philosophy) feels the necessity to ground in a more originary form of self-evidence: the originary self-evidence is precisely that beings, in their essence, are movement. Idealism, *qua* recognition of the impossibility for beings to be something external to thought, then establishes the identity between beings and the Concept, and the method is therefore not a 'merely external form' (*ibid.*) to beings but coincides with their very essential processual nature (*pro-cedere* = μέθ-οδος).

Movement, however, is such only insofar as there exists a beginning that, as such, differs from the result of that movement, and is therefore 'only a moment' (*ibid.*). Insofar as it differs from that result, this beginning is 'deficient' (it is what is 'in its own self deficient', *ibid.*); however, *qua* beginning of the movement that produces that result – namely, *qua* beginning of the production of that result (i.e of the 'realisation of the Concept') – that beginning is already 'in itself' that result: it 'is *in itself* the *concrete totality*, though that totality is not yet *posited*, is not yet *for itself*' (*ibid.*). It is therefore the 'universal' and the 'simple'. Precisely because the beginning is an '*in-itself*' that is without a *being-for-self*, 'this *in-itself* is only an abstract, one-sided moment'. The beginning for-itself, the 'advance' [*Fortgang*] beyond the beginning, is therefore not 'a kind of superfluity', but the accomplishment of something deficient.

Precisely because, as part of the beginning, the result is only something in itself, as part of that beginning the being-for-itself of the result is, *qua* being-for-itself, still a nothingness. This does not mean that the beginning is nothing and that the result is not, in itself, already in the beginning; rather, it means that, as part of the beginning (which is not a nothingness, but it is in itself already the result), the being-for-itself of the result, *qua* being-for-itself, is still a nothingness. (In the same way, in Aristotelian ontology, the beginning of becoming is not a pure nothingness, but it is the potentiality for a being – as part of which the result, i.e. the actual being, is already 'in itself'; and yet, as part of the potentiality for that being, the actuality of the result is, *qua* actuality, still a pure nothingness.) The advance beyond the universality of the beginning is certainly a determination of the universal, which is in fact a *self*-determination of the universal (i.e. a determination of the universal does not arise within the universal as something external: 'The essential point is that the absolute method finds and cognises the *determination* of the universal within the universal itself', *ibid.*); accordingly, the method is 'analytic'. The determination of the universal, however, (the 'further' determination, *die weitere Bestimmung*, relative to the immediate determination of the universal *qua* beginning and simple universality) – a determination that the method 'finds' within the universal itself – is 'an other' [*ein Anderes*] of the universal itself: that is to say, the beginning, 'as a simple universal', in its determining its own immediate simple universality, 'exhibits itself as an *other* [*als ein* Anderes *sich zeigt*]'; it appears as something other than its own immediate simple universality, and the method is therefore 'no less synthetic'. 'This no less synthetic than analytic moment of the *judgement* [the judgement being precisely the "process of determining in general", "the emergence of real difference", *das Hervortreten der Differenz*, relative to the beginning], by which the universal of the beginning of its own accord determines itself as the *other of itself* [*aus him selbst als das Andere seiner sich bestimmit*], is to be named the *dialectical* moment' (*ibid.*). As part of this determining itself as something other than itself, the method, *qua* 'immanent principle' of what is being determined, finds the other of the beginning within the beginning itself ('takes the determinate element from its own subject matter'); it can find it, however, only as something in itself, for, otherwise – namely, if it were to find it as something for itself, and not only in itself – the beginning would not be 'the beginning of the advance and development [*der Anfang des Fortgehens und der Entwicklung*]' – i.e. the beginning of the 'emergence of real difference' (this difference being precisely the other of the beginning) – but it would have already advanced beyond and developed into that difference. That is to say, the method is analytic in a different way than it is synthetic. The fact that the other of the beginning is only in itself within the beginning means that, *as part of the beginning*, that other, *qua* other – *qua* determination introduced by that advancing and developing, and *qua* difference that has emerged – is still a nothingness. That advancing beyond the beginning is the very issuing from its own nothingness of the other of the beginning *qua* difference that has emerged: i.e. it is the very issuing of that other from its own having been a nothingness.

Precisely because the method is the 'movement of the Concept'; however, the beginning is the beginning of the Concept: that is to say, it is not something that exists outside of the Concept. When the Hegelian text remarks that 'what is in-itself is the Concept' (*ibid.*), this remark has nothing to do with the assertion that the being-in-itself of the beginning is something that has not been cognized yet, and that this cognizing is only produced through the result of that movement – i.e. with the becoming for-itself of Concept – but it rather means that, within the beginning, cognizing does indeed cognize the Concept, but does not yet cognize it *as* the Concept, but as a content that is still only 'the immediacy of the universal', and that is therefore 'only an abstract, one-sided moment'. In the preliminary exposition of the method (i.e. of the 'logical' – *das Logische*), included in §§79–82 of the *Encyclopaedia*, the 'abstract, one-sided moment' of the being-in-itself of the beginning is qualified as the 'moment' or 'the side of abstraction or of the understanding' (§79). That is to say, the being-in-itself of the beginning is a cognizing or thinking *qua* understanding: *das Denken als Verstand* (§80). 'Thinking, as understanding, stops short [*bleibt… stehen*] at [*bei*] the fixed [*festen*] determination and its distinctness vis-à-vis other determinations' (§80). This 'determination' and this 'distinctness' are to be understood as a determination and a distinctness *in-themselves* (they are 'the Concept that is still indeterminate, i.e. determined only in itself or immediately', *Encyclopaedia*, §238), and they therefore constitute the immediacy of the simple (or relatively simple) universal of the beginning. That 'stopping short' of the understanding and that 'fixity' of the determination in itself are correlated: the understanding stops short at the determination because it is fixed, and that determination is fixed because the understanding stops short at it. It is by virtue of this correlation that the Hegelian method is, at the same time, the content of a theory of becoming and of a semantic theory.

The determination in itself is 'fixed', or 'firm', precisely because it is the beginning of a movement: it is possible to 'advance' only if that beyond which one advances succeeds first of all in standing and remaining firmly by its own self. That movement is, precisely, a negation and an overcoming of this initial fixity; the latter precisely exists in order to be negated. But if the latter does not exist at all, nor does the movement of its negation. However, precisely because the fixity of the beginning exists in order to be negated by that movement, the negation of the beginning does not appear as part of the beginning as such, and that 'abstract, one-sided moment', 'this restricted abstraction, counts for the understanding as one that is and subsists on its own account' (*Encyclopaedia*, §80). Relative to the entire movement of the Concept (which consists in the becoming for-itself of the concrete totality in-itself), the beginning is an abstract moment that is inevitably isolated from the totality of the movement. This isolation is precisely the 'stopping short' of the understanding at the fixed determination of the beginning. The understanding stops short at the fixity of the beginning because the difference produced by the advancing beyond the beginning has not yet appeared.

The fundamental meaning of the dialectical method is therefore to be expressed as follows: *since* the abstract, i.e. the isolation of the abstract by the understanding, constitutes the beginning of the movement of the Concept, it follows *for this reason* that the abstract, advancing beyond itself, 'exhibits itself as its own other'. Or: *since* the abstract – the 'universal of the beginning' – is the beginning of the movement, it follows *for this reason* that, in moving itself, 'the universal of the beginning of its own accord determines itself as the other of itself' (*Science of Logic*, ibid.). Or: *it is because* the understanding that isolates the abstract constitutes the beginning of becoming that, *precisely for this reason*, the abstract is a 'self-sublation' [*das eigene Sichaufheben*] and a 'passing [*übergehen*] into its opposite' (*Encyclopaedia*, §81). *It is because* the abstract constitutes the beginning of becoming that *it* becomes something other than itself – and, in becoming this other of itself, *is* this other of itself: i.e. it is a 'dialectical contradiction'. *It is because* the abstract constitutes a beginning that the isolation of the determination, operated by the understanding, *produces* the dialectical contradiction – as part of which the determination (i.e. the universal of the beginning), in advancing beyond itself, 'exhibits itself as its own other'. Becoming is the ground of the ensuing of the contradiction of the abstract. (That is to say, the positing of the existence of becoming is the ground of the positing of the contradiction of the abstract.)

Positing becoming as ground means positing becoming as the very originary self-evidence. Becoming is the originary self-evidence of the West, and it is as such that it is testified to by the great thinkers of the West. In asserting that 'no object [...] could offer resistance' to the 'absolutely infinite force' of the method and 'could not be penetrated by it' – and that everything 'is completely subjugated to the method', because the method is the 'soul and substance' of everything (*Logic*, ibid.) – Hegel does not formulate a theorem that is open to receiving its ground from elsewhere, but he expresses the fundamental faith of the West: namely, the belief that the essence of beings *qua* beings coincides with that method, *i.e.* with becoming itself.

This faith still constitutes that ground even when Hegel attempts to present the becoming of beings as a *necessity*, rather than as a simple *fact*. It is precisely as part of this attempt, however, that the Hegelian dialectical method comes to appear as a theory of meaning that leaves behind, or only in the background, a meaning of method *qua* becoming; and it is to this aspect of the Hegelian dialectical method that *The Originary*

Structure turns as to a conceptual material that – even if radically reconsidered – may be traced back to the relation between the concrete and the abstract, as this is constituted in and as the originary structure of Necessity. The conviction that the becoming of beings *qua* beings constitutes the ground and the originary form of self-evidence holds sway in Hegel's language, too; this dominant conviction, however, tends to remain implicit. That is to say, the connection that we have emphasized above tends to remain implicit: namely, that *it is because* the isolation of the abstract by the understanding constitutes the beginning of becoming that the abstract, thus isolated, contradicts itself, and becomes. This other connection tends instead to come to the fore in the Hegelian text: that *it is because the abstract is isolated by the understanding that the abstract contradicts itself and becomes*.

In the first case, it is simply asserted that the beginning of becoming develops into becoming itself, *qua* becoming – this assertion expressing simply the structure of becoming. In the second case, instead, the contradiction and the becoming of the abstract are presented as a necessary consequence of the isolation of the abstract. The aim is here to present becoming and the contradiction not as a fact or a presupposition but as a necessary determination of the abstract: as a determination that the abstract has in and of itself: 'That is what everything finite is [the finite coinciding precisely with the abstract]: its own sublation' (*Enciclopaedia*, §81). Here, the finite is not self-sublating insofar as it is, precisely, the beginning of its own sublation, but insofar as the finite is finite. *Once the initial abstract of the beginning has been posited*, 'the system of concepts as such has to [… *hat… zu*…] be formed – and has to complete itself in a purely continuous course in which nothing extraneous is introduced' (*Logic*, Introduction). The purity of that 'course' consists in letting the initial abstract necessarily develop itself *by itself*. The ground of the ensuing of the dialectical contradiction is not here indicated by the factual existence of becoming but by the abstract character of the finite.

What is particularly explicit in the configuration of this second stance of the Hegelian text is the way in which, in the last chapter of the *Logic*, Hegel clarifies that 'the immediate of the beginning must be *in its own self* deficient and endowed with the *urge* to carry itself further [*sich weiter zu führen*]' (*Logic*, ibid.). Insofar as the method posits itself 'as the consciousness of the Concept', i.e. as the consciousness of the Concept in its movement, within this consciousness it appears that the beginning is only a simple universal, and that it is therefore 'deficient'; that is to say, it appears that 'the universality is only a moment, and that, in it, the Concept is not yet determined in and for itself'. As part of the consciousness of becoming, it thus appears that the beginning is only a moment of becoming – a moment that, on the one hand, is deficient in relation to the result of becoming (i.e. the Concept in its being determined in and for itself), and that, on the other hand, *qua* beginning of becoming, possesses an urge to carry itself further. This 'consciousness' of becoming (which is the self-consciousness of the method – the consciousness that becoming has of itself) is the very originary self-evidence of Western thought. *Except that* the Hegelian text continues in the following way: 'But with this consciousness that would carry the beginning further only for the sake of the method [*das den Anfang nur um der Methode willen weiter führen wollte*], the method would be a formal affair, something posited in external reflection. Since, however, it is the objective immanent form, the immediate of the beginning must be *in its own self* [*an ihm selbst*] deficient and endowed with the *urge* to carry itself further.'

That is to say: it is not on the grounds of the consciousness of becoming that the beginning appears as a carrying itself forward, but it is the very immediate content of the beginning that is *in its own self* an urge to carry itself forward. It is not because the abstract ('the immediate of the beginning') appears as the beginning of an advancing that it is possible to affirm the advancing of the abstract; it is rather because the abstract is abstract, i.e. by virtue of what it is 'in its own self', that it advances beyond itself. In the first case, the abstract would be carried forth (i.e. it may be posited as an advancing) by an 'external reflection' – namely, by the consciousness of becoming, which is 'external' to the beginning of becoming – and the method would only be something formal. It is instead only in the second case that the method constitutes itself as a form that is immanent to the beginning.

The interpretation given above of the Hegelian dialectical method *as an expression of becoming*, i.e. as consciousness of becoming, thus holds the Hegelian method at a level at which it explicitly does not intend to position itself – namely, at a level at which it merely consists of an 'external reflection'. However, it is precisely to the extent that the Hegelian method does not intend to remain at that level that it appears as a theoretical apparatus that is significantly inadequate with respect to its own intentions. The main structure of this apparatus may be indicated in the following way (as already outlined at the beginning of this section).

The dialectical method, as a will for becoming and the contradiction to originate from the abstract as such (i.e. from the isolation of the determination), appears as the essence of the last grand form of the ἐπιστήμη of Western thought – namely, as the positing of the *necessary connection* of the determinations of the *world* (i.e. of reality itself insofar as it primarily manifests itself as becoming). Precisely because the finite sublates itself, dialectic is 'the principle through which alone *necessity* and the *immanent connection* enter into the content of science' (*Encyclopaedia*, §81). The self-sublation of the finite (i.e. of the abstract determination) – namely, its determining itself 'of its own accord as the other of itself' – does not indeed aim to present the simple *factum* of becoming, but to constitute the contradiction that is *necessarily* produced by the isolation of a determination from the other determinations (i.e. from its opposite). The superseding of a contradiction is the superseding of what produces that contradiction: that is to say, it is the superseding of the isolation of the determination. If the contradiction is given by the determination that, in its being isolated, appears as something other than itself, the contradiction is superseded only if that other develops, in turn, into its own other, and itself appears as 'the other of the other' and 'negation of the negation'. That is to say, the contradiction is superseded only if the determination that has appeared as being something other than itself appears as being the other of its other, and the negation of its negation. As part of the superseding of the contradiction, the appearing of the determination as the negation of its negation means that the superseding of the contradiction is a superseding of the isolation of the determination: namely, it is a positing of the necessary unity of the determination and its opposite (i.e. its negation), insofar as the determination, *qua* negation of its negation, is no longer isolated from its negation – granted that that from which the determination is isolated is precisely its negation (i.e. its other).

As part of the contradiction, in which the determination appears as its own other, there precisely appears that very other from which the determination has been isolated; that is to say, as part of the contradiction, the unity of the determination with its other is already established. This unity, however, is precisely established as a contradiction: i.e. in the form of 'untruth'. 'The first two moments of the triplicity are *abstract*, untrue moments [*die abstrakten, unwahren Momente*], which for that very reason [*die eben darum*] are dialectical' (*Logic*, ibid.). The unity of the determination and its other – the unity of the opposites – must therefore realize itself in the form of truth: that is to say, in the form of the superseding of the contradiction. 'This result is therefore the truth [*Dies Resultat ist daher die Wahrheit*]' (ibid.). Precisely for this reason, this result includes 'the unity of the determinations in their opposition', and it is 'the *affirmative* that is contained in their dissolution and in their transition' (*Encyclopaedia*, §82). What is affirmative in their dissolution and in their transition, i.e. in their advancing, is precisely the superseding of the contradiction encountered at first by that advance – i.e. the contradiction that precisely constitutes what is *negative* in the advance of the determination. The result of the method – the unity of the opposites – *qua* superseding of the necessary self-contradiction of the isolated determination, constitutes the *necessary* connection between the determinations.

According to this structure, the Hegelian dialectical method is, at the same time, a theory of meaning and a theory of becoming: a theory of meaning *qua* becoming. As a theory of meaning, it essentially consists in the principle according to which an isolated meaning (i.e. a determination, the abstract) is meaningful as what is other than itself, and this contradiction is superseded by superseding the isolation between that meaning and its other. This is the aspect of the Hegelian method that is continuously addressed in *The Originary Structure*. In *Gli abitatori del tempo*, too, the analysis addresses for the most part this aspect of the dialectical method. In *The Originary Structure*, however, this aspect of the dialectical method is isolated from its other aspect (namely, its being a theory of becoming), and the Hegelian dialectic thus appears as something that, albeit through a radical rethinking, may be retraced to the meaning that dialectic has as part of the originary structure of Necessity.

First of all, the method must be turned on its head: namely, the necessary connection between determinations must not be a result, but the originary itself. Only in this way can the isolation of the determination be the ground of the arising of the dialectical contradiction, and only in this way can that contradiction succeed in freeing itself from the presuppositional character that it instead possesses in the Hegelian text. (This reversal has nothing in common with Marx's reversal of Hegel's dialectic, which aims to 'turn it on its head in order to discover the rational kernel within the mystical shell'. It is effectively the case that, in Marx's writings, that necessary connection actually appears as an originary whose violation produces a dialectical contradiction, and not as the result of the supersession of the contradiction – cf. *Gli abitatori del tempo*, 'Tramonto del marxismo', 2. According to Marx, however – and to the entirety of Western thought – 'necessity' is the content of a faith: that is to say, it consists in the will to power in its setting out to dominate becoming by creating an immutable meaning of the world.)

Secondly, the arising of the contradiction does not constitute a 'second' moment relative to the originary: as negated, the contradiction belongs to the essence of the originary, for the originary (the concrete concept of the abstract) is such only insofar as it is a negation of the abstract concept of the abstract (this latter concept precisely consisting in the isolation of the abstract).

Thirdly, the terms of the dialectical contradiction may not be the isolated abstract and its other, but they must be the abstract as a determination (A) that is *concretely* distinct – i.e. the abstract *qua* content of the concrete concept of the abstract – and the abstract in its being abstractly conceived of as isolated from the originary concrete (and thus consisting of a non-A). The terms of the dialectical contradiction are therefore not two contraries, as in the Hegelian method, but the two contradictories A and non-A (without thus ruling out the possibility of determining this contradictory of A).

Fourthly, however: if, on the one hand, the term A (the abstract term constituted by A) may appear as part of the contradiction that constitutes the abstract concept of the abstract only insofar as A is a content of the concrete concept of A, on the other hand, non-A may appear as part of the contradiction only if A is not simply isolated (i.e. only if A is not simply abstractly conceived), but only if the isolation of A is itself abstractly conceived (namely, only if the separation of A from the concrete consists in the abstract concept of the abstract concept of A; cf. Chapter 9, §9).

For, indeed, concerning this last point, the isolation of A from the originary concrete – namely, the positing or abstract concept of A (the appearing constituted by that positing or concept) – *immediately* includes in its actual content a non-A. This 'immediacy' means that any becoming in which there would first still appear A, followed by a non-A, is to be ruled out. Only a non-A appears within the isolation of A (and – as already remarked – it does not appear *as* a non-A, but as a content that is a non-A *from the standpoint* of the concrete concept of A). If the abstract concept of A simply consists of this isolation, there arises no contradiction in appearing. The concrete concept of A, in turn, may simply assert that the content of the isolation of A is a non-A; here, however, there is no identification between A and non-A. In order for a contradiction to appear – namely, in order for A to be identified with non-A – it is precisely necessary that the non-A that is the actual content of the abstract concept of A should be posited as A. This positing of that non-A as A is precisely the abstract concept of the isolation of A: i.e. it is the abstract concept of the abstract concept of A. It is within this abstract concept of the abstract concept of the abstract – as part of which A and non-A are identified (i.e. as part of which this identity appears, and therefore so do the terms that constitute it) – that, as already remarked, the appearing of A necessarily entails the appearing of the concrete originary meaning within which alone A is meaningful as A: a concrete meaning of which, however, the abstract concept of A (i.e. the isolation of A) affirms to be independent. The abstract concept of the abstract concept of A affirms that this being-independent of A – posited by the isolation, i.e. by the abstract concept of A – (a being-independent that is in truth a non-A) is A; the abstract concept of the abstract concept of A thus implies that from which its content (i.e. the abstract concept of A) is abstracted.

The analytic development of *The Originary Structure* concerning the meaning of dialectic is centred around these elements, and extends beyond Chapter 9, explicitly devoted to dialectic, and involves the entirety of the enquiry. The actual point of contact between *The Originary Structure* and Hegel's thought is reduced to the *abstract thesis* that the isolation is the ground of untruth. (For, indeed, what constitutes an isolation is not only the abstract concept, but also the abstract concept of the abstract concept of the abstract, since it is only by isolating A from the originary that it is possible to identify A with the non-A that is the content of the abstract concept of A. This means that the abstract concept of the abstract concept is and *at the same time* is not an isolation: it is an isolation in that it consists in the identification just discussed; it is not an isolation in that, within that concept, A may appear as A – i.e. as that concrete meaning of A with which non-A is identified – only insofar as A is not isolated from the originary concrete; that is to say, it is an isolation *in actu signato* and it is not an isolation *in actu exercito*.) This is an *abstract thesis* because Hegel's isolation is an isolation from becoming (the determination, *qua* negation of the negation, consisting in a 'consummated' becoming [*das Fortgehen... in seiner Vollendung*]), while in *The Originary Structure* the isolation is the isolation from the originary structure of Necessity, as part of which beings appear in and through the Necessity of their always already and forever being saved from nothingness. *The Originary Structure* thus performs a form of violence on both Hegel's thought and on the entire trajectory of Western philosophical thought; this violence, however, is a symptom of the fact that this book starts to testify to something that is absolutely alien to Western thought.

And yet, the Hegelian dialectical method exposes itself to the violence of *The Originary Structure*, in that it does not intend to be a pure faith in the existence of becoming – a pure consciousness of the fundamental 'self-evidence' of becoming – but a demonstration of *the necessity* for the abstract, *qua abstract*, to be an advance: i.e. a becoming. That is to say, that method aims to *infer* the becoming of a determination from that determination *as such*; it aims to *infer* that 'the universal of the beginning of its own accord [i.e. as such, *qua* universal of the beginning] determines itself as the *other of itself*. This inference or deduction of becoming, however, operates by precisely presupposing the becoming that it wishes to infer and deduce.

Indeed, if one remains at the explicit form of that deduction, each step of the method appears to be unexplainable. Why does the determination (i.e. the universal of the beginning) *linger* in its immediacy and succeeds in being something 'fixed' that has not yet advanced beyond itself? That is to say, why is it not an originary *staying* beyond itself? What holds the determination to its own immediacy (even if only provisionally)? And why does the determination, in advancing beyond itself, linger once again by the contradiction constituted by this advance – i.e. linger by the contradiction *as a contradiction that has not yet been superseded*? And is the contradiction superseded by the negation of the negation constituted by the unity of the opposites only after the contradiction has succeeded in fixing itself as a contradiction that has not yet been superseded? Why is the determination not *originarily* a negation of its negation? Why does the determination 'first' linger by its isolation, and then by the contradiction produced by that isolation – namely, why is the supersession of the contradiction, i.e. of the isolation that produces it, instead not an *originary* supersession? There is no doubt that, according to Hegel, the moments of the method are not to be separated from one another ('All of them together can be put under the first moment, that *of the understanding*; and in this way they can be kept separate from each other, but then they are not considered in their truth'; *Encyclopaedia*, §79); their unity, however, does not preclude each of their being set apart, and it is therefore insofar as a determination succeeds in the first place in fixing itself that it contradicts itself – and it is insofar as, in turn, the contradiction succeeds in constituting itself as not having yet been superseded that it is then superseded.

The hidden ground by virtue of which, within the Hegelian method, the determination (= the simple universal, the isolated abstract, the immediate, the beginning) succeeds in lingering by its own immediacy, rather than being an originary *staying* beyond itself, thus lies in the fact that this originary *staying* would not afford the opening of any becoming – which precisely consists in an advancing, starting from an immediacy that, in being fixed, lingers by its own self and has not yet advanced. As a result, the immediate, which is supposed to contain 'in its own self' an 'urge' to advance, constitutes itself in the way that it does (i.e. as a lingering by its own fixity) precisely insofar as it is originarily conceived *as part of* that very advancing: i.e. as part of a becoming that is instead supposed to originate from it. It is only insofar as the immediate lingers by its own self that it may *advance* beyond itself; but since the Hegelian text does not indicate why the immediate lingers by its own self rather than immediately *staying beyond* itself, it follows that the only reason for that lingering is precisely given by the fact that this lingering constitutes a precondition of that advancing; accordingly, it is because that advancing *must exist* that the deduction of becoming assumes the immediate as a lingering – i.e. as a beginning. Hegel's attempt, too, at *inferring* becoming – i.e. at showing that 'the universal of the beginning of its own accord determines itself as the other of itself' – is therefore grounded in a faith in the originary 'self-evidence' of becoming. The fundamental faith of the West defies all attempts at making it something derived from, and grounded in, something else.

In the same way, the Hegelian text does not indicate why the contradiction – namely, the determination's advancing beyond itself in showing to be other than itself – is in turn a lingering by its own not having yet been superseded, rather than being an originarily superseded contradiction: i.e. rather than being an originary staying beyond itself *qua* originarily superseded. According to Hegel, the superseding of the contradiction is the very *consummation* of becoming (the being-in-itself of the Concept 'is only an abstract, one-sided moment'; the 'absolute' is a being-in-and-for-itself; 'the advance consists rather in the universal [the Concept in-itself] determining itself and being for itself [...]. Only in its *consummation* is it the absolute', and this consummation is 'the negative of the negative' *qua* 'sublating of the contradiction' [*das Negative des Negativen... ist jenes Aufheben des Widerspruches*]); as a result, if the contradiction did not exist as not superseded (i.e. as lingering by its not having yet been superseded), and existed only as immediately superseded, becoming would not exist. Once again, however, Hegel's text does not indicate why the contradiction is inferred in the form of its not having been superseded, rather than in the form of its having been superseded – as a consequence of which the only ground of the lingering of the contradiction by its own not having been superseded lies in the originary faith of the West: namely, in the will that wills the existence of becoming.

In its objective character, the Hegelian dialectical method is the expression of that will, and it is as such that it becomes completely transparent. Becoming is the movement of the Concept, i.e. of meaning, 'in its determining and realising itself'. The beginning of becoming is therefore a simple meaningfulness, which is an 'abstract, one-sided moment' (i.e. which is isolated by the understanding), insofar as what exists beyond it is not yet realized, but must also necessarily realize itself (for, otherwise, the simple would be immutable); as a result, the consciousness that stops short at the beginning (i.e. that stops at the stopping short constituted by the beginning) is a form of understanding that isolates a part from the self-realization of the whole. Precisely because the simple is the beginning, it is necessary that its lingering by itself should be provisional and transitory, and it is therefore necessary that the simple should become. The simple cannot but become something *other*, i.e. it cannot but advance beyond itself exhibiting itself as an *other*. This exhibiting of itself as an other is the contradiction ('it is only insofar as something has a contradiction within it that it moves', *Logic*, II, Section One, Chapter 2, C, Remark 3). The 'first stage of the movement onwards', 'the emergence of real difference', is the 'judgement, the process of determining in general' (*Logic*, III, Section Three, Chapter 3). The judgment, *qua* contradiction, is *at the same time* 'positive' and 'negative': as a positive judgement, it consists in the identification between the simple and its other; as a negative judgement, it consists in the positing of that other as a negation of the simple. The contradiction, however, is not the *result* or *consummation* of becoming: it is not the Concept in and for itself. The Concept, *qua* beginning, must be something positive; as part of the contradiction, however, the positive is not positive but 'allows itself to be dominated by the contradiction': 'in the contradiction, it falls to the ground'. That is to say, the simple does not carry itself forward only as far as its other, but even farther – as far as the other of its other, which is to say, as far as its own self: 'as self-sublating contradiction [*als der sich aufhebende Widerspruch*]', 'the other of the other, the negative of the negative, is immediately the positive, the identical, the universal' (*ibid.*). Isolated from its other, the simple becomes an other, and the contradiction is superseded insofar as the simple becomes the other of its other (i.e. the other of the simple becomes itself an other: that other that is the simple itself) – namely, the contradiction is superseded insofar as the isolation of the simple from its other is superseded.

As part of the method – which is a will for becoming to constitute the originary 'self-evidence' – the necessary connection between determinations consists of becoming itself; the contradiction must constitute a 'second' moment relative to the beginning; the terms of the contradiction must be two contraries, and *not* two contradictories (Aristotle had already remarked that becoming takes place between contraries, and not contradictories); the arising of the contradiction does not require the abstract concept of the abstract concept of the abstract, but only the abstract concept of the abstract (i.e. the isolation of the determination). This means that the paralogisms that beset the Hegelian dialectical method – insofar as it claims to *infer* becoming from the finite *qua* finite – altogether disappear when that method is reduced to an expression of the fundamental faith of the West: namely, to the will that wills that becoming (understood in a nihilistic way) should constitute the originary self-evidence.

6. Aporias and dialectic

In *The Originary Structure*, however, the meaning of dialectic also presents a second side, which is essentially connected to the one recalled above. The side that has been recalled above consists in affirming that the (abstract) concept, which regards the abstract determination as being independent of and isolated from the originary concrete, is contradictory. The terms of this contradiction have also been recalled (even though this mention has remained at a generic level compared to the determinate analysis of *The Originary Structure*).

However, the fact that the terms of that contradiction have been indicated in that first side of the meaning of dialectic by means of variables (A, non-A) means that what is being considered is the abstract concept (i.e. the abstract concept of the abstract concept of the abstract determination) *as such*, and not a *specific* abstract concept; it means that the dialectical contradiction is also considered *as such*, and not insofar as it is *a specific* dialectical contradiction. The originary, however, is the negation *of all* abstract determinations (namely, of all the abstract determinations that constitute it) in their being abstractly conceived: that is to say, it is a negation of the totality of the *specific* contradictions of the abstract concepts.

One of the specific modes of the contradiction already appears by expressing the determinate values of the variables – for instance, in letting A be this lamp that is on the table. Insofar as it is isolated from the concrete (namely, insofar as it is abstractly conceived), this lamp is not this lamp, i.e. it is a non-A – and the abstract concept of this isolation (i.e. of this abstract concept) identifies A (i.e. that concretely conceived element of the concrete) with that non-A. This specific mode of the contradiction obtains even if the testimony of the originary structure is not yet able to express the specific meaning of that non-A – which at present remains a contradictory of A, the determinate content of which still constitutes a problem.

In this instance, however, the specificity of the dialectical contradiction is given by the specificity *of the terms* of the contradiction, and not by the specificity *of the contradiction*; the contradiction itself is always *the same*: namely, it is always the identification of the contradictories that appears in the abstract concept of the isolation of a determination. What, in this instance, makes the contradiction a specific contradiction is only the specificity of the isolated determination.

A second side of the meaning of dialectic (a second side *of the same meaning*, not a second meaning), however, runs through the entirety of *The Originary Structure* – a side as part of which the specificity of the dialectical contradiction does not simply consist in the specificity of the terms of the contradiction, but in the specificity *of the contradiction* itself (and as part of which that specificity comes at the same time to solve the problematic character of the meaning of non-A, which instead still remains an open problem for the first side of the meaning of dialectic). The contradiction, *as such*, is an identification of the non-identical and a differentiation of the identical: in this respect, there is no 'specificity of the contradiction'. That is to say, this expression does not indicate the possibility that a contradiction may be contradictory in a different way in addition to the one constituted by its being that identification-differentiation; on the contrary, it indicates a circumstance in which a specific content is posited as a contradiction because it is *that specific* content, and not because of that single reason that constitutes the first side of the meaning of dialectical contradiction – this reason being given by the identification of the contradictories performed by the abstract concept of the abstract concept of the abstract (this latter concept consisting in the affirmation that a specific determination of the originary is independent of or indifferent to its relation with the originary concrete). This does not mean that, in this second side, the specific contradictions are not determined by the isolation of a determination, but that these contradictions (while being determined by an isolation) do not consist in the contradiction constituted by the abstract concept of that isolation (which constitutes what we have called the first side of the meaning of dialectic).

These specific contradictions are the 'aporias' considered and solved in *The Originary Structure*. For instance, in Chapter 2 (§§11–17, 18–19, 21–2, 23), in Chapter 3 (§§9–10, 11, 12, 16, 21, 23), in the entirety of Chapter 4, in Chapter 5 (§§20–1, 26–7, 30–4), in Chapter 6 (§§9–10, 17), in Chapter 8 (§§4–7), in Chapter 10 (§§4, 13–18, 22–4). Each of these aporias is a specific and determined contradiction: i.e. the determinate contradiction entailed by the isolation of *a specific* determination of the originary from *another specific* determination (or from *other specific* determinations) of the originary, or from the totality of the determinations of the originary. This determinate contradiction is *entailed* by that isolation, but, let us repeat, it does not consist in the contradiction constituted by the abstract concept of that isolation.

As part of the language of *The Originary Structure*, the presentation of an aporia usually precedes the presentation of its resolution. The originary structure itself, however, consists in the *originary* relation between the concrete concept and the negation of the aporia: i.e. between the concrete concept and the isolation that determines the aporia. This originary relation constitutes the resolution of the aporia – which is therefore an originary resolution.

In order to highlight the specificity and determinateness of the specific contradictions that constitute the aporias considered in this book, we may take advantage of the fact that, in the previous pages (§2), one of the most relevant of these aporias has already been considered. Namely: the originary consists of a necessary predication, but a predication is an identification of a subject and a predicate – i.e. it is an identification of non-identical terms (for, even in the predication 'A is A', the two *A* are, precisely, two, and they therefore differ from one another). The analysis of this aporia does not thus consist in observing that the subject (A), as separated from its predicate, is *other* than itself (i.e. it is a non-A), and that the abstract concept of the separation of A is an identification of A and non-A (an analysis of this kind representing the first of the two sides of the meaning of dialectical contradiction): the analysis of this aporia consists instead in identifying the specific contradiction *of the predication* (consisting in the fact that a predication is an identification of the non-identical), and in observing that *this* contradiction is determined by the mutual isolation of those specific determinations of the originary that are the subject and the predicate of the predication. The equation $(x = y) = (y = x)$ constitutes the predicative structuring of the originary only insofar as it is an originary negation of the mutual isolation of x and y; considering the aporia, however, the contradiction of the isolation does not result from an analysis of the abstract concept of the isolation (this, let us repeat, being the first side of the meaning of dialectic; moreover, it is precisely insofar as this generic contradiction results from that analysis that it may remain indeterminate – i.e. that the semantic content of non-*A* may remain an open problem); on the contrary, that contradiction is a specific contradiction: that is to say, it is the contradiction that arises from the analysis of the concept of predication insofar as in that concept the subject remains isolated from the predicate. A specific contradiction thus arises from the analysis of a concept governed by an isolation, but it does not arise from that concept insofar as the latter is thus governed, but insofar as it has a specific and determinate content (which, in this instance, is given by the being-predication of the predication).

This and every other aporia consist of a contradiction whose terms are mutually contradictory affirmations, i.e. contents that are *both* determined: the non-*A* that is here in contradiction with *A* is not a contradictory of *A* that still remains indeterminate as to its content, but it precisely consists of a determinate affirmation that negates another determinate affirmation. For instance, in the aporia of predication, the two contradictory affirmations are the affirmation of the difference of the different terms (i.e. the subject and the predicate) and the affirmation of their identity (this affirmation precisely consisting in the predicate's reference to the subject). That is to say, the *contradictory affirmation*, in the aporia, is not simply the indeterminate *contradictory* of the determination (i.e. a contradictory whose determination remains an open problem).

The two sides of the meaning of dialectic that appear in *The Originary Structure* may thus be presented: according to one side, the analysis of the isolation of a determination (e.g. *A*) shows that *the abstract concept of that isolation* is a contradiction in which that determination (*A*) comes to be identified with what it is not (i.e. to non-*A*); according to the other side, the analysis of a specific determination (for instance, the predication) shows that *this determination* is a specific contradiction, and that this specific contradiction is (originarily) superseded insofar as the very isolation in which that determination has been confined is superseded.

Another relevant example of a specific contradiction (and, in fact, of a set of specific contradictions) is given by the aporia considered in §§11–23 of Chapter 2. Let us recall here the central aspects of its formulation. The affirmation of the existence of appearing beings is part of the originary structure of Necessity only if the appearing of those beings – i.e. their Ph-immediacy – is itself affirmed. However, the existence of that appearing, too, may be affirmed only if the appearing of that appearing is affirmed. And, in turn, and *in indefinitum*, the appearing of that appearing may be affirmed only if its appearing is affirmed – in such a way that, in the originary structure, the appearing of beings is, on the one hand, part of Necessity, and, on the other hand, it is something groundless that endlessly pursues its necessity without ever being able to reach it. This is the content of the specific contradiction that constitutes this aporia.

And this is an aporia from which the thinking of phenomenology (for instance, Husserl's) is inherently unable to escape. The thinking of phenomenology precisely consists in the abstract concept of Ph-immediacy, which, in isolating this Ph-immediacy from the concrete totality of the originary, remains altogether oblivious to the dialectic between the concrete and the abstract concepts of the abstract. The aporia recalled here is indeed a consequence of the isolation of the positing of appearing beings from the positing of their very appearing, in such a way that this second positing comes to be constituted as something *additional* relative to the first one – and, therefore, as the positing of something (i.e. that appearing) whose affirmation once again requires the affirmation of its appearing (and so on, *in indefinitum*). The originary structure is the originary negation of this isolation and of the specific contradiction that ensues from it. This means that the totality of appearing beings originarily includes its own appearing (i.e. it originarily includes that being constituted by its appearing), in such a way that the positing of the appearing of appearing beings is *originarily* a positing of the appearing of this appearing (i.e. a positing of a self-appearing) – that is to say, in such a way that the affirmation of the existence of appearing does not need to seek its ground in the affirmation of the existence of the appearing (a') of appearing (a), where the appearing a' would be different from the appearing a of beings. The appearing a of beings is, at the same time – originarily – the appearing *of itself*, and it therefore does not need to endlessly pursue its Necessity.

The originary superseding of this aporia also coincides with the originary negation of the logico-mathematical concept of 'class'. According to this concept, a 'class' is a set of *homogeneous* elements: namely, it is the set of elements that satisfy a single specific property. What that homogeneity *presupposes* is, on the one hand, that a property should be a sufficient and necessary condition for the determination of a class, and, on the other hand, that in a class the only necessary connection should be the one obtaining between the elements that satisfy a specific property and that very property. As a result of this presupposition, a class is constituted as something *isolated*: precisely in that it is assumed that the constitution of a class does not involve anything other than its intension and its extension.

It is only as a result of this *presupposition* that Russel's 'paradox of classes' appears as something unsolvable, or as something that may only be solved through the introduction of certain expedients such as his theory of 'types'. If a class is 'normal', if it does not include itself as an element, and 'non-normal' if it does, and if K is the class of all normal classes, then the 'paradox of classes', as is well known, consists in noting that if K is normal then K is one of its own elements – that is, it includes itself as an element – and it is therefore non-normal; and if K is non-normal, then, insofar as it includes itself as an element, it must be one of the normal classes that it includes.

Except that the pertinence of the paradox is a consequence of the *presupposition* indicated above; and, at the same time, it is precisely this paradox that leads to the elimination of that presupposition (the authentic elimination of which, however, only obtains as part of the originary structure). For, indeed, K is, *at the same time*, normal and non-normal – but relative to two *different* meanings of its own self-inclusion. The fact that K may not include itself as an element depends on the presupposition that the elements of a class must all be homogeneous: namely, that the only condition of their being part of the same set should be constituted by the fact that each of them satisfies the same property. If this presupposition is not regarded as an incontrovertible foundation, then K must necessarily include itself – precisely because if K did not include itself it would be a normal class, and its elements would not consist of *the totality* of the normal classes. This means that the totality of the homogeneous elements of K (i.e. the set of its normal classes) is necessarily a subset of the set consisting of that subset and of *K* itself, *qua* element that is heterogeneous with respect to the elements of that subset (and that is heterogeneous precisely because *K* is not a normal class). That is to say, it is self-contradictory for that subset to be constituted independently of its being part of a set that also includes *K*, which is heterogeneous with respect to that subset. Therefore, *K includes* itself as an element – and, in this respect, it is non-normal – but not as an element of that homogeneous subset, but as an element that is heterogeneous to that subset. *At the same time*, however, *K* does *not* include itself as an element – and, in this *other* respect, it is normal – but it does not include itself as an element of that homogeneous subset, and not as an element that is heterogeneous to that subset. That is to say, *K* is not an element of that homogeneous subset precisely because – as per the paradox – *qua* element of that subset, it would be a heterogeneous element.

The appearing of beings is part of the originary structure of Necessity, provided that the totality of appearing beings (i.e. of the beings of which appearing is predicated) should not be regarded as a 'class', in which the homogeneity of the terms would be given by their being beings that are not, in turn, the appearing of a being. It is on the basis of the notion of 'class' that – in particular within the empiricist and neo-positivist perspectives – appearing has been understood in terms of 'experience', to be referred in the last instance to 'individual elements', 'simple objects', 'atomic facts' (categorically or hypothetically regarded as 'simple' and 'atomic'), and, in any case, to objects that are not in turn the appearing of other objects. However, the very isolation that separates the affirmation of the existence of the appearing beings from the affirmation of their appearing is present within the presupposition that the beings that appear are a homogeneous class in the indicated sense. The homogeneity of a class is the result of the isolation that separates the affirmation of the existence of what appears from the affirmation of what (i.e. the appearing, the Ph-immediacy of what appears) makes that first affirmation an element of the originary structure. As part of that structure, the beings that appear therefore constitute *heterogeneous* sets of elements that, in addition to those beings that are not in turn the appearing of a being, include as elements the very appearing of those sets. It is not here a matter of choosing a different definition of 'class': it is rather only insofar as the totality of what originarily appears includes its own appearing that this very totality belongs to the originary structure (i.e. to that the negation of which is self-negating) – and that the logico-mathematical notion of 'class', in its application to the appearing beings, is revealed as a groundless presupposition, as part of which the homogeneity of the elements of a 'class' results from the isolation of the homogeneous elements from what renders the affirmation of their existence necessary.

The presupposition of the extensional homogeneity of a 'class' explicitly appears in Russell's theory of 'types', which is supposed to eliminate the 'paradox of classes', but which in fact is itself a conceptual development to which that paradox may be applied. 'Types' are precisely homogeneous classes that are arranged in a hierarchy in which the class of objects that are not properties of other objects (type 0) is sub-ordinated to the class (type 1) of the properties of the objects of type 0, and in which the class of type 1 is sub-ordinated to the class (type 2) of the properties of the objects of type 1, and so on. The theory of 'types' thus aims to eliminate the paradox of the class *K* by stipulating that a property of type n should only be predicated of objects of type n-1; in this way, it is not possible to assume that a class should include itself as an element, for that would entail that a property K (i.e. the property that defines this class) is predicated of itself: namely, of something that belongs to the same type of that property.

Aside from the fact (among countless others indicated by the logico-mathematical reflection on this theory) that, in this way, it would only be possible to assert that this green is a colour, but not that a colour is a colour (i.e. it would only be possible to assert that an element belongs to a class, but not that a class is a class), the theory of types is subject to the very logic of the paradox that it aims to eliminate. If, indeed, T indicates the theory of types, then T presents itself as a property that may be predicated of all other properties. If one asks whether T may be predicated of T, the answer is that if T cannot be predicated of T, then there exists a dimension in which the theory of types is not valid (i.e. a dimension of type lower than the type of T), and T may therefore be predicated of T; if, instead, T can be predicated of T, then (since this predication precisely states that a property of the type to which T belongs may not pertain to T), T may not be predicated of T.

What we wanted to emphasize here is that the originary structuring of the appearing of beings constitutes the authentic refutation of the theory of types: precisely in that the totality of appearing beings originarily includes the appearing of that totality, in such a way that the positing of the appearing of beings leaves no margin for asking for the ground of the positing of appearing – precisely because the positing of the Ph-immediacy of appearing beings *is already*, originarily, a positing of the Ph-immediacy of Ph-immediacy itself.

While the aporias considered in *The Originary Structure* are determined by the isolation of a determination (of the originary), every determination (of the originary) is essentially connected to its own isolation *qua superseded* in the originary: that is to say, to each determination there corresponds an aporia (in the same way in which to each determination there corresponds, *qua superseded*, an abstract concept of the isolation of that determination, i.e. a contradiction in the first of the two determined senses of the dialectic of the originary). The aporias considered in this book thus constitute only a part of the aporias of the originary: that part whose absence from the language that testifies to the originary might have perhaps compromised its 'intelligibility'. (As part of the originary, however, it still remains an open problem how to determine which elements should be included in the language that testifies to it in order to be 'intelligible' or 'comprehensible' to a heeding that differs from the one constituted by the originary structure of Necessity – a heeding that, however, if it is a heeding, cannot but be a heeding of Necessity, i.e. of the Destiny to which every heeding is destined. That problem is primarily determined by the problematic character of the very existence of such another heeding.) Particularly relevant, in this sense, are the aporias concerning the appearing of nothingness (Chapter 4) and the (unavoidable) appearing of what is affirmed as necessarily not belonging to the totality of appearing (Chapter 10, §4) – which, in its most comprehensive form, consists of the immutable whole in its surpassing what, of it, appears as part of the originary structure.

Even more relevant is certainly the aporia of becoming considered in Chapter 13. The presence of nihilism in this book, however, essentially consists precisely in the way in which this aporia is solved. It is formulated as follows: logical immediacy consists in the affirmation of the immutability of beings *qua* beings, and, therefore, of every being; phenomenological immediacy consists in the affirmation of the becoming of appearing beings, i.e. of their issuing from nothingness and returning to it. In *The Originary Structure*, the superseding of this aporia consists in the affirmation that the totality of beings, as immutable, *does not coincide* with the totality of beings that appear, and that appear in their becoming. From a formal point of view, the way in which this aporia is superseded is identical to how the other aporias are themselves superseded: namely, by superseding the isolation (of the determination) that causes the aporia. In this instance, the isolated determination is precisely the *otherness* of the immutable totality of beings, which separates it from the totality of the appearing of becoming beings (in such a way that the contradiction of the aporia obtains insofar as, in and through the isolation of that otherness, the being that is posited as immutable is *the same* being that is posited as becoming). Nihilism, however, governs the superseding of this aporia, in that the very conviction that beings appear in the form of an issuing from and returning to nothingness is nihilistic. Outside of nihilism, the appearing of becoming is the appearing of the disclosing and concealing of the immutable whole (i.e. it is the appearing of its entering and leaving appearing), and the superseding of that aporia consists in the superseding of the isolation of the authentic determination that causes the aporia: namely, the determination constituted by that conviction. That conviction is itself – however, *in its being superseded, negated* – a determination of the originary structure. Isolated from its connection to the originary, this determination is at the same time isolated from its being superseded and negated by the originary; appearing as posited and affirmed in this isolation, it therefore contradicts the affirmation of the immutability of beings *qua* beings, and it causes the aporia.

Each aporia determines a conceptual situation in which the originary structure itself appears as a negation of logical immediacy, and, therefore, as a self-negation. However, since the originary structure is Necessity itself, the negation of which is self-negating, the fact that the originary structure negates itself can only be an appearance. That appearance is determined by the isolation of the determinations of the originary. This does not mean that this isolation determines the contradiction of the aporia only apparently (the implication between isolation and aporetic contradiction being in fact necessary), but it means that this contradiction is only apparently a self-negation of the originary structure, and that the isolation of a specific determination of the originary is precisely the cause of that appearance.

This is the case regardless of whether the identification or recognition of the isolated determination already appears within the originary structure or not. Affirming that the aporias considered in this book are a part of the total aporias of the originary does not indeed mean that the originary is the originary supersession of the totality of the aporias in which it might come be involved: Chapter 1 (§4) already establishes the meaning of the possibility of the arising of a negation of the originary that, while being originarily superseded *qua negation* (*qua* 'universal negation'), may not be originarily superseded in its specificity (i.e. *qua* 'individuation' of that universal negation of the originary). The fact that the specificity of that negation should appear as part of the originary as not superseded does indeed mean that the originary constitutes an originary positing of the *appearance* of the (i.e. of any) support of that negation (namely, of the support that allows the appearing of that negation, as part of the originary, in its not being superseded as to its specificity); that fact, however, also means that, in the originary, there does not yet appear the identification (or recognition) of the determination whose isolation precisely constitutes the apparent support of that specific negation – i.e. precisely determines the aporia. The self-negating negation of the originary is a universal negation: that is to say, the originary consists of an originary supersession of the totality of the aporias *qua* universal negation. The originary, however, does not yet consist of a supersession of the totality of the aporias *qua* totality of the individuations of that universal negation.

The aporia of becoming is instead part of the set of the aporias that are originarily superseded by the originary. However, the contradiction of this aporia, too, is itself determined by the isolation of a specific determination of the originary (that is to say, by the isolation of the conviction that beings' issuing from nothingness and returning to it appears); therefore, that contradiction, *qua* self-negation of the originary, is a merely apparent contradiction. The appearance of this contradiction coincides with the very appearance of the self-contradictoriness of becoming as part of its appearing. That is to say, becoming, as part of its appearing, contradicts the immutability of beings – this contradiction giving rise to the aporia of becoming – insofar as becoming is regarded as entailing the being-nothing of those beings that issue from nothingness and return to it: i.e. insofar as becoming is regarded as a self-contradiction. *As element of the originary structure*, however, this self-contradictoriness of becoming is a merely apparent self-contradictoriness (even though the fact that the nihilistic concept of becoming should be self-contradictory is *necessary*), and this appearance is determined by the isolation of the nihilistic concept of becoming from its being superseded as part of the originary, i.e. from its being superseded by that appearing of becoming in which becoming appears as the appearing and disappearing of the immutable. It is in this sense that one should understand the connection established in *The Essence of Nihilism* ('Returning to Parmenides (Postscript)', I) between the 'formal meaning of the situation in which truth find itself in an aporia' (that meaning, in *The Essence of Nihilism*, being essentially resumed from *The Originary Structure*, and, explicitly, from *Studi di filosofia della prassi*)[9] and the way in which the aporia of becoming is addressed in *The Essence of Nihilism*.

In the meantime, it has become clear from the above that the two sides of the meaning that pertains to dialectic as part of the originary structure are, respectively, the very meaning of dialectic in its universality and one of its relevant specifications – this relevance being given by the fact that this specification is in turn a universality that gathers in itself a multiplicity. The meaning of dialectic, in its universality, is the one that appears in the constitution of the aporia: *the isolation* of a specific determination of the originary entails a specific contradiction, and dialectic, as such (i.e. in its universal meaning), consists in the ensuing of a specific contradiction on the grounds of the isolation of a specific determination of the originary.

The other side of the meaning of dialectic – namely, the relevant specification of that meaning – is the one that above has been considered first, which consists in *the abstract concept of the isolation* (i.e. of the abstract concept) of a specific determination of the originary. Indeed, the abstract concept of the isolation consists in the isolation of the isolation of a determination. The isolation of the determination precisely consists here in the determination of the originary that is isolated – that determination belonging to the originary as negated. As a result, the dialectic of the isolation of the isolation is a specification of the dialectic of the isolation of a determination of the originary. That isolated isolation is a specific determination of the originary, and the isolation of the isolation entails a specific contradiction: namely, the identification of non-A – i.e. the determination A that is isolated and that, thus isolated, is a non-A – with A. The contradictory character of this identification consists in turn of a universality that gathers in itself a multiplicity, for the determinations that are identified with their contradictories as part of the isolation of the isolation consist, in addition to A, of all the determinations of the originary. This specification of the meaning of dialectic, too, is therefore an aporia caused by an isolation, and this aporia, too, is superseded by superseding that isolation (namely, by negating that A, *qua* isolated, is A – the isolation of A being precisely the determination that is isolated from the isolation that constitutes the aporia).

7. The whole and the contradiction of the originary

The authentic meaning of dialectic, however, extends even further into the structuring of the originary. The originary structure of Necessity is the originary negation of the totality of the contradictions determined by the isolation (i.e. by the abstract concept of the determinations of the originary). And yet, the originary structure of Necessity is *itself* a dialectical contradiction: namely, an isolation and an abstract concept. The originary superseding of the contradiction is a contradiction. (Even though it is originarily impossible that the originary should be contradictory *insofar as* it is a superseding of the contradiction.) And this is not an assertion brought about by an external reflection on the originary structure, but it is this very structure that posits *itself* – i.e. that manifests *itself* – as a contradiction. Chapter 8 (titled precisely 'The Ground *qua* Contradiction'), as well as Chapters 10 and 11 – together with Chapter 9, explicitly devoted to dialectic – expresses the concrete meaning of the assertion according to which the originary structure is a contradiction. The contradiction that encloses the originary itself – which in this book is called 'C-contradiction' – is a dialectical contradiction (namely, it falls within the authentic meaning of dialectic), but it singularly pertains to the originary. The concrete meaning of this assertion may be recalled as follows.

The originary structure is the meaning the negation of which is self-negating. It consists in the appearing of beings and in the impossibility for beings, *qua* beings, not to be. That is to say, the Whole is eternal as Whole and as each of its parts, including the smallest and most insignificant one. The beings that appear, however – namely, the beings that appear in (and as) the originary structure – are a part of the Whole. This latter assertion has a twofold meaning in this book: the one appearing in Chapter 11 and the one, more relevant, appearing in Chapter 13. In Chapter 13, however, the assertion that states that the beings that appear are a part of the Whole is grounded in the nihilism of the conviction that an issuing from nothingness and a returning to it appears. That assertion stands instead outside of nihilism in *The Essence of Nihilism* ('The Path of Day', XX), and it is in relation to this standing outside of nihilism that the positing of the originary structure as a dialectical contradiction preserves its necessity. (It also preserves this necessity when considering only the first of the two meanings that pertain to it: namely, the one appearing in Chapter 11.)

Moreover: Chapter 7 introduces the concept of 'constant' (in opposition to the one of 'variant'): a 'constant' of a determination x is a determination y, the appearing of which is necessarily implied by the appearing of x insofar as y is a determination that is necessarily predicated of x, or insofar as it is an element of the semantic content of x or y. Chapter 10 shows that the determination, i.e. the meaning, 'Whole' ('the Whole', 'the Totality of beings') – the infinite semanteme – is a constant of every determination (i.e. of every meaning) and that every determination is a constant of the infinite semanteme. That is to say, the concrete and complete Whole of beings – the infinite semanteme, not *qua* simple formal meaning of the infinity of meaning, but *qua* concrete and absolutely comprehensive determinacy of this infinity (which is therefore not 'this', but includes in itself every 'this-ness') – is a constant of every meaning, and it is originarily a constant of that meaning constituted by the very originary structure of Necessity. It thus appears, on the one hand, that a necessary connection links the originary structure to the Whole – granted that the Whole *is* the concrete meaning of the originary structure – and, on the other hand, that the Whole conceals itself in the originary structure and does not completely manifest itself in it. The Whole is a constant of the originary, and the originary may therefore appear only if the Whole appears; and yet, the Whole does not appear, it conceals itself from the originary, and, at the same time, it gradually discloses itself – it conceals itself precisely insofar as it gradually discloses itself, and vice-versa.

The gradual manifestation of the Whole in the originary consists in the arising of the constants of the originary as part of the appearing of the originary itself. Chapter 8 shows the meaning and the determinate mode of this arising – which are precisely the meaning and the determinate mode according to which the originary structure itself is a dialectical contradiction. In the same way in which every determination of the originary is linked through a necessary connection to the originary – i.e. to the concrete totality of the originary (the necessity of that connection consisting in the fact that this connection is that the negation of which is self-negating) – so is the originary itself linked to the complete Whole of beings through a necessary connection. And in the same way in which the isolation of a determination of the originary (from the originary) entails a dialectical contradiction, so is a dialectical contradiction entailed by the isolation of the originary from the Whole. The isolation of the originary from the Whole consists in the Whole's concealing of itself from the originary – namely, in its not completely disclosing itself in the originary. The (C-)contradiction of the originary thus lies in the fact that since the originary is and means what it is and means only as part of its connection with the Whole (this being and meaning of the originary being indicated in this book by the symbol S), as part of the isolation of the originary from the Whole (i.e. insofar as the Whole does not manifest itself in the originary), the originary is not the originary: S is not S.

The way in which the originary is a contradiction, however, singularly pertains to the originary itself. First of all, it is the very originary structure that shows its own contradictoriness; it is the originary structure itself that shows *itself* as a contradiction. (On the contrary, the contradiction of the isolation, which is originarily superseded in the originary, does not show itself as part of the isolated determination, but outside of it: namely, precisely as part of the originary.) The originary is the structure the negation of which is self-negating – it is the structure of Necessity; the fact that this structure shows itself as a contradiction may not therefore mean that the structure of Necessity shows that its own negation is *not* self-negating. In fact, precisely because that negation is self-negating, the negation of the fact that the originary is a dialectical contradiction is self-negating. At the same time, stating that the originary is a contradiction means precisely that the negation and superseding of this contradiction, i.e. the negation of the originary *qua* contradiction, is not self-negating.

The concurrent possibility of these two aspects is given by the specificity of the contradiction of the originary.

For, indeed, the originary is not contradictory because it *affirms* that it is other than itself (namely, that S is non-S), but for a different reason. Insofar as it shows itself to be surrounded by a self-concealing Whole – insofar as it shows itself to be isolated from the Whole – the originary shows that its own being meaningful *qua* structure of Necessity coincides with the meaning (the being meaningful) of what is not the structure of Necessity; this latter meaning is not the structure of Necessity because this structure is and means what it is and means only as part of its necessary connection with the Whole: namely, as part of the appearing of this connection and as part of the appearing of the Whole. The originary, however, in showing that its meaning does not coincide with the originary itself – in showing that it is other than itself – does not let this contradiction appear as something that is affirmed, *but lets it appear as negated*. That is to say, not only does the originary show itself as a contradiction, but it is also the superseding of this contradiction.

This superseding, however, remains a *formal* one. If the contradiction of the originary lies in the fact that the originary appears without the appearing of the Whole in the totality of its determinacy, the superseding of this contradiction would consist in the complete appearing of the Whole as part of the originary: namely, in an extending of the originary that would reach the extreme ends of the Whole. Insofar as the Whole continues instead to remain concealed, the superseding of the contradiction of the originary is therefore a *formal* one: namely, it is such that it leaves the originary in its being the appearing of a part of the Whole (i.e. an abstract determination of the Totality of the concrete), in such a way that this part continues to appear as a being-the-originary-structure of something that is not the originary structure. Within the originary, the contradiction of the originary is superseded formally, not concretely.

The originary is therefore the structure the negation of which is self-negating in that it consists of a formal superseding of its own contradiction (that is to say, not in that it conforms with it or submits to it); and the negation of the originary, insofar as the latter is contradictory, is not self-negating in that it constitutes a concrete superseding of the originary contradiction: that is, in that it does not negate the originary insofar as this is a *saying* (i.e. on the grounds of what it says) but insofar as it is a *not saying* – i.e.

on the grounds of what it *does not say*, insofar as it does not say the Whole, but only a part, and thus says the Whole only in a formal way. As a result, the superseding of the contradiction of the originary would coincide with the very disclosure of the Whole within the originary.

It is effectively the case that, precisely insofar as the originary *does not say* the Whole, the very *saying* of the originary is contradictory (but, precisely, it is not contradictory insofar as it says what it says, but insofar as, in saying what it says, it does not say), in such a way that the superseding of the contradiction of the originary *qua* not-saying is at the same time a superseding of the originary *qua* saying. The originary, however, says Necessity itself – that the negation of which is self-negating. As part of this saying, the originary says that it is itself isolated from the Whole (namely, it says that precisely because it is necessarily connected to the Whole, the non-appearing of the Whole leaves it isolated from the Whole). In other words, the originary says the *difference* between itself *qua* isolated from the Whole and itself *qua* manifest as part of the Whole (i.e. *qua* appearing of the connection between itself and the Whole), but, at the same time, it says the *identity* of these two different terms: the identity that they must necessarily share. (Even if in a more specific context, this identity is indicated in Chapter 9, §8, e, by means of the symbol Ŝ.) This identity consists of Necessity in its being originarily said: *precisely because it consists of this Necessity*, the negation of which is self-negating, it must not only be part of the originary *qua* isolated but also of the originary *qua* manifest as part of the Whole. *This identity* of the differents, which coincides with Necessity itself in its being part of these differents, constitutes the saying of the originary – a saying that, *qua* saying, must necessarily not be a contradiction and something to be superseded and negated. However, insofar as this identity is in a synthesis with that different term constituted by the originary *qua* isolated – i.e. insofar as it is in a synthesis with a saying that is at the same time a not-saying – this synthesis is the saying constituted by the contradiction of the originary, which is therefore negated *qua* saying, without this negation of the originary being itself self-negating.

This distinction between the isolated originary *qua* identical and *qua* different is precisely what makes the contradiction of the originary possible – this contradiction being precisely a predication that refers an identity (the identity of Necessity) to what (the different term constituted by the isolated originary) is not an identity. The latter is not an identity insofar as that to which that identity is referred (i.e. that of which it is predicated) is an identity (or: the originary that is posited *qua* Necessity is Necessity) only insofar as this reference appears as part of the appearing of the Whole: that is to say, only insofar as the synthesis between Necessity and the originary appears as part of the appearing of the Whole. In other words, the originary may say to be other than itself (i.e. to be, *qua* isolated, other than itself *qua* not isolated from the Whole) only insofar as there must necessarily exist an identity shared by the originary *qua* isolated and the originary *qua* not isolated – this identity consisting in the Necessity of the originary. The gradual appearing of the Whole in the originary is the persisting of this identity – and, at the same time, the concrete and gradual superseding of the contradiction of the originary. This gradual superseding, in turn, is the very gradual appearing of the concreteness of the originary Necessity. The surpassing of the originary consists in the arising of its concreteness. This means that while the superseding of the contradictions superseded *by* the originary consists in the *negation* of their predicative content, the superseding of the contradiction *of* the originary consists instead in the concrete and determinate *affirmation* of the originary predicative content: that is to say, in an affirmation that does not negate what the originary says, but negates the very lack of determinacy and abstractness of its saying, due to which it is contradictory.

8. The appearing of the never-setting

The originary structure of Necessity is, as such, a structure of *constants* – a constant of a determination being a determination that is *necessarily* part of the meaning of the determination of which it is a constant. The structuring of these constants is an emergent mode of the co-originarity of L-immediacy and Ph-immediacy. It is indeed insofar as a specific determination *y* is a constant of another specific determination *x* that the appearing of *x* must necessarily entail the appearing of *y*. The content of appearing (the configuration of the spectacle that appears) may not be established by a *simple* phenomenological reflection: that is to say, by a phenomenology that would be isolated from the logical element, i.e. from the originary meaning of the necessity of the connection (= predication). A *simple* phenomenological reflection must necessarily overlook the necessary connections that link what appears, and that make every determination into a constant of every other determination; the appearing determinations appear in and through their mutual isolation, and, therefore, they appear *as being other* than what they are and mean. If it relies solely on itself, even the most rigorous phenomenological enquiry is altogether unable to say what appears: it must *essentially* alter and corrupt what appears. The critique that the philosophy of phenomenology addresses to the distorting and reductive character of scientific 'experience' is the expression of as radical a distortion and a reduction. The spectacle that authentically appears is the one that is manifest in and as the originary structure.

The language of *The Originary Structure* takes an essential step forth in the testimony of the authentically appearing spectacle (αὐθ-εντικῶς, i.e. by and from itself, not from other). Chapter 10 presents, firstly, the broadest form that pertains to the contradiction of the originary insofar as the latter is not an appearing of the Totality of its constants (i.e. insofar as it is not the appearing of the Whole); secondly, Chapter 10 indicates the field of the constants that must *necessarily* appear: namely, the constants whose non-appearing does not simply entail a self-contradiction of the originary, but the very impossibility for anything in general to appear – and therefore the impossibility for the originary itself to appear. The field of these constants is the 'persyntactic field' (Chapter 10, §19): that is to say, the field of those constants that are 'syntactic constants' *of every* meaning (i.e. of every being). The syntactic constants of a specific meaning are those constants whose non-appearing necessarily entails the non-appearing of that meaning as such (rather than only entailing its appearing as a contradiction), in that they are necessary determinations of the 'syntax' – i.e. of the essence or form as such – of that meaning. For instance, not being non-*x* is a syntactic constant of *x*. Being a being, which is a syntactic constant of *every* meaning, is therefore a persyntactic constant. Appearing, *as such* – i.e. both as the appearing of truth and as the appearing of untruth, as the appearing of mortals and of immortals, as finite and as infinite appearing – thus necessarily consists in the appearing of the persyntactic field.

This book, however, rules out the possibility that the originary structure should itself be part of the persyntactic field. *The Essence of Nihilism* shows that the ruling out of that possibility is determined by a persistence of nihilism. 'In *The Originary Structure* it is still asserted that the content of philosophy does not belong to the 'background of appearing' (i.e. to the 'persyntactic field'). However, if something belongs to that background by being the necessary predicate of every being – in such a way that nothing may appear unless that predicate appears – the only site in which every necessary predication, as well as the very meaning of necessity, may constitute itself is the truth of being (and the 'originary structure' precisely coincides with the originary structure of the truth of being). The truth of being is therefore the predicate of every being: not in the sense that beings lie outside the truth of being but rather in the sense that the truth of being consists in this very predication, i.e., in the veritable unity of a being and its predicate, as part of which the subject may only exist in this unity with its predicate. The truth of being – which is the content of philosophy – is therefore the background of every appearing, or of appearing as such. In the most irrelevant as in the most anomalous of human situations – in the farthest remove from the truth of being – what stands before us, never-setting, is the very content that the philosopher, as keeper of the truth of being, brings to language. *The Originary Structure* holds that appearing 'attests' the existence of human situations in which the structure of the truth of being is not present (Chapter 10, §13). This 'attestation' then induces one to seek the conditions that permit such an absence (*ibid.*, §§23, 24). This 'attestation', taken as ground, constitutes the principle of phenomenology. Phenomenology, however, is part of the history of metaphysics. According to Husserl, the 'principle of all principles' states that everything that appears constitutes 'a legitimate source of cognition, i.e. everything is to be accepted simply as what it is presented as being, but also only within the limits in which it is presented there' (*Ideen*, §24). Yet, here as well, the limits of what is given are marked out by the isolation of the earth; the ground of the assumption that affirms everything that appears and to the extent that it appears consists in the conviction that the earth is what securely appears. Phenomenology does not testify to everything that appears, but to what from the outset has been isolated from the appearing whole and has itself been posited as the appearing whole. If the testimony of the truth of being still lets itself be accompanied by the principle of phenomenology (which is precisely what takes place in *The Originary Structure*), then it will inevitably be affirmed that appearing itself 'attests' the existence of human situations, i.e. of forms of appearing, in which the structure of the truth of being does not appear. Once the earth has been isolated from that which, through its appearing, makes the appearing of every thing possible, it is inevitable – even while testifying to the truth of being – that whenever one aims to indicate what appears one should affirm that, at times, the earth appears without the appearing of the truth of being' (*The Essence of Nihilism*, pp. 229–30). The footnote then adds:

> With reference to the specific determinations of *The Originary Structure*: while in that work the background is understood as consisting of "persyntactic constants"

and the content of philosophy (the truth of being) as consisting of the set of "metasyntactic constants" (Chapter 10, §23) – which may therefore be absent from the content of appearing – the difference between these two types of constants must instead be superseded, and the "persyntactic field" must be identified with the truth of being.

That is to say, *The Essence of Nihilism* states that the appearing of a being is necessarily entailed by the appearing of another being if the first one is a 'necessary predicate' of the second one; and since the truth of beings is *the* necessary predicate of every being *qua* being – for it is the very unitary dimension of the necessary predication that pertains to beings *qua* beings – something may appear and there may be an appearing only if the truth of beings appears: only if the originary structure of the truth of beings appears. (In *The Originary Structure*, Chapter 7, §12, Chapter 8, §12–14, Chapter 13, §§9–12, it is shown in which sense the articulation between immediacy and mediation is internal to the originary itself. For an understanding of this central issue, we can but refer directly to the text itself.) The 'necessary predicates' of the passage from *The Essence of Nihilism* quoted above are the syntactic constants.

Stating that the originary structure is *the* predicate of every being does not mean that this lamp *is* the originary structure, and that every determination, i.e. every being, *is* that structure; rather, it means that this structure is the very dimension in which the set of predicates that necessarily pertain to this lamp and to every other being necessarily resides. This dimension is the originary structure of Necessity, as part of which every necessary predication is necessary and appears as necessary. It is therefore not correct to state that this lamp is the originary structure; it should be stated that it is that whose necessary predicates necessarily constitute themselves as part of the originary structure of Necessity. 'That whose necessary predicates [= that being-a-being whose necessary predicates] necessarily constitute themselves as part of the originary structure of Necessity' is therefore the predicate that properly pertains with necessity to every being – and that pertains to it in the form of the equation $(x = y) = (y = x)$. At the same time, if the originary structure is a 'part' of the meaningfulness of that predicate, this part is also a dimension that includes not only the entire meaningfulness of that predicate but also the very relation between subject and predicate.

The difficulties that may be encountered in positing this lamp, or any other being, as that to which that predicate L-immediately pertains may once again be ascribed to the isolation of this lamp (or of any other being under consideration) from the originary structure, for, as part of this isolation, it appears to be impossible that an analysis of this lamp should include the categorial complexity of that predicate. This lamp, however, may be a content of a necessary saying only outside of the isolation of the originary structure; this necessary saying (the originary structure of Necessity) says that this lamp ('this lamp' being an *interpretation* that regards a specific set of empirical determinations as the *aspect* of this being-a-lamp) is a being that belongs to the content of the appearing of the originary and a being whose necessary predicates constitute themselves in their necessity only as part of the structure of Necessity; accordingly, as part of its synthesis with the originary, this lamp is identical to every predicate that, if isolated from that lamp, must instead necessarily not pertain to it. That is to say, it is to that (*x*) to which this predicate (*y*) pertains that this predicate pertains: *y* pertains to *x* insofar as $(x = y) = (y = x)$. At the same time, this lamp (*x*), *as a meaning that is distinct* from its predicate (*y*), is not identical to its predicate (while *x*, as a meaning that is distinct and concretely distinct from *x*, is identical to *x*), in such a way that, in the language of *The Originary Structure*, the pertaining of *y* to *x*, *qua* distinct meaning, is not analytic (L-immediate) but synthetic *a priori* (L-mediated).[10]

Consider this other remark concerning the passage from *The Essence of Nihilism* quoted above. That of which the originary structure is a necessary predicate is the Whole of beings; and the Whole that in truth appears as that of which the originary structure is predicated is the Whole that, in concealing itself, appears *as part of* the originary structure: that is, *as part of* its gaze. If the Whole is part of the gaze of the originary, the originary is *part of* the Whole. The originary is *one of the beings* of which it, itself, is predicated; it is not the only one. The originary is originarily predicated of everything that, of the Whole, appears – and, therefore, also and in a certain sense primarily of all the beings that enter and leave appearing (and that, through this unfolding, constitute what the inhabitants of the West call 'history' and the 'cycles of nature'); the latter are therefore 'variants' of the appearing content, thus distinguishing themselves from the 'constants' of that content. (This is the case even though the distinction between variants and constants is internal to constants themselves, understood in a broader sense – cf. Chapter 10, §9.) In *The Essence of Nihilism*, the totality of variants is called 'the earth'. What, of the earth, appears is part of the content that appears as part of the originary structure: that is to say, the variants are part of the originary structure. However, in stating that this structure is the necessary predicate of the Whole, and that nothing may appear without its appearing, this structure is not regarded as to its including those variants, but as to its being distinct from them. The originary structure is the necessary predicate of every being – but not *insofar as* it is the necessary predicate of a specific being: namely, of that specific dimension of beings constituted by the set of variants. The originary structure is a syntactic constant of every being (that is to say, it is a persyntactic constant) – but not insofar as it includes the variants.

This does not mean that it constitutes itself as what it is independently of the variants – of which it constitutes the appearing – but that, within *itself*, it distinguishes itself from what, on the one hand, is not the totality of which it is predicated, and, on the other hand, is something that, while appearing (and therefore essentially belonging to the *actual and present* configuration of the originary structure), has, however, arisen as part of appearing, and is therefore not that without which the originary would not be able to be predicated of every being – i.e. Necessity itself, the negation of which is self-negating. Moreover, contrary to the Hegelian dialectic, the dialectic of the originary structure does not simply concern the 'categorial' element, to the exclusion of the 'sensible' one – if an analogy is to be established between variants (and, more precisely, that specific kind of variants that in *The Originary Structure* are called 'hyposyntactic variants') and the 'sensible' element, and between syntactic constants and categories. Undoubtedly, in *The Originary Structure*, this red's not being non-red is not necessary insofar as this red is this red, but insofar as this red is a being (Chapter 7, §18) – which may be stated: not insofar as the sensible is sensible, but insofar as the sensible is subordinated to the categorial. In this respect, there exists no dialectic of the sensible *as isolated* from the categorial. (The fact that this red, isolated from its not being non-red, is a non-red is a predication that belongs to the originary structure only if the connection between this red and its not being non-red appears as an individuation of the connection between beings and their not being non-beings, i.e. as an individuation of a categorial connection.) At the same time, in the originary structure, dialectic does not simply concern the categorial element, as in Hegel's thought, but also the sensible insofar as it is not isolated from the categorial. Furthermore, a dialectic of the sensible that would be isolated from the categorial is as impossible as a dialectic of a pure categorial isolated from the sensible. A being's not being a non-being is a necessary connection only if that 'being' does not simply consist of a synthesis between a general determination – the universality of the determination – and its 'is' (namely, it does not consist of a synthesis of purely categorial elements), but it is a synthesis between the 'is' and the concrete and specific totality of determinations that appears while concealing itself. Each of the specific determinations of the totality of beings is a 'being' that necessarily negates its non-being; isolated from the appearing of those determinations, that 'being' is a determinacy of nothing, in such a way that it is of this determinacy of nothing – i.e. of this nihil of determinacy – that one states that it 'is'. That 'non-being', on the other hand, is the totality of the specific content that is not each of those determinations.

Now, in *The Originary Structure*, 'variants' consist of syntactic but non-persyntactic constants, as well as of hyposyntactic constants and metasyntactic ones. The passage quoted above from *The Essence of Nihilism*, instead, rules out the possibility that metasyntactic constants should be variants.

Hyposyntactic constants are individuation of syntactic constants. The meaning not-this-red is, *qua* negated, a syntactic constant of this red (and, therefore, it is not a persyntactic constant). This green is a hyposyntactic constant of not-this-red, for it is not part of the formal essence of not-this-red and it does not syntactically determine the latter's syntax, but it is subordinated to it – it determines it hyposyntactically (in the way in which a specific content determines its own form). And yet, the isolation from any hyposyntactic constant, even the most irrelevant one, (or from its non-appearing) determines the self-contradiction of any appearing content – thus including, and in fact originarily, the originary structure itself.

As stated in *The Essence of Nihilism*, the opposition between metasyntactic and persyntactic constants established in *The Originary Structure* takes place under the sway of the isolation of the earth from the truth of being. In §22 of Chapter 10, however, that aporia is presented in the most explicit way (and by means of elements that belong to the authentic resolution of this aporia) as follows. It is the originary structure itself that affirms the existence of the persyntactic field; it is as part of the horizon of Necessity that this existence is posited (even though, as part of that horizon, it is asserted that the persyntactic field is a content that also necessarily appears in all the other horizons, i.e. also in all the horizons of the appearing of untruth). The originary structure is therefore a structure of constants of the persyntactic field, and it is thus itself a persyntactic structure. This, however, entails that if something appears – if there is an appearing – this appearing is an appearing of the originary structure of Necessity: i.e. it is an appearing of truth. Accordingly, an appearing that is only an appearing of untruth – of the error, of the alienation, of common sense, of a pre-philosophical existence that is indifferent to the philosophical element (provided that this 'philosophical' element should precisely consist in the appearing of truth) – is therefore impossible: its existence is impossible. The only possible appearing is the appearing of truth. At the same time, however, untruth appears: 'The totality of the immediate attests [...] the opening of pre-philosophical positional horizons' (*ibid.*). (In a different context, cf. Chapter 5, §29 and Chapter 7, §2.)

The Essence of Nihilism does not deny the appearing of untruth – in fact, the fundamental aim there is precisely to establish the *essence* of untruth, the essence of *nihilism*, as an essence that has by now pervaded the appearing of the earth. *The Essence of Nihilism* does not deny that appearing attests untruth itself, and, in fact, the domination of untruth as part of appearing; the appearing of untruth and its domination of the earth are affirmations that belong to the structure of truth. *The Essence of Nihilism* (cf. 'The Earth and The Essence of Man') shows the impossibility for any content whatsoever to appear without the appearing of truth – i.e. the originary structure of Necessity – and it shows that the appearing of the domination of untruth, too, is an appearing of truth: namely, it is the appearing of the *contrast* between truth and untruth. Moreover: since the appearing of truth, too, is an eternal being, the possibility of the dissolution and non-being of (this) appearing is originarily contradictory (i.e. it is itself an expression of nihilism); accordingly, truth – the structure of Necessity – is a spectacle that necessarily appears, never setting, as part of the eternal appearing of beings: an eternal appearing that consists of *this* actual and present appearing of beings – *this* appearing that includes the appearing of the occurrence of mortals, of the isolation of the earth and of the history of the West.

The Originary Structure, instead, letting itself be reached and enclosed by the isolation of the earth, convinces itself that if appearing 'attests' the opening of horizons of the appearing of untruth as part of the originary structure, this 'attestation' is at the same time an 'attestation' of the fact that truth does not appear as part of those horizons. In isolating the earth from the truth of the earth, and in looking at what appears, it is not possible to realize that truth accompanies (or opposes) every spectacle that appears. This book, which nonetheless takes an essential step forth in refuting the possibility that pure phenomenology (i.e. a phenomenology isolated from the originary structure) should be able to determine what authentically appears, still lets itself be guided by that very pure phenomenology in the determination of the content of the appearing of untruth (that is to say, it lets itself be reached by the isolation of the earth that entrusts phenomenology to phenomenology alone). It thus sets out to enquire into the conditions that make the non-appearing of truth possible (namely, those conditions that make it possible for the originary structure to be a non-persyntactic structure, i.e. something that must not necessarily appear as part of every appearing, while nevertheless being a structure of the constants of the persyntactic field). In this way, it is inevitable that the conditions thus uncovered should be merely apparent ones (namely, that the solution of the aporia should only be a merely apparent one) – even if that uncovering is altogether consistent with the unknowing decision to let pure phenomenology have the last word concerning this issue.

Section 23 of Chapter 10 is titled: 'Solution of the Aporia: Metasyntactic Constants'. The underlying principle of this resolution lies in the claim that the originary structure is not a syntactic determination of the persyntactic field, but it is a metasyntactic determination of that field: that is to say, its absence does not entail the absence of the syntax of that field. This is a principle that refutes one of the most recurring themes of *The Originary Structure*: namely, that the truth of saying necessarily determines the *formal* (= syntactic) *meaning* of every saying; that the ground of an affirmation determines the *formal meaning* of that affirmation; that the originary structure is a *syntactic* determination of its own content, and, therefore, also of the persyntactic field. It is indeed from within the originary structure that this field is posited as the background of every appearing – as the underlying content that appears as part of the appearing of every content. That is to say, it is in its being determined by the originary structure (in its structuring itself as part of that structure) that this field is posited as a persyntactic field. In determining that field, the originary structure (as noted in this book, cf. Chapter 10, §§20 ff.) is a structure of the *syntactic* constants of that field. If that field is separated from the originary structure (its appearing, without the appearing of that structure, being precisely its being isolated from it), that field is something *other*: its meaningfulness is something other than the meaningfulness that pertains to it insofar as it is linked to the originary structure. Even if this otherness were a *syntax* that differs from the one wherein that field consists insofar as it is not separated from the originary, this different syntax would precisely differ from the syntax that, as part of the originary structure, is posited as the syntax *of every* meaning – i.e. as a hyper-syntax. (The reason why it is not possible to establish an analogy with the relation between mathematics and metamathematics – namely, an analogy with the assertion that mathematics, separated from metamathematics, has a syntax that differs from the one that pertains to it insofar as it is a content of metamathematics – lies in the fact that metamathematics is a determination of the meaning of the content of mathematics that takes place, like every other determination, outside of the Necessity that appears in the originary structure of Necessity.) If separated from the originary structure, the persyntactic field is no longer a persyntactic field. This means that the originary structure is the authentic content of the persyntactic field – namely, that truth constitutes the background and the never-setting content of every appearing. The isolation of the earth and the coming to pass of mortals, too, and even the nihilistic alienation of the West, appear as part of truth.

All of this does not entail a negation of the distinction between syntax and metasyntax; rather, it means that this distinction is internal to the very persyntactic dimension constituted by the originary; that is to say, this distinction may not be used in the direction of §23 of Chapter 10. (In other words, that distinction is negated, as it precisely takes place in *The Essence of Nihilism*, insofar as it is equivalent to locating that metasyntax outside of the persyntactic field.)

At the same time, the language of Chapter 10 is also altogether aware of the meaning and the scope of the 'resolution' of that aporia. Section 24 states that the 'superseding [of that aporia] did *not* consist in showing that the proposition: "The outcome of the positional *steresis* of a metasyntactic constant of the persyntactic field is an absolute positional annulment [i.e. the non-appearing of such a constant entails that nothing appears]" is *self-contradictory*, but it consisted in showing that the proposition: "The outcome of the positional *steresis* of a metasyntactic constant of the persyntactic field is not an absolute positional annulment" is not self-contradictory'. This means that, according to *The Originary Structure*, the assertion included in *The Essence of Nihilism*, according to which truth also appears as part of the appearing of untruth, is not a self-contradictory assertion. (This is the case even if it is not yet realised that not only is this assertion not contradictory, but that it is in fact necessary – and it is not possible to realise this precisely because it is still believed to be possible to 'see', i.e. to 'attest', the absence of truth from the appearing of the contents of untruth).

9. The actual presence of truth and the domination of the negation of truth

Originary truth is the only site as part of which untruth itself may appear (that is to say, it is the only site as part of which the assertion of the existence of untruth is itself truthful). The *actual and present* appearing of the originary (the appearing that has the originary as content and, at the same time, is an element of the originary itself) includes as part of its own content the difference between truth and untruth; this difference appears as part of truth itself – that is to say, as part of the actual presence of originary truth. The very appearing and disappearing of beings, i.e. 'time', appears as part of truth – if that word is removed from the nihilistic meaning of the separation (*tempus* = τέμνειν) of beings from their being. 'Time' belongs to the content that appears as part of truth. In *The Originary Structure*, however, untruth (as well as 'common sense', which is a form of untruth) is a past, a possibility or a future (cf. Chapter 1, §§23–4). The appearing of untruth exclusively as a past or a possibility is not simply a *fact*: the actual presence of truth necessarily rules out the actual presence of untruth. The actual presence of truth entails that untruth is present *as negated*. As non-negated, untruth may therefore be present only as a past or as a possibility. That is to say, as part of truth, within which untruth appears as negated, there appears a time in which untruth exists as non-negated: truth is also a negation of untruth insofar as untruth belongs to that time; in that time, however, untruth exists as non-negated, and it is as thus non-negated that it appears as part of the truth that negates it. As already remarked, the shortcoming of *The Originary Structure* lies here in regarding the time of untruth (the past and the future) as the appearing of a dimension *in which* truth itself *is absent*, and *in which* untruth (which appears as non-negated) is therefore not countered by truth (even if this is a truth that is not testified to *by language* and that is absent from it). That shortcoming does *not* lie with the assertion that untruth is present as negated as part of truth. (Moreover: if the negation of untruth does not simply consist in the meaning or the meaningfulness of that negation, but consists in the language and the testimony through which that meaning expresses itself, then it must be the case that untruth is actually present, as a past or a possibility, not only as non-negated but also as not addressed and countered by the language that testifies to truth.)

Therefore when, starting with *The Essence of Nihilism*, it is asserted that untruth is not only a past or a future but dominates the earth – and, in fact, continues to expand its domination – this assertion does not refute (as it might appear) the assertion of *The Originary Structure* according to which untruth is present as negated but *determines* this assertion. That is to say, it is *as part of truth*, within which untruth is present as negated, that there appears the present and expanding domination of the concrete form of untruth: i.e. the domination of the alienation of the West.

For, indeed, in *The Originary Structure*, the negation of truth – i.e. the relation between the universality and the specificity or individuation of the negation – is considered (starting with Chapter 1, §4 up to Chapter 9, §§2–5 – but, also, throughout the whole enquiry) as a concrete system whose relation with the factual-historical occurrence of that negation is, however, only indeterminately posited. This lack of determinacy is not accidental but follows in an essential way from the meaning of the structuring of the originary. If, indeed, every negation of truth is a meaning that appears as such as part of truth itself, however, *that* this meaning should structure the meaning of specific factual-empirical events – the events constituted by what is referred to as the language and the works of humans and peoples – is the result of an *interpretation*: i.e. it is not a content that appears in the same way as that meaning and those events. As part of the originary structure of Necessity, the fact that a meaning – thus also including the meaning constituted by a specific negation of truth – should be the meaning of a determinate factual-empirical event (i.e. the meaning of something that immediately appears as having its own meaningfulness, which, however, differs from that meaning) is a *problem*. (It is a connection that, as part of the originary, appears as having a problematic character.) An interpretation is a will that wills the non-existence of the problem: i.e. it is a *decision* to regard that historical-empirical event as the sign of that meaning. It is as a result of this decision that the immediate meaning of factual-empirical events is linked to an additional meaning – and, through this link, it appears in the form of the language and the works of mortals. For instance: phenomenology's isolation of the originary is a negation of truth, and this negation is a meaning that appears as part of truth itself. *That* this meaning, however, should be the meaning of those factual-empirical events (or objects) referred to as 'Husserl's writings' is the decision of an interpretation: that is to say, it is the result of the decision to link specific empirical events to specific meanings, based on a determinate system of rules (cf. *The Essence of Nihilism*, Part II).

A second example: thinking and living the earth as a place in which things issue from nothingness and return to it constitutes a negation of truth, and this negation is a meaning that appears as part of truth. However, *that* this should be the meaning of a specific and extremely complex set of factual-empirical events (which, as such, already appear as having a meaning of their own: forms, volumes, colours, sounds, transformations thereof, etc.) – i.e. *that* this set should constitute what is referred to as 'the civilization of the West' – this is once again the result of an interpretation: the result of a will to posit the meaning that affords the comprehension (*pret*, φράζει) of the meaning of an empirical event between (*inter*) that event and its comprehension. The 'West', to which *The Essence of Nihilism* and the later writings refer, is *the content of an interpretation*: the West appears as part of truth insofar as it is a content of that interpretation, and not as a determination that is distinct from the latter. The *result* of the interpretation is an open problem for truth itself – it appears as an open problem as part of truth – but the *existence* of that interpretation is not a problem for truth, but a 'fact' that appears: the fact that gathers in itself the totality of empirical facts. As a will to unify different meanings, an interpretation is therefore itself the opening of a broader meaning. It is of this broader meaning that truth *establishes the structure* – the structure of Western civilization – reaching deep beneath what, as part of that interpretation, the West appears to know of itself. (That establishing is not in turn an interpretation, but an element of Necessity itself: *if* the West is what appears as part of that interpretation, then *it is necessary* that the West should consist in the land of nihilism and of the negation of truth.) *As part of that interpretation*, the West is a form of *consciousness, appearing* (of gods, humans, peoples, societies), and this appearing does not simply consist of a past or a possibility, but it is the dominant appearing – the actual and present appearing that keeps every other form of appearing at the margins. That is to say, *as part of that interpretation*, untruth (the alienation of truth, nihilism) is present *as not negated*. This is the case, however, precisely *as part of that interpretation*. This means that, as part of the actual presence of truth, within which untruth is present *as negated*, that interpretation – the will that wills the existence and the domination of the West – appears, and, as part of this will or interpretation, untruth is present *as not negated*: and, in fact, as dominating. That is to say, that will wills a content – which is a content of untruth only to the eye *of truth*, not to the eye *of that will* – as part of which something that is untruth in the eye of truth is a non-negated presence. It is in this sense that the way in which the negation of truth is considered in *The Originary Structure* is not refuted but *determined* by the later writings. This determination precisely consists in a reference to the interpretation that leads the West – namely, the domination of the alienation of truth over the earth – into the appearing of truth. Insofar as untruth, namely, the pre-philosophical, common sense, faith and the very existence of mortals are determinations that *appear* as part of truth – i.e. determinations whose existence is affirmed with necessity – they are present, as non-negated, as a past, and, in fact, as 'my' past. As non-negated, their actual presence is not simply a past, but, precisely, what dominates – in that they are what is willed as part of that interpretation, and in that, as such, they are not something whose existence is affirmed with necessity.

The *actual presence* of truth constitutes the essential meaning of the *mine-ness* of truth. The assertion at the end of §17 of Chapter 1: 'I am the only philosopher, and mine is the only philosophy' means that the actual and present appearing of the originary structure is not surrounded by other dimensions of present appearing – i.e. that its being thus surrounded does not presently appear (or, which is the same: all the dimensions of present appearing are *unified* in and by the totality of appearing). Therefore, if the term 'philosophy' indicates the originary structure in its being testified to by language, the actual and present appearing of that structure originarily constitutes the oneness and uniqueness of philosophy (a oneness that does not preclude the project of a multiplicity). If stating that truth is mine means that it is the making of a human individual, or something that mortals may in certain ways have at their disposal (at least to the extent that they *may* approach it, they *may* tarry with it or they *may* turn their back on it), then nothing could be farther removed from this statement than the content of *The Originary Structure*; in this respect, it should, on the contrary, be stated that truth is such only insofar as it is not mine, yours, of a social group, of a people or of a god. If, instead, that 'mine-ness' signifies in its originary meaning the actual presence of the appearing of what is said to be 'mine', then truth cannot but be mine, for the originary structure of Necessity is its own present and actual appearing.

Analogously, the assertion according to which I am the only philosopher, considered as to its radical meaning – namely, regarding that 'I' as the self-reflection of the appearing of truth (cf. *The Essence of Nihilism*, 'The Earth and the Essence of Man', XVII–XVIII; the meaning of this self-reflection, however, being already explicitly determined in *The Originary Structure*, cf. Chapter 2, §§16–23; Chapter 5) – that assertion signifies nothing but the oneness of the actual and present appearing of the originary; even though the context in which that assertion appears in *The Originary Structure* hints at something different, namely at the oneness and uniqueness of the relation that obtains between the originary and that particular content of the originary that 'I' am as a human individual: that is, as that set of human convictions that constitute a *faith* (and that are grounded in the isolation of the earth, i.e. in the occurrence as part of which my being mortal occurs).

In this sense, stating that I am the only philosopher means that, originarily, I am the only faith that, as part of truth, appears as a heeding of truth – a heeding that, precisely insofar as it is a faith, is *destined* to fail to heed that truth. Insofar as it is heeded 'by me', i.e. by the faith in which 'I' consist as a mortal individual, truth cannot be truth, and I am destined to remain only the desire, *in indefinitum*, for that truth – i.e. precisely, and to the letter, a philo-sopher. The originary structure of truth is not the end point reached by philo-sophy understood in this way: philo-sophy is destined to remain outside truth, for the path along which it wishes to reach truth cannot but proceed as part of untruth. The originary structure of Necessity is not the end point of any 'enquiry': the originary structure is always already open outside of every enquiry, containing it and knowing that it constitutes an impossible attempt, by a mortal individual or by a social group, at becoming the 'site', the 'keeper' or the interlocutor of truth. As a mortal individual, I am 'part of' truth – I am one of the determinations that appear as part of the appearing of truth; in my being part of truth, however, I *am* one of the forms of untruth (that is to say, I am a 'mortal' – according to the specific meaning that this word takes starting with *The Essence of Nihilism*). It is Necessity itself that determines that being that says 'I' as a form of untruth and as a mortal being.

10. What is called thinking

The Originary Structure also takes a crucial step forth along the path that leads the Western concept of 'thinking' to its twilight. For the West, thinking is a 'gesture', an 'act', an 'action', an 'operation'; it is in fact a gesture in its absolute purity and agility. A gesture is something that arises (*gestus*, from *gerere*, means 'to act towards the accomplishment of something'), namely, something that is done, interrupted, done again, repeated and controlled. As such, thinking is the most impermanent and unstable of things. Thinking may even think the eternal, but it is nevertheless an act that comes and goes, is interrupted, is an object of the will. 'We' – the inhabitants of the West state – '*want* to think'. Even when idealism understands thinking as a 'pure act', or as transcendental thinking, thinking still preserves an essential feature of gestures: the agility of self-production. In both classical and modern metaphysics, God's thinking is not immutable insofar as it is thinking, but insofar as it is godly. The imagination of mortals associates thinking with the flash of a lightning or a series of lightnings in the night of un-thinking: a flash that may last for a longer or a shorter time, but a light that is as impermanent as it is intermittent, in which it is possible to identify a first and a last term of the series – first, the darkness that precedes the birth of mortals, then the darkness of their death. According to Christian theology, the soul – the subject of thinking – is immortal, but it is created as part of time and it is sustained in its eternal life by God's will. Without this will, the soul, too, would be extinguished, like every lightning and every bolt.

Outside of the nihilism of the West, the essential meaning of thinking is the appearing of the Whole. This appearing is eternal, like every being, and it coincides with the appearing of its eternity. This eternal appearing is not something to be sought afar – it is in fact what is nearest: it is the very dimension with respect to which things may be said to be near or far. In this sense, it consists of the *actual and present* appearing – without this actual presence having anything to share with the Western meaning of 'act'. The actual and present appearing is the appearing that appears; if it is said to be 'actual and present', its 'actual presence' indicates its difference from the appearing that remains concealed. (This latter appearing consists exactly in the appearing in which the Whole does *not* appear while concealing itself – this appearing while concealing itself being precisely the actual and present appearing – but appears in and through the concrete and full volume of its determinations; cf. *The Essence of Nihilism*, 'The Path of Day', XVII ff.) *This* actual and present appearing of the Whole is the appearing that for millennia and always already and forever illuminates the Whole. *This* appearing: in which our world appears, and so do the history of the West and the entire sequence of mortal occurrences. *This* appearing: which is not the doing of any human or god (and as part of which the alienation of every doing appears). All millennia of history unfold within it.

As part of the Necessity of this meaning, thinking is not a gesture, an act, a doing or an action, but the site in which all gestures, acts, doings and actions arise (which, in their essence, consist in the *conviction*, the *will* and the *faith* of handling, acting and doing). Thinking is in fact the site in which the earth itself arises: which is to say, everything that may come to arise. Insofar as it is the appearing of everything that appears, thinking does not arise and does not take leave, for every arising and taking leave mean entering appearing and taking leave from it. Thinking is not a gesture or a lightning but the firm will of the heavens in which the constellations of being proceed one after the other, taking their turn: these are the eternal stars of the 'Path of Night' (the eternal stars of the sequence of the occurrences of mortals and of the history of the West), and, should their appearing be necessary, the eternal stars of the 'Path of Day'. What the language of mortals refer to as 'our thoughts', 'our feelings', 'our moods' or 'the acts of our will', too, are themselves eternal stars of being, which enter and leave the eternal vault of appearing: the firm circle that constitutes the authentic meaning of thinking. Not guided or willed by any human or god (hence not even by Jesus' god), they belong to the earth, which is accompanied by Destiny through the vault of appearing. The vault of the heavens, *qua* firm ground, possesses no 'agility' – it is not a form of *agere*, of 'setting itself in motion' or springing into flight. Every flight takes place as part of that vault, and it is not 'sprung' – namely, detached from Destiny, which leads the eternal stars of being into appearing.

The necessity, however, that this should be the authentic meaning of thinking is the necessity that thinking should consist in the appearing of the originary structure of Necessity. One of the central points of this book is that thinking is a *structure* – in a sense that is altogether alien to structuralism itself (also for chronological reasons, since *The Originary Structure* is published in the same year as Lévi-Strauss's *Structural Anthropology*). Structuralism comes to recognize specific constant structures in the behaviour of social groups through empirical investigations, i.e. through a scientific process. In *The Originary Structure*, thinking, *qua* appearing, is a structure because in the originary structure of Necessity *appearing originarily includes itself as part of its own content* (i.e. as part of the totality of appearing beings). Necessity is not such without this originary self-comprehension of appearing (cf. Chapter 2, §§11–23). *The Essence of Nihilism* ('The Earth and The Essence of Man', XVII) precisely refers to those sections of *The Originary Structure*. Self-comprehension or 'self-consciousness'.

The self-consciousness of idealism, however, is the result of the process of the self-realization of being. Outside of the nihilism of the idealistic interpretation of thinking, the self-comprehension of appearing is not a movement that returns to itself, a gesture that indicates an already performed gesture or an act that increments itself, but an immutable standing: an eternal iris. This eternal iris consists of the *actual and present* appearing. In the history of the West, if thinking is *this* actual and present thinking, it is not an immutable thinking (the very eternity of thinking consisting in the eternal process of creation and destruction of all things); conversely, if thinking is immutable, it is not *this actual and present* thinking. As part of the originary structure of Necessity, thinking, *qua* appearing, is the firm iris in which the eternal spectacle of Necessity comes to light and the eternal star of the earth, and of its isolation, comes to pass.

The language that speaks of the originary structure neither encloses it nor reaches it from without. This language – which comes and goes, which speaks about the originary structure, but also stops speaking about it, to then come back to speak about it again, and so on, in an alternating sequence – is itself one of the beings of the earth that proceed into the vault of appearing: a being that in a certain way accompanies all other beings, placing them on the pedestal of a noun. By no means does language make us turn to the originary structure, to then make us turn away from it and then make us return to think it. By no means does one, through language, begin, stop and return to think Necessity: it is the words of language, and, therefore, of the language that speaks of the originary structure that *return* as part of *the same* thinking – i.e. as part of the appearing of the originary structure. By no means do words approach that structure from without, gather it and carry it on themselves: words, too – thus including the words that speak of the originary – are eternal stars of being that enter and leave the eternal circle of the appearing of the originary. The originary sees within itself the language by which it is spoken and sees within itself the arising of that language.

It is therefore the originary itself that sees *itself*, within *itself*, as a form of self-comprehension. This self-seeing consists in the appearing of the appearing of itself: namely, in the consciousness of its self-consciousness. The language that, in Chapter 2, expresses the self-comprehension of appearing precisely arises within the consciousness of this self-comprehension. The firm iris of appearing is thus a structure, in that it consists of the appearing of the appearing of appearing. These three, however, *are the same* appearing: this is what is concretely clarified in Chapter 2 (where, however, the emphasis is placed on the sameness that constitutes itself as part of the self-comprehension of appearing), as well as in the passage quoted above from *The Essence of Nihilism*. Precisely because it is necessary for appearing to originarily be the appearing *of itself*, the circle of appearing includes its own self – but not in the way in which a circle with a larger area includes a circle with a smaller one: the appearing (let this be A_2) that appears is *the same* appearing (let this be A_1) in which it (i.e. A_2) appears. The appearing (let this be A_3) of this self-identity of appearing is *that same* self-identical appearing: $A_3 = A_2 = A_1$. This means that A_3 is not a reflection (an act of reflection) that would arise while taking as content the identity between A_1 and A_2: A_3 is A_2 itself, *that is to say*, A_1 itself.

This, however, does not mean that there only exists one of these three terms – precisely in that appearing does not only consist in the appearing that comprehends but also in the appearing that is comprehended: i.e. it exists both as comprehending and as comprehended, in such a way that, in this sense, the identical distinguishes itself. This distinguishing, in turn, appears: it is itself comprehended by appearing (that is to say, by the appearing in which this speaking of a distinction is grounded – an appearing that, in comprehending that distinction, is distinct from the terms that are distinguished). Precisely because appearing is such – namely, appearing *of* something, and, therefore and necessarily, appearing *of* itself – this reference *to itself* consists, at the same time, in the identity and in the difference of the terms of the reference. The *reference* entails a difference, the reference *to itself* entails an identity. (This difference is not to be confused with the one that must also exist in order for any determination d to be self-identical – cf. Chapter 3, §11: d is self-identical only insofar as d does not appear as isolated from its being self-identical, but appears as $(d = d) = (d = d)$; as isolated from the appearing of its being self-identical, d is not d and does not appear as d, but as non-d. Appearing, too, is a determination that is self-identical in the way in which every determination is, and, in this sense, it requires a *difference* between d and the concrete equation that expresses its identity. *In addition*, however, appearing is that specific determination that consists of a *self-reference*, whereby the *reference* entails a difference between what refers and that to which this refers, and the *self*-reference entails an identity of the differing terms. The two terms are thus identical in that they are the same determination – namely, in that, as part of that reference, what refers refers to itself – and they are different in that this determination is a reference to...: i.e. it is the appearing of...).

It is in and through this firm and threefold unity of appearing that the eternal star of the earth proceeds. The threefold unity of appearing is the eternal and never-setting vault of thinking, as part of which the eternal and never-setting star of Necessity comes to appear, and as part of which the eternal stars of the earth come to rise and set.

In Chapter 3 of this book, it is completely explicit that the appearing of appearing, *qua* element of the originary structure of Necessity, cannot consist of a free act of reflection, which would come to be performed on a previous reflection, and which could then, in turn, come to be the object of a new reflection. Chapter 5, however, considers the meaning of this reflection regarded as a *possibility* (§§31–4), rather than as that to which the constitution of the originary structure of Necessity is entrusted. Overall, the argument that this book makes on this point consists in claiming that while the appearing of Necessity is the structure of the firm and threefold unity of appearing (Chapter 3), a *reflection* – and, in fact, a 'series' of reflections (Chapter 5, §§6–16) – on that structure is nevertheless *possible*. It is in this second part of the argument that the notion of thinking *qua* 'gesture' or 'act' appears again in *The Originary Structure*, despite the fact that it is precisely this notion that is radically put into question by the fundamental meaning of this book.

Chapter 5 is completely explicit in stating that *the same structure persists* through the unfolding of the series of reflections – this persisting structure being precisely the 'originary judgement' *qua* self-positing of the originary structure (§17). (Indeed, stating that the same structure persists through the unfolding of that series means stating that this structure constitutes the site in which that series arises.) Chapter 5 also explicitly asserts that the unfolding of that series does not involve the *form* of the totality of appearing (i.e. the form of appearing *qua* totality), but the *content* of that totality (§§2, 16, 21, 27). That is to say, what arises in the series of reflections is not appearing *qua* totality of appearing, but appearing *qua* content of that totality. What is instead not determined in that chapter is the way in which the unfolding of the series of reflections on the originary structure may involve only the content and not the form of the totality of the originary – given that this series is precisely a series of reflection *on* the originary: i.e. a series of dimensions, each of which constitutes itself as *the totality* of what appears. The originary structure is the totality of appearing; the arising, in that series, of a *reflection* on the originary structure thus consists in the arising of an appearing that constitutes the new total dimension of appearing. The concept of persistence (through the unfolding of the series of the reflection) of the form of the totality is thus in contradiction with the concept of the arising of a reflection on the originary. However, it is precisely in and through this second notion that the originary becomes the content of a 'gesture'. It is impossible for the form of the totality of appearing – i.e. for appearing *qua* totality (referred to as 'transcendental appearing' in *The Essence of Nihilism*) – to be something that arises; it must necessarily be the site in which everything that arises is received and from which everything that departs takes leave.

The unfolding of a *possible* series, in which the threefold unity of appearing appears, and in which this latter appearing itself appears, and so on, must therefore, of necessity, *not* be a *reflection on* the threefold unity of the appearing of the originary, but an unfolding *of the analysis of the content* of that unity. There arises no new gesture, which includes within itself what *was* the totality of appearing – that new gesture being now the new totality that is itself able to be included into a more comprehensive gesture; rather, it is as part of the firm will of the threefold unity of appearing that the analysis of what that vault encloses unfolds. No new light (or series of new, ever-expanding lights) is shone *on* the light of the originary; no new and ever-wider circles are traced *around* the three identical and mutually encompassing circles of the threefold unity of appearing; rather, there appears an unfolding of the analysis of the internal structure of the firm light of the originary: i.e. of its three circles. It is not the vault of appearing that rises upwards, or is included in a higher vault, but the elements of the content that this vault protects that come to be articulated and enriched. While, as part of the structure of Necessity, the identity of A_1, A_2 and A_3 rules out every *regressus in indefinitum* in the self-foundation of the originary, an analysis may attest that, as part of that identity, which is structured as a consciousness of self-consciousness, the consciousness that *is the content* of self-consciousness is *the same* consciousness *of* self-consciousness – in such a way that the consciousness of self-consciousness is the consciousness of a consciousness whose content is the consciousness of self-consciousness. An unfolding certainly takes place in this way, but it is an unfolding of the analysis that shows how the consciousness of the consciousness whose content is the consciousness of self-consciousness is *the same* as the consciousness of self-consciousness, rather than an unfolding of the reflection of appearing *on* the appearing of the originary. That analysis may unfold without any limits, but precisely in showing how the multiplicity of the terms that – ever more numerous – arise as part of the originary is *the same* as the threefold unity of the appearing of the originary. If the unfolding of this series is regarded as an unfolding of the *analysis of the content* of the originary, rather than as an unfolding of the *reflection* on the originary (or, equivalently, if by 'unfolding of the reflection' one understands the unfolding of the analysis of that content), then the entirety of Chapter 5 is freed from the contradiction noted above.

11. The necessities of the West, and Necessity itself

The ground of every form of erring is the isolation of the earth from the Necessity as part of which the earth proceeds. Thus isolated from Necessity – i.e. from the originary structure of Destiny, in which the meaning of every being is determined – the eternal star of the earth appears as a nothingness precisely because it is willed as the secure whole with which mortals have to do (cf. *The Essence of Nihilism*, 'The Earth and the Essence of Man'). The nihilism of the West consists in the testimony of this nothingness of the earth; as part of this nothingness, language allows the availability of the things of the earth for being and non-being (i.e. becoming, temporality, the historicity of things) to surface in the word, but withholds in the domain of the unexpressed what is necessarily connected to this availability of things: that is to say, the latter's being nothing insofar as they are things – i.e. not nothing.

In turn, however, the isolation of the earth, which constitutes the ground of every erring and, at the same time, the occurrence of the being-mortal of mortals, is grounded in the isolation of the originary Necessity of the Whole: it is only insofar as the originary structure of Necessity does not coincide with the appearing of the concrete and determinate completeness of the Whole that, in the structure of the

Necessity, the earth may proceed in its being enclosed by the isolation that separates it from Necessity. The meaning of the difference between the isolation of the earth from Necessity and the isolation of Necessity from the Whole has already been indicated in §7 of this Introduction. The overcoming of the dialectical contradiction that surrounds Necessity, in its being isolated from the Whole, is given by the gradual appearing of the Whole within that very Necessity. In this sense, the isolation of the earth, too, as well as the occurrence of mortals and of the 'houses of the Night' (δώματα Νυκτός, Parmenides, Fragment 1, 9), inhabited by mortals and by the nihilism of the West – that is to say, the appearing of this essential alienation, too – belongs to the path that leads outside of the dearth of originary Necessity, which is isolated from the Whole. The 'Path of Night' is a segment of the way along which the Whole manifests itself in the circle of Necessity. The overcoming of the dialectical contradiction that encloses the earth in its isolation from the originary Necessity, however, is given by the consummation and the twilight of the 'Path of Night' traversed by mortals and by the West, and by the stepping forth, in that Necessity, of the 'Path of Day', which leaves behind not only the thoughts but also the works of the Night, and which is no longer traversed by any mortal traveller.

Isolated from Necessity (which is at the same time the Necessity of the earth), the earth itself appears as a nothingness: i.e. as that other of itself that cannot be a being (for Necessity, on which the isolation of the earth turns its back, is the Necessity *of every* being), and is therefore nothing. In the same way in which the isolation of the earth is already a form of nihilism (which, however, awaits to be testified to by the West), so nihilism itself is an isolation: namely, that separation of beings from their being that leaves them available for being and nothingness. These two fundamental aspects – the dialectic of the isolation and the impossibility of separating things from their being – constitute the themes developed in *The Essence of Nihilism* and in the later writings; it is, however, in *The Originary Structure* that these two aspects are not only expressed for the first time but also receive the analytically most determinate formulation of the meaning of their inscription in the originary structure of Necessity.

The Necessity of which this book begins to speak has nothing to share with the various forms of 'necessity' invoked by Western culture and civilization. In the history of the West, 'necessity' consists in the will to power's 'not ceding' (*ne-cedit*) to becoming, thus overpowering it. It overpowers it, however, precisely insofar as it feels threatened by it. This feeling threatened and not ceding are one of the most radical forms of acknowledgement of the existence of becoming. Precisely insofar as 'necessity' does not cede to becoming, it acknowledges the fact that becoming does not cede its own existence. In the history of the West, 'necessity' appears from the outset as being internally split: it appears as the 'necessity' of the immutables that dominate the insurgence of becoming, and as the 'necessity' of becoming, which continues to survive under the domination of the immutables of the West, while laying the groundwork for their destruction. The will to power lies at the foundation of this split of 'necessity': the will to power requires the existence of what is to be dominated and secures it by separating the earth from Necessity – i.e. by separating things from their being, thus making them available for a domination that delivers them to being and nothingness.

In the history of the West, the originary form of the will to power is the will that wills the existence of the becoming of things: i.e. the will that wills the existence of the separation of things from their being.

The will to power, however, by invoking the becoming of things releases the unpredictable forces of that very becoming, from which it must defend itself by invoking the 'necessity' of the immutables, which dominate and anticipate becoming itself. It is in this essential sense (a sense that is in its essence unknown to Nietzsche) that, in the history of the West, the remedy has been worse than the ill – 'worse', from the standpoint of the will to power, for the remedy of the immutables has ended up making unthinkable and impracticable the very field of domination constituted by becoming. Becoming, *qua* absolute unpredictability, does indeed determine the ill of the threat, but, to the very eye of the will to power that invokes the forms of 'necessity' of the West, it also constitutes the ultimate form of self-evidence. Precisely because the remedy has been worse than the ill – in that it has come to threaten to stifle the very life of becoming (namely, in that the threat constituted by 'life' has resulted in a threat to that very 'life') – the will to power has gradually destructed the immutables and the ἐπιστήμη as part of which they have been erected. The will to power has thus begun, and continues to this day, to defend itself from the threat of becoming not by means of a form of 'necessity' – i.e. a form of not ceding to becoming – but by relinquishing the very will to constitute itself as a force that is external to becoming (thus being threatened by the latter), and by identifying with that very becoming as a force that drives it from the inside. Accordingly, this force does not have the character of a 'necessity' to which becoming must submit, but that of a 'hypothesis' that awaits its confirmation from becoming itself. Modern science and the technological organization of the earth are grounded in this hypothetical character, which drives becoming from the inside by *ceding* to its indications.

An abyss separates the Necessity that begins to be testified to in *The Originary Structure* from the forms of 'necessity' of the West. That Necessity is not a will to dominate becoming, a will that is grounded in the originary form of the will to power: i.e. in the will that wills the existence of becoming and the availability of things for being and nothing. Outside of the isolation of the earth, Necessity is the appearing of the inalienable accord between every thing and its being; Necessity is not a force that imposes itself and succeeds in dominating becoming, but it consists in the appearing of the self-negation of the negation of what it says, and, therefore, it consists in the appearing of the alienation of the faith that wills the existence of the becoming of things and the isolation of the earth. Only outside the history of the West is a testimony of Necessity possible. The forms of 'necessity' of the West are destined to their twilight. If 'philosophy' does not indicate a setting out on a path towards truth, proceeding from untruth and moving along its broken paths – if 'philosophy' does *not* indicate a process of real transformation of humans and of the world, which would lead from untruth to truth, or from truth to truth, or from a problem to its temporary solution – but indicates a *care* (φιλία) for the *clearing* of Necessity (in tracing σοφία to σαφήνεια), namely, the care that expresses itself in and through the testimony of Necessity, then philosophy is only possible outside of the West (and outside of the domination of the entirety of the earth operated by the West): and, through that philosophy, a first step is taken along the 'Path of Day'.

The Necessity that is always already open outside the isolation of the earth and the history of the West is not a doctrine that may be handed over by one person to another, and nor is it something that may be 'understood' by one person or by many. Insofar as it is 'understood' by one person or by many, Necessity simply becomes a 'perspective' of the one or of the many, i.e. something that cannot be Necessity. The testimony of Necessity may be 'heeded'. If, however, as part of that heeding, Necessity appears as such, the heeding one may not be 'one of us', a mortal or a god; it may not be 'my neighbour'. If Necessity may not be what 'one' uncovers, which is thus confined within the limits of the gaze of that one, neither can Necessity be what is heeded by an 'other', or 'others'. If, as part of this heeding, Necessity appears as Necessity, the heeding one cannot but be Necessity itself, and that heeding constitutes once again its appearing.

12. Note

Completed in the first months of 1979, this introduction makes no mention of *Destino della necessità* (Emanuele Severino, *Destino della necessità*, Milan: Adelphi, 1980), published a year later. The work on the preparation of this book, however, which had begun almost ten years earlier, was precisely interrupted to prepare the second edition of *The Originary Structure* – which, in the initial editorial project, was supposed to be published before *Destino della necessità*. This is mentioned in order to note that if no explicit reference is made in this Introduction to the themes of *Destino della necessità*, this book nonetheless constitutes the clearly discernible milieu in which this Introduction has been written.

The meaning of the relation *between the contents* of the two books may instead be thus formulated: *The Originary Structure* indicates the originary structure *of the Necessity* to which *Destino della necessità* refers.

The text of this second edition of *La struttura originaria* replicates the text of the first edition (Brescia: La Scuola, 1958). The fifteen chapters have become thirteen, for the fifth has been joined to the first and the seventh to the sixth. The most substantial additions consist in the paragraphs following the first two paragraphs in point a of §11 of Chapter 4 and in the last paragraph of §10 of Chapter 13. The purpose of these and all other additions was to clarify the language of *The Originary Structure*, and not to trace it back to the language of the later writings. All the other revisions, too – which modify or reduce the text of the first edition – have this aim. Sections 2–11 of Chapter 12 (corresponding to Chapter 10 of the present edition) have been removed because the result they sought to achieve had already been correctly and adequately obtained in the previous section. The content of §9 of Chapter 5 (corresponding to §9 of Chapter 6 of the first edition) has also been modified.[11]

Spring 1979–Spring 1981

The originary structure

Note

This volume presents a first group of investigations into the originary structure (through which we intend to arrive at a concrete meaning of this term). The discussion remains thus open to an extension and a further development – in such a way, however, that it remains at the same time established what it means to refer these two notions to an investigation into the originary.

The present essay, then, does not so much stand alongside the author's previous works, but it rather intends to stand as an exposition of the domain from which their validity may be determined, and their revision carried out. Furthermore, however – more importantly – this domain constitutes that in relation to which alone the validity of any assertion may be determined: the authentic meaning and grounding of the theoreticist attitude. The investigations contained in this essay do not therefore intend to move within a pre-established or presupposed logical horizon. One would wish for their validity to be sought solely in them. For, indeed, these investigations may be able to indicate in which direction the theoretical use and valorization of the historical material are to be carried out, and in what sense they themselves constitute an aspect of that valorization.

It is likely that the reading of this essay will be inconvenienced by the fact that, from the very first pages, we refer to the last chapter. This, however, could not be otherwise; that is to say, it appeared that this was the only way to avoid a greater number of references. For the discussion is not, so to speak, centred on a logical segment, but on a logical point; hence all the elements of the exposition are, from the outset, required in the same way. The reading of that chapter may, however, be anticipated, if desired, although it only achieves a sufficient degree of intelligibility through a knowledge of the preceding chapters...

Summer 1957

NB: When only the section is indicated in an internal reference, this means that we refer to the section belonging to the same chapter in which the reference is found.

1

The exposition of the originary structure

1. The originary structure (formal definition)

The originary structure is the essence of the ground. In this sense, it is the anapodeictic *structure* of knowledge – the ἀρχὴ τῆς γνώσεως – and, therefore, the *self-structuring* of the essence of principality, *or* immediacy.

This entails that the essence of the ground is not something simple, but a complexity, or the unity of a multiplicity.

2. The ground and the negation of the ground

What Aristotle observes concerning the principle of non-contradiction pertains to the originary structure – leaving here aside the clarifications that will have to be made regarding this point: namely, that the negation of that very principle, in order to hold itself firm as such, must presuppose it. As a result, that negation negates and at the same time affirms that principle: it negates it *in actu signato*, and it affirms it *in actu exercito*; therefore, precisely insofar as it affirms it and negates it *at the same time*, it fails to negate it.

An explicit presentation of this fact, however, requires an exposition of the originary structure (that is to say: exhibiting that the negation of the originary structure is possible only by presupposing this very structure – or that the condition of that negation is precisely what is negated – entails above all that the originary structure should have been exhibited and exposed); this therefore requires a considerable discursive development.

3. Note on the history of the ground

a. While in the history of philosophy the elements of the structure of the ground do not realize themselves as constants, they nevertheless present remarkably low indices of variation. Consider, for instance, the persistence – as relevant as ever in modern philosophy – of the Aristotelian pair '*principle of non-contradiction-immediate knowledge*' (experience, ἐπαγωγή), in which these two terms precisely stand as elements of the structure of the ground. (This becomes more plausible if one takes care not to conflate these elements with general 'categories'. The extreme variability of the latter takes indeed place within a relative persistence of those elements.) From a general standpoint, it may be claimed that the task of ascertaining the elements of the structure of the ground is already complete with Aristotle.

These elements, however, are nothing but the abstract moments of the ground. At the same time, while the *structuring* of the abstract is most prominent in modern philosophy, the uncovering of this structure carried out is in that case under certain preconceptions, due to which a grounding dimension is presupposed to the ground itself. Epistemological presupposition: reversal of the ground into something grounded. (The transition from dogmatism to critical philosophy is a development – however, prominent – which takes place as part of that reversal.) The 'end of the philosophy of knowledge' – which nevertheless takes place as part of a temporal process or adjustment – affords today an uncorrupted opening of the question of the ground. Contemporary philosophy itself, considered as a whole – in its *self-structuring!* – may with good reason be regarded as realizing that opening, albeit with a proviso that we are shortly to make explicit. Accordingly, the *resistance* that the single philosophical movements may offer to the structuring that supersedes them in a higher speculative dimension should not be ascribed to their positive contributions (which are positive precisely insofar as and to the extent that their content, as such, does not require that resistance), but, in an Hegelian way, to the claim of the single movements to each stand as the whole of that opening.

At the same time, however, it is also not the case that, in relation to the opening of the ground, philosophy is left with no other option than to merely draw the conclusion of present history, relying on a simple repetition and juxtaposition of elements that have already been introduced. We, too, in a certain respect, can state that if recent philosophy had provided the content or the elements of originary knowledge, it would now be a question of conferring a *form* on that content – but, as it is clear, a form does not join a content from the outside but permeates it in its entirety, down to the last element, and *renews* it.

b. Furthermore, however, it is not merely a question of conferring a form upon a content, but to carry out an essential integration of the content itself; as a result, in this respect, it will not be possible to claim that contemporary philosophy, in its unitary structure, may be regarded as the opening of the ground. Indeed, the authentic meaning of the originary content remains concealed not only if this is understood as a negation of metaphysics (namely, as the impossibility, meaninglessness and lack of theoretical stance of metaphysics), but even if it is entrusted with the role of a methodological foundation of metaphysical knowledge, thus regarding it as the *problematic* opening of the metaphysical horizon. The concrete exposition of the originary structure precisely shows that metaphysics, *in its theorematic or categorical character*, belongs to the very structure of the immediate. Relative to the ground, metaphysical *knowledge* is not something to be pursued additionally, but it belongs to the very essence of the ground; that is to say, it leaves no respite, or any possibility of retreating on a plane that might serve as a foothold from which one may then set out on the metaphysical journey. Or, in fact, something like a 'starting point' certainly exists, *but as an abstract moment of the originary structure* – in such a way that the journey is originarily completed.

All of this, it is clear, will have to be adequately determined. Here, let us only state that if humans are originarily 'at home', this is not simply to be understood according to the vantage point secured by contemporary philosophy, to the extent that the latter constitutes an elimination of every naturalistic realism – in a way that this being at home would here simply indicate a negation of the immediate distinction between certainty and knowledge (that negation only being able to turn itself into a simple and formal affirmation of the identity of those two terms); and nor is that being at home to be understood as the bestowing of a metaphysical value on that elimination (which actual idealism may, with good reason, be argued to have done), thus giving rise to a kind of 'immanentist metaphysics'. Considered from a historical standpoint, the originary theorematic character of metaphysics consists instead in a return to the pure essence of metaphysics, as this is realized in Parmenides' thought – with, in addition, a knowledge of the originarity of that pure essence. Accordingly, a return to the ground of metaphysics – as instead put forth by Heidegger – regarded as something originarily preliminary to metaphysics itself, is thus possible only if metaphysics is not regarded as to that pure essence.[1]

4. The ground and the history of the ground

The history of the ground is an essential element or moment of the ground itself (in the same way in which, more generally, every logical structure that must proceed from the ground must also *essentially* include its own history within itself). Furthermore, it is not simply the history that has taken place that belongs to the ground, but also the possible one. The history that has occurred only constitutes one section of the possible ways of standing in relation to the ground. This system of possibilities, which also includes what has effectively taken place, is precisely to be understood as the possible history of the ground. All of this is then to be briefly elucidated.

All the possible ways of (explicitly or implicitly) standing in relation to the ground – *except one* – constitute as many negations of the ground. There are different kinds of negation: for instance, the ground may be negated insofar as its content is not recognized as having the value of ground; or, insofar as this value is recognized only for a part of that content (even if to the extent that the remaining part is disregarded); or insofar as it is denied that knowledge should have a ground; or, simply, insofar as the ground is not known in terms of both its concrete content and its very formal meaning. A logical content has a 'history' insofar as, in one way or another, it has been negated. (We do not intend to exhaust the meaning of the term 'history' in this way, but we only aim to take note of a determination that essentially belongs to history *qua* becoming.) If that logical content had never been negated, there would only be a history *per accidens* of that content (or its historicity would belong to the future): in the sense, for instance, that there would only be a history of those who have kept affirming it. The historical and factual occurrence of that negation is therefore included in the system of possible negations of the content under consideration, and it is to this system that we refer as the possible history of that content, or – given the matter at hand – as the possible history of the ground. (Whether or not, in that system, those negations should be found to be arranged according to a determinate logical order is a question that, at this point, may be left aside without any consequences.)

Within the system of possible negations, the ones that have *occurred* – let us add – distinguish themselves from the ones that have not occurred to the extent that the former ones are the object of concerns, interests or passions, due to which either the logical basis on which those negations rest is regarded as the ground itself or, more generally, they become, as such, the content of a *certainty*. The 'cunning of reason' precisely consists in fully engaging the individual (since individuals precisely consist of those concerns, interests and passions), making the work or task entrusted to them appear as something positive, and as the whole of the work or task: even when it is something negative, or only a moment of the positive.[2]

As a way of provisionally approaching or elaborating the question, it may therefore be stated that the positing of the ground entails in an essential way the superseding of the negation of the ground; or it may be stated that the ground only realizes itself as the originary opening of truth insofar as it is able to supersede its negation, and, therefore, only insofar as it is in relation with the latter. Accordingly, the ground is only posited insofar as its negation is also posited (*qua* superseded). If it were to be argued that, while admitting that the ground is that which must be able to absolutely supersede its negation, it is nevertheless possible *to posit* (i.e. to have before oneself in its manifestness) the ground without the necessity of positing its negation, we would have to remark that the content that is posited *is* the ground precisely insofar as it *exhibits* its ability to absolutely supersede its negation (i.e. insofar as this ability is posited); equivalently, one would have to remark that it is possible to affirm that this content is the ground only insofar as that ability *is posited*: for if that ability is instead not posited – and that must be the case if the ground is posited without the positing of its negation – then not only does that content not *exhibit itself* as the ground, but it *is* not the ground either. Instead, it *is* only an *abstract moment* of the ground – the whole or concreteness of the ground precisely consisting in the positional relation between that moment and its negation.

Accordingly, that negation is not an abstract universality, but the concrete system of possible negations. Furthermore, this system precisely consists in the possible history of the ground – the term 'history', as already mentioned, including in its meaning the arising of difference, and, therefore, of the respective negation. Since the ground is such only insofar as it entails its negation as superseded, this system of negations is therefore essential to the ground itself.

While a negation of the ground certainly presents a character of definitiveness and completeness also to the extent that it is regarded as a formal negation – namely, as a universality in which the particular is only 'in itself' – this formal negation is, however, only something abstract: the concrete, as already mentioned, being here the system or the organism of the negations of the ground. This is a system that realizes itself in and through a process, or a becoming, whose content consists in the individuation of a universality or in the actualization of a particular, i.e. in its becoming 'for itself' within the horizon of that universality. This process or becoming is the very act of the – actual and non-actual – manifestation of the system of the negations of the ground; or, equivalently, it is the mode of being of that system. In accordance with that mode of being, the positing of the horizon of a negation coincides at the same time with a projecting of those individuations of that negation that are not included in the present and actual horizon of the latter; that is to say, these individuations are such that their potential realization increases the process of the manifestation of that negation.

In and through this becoming, the universality of the negation *concretizes itself*. Accordingly, the superseding of that negation, too, concretizes itself – and, therefore, so does the very ground that implies its own negation as superseded. If the ground negatively implies its negation, it cannot be indifferent to the concretization of that negation. This does not mean that the opening of the ground is foreclosed until the consummation of the process in which that negation realizes itself has taken place: the ground, in its opening, does not (negatively) entail a *quantum* of that negation, but the *totality* – or, precisely, the universal – of that negation. As a result, the exclusion of that negation is infinite and universal. Accordingly, the unpredictability presented by the negation, in its individuating itself, is absolutely superseded. In this respect, the ground originarily pre-empts every surprise. Or: the opening of the ground originarily resolves in itself the development of its own negation; that is to say, it does not depend upon it (in the sense that it does not await the conclusion of that development in order to posit itself).

At the same time, however – as already mentioned – this does not entail an *indifference* of the ground with respect to the processual self-manifestation of the individuation of the universality of its negation, for, on the contrary, it pertains to the ground, per its own essence, that it should affirm itself as such a ground with respect to every increase of that negation: exhibiting that increase and recognizing it precisely as something that is *already superseded* – i.e. including it in the superseded horizon of the universality of its negation.

The abstraction of the ground from the development of its negation can either mean that the ground lets that development unfold without asserting itself upon it, and without resolving it within itself, or that the development of that negation takes place outside of the cognition of the ground (that is to say, outside of the cognition wherein the ground consists). In the first case, the ground, letting its negation subsist, would not constitute itself as ground. In the second case – the discussion here, however, suffering from the inadequacy of the exposition of the ground at this point – the positing of a development of a negation that is not known is a *project* produced by the ground itself: and, therefore, it is an element of the structure of the latter. (That project consists in the project of the non-conforming of the known quantum of the individuation of the universal negation to the universality of the negation.) To the extent that this project is posited, and known, it is superseded – for, otherwise, what has been ruled out in the first of the two cases mentioned above would apply to that projected content.

Insofar as the ground is essentially involved in its own history, the ground 'eternalizes' itself to the extent that it 'historicizes' itself. Since the history of the ground consists in the concretization of the universality of its negation, it is precisely in relation to the development of that negation that the ground asserts its significance. The condition of possibility of the historical development of philosophical knowledge lies precisely in that structure, in accordance with which the ground – as well as every logical positing that rests upon it – (negatively) implies the concreteness of its negation. Phenomenology is thus essentially subsumed within science itself; or: science is the unity of phenomenology and science. It is therefore in relation to the development of that negation (i.e. the phenomenology of the error) that the ground *stands firm*; it is by standing firm in this way that it is always *the same*. This standing firm relative to the development of that negation, however, is also a movement: the movement of the negation of what gradually arises in opposition to the ground (i.e. the movement of the negation of the processual negation of the ground). Accordingly, in this respect, the ground consists in a form of unfolding, a novelty, a progress.

> The progress is not an addition that is appended to the past: $A + a$, where the new (a) leaves the old (A) intact, and the past and the present co-exist, awaiting the future. Traditionalists admit this form, but they do not confute the real idea of progress, which, according to the renowned formulation of logical dialectic, negates in preserving or preserves in negating. What is truly preserved must transform, renew, transfigure and empower itself: A^2 – in which A persists, but as the root of its own power, which alone is real, for A has multiplied itself by itself. (Giovanni Gentile, *Sistema di logica*)

5. Formulation of the originary judgement

Let the 'originary judgement' be the affirmation in and through which the originary structure realizes itself.

The originary judgement may be formulated as follows: 'Thinking is the immediate'. Or, more precisely, in relation to the clarifications to be made in due course: 'Everything that – in the way that pertains to it – is immediately known is the immediate.'

6. Preliminary definition of the subject of the originary judgement

With the term 'thinking' we indicate here – as a preliminary characterization – the actual or immediate presence of being, regarded in relation to the semantic structures that are *immediately* implied by the positing of the actual or immediate presence of being. (As a provisional determination, let us accept an altogether generic definition of these structures, and let us note that the very designation of these structures in terms of a plurality belongs to the indeterminacy of that generic character.) If that actual presence is referred to as 'experience' (or 'ontic horizon', in Heidegger's terminology), the term 'thinking' is then defined as the immediate implication that obtains between experience and those structures (or between the ontic horizon and the 'ontological' one – understanding with this expression the plane of the manifestation of those structures).

A definition of this kind of the subject of the originary judgement is, however, to be held firm in its simply preliminary value, for the term 'thinking', defined as the immediate presence of being, only indicates an aspect or a value of the immediacy that constitutes the subject of the originary judgement – this immediacy (or originarity) having to be understood as the structuring of the meanings that pertain to it, according to what the present enquiry will gradually make explicit.

7. First note

To the extent that the ontological horizon is *immediately* implied by the ontic one, the ontological horizon is once again part of the ontic horizon, while nevertheless distinguishing itself from it. (The reason for this distinction is given by the very content of the two horizons, a content that will have to be concretely determined – together with the meaning of that 'immediate implication'.) For, indeed, the term that is immediately implied is, as such, something that is immediately present – even though, as already mentioned, it distinguishes itself from that immediate presence by virtue of its content – and it is once again included in the ontic horizon to the extent that this is the horizon of immediate presence.

In this respect, the originary judgement may also be formulated by simply stating that experience, or immediately and actually present being, is the immediate, or that being that is known for itself is known for itself.

8. Second note

In relation to the definition that has been given of the term 'thinking', it should be noted that this does not mean that, should the development of knowledge come to present a specific content *in a mediated way*, this presence would not be a form of 'thinking'; in this case, there would take place an internal determination of thinking, due to which 'thinking' would come to designate the generic structure that includes the dimension that is presently indicated by the term 'thinking' as a moment.

9. Clarification of the meaning of this enquiry

The following reflections do not form a 'demonstration' or 'grounding' of the originary judgement, which would posit it as a structure that is extrinsic to the structure of positing; rather, they are the *self*-exposition of the originary judgement.

This does not imply in any way an accidental character of the exposition. For, on the contrary, that judgement consists in its manifestation, and it is its own ground only insofar as it manifests itself.

That accidental character rather concerns the form taken by the exposition insofar as this is directed to a potential communication; that is, insofar as the demands of a dialogue arise and assert themselves, and the exposition and manifestation of the originary judgement become language and writing.

10. Analysis and synthesis of the originary judgement

To the extent that the originary structure realizes itself as a semantic complexity, the exposition of the originary is an *analysis* of the terms that constitute that complexity.

Here, it should be noted that the groundedness of this analysis is provided by the concomitant presence of the corresponding synthesis. That is to say, the groundedness of the mode of presentation of the originary structure – consisting in the gradual positing or consideration of the individual terms of that structure, insofar as they are such or insofar as they are what they are – is provided by the concomitant presence of the mode of presentation of that structure that consists in the positing of the relation between those very terms. That co-presence is the concrete mode of presentation of which the previous modes, as formally distinct, are abstract moments.

The manifestation of the originary is thus not a result that is only realized at the end of an analysis, but rather, it is immanent in each moment of the latter: in such a way that each moment of the analysis belongs to the originary – and, in and through this belonging, enjoys the absolute and intrinsic groundedness of the originary – only insofar as that belonging *is posited*: that is to say, only insofar as the totality or concreteness of the originary, in which that moment is included, is itself posited. Exhibiting the validity of the positing of a moment of the originary thus means exhibiting and making explicit the content that originarily includes that moment. Hence, it should precisely be stated that the validity of an analysis entails that this making explicit should be something that has already originarily taken place.

The co-presence of synthesis and analysis – which precisely constitutes the concrete manifestation of the originary – is the synthesis itself insofar as it includes the analysis, and, equally, it is the analysis itself insofar as it includes the synthesis. That is to say, each of the two terms includes the other one and distinguishes itself from it: to the extent that it includes it, it is precisely the concrete presentation of the originary judgement (i.e. the unity and inseparability of synthesis and analysis); to the extent that one term is instead distinct from the other one, and it is held firm as something distinct, it is that abstract mode of presentation mentioned above – *either* a synthesis *or* an analysis.

It should be noted that if that inclusion-distinction has been posited as a mutual one – namely, as pertaining to 'each of the two terms' – it should, however, be remarked that, strictly speaking, these are not *two* terms but a unity that distinguishes itself within itself: in such a way that the inclusion and the distinction are twofold (and there are two terms) only from the standpoint of that distinction, i.e. from the standpoint of the abstract.

11. The concrete and abstract concepts of the abstract

The formal distinction between analysis and synthesis does not entail that the analysis is a negation of the relation of the terms or that the synthesis is a negation of the terms themselves. That formal distinction simply entails that that relation is not posited, or that it is not part of the positional domain covered by the analysis as distinct from the synthesis, and that the terms themselves are not posited, or that they are not part of the positional domain covered by the synthesis as distinct from the analysis. Insofar as that relation and those terms are not posited in that way, they are not negated either – this negation being understood here as the positing of something as superseded.

What has been asserted concerning the formal distinction between synthesis and analysis is also valid in relation to the formal distinction between any two moments of the originary.

To the extent that the analysis and the synthesis are not realized as a negation of, respectively, that relation and those terms, the abstract character of that analysis and that synthesis, as distinct from one another, is not a contradiction. In other words (and more generally): the concrete concept of the abstract differentiates itself from the abstract concept of the abstract. (This is not to claim that this second concept exhausts the meaning of contradiction, but that it is at least a fundamental determination or specification of that meaning.)

Indeed, the concreteness of the abstract consists in its being posited *as such*: namely, as something abstract. This necessarily entails the positing of a semantic excess relative to that of which the abstractness is predicated, and it is in relation to this excess that the abstract can be posited as such. The originary precisely consists in this originary passing of the abstract into something else: namely, in the excess – or, more precisely, the totality of the excess – that originarily surpasses the abstract; the abstract passes in this way into an other because its remaining by itself is contradictory.

On the contrary, the positing of the originary volume of that excess necessarily entails the positing of what is in that way surpassed: in the sense that the concrete presentation of the originary judgement is posited as the concrete in relation to the formal distinction between synthesis and analysis: that is to say, in relation to the abstract that the concrete supersedes in itself by positing it as such. This relation is therefore not something extrinsic to the concrete but defines it in an essential way and constitutes it as such. The content of the concrete is the abstract; or, equivalently: the concrete is precisely the concrete concept of the abstract.

The positing of the abstract as such coincides furthermore with the very superseding of the abstract concept of the abstract: namely, of that concept that contradictorily negates the concrete, and that negates it insofar as it posits something, which from the standpoint of the concrete is abstract, as this thing or that thing – or even as the concrete itself – and not as something abstract.

(On the other hand, the concrete is posited by virtue of the actual and present absence of a term in relation to which the concrete would in turn be reduced to an abstract moment. Here, the concrete is once again what presently withdraws from that relation, and it is therefore what stands in relation with that relation as superseded.)

Therefore, the *matter* or logical element of the abstract is not *as such* a negation of the ground: it becomes such a negation only insofar as it is regarded as the content of the abstract concept of the abstract. It is therefore the system of these concepts that belongs to the system of the negations of the ground. (While the abstract is indeed considered here as an analytic moment and as a synthetic one, it should be remarked that each of these two moments is, in turn, a complexity that includes a multiplicity of moments that can be more or less abstract.)

Insofar as the abstract passes into something different, it is at the same time preserved and confirmed as part of that into which it has passed; what is thus confirmed is precisely the matter or logical content of the abstract. What is superseded is instead the *form* that pertains to the abstract insofar as it has not passed into the horizon that originarily includes it. That is to say, it is of this form (= abstract concept of the abstract) that the abstract is divested insofar as it passes [*nel suo passare*], and it is this form what becomes a 'past' ['*passato*'], a no longer (originarily) being – a no longer being part of truth, however, not of time (for, otherwise, it would be meaningless to speak of a 'no longer *originarily* being', this expression thus indicating that the error is originarily superseded, or sur*passed* [oltre*passato*]).

What has been asserted in these last two sections is immediately included in the concept of the manifestation of a semantically complex content – such as, precisely, the originary structure. Indeed, the manifestation of that content entails, on the one hand, that *all* the elements that constitute it should be manifest, and, on the other hand, that *each* of these elements should be manifest as a moment or something abstract, in such a way that the manifestation of the whole content consists in the positing of the abstractness of the single elements. Then: if the content in question is the ground, the validity of the analysis of the single elements – or the validity of the positing of a single element – is given by the co-presence of those elements, i.e. by the positing of their totality, which precisely constitutes the ground. Equivalently, as already stated, the validity of the analysis is given by the fact that the analysis itself is posited as the content of the synthesis.

12. Discursivity *qua* realization of the abstract

The character that the manifestation of the originary judgement acquires in determining itself as discursivity – and, therefore, as those enhanced forms of discursivity constituted by language and writing – suggests the appropriateness of the observations presented above. Discursivity, as such – and, therefore, as the development or processual character of that manifestation – consists indeed in the very formal distinction between analysis and synthesis (and, more generally, between all the single moments of the originary) *as something that has been realized*. For, indeed, as part of discursivity, as such, the single moments of the originary realize themselves in their simply being external to one another, or, precisely, in their simple formal distinction. Accordingly, it is therefore in relation to this realization, and due to its significance, that there arises the *possibility* of understanding the analytic positing of the terms of the judgement and the positing of their synthesis as being mutually unrelated or independent.

That possibility is to be understood as the presence of a condition of possibility; it is in this sense that it is asserted that it pertains to the manifestation of the originary *qua* discursivity, and not to that manifestation as such. Furthermore, insofar as the realization of the formal distinction between analysis and synthesis determines itself in the form of language and writing, this determination gives rise to an enhanced form of the possibility of that understanding – which, as already mentioned, does not obtain with respect to the manifestation as such of the judgement. This manifestation thus constitutes the horizon that withholds that possibility to itself, preventing it from becoming real as a contradictory understanding of the unrelatedness of analysis and synthesis (or, more generally, of the single moments of the originary). The logical tension exerted by that horizon on that possibility, constraining it within itself, does not, however, consist in a superseding of that possibility as such, for that superseding would be equivalent to the superseding of the very discursivity that comes to be defined by that possibility, albeit in a negative way.

In other words: if the content that is manifest (= the manifestation as such of the originary judgement) distinguishes itself from its mode of manifestation (= discursivity), it is once again necessary to keep in mind that the value of that distinction is grounded in the concrete unity of those two moments. If, indeed, that discursivity consists in the self-realization of the abstract, and if the concrete is thus defined by its relation to the abstract – in such a way that the concrete is the unity of the concrete and the abstract – the meaning of the unity of discursivity and manifestation becomes clear.

It should therefore be stated that, in the same way in which that manifestation as such includes that discursivity and distinguishes itself from it, so this discursivity includes that manifestation as such and distinguishes itself from it (i.e. it includes that manifestation as such insofar as the latter becomes the object of a discourse). Furthermore, insofar as each of the two terms includes the other one, that term is the whole (it is the unity of the manifest content and of its mode of manifestation), whereas insofar as each term distinguishes itself from the other one, that term is an abstract moment. (It should be noted that the abstract, in distinguishing itself, is the distinct as such, for the distinction, as the unity or relation of the distinct terms, is the whole *qua* concrete inclusion of the distinct terms.)

13. Corollary: Logical and discursive orders

As part of the analytic exposition of the originary judgement, in which the exposition of the structure of the predicate is anticipated by the exposition of the structure of the subject, and the exposition of the relation between the two terms is anticipated by the exposition of those very two terms, that anticipation does not therefore express a logical precedence. That is to say, that anticipation must be preserved as to its discursive nature, as a contingency of discourse (a contingency of the 'order' of discourse, not of discourse as such), due to which one is compelled to *say* 'one thing after the other' (and, therefore, one thing outside the other), without that 'after' expressing anything concerning the nature of the logical relation between the two things. If the logical order of the exposition is often not followed, this is due to the particular conditions of the cultural setting in which the author (i.e. the one who is communicating) finds themselves and which they must somehow take into account.

This divergence between the logical order and the discursive one may be regarded as a variant – of a significant importance when dealing with the nature of language – of the Aristotelian observation according to which not everything that is prior in discourse is also prior in substance: this substantiality, in our case, precisely expressing the logical-methodological relation between terms.

14. Discursivity and the present essay

The observations that we are now making, together with the ones that will be made later on, therefore coincide, as already implicitly remarked, with that very discursivity at work. As part of that discursivity, however, more or less emphasis is placed – for the purpose of communication, or in relation to the present philosophical culture – on certain elements that are considered to be more relevant, or in any case more suitable for reaching an agreement, and on which it is deemed appropriate to focus; on the contrary, other elements, whose communication is deemed unnecessary or self-evident, are omitted despite being of equal importance as to their content. It is nevertheless the case that this choice of elements in the communication – a choice that is virtually unavoidable – constitutes one of the main sources of misunderstanding and disagreement.

The present observations therefore constitute a realization of the abstract content of the originary – this, however, being concretely rather than abstractly conceived: realization of the concrete concept of the abstract. These observations will therefore be valid from the standpoint of the reader to the extent that the latter will be able to rise to a concrete comprehension of the originary structure. For, indeed, in the order of communication, the reader who has not already come to a disclosure of the originary structure by themselves will come to a manifestation of the latter at the end of the analysis of the originary (that analysis consisting in the present exposition); that is to say, the conditions that determine the validity of the analysis are not fulfilled (since, precisely, the immanence of the totality of the originary in that analytic development does not take place): the analysis realizes itself independently of the synthesis, or outside of its relation with the latter. In this sense, the exposition of the originary is necessarily misconstrued, and one necessarily fails to recognize the groundedness of the single moments of the analysis. It is, however, equally necessary that, in rising to a concrete comprehension of the originary – i.e. of the relation of synthesis and analysis – every misconstruction and every groundlessness should come to disappear. The acceptance or approval that pertains to the exposition of the originary does not therefore take place step by step: the exposition is accepted all at once and all together. However, insofar as language, as expression of the originary, seeks an 'other' in order to realize the originary communication or dialogue, it enters an adventure, or a danger – to which it is nevertheless immune as long as it is confined to the simple role of an expression, *simpliciter*, of the originary.

According to Fichte, too – let us remark – the *Wissenschaftslehre* consists of a single and indivisible 'gaze'. Except that the exposition of that 'gaze' is regarded by Fichte as something accidental relative to the 'gaze' itself. This is a residue of that naturalistic realism due to which something – even the *Wissenschaftslehre* – is presupposed beyond the present and actual knowing, which precisely constitutes its exposition. Upon conceiving the unity of intuition and discourse, however – asserted above all by Hegel – that discourse comes to be something essential for intuition. At the same time, the Fichtean intuition or 'gaze' corresponds to the (less explicit) originarity of the speculative whole in Hegel – a whole that may be a result not insofar as, at first, it is not and then it arises, but insofar as, in being originarily (this being the Fichtean 'gaze'), it may retrace its own path by virtue of that originarity.

It should also be remarked that insofar as the abstract is held firm as a content of the concrete, and the realization of the abstract acquires a propositional structure, all the propositions that constitute that realization agree in general in this: that their logical negation, regardless of how it may be determined, is contradictory. Or, equivalently: the negation of each of those propositions entails at least one contradiction. (The various propositions differentiate themselves in a negative way according to the different structure of contradiction determined by their negation.)

Once again, therefore, the structure of the contradiction of the negations of 'significant' propositions will be determined and indicated in a more or less explicit way, while omitting this determination and leaving it implicit for all other propositions. One of the significant forms of this omission consists in the arising – as the exposition proceeds and is gradually completed – of the contradictoriness of the negation of propositions that have already been expressed: for instance, of the propositions outlined up to that point. (Needless to say, the discussion remains abstract – *abstract* precisely in the indicated sense – insofar as it here leaves aside the most important aspect of the question: namely, the determination of the meaning and value of non-contradictoriness itself. The identification of contradictory structures carried out before that determination thus receives its authentic meaning and value from that determination.)

15. The aim or end of the abstract and of the concrete

a. Whereas the content of the originary judgement is discursively manifest, the end or aim of discourse [*discorrere*] is not simply its 'course' [*scorrere*] as such, but it is what is disclosed as part of that course: that is, precisely the manifestation of the content. The end of discursivity thus appears to consist in the very consummation of discourse, or in its subsiding in the form of an intuition. The intuition that supersedes discourse is the presence as such of the originary structure.

Discursivity itself, however – or expression (discourse being able to be regarded as the expression of intuition) – has as its end a term that differs from itself only insofar as it is kept distinct from this very term: that is to say, only insofar as that discursivity is regarded as an abstract moment.

For now, it should be noted that the aim or end of discursivity, regarded as an abstract moment, may be understood either as being itself the other side of abstractness (i.e. as simple intuition) or as the concrete itself: as the unity of discourse and intuition. In the first case, the end itself is something abstract. In the second case, the terms that are part of the final relation distinguish themselves in such a way that one of the distinct terms does not lack – *qua* distinct term – what it is distinct from: that is to say, it consists in that very distinction as posited; it is that very distinguishing – or, precisely, the concrete itself. Therefore, while in the first case – in which the distinct terms (discourse and intuition) lack one another and stand outside of each other – there obtains a mutual symmetry in the final relation, in the second case the relation between the two distinct terms is asymmetric: in that the concrete, *qua* unity of discourse and intuition, does not have its end in the abstract (to the extent that the latter is to be kept distinct from that unity), but has its end in itself.

b. The concrete, *qua* unity of those two abstract moments, is therefore itself an end to itself. Accordingly, discursivity itself is resolved or superseded in that end only to the extent that the latter is retained as an abstract moment, which, as such, simply allows that discursivity to be consummated within itself. Concretely, instead, the consummation of discourse in intuition entails at the same time a persistence of discourse – or, this persistence is the condition of that consummation. Accordingly, once that persistence is superseded – abstractly superseded, i.e. superseded and not at the same time posited and preserved – what is consummated is the very consummation resulting in intuition.

It can then be stated that that in which discourse is consummated is 'meaningful' insofar as that which is consummated persists, or insofar as that in which it is consummated is determined as the *result* of that consummation. (This is not contradictory to the extent that discourse consummates and supersedes itself in a different sense compared to the one in which it persists and posits itself; or, in other words: it does not consummate itself insofar as it persists, and it does not persist insofar as it consummates itself.) If, therefore, discourse must be consummated or superseded in its entirety as part of the presence of the concrete, and if, at the same time, that consummation is meaningless or abstractly immediate if it is not posited as the result of a process – and if that process is not retraced every time the result is to be concretely achieved – there arises in this way that unfolding or essential historicity that may not be disposed of once the content has been disclosed in its entirety.

Conversely, discourse – which nevertheless gravitates towards its own consummation as towards its own end – is meaningful insofar as it is posited as the result of an intuition, or as the aim or end of its end (that is to say: intuition, too, *must express itself*, and has therefore its end in discourse). Accordingly, the end is such insofar as it converges back on its means, withholding it within itself and including it in the domain of ends.

It should be noted that the *resulting* that has been mentioned above belongs to and in fact constitutes the originary: intuition *originarily* or *immediately* results from discourse, and the latter from the former. This means that this resulting is the vey 'being in relation' of each of the two moments – this relation precisely consisting in the supersession of their abstract immediacy. This supersession is therefore the very opening of that concrete immediacy that constitutes the originary.

16. The history of philosophy and the multiplicity of subjects

If, in the development of that discursivity, any moment of the latter is held firm in such a way that the form of discourse is posited as its content – namely, if it is held that the form acquired by discourse until that moment should be a property of the content as such – there arises an abstract concept. This concept separates its content from the global context, giving it the character of a release from the whole, or the attainment of an autonomy relative to the latter. This release of the particular is not to be conflated with that absence of the whole as such that, in being made possible by the very *positing* of the latter, consists in the abstract itself *qua* concretely conceived; the release that we are considering is a simple disregard or forgetting of the whole, or it is that very absence, but not posited as such; as a result, the whole is absent from the abstract moment, but it is not known as absent. As already mentioned, the particular thus becomes the object of a concern, which constitutes that very interest without which, as Hegel recalls, humans would not do anything. There thus arises the taking place of 'a' philosophy.

This taking place, however, does not have a naively realist meaning – almost as if the reality of abstract consciousness were regarded as being 'independent' or 'outside' of the concrete consciousness. For, indeed, what has been presented here is simply the concrete concept of the abstract concept of the abstract; or: that abstract consciousness has been considered as a content of the concrete consciousness – or, which is the same, as a moment of the originary structure.

The taking place of the 'many philosophies' that in their mutual relations constitute themselves as the 'history of philosophy' thus coincides with the very deduction of the history of philosophy as an eternal ideal history (to the extent that it is not conditioned by time), or as the necessity for history to be in time. This eternal ideal history thus consists in the very structuring of the abstract concepts of the abstract.

There exists no content difference between the development of the content of the concrete concept of the abstract concept of the abstract, *qua* ideal history, and its development *qua* temporal history – since this temporal history is the realization of that ideal historicity. There only exists a difference as to the mode of positing: in that there pertains to that temporal history a factual existence (i.e. a mode of existence) that, *qua* excess relative to a purely ideal positing (i.e. to that mode of existence that pertains to what is ideally posited), constitutes the non-deducible element of that historicity. In other words: the opening of the system of the negations of the originary (§4) – a system that either coincides with or includes, as will be determined in due course, the system of the abstract concepts of the abstract – is not necessarily conditioned by an actual verification of those negations; that is to say, it can realize itself independently of that verification. Whether or not a negation has occurred as a matter of fact may, however, not be established – or, in any case, we are not at present able to establish it – independently of a presentation of the plane of factual existence.

The distinction between eternal and temporal history thus falls entirely within the concrete itself: that is to say, it does not in any way correspond to the distinction between abstract consciousness, regarded as a content of the concrete, and abstract consciousness *qua* potentially shown to be different from and independent of the concrete consciousness. As already noted, what differentiates that ideal historicity from the temporal one is therefore a situation that is altogether empirical – such as the presence of written documents, or the presence of a language of human individuals who act as the owners or authors of what they write and state: signs, sounds and behaviours that are to be understood as a manifestation of those concerns or interests mentioned above.

As long as there has been no demonstration of the otherness or independence of a – concrete or abstract – consciousness relative to the concrete one, what those signs, sounds and behaviours mean (as well as the relations between these meanings) is nevertheless a content that is internal to the concrete consciousness. Furthermore, those concerns or interests do not appear as something additional relative to the empirical situation that would claim to constitute their manifestation, but they are posited as that very situation and they are exhausted within it – even though the project of that additional meaning persists as the problematization of that identity or consummation.

Pending a demonstration of the independence of another consciousness relative to the concrete one (a demonstration that coincides with, or specifies, a demonstration of the existence of a multiplicity of subjects), the positing of that independence – to the extent that it is not restricted to the simple level of a project – constitutes a type of abstract concept of the abstract concept of the abstract.

17. Philosophy and philosophies

For, indeed, a multiplicity of subjects or instances of consciousness is not immediately present, and it is therefore not part of the originary structure (it is not part of it as a matter of fact; whether it *may not* be part of it is a question that can be left aside here). The immediate instead includes the project or the supposition of such a multiplicity: which is to say, the latter is part of the originary structure, but, precisely, *qua* part of a project. Insofar as one therefore keeps to the level of originarity, and insofar as this is the very originary opening of philosophizing, it is to be stated that philosophy and philosophizing cannot but be *my* philosophy and *my* philosophizing. This character of 'mine-ness' does not have a restrictive value – as if it were equivalent to the common expression 'everyone has their philosophy', and so I have mine. It does not have that restrictive value and that equivalence does not obtain because, as a matter of fact, *there simply is not* another philosophy, or other philosophies, that is not my philosophy – there is not: meaning precisely that it is not part of what is immediately present. Equivalently, the existence of other philosophies is, originarily, a *possibility*. These other philosophies are therefore negated in a twofold sense: in that, remaining at the level of the originary knowledge, it is not possible to affirm their existence, and in that, even if it were possible to affirm that existence, they – *qua* philosophies 'other' than mine – would be negations of the originary structure.

It should then be added that the set of events constituted by philosophical writings and discourses is certainly part of the immediate – and it is only insofar as it is thus part of the immediate that it can be affirmed, and its affirmation has a ground; furthermore, that set certainly includes more or less complex propositional structures that are posited as a negation of the originary structure (and it is precisely due to this negation that a philosophy is said to be 'other' than mine). And yet, it is also true that this set of negations – insofar as it is posited as an immediate content, or as being part of the horizon of what is immediately known – is originarily posited *as superseded*; or, equivalently: the *form* that originarily pertains to that set consists in the negation or superseding of the terms that constitute it (these terms being precisely the negations of the originary). Furthermore, it is true (= it is immediately known) that those philosophical writings and discourses – explicitly or implicitly – state and argue that they aim to be negations of the originary structure, and, therefore, that they aim to take the form of a negation of that structure (rather than the form of a negation of the negation of that structure); it is true that there are individuals who – explicitly or implicitly – refuse to agree with the originary structure and exhibit a particular determination and tenacity as part of this refusal; however, it is nevertheless the case that those statements, arguments and refusals originarily take the form of their own being superseded: or, equivalently, they stand as something that is originarily negated precisely to the extent that it is a negation of the originary. The many philosophies whose existence is immediately known, as well as their arrangement within a logical system that is referred to as 'the history of philosophy', are therefore part of the originary as a particular dimension of its *content* – and, regardless of their constitution, they *cannot* stand in opposition to (my, originary) philosophy: precisely because they fall *within its content*, in such a way that the terms that were supposed to stand in opposition are placed on two different levels, and their opposition disappears (and those philosophies are not 'other' than mine). Stating that the immediate does not include within itself a multiplicity of subjects is therefore equivalent to stating that there are originarily no philosophies other than mine, or that the only form taken by the negations of the originary structure insofar as they are part of the immediate is that of their own being superseded. The existence of other philosophies is then a possibility in the same sense in which – remaining at the level of the originary – it is a possibility that there should be other instances of consciousness beyond the originary one (or beyond 'mine), or that the negations of the originary structure should not take the form of their own being superseded. This precisely means that those other philosophies are originarily real *qua* superseded, and, therefore, *qua* part of the *content* of philosophizing – and it is in this sense that, above, we discussed the concrete concept of the abstract concept of the abstract.

That being said, the fact that a negation of the originary structure exists as not superseded may be affirmed in two ways: (1) insofar as the originary includes the recollection of positional horizons (i.e. of situations of awareness) in which that negation was not superseded – for instance, insofar as the originary includes the presence of a past time in which the originary structure had not yet been posited, and was therefore implicitly negated; (2) insofar as one could demonstrate the existence of instances of consciousness, other than the originary one, in which the negation of the originary structure is not superseded. In the first case, there is no departure from that originary knowledge; in the second case, this knowledge is surpassed through the process of a mediation. Here, let us only remark that, in both cases, the positing of a negation of the originary, as a negation that is not superseded, is carried out on the basis of the originary itself. Indeed, as in that first case the validity of the positing of that recollection is determined by the belonging of the latter to the structure of the originary, in the same way, in the second case, that potential process of mediation is constructed on the basis of the structure of the immediate – which is, precisely, the originary structure. It is therefore not only the case that the negation of the originary is originarily superseded insofar as it is inherently contradictory – that is, insofar as it must presuppose the originary structure in order to realize itself (and this will have to be adequately elucidated) – but that negation presupposes what it negates even if one is able to demonstrate that it exists, in another consciousness, as something not superseded.

To conclude: the existence of others, who think differently from me or who have a philosophy that differs from the originary realization of philosophizing (i.e. a philosophy that thus differs from my philosophy), is not originarily manifest: that is to say, it does not belong to the ground of every possible knowledge. The behaviour of other people certainly *hints*, both in speech and in writing, at convictions that differ from mine. However, it cannot be more than a hinting: that is to say, the hinting is present, but the plane (the different convictions) at which it hints is not. There always remains open the possibility of suspecting that this plane does not exist at all; and one may even suspect the legitimacy of the hinting. (As long as it is not demonstrated that it is inherently contradictory to negate the legitimacy of that hinting, the plane to which the latter refers can indeed be negated without any contradiction.) If, then, the plane to which that hinting refers is truly demonstrated – i.e. if it is truly demonstrated that there exist convictions that differ from mine – this demonstration precisely relies on that originary structure that constitutes the content of my conviction. In other words, the wonder and the disingenuous awe before the fact that philosophers think differently from one another are, also in this respect, shown to be inconsistent: for, precisely, it is to be originarily stated that I am the only philosopher, and mine is the only philosophy.

18. Note

It should also be noted that, since here 'philosophy' cannot but indicate the very opening of originary knowledge, those 'other' philosophies are originarily superseded in that they are a negation of the originary, and not in that they are determinations of a knowledge that exceeds the originary one. For, indeed, the originary governs the logical determinations that take a stance in relation to the originary itself – or, equivalently: philosophizing is originarily active and excluding in relation to the negations of the originary. However, it leaves the discourse undetermined, or it does not take a stance, in relation to those affirmations and negations that do not concern the positing of immediacy – while nevertheless including them within that very immediacy in their being thus undetermined or problematized.

19. The originary concept of philosophy

If the originary arising of philosophy consists in the presence or consciousness of the originary structure – or if by philosophy one originarily means the interest in what is originarily present – the unfolding of this enquiry, *qua* development of that interest, is therefore an unfolding of the concept of philosophy. The latter thus has an adequate concept of itself only at the very end – if the meaning of such a definitiveness can be constituted. Every excess relative to the originary concept of philosophy – as this has been indicated here – must derive from this concept. That is to say, starting from this concept, it is possible to recuperate that excess. (Furthermore, the project of that excess belongs to the originary concept of philosophizing, and it consists in the originarity or immediacy of the project of a knowledge that exceeds the one constituted by the originary judgement.)

20. Meaning

The originary structure is the originary meaning itself; that is to say, it is the originary opening of meaning. In this respect, the originary judgement is to be formulated by stating that meaning is meaningful for itself. 'Meaning' precisely means here: being that is immediately known. The meaningfulness constituted by the horizon of immediacy is meaningful for itself. Accordingly, meaning is not affirmed in an indeterminate way, but it is a *structure*: the originary structure or 'syntax'. (The affirmation of the 'conventional character' of the originary structure is one of the many modes of the negation of the immediate, and it is superseded by the superseding of that negation. The most relevant syntactic configuration identified up to this point is the one by virtue of which it is stated that the plane of meaning consists of that which is posited as being meaningful for itself, i.e. as an immediate meaning; accordingly, meaning is what is posited in this way, rather than anything arbitrary or imaginary that would lie beyond this positing.)

The very linguistic structure that expresses the originary – namely, the terms that are being used here to communicate the originary – thus draws its meaning from what it expresses.

21. Originarity and conventionality

Proposition 6.54 of Wittgenstein's *Tractatus* reads: 'My propositions serve as elucidation in the following way: anyone who understands me eventually recognises them as nonsensical, when he has climbed out through them, on them, over them. (He must, so to speak, throw away the ladder after he has climbed up on it).' This proposition constitutes the very self-confutation of Wittgenstein's philosophy. (It may also be considered as one of the main points of divergence between the neo-positivist logic and the idealist one.) That proposition asserts that the process through which the meaningfulness of (only) non-philosophical propositions is established is meaningless. It is clear that: either the meaningfulness of non-philosophical propositions is a *result* of that process of signification, in such a way that this process must be *retained* as that in relation to which the meaningfulness in question is a result or that meaningfulness is not regarded as such a result, and it is then as though Wittgenstein's philosophical proposal had not even been advanced.

This aporia of the *Tractatus* is determined by the influence of the underlying framework of modern axiomatics and meta-mathematical enquiries. If, indeed, the principles according to which a specific logical system or 'language' is constituted have a conventional value, as in the case of mathematical languages, that very convention – i.e. the choice of those rules that function as principles of the system under consideration – takes place at a different linguistic 'level' relative to the one at which the system takes place. The criterion of that choice belongs to a different level relative to the one constituted on the basis of the rules that have been agreed upon. This level difference precisely exists by virtue of the conventional nature of those rules. If the new level that is thus obtained is in turn structured according to conventional rules, the determination of these rules will take place as part of a third linguistic level. Wittgenstein has believed to dispose of the *regressus in indefinitum* in the introduction of these levels by acknowledging the meaninglessness of the base level. Signification itself is thus exclusively understood as a form of casting light on something else, giving it a meaning, while, however, remaining in the shadow, or outside meaning. Otherness of *signification* (or meaningfulness) and *meaning*.

Signification, instead, originarily affects uniquely itself; hence, as already mentioned, meaning is what is meaningful for itself: self-signification.

For what concerns Wittgenstein, it should be noted that, aside from the self-confutation mentioned above, there arises a logical situation by virtue of which the very proposition 6.54 of the *Tractatus* must be meaningless, thus reproducing in this way the *regressus* that was supposed to be eliminated. That is to say: if only the propositions of the science of nature are meaningful, not only is the proposition: 'Only the propositions of the science of nature are meaningful' (let this proposition be P_1) meaningless, but so is the proposition: 'The proposition P_1 is meaningless' (let this proposition be P_2), as well as the proposition: 'The proposition P_2 is meaningless', etc.

The other attempts made by the other leading figures of neo-positivism, as well as by Wittgenstein himself, to eliminate this aporia are well known. Here it should only be remarked that, in general, these attempts always operate from a conventionalist standpoint. The very introduction of unlimited operators, advanced by Carnap, has a conventional character, and simply addresses the need to give meaning, through appropriate technical expedients, to the propositions of both objective and syntactic language, so as to achieve a conventional logical structure that would not be affected by Wittgenstein's aporia. That is to say, these attempts leave beside themselves their negation, as not superseded. Carnap's more recent studies, aimed at a determination of a 'neutral' language, in which the criterion for the choice of rules would be given by language itself in its self-structuring in accordance with those rules, may be considered as a need or desire to leave the conventionalist perspective behind.

It is clear, however, that if the criterion for the choice of a specific semantic structure is given by that very structure, the departure from the conventionalist perspective is achieved to the extent to which that structure qualifies as the structure of the immediate. The choice of the immediate has a different meaning relative to the previous choices, for, in this case, it is the immediate itself that *makes itself be chosen*, and this making itself be chosen coincides with the very recognition of the immediacy of the immediate, or the originarity of the originary meaning. Or, equivalently, if the term 'choice' is uniquely defined, there is in this case no longer any choice, for the immediate is what asserts itself by itself, and, in this asserting, constitutes itself as the originary structure.

If one insists that there still remains the freedom to think of other things, to take care of or choose other things, which are not philosophy, this freedom is the freedom to find oneself without a ground, or, even, in a contradiction. In this respect, philosophy, too, is the object of a choice: not, however, insofar as philosophy is philosophy (philosophy being, as such, the exclusion of any other choice), but insofar as philosophy is regarded in relation to that being – the human – who believes to be able to choose, and, therefore, to choose philosophy or reject it (or disregard it).

22. Meaning and meaninglessness

If one wishes to disregard the originary structure, one places oneself in the domain of meaninglessness. It is therefore only insofar as *one already is* within the originary opening of meaning that the very *question* concerning meaning acquires a meaning; by acquiring it, however, that question is superseded, *qua question*, by the originary answer. That is to say, the question is authenticated (= made meaningful) as soon as it is answered. This very 'answering' consists in the very conferring of a meaning on that question. Accordingly, the originary answering does not answer anything, or, equivalently, it does not presuppose anything that it has not itself posited.

At the same time, however, that 'meaninglessness' is nothing but the 'groundlessness' or 'contradictoriness' of a propositional content. In other words: there is nothing *simpliciter* meaningless; everything that is meaningful in its own way. Only nothingness itself, *qua* absolute negativity, is meaningless. (This absolute meaninglessness, however – cf. Chapter 4 – is itself positively meaningful.) In affirming that meaning constitutes itself only in and through the positing of the immediacy of meaning – or that if one does away with the originary structure, one places oneself in the domain of meaninglessness – one is therefore considering the *value* or the *ground* of meaning; and one must therefore state that every knowledge that does away with the originary structure is either groundless or contradictory. (Furthermore, contradictoriness is itself a form of groundlessness: what is contradictory is what *cannot* have a ground, as opposed to what simply, or *as a matter of fact*, does not have a ground.)

Neo-positivists generally distinguish two kinds of 'meaningless' propositions: those constituted by words that, while being meaningful in a specific semantic context, are meaningless as part of the connection in which they are found in the proposition under consideration – this kind of meaninglessness arguably including most of metaphysical and philosophical questions; and those that, for instance, can be obtained by randomly typing on the keys of a typewriter. As for the first kind of propositions, it should be noted that they can be traced to *contradictions* (when they are such). In stating that 'Caesar is a quadratic equation', one does not utter a meaningless proposition, but a proposition that, after having defined the terms that comprise it, is revealed to be self-contradictory – since the definition of the predicate implies a negation of the definition of the subject. As for the second kind of propositions, even though they are meaningless *to the extent that they are understood* to count as propositions, they are, however, meaningful as things or graphemes, i.e. as empirical contents. Once again, however, that side of meaninglessness is strictly speaking a contradiction. The contradiction lies in this: that *one understands* that something that is not a proposition – but is a sign, a sound, etc. – should count as a proposition. (If this understanding or intending does not exist, however, neither does that contradiction, and those signs belong to the present content just as this sheet of paper or this colour do.) With this in mind, it is nevertheless perfectly acceptable to refer to a contradiction as a 'meaninglessness'; and, as already noted, groundless propositions can then be said to be meaningless.

Pre-philosophical consciousness (which includes the religious, scientific, aesthetic, etc. forms of consciousness) undoubtedly constitutes the opening of a semantic plane. One speaks, precisely, of common *sense* [*senso*]. To the extent that this signification, however, is not able to assert itself – i.e. to show its ground – it carries alongside itself its negation or leaves its opposite meaning beside itself. Instability of meaning; or, precisely, meaninglessness. Meaninglessness, understood as groundlessness, is accompanied as part of certain aspects of common sense by meaninglessness *qua* contradiction. If the sophists – in keeping with Hegel's observation – took on the task of bringing to light this self-annihilation of common sense, it is nevertheless the task of philosophical knowledge to show to what extent pre-philosophical knowledge is something groundless, and to what extent it is a contradiction.

The fact that one way or another common sense keeps persisting as something stable is therefore the result of the intervention of a pragmatic component, whereby *one wants*, in order to achieve certain ends, to hold firm a certain semantic content rather than its negation. Religious *faith* constitutes a prominent moment of this pragmatic stance. Christianity wants, above all, to save from the meaninglessness of the 'world' – that is, from the meaninglessness of common sense itself. However, it is possible to save oneself through an act of *absolute* faith in a determinate meaning (the content of the revelation). In this respect, it may be stated that the philosophical stance is an *exception*: normality consisting in the internal differentiation of the fideistic stance (which is the stance of those who simply *do not want* to contradict themselves or be contradicted – or *do not want* for what they say to be groundless).

23. No knowledge precedes philosophical knowledge

Hegel states that while philosophy cannot presuppose its objects, it must nevertheless presuppose a certain knowledge of them, '[the reason being] that, in the order of time, consciousness produces *representations* of objects before it produces *concepts* of them; and that the thinking spirit only advances to thinking cognition and comprehension by going *through* representation and by converting itself *to* it.'[3] (Husserl's notion of *Lebenswelt* essentially remains at this level of considerations.) This is correct, however, only if one bears in mind that the very precedence of pre-philosophical knowledge relative to philosophical knowledge (of representation relative to the concept) is a particular content of what is posited as the immediate. Hence, that precedence (the 'order of time') is posited – i.e. it may be held firm, or one may speak of it on the basis of a ground – only through the positing of philosophizing. This positing is not a superseding of that precedence, to the extent that the order of time is distinct from the order of the concept. Accordingly, relative to that dimension of pre-philosophical knowledge in which the latter is posited as being not only temporally *but also* conceptually prior, the positing of that precedence coincides with its being superseded. Rigorously speaking, philosophy does not even presuppose the 'disclosure' of its objects: this presupposition would be equivalent to the positing of a semantic plane that, in being external to the domain of self-signification, would coincide with the very plane of meaninglessness – upon which philosophy would let itself rest as though on a basis or a ground.

24. Pre-philosophical and philosophical knowledge

Since the precedence of any kind of knowledge (and, therefore, any kind of reality) over philosophical knowledge may only be established within this latter knowledge, it follows that, should that precedence be established in another way, this establishing is no more grounded than what is established as that precedence, and it is itself included as part of the horizon of the latter.[4] Hence this can itself be posited only within the opening of philosophical knowledge – which, in positing that precedence, posits the meaninglessness or groundlessness of what is prior, *to the extent that it is prior*.

Strictly speaking, what is prior in that way is posited – insofar as it is prior – as a *possibility* of being grounded: and, therefore, as a possibility of being groundless.

Within pre-philosophical knowledge, groundlessness is not *posited*: that is to say, it is not 'for' that knowledge. That knowledge *is* groundless, but it is such only for philosophical knowledge. (The mere suspicion of groundlessness, in which sometimes common consciousness indulges, is no less groundless than what that consciousness suspects.) According to common knowledge, there instead exists that set of contents of knowledge that are 'certain', to which it refers as 'world', 'life', etc. Pre-philosophical knowledge is groundless because, as already remarked, it consists *per its own essence* in letting its negation subsist – both *qua* general negation and *qua* negation of those specific statements in which that knowledge realizes itself. Or, at most, the *intention* of not letting that negation subsist pertains to that knowledge. For, indeed, the way in which pre-philosophical knowledge disposes of the negation that confronts it consists in a practical intolerance of the latter: an intolerance that realizes itself in a variety of attitudes that ranges from a simple refusal of that negation – i.e. from simply rejecting it away into oblivion ('not wanting to hear about it') – to the physical elimination of its bearer. Furthermore, this cannot be any different: for if pre-philosophical knowledge were to justify to itself its negating its negation, if it were truly able to hold itself firm against the negation that is placed before it, that knowledge would no longer be pre-philosophical, but actual philosophizing – provided that 'philosophy' indicates the opening of the ground of every possible knowledge. Pre-philosophical knowledge, on the contrary, cannot but leave its own negation beside itself, without being able to state why it itself should be held firm rather than its negation. In the same way, the negation of that knowledge, to the extent that it does not constitute itself as a negation performed by philosophizing, is a mode of pre-philosophical knowledge, and, therefore, it also leaves what it negates beside itself. Outside the domain of philosophizing, no affirmation is able to exclude its negation, and nor is the latter able to exclude the former. Since, however, the urgency of life and praxis requires a decision – i.e. the choice of one of the two sides – choices must be based on a mere *volition* or *will* that is directed towards one of the two sides, determined by its greater 'convenience' (taking this term in its broadest significance). The will constitutes the practical resolution of the aporia – or: that groundlessness is superseded in a practical way, in that the ground of one of the two sides precisely consists in the fact that it is chosen by virtue of its greater convenience. The *agreements* realized by pre-philosophical knowledge are therefore due to a 'good will' – namely, a will that is only 'good' insofar as it is a will to agree. Willing to agree means deciding or choosing in such a way that what is realized is 'convenient' for all those who have so chosen. Naturally, when the choice is no longer convenient for someone, or when others come along for whom that choice has never been convenient, the agreement reveals all its gratuitous character, whereby it is altogether indifferent to choose the affirmation or the negation (and one as much as the other finds someone for whom that choice is convenient). The crises of meaning from which the contemporary world suffers – no more and no less than any other historical epoch – are crises of that good will: but, at the same time, more importantly, they are the natural consequence of the oblivion of philosophy.

Concurrently, however, the horizon disclosed by the originary structure constitutes the *originary determination* of that 'possibility of being grounded' (mentioned in the second paragraph of this section), which pertains to pre-philosophical knowledge. From the standpoint of that originary determination, that *possible* groundedness is originarily posited, in a *categorical* way, either as a groundedness or as a groundlessness. That is to say: if pre-philosophical knowledge, insofar as it is regarded as a temporal antecedence, is posited as a possibility in the sense just described, at the same time, *with regard to a specific dimension* of that knowledge, the positing of that possibility is co-originary with the *determination* of that possibility (namely, with the resolution of the latter in a categorical way), to the extent that the temporal antecedence is originarily superseded. As mentioned, this is limited to that dimension that the originary structure is able to posit as being either grounded or groundless. The determination of the possibility in question therefore means: on the one hand, that a set of statements that are held firm by pre-philosophical consciousness is originarily *retained* as also being grounded according to philosophical consciousness; on the other hand, that a set of other statements of pre-philosophical consciousness are either posited as contradictions or they are allowed to stand as possibilities of being grounded. The most familiar example of a determination of that possibility, *qua* confirmation of the statements of common consciousness, consists in the positing of the groundedness of those statements of common language that express an immediate content.

That *retaining* of the statements of pre-philosophical consciousness coincides with their very originary grounding or signification. In this respect, since a statement that is considered outside of its relation with the ground is *essentially* different from what one refers to as the 'same' statement 'but' considered as part of that relation – whereby the process of verification or grounding coincides with the very process of signification of what is verified[5] – it is instead necessary to state that there is *nothing* of pre-philosophical knowledge that is 'retained' as part of philosophical knowledge: or, equivalently, that what is retained in the latter is only the abstract *matter* of the former. It is therefore not possible to state that philosophy verifies that, at times, good or common sense 'is right' ['*ha ragione*']: this cannot be stated precisely because pre-philosophical knowledge is unable to hold itself firm – i.e. it *has no reasons* [*non ha ragioni*]. These 'reasons' are all conferred upon it by philosophy; since, however, pre-philosophical knowledge as such does not accept them, or make them its own – for if it did, it would no longer be pre-philosophical knowledge, but philosophizing itself – it is strictly speaking only philosophy that 'is right'. That is to say, *one is* right when one knows to be so: namely, when one knows one's reasons; for it is precisely by knowing these that it is possible to show the untenability of the opposite statements.

This, however – let us repeat – does not rule out the possibility that the philosophical horizon should be able to retain those *contents* of the pre-philosophical moment, whose groundedness should be successfully established. Pre-philosophical knowledge, however, does not only consist in a content but also in the mode in which that content is regarded. That mode constitutes the *form* of pre-philosophical knowledge. Regardless of the content, that form, as already noted, indicates a lack of groundedness: in that it pertains to it, as such, to leave beside itself the negation of its content; or, more generally, to leave beside itself the negation of the synthesis constituted by that form and that content – the negation of the unity-totality of pre-philosophical knowledge. That synthesis constitutes pre-philosophical knowledge in its character of totality, or insofar as it claims to stand as a unitary system. (The negation of pre-philosophical knowledge, considered in this way, is always grounded – provided that, of course, it should be performed by philosophy.) It is for this reason that the originary structure includes pre-philosophical knowledge as a past and as a future: the temporal present being indeed filled – at least until the existence of other thinking subjects should come to be demonstrated – by the act or form of philosophizing. As already mentioned, it is insofar as one only considers the content of pre-philosophical knowledge that it may occur that specific moments of that content should be retained by philosophy. What is retained, however, is simply the content – and this content is retained not for what it is, but by virtue of its being adopted as the content of the form of philosophy. *Being* part of truth (i.e. part of the ground) – i.e. merely *being* so – therefore means not being part of truth. For being part of truth – being in a way that, at the same time, is not a non-being part of it – means *possessing* this truth, knowing it, comprehend it (whereas, on the contrary, it is possible to only *be* in the error, for as soon as the latter is known, one is already outside it, and part of truth).

The dialogue between 'people' and 'philosophers' – often insisted upon, in particular in relation to the so-called 'questions' and problems that common consciousness addresses and puts forth to philosophy – is in fact a misconception; for the meaning of the terms that constitute those questions and problems *necessarily* differs from the meaning that those 'same' terms acquire insofar as they are part of the answer or the solution. It should furthermore be noted that this misconception does not take place insofar as philosophy establishes the meaninglessness of pre-philosophical consciousness, but insofar as it is stated that the assertions of the latter are 'retained' as part of philosophy; hence the reluctance of 'philosophers' to communicate the *results* of their toil to 'people', and hence the discouragement of those 'people' in learning them. The former are reluctant because they know that their words will be translated into a different semantic horizon (the primary occurrence of this being provided by philosophers themselves, insofar as they give in to the temptation of that communication); the latter are discouraged because, precisely due to that translation, they either come to learn something that they 'more or less' already knew, or find what is being communicated to be completely alien to them, thus immediately disposing of it. In this respect, the task of the philosopher therefore lies – negatively – in *not accepting* that dialogue, regarded as a one-to-one relation between two semantic planes, and – positively – in *transforming* those people into philosophers: establishing of logos, and, therefore, transformation of the world.

Originarily, however – namely, as part of the horizon of the originary structure – common knowledge is always *pre*-philosophical: namely, a past. For, indeed, common knowledge originarily belongs only to 'my' past: that is to say, it only appears as 'my' past. As an ultimate form of knowledge (namely, as affirmed, and not as a content negated by a different form), common sense only appears as the past of the actual and present content of knowledge (i.e. of the content whose form is the originary structure): that is to say, it appears as a past of 'my' knowledge – this 'mine-ness' of knowledge precisely consisting, above all, in the actual presence of knowledge. The existence of a common knowledge that co-exists or exists simultaneously with philosophical knowledge precisely constitutes what originarily does not appear. It does not appear in that, on the one hand – relative to the actual and present form of knowledge, which is the form of philosophy – its existence is contradictory, and, on the other hand, in that a multiplicity of 'subjects' does not originarily appear.

If 'another' individual – or an entire historical epoch – manifests a disagreement with the originary discourse, this disagreement is *immediately* met with a negation, in such a way that this disagreement does indeed exist simultaneously with philosophical knowledge, but *as negated*. (The same is to be argued for any disagreement that appears to be justified by philosophical considerations.) Its simultaneous existence, *as affirmed*, is what is to be mediated: by demonstrating the existence of other centres of consciousness, and, therefore, by moving beyond that originary immediacy.

25. The impossibility of a problematization of the originary meaning

If someone were to enquire into the meaning of the originary self-signification, they would have to be urged, following Aristotle's suggestion, to give a meaning to their own question. If the question aims to be meaningful, its meaning must in any case be traced back to the very originarity of meaning.

In this way, every problematization of the originary meaning contradictorily presupposes what is being problematized: that is to say, it is and at the same time it is not a meaning. It is a meaning to the extent that it presupposes the originary meaning; it is not a meaning to the extent that it calls the latter into question. The problematization of the originary meaning constitutes a mode of the negation of the structure of immediacy, and, therefore, it is superseded in the very act in which that negation is superseded.

The request for the meaning of the negation of the originary meaning is a call for that negation to break out of the *indifference* of 'negating for the sake of negating', or 'asking for the sake of asking': an indifference that in being, as such, an indifference relative to that asking or negating – whereby asking and not asking or negating and not negating are equivalent – does not even succeed in constituting itself as an actual asking or negating. The latter, as a result, if left to that indifference, annul themselves by themselves. Their acquiring a meaning thus consists in their breaking out of that indifference.

Breaking out of this indifference consists in their insisting on or going into themselves, in such a way that their supersession, as already noted, is brought about by something other than their immediate inability to hold themselves firm by themselves. This is the case even if their meaningfulness coincides with the verification of their contradictoriness: for, in that case, their supersession (originarily) results from the positing of the impossibility of their acquiring a non-contradictory meaning.[6]

2

The immediacy of being

1. The immediate

Being that is immediately present – the 'immediate', as that which comes to constitute the subject of the originary judgement, or, more precisely, as an element of that structuring of the meanings of immediacy that precisely constitutes the subject of the originary judgement – is what, in order to be affirmed, does not require or presuppose anything other than its own presence, or does not presuppose anything other than itself *qua* present: τὸ δι' αὐτὸ γνώριμον; the *per se notum*.

Its affirmation or positing is the very presence, manifestation and actuality of that being. That is to say, the presentation or manifestation of being is precisely the affirmation: 'being is'. We are then precisely asserting that, in order to affirm that being is, there is no need nor can there be any need to introduce a *different* term from the one that is affirmed; that is to say, in order to affirm that being is there is no need nor can there be any need for any mediation, demonstration or *apodeixis*.

'In order to affirm that being is there is no need nor can there be any need for any mediation'; this means: 'It is known for itself that being is.' Known for itself: namely, it is not known for or through something other. If that for which being is known is the very being that is known, the fact that being is is *immediately* known or present: phenomenological immediacy.

2. Note on the meaning of the term 'being'

The term 'being' indicates a synthesis – to be precisely determined – between the meaning 'being' (*formal being*) and the meanings constituted by the *determinations* that, precisely, *are*. Or, equivalently: the term 'being' indicates a semantic complexity or concreteness, the abstract moments of which are that formal being and the determinations of this formal element.

3. Principium cognitionis

If, at this point, one wished to argue that 'that for which' it is known that being is is something akin to 'consciousness' (or the 'subject', the 'I', etc.), it should be observed that not only is consciousness that by virtue of which *it is affirmed* that being is, but it is also that by virtue of which it is possible to *negate* that being is.[1] Consciousness (or the equivalent terms), as such, is therefore not that by virtue of which an affirmation, rather than a negation, is held firm. 'That for which' it is known that being is has therefore a *different* meaning from 'that for which' both the affirmation and the negation of being may obtain: this difference precisely exists to the extent that that for which it is known that being is excludes the possibility that being should not be. We shall therefore state that 'that for which' it is affirmed that being is is the *principium cognitionis* – with the proviso, however, that this 'principle', or ground, is here cognition itself (i.e. the affirmation that being is).

4. The determination of the meaning of the immediacy of being

a. Stating that being is known means that, of being, it is known that it is. (Every other knowledge that may be realized concerning being is an internal determination of the knowledge that being is.) Or, equivalently, as stated in §1, the presentation of being realizes itself in and through the affirmation that 'being is'. It must then be remarked that the proposition: 'It is known for itself that being is' is not meant to affirm the immediacy of the connection between the subject and the predicate of the proposition: 'Being is', but the immediacy *of the disclosure* (i.e. the presence, or positing) of that connection. The latter is therefore not of interest here as such, but as a positivity (= being) that is a content of that presence. (It is for this reason that the propositions: 'It is known for itself that being is', and 'Being is known for itself' have been used interchangeably.) In other words, in stating: being is, *because* the fact that being is is known for itself, that 'because' (i.e. the ground) is not here the because of the being of being (i.e. it is not the because of the connection between the subject and the predicate of the proposition: 'Being is'), but it is the because of the 'that' (*dass*) being is: phenomenological immediacy.

The content of the proposition: 'Being is' may also be expressed in this other way: 'The set x, y, z is' – where the symbols x, y, z indicate all the determinations of that being that is known for itself. Insofar as these determinations are designated in accordance with that determination – 'being' – which includes every other determination, or which is able to express every other determination, one precisely obtains the proposition: 'Being is'.

Lastly, it should be noted that if the proposition: 'It is known for itself that being is' is not meant to affirm the immediacy of the connection between the subject and the predicate of the proposition: 'Being is', this does not mean that this immediacy does not obtain. The immediacy of that connection is indeed the immediacy of the *identity* or *non-contradictoriness* of being (logical immediacy), and it will be considered in this sense in Chapter 3. (This concludes the outline of that structuring of the meanings of immediacy that, as already remarked, constitutes the subject of the originary judgement.)

b. That non-contradictoriness represents the formal side of the very proposition: 'Being is' (this, however, does not mean that the meaning of non-contradictoriness is exhausted by this formal function). For what concerns the content – of which that non-contradictoriness is the form – that proposition expresses the concrete configuration or determination of that being that is known for itself: hence, as already noted, the equivalent proposition: 'The set x, y, z is' obtains. In this respect, affirming that being is means affirming that being is in that mode whose pertaining to being is known for itself (non-contradictoriness being the form of that mode or configuration).

It is therefore clear that the negation of the proposition: 'Being is' is a negation of the pertaining to being of that concrete configuration or determination whose pertaining to being is known for itself. (The very being known or the very presence of being belongs to that configuration; that is to say, the fact that being is known is a – distinctive – determinacy of the horizon of what is known for itself. Accordingly, the negation of the fact that being is known is a particular aspect or moment of the negation of that being that is known.)

Once again: that the negation of that proposition should have the meaning that has been indicated does not mean that the negation (*qua* superseded) of the indicated formal value of the proposition in question does not exist: in this respect, that negation is a negation of the identity or non-contradictoriness of being.

5. The positing of being and the ground of this positing

That for which being is known – the ground of the disclosure of being – is the very being that is known. If, therefore, one merely affirms that being is, this affirmation – to the extent that one affirms the being of the being that is known for itself – *is* certainly its own ground; precisely, however, it only *is* so; the ground is only *in itself*: it is not posited; it is not known. Or, equivalently, it is known (in that the being that is known is known), but it is not known as ground: precisely because it is not known that the affirmation that being is is its own ground – and, therefore, because *it is not posited* that being is known *for itself*, i.e. because the immediacy of the presence of being is not posited. As long as one remains at this moment of the in-itselfness or implicitness of the ground, the affirmation that being is is not able to assert itself (i.e. it is not able to *exhibit* its own groundedness), and it thus leaves beside itself the negation of the fact that being is. It is not able to supersede it, and it therefore lets itself be superseded by it. This means that if the ground (simply) *is* the ground, the ground *is not* the ground.

6. Note

That negation, in turn, lets itself be superseded by that affirmation to the extent that it merely states that being is not (i.e. it merely negates the horizon of what is known for itself). Neither the affirmation nor the negation is in any case able to rule the other out, or to hold itself firm in opposition to the other one, and they thus stand together as an infinite vanishing of the one into the other. That is to say, they each infinitely vanish by virtue of the simple existence of the other one.

This vanishing, in turn, is infinite because it does not have a result that posits itself beyond the very movement of that vanishing. This result would constitute the *definitiveness* of the vanishing of the opposite terms: a vanishing that would no longer let each of those terms arise in opposition to the other one. This may only take place by overcoming the contradiction.

This overcoming, however, does not realize itself as a 'setting aside' of the opposition, but as the groundedness or value of one of the two terms that comprise that opposition: that is to say, the overcoming of the contradiction does not consist in the arising of a *middle term* between the affirmation and the negation – whereby the vanishing would encompass both of them – but it once again consists in the arising of the ground of one of the two opposed terms; it consists in the coming to stand firm of one of the two terms.

It is clear that the other of the two terms is not superseded by the term that is simply opposed to it, but by the one that is now able to hold itself firm, and that is therefore no longer the one that, in the opposition, was vanishing together with its opposite.

7. Resuming

As long as one merely affirms that being is, this affirmation therefore lets itself be superseded by its negation. Remaining with the affirmation thus means leaning or *tending* 'in unam partem contradictionis *cum formidine alterius*'. That is to say, thinking subsides by the thesis only by virtue of an *intention* – which is, a practical act – but, precisely for this reason, *it fears* the opposite thesis.

The opposite – the negation of the fact that being is (and that it is in that mode whose pertaining to it is known for itself) – is only superseded insofar as *it is noted, i.e. posited* that being is *immediately* present: *which is*, only insofar as it is noted that in order to affirm that being is there is and there can be no need for any demonstration.

The singular and timeless merit of Greek philosophy is to have *disclosed* the meaning of immediacy. This disclosure is therefore not something ancillary relative to that immediacy, but it is precisely that by virtue of which the latter stands as the ground. Or, equivalently: immediacy is the ground only insofar as it is disclosed, or *posited*, as immediacy.

8. Observations concerning the concrete meaning of immediacy

Note: it should not be stated: 'Being is immediately present *for the reason that* in order to affirm that being is there is no need for a demonstration'; nor should it be stated: 'There is no need for a demonstration *for the reason that* being is immediately present'. Or, equivalently: if being is immediately present for the reason that there is no need for a demonstration (or vice-versa), it is, however, necessary to note right away that there is no need for a demonstration for the reason that being is immediately present (or vice-versa). We are remarking that 'that for which' it is affirmed that being is is something *concrete*, whose *abstract moments* are that (posited) immediate presence, as distinct from that (posited) lack of need for a demonstration, and this lack of need, as distinct from that immediate presence.

Indeed, by immediate presence we mean: being that is known or affirmed for itself and on the basis of itself. Stating that being is known for itself means excluding that it should be known for something other. On the one hand, the fact that being is is known for itself *in that* it is not known for something other, and, on the other hand, the fact that being is is not known for something other *in that* it is known for itself: mutual determination.

If *only* the first side of this mutual relation were present, the term 'not known for something other' would be *independent* of the term: 'known for itself', and it would therefore be *indifferent* to the negation of the term: 'known for itself'. That is to say, the negation of 'known for itself' would not entail the negation of 'not known for something other' – and this is immediately self-contradictory. Conversely, if *only* the second side of that mutual relation were present, 'known for itself' would be *independent* of 'not known for something other', and it would therefore be *indifferent* to the negation of 'not known for something other' – and this is immediately self-contradictory.

9. First note

It must be observed that this mutual determination is not *demonstrated* or *mediated*. For, indeed, the two sides of that mutual relation are constituted by two analytic (identical) judgements, in which the predicate pertains to the subject on the basis of a simple analysis of the predicate – which is to say, it pertains to it immediately. These judgements may also be formulated as: '*Known for itself* (subject) is that which is determined by *not known for something other* (predicate)'; '*not known for something other* is that which is determined by *known for itself*'. In the first of these two judgements, for instance, 'that which is determined by *not known for something other*' means 'that which is negated by negating *not known for something other*'. Stating that 'known for itself' is *insofar as* 'not known for something other' is, or that it *depends* on 'not known for something other', precisely means that the negation of 'not known for something other' immediately entails the negation of 'known for itself'; accordingly, 'known for itself' is not something grounded by 'not known for something other' – if the ground is understood as being logically prior to what is grounded. The same holds for the second judgement.

The appearance of a mediation, which might have arisen above, is merely the explicit realization of the analysis on the basis of which it is possible to discern the identity of the subject and the predicate. The realization or emergence of that analysis is a logical increment only from a merely discursive standpoint, or from the standpoint of communication as such. Looking at *both* those judgements, it should be remarked that 'known for itself' and 'not known for something other', insofar as they are regarded *as distinct* from one another, are only *abstract moments* of the concrete. If the negation of one entails the negation of the other, the concrete precisely consists in this mutual determination. This means that each of them is what it is insofar as it is part of this mutual determination or relation. It is therefore only as part of this relation that what is 'known for itself' is distinct from what is 'not known for something other'. Or, equivalently: *that which* is determined by 'not known for something other' and *that which* is determined by 'known for itself' – the 'that which' that appear in the predicates of the two judgements – respectively, stand as 'known for itself' and 'not known for something other' only insofar as they are determined in this way.

10. Second note

Furthermore, it should be observed that this mutual determination is not a contradiction only insofar as that determination is not understood as a 'grounding' in which the ground stands as something logically prior to what is grounded. If that determination is understood in this way, it is indeed contradictory that one of the two moments of that mutual determination should at the same time determine the other one and be determined by it. The two moments, determined in this sense – i.e. such that they each have their ground in the other of the two, regarded as something logically prior – are only abstract moments of that mutual relation *insofar as they are abstractly conceived*: that is, insofar as each of them is not seen to be part of the essence of the other one. In this case: on the one hand, insofar as each of the two terms is prior to the other one, their mutual determination constitutes a contradiction; on the other hand, insofar as each of the two terms, as prior to the other one, *does not immediately exclude* the negation of the other – for if this *immediate* exclusion of the negation of that other were present, that very other would not exist as something logically *subsequent* – it therefore does not even exclude its own negation, since the negation of the other one entails its own. In this way, the grounded term has its ground in a term that is not able to stand as an exclusion of the negation of that very grounded term.

Having excluded that contradictory meaning of that mutual determination, this concept indicates the *immediate relation* of the distinct terms by virtue of which each of the two terms is not without the other one. Relative to each of the two distinct terms, however, the other one is not something logically prior (whereby the subsequent term would require a ground), but, precisely, it is an immediately related term; accordingly, neither of the two terms is something mediated, but the two terms constitute the structure of logical immediacy (taking for granted that the immediacy that has been discussed in this last section is precisely the logical immediacy. The question of the difference, and therefore of the relation, between logical immediacy and phenomenological immediacy will be considered further on. This second kind of immediacy is the subject of the present chapter).

11. Aporia: The ground of the positing of being constitutes itself as an indefinite process

Resuming: being is because *that* being is is immediately known. (Once the concrete meaning of immediacy is held firm, it is irrelevant, from a discursive point of view, if one expresses this concreteness through one or the other of its two moments.) That immediate disclosure coincides with the very affirming that being is: the ground of this affirmation is its very being posited as immediate knowledge.

It appears to be relevant, at this point, to consider an aporia of significant interest, determined by the unchecked use of the *abstract understanding*. It may be formulated as follows.

It is immediately known that being is. On what basis, however, is it affirmed that it is immediately known that being is? The answer will be: it is immediately known because it is immediately known that it is immediately known. That is to say: in the same way in which the positing (affirmation) of being was first grounded in the positing of its immediacy, so is now the positing of this immediacy grounded in the positing of the immediacy of immediacy itself. It is clear that, in this way, one could then ask for the basis of the positing of the immediacy of immediacy, thus giving rise to a *regressus in indefinitum* in the justification of the positing of being. If, indeed, being may only be posited insofar as the immediacy of this positing is posited, and this immediacy may only be posited insofar as the immediacy of the positing of immediacy is posited, and since it is possible to ask for the ground of every positional level that is effectively achieved, and since the positing of its ground leads beyond that level, the positing of the ground will in any case be sidestepped, and the positing of being will have a simply unwarranted or conventional value.

12. Transition

A first kind of solution to this aporia may be given by remarking that, even if that *regressus in indefinitum* were to arise, the positing of being would not be unwarranted, since the proposition: 'Being is not' (the negation of the being that is known) is inherently self-contradictory.

Since, however, the exposition has not yet considered this inherent contradictoriness of the negation of present being (cf. Chapter 12), and since it would be contradictory to let something that is not an indefinite process stand as an indefinite process, the aporia must be precisely resolved by showing that this process does not arise.

13. Negative solution of the aporia

Let us then begin by considering the meaning of the request to ground the positing of the immediacy of being. That is to say, let us elucidate the meaning of asking on what basis it is affirmed that it is immediately known that being is: namely, the meaning of asking on what basis it is affirmed that in order to affirm that being is there is and there can be no need for any mediation.

Let us state right away that the meaning of this question is a *contradiction* to the extent that the question requires the introduction of a term that *differs* from those that constitute the proposition: 'Being is, because it is immediately known that being is.' Or, more precisely: what the question asks for or requires is a contradiction if what is asked for is a term that differs from the terms of that proposition.

If, indeed, one posits that *that for which* it is affirmed that being is immediately known is x, with x being a term that *differs* from the terms of the proposition in question, the affirmation: 'Being is' (i.e. the disclosure of being) will be, at the same time and in the same respect, something immediate and something mediated; that is to say, that affirmation will be at the same time something that requires no demonstration and something that is demonstrated. It will be something immediate, or something that does not require a demonstration, insofar as, on the basis of that x, it is precisely established that it is something immediate. It will be something mediated, or something 'demonstrated', precisely insofar as it is established that it is something immediate *on the basis of that x*. As a result, in this second respect, being is not *known for itself*, but *for something other*: i.e. for and through that x, since it is possible to hold firm the affirmation of being only insofar as that x is established.

Therefore, *demonstrating* that the positing of being requires no demonstration is contradictory. If one asks on what basis it is affirmed that the positing of being requires no demonstration – and as long as what serves as that basis is an x in the indicated sense – what is thus asked for is a contradiction.

The reason why what has been stated here is a 'negative' solution to the aporia is made clear further ahead (§15).

14. Another aspect of the aporia

In the meantime, one may counter as follows: if that contradiction is eliminated by eliminating the x (namely, by negating that it is possible to demonstrate that the positing of being requires no demonstration), that contradiction may also be eliminated by negating that being is, or also by negating that it is known for itself that being is. In other words, affirming that the contradiction may *only* be eliminated by negating the possibility of that x – in such a way that the outcome of this negation should be the *standing firm* of the positing of the immediacy of being (i.e. in such a way that the outcome of that negation is the persistence of the positing of being, posited as an immediate positing) – means *presupposing* what one wants to achieve: namely, the validity or standing firm of the positing of the immediacy of being. By *presupposing* that this positing is something absolutely grounded, the contradictoriness of the concept: 'Demonstration of the positing of the immediacy of being' may only be eliminated by letting this positing stand as an absolute self-foundation. Since, however, what we are trying to establish is precisely the validity of the affirmation: 'It is known for itself that being is' (i.e. the positing of immediacy), the contradictoriness of that concept, as already stated, may also be eliminated by negating this very affirmation.

15. Radical formulation of the aporia

This new aspect of the aporia effectively presents a positive side. Namely: the reason for holding firm the positing of immediacy may not be given by the contradiction that would ensue in introducing the *x* – precisely because this contradiction may also be eliminated by negating the immediacy of being.

At the same time, however, if this immediacy is to be held firm, it may not be held firm through the introduction of that *x*: precisely because, as already seen, this entails a contradiction. It is in this sense that above we referred to a 'negative' solution of the aporia.

The aporia acquires at this point a greater significance. It may be formulated as follows:

The positing of the immediacy of being – i.e. affirming that being is known for itself – has its ground either in itself or in something other. Or, equivalently: that immediacy is known or affirmed either for itself or for something other. That it should be known for something other (for that *x*) is contradictory (§13). If, instead, it is known for itself – i.e. if that immediacy is affirmed on the basis of its own immediacy – there arises a *regressus in indefinitum* (§11), since if being can only be posited on the basis of the positing of the immediacy of this positing, and if this immediacy can only be posited on the basis of the positing of the immediacy of that immediacy, one will again and always be able to ask for the basis of the positing of the immediacy of immediacy.

16. The superseding of the aporia

The responsibility for the aporia lies – as already mentioned – with the abstract understanding. This becomes clear if we retrace the fundamental moments of the argument. Being is: as long as one remains at this affirmation, it is not possible to eliminate the negation of that being that is known for itself; this negation therefore overthrows the affirmation. The negation is superseded because *that* being is is immediately known or known for itself; that is to say, because the negation negates what is known for itself: i.e. that which is the very ground or basis of its own being affirmed.

Being that is known, however, *insofar as it is regarded as the basis* of the affirmation that being is – or *insofar as it is regarded as that for which being is affirmed* – does not lie outside of the horizon constituted by the being that is thus affirmed, but it is included in it. That is to say, the immediacy of immediate being belongs to the horizon of immediate being: it is *not only* known for itself that being is, *but it is also* known for itself that the being that is known is that for which it is affirmed that being is. The fact that the being that is known should be that basis or ground of the affirmation of being is itself a moment of that being that is known for itself (a moment, moreover, to which it pertains to be the form of the other moments). Being, *qua* ground or basis, is a moment of what is known for itself.

What needs to be correctly understood, however – this being the main point – is the meaning of that 'not only... but also'. Namely: *the fact that immediate being, qua* (i.e. posited as) *basis of the affirmation of being, should be included in immediate being itself* (i.e. in what is known for itself) *does not constitute a moment that is logically distinct from the moment in which it is posited that being is known for itself;* the positing of that inclusion is not a moment that is additional to or logically distinct from the positing of the immediacy of being. This means that *in the very act* in which the being that is known is posited as that for which it is itself affirmed, *in this same act*, being (i.e. precisely the being that is known), regarded *as* that for which being is affirmed, is included in that being *that* is known for itself; *in this same act*, being *as* the basis of the affirmation of being is included in the being *that* is the basis of its own affirmation.

Granted this, if one asks on what basis it is affirmed that being, which is asserted to be known for itself, is the basis of its own being affirmed – i.e. on what basis it is affirmed that this being is, precisely, known for itself – one calls into question what has *already* been posited as being known for itself. Accordingly, the problematization caused by the question constitutes itself as something *already superseded*; or, equivalently: the negation of the fact that being (that is known for itself) is the basis of the affirmation of being is something already superseded – already superseded by the positing of the for-itselfness or immediacy of that basis value.

Naturally, the *discursivity* of thinking says *over time* – one thing after the other – what is not temporal. The reasoning therefore takes this course: '"Being is". This is affirmed because being is known for itself; it is affirmed that being is known for itself because it is known for itself that being is known for itself'. In this way, the abstract understanding, which precisely consists of an inability to rise above the *technique* or external form of discourse, gives rise to a *regressus in indefinitum*. The *word*, as such, is not responsible for this: time is the destiny of the word. That discursive 'course' is correct – provided, however, that what counts as a single logical moment should not be regarded as two separate moments (i.e. as the positing of immediacy and as the positing of the immediacy of immediacy); namely, provided that that '*not only* (is being known for itself)' should not be regarded as being logically prior to that '*but also* (it is known for itself that being is known for itself)'.

The moment of the positing of (immediate) being as basis and the moment of the inclusion of this basis value (possessed by that immediate being) in the immediate being that is the basis are, certainly, *qua* distinct from one another, abstract moments of the immediate content. That is to say, that domain of the immediate that does not include immediacy itself as posited and that domain of the immediate that is constituted by the posited immediacy of the immediate are certainly abstract moments of the immediate. However, to the extent that one *only* considers that first moment – i.e. to the extent that the immediacy of being is not regarded as being immediately included in being (which is posited as being known for itself) – one loses sight of the concrete: that is to say, the concrete concept of the abstract moments is replaced by the abstract concept of the abstract. By *turning* from this moment of the isolation of the abstract to that other moment – namely, as soon as the need for the concrete arises, and one sets to reflect on the immediacy of immediate being – this is not found as something that is *already included* in the immediate itself, but as something that *is to be included in it*, and that is therefore to be included through an additional and *different* step relative to the one constituted by that first moment. Insofar as immediacy itself is not already included in the immediate, the question into the ground of the affirmation of that immediacy is not manifested as something already superseded, but as something to be superseded. This is precisely superseded by including that immediacy in the immediate as indicated: that is, by stating that it is known for itself that being is known for itself.

If, at this point, one *once again* does not regard the immediacy of that inclusion (i.e. the immediacy of the immediacy of the immediate) as being *already included* in the immediate thus constituted or augmented by that inclusion, one, in setting to reflect on this inclusion, will ask on what ground it is admissible: and, once again, this question will be solved by including the inclusion of the immediate. *Et cetera.*

As already indicated, this aporetic development is eliminated by remarking that the concrete content of that being that is known for itself *immediately* includes this very immediacy or for-itselfness, by virtue of which it is precisely possible to affirm that being is (being: with all the determinations whose pertaining to being is known for itself – thus including that determination that consists in the very immediacy of all these determinations).

It is therefore clear from what has been said that the aporia only arises insofar as one holds firm the *impossibility* for the immediacy of immediate being to be *immediately* included[2] in the horizon of immediate being itself – i.e. the impossibility that this immediacy should be included in this horizon in the very act in which the latter is posited, in such a way that this inclusion should come to be realized in an additional logical moment. Since, as part of this additional moment, there ensues the previous situation (i.e. the affirmation of the immediacy of a content – a content that, however, is already determined as the affirmation of the immediacy of a content), a *regressus in indefinitum* is thus initiated: a regress that, in other words, consists in affirming that the affirmation of the immediacy of any content has no ground. That *impossibility* is then to be held firm only if the positing of the immediacy of being and the positing of the inclusion of that immediacy in that immediate being are abstractly conceived or abstractly separated: in such a way that, by definition, the immediacy of immediate being cannot immediately manifest itself as part of the horizon of immediate being, or, precisely, in such a way that it manifests itself in an additional logical moment relative to the one constituted by the realization of those two acts of positing. By superseding the abstract concept of these two acts of positing, that impossibility is also superseded, and the aporia is resolved in showing that the positing of the immediacy of being stands as the ground only if the immediacy of the horizon of the immediate is immediately included in that very horizon. This does not mean that a positing of that horizon, which would not include its immediacy, is *impossible*; rather, it means that if a positing of this kind is realized, it is something groundless, since, precisely, the affirmation that this horizon stands as an immediacy has no ground.

17. Corollaries

The following corollaries result from what has been said:

1. The *regressus in indefinitum* (§11) does not arise as a result of *a single* intervention of the abstract understanding, but as a result of a *repetition* of this intervention. That is to say, at every moment of the *regressus* the immediacy of the immediate content is abstractly separated from that very content, and, receding into the background the very moment that one loses sight of the concreteness of the content, it must *each*

time be reintroduced as part of the immediate content – this re-introduction standing precisely as a logically different and subsequent moment relative to the one in which the immediate content is posited. Aside from the psychological difficulties of positing a significantly reflexive content ('the immediacy of the immediacy… of the immediate') as something that is known for itself, it is clear that the *regressus in indefinitum* may be superseded *at every moment* of the regress: as already mentioned, by concretely conceiving the relation between the positing of the immediate content (of a higher or lower reflective order) and the positing of the immediacy of the immediate. The concrete superseding of the abstract positing of the immediate therefore recognizes that abstractness from the first moment of the *regressus*, and does not allow the request for the ground of the positing of immediacy to be constituted as something that has not yet been superseded or resolved.

2. If the immediacy of the immediate content is not originarily (i.e. immediately) included in this content – if, therefore, the grounding of the former *follows* the grounding of the latter – the grounding of the positing of the immediacy of the immediate (a grounding that consists in the inclusion of that immediacy in the immediate horizon) constitutes itself as that x that has been discussed in §13. If, indeed, the immediate may only be held firm insofar as its immediacy is held firm – and if the grounding of this immediacy constitutes a moment that is logically distinct from the grounding of the immediate – it precisely follows that the grounding of the immediacy of the immediate stands as that x. That is to say, it follows that one states that there is no need to demonstrate that being is, in that the fact that there is no need to demonstrate it results from that x. This x consists, on the one hand, in the verification that there is no need to demonstrate that being is – and, in this sense, i.e. insofar as the immediacy is included in the immediate, that x does not stand as a different term relative to the terms of the proposition: 'There is no need to demonstrate that being (which is known for itself) is' – but, on the other hand, that verification is regarded as being logically additional relative to the positing of the immediate, in such a way that, in this respect, that x retains its contradictory character. That is to say, that x does indeed consist in the acknowledgement of the fact that there is no need to introduce a different term, but since this acknowledgement is regarded as something logically additional relative to that moment, which includes the terms in relation to which that x seeks not to stand as something different, that very acknowledgement precisely constitutes the 'different term' that gives rise to the contradictory concept of a demonstration of something that cannot be demonstrated.

18. New aporia: The fact that being is is both immediate and mediated

Let us now consider an aporetic structure that makes use of already known elements.

It has been established that it is contradictory to justify the positing of the immediacy of immediate being *by means* of an x. Since the immediate includes the immediacy of the immediate the very moment the immediate is posited, the immediacy of the immediate is not known for anything else (i.e. for x), but for itself.

And yet, it seems that in this way, too, it is not possible to avoid the fact that being, which is immediately known, should be something immediate and at the same time something mediated. It has indeed been stated that the affirmation: 'Being is' may only be held firm insofar as it is noted, or posited, that being is known *for itself*. That is to say, *the ground* of the positing of being consists in the positing of the immediacy of that positing. From this it follows that the positing of being (= the affirmation: 'Being is') is something *mediated*, insofar as that for which being is posited is the positing of the immediacy of that positing; and, at the same time, it is something *immediate*, precisely because that for which being is posited is the acknowledgement of the immediacy of the positing of being. That is to say, the fact that being is does not necessitate a demonstration – precisely because being is known for itself – and, at the same time, it is demonstrated, because in order to hold firm that being is *it is necessary to acknowledge* that there is no need to demonstrate that being is, and this acknowledgement is *something other* (i.e. that *x*) relative to the positing of being. (The positing of being is indeed formally distinct from the positing of the immediacy of being.)

19. The superseding of the aporia

In this case, too, the abstract understanding is responsible for the aporetic situation. That is to say, the aporia arises insofar as the moments of the concrete are abstractly considered outside of their relation. In this case, what is considered abstractly is the positing of being and the positing of the immediacy of that positing. The concrete concept lets itself be unseated by the abstract concept of these two abstract moments.

Those two acts of positing are certainly distinct from one another. Concretely, however, their distinction is at the same time their relation. Insofar as the positing of being is instead considered outside of its relation with the positing of the immediacy of the positing of being, the positing of being does not appear as an immediacy, and it therefore leaves the negation of being beside itself; that is to say, it manifests itself as something groundless. It follows that when the positing of that immediacy *supervenes* – when the two abstract moments come to be related to one another – one attests that this new positing *mediates* and *grounds* the positing of being. As a result, this latter positing effectively comes to stand as something mediated and immediate.

The contradiction therefore arises to the extent that the positing of being logically precedes the positing of the immediacy of that positing. That precedence precisely constitutes that positing's standing outside of its relation with the positing of that immediacy: namely, it constitutes a presupposition of that former positing to this latter one – i.e. the abstract separation of the two acts of positing.

Once again, the aporia arises due to the power of suggestion of the word (that is to say, the abstract concept of the abstract is determined by the power of that suggestion). Since discursivity places those two acts of positing one after the other, this property of discourse is conferred upon the content itself.

The aporia is therefore resolved by noting that the positing of immediacy *is not* the positing of the immediacy of the positing of being as long as this latter positing is conceived of as being *prior* to the positing of its immediacy: insofar as that positing is thus prior, not only can it not be posited as an immediate positing, but it is in fact superseded – it is superseded to the extent that, *qua* prior, it is something absolutely groundless. (Furthermore, the act that supersedes or negates the positing of being, regarded as something prior to the positing of its immediacy, coincides with the very act that posits or affirms the immediacy of the positing of being, regarded as being co-originary with the positing of being.)

In other words: what is posited as ground – i.e. being that is posited as the immediate – is not something that *was* without a ground: that is to say, it is not the positing of being as prior to or abstractly separated from the positing of its immediacy. What is posited as ground is what is posited – vis-à-vis the determinations that pertain to its content – *in the very act* in which it is posited as ground: or, more precisely, what is posited as ground is not a content that is presupposed to or separated from its being posited as ground, but it is precisely something that is in relation with (or, as stated, that is posited 'in the very act' as) its being posited as ground. (It should be clear that this co-originarity of the two acts of positing does not have a psychological or discursive character – for, on the contrary, discursivity constitutes the dimension in which what is co-originary appears as a sequence – but concerns the content as such.) Accordingly, the positing of being appears as something mediated only insofar as it is abstractly separated from the positing of its immediacy.

The positing of being is not therefore something mediated and at the same time something immediate, but – concretely conceived – it is *only* something immediate. For, on the contrary, the positing of being, *qua* co-originary with the positing of its immediacy, is not something that – to the extent that this immediacy is not yet posited (and, therefore, to the extent that the positing of this immediacy is not co-originary with the positing of being) – stands as something groundless, which therefore requires a mediation. Precisely insofar as the positing of being is thus co-originary, it does not precede the positing of its immediacy, and it therefore simply and only stands as the immediate: as that of which, precisely, immediacy is predicated.

This co-originarity – let us add – is not an identity: the positing of being is distinct from the positing of its immediacy. This distinction, however, is precisely the content of that co-originarity. What produces the aporia is the separation or the abstract isolation of the distinct terms.

20. Note

From what has been said, it appears that the positing of immediacy is not the result of a form of discursivity, but it is immanent to the *whole* discursive process. It is by virtue of this immanence that the very *question* concerning the ground of the positing of being may be held firm. Let us clarify this point. The *discourse* relative to the affirmation of being has unfolded as follows: at first, being has been posited; secondly, it has been noted that this simple positing is not able to hold itself firm, and we have therefore 'asked' for the ground of that positing; thirdly, the immediacy of the positing of being has been posited (thus ruling out the negation of being).

We are now stating – confirming what has been discussed above – that this latter positing is not the result of the question indicated above, but it is what, in being co-originary with the positing of being, makes that very question possible. For, indeed, also in relation to the question concerning the ground, one may ask on what basis that asking is held firm in opposition to a not-asking. This question, however, is possible insofar as it is *already resolved*: that is, insofar as the positing of being is already seen as the ground itself, or insofar as the need leading to that question is already originarily fulfilled. Accordingly, that question does not affect the concrete – i.e. the co-originarity of the positing of being and of the positing of the immediacy of that positing – but the abstract, i.e. the positing of being regarded as distinct from the positing of its immediacy.

That question is therefore an act of the concrete itself, which, calling into question one of its moments, precisely recognizes it as a moment of the concrete. This means that the question only exists from the standpoint of discursivity. (For a development of the themes mentioned in this section, cf. Chapter 5, §§10 ff.)

21. Resuming: Another aspect of the aporia presented in §18 and its solution

The remarks developed in §10 make it possible to eliminate a difficulty analogous to the one presented in §18.

The immediacy of the positing of being is immediately included in the content of that positing, i.e. precisely in the horizon of which one posits the immediacy (§16). That is to say, the immediacy of this horizon is itself one of the determinations that constitute that horizon – a determination that, as already mentioned, while being one 'among others', has the specific property of being the form of all other determinations. In this way, however, it appears that the immediacy of the positing of being stands at the same time as ground and as something grounded (i.e. not as ground). Indeed, the immediacy that is *included* in the horizon of the immediate is *the very* immediacy *of* that horizon. (The immediacy that is included is that same immediacy whose positing is the ground of the affirmation of that horizon.) Accordingly, insofar as that immediacy is thus included, it is something that, together with all the other determinations of that horizon, may only be affirmed insofar as the immediacy of that affirmation is posited – and, therefore, it is something *grounded* by that positing. Insofar as it is instead the immediacy *of* the horizon in question, that immediacy is, on the contrary, the positing *on the grounds of which* it is possible to affirm everything that is part of that horizon. The positing of immediacy is therefore, at the same time, ground and not ground.

It is clear that, also in this case, the aporia arises insofar as the distinction between the positing of being and the positing of the immediacy of that positing is not concretely conceived, in such a way that that former positing is considered as being logically prior to the second one, and, therefore, as something *grounded* (§19). The positing of that immediacy, too, therefore appears as something grounded: precisely to the extent that this immediacy is included in the content of that first positing. (Furthermore, given that logical antecedence, i.e. given the abstract separation of the two acts of positing, the second one arises as a positional dimension that lacks the positional positivity constituted by the first positing.) If, instead, the co-originarity of the two acts of positing is held firm, that immediacy is not, at the same time, the ground and something grounded, but only the ground: precisely because the content of the first positing (the 'horizon' discussed above) is the ground, i.e. precisely what is known for itself – the immediate.

22. Clarifications concerning the meaning of the relation between P_1 and P_2

It is thus clarified that, in the same way in which the positing of being (let this be P_1) is something merely grounded (and, in fact, *qua* mere antecedence it is something superseded by the ground) only insofar as it is abstractly separated from the positing of the immediacy of P_1 (let P_2 be the positing of this immediacy), so P_2, insofar as it is abstractly separated from P_1, *is not* the ground of P_1, but, on the one hand, P_2 itself – insofar as it is referred to or predicated of P_1 – requires a ground, and, on the other hand, it is inherently contradictory.

In other words: the abstract consideration of the two acts of positing entails that the originary positional whole ($= I$) is such that

$$I = P_1 + P_2$$

(with P_1 being a positional positivity that is not included in the positional positivity constituted by P_2, and vice-versa). A concrete consideration entails instead that:

$$I = P_2$$

Indeed, insofar as P_1 and P_2 are abstractly separated, or not part of their relation, P_1 is not posited in P_2 – for, if in the positing of the immediacy of being that immediacy were posited as the immediacy *of being*, P_2 would include P_1, and P_1 and P_2 would no longer be unrelated. Insofar as P_2 (regarded as unrelated to P_1) claims, standing as ground, to find before itself P_1, P_2 is therefore the positing of the immediacy of nothing: it is the positing of what is known for itself without thus positing what is known for itself, and it is therefore the simple positing of the formal meaning of immediacy; accordingly, the question remains as to why this formal meaning is predicated of the positing of being.

The answer to this question may only consist of noting that the immediacy of immediately present being is included in this being – this inclusion thus coinciding with that very co-originarity of P_1 and P_2 that is supposed to be disregarded. Or, equivalently: once P_1 and P_2 have been conceived of as being unrelated to one another, the ground of their *coming* into a relation can only be their originary relation. More precisely, however, it is once again not a question of grounding the lack of relation between the two acts of positing, but to observe that the lack of their relation is *superseded* by their co-originary positing – in the same way in which, above, it was not a question of grounding P_1 *qua* logically prior to P_2, but of seeing that the co-originarity of P_1 and P_2 negates and supersedes P_1 *qua* logically prior in that way.

To conclude: P_2 is not the ground of P_1 insofar as $I = P_1 + P_2$, but insofar as $I = P_2$, i.e. insofar as P_2 *includes* P_1, and it is the whole of which P_1 – *qua* positional domain that does not include the positing of its own immediacy – is a moment. This means that the ground of a moment of the originary whole consists in the positing of the relation of that moment with all the other moments of the whole. Moreover, if P_1 is not regarded as a moment that is simply distinct from P_2, in the indicated sense, but as to its including the positing of its own immediacy – i.e. as to its including P_2 – then, concretely conceiving this inclusion, one obtains

$$P_1 = P_2 = I$$

That is to say, if P_1 includes P_2 (in the sense that P_2 stands as one of the determinations posited by P_1), P_2 in turn, *and in its specific way*, includes P_1 (in the sense that the positing of the immediacy of the positing of being is the form of the positing of being, whereby P_1 is the content of P_2), and it includes it in its including, in its specific way, P_2 itself. If P_1 and P_2 are therefore concretely considered, one obtains $P_1 = P_2$, and the difference in the subscripts simply points to the twofold aspect *of a concrete sameness*: a twofold aspect that consists in the different meaning of the inclusion of P_1 in P_2 and of P_2 in P_1. In this sense, the ground is $P_1 = P_2$, or the concrete unity of the distinct terms.

23. Corollary: Self-grounding

The development of these remarks makes it possible to do away with the objection that is at times raised to the concept of immediate knowledge.

One states: the immediate is the ground *of itself*, and, therefore, it is at the same time the ground and something grounded.

This objection will not be discussed here in general, but only to the extent that it negates the concept of immediacy that has been advanced.

We respond by stating that the *sameness* of the ground is not a *result*, but it is itself the ground or the immediate. The ground is also something grounded – and that self-grounding thus becomes the identity of ground and non-ground – only if what the ground finds at the closing point of the circle of self-grounding (what it finds being *its own self*) is conceived of as pre-existing the moment in which the ground finds *itself*. (This pre-existence precisely consists in P_1 *qua* logically prior to P_2.)

Self-grounding consists in this: that the being, which is known in P_1, is posited as being *known for itself*. We have seen how the being that is known in P_1 is known for itself, or stands as that for which it is itself known, precisely and absolutely in the very act with which it is posited as being known for itself – i.e. in the very act with which P_2 is realized. If, indeed, P_1 is regarded as being logically prior to P_2, the positing of being leaves beside itself the negation of being, *qua* not superseded; what is therefore posited in P_1 is not able to stand, itself, as that for which it is itself known. In other words: if what is posited in P_1 is not known or posited as the very being for which it is posited, it is not even possible to exclude the negation of what is posited in P_1. In this case, what is posited in P_1 'is' (i.e. it *only* 'is': it is not 'posited as') that very being for which it is known: and it is clear that if the content of P_1 only 'is' that very being for which it is known, that content is not (i.e. it is not able to stand as) something that is known for itself. The content of P_1 therefore 'is' what is known for itself only insofar as 'it is posited as' what is known for itself – and, insofar as it is thus posited, it is not something grounded, but it is the ground itself, i.e. precisely what is known for itself. Therefore, self-grounding does not mean: 'Ground and, at the same time, grounded', but it indicates the sameness of the content of P_1 and of that for which P_1 is posited.

What has been said may be confirmed through an analysis of the concept of self-grounding. Self-grounding means that a term *X* is that for which and by virtue of which *X* is affirmed. If one of the two *X*s were the *ground*, and the other one the *grounded*, the two *X* would not be *the same*, and there would therefore be no *self*-grounding. The objection formulated at the beginning of this section is then exactly to be turned on its head: *precisely because* the immediate is *its own* ground, it cannot at the same time be the ground and what is grounded.

24. Concerning a critique of the concept of immediacy

The originary structure constitutes the horizon within which the different movements of contemporary philosophy operate, according to different degrees of self-awareness. 'Phenomenology' constitutes one of the moments of greatest awareness of the value of the originary. The 'principle of all principles' of phenomenology reads as follows: 'No conceivable theory can make us err with respect to the principle of all principles: that *every originally presentive intuition is a legitimate source of cognition*, that *everything originally* (so to speak, in its corporeal actuality) *offered to us in "intuition" is to be accepted simply as what it is presented as being*, but also *only within the limits in which it is presented there*.'[3]

In the very domain of contemporary philosophy, however, it is also possible to discern standpoints that are in opposition to the concept of originarity. One of the most significant examples of this negative stance is constituted by the critique that Dewey advances to the concept of immediacy. In general, it should be noted that the immediacy criticized by Dewey is not the immediacy in support of which we are arguing here; accordingly, Dewey's critique, thus delimited, is in fact perfectly valid. The inadequacy of that critique lies in claiming that this confuted notion of immediacy exhausts or includes every meaning of immediacy.

The observation that underlies Dewey's critique is the following: 'The immediate *use* of objects known in consequence of previous mediation is readily confused with immediate knowledge.'[4] For instance: every time I use a typewriter, I do not set out on an enquiry aimed at establishing the conditions of the use of this object (to which I refer as 'a typewriter'): I *immediately* make use of this object *as* of a typewriter. It then happens that this *immediate use*, whose cognitive counterpart is the 'familiarity' that one has with the object, is mistaken for an *immediate knowledge* of this object as a typewriter. Except that it is clear that, in order to establish that this object is a typewriter, a series of approaches or 'mediations' has been necessary, on the side of the user, that have 'resulted' in the consideration of that object as a typewriter. That object, considered in that way, is certainly apprehended in a direct or immediate way, but this immediacy is 'a product, mediated through certain organic mechanisms of retention and habit, and it presupposes prior experiences and mediated conclusions drawn from them'.[5] Regardless of the determining value that the previous mediations might have had in view of a future use of that object, the latter cannot by itself guarantee to be able to also meet in future situations all the demands that it satisfied in one or many previous situations. 'One of the commonest sources of error is the premature assumption that a new situation so closely resembles former ones that conclusions reached in these earlier cases can be directly carried over.'[6] The history of physics and the history of mathematics confirm this.

This critical remark is very accurate. However, it only highlights that the *content* of immediacy is a *process, becoming or development*: and, in this sense, a 'mediation'. This kind of mediation is not the *counterpart* of the immediacy that we have been discussing, but its content. Only someone who were to insist that immediate reality consists of an absolute persistence or immutability may refuse to accept Dewey's standpoint; in that case, apprehending an object may certainly not consist of apprehending the process through which that object constitutes itself in its meaningfulness. The correct meaning of immediacy therefore only demands that the process of constitution of meanings should not itself be known in a processual way – this processual character only pertaining to the discursive exposition of the structure of the immediate.

It should, however, be noted that if the process of constitution of the meaning of a certain object is not known, the meaningfulness of that object is not thereby reduced to nothing, but the object loses the quantity of meaning that pertains to it insofar as it is regarded as the result of a process.

(It may further be noted that the critique that Dewey advances to the stance of logical atomism, insofar as the latter affirms an immediate form of knowledge, is perfectly valid to the extent that one regards atomic meanings as no longer being susceptible of analysis, in such a way that their 'immediacy' would consist of their simplicity. We shall, however, have to return to this last point with particular attention.)

25. The determination of the positing of being

The negation of being is (immediately) superseded because being is the very ground of the affirmation that posits it. This means that the negation of being is superseded *to the extent that* it negates the being that is the ground of the very affirmation that posits it – that is to say, to the extent that it negates that being that is known for itself. Or, equivalently, being is, to the extent that it is such a ground of the affirmation that posits it: i.e. to the extent that it is known for itself. (It will become clear further on in which respect it is possible to speak of a *quantification* – or 'measure' – of being when dealing with present being). The positing of being is therefore not something indeterminate, but determinate – i.e. precisely determined by the quantity of being that is known for itself.

The authentic meaning of a most seminal principle is in this way established. For, indeed, the meaning of the proposition: 'Being is' is determined by the method of its verification. In this case, the verification consists in positing the immediacy of the affirmation expressed by the formulated proposition. Stating that the meaning of that affirmation is constituted through the verification or foundation of the latter precisely means that being is, in the sense that the being that is (or exists) is that being – all being and only that being – that is known for itself. Or, equivalently: being that *is* is the whole and only being that *there is*. This is not to be taken in the sense that being that is not known is not, but in the sense that being, whose being can be immediately affirmed, is precisely that being that is known for itself (in this respect, cf. §26). This may also be stated: the meaningfulness at stake here is not the meaningfulness of the connection between the subject and the predicate of the proposition under consideration, but it is the meaningfulness of the subject of the latter (i.e. being), and, in this sense, of the connection between the subject and the predicate.

Furthermore, in this case, the assertion that is verified includes the verification itself (i.e. the immediate includes the immediacy of the immediate), in such a way that the verification of the assertion constitutes the very meaningfulness of that verifying. (That meaningfulness does not rule out the possibility of a further determination of the meaning of verification or of the meaning of ground.)

26. Prospective note

The extent to which what has been put forth in the previous section – 'being that *is* is the whole and only being that *there is*' – is to be amended, or, rather, accommodated within a broader speculative dimension, will be clarified in Chapter 13. If immediacy, regarded as the immediate presence of being – phenomenological immediacy – is only one element of that structuring of the meanings of immediacy that constitutes the concrete value of immediacy, it is, however, already possible to note that that whose being can be immediately affirmed does not simply consists – as instead envisaged above – in the totality of the phenomenological immediate, but it also consists in all that positive being that can be immediately affirmed in accordance with all the other meanings of immediacy that are distinct from the one of phenomenological immediacy. This remark must at this point appear obscure to the extent that: on the one hand, those other meanings of immediacy have not been determined (even though we have already pointed to that logical immediacy constituted by non-contradictoriness itself); and, on the other hand, it has not been shown in what way the totality of the phenomenological immediate may let itself be surpassed by a positive element – a being – that is nevertheless immediately affirmed. While this is the case, it is also true that, were we to make explicit what at present remains unexpressed, the proposition: 'being that *is* is the whole and only being that *there is*' ('Being whose being can be immediately affirmed is being that is known for itself – i.e. the phenomenological immediate') would have to appear as an *abstract concept of the abstract*: i.e. the abstract concept of that abstract constituted by phenomenological immediacy relative to that concrete that consists in the structuring of the different meanings of immediacy. It is indeed only insofar as that abstract is abstractly separated from the context that pertains to it as part of that structuring that it is possible to affirm that the totality of the immediate coincides with the totality of the phenomenological immediate, or that what is not part of the latter lies outside the totality of the immediate – and it is therefore something that from the standpoint of immediacy is only a possibility, a project and therefore something that, if categorically affirmed, is constituted as something *grounded*, mediated by that phenomenological immediacy. The proposition: 'what *is* is all and only that which *there is*' does not thus stand as an abstract concept of the abstract, and it is only posited as the concrete concept of the abstract insofar as it is regarded in the following way: 'On the basis of – *relative, limited to* – phenomenological immediacy, it can and must be stated that the being that *is* is the whole and only being that *there is*: i.e. precisely all and only that being that is phenomenologically immediate.'

At the same time, – as already implicitly remarked in the note in §3 of Chapter 1 – the exposition of the originary allows a development of that abstract concept of the abstract (i.e. of that *element* of the structuring of the meanings of immediacy) throughout the present enquiry, in its fundamental corollaries and implications, despite the fact that this development is one of the most significant forms of the negation of the ground (cf. Chapter 1, §4): namely, it is something that the ground (the structure of the originary, or the structure of the immediate) necessarily implies *as superseded*, and, therefore, *as posited* (developed, presented, made explicit) precisely in order to be superseded.

Given the significant complexity of this logical situation, the reader will agree that each time the exposition will come across a development or an articulation of that abstract concept of the abstract – or at least in those instances that present a particular interest – we shall remark, thus repeating each time the same remark (even though in relation to different contexts), that the exposition is presenting an abstract concept of the abstract. This remark consists in the very check operated by the concrete on that abstract concept – a check that precisely consists in the concrete concept of that abstract concept of the abstract. The abstract concept of the abstract considered above will be indicated by the expression: 'concept Γ_a.'

It is clear that *to the extent that it is not known* in which way a positive element, which is not part of the totality of the phenomenological immediate, might nevertheless be the content of an immediate affirmation, the fact that the proposition: 'being that *is* is the whole and only being that *there is*' should be an abstract concept of the abstract is only a project.

In this respect, it can simply be stated that the concept Γ_a consists in that structuring of the originary, or that mode of being of the originary structure, by virtue of which phenomenological immediacy is held firm as the totality of immediacy: i.e. as the horizon of *everything* whose being can be immediately affirmed.

It should also be clear, from what has been said, that affirming that the concept Γ_a posits phenomenological immediacy as the totality of immediacy *does not mean* that Γ_a negates the fact that beyond this phenomenological immediacy there are other forms of immediacy (this negation giving rise to an abstract concept that is distinct from Γ_a); on the contrary, it means that, from the standpoint of Γ_a, these additional forms of immediacy are not able to affirm the being of a content that is not part of the totality of the phenomenological immediate.

27. The factual superseding of the negation of being

It is affirmed that being is insofar as the negation of being negates that which is the very ground of the affirmation of being. Or, equivalently: that negation is superseded insofar as the positing of being is posited as an immediacy. Furthermore, since the immediacy of the immediate is included in the immediate itself, the superseding of the negation of immediate being is, or includes, the very superseding of the negation of the immediacy of being.

Up to this point, being is not therefore affirmed because the negation of being is superseded; rather, this negation is superseded because it is known for itself that being is. This means that, given what has been said so far, the negation of being is not *inherently* contradictory, but it is in contradiction *with* the immediacy of being. The two sides of the contradiction are not here part of a single term, but they precisely consist in the affirmation and in the negation of being. The negation of being is therefore *de facto* superseded – or, equivalently, it is superseded *by a fact*: precisely by that 'fact' that consists in the immediate being-there of being itself. It should, however, be noted that this superseding will appear as a moment of the concrete superseding of the negation of being (Chapter 12).

28. Note on the modes of the negation of being

The negation of the immediate realizes itself in different ways or modes: as an *explicit* negation of a part or the totality of the immediate – this negation being *posited* – or as an *implicit* negation. The limiting case of an implicit negation is that in which nothing is posited: nullity of the positional domain. Non-limit cases consist of positional horizons in which only a part of the immediate determinations is posited, in such a way that the residual part is not posited. Among those horizons, some are not even a positing of the immediacy of their content (e.g. common, religious, scientific forms of consciousness); others are a positing of the immediacy of their content, but, precisely, what is posited as the immediate is not all whose immediacy must be posited. All these horizons, however, share the fact of *being in contradiction with* the immediate: precisely insofar as they do not posit everything that is to be posited – whereby the negation of being only *is*: i.e. it is not *posited*.

(Care should be taken not to conflate these horizons, which are abstract concepts of the abstract, with the corresponding concrete concepts of the abstract; while the latter let themselves be superseded by the concrete, i.e. by the positional whole, those former horizons – while being a part of the originary positional whole – aim instead to posit themselves as the positional whole.)

29. More on the meaning of the negation of being

As anticipated in §27, the factual superseding of the negation of being is a moment of the concrete superseding of that negation. This concreteness will be achieved by exhibiting the inherent contradictoriness of that negation. It should be reiterated here (cf. §4) that since the affirmation of being has not been regarded up to now as to its value of positing of the non-contradictoriness of being, but as the affirmation of a positive content, the corresponding negation does not negate that non-contradictoriness, but the being of that positive content: that is, it negates the being of what is said to be immediately known. The verification of the inherent contradictoriness of this negation is therefore not a verification of the self-contradictoriness constituted by the negation of that non-contradictoriness.

30. The analytic character of the originary judgement

The way in which the originary judgement has been formulated in Chapter 1, §5 makes it explicit that the immediacy of the immediate is included in the immediate itself in the very act with which being is posited as the immediate. 'The totality of immediately present being is the immediate' ('Thinking is the immediate') means that the totality of being that is known for itself immediately includes its being known for itself; accordingly, the totality of being that is known for itself is what is known for itself. This formulation is determined by the *necessity* of the inclusion of the immediacy of the immediate in the immediate itself; in the very act in which being is posited as the immediate, that being (= that horizon of determinations) that is thus posited, *insofar as* it realizes itself as the originary structure, cannot fail to include its own being posited in that way. Since this inclusion constitutes the ground of the affirmation of the very immediacy of being, the originary judgement is not to be formulated by stating that being is the immediate, but that the immediate is the immediate. Or, equivalently: since being that is not *originarily* posited as the immediate is *not* the immediate, the originary judgement precisely states that being, whose immediacy is predicated, is precisely that being that is immediate (and not that being that is considered to be presupposed to the predication of its immediacy or to be abstractly separated from it). The predicate of the subject is here the subject itself; or, equivalently: the originary judgement, in this formulation, is an analytic proposition.

This is a significant conclusion, particularly if one relates it to what has been affirmed in §27. Indeed, while in that section we remarked that the negation of immediately present being does not appear as something self-contradictory – in such a way that the affirmation of the immediate may not give rise to an analytic proposition – we are now affirming that the originary judgement, *qua* affirmation of the immediate, precisely gives rise to an analytic proposition. The aporetic situation that arises in this way will be resolved in the course of this enquiry: on the one hand, by showing how *every* judgement is analytic in the sense in which the originary judgement appears here as an analytic proposition (cf. Chapter 6, §10, b); on the other hand, by showing that, despite this fact, there remains a distinction between those propositions whose negation is inherently contradictory and those propositions whose negation is not (cf. Chapter 6, §11).

It should furthermore be observed that since the mode of formulation of the originary judgement indicated above only expresses an aspect of the notion of originarity (cf. Chapter 1, §6), the analytic character of the originary judgement that has been discussed is precisely the analytic character of that aspect.

31. Notes

It is by now widely affirmed, and not disputed here, that the positing of the immediacy of thinking finds its first explicit assertion in Descartes' philosophy. It should, however, be noted – and this remark, too, is now widely supported – that for Descartes the term 'thinking' (as soon as thinking is posited as the immediate) stands as the simply 'subjective' or 'ideal' side of thinking. At the level of immediacy, certainty is thereby kept distinct from truth – or, equivalently, being is *presupposed* as something additional, to which it is then necessary to gain access setting out precisely from the immediacy of thinking. The superseding of this epistemological presupposition confers upon thinking its proper character: namely, that of being the unity of the subjective and the objective, the ideal and the real – or, in less compromised terms, the totality of immediately present being.

It is thus also clarified that the immediate is a *mediation*, in the sense that present being consists of a superseding of the abstract immediacy of pure being in itself.[7] This superseding is that very being-for-other (*fieri aliud*, ecstaticity, intentionality) in which the presence *of* being consists. The negation of this mediation is therefore not the immediacy of the totality of the immediate, but the abstract immediacy of a being that is not thought, or of a presence that is not the presence *of* being. That is to say, that mediation is that typical relation constituted by presence *qua* being-for-other, in which the *being* of this being-for-other is consummated in its letting that other – i.e. being, reality – appear.[8]

3

The immediacy of the non-contradictoriness of being

1. The positing of being and the positing of the non-contradictoriness of being

The negation of being is superseded insofar as it *contradicts* the immediacy of being. It follows from this that the positing of the non-contradictoriness of being belongs in an essential way to the positing of being. That is to say, the groundedness of that positing requires the positing of the non-contradictoriness of being.

This remark gives rise to an aporetic development that will be considered further ahead (cf. §§22 ff.). Here, suffice it to note that, in the same way in which the positing of that non-contradictoriness belongs in an essential way to the groundedness of the positing of being, so this positing belongs in an essential way to the groundedness of the positing of the non-contradictoriness of being. This means that these two acts of positing, insofar as they are each distinct from the other, stand as *abstract moments* of a single structure (i.e. the structure of the immediate).

2. The principle of non-contradiction

Of the principle of non-contradiction and of the affirmation of being (Chapter 2) it is to be asserted that 'proprium est horum principiorum, quod non solum necesse est ea per se *esse* vera, sed etiam necesse est *videri* quod sint per se vera (Aquinas, *Expositio libri Posteriorum Analyticorum*, nineteenth, our emphasis).[1] This – as we have interpreted it – has already been remarked for what concerns the affirmation of being, which is able to exclude the negation of being if it *is* not simply an immediacy, but if it *is posited* as the immediate positing of being: that is to say, if in addition to 'per se *esse* vera', '*videtur* quod est per se vera'. The 'necessity' (*necesse*) for that affirmation to be *posited* as the immediate positing of being is precisely given by the fact that the *steresis* of the positing of that immediacy allows the negation of being to persists as something that is not superseded. What has been stated concerning the affirmation of being is then to be repeated for what concerns the non-contradictoriness of being. The principle of non-contradiction – which is precisely the expression of that non-contradictoriness – may be formulated as: 'Being is not non-being.'

Once again, here, as long as it is only affirmed that being is not non-being, this affirmation is therefore not able to exclude the corresponding negation. (And that negation is not able to rule out that affirmation.) This is the point at which the need for the reason for holding firm the non-contradictoriness of being, as opposed to its contradictoriness, is simply evaded.

There arises in this way a logical structure that is analogous to the one established in §6 of Chapter 2. The reader may further develop this point independently.

3. The immediacy of the principle of non-contradiction

The affirmation of the contradictoriness of being is superseded insofar as the positing of the non-contradictoriness of being is posited as an *immediacy*. The fact that being is not non-being is known for itself. The negation of this non-contradictoriness negates that which is the ground of the affirmation that posits it. Being is not non-being because the fact that being is not non-being is known for itself.

It should, however, be noted – thus coming to determinately address that structuring of the meanings of immediacy mentioned in the previous chapters – that the sense in which the affirmation of being is an immediate positing is not the sense in which the principle of non-contradiction is, as such, an immediate positing. For, indeed, this immediacy is in the first case the *immediate presence* of the content – i.e. a phenomenological immediacy – while in the second case it is the *immediacy of the connection* between two determinations: a logical immediacy. This latter immediacy is, however, itself immediately present, and, that is, it belongs – even if in a particular way – to the horizon of immediacy understood in the first sense.

In other words: the reality that is immediately present constitutes itself as an extremely complex organism of connections (or predications). A set of these connections are immediate precisely and *only insofar as* they are immediately present: that is to say, only insofar as the predicate pertains as a matter of fact to the subject. The expression of this kind of connections thus gives rise to synthetic *a posteriori* propositions. A second set of those connections are immediate *both* insofar as they are immediately present *and* insofar as one of the two connected determinations (the predicate) immediately pertains to the other one (the subject). This immediate pertaining is determined by the *identity* of the subject and the predicate. By expressing this identity in a universal way, one obtains the proposition: 'Being is being' – or, *which is the same*: 'Being is not non-being.' (Let us set aside for the moment the determination of the meaning of the 'sameness' of these two propositions.) The expression of this second set of connections thus gives rise to analytic propositions.

(It is clear that, while on the one hand this analytic character concerns *a set* of connections, on the other hand *every* connection, i.e. *every* relation according to which the immediate content is realized, is subject to that analytic character – in that every synthetic connection stands as the subject of an identical affirmation.)

If, therefore, there exists a phenomenological value of the originary judgement, according to which the latter is formulated by stating that thinking is the immediate (phenomenological immediacy), there also exists a logical value of that judgement, according to which the latter is formulated by stating that non-contradictoriness itself is the immediate (logical immediacy).

4. Note

While we shall have to return to this issue with particular attention, it should be noted here that a formulation of the concept of *a posteriori* synthesis requires a distinction between the individuation and the persistence (in an Aristotelian way one would say: the *essence*) that is individuated. (Essence is a form of persistence precisely in relation to the becoming to which it is subject insofar as it individuates itself; accordingly, in this respect it is not a persistence that individuates itself, but an essence, or a meaning, that, in individuating itself, *persists*: it precisely persists in relation to the process – the becoming, development – of the individuation.) If, indeed, one asserts: 'This book is on the desk', one is dealing with an analytic proposition, in that this book's being on the desk is formally included in the concept of *this* book, *hic et nunc*. That proposition has instead a synthetic value if the term 'This book' refers to an object (essence, meaning) that *persists* despite a specific series and a specific kind of past variations of the immediate content, and possibly in relation to a specific series and a specific kind of future variations. The determination or characterization of the variations of the immediate context, in relation to which that persistence is realized as such, is not immediately included in the concept of this persisting object. Since every variation of the context determines a different individuation of that form of persistence, the relation between a persistence ('this book') and its individuation – and, therefore, between a persistence and a particular aspect of its individuation ('being on the desk') – is therefore a synthetic *a posteriori* relation.

In general, however, the terms 'analytic' and 'synthetic *a posteriori* propositions', which appeared in the previous section, will need to be subject to closer scrutiny.

5. The negation of the non-contradictoriness of the immediate and the negation of the immediate

Insofar as the negation of the non-contradictoriness of being is in contradiction *with* the immediacy of that non-contradictoriness, that negation is inherently contradictory; conversely, insofar as that negation is inherently contradictory, it is in contradiction with the immediacy of that non-contradictoriness.

Up to this point, instead, the negation of the phenomenological immediate has appeared as something that is in contradiction *with* the immediacy of manifest being. As already mentioned, it will be verified that the negation of the phenomenological immediate is also an inherent contradiction; the fact, however, that the negation of phenomenological immediacy should also have a value by virtue of which that negation is not an inherent contradiction, but it is – simply – in contradiction *with* what is immediately manifest, is something that is required by the very structure of the originary. If the impossibility of holding firm the negation of the phenomenological immediate simply and absolutely consisted in the inherent contradiction of that negation, the *immediacy* of manifest being would indeed be something *mediated* by the superseding of that inherent contradictoriness. In other words, the positing of the immediacy of being is such only insofar as it is also a superseding of the negation of immediately present being; but if this negation were *only* superseded insofar as it is inherently contradictory, that immediacy would be something mediated by the principle of non-contradiction (to the extent that the positing of non-contradictoriness is distinct from the positing of manifest being).

It is therefore necessary for the negation of the immediate to *also* be superseded insofar as it is *simply* in contradiction *with* immediacy itself; that is to say, there must necessarily exist an aspect of that negation by virtue of which that negation is not inherently contradictory. (If, moreover, one wanted to posit the immediacy of non-contradictoriness as the only kind of immediacy, the question concerning the ground of the *disclosure* of that non-contradictoriness would remain unanswered.)

It is clear that the negation of the immediate is superseded in that it is not possible to affirm and at the same time negate the immediate; this impossibility, however (that is to say, the principle of non-contradiction), does not constitute – as will be made clear further on – the ground in relation to which the affirmation of the immediate is something grounded, but it constitutes the *form* of this affirmation.

6. Determination of the meaning of the negation of non-contradictoriness

In order to realize itself as a negation (and not as a non-negation), the negation of the non-contradictoriness of being must implicitly allow that non-contradictoriness to exist as non-superseded – precisely in relation to that positive element constituted by the negation itself. Accordingly, as soon as that negation realizes itself, that non-contradictoriness is negated *in actu signato* and affirmed *in actu exercito*. There is therefore only an *intention* to negate that non-contradictoriness; for as soon as non-contradictoriness is negated, non-contradictoriness itself – precisely insofar as it is truly negated – is at the same time affirmed.

It is clear that the negation of non-contradictoriness is self-contradictory for a twofold reason: (1) because the positional domain of that negation is a self-contradiction (the content of that negation being precisely expressed by the proposition: 'Being is non-being'); (2) because that negation, in realizing itself, implicitly affirms what it explicitly negates. (While the first side of that self-contradictoriness is *for itself* – is posited – as part of the positional domain of that negation, the second side of that self-contradictoriness is *for itself* as part of the originary positional domain that supersedes that negation; or, equivalently, that negation only *is* this second side of that self-contradictoriness.)

In order to successfully realize that negation as a negation – that is, in order to avoid that that negation should at the same time be an affirmation, in such a way that non-contradictoriness itself should come to be reduced to the first of the two sides mentioned above – one can only fall back on the affirmation that the non-contradictory (i.e. that which is, rather than being and at the same time not being) precisely consists in the negation that being is being – 'being' standing as 'all that is not this negation'. The second side of self-contradictoriness mentioned above is certainly superseded in this way, but one is then no longer even dealing with the negation of non-contradictoriness, but rather with an absolute or exhaustive determination of the non-contradictory: since, precisely, the non-contradictory is identified with the negation of the fact that being, which differs from the being of this very negation, is being – an identification that takes place on the basis of an arbitrary act, which of the totality of the non-contradictory positive only holds firm the non-contradictoriness of that positive constituted by the restricted negation of non-contradictoriness. It is, however, clear that in this case, too, a twofold kind of self-contradictoriness persists, for that arbitrariness consists in regarding that positive element – which realizes itself *both* in that restricted negation of non-contradictoriness *and* in everything that is distinct from that negation – concurrently as non-contradictory and as self-contradictory.

7. The principle of identity and the principle of non-contradiction

Insofar as the principle of identity and the principle of non-contradiction are kept distinct from one another, they stand as abstract moments of the concreteness of *the* principle. Concerning this concreteness, it is indifferent whether that principle is referred to as the principle of identity (or of determination) or as the principle of non-contradiction. For, indeed, being is not non-being because being is being, and, vice-versa, being is being because being is not non-being. (When the Scholastics state that the principle of identity is less suitable *ad demonstrandum*, they consider the principle of identity as an abstract moment, i.e. as a moment that is held firm as distinct from the principle of non-contradiction.)

In the same way, the logical priority of either of the two principles relative to the other one is to be excluded: the two sides of the principle are immediately connected, and, therefore, neither of them is something mediated by the other (cf. Chapter 9, §22).

More generally, it may be stated that the abstract concept of the principles of identity, non-contradiction and excluded middle allows a dialecticization of these principles akin to the one advanced by Hegel in his *Logic* – as long as it is clear that the critique that Hegel moves to these principles only refers to their abstract concept.

When it is affirmed that it is known for itself that being is not non-being, one is therefore referring to the principle of non-contradiction (or to the principle of identity) regarded as the concrete relation of these two abstract moments.

8. The modes of formulation of the principles of identity and non-contradiction

a. The proposition: 'Being is being' is equivalent – in a sense that is to be thoroughly determined – to the proposition: 'Being is'. This 'is' is indeed – or, better, belongs to – the semantic structure of that 'being' that appears as predicate in the other proposition (cf. Chapter 13, §1).

b. The distinction that may be made between the 'impossibility for the same to be and not to be' (*impossibile est idem simul esse et non esse*) and the 'impossibility for the same to be and not be *something*' is altogether ancillary, since – in this second case, too – it is stated that it is impossible for that 'something' *simul esse et non esse* (the condition expressed by that '*simul*' including here the positing of that something as predicate *of the same term*). The difference between the formulation of the principle of non-contradiction that Aristotle first states in the fourth book of his *Metaphysics* (τὸ γὰρ αὐτὸ ἅμα ὑπάρχειν ἀδύνατον τῷ αὐτῷ καὶ κατὰ τὸ αὐτό) and the Scholastic formulation (which translates the ἀδύνατον ταὐτὸ εἶναι καὶ μὴ εἶναι) is therefore merely apparent. The τὸ αὐτό of the Aristotelian formulation may indeed take on not only the value of a particular determination (of which it is stated that it is impossible that it should pertain and not pertain to the same term) but also that of εἶναι itself – this second value thus determining the explicit coincidence with the Scholastic formulation. The latter, in turn, does not only have the value by virtue of which the '*esse*' and the '*non esse*' constitute the predicate of the '*idem*', but it also rules out the possibility that *a determinacy* should pertain and not pertain to another one, by regarding that '*esse*' as a formal predicate that is able to take on the value of every possible determinacy.

c. The term 'impossibility', which appears in these formulations, is to be regarded as the very *positing of the immediacy* of non-contradictoriness itself; accordingly, stating: 'It is impossible for being not to be' is equivalent to stating: 'It is known for itself that being is.'

9. Resolution of an aporia concerning the formulation of the principle of identity: The concrete meaning of identity

a. In relation to the proposition: 'Being is being', it may be objected that the recognition of the identity of subject and predicate requires a comparison – and, therefore, a *distinction* – between being, *qua* subject, and being, *qua* predicate. The condition of possibility of the principle of identity would in this way consist in the negation of the principle of non-contradiction, since, in order to affirm that being is being, being must in some way be different from being.

b. In this case, too, the objection arises due to the abstract understanding, which presupposes the two terms to their relation – a relation that, in this case, is the very identity of what is therefore not two, but one. Accordingly, if the being of the subject and the being of the predicate are presupposed to the positing of their identity, to the extent that they are thus presupposed they certainly cannot be posited as being *the same* – precisely because this positing is the positing of their identity, i.e. it is that relative to which they are presupposed. If they are therefore posited as *the same*, there arises a logical structure due to which in a first moment they are found as two, or as an otherness, and, in a second moment, this duality or otherness is posited as an identity. If one is not able to rise above the abstract understanding, one will therefore conclude that the condition of identity is the negation of non-contradictoriness: that is to say, that being can stand as the same only insofar as it is other than itself.

Overcoming the perspective of the abstract understanding, we shall therefore state that the positing of identity does not arise in a second moment relative to the positing of being, and certainly not relative to the positing of being as subject and as predicate. (For what concerns the first of these two cases, it should be noted that a positing of being that is not already a positing of the identity of being would not even exclude that being differs from itself: that is to say, the affirmation of that difference is left beside that positing *qua* non-superseded. With the arising of the positing of the self-identity of a being presupposed in this way, it would follow that being that is being – i.e. being that rules out the possibility of being self-different – would coincide with a being that does not rule out the possibility of being self-different. We have thus indicated a further aspect of the aporias that arise from the abstract presupposition of being to the positing of its identity.)

The positing of identity is therefore *originary*. Accordingly, originarily stating that being is being does not entail establishing a comparison, and therefore an identification, between being *qua* subject and being *qua* predicate, both of which would be presupposed to that identification – for, in fact, given this presupposition, being (subject) is not being (predicate). Or, equivalently: being that is being (i.e. being that stands as subject of the proposition: 'Being is being') is being-*that*-is-being: namely, it is being *that* is posited as an identity, and not being that, having been posited (presupposed), is *then* posited as an identity (whereby this identity would constitute itself as the identification of an otherness). The identity of being with itself is therefore absolute. This point is further developed in §10.

c. From what has been said, it thus follows that, of the principle of identity/non-contradiction it is not possible to state that '*fundatur super rationem entis et non entis*', but that the '*ratio*' realizes itself in the very moment of the apophansis, i.e. only to the extent that it is in relation with the latter. The noetic moment, in which the *operatio prima intellectus* is realized, cannot therefore be presupposed to the dianoetic moment, which therefore cannot be *grounded* in the former. At the same time, however, negating this presupposition does not mean negating the distinction between noesis and dianoesis, between the semantic and the apophantic, between *being* and the *being of being*; for that noesis is distinct from that dianoesis in the same way in which the abstract is distinct from the concrete, or the moment from the whole. That is to say, that distinction is the very internal articulation of identity. (For an elucidation of this distinction, cf. §11.)

10. The concrete meaning of identity

a. Both the subject and the predicate of the proposition: 'Being is being' are not simple noetic moments, of which the judgement (expressed by that proposition) is a synthesis; rather, they are that very judgement, or the identity itself, in its being posited.

The fact that the subject and the predicate of the judgement themselves have an apophantic value is to be affirmed with respect to every judgement. This development of the matter will be considered further on (Chapter 6, §11).

The theorem that we are trying to elucidate here therefore states that the concrete identity of being with itself is not the identity of being, regarded as a noetic moment, with being, once again regarded as a noetic moment; that concrete identity is not such an identity both if the noesis (which comes to constitute the identity conceived of in this way) is conceived abstractly, and if one claims to conceive it concretely; the concrete identity is instead the identity of being, which is itself already the identity of itself with itself, with being that, once again, is itself already this identity. (It should be noted that here the noesis is assumed as such *relative to* the dianoesis – this being regarded as the positing of the identity of being with itself – without thus ruling out the possibility that the concrete content of that noesis should be an apophantic structure. This structure is a noesis *relative to* that identity, and not absolutely so.)

It has already been noted in the previous section that if the subject and the predicate of an identity are presupposed to the identity itself (which is, precisely, their identity), they come to be constituted as a form of otherness, due to which it will be necessary to affirm that being (subject) is *not* being (predicate).[2]

Insofar as being (subject) and being (predicate) are presupposed to their identity, they are manifestly presupposed as noetic moments – since their dianoesis is precisely that with respect to which they are presupposed.

The logical situation that must then be remarked upon is the following: it is only possible to affirm that 'being is being' insofar as being, which stands as the subject of this proposition, is regarded (= is posited) precisely *as being that is being*, as well as insofar as being, which stands as predicate, is precisely regarded as predicate – i.e. once again, as being of being. This means that the subject as well as the predicate do not simply have a noetic value, but they are both already, as such, a realization of an apophansis, i.e. of an identity.

In other words: if the subject and the predicate of an identity simply stand as noetic moments (and the identity itself stands as the simple reference of a noesis to a noesis), the semantic domain constituted by each of them does not include, as something posited, the fact that each of them is the other, for the positing of this is the positing of an identity, i.e. of an apophansis. If the subject and the predicate are conceived in that way, it is not even possible to affirm: 'Being is being' (i.e. this affirmation only exists as a mere verbal expression), since that affirmation precisely *posits* the fact that the predicate is the subject, i.e. it *posits* the relation between these two terms. This is not only a relation that cannot be included as posited by a noesis, but one that cannot be included in or even constitute an identity, understood as a mere reference of a noesis to a noesis. There thus arises a contradiction between the intention of positing that affirmation and the impossibility for that affirmation to be posited if the subject and the predicate are given a simply noetic value. It is, however, also contradictory to regard the subject as a noesis and the predicate as a dianoesis (or vice-versa), for, in this way, the connection between the subject and the predicate would be constituted as the self-contradictory affirmation that a noesis is a dianoesis, and there would no longer be any identity of being with itself.

As already remarked, if identity is regarded in this way, the proposition: 'Being is being' therefore becomes a self-contradictory affirmation, since the subject and the predicate are posited as being the same, while each of them, *qua* simple noetic moment, is other than the other one, in such a way that an otherness is posited as a sameness. If the subject and the predicate are presupposed to their identity, they stand as noetic moments; and if they are regarded as noetic moments, they are presupposed to their identity.

b. Concrete identity is therefore the identity of identity with itself. As already noted, negating this entails that the principle of identity is a self-contradictory affirmation. Let us now concretely consider the meaning of this identity of identity.

'Being' (E'), whose 'being' (E'') is predicated, is precisely 'being-that-is-being':

[1] $$E' = E'';$$

and the 'being' (E'') that is predicated is precisely the 'being-of-being':

[2] $$E'' = E'.$$

The formula for this concrete identity is therefore:

[3] $$(E' = E'') = (E'' = E').^3$$

Except that the argument may at this point be developed as follows. In the same way in which the identity of being with itself is, concretely, the identity of identity with itself, it will be necessary to state that it is of that identity-that-is-identity that it is possible to predicate the identity, and this identity is predicated precisely as the identity-of-identity. Accordingly, the formula of identity will be:

[3ª] $$[(E' = E'') = (E'' = E')] = [(E'' = E') = (E' = E'')].$$

For, indeed, in relation to their identity, both $E' = E''$ and $E'' = E'$ stand as noetic moments, in such a way that – once again, as above – one will have to exclude that an identity obtains between a noesis and a noesis. According to the argument developed above, it is clear that equation [3] has an infinite development: that is to say, the principle of identity has an infinite formulation, and it cannot therefore be affirmed, since its affirmation is a contradictory affirmation – every moment of that infinite development being an identity of two different determinations (which are different precisely insofar as each of the two must additionally be regarded as being identical to the other one). Affirming that something is its own self is therefore contradictory: precisely because being is not a self-identity, but an infinite identification of itself to itself, such that the terms that are being identified at each step of the identification differ from each other.

We reply by observing that the equation $(E' = E'') = (E'' = E')$ *is not* an identity of two distinct semantic contents, in which one is not posited in the positional domain of the other one. Indeed, on the one hand, E'', which appears in the first part of the equation, is precisely the E'' that appears in the second part of the equation, and it is posited or known precisely as this 'second' E''; on the other hand, E', which appears in the second part of the equation, is and is known as the very E' that appears in the first part of the equation. This is the concrete meaning of the equation. If, therefore, the semantic domain constituted by $E' = E''$ is kept distinct, in the indicates sense, from the domain constituted by $E'' = E'$, and vice-versa, it follows that neither the E'' that appears in the first domain may be posited as the E'' that appears in the second domain, nor the E' of the first domain may be known as the E' of the second domain. Through this distinction, however – namely, regarding that equation as an identity of determinations distinct in this way – the meaning of $(E' = E'') = (E'' = E')$ is conceived abstractly, since in this way it is not possible to posit the concrete meaning of the equation.

It is then precisely as a result of this abstract conception that, in order to retain that equation, one is forced to develop it into equation [3ª], in the same way in which in order to affirm $E' = E''$ it is necessary to understand this equation as $(E' = E'') = (E'' = E')$.

The infinite development of this equation therefore arises insofar as the abstract understanding *at first* posits that identity as $E' = E''$ – in such a way that the terms of that identity are constituted as being different from one another – and, *in a second moment*, it develops that equation as $(E' = E'') = (E'' = E')$ (precisely with the aim of coming to an identification of those different terms). As a result, the two terms of this equation appear as something that must be developed in the same way in which $E' = E''$ has been previously developed; and so on, *ad infinitum*.

It is clear, however, that insofar as $E' = E''$ is abstractly presupposed to its concrete identity, it does not find in equation [3] its *development* (= grounding), but its *negation* (precisely because the concrete is not a grounding of the abstract concept, but a negation of the latter). It follows that this development must be regarded as being co-originary with what is being developed, which does not therefore at first realize itself as something that is to be grounded.

There thus arises an infinite development only because one *repeats ad infinitum* the abstract presupposition of identity to the identity of identity with itself.

c. An infinite development may also be determined by another kind of intervention of the abstract understanding. Upon considering equation [3], $E' = E''$ – or $E'' = E'$ – is abstractly separated from the concrete; as a result, $E' = E''$ appears as something that must in turn be developed as

$$(E_1' = E_1'') = (E_1'' = E_1')$$

$$[(E_2' = E_2'') = (E_2'' = E_2')] = [(E_2'' = E_2') = (E_2' = E_2'')]$$

This development of $E' = E''$ arises insofar as $E' = E''$ *is and at the same time is not* regarded as an abstract moment of equation [3]: it is not regarded as an abstract moment of that equation precisely insofar as it is separated from it, in such a way that by developing $E' = E''$ into $(E_1' = E_1'') = (E_1'' = E_1')$ one *repeats* the development that gives rise to equation [3] (that is to say: it is insofar as $E' = E''$ is abstractly separated from the concrete that one proceeds to unfold that development that would be seen as having already been realized in equation [3], were $E' = E''$ not thus abstractly separated); and it is regarded as an abstract moment precisely insofar as, in order to establish that infinite development, one aims for $(E_1' = E_1'') = (E_1'' = E_1')$ to stand as an abstract moment of equation [3]. This – let us note – has been clearly seen by Gentile, who, however, rules out the possibility that the concrete identity should be understood in the form of

$(E' = E") = (E" = E')$. It should also be noted that the concrete development of $E' = E"$ is not the abstract development

$$(a = a) = (a = a),$$

which is excluded by Gentile.[4]

d. From what has been said, it is clear that the infinite development is immediately superseded insofar as it is a negation of the *concretely conceived* identity, and not insofar as the very identity that makes the realization of that development possible is held firm in opposition to it: for not only must this identity not be held firm in opposition to that infinite development, but it must in fact be negated – that infinite development being precisely the necessary consequence of an abstract identity. It therefore cannot simply be stated that an infinite development cannot be affirmed because it negates identity, but it must be concretely shown, as we have done, that a concretely conceived identity does not permit the realization of that infinite development.

More generally: if there arises an aporetic argument, due to which one is forced to admit the negation of the immediate, the immediate that must be held firm, and on the basis of which its negation is superseded, is not the immediate that allows the arising of its negation, but it is the concretely or authentically conceived immediate. Returning to the question at hand, it is therefore certainly correct to rule out that infinite development to the extent that it constitutes a negation of identity, but only insofar as this identity is concretely seen as something that does not permit the arising of that infinite development.

e. If the equation $(E' = E") = (E" = E')$ is concretely conceived, there arises no infinite development in the formulation of identity. While that development is not necessary, it is not impossible either. As it is phenomenologically attested, the content of self-identical being is indeed not an absolute immobility, but a process; accordingly, if the term 'being' is regarded as to its determining itself as a 'self-identity', i.e. as $(E' = E") = (E" = E')$ – i.e. if by 'being' one understands this equation – this semantic content, like any other content, coincides with itself only insofar as it is conceived of as

$$\{[(E' = E") = (E" = E')]' = [(E' = E") = (E" = E')]"\} =$$

$$\{[(E' = E") = (E" = E')]" = [(E' = E") = (E" = E')]'\}.$$

In this way, the infinite development that may arise through a gradual increment of the meaning 'being' (as the one indicated) is not something that does not allow the positing of identity – i.e. it is not something due to which identity, as such, realizes itself as a contradiction – but it is precisely an increment of the content of the originarily posited identity.

11. The concrete meaning of the distinction internal to identity

a. The observations developed above make it possible to formulate a corollary that offers a significant clarification of what we have stated in Chapter 1 concerning the concrete concept of the abstract. It has indeed been seen that an abstract comprehension arises not only if being (subject) and being (predicate) are presupposed to their identity (§9) but also if an identity is simply regarded as obtaining between two distinct determinations that have a simply noetic value. That is, if one were to claim to not want to presuppose a noesis to its dianoesis, but then conceived of this dianoesis as an identity between a noesis and a noesis, this identity would not be posited, since neither the subject nor the predicate – conceived of as noetic moments – would be able to be posited as part of their relation (this relation being precisely that dianoesis, which cannot be included as posited by the noesis). Despite the intention not to presuppose the noesis to the dianoesis, that presupposition would nevertheless take place. The simple positing of the distinct determinations that constitute the concrete thus rules out the possibility of positing the concrete and does not allow its positing, in such a way that the positing of that distinction constitutes an abstract comprehension of the distinct. The abstract (= the distinct = the terms of the identity) is indeed concretely conceived if its positing does not negate the concrete. However, if the subject of the identity is understood as a noetic moment, and so is the predicate, the positing of these two abstract moments is a negation of the concrete.

Not even Gentile's *Logic* – which has nevertheless the greatest merits in determining the concrete meaning of identity, and more generally the meaning of the concrete – has been able to free itself from this abstract defect.

How are therefore the abstract moments of the concrete identity to be conceived? For, if it is to be ruled out that the subject and the predicate of that identity should have a simply noetic value, a distinction between noesis and dianoesis cannot be excluded. Accordingly, what needs to be clarified now is precisely the nature of this distinction.

b. If the concrete meaning of equation [3] does not consist in the identity of the two distinct semantic domains, respectively, constituted by $E' = E''$ and $E'' = E'$ (distinct in such a way that each of the two does not appear as part of the other; §10, b), an analysis of that equation nevertheless comes to recognize both $E' = E''$ and $E'' = E'$ as meanings that are *distinct* from the meaning constituted by the whole equation.

Furthermore: the analysis of $E' = E''$, or of $E'' = E'$, *qua* meanings that are distinct from the whole, comes in turn to recognize both E' and E'' as meanings that are *distinct* from the meaning constituted by the equation $E' = E''$, or $E'' = E'$.

c. Let us regard $E' = E''$ and $E'' = E'$ as meanings that are distinct from the concrete identity of which they are abstract moments.

It should first of all be remarked that if $E' = E''$, as well as $E'' = E'$, may be regarded as meanings that are distinct from the meaning constituted by the concrete identity, the meaning $E' = E''$, as distinct from that concrete identity, *is nevertheless not distinct in any way* from the meaning $E'' = E'$, itself regarded as distinct from that concrete identity. Accordingly, the positing of this 'second' meaning is nothing but a *repetition* of the positing of that first meaning.

Let us assume $E' = E''$ as a meaning that is distinct from the concrete identity. Insofar as it is concretely distinct from the latter, rather than being abstractly separated, that meaning precisely coincides with that $E' = E''$ that appears in equation [3]: except for the fact that, while in that equation E' and E'' – which form $E' = E''$ – are *posited as* the E'' and E' that appear in the second part of the equation, this cannot be the case if $E' = E''$ is held firm in its being distinct from equation [3]; the semantic domain constituted by $E' = E''$ only includes the identity of the noesis with itself. (Furthermore, insofar as $E' = E''$ is concretely distinct and not abstractly separated from equation [3], it does not in turn develop into $(E_1' = E_1'') = (E_1'' = E_1')$; cf. §10, b.) What has been stated concerning $E' = E''$ is also to be repeated concerning $E'' = E'$, to the extent that this is also regarded as a meaning that is distinct from the concrete identity.

d. The analysis of $E' = E''$, or $E'' = E'$, presents in turn E' and E'' as being distinct from $E' = E''$. There arises here a situation analogous to the one considered above: for if both E' and E'' may be regarded as meanings that are distinct from $E' = E''$, *there is however no distinction* between E' and E'', in such a way that the positing of E'', as distinct from $E' = E''$, is nothing but a repetition of the positing of E', as itself thus distinct. The subject and the predicate of the proposition: 'Being is being', as distinct from their identity, are not two terms, but a single repeated term. (As in the previous case, insofar as E', or E'', is concretely distinct and not abstractly separated from $E' = E''$, it does not in turn develop into $E_1' = E_1''$.)

e. The following objection must, however, be taken into account at this point. Even if – one objects – the positing of identity is originary, or the positing of being may not be presupposed to the positing of identity, it is nevertheless the case that, in order to affirm that being is being (i.e. $E' = E''$), it is necessary to *distinguish* in some way being from being (E' from E''); for if this distinction were not present, one would simply be stating being, rather than stating that being is being – since a mere *repetition* of that stating is not equivalent to the *affirmation* that posits being as the predicate of being. In the same way, in order to affirm $(E' = E'') = (E'' = E')$, it is necessary to distinguish in some way $E' = E''$ from $E'' = E'$; for if this distinction were not present, one would not be positing the identity of identity with itself, but simply an identity.

Positing $E' = E''$ and positing $(E' = E'') = (E'' = E')$ certainly means positing a certain difference, since it is not simply E' that is posited in the first case or $E' = E''$ in the second one. At the same time, however, affirming that being is being precisely means *superseding* every distinction or difference between being and itself, both in case being is regarded as a self-identity, i.e. as $E' = E''$, and in case it is regarded as a noesis, E'. And yet, it must at the same time be noted that this superseding does not indicate a superseding of that distinction by virtue of which, in affirming that being is being, it is not simply being that is affirmed, but the identity of being with itself; it does not indicate this because, in this way, the positing of identity would constitute a negation of the condition by virtue of which identity realizes itself as such, rather than simply as being that has not yet advanced into itself.

Identity is therefore certainly identity of a difference. But how is this difference determined? For the difference between being and being may not count as a simple repetition of the subject in the predicate. The repetition of being does not determine any difference between being and itself, and it does not determine any difference because it is not even able to constitute an identity. As part of its identity, being is predicated of being itself; in a repetition, no predication takes place (the repeated term, insofar as it is repeated, not being posited as the predicate of the term itself), and, therefore, no identity or sameness is realized.

Let us then respond by stating that the difference – the only difference – immanent to identity is the very difference between the abstract moment and the whole, i.e. between $E' = E''$ and $(E' = E'') = (E'' = E')$; and between E' and $E' = E''$. Or, equivalently: identity is constituted by difference precisely insofar as the abstract moment (noesis) is distinct from the concrete (dianoesis). (It should be noted that in the same way in which E' is a noesis relative to $E' = E''$, so is $E' = E''$ a noesis relative to $(E' = E'') = (E'' = E')$).

Let us consider $(E' = E'') = (E'' = E')$. If, in considering this, one assumes $E' = E''$ as a meaning that is distinct from $(E' = E'') = (E'' = E')$, the 'remaining' term, the 'residue' – i.e. $E'' = E'$ – is not simply $E'' = E'$ (*qua* itself distinct from the concrete identity); it is not a 'term', but it is the very concrete identity $(E' = E'') = (E'' = E')$, namely, it is $E'' = E'$ *regarded as the predicate of $E' = E''$*; or, equivalently, it is $E' = E''$ *regarded as that of which $E'' = E'$ is predicated*. If the 'remaining' term is considered in turn as something distinct from the concrete identity – i.e. if *both $E' = E''$ and $E'' = E'$* are considered as being distinct from the concrete (the analysis of the concrete resulting in these two terms thus distinct) – the concrete (i.e. the identity, the predication) is no longer posited: what is posited is only a repetition of the abstract moment – and, as already stated, a repetition is not a predicative relation between a term and the repeated term. If, in considering $(E' = E'') = (E'' = E')$, both $E' = E''$ and $E'' = E'$ are considered as meanings that are distinct from the concrete, this consideration is therefore the abstract concept of those distinct terms: precisely insofar as the concrete cannot be posited in this way. However, precisely insofar as one does not aim to abstractly separate $E' = E''$ from $E'' = E'$, but aims to keep both of these terms distinct from the concrete, these two terms are not in any way 'two': they do not distinguish themselves in any way, and the 'second' is not *identical* to the 'first' one – it is not the *same* as the 'first' one – but it is a repetition of the first one. In this way, it is not possible to determine the difference that constitutes the identity, since if a repetition of the first term cannot count as a predication, it is instead precisely of a predication – i.e. of an identity – that we are to establish the internal difference.

It should therefore be emphasized that the abstract concept of the abstract arises in this case insofar as one aims to produce a concrete concept of the abstract that would regard *both* the subject *and* the predicate of $(E' = E'') = (E'' = E')$ as abstract contents – that is, insofar as one aims to (concretely) conceive of *both* the subject *and* the predicate of that equation as abstract moments. Therefore: if $E' = E''$ is abstractly separated from $E'' = E'$ – or E' from E'' – whereby the terms thus separated are presupposed to their identity, these terms distinguish themselves from one another in such a way that, as discussed in §9, it must be stated that each *is not* the other. If, instead, one aims to concretely conceive the abstract, but in a way that, having regarded $E' = E''$ as being concretely distinct from the concrete, one would *also* aim to regard $E'' = E'$ as being concretely distinct from the concrete, the elimination of the difference between $E' = E''$ and $E'' = E'$ even entails that the positing of this 'second' term should be nothing but a repetition of the 'first' one. It should be noted that in this second case an abstract concept only arises if one considers that the positing of $E' = E''$ and the positing of $E'' = E'$, *qua* meanings respectively distinct from the concrete, *exhaust the analysis of the concrete*, in such a way that the latter *consists* of the positing of those two distinct meanings.

Accordingly, it must be stated that the subject of identity is not distinct from the predicate of the latter insofar as both subject and predicate are regarded as being distinct from that identity, but insofar as the subject is considered as an abstract moment and the predicate as the whole predication or the identity itself. If one regards $E' = E"$ as a distinct meaning, it is then $E" = E'$ that stands as the whole predication; if instead one regards $E" = E'$ as a distinct meaning, it is then $E' = E"$ that stands as the whole predication. That is to say, the predicate is the subject itself but posited as the predicate of itself.

What has been stated concerning the difference that arises in positing $(E' = E") = (E" = E')$ must be analogously stated concerning the difference that arises in positing $E' = E"$: E' distinguishes itself from $E"$ insofar as, having regarded E' as a meaning that is distinct from $E' = E"$, the semantic domain constituted by $E"$ stands as the whole predication $E' = E"$. The distinction entailed by the proposition: 'Being is being' is therefore the distinction between the abstract (noesis) and the concrete (apophansis).

If, therefore, the subject is posited as a meaning that is distinct from the identity, the predicate is certainly something that does not distinguish itself in any way from the subject – but this something that does not distinguish itself from the subject is precisely posited as the subject *itself*, i.e. it is posited as the predicate of itself.

f. Taking stock of the fundamental points of this discussion: the concrete positing of equation [3] rules out the possibility that the concrete identity should be the identity of $E' = E"$ and $E" = E'$ as determinations that are distinct in such a way that the semantic-positional domain of the one does not include the domain of the other; $E"$ and E' that appear in the first part of the equation are indeed posited as the same $E"$ and E' that appear in the second part of the equation.

At the same time, however, the analysis of the identity is able to distinguish both $E' = E"$ and $E" = E'$ from the concrete. The same should be stated of E' and $E"$ with respect to that relative concreteness constituted by $E' = E"$. Insofar as they are thus distinct from the concrete, $E' = E"$ is not distinct from $E" = E'$, and E' is not distinct from $E"$.

The distinction – which is nevertheless required upon positing equation [3], or even simply $E' = E"$ – is then the very distinction between the abstract and the concrete: there is here – i.e. when dealing with identical propositions – no distinction between the abstract and the abstract.

The analysis of the concrete certainly finds the abstract repeated; the concrete, however, is not simply the repeated abstract, for what is posited in the repetition is at the same time posited as the predicate of itself. Negating that the repetition exhausts the analysis of the concrete does not indeed mean negating the repetition of the abstract: the repetition is the matter of the predication; or, the predication is the form of the repetition.

For what concerns the concrete meaning of 'non-identical' propositions, cf. Chapter 6, §11.

12. Aporia and resolution

The observations developed in the previous section make it possible to solve an aporia that is arguably among the most insidious caused by an abstract comprehension of the principle of identity. Keeping firm the fact that, in order to affirm that being is being, it is necessary to *distinguish* being from being, one concludes that this distinction contradicts the affirmed identity; that is to say, once again (§9), in order to affirm an identity it is necessary to negate the non-contradictoriness of being. It should be noted that this aporia is a new one with respect to the one formulated at the beginning of §9, for now the noesis – which may be regarded either as E' or as $E' = E''$ – is not abstractly presupposed to the identity; accordingly, the distinction, and therefore the ensuing contradiction, appears as the distinction required by the very formation of the concretely conceived identity.

Let us state that the aporia is completely valid if the analysis of an identity is regarded as resulting in two simple and distinct moments; namely, if the subject *and* the predicate of the identity are regarded as determinations that are distinct from the identity itself. It is precisely in this way that Gentile, in his *Logic*, conceives of the analysis of the proposition $A = A$: i.e. as resulting in A, A.[5] Let us observe that what poses a difficulty in this logical situation is precisely what, according to Gentile,[6] stands before us as something easily comprehensible: the *difference* of the identical. For, indeed, once the subject and the predicate are not presupposed to their identity, the fact that being is being – i.e. that being is not distinct from itself – is the most easily discernible aspect of the matter. But – and here lies the real difficulty – what does that difference, which is nevertheless necessarily required by the very constitution of identity, consist in? A and A are absolutely the same. However, despite the impossibility of affirming a difference between A and A, since a difference that is immanent to identity must still be admitted for the identity to be such, it follows that this difference – which must be recognized to be immanent to the identity – is simply permitted to stand beside the identity, in opposition to it (insofar as the latter absolutely excludes difference); the identical, insofar as it is identical, is different, and vice-versa. This being the case, propositions such as: 'A is A insofar as each of these terms is different from the other one, but in its being identical with it' or 'must be different, but in order to be identical with it'[7] do nothing but render the contradiction explicit, and in no way do they resolve the aporia.

The latter is resolved as already indicated in the previous section: the distinction entailed by the proposition: 'Being is being' is the distinction between the abstract and the concrete, and not – as per the aporetic argument – between being and being, both regarded as abstract moments. If identity is understood as an identity of abstract moments, one can only affirm that the condition of identity is a contradiction, since the difference required by the constitution of identity may only be referred to the identical as such.

13. Note

E', as concretely distinct from $E' = E''$ and from $(E' = E'') = (E'' = E')$ *is*, however, E'', and it *is* what is concretely posited as $(E' = E'') = (E'' = E')$; in the same way, $E' = E''$, as concretely distinct from $(E' = E'') = (E'' = E')$, *is* what is concretely posited as $(E' = E'') = (E'' = E')$: what is not included in E' and in $E' = E''$, insofar as these are distinct from the concrete identity, is the *positing* of that *being*.

14. Identity as the identity of identity and non-contradiction

a. From what has been said, it appears that the concrete meaning of the principle of non-contradiction requires this formulation: 'Being that is not non-being is not non-being – this not being non-being pertaining to being itself.' In symbols:

[4] $\qquad (E = \text{nn}E) = (\text{nn}E = E),$

in which '$E = \text{nn}E$' means: 'being is not being non-being'. The reader may unfold the corollaries analogously to what we have done for equation [3].

What is now to be remarked, however, is that if identity and non-contradiction are the abstract moments of concrete identity (or non-contradiction) (§7), the ultimate formulation of identity is the positing of the identity between identity (I) and non-contradiction (nC): 'Stating that being is being is *the same* as stating that being is not non-being.' Therefore:

[5] $\qquad (I = nC) = (nC = I).$

b. It may be object that the identity (i) between $I = nC$ and $nC = I$ is *the same* non-contradictoriness (nc) by virtue of which it is posited that '$I = nC$ is not non-($nC = I$)'; accordingly, it will be necessary to posit the identity (i') between i and nc:

[5ª] $\qquad (i = nc) = (nc = i).$

And, once again, since i' is the very non-contradictoriness (nc') by virtue of which it is posited that '$i = nc$ is not non-($nc = i$)', it will be necessary to posit the identity i'' between i' and nc'; and so on, *ad infinitum*. As a result, it will not be possible to posit the identity.

Let us respond by stating that this infinite development only arises insofar as one understands that it is *necessary* for i not to be posited as immediately belonging to the content of I, in such a way that the positing of this belonging necessarily determines a logical development with respect to the positing of I. For, indeed, I is not a simple abstract universal, but a universality that is immediately determined: that is to say, it has, as its immediate content, all the immediately present identities, thus also including i – which, strictly speaking, is not *one identity among others*, but it is the *form* of every identity, in such a way that the concrete positing of i (i.e. the positing in which that form is regarded in its relation to the content) is the same concrete positing of I. This means that the positing of equation [5] *immediately includes* the positing of equation [5ª], as long as i is regarded as to its value of form (in such a way that, by virtue of this being assumed as *form*, it can be *included* in the concrete); furthermore, if i is regarded as to its concrete relation to its content (i.e. if it is regarded as the form *of* that content), the positing of equation [5] is not distinct from the positing of equation [5ª] in any way. The form of identity is *immediately* posited as the content of itself, in such a way that it does not follow that, *in becoming* the content of itself, this becoming (i.e. this appearing as part of its own content in a logical moment that is additional relative to the moment of the positing of the content) realizes the first step of an infinite development. *Requiring* the development of equation [5] into equation [5^a] thus means requiring something that is already immediately achieved with the positing of equation [5], and it therefore means negating what is immediately posited.

Once again, it must be stated (cf. Chapter 2, §16) that the affirmation of the *impossibility* for the semantic-positional domain of equation [5] to *immediately* include the domain of equation [5^a] is responsible for that infinite development, i.e. for affirming that the positing of identity has no ground. That impossibility, however, is determined by the abstract separation (the abstract concept) of the positing of equation [5] from the positing of the inclusion of equation [5^a] in the concrete content of equation [5]. Once this abstract separation is superseded, so is that impossibility; namely, what is superseded is the element that precludes the affirmation that equation [5^a] is *immediately* included in the content of equation [5].

15. Two aspects of the principle of non-contradiction

a. Turning now to a consideration of the semantic content of what constitutes itself as identity or non-contradictoriness, it is possible to note two aspects of the principle of non-contradiction. This twofold character is precisely given by the different meaning that may be ascribed to the term 'being'.

Since being, of which it is possible to immediately speak, is precisely immediate being (the totality of the immediate) – i.e. since the immediate determination of being is the immediate – in this respect the principle is to be formulated as follows: 'Immediate being is not non-being' (or, in the form of identity: 'Immediate being is being'). This formulation only differs *materialiter* from the previous one ('Being is not non-being'): in the sense that while that first formulation might appear to leave the content of the term 'being' undetermined, this second formulation makes it instead explicit that the content that is immediately addressed by the principle is immediate being, or that non-contradictoriness originarily (i.e. immediately) determines itself as the non-contradictoriness of the immediate.

At the same time, however, to the extent that the meaning 'being' is formally distinct from the meaning 'immediate being', the principle is to be formulated in terms of *being* and *non-being*: i.e. it is posited as the structuring of *being qua being* (Aristotle, *Metaphysics*, 1. IV, Ch. III). By this we mean that that being that is immediately known is, precisely, 'being'; and that, *qua* being, it distinguishes itself from its being immediately known. This distinction is itself immediately known.

(Even if the *extension* of the meaning 'being' did not differ from the extension of the meaning 'immediate being' – i.e. even if the immediate coincided with the totality of being – the *comprehension* of those two meanings would nevertheless differ. The difference in that comprehension would indeed be determined by the very exclusion of a 'being' that is not part of immediately known being; that is to say, what is excluded – non-immediate being – must be posited as formally distinct from immediate being, and it is precisely insofar as it is posited as thus distinct that it can be superseded.

The Immediacy of the Non-contradictoriness of Being 141

That is to say, the condition of that superseding is the distinction between 'being' and 'immediate being').

Considering then immediate being as being, or discerning being within immediate being, the principle of non-contradiction is to be formulated as follows: 'Being is not non-being.' The term 'being' is therefore not, as it might have appeared, something indeterminate, for it has immediate being as its content.

It is important to note that this formulation is not ancillary with respect to the previous one, but it is co-essential to it. For, indeed, immediate being is not non-being precisely insofar as immediate being is 'being'. If the immediate were not posited as being, the exclusion of the non-being of the immediate would have no ground.

From this, however, it does not follow that the proposition: 'Immediate being is not non-being' is *inferred* from the proposition: 'Being is not non-being.' The subject of the former proposition is indeed the immediate content of the subject of the latter, in such a way that the predicate pertains to the subject of that former proposition *in the very act* in which the predicate pertains to the subject of that latter proposition. It is in this sense that a 'co-essentiality' was mentioned above. If, on the one hand, the immediate is not non-being precisely insofar as the immediate is being, on the other hand, it is possible to affirm that being is being precisely insofar as the immediate is available *qua* immediate content of being.

b. It is clear that if the terms 'immediate being' and 'totality of the immediate' are regarded, respectively, as 'phenomenological immediate' and 'totality of the phenomenological immediate', everything stated in a. has been stated from the standpoint of the concept Γ_a (cf. Chapter 2, §26), i.e. from the standpoint according to which the totality of immediacy is the phenomenological immediacy – i.e. from the standpoint in accordance with which everything whose being can be immediately affirmed is the phenomenological immediate. Instead, from the standpoint for which phenomenological immediacy is only a moment of the totality or structure of the immediate – this being a standpoint that at this stage of the exposition has only been anticipated – it must be stated that the content of the principle of non-contradiction does not immediately consist of the phenomenological immediate, but of everything whose being, in one way or another, is immediately affirmed.

Point a., instead, is *not* developed from the standpoint of the concept Γ_a if 'immediate being' and 'totality of the immediate' indicate the concrete structuring of the different meanings of immediacy – whereby it is this very structuring that stands as the immediate determination of being.

One may use the expressions 'L-immediate' ('L-immediacy') and 'Ph-immediate' ('Ph-immediacy') to indicate those logical and phenomenological immediacies.

c. As a corollary of what has been stated at b.: keeping in mind that, as seen in the previous sections, the positing of the non-contradictoriness of being is a form of immediacy, it is already possible to anticipate here that, if a positive element that does not belong to the totality of the Ph-immediate is L-immediately affirmed, this immediate positing of that positive element will have to consist of the very principle of non-contradiction. It will therefore be stated that this principle has as its immediate content a positive element that exceeds the Ph-immediate, precisely insofar as that very principle constitutes the immediate positing of that positive element. (The reader, however, should consider what is stated in this last point as a simple guideline.)

16. Note on the outcome of the abstract consideration of the two aspects of the principle

The two aspects remarked above are the abstract moments of a concreteness that is given by their very relation. A loss of this relation constitutes the emergence of an abstract concept of the abstract.

If, while considering the non-contradictoriness of immediate being, one believes to be able to *project* the contradictoriness of what is not part of the immediate, this entails that the non-contradictoriness of the immediate is not considered to be in relation with the non-contradictoriness of being: i.e. it entails that the immediate is not regarded *qua* being. It follows from this that, contrary to what has been assumed, one is not even able to exclude the non-being of the immediate.

Instead, to the extent that being is regarded as part of the immediate itself, the project of the contradictoriness of a being that is not part of the immediate is immediately superseded.

If, instead, one considers the non-contradictoriness of being as something isolated – i.e. if being is not regarded as immediate being, but it is held firm as pure being (Parmenidean position) – the affirmation of being no longer has any content ('nothing exists', states Gorgias), and, therefore, non-contradictoriness itself cannot be affirmed because the non-contradictory content does not exist.

A formal consideration of the principle of non-contradiction has its most customary aspect in those formulations of the principle that express that non-contradictoriness as a relation that obtains between two variables that are in themselves indifferent as to whether the relation should have an ontological value: 'A is not non-A'; 'for every value of A, A is not non-A'. The one who were to posit this proposition as such as the ground and foundation of knowledge would need to be asked for the meaning or the ground of A's very coming to take any value – or, equivalently, for the meaning of this absolute possibility of acquiring values, by virtue of which the possible variation of A would be limitless. An answer to this question is necessary in order to retain the principle, for if one were to rule out the possibility that A should be able to take any meaning whichever, the affirmation that A is not non-A would no longer be meaningful. On what basis is it instead excluded that A could be meaningless? And, admitting that A should have a meaning, what would be the ground of this determination? An answer to this question leads to the level of the *determination* or the *content* of the principle, and this level is not something accidental or external to the structure of the principle, but it essentially belongs to it. The classical formulations of non-contradictoriness, according to which the latter *dependet ex intellectu entis* (i.e. it is the non-contradictoriness *of being*) are in general superior to the rationalist formulations, as well as to more recent logical analyses. It may also be added that the logic of idealism, too, aims to meet a need for concreteness in direct opposition to the abstract logic of rationalism. For instance, one of the meanings that may certainly be attributed to Fichte's identity '$I = I$'

precisely consists in the affirmation of an identity that is not simply formal, but that is the identity of an originary *content*.

17. Note on the synthetic value of the principle of non-contradiction

a. Kant observes that it is meaningless to ground an analytic judgement in experience, since it is not necessary to go outside the concept of the subject in order for the predicate to pertain to the subject. Considering then the analytic character of the principle of non-contradiction, it is clear that Kant's observation cannot mean that this principle has no synthetic *a posteriori* significance, i.e. that the connection of the subject to the predicate has no synthetic value. Negating this value would indeed mean negating that that being that is manifest as part of the phenomenological horizon is non-contradictory; it would mean affirming that the actuality or being-there of being refutes the non-contradictoriness affirmed by that principle (and it would therefore mean negating the analytic character of the latter). It must therefore be stated that the principle of non-contradiction, too, has a synthetic value (i.e. that non-contradictoriness is an immediacy also *qua* phenomenological immediacy), but that this value is only a moment of the value of that principle.

Considering this abstract moment of the value of that principle, it must therefore be stated that it is immediately present (phenomenological immediacy) that being is not non-being: for instance, that this sheet of paper is not what this sheet of paper is not. That is to say, it is immediately present – in the same way in which any other Ph-immediate content is present – that being is non-contradictory, or that the form of being is its non-contradictoriness. This means that being is Ph-immediate *qua* non-contradictory being. In this respect, non-contradictoriness itself, while constituting the formal aspect of the Ph-immediate, is one of the many determinations of the latter.

b. If, on the basis of what has been stated, one should believe that it is legitimate to conclude that it is possible to project that the immediate should be constituted as something contradictory, this means that, once again, one has moved from the concrete concept of the synthetic moment of the value of the principle of non-contradiction to its abstract concept. That concrete concept, while still considering the synthetic character of that principle, retains this character in its relation with the analytic character of the principle. The abstract concept severs that relation and holds firm the abstract moment as the entirety of that value.

18. Being *qua* abstract universal and *qua* concrete universal

To the extent that 'being' is regarded as a meaning that is indifferent to the *quantity* of its determination (differentiation, individuation) – that is, to the extent that it is posited as something that is able to stand both as the totality and as a part (and as any part) of being – 'being' is posited as an *abstract universal*. It is formal being itself (Chapter 2,

§2) *in its being in relation* with 'any' determinacy, or insofar as the determinacy with which it is in relation is a variable. (The maximum limit of this possible variation consists in that value of the variable for which being is determined as the totality: as the consummation and therefore surpassing of every quantification of its differentiation. The minimum limit of that variable may be regarded as that quantification for which it is contradictory that there should exist a middle term – or quantification – between it and nothingness.)

The abstract character of that abstract universal is determined by the fact that that with which formal being is concretely related is the very totality of determinations: this totality not simply standing as one of the values that may be taken by a variable, but as the horizon of every variation – a horizon that is therefore posited as the constant determination of the content with which formal being is concretely related. This concrete relation is precisely the totality of being. The indifference or possible variation of the content of the abstract universal thus constitutes a moment in which formal being is in relation with something determined, but in such a way that this relation is distinct from the moment in which the concrete determination of what is determined is posited *qua* determinacy that exceeds its simply being determined as 'determined'. The abstract character of the abstract universal therefore lies in the fact that the content of being is only determined as 'determined', thus being valid for *every* determined being.

Insofar as being is instead in a concrete relation with the totality of determinations, and therefore counts as the *concrete universal*, it is not able to count as 'every' determination of being, but simply as *that* (whole) determination that is the horizon of every determination. Accordingly, while the abstract universal realizes itself in a multiplicity of individuations, the concrete universal is itself the one individuation of itself; or, to the extent that the individuation of the concrete universal entails the constitution of a multiplicity, that individuation is not the contradictory individuation of the form or essence of the whole, but it is the whole itself in its particularizing itself. The individuation of the concrete universal conforms with and exhausts essence itself, in such a way that it necessarily posits itself as a single and unique individuation.

While it is in relation to the concrete universal that the abstract universal may be posited, the positing of the concrete universal entails, on the contrary, the positing of the abstract universal as that in which all determinacies agree: i.e. in being a determinacy of being. It is insofar as this concurrence or sameness is posited that it is possible to posit something like the 'totality of being'.

The distinction between abstract and concrete universal does not entail that the positing of the concrete universal, as this is realized as part of the originary structure, consists in the actual positing of the totality of determinations in their concrete semantic value; it will indeed be shown that the originary positing of the concrete universal – i.e. of the whole – is a *formal* positing of the whole: namely, such that the concrete semantic value of what is determined is not posited. Despite this, the distinction between abstract and concrete universal persists unchanged: in that (formal) *being*, in its being posited in relation to 'any' determination, is distinct from (formal) *being* in its being posited in relation to the totality of determinations – even if this is formally posited. It can therefore be stated: even if the positing of the concrete universal, *qua* formal positing of the whole (but this, let us reiterate, is a statement that will have to be adequately justified), is an indeterminate positing of the totality of determinate being, the positing of the abstract universal is that indeterminate positing of determinate being that is already indeterminate with respect to that indeterminate positing of determinate being constituted by the positing of the concrete universal.

19. Note

'Being' may therefore be considered abstractly or concretely. It is clear, however, that the abstract universal is not to be conflated with formal being itself, since the semantic content of the latter does not include, as posited, the relation with the determination (be the latter abstractly or concretely conceived), but it includes – or, more precisely, it is constituted by – the simple meaning *being*. Insofar as this meaning is posited in relation with determinate being, formal being is structured as a concrete universal and as an abstract universal. The latter are therefore meaningful insofar as that meaning is posited. Both the abstract and the concrete universals therefore each stand as a synthesis of a formal and a material positing of being, i.e. of the positing of formal being and of the positing of a determination; the first term of the synthesis is the same for both universals and constitutes a formal positing (since *being*, which is concretely related with the determination, *does not mean* anything other than *being*, which is abstractly related with the determination; indeed, strictly speaking, these are not two relations, but two aspects of a single relation); the second term of that synthesis is different, and this difference constitutes the formal and the material aspects of the material positing (i.e. of the positing of the determinations of being).

Analogously, both the positing of a determinate being (of a particular being) and the positing of the totality of being consist in a synthesis of a material and a formal positing: since, once again, these two acts of positing distinguish themselves internally into a positing of pure being and a positing of a determination – the first distinct term being the same in the two acts of positing, whereas, concerning the second distinct term (which is different in the two acts of positing), the first positing stands as one of the particular moments of the material positing, while the second positing stands as the whole of the material positing.

Stating that formal being has the same semantic value both insofar as it is in relation with an abstract determination and insofar as it is in relation with a concrete determination – and both insofar as it is in relation with the totality of determinations and with a moment of this totality – means emphasizing that aspect of univocity that the analogical character of being nevertheless *includes* to the extent that being is predicated *secundum rationem eandem*. In other words: if 'beings' are a synthesis between (formal) *being* and a determination, the analogical concept is the one of *beings*, rather than that of *being* (which is univocal). (It should be noted that the term 'being', when used without any specification, means 'beings', i.e. being in its concrete determining itself.)

20. Formal and concrete values of the principle of non-contradiction

The principle of non-contradiction has therefore a formal or a concrete value depending on whether 'being', which enters into the formulation of the principle, is regarded as an abstract or as a concrete universal: on the one hand, this consists in non-contradictoriness *qua* universal that realizes itself in a multiplicity of individuations; on the other hand, it consists in non-contradictoriness *qua* universal that is its own single individuation.

Concerning the value of this distinction in the formulation of non-contradictoriness, cf. Chapter 9, §17.

21. Concerning the aporia of non-contradictoriness

The positing of the immediacy of non-contradictoriness gives rise to aporetic structures analogous to the ones that arise in relation to the positing of the phenomenological immediacy of being (cf. Chapter 2).

Indeed, it may once again be held that the positing of the immediacy of non-contradictoriness determines a *regressus in indefinitum*. Indicating this non-contradictoriness by the expression $(I = nC) = (nC = I)$ (to be understood as indicated in §14), $(I = nC) = (nC = I)$ is affirmed on the basis of $(I = nC) = (nC = I)$ itself. However, in the same way in which this equation may be held firm vis-à-vis its negation only insofar as its immediacy is posited (i.e. insofar as it is posited that $(I = nC) = (nC = I)$ is that on the basis of which $(I = nC) = (nC = I)$ is affirmed), so that very immediacy may only be held firm by positing the immediacy of that immediacy; and so on, *ad infinitum*. The positing of the immediacy of non-contradictoriness will therefore be an affirmation that has no ground.

Once again, we respond that this aporetic conclusion only arises if the positing of the immediacy of $(I = nC) = (nC = I)$ is presupposed to, or abstractly separated from, the positing of the inclusion of that immediacy in the immediate content constituted by non-contradictoriness itself. $(I = nC) = (nC = I)$ therefore stands as the ground – it is the basis of its own affirmation – only insofar as it is originarily considered or posited as the basis of its own being affirmed. That is to say, what is known for itself is not simply $(I = nC) = (nC = I)$, but it is $(I = nC) = (nC = I)$ *in its originarily standing* as something known for itself, as part of which this very standing is one of the determinations that constitute the content of identity (I), i.e. of non-contradictoriness (nC). That is to say, the content of immediacy includes *its very* immediacy: it is not a content in which the value of immediacy is introduced *in a second moment*. The *regressus* arises to the extent that – due to that abstract separation of the positing of immediacy from the positing of the inclusion of immediacy in the immediate content – the positing of immediacy cannot be regarded as being originarily part of what is known for itself, and it therefore requires an *additional* logical moment, in which the immediacy of immediacy is posited (i.e. in which immediacy is included in the immediate content).

The aporia that consists in observing that the positing of the immediacy of non-contradictoriness entails that non-contradictoriness itself stands at the same time as something immediate and as something mediated (cf., similarly, Chapter 2, §§18, 21) is also to be resolved in a manner analogous to the one developed in §§19, 21 of Chapter 2. The reader may independently develop these implications.

22. Transition

From the point of view of the exposition, the two kinds of immediacy have appeared so far in different ways. For, indeed, while Ph-immediacy has appeared as the affirmation of a specific positive content – i.e. as the affirmation of a specific dimension of being, or as an existential affirmation – (immediacy being here precisely the immediacy of that affirmation of being), L-immediacy has not yet appeared as to its existential value, by virtue of which a dimension of being exceeding the one affirmed by Ph-immediacy would thus be affirmed (and, therefore, immediately affirmed). This existential value of L-immediacy has only been *anticipated*, but it has not been concretely posited. *Up to this point*, therefore, L-immediacy has appeared as to its value of *formal property* of being – and, therefore, originarily of that being that can be immediately affirmed: i.e. of what *up to this point* has been constituted as Ph-immediate being. That is to say, up to this point, L-immediacy has not appeared as the immediacy of the affirmation of a positive element, but as the immediacy of the identity or non-contradictoriness of every positive element; accordingly, the positive content that at this point of the exposition is available as the content of L-immediacy is the Ph-immediately positive content. It is here clear that, by affirming this fact, one does not assume the standpoint of Γ_a, for we are not here affirming that the Ph-immediately positive content constitutes the totality of the positive content that may be immediately affirmed, but we are only pointing to a configuration that obtains at this point of the exposition of the originary. The following remarks are to be referred to the relation between Ph-immediacy and L-immediacy – the latter being regarded as to its formal value; (or, strictly speaking, the following remarks are to be referred to the aporia determined by an abstract comprehension of that relation). These remarks are not made from the standpoint of Γ_a, since – let us repeat – the formal value of L-immediacy is posited as a moment of the very concrete value of L-immediacy (even though, from the point of view of the exposition – and, therefore, of the reader who is not aware of the concrete – it is precisely this concreteness that appears as something abstract and simply anticipated). L-immediacy, regarded as to its simple formal value, may be indicated by the expression: 'Ph-L-immediacy'.[8] When the terms 'immediacy' and 'immediate' are used without any prefix – unless the meaning of these terms were to appear so clearly from the context as to make the use of a prefix unnecessary, or unless the task of the text is precisely to determine the prefix to be adopted – this will indicate that we are not considering this or that mode of immediacy, but immediacy itself in its concrete structure. (Concerning the concrete meaning of L-immediacy, cf. Chapters 7, 13.)

23. Concerning the aporia of the relation between the positing of Ph-immediacy and the positing of L-immediacy

a. For what concerns the set of aporetic structures determined by a consideration of Ph-immediacy *qua* unrelated to L-immediacy (the latter, as discussed, being regarded as to its simply formal value, i.e. as Ph-L-immediacy), it should be noted here that, due to that lack of relatedness, each of the two immediacies may be posited as the ground of the other one – whereby each of the two is constituted at the same time as something immediate and as something mediated (i.e. as the positing of the immediacy of what is posited, and as a form of letting what is thus posited be something mediated).

The aporia that originarily affects the originary structure is more generally precisely superseded by highlighting the *structural* character of the originary, i.e. its being a *semantic complexity*. This complexity is the concrete in which the abstract moments are superseded – or, equivalently, in which the abstract moments are retained in their realizing themselves as part of their relation. Furthermore, as already discussed, the aporia arises more generally as soon as one confers on the content of the concrete that form of discursivity, due to which the moments of the concrete are posited one after the other – i.e. as soon as a discursive sequence is regarded as a logical sequence. This takes place insofar as the abstract moments of the concrete are abstractly separated.

For what concerns the moments constituted by the positing of Ph-immediacy and of Ph-L-immediacy, it must therefore be stated that if one of the two acts of positing is regarded as being logically prior to the other one (this being the case if the two acts of positing are abstractly separated), both of them are constituted as something groundless. For, indeed, that logical antecedence entails that the prior positing should realize itself without that other positing – and that therefore this other positing, too, should arise as something that, as such, lacks something already realized. (Once this abstract separation has taken place, it makes no difference which of the two separated terms should be regarded as being prior to the other one: it is precisely the term that has been separated, *qua* separated, that is prior to the other one.) Each positing therefore stands in relation to the other one as to something without which it is itself something groundless: namely, as a content (being) that is posited without the form of non-contradictoriness, and as this form, which is posited without a content. It thus follows that the logical moment in which that form is said to pertain to that content, and this content is said to pertain to that form – i.e. the logical moment in which the grounding of the form and content in question is realized – is distinct from the moments, respectively, constituted by the positing of that form and by the positing of that content. Since each of these two acts of positing is the positing of the immediacy of what is posited, however, it follows that the other of each of the two acts of positing stands as the x discussed in §13 of Chapter 2; accordingly, what in each of the two acts of positing is posited as the immediate is then mediated by the intervention of the other positing.

b. Let us add that if one were to consider superseding this contradiction through the simple *mutual determination* of the two acts of positing, not only would the contradiction in question remain unsolved, but, as explained below, an additional contradiction would be allowed to persist.

Let us, however, state right away that, strictly speaking, a mutual determination does not constitute anything new in relation to the aporetic situation (outlined above) determined by the affirmation of a logical succession of the abstract moments of the originary. It has indeed been stated that, precisely due to that logical succession, *each* of the two acts of positing stands as the ground of the other one, in such a way that here a mutual determination already takes place.

The observation that we now wish to make therefore aims to note that a mutual determination – abstractly considered (which was expressed above through the mention of a 'simple' mutual determination) – does not only entail that already noted contradiction but also the following one: namely, that each of the two acts of positing is, relative to the same term – i.e. relative to the other one of the two – something mediated and something mediating (something grounded and something grounding). (The first contradiction, on the contrary, consisted in the fact that each of the two acts of positing affirms the immediacy of something that is mediated by the other positing.) This second contradiction obtains to the extent that the two acts of positing stand as part of that mutual relation as each lacking the positive element that pertains to the other one.

c. The aporetic structure just outlined is solved as follows:

By first of all realizing, as already noted, that a discursive sequence does not entail a logical sequence of what is manifested by discourse in time; or, equivalently, that the distinction of the moments – a distinction that is seized upon by discursivity itself, leaving each of the distinct terms outside the other one – is not their abstract separation. The positing of Ph-immediacy and the positing of Ph-L-immediacy are thus *co-originary*, i.e. they constitute the structuring of the originary. By virtue of this co-originarity, neither of the two acts of positing must be said to pertain to the other one in a distinct or additional logical moment relative to the one in which those acts of positing are realized. Their mutual pertaining is originary, immediate, and it does not therefore arise as something that must supersede the groundlessness determined by their not pertaining to one another.

Something that may thus be superseded, i.e. that may be grounded or mediated – and that in and through this mediation constitutes itself as a contradiction (that mediation being precisely a mediation of the immediate) – is an abstract positing of immediacy; it is a positing that keeps the two forms of immediacy separate, in such a way that their synthesis constitutes an additional moment with respect to their positing. Insofar as the positing of these two immediacies constitutes instead an originary synthesis, the moments of this synthesis are not something that needs to be grounded – precisely because they *are already* (originarily, immediately) part of that synthesis, the arising of which (relative to the moment in which the terms of the synthesis are posited) would instead determine a grounding of the moments presupposed to the synthesis.

That synthesis is the concrete concept of the abstract – this abstract precisely constituting itself as the *two acts of positing* of immediacy. It is therefore a concrete concept of distinct terms, since the originarity of the synthesis does not negate the distinction between the form of non-contradictoriness and the content of this form.

These distinct terms, however, are not unrelated: in conceiving that distinction as a lack of relation, one moves from the concrete concept of the abstract to the abstract concept of the abstract; or, equivalently: holding that the distinction entails that each of the distinct terms should be something that, as such, is to be mediated indicates that a distinct term is no longer regarded as distinct, but as unrelated. What is distinct is indeed precisely something that is *co-originary* with the other distinct term, whereby it immediately pertains to it.

From what has been said, it becomes clear that the originary synthesis of the two acts of positing of immediacy differs from a mutual determination of those acts of positing, both regarded as moments that are originarily unrelated to one another. That mutual determination constitutes an abstract synthesis, whereby, as discussed, the distinct terms are regarded in such a way that each of them is mediated by and mediating the other one – from which it follows that not only is the immediate something mediated, but that the mediated is also something mediating (relative to the same term). That mutual determination precisely negates the immediate pertaining of each positing to the other one – by virtue of which non-contradictoriness is immediately the non-contradictoriness *of the immediate content*, and this content immediately appears through the form of non-contradictoriness. (This immediate pertaining constitutes that by virtue of which, on the one hand, the affirmation of the immediate content is such that it entails the superseding of the negation of that content, and, on the other hand, non-contradictoriness itself does not vanish as a result of the vanishing of its content.)

24. Notes

The negation of Ph-immediate being is superseded insofar as it contradicts the immediacy of this being (Chapter 2, §27). This means that, as already stated at the end of the previous section, the affirmation of Ph-immediate being may not be held firm in opposition to its negation *simply* because that being is known for itself, but because it is known for itself as something non-contradictory. It is precisely insofar as being is immediately present as something non-contradictory that it is possible to immediately exclude the negation of immediately present being. That is to say, it is insofar as Ph-immediate being is not non-being that the positing of Ph-immediacy may stand as the superseding of the negation of Ph-immediate being.

Here, however, the following must be noted: in the second paragraph of §27 of Chapter 2, we stated that being is not affirmed *because* the negation of being is superseded, but this negation is superseded *because* the fact that being is is known for itself. This was stated in order to clarify the difference between 'being in contradiction with…' and 'being inherently contradictory'. Let us now point out that – since being is immediately present as something non-contradictory – the superseding of that negation does not belong to an additional logical moment relative to the positing of the immediate, but it is immediately connected to that positing. That is to say, the latter is the ground of the superseding of that negation, but not in the sense that this ground constitutes itself as a moment in which that superseding is not already included. This would entail that, within this moment, that negation would be able to exist, in such a way that the superseding of that negation would take place on the basis of something that allows the existence of that negation. In this respect, it is therefore not correct to state that that negation is superseded *because* of the fact that being is is known for itself: these two sides are immediately connected, and, therefore, neither of the two mediates the other.

25. Prospective reference

As stated in §22, this chapter has emphasized only one aspect of the concrete meaningfulness of the principle of non-contradiction. Chapter 13 will consider the concrete value of this principle: namely, the value that constitutes its *metaphysical* aspect, i.e. the aspect by virtue of which the principle of non-contradiction – *qua* immediate affirmation of a positive element that is not part of the totality of the phenomenological positive – *coincides with the metaphysical discourse itself* in act.

4

The aporia of nothingness and its resolution

1. The formulation of the aporia

The positing of the principle of non-contradiction requires the positing of *non-being*. Not only: this 'non-being' is part of the very meaning of 'being'. This belonging of non-being to both the dianoetic moment (whereby the principle of non-contradiction is constituted) and to the noetic one (whereby the meaning 'being' is constituted) constitutes a twofold aspect *of the same* logical situation. This will be discussed in Chapter 12. Here let us only consider the belonging of non-being to that dianoetic moment, keeping, however, in mind that the aporias determined by this belonging may be formulated in terms of the belonging of non-being to the meaning 'being' – and keeping also in mind that the solution that we provide here to this aporia is a solution for both ways in which the aporia may be formulated.

The aporia that we wish to consider does not pertain to non-being to the extent that this is *a specific* non-being, i.e. *a specific* being (a determinate being), but insofar as non-being is a '*nihil absolutum*' – what is *absolutely other* than being and, therefore, insofar as it is what lies *beyond* being, regarded as the *totality of being*. An age-old aporia – of which Plato was already fully aware – but an aporia that, one way or another, has always been avoided, eluded and ultimately left unsolved.

Therefore, precisely insofar as it is excluded that being should be nothing – precisely in order for this impossibility to hold – nothingness itself *is posited*, or *present*, and it therefore *is*. There is a reasoning about nothingness, and this reasoning attests the *being* of nothingness; or, equivalently, there is a disclosure or awareness of nothingness, which attests its being. Accordingly, it appears that one should conclude that the ground upon which the very principle of non-contradiction may be realized consists of a contradiction. The lucidity with which Plato presents this aporia in the *Sophist* is well known; it is, however, also well known that the aporia is there only presented, and then once and for all set aside. For Plato certainly shows which kind of non-being may be said to be – that is to say, non-being is as *a certain* being – but he leaves unresolved the difficulties advanced at a first stage of the dialogue (236e–239a), which arise from the impossibility of excluding non-being (regarded as absolute non-being) from being, without however including it. In order to refute the sophist's standpoint – but, above all, in order to show that being does not entail a negation of multiplicity, as held by Parmenides – Plato's analysis is certainly sufficient; the aporia, however, persists for what concerns absolute non-being, which Plato, following Parmenides, holds firm as non-being: for it is precisely this absolute non-being that, in manifesting itself, testifies to its own being.[1]

A singular position in relation to this aporetic situation is the one held by Fridugisus of Tours, who in his *Epistola de nihilo et de tenebris* uncompromisingly asserts the being of nothingness: '*Quaestio autem huiusmodi est nihilne aliquid sit, an non. Si quis responderit "videtur mihi nihil esse", ipsa eius quam putat negatio compellit eum fateri aliquid esse nihil, dum dicit "videtur mihi nihil esse". Quod tale est quasi dicat "videtur mihi nihil quiddam esse."*'[2] It therefore follows that nothingness, too, is. The principle of non-contradiction is thus explicitly negated.

2. Concerning certain ways of superseding the aporia

It has been held that the aporia may be solved through Frege's distinction between the *reference* or *meaning* (the logical content or the manifest object) of a concept and its *sense* (the mode of positing of a reference or meaning): nothingness, while having no reference, has however a sense, in that the logical operation of negation has a sense. Aside from the fact that Frege's distinction repeats one of the most distinctive motifs of the Scholastic tradition, that distinction, as such (i.e. as a simple distinction), does not solve the aporia, which once again appears with respect to the *lack of reference* of the term 'nothingness'. For, indeed, that absolute lack is posited, and, as such, *quiddam est* – in which its *being* is its being *meaningful* as an absolute *steresis* of meaning or reference. The cogency of the argument that leads Fridugisus to admit the being of nothingness thus remains unaltered.

And nor may the aporia be eliminated by *absolutely not positing* nothingness (i.e. through an oblivion of nothingness). Indeed, if nothingness is not posited, the principle of non-contradiction cannot be posited either: not positing nothingness means that it is impossible to exclude that being could be nothingness. Not only: it is not possible to posit being either. It has indeed been mentioned above that 'nothingness' belongs to the meaning 'being'; accordingly, if not positing nothingness entails not positing being either, not positing being entails not positing anything. Negating the positing of nothingness thus entails negating the horizon of the totality of the immediate. The belonging of the meaning 'nothingness' to the meaning 'being' can be attested *immediately* – and so can the fact that the positing of any meaning entails the positing of the meaning 'being'.[3] However, the *explication* or the *expression* of the structure of the immediate is in general considerably complex – and particularly complex is the explication of that twofold immediacy that is here in question. If, therefore, on the one hand we must refer to the analytic development of the exposition – cf. Chapter 10 – on the other hand, it is already possible to observe here that if being is in its essence what is not non-being, positing being without positing non-being also means not positing being: since, precisely, being is in its essence what is not non-being. (Equivalently, even supposing that the positional *steresis* of non-being did not entail the positional *steresis* of being, a positional horizon that in its essence does not include non-being as posited is not able to negate the identification of being and non-being, and it is therefore itself part of a contradictory situation – precisely to the extent that it is separated from the negation of that contradiction.) Not positing being, however, means not positing any other determinate meaning, since – we shall, however, have to return to this point with particular attention – positing a meaning is equivalent to positing *a specific positivity* or a specific determination *of the positive*, i.e. of being.

Furthermore, the aporia may not be solved in the same way as aporetic situations with a similar structure are resolved in other logical dimensions. We are referring to the aporia of the 'presence of the absent', which is solved – the solution precisely consisting in exhibiting the non-contradictoriness of this expression – by observing that what is absent is certainly present but *as absent*. In the same way, in the case at hand, one might think of repeating that non-being certainly is, but *as non-being*. In this respect, it must then be observed that this solution constitutes nothing but an explication of the contradictoriness of the aporia, for while in the case of the presence of the absent the fact that the absent is present is not contradictory, to the extent that it is possible to verify that it is not contradictory to negate that presence is coextensive with being – whereby there exists a dimension of the absent that is not present, and the absent is not present to the extent that it is absent, but to the extent that it is present – the affirmation that non-being *is as non-being* is instead the contradiction itself, *simpliciter*. This is the case since, to the extent that what is referred to as 'non-being' is, it is not possible to affirm that it is *as non-being* – but, for instance, as the idea or presence of non-being; and to the extent that non-being is not, it cannot even *be* as non-being.

3. Another formulation of the aporia

Nothingness, *qua* absolute non-being, constitutes the *horizon* of being: nothingness is indeed what is absolutely *other* than being, what is *over and above* being, *beyond* being.[4]

The principle of non-contradiction precisely expresses the nature of the relation between being and the horizon of nothingness. According to this relation, on the one hand, being implies the horizon of nothingness – precisely insofar as it is affirmed that being is not non-being – but, on the other hand, since that horizon is nothing, being does not imply anything or any horizon. Accordingly, the principle of non-contradiction, which is supposed to express that implication, cannot constitute itself. (At the same time, however, it is precisely this recognition of the fact that being as such does not imply anything beyond itself that requires that being should refer to nothingness, i.e. that requires the implication of the latter by the former.) In other words, if non-being is not, it is not even possible to *affirm* that being is not non-being, because in this affirmation, in some way, non-being is.

4. The general structure of the aporia

The aporia of non-being can therefore be unfolded in two directions: either by showing that non-being is (§1) or, holding firm the non-being of non-being, by showing that those logical structures that imply the *positing* of non-being cannot constitute themselves (§3).

5. Clarification of the sense in which nothingness is

In order to resolve the aporetic situation outlined above, let us begin to observe – but this is in fact the fundamental observation – that, in affirming that the positing of non-being attests to the being of non-being, one cannot intend to be affirming that 'nothingness' means, as such, 'being', but that nothingness, which is meaningful as nothingness, is. The appearing of nothingness does not attest that 'nothingness' means 'being', but that 'nothingness', which is meaningful as nothingness, is. And, conversely, this 'being' of nothingness is not meaningful as 'non-being', but, in being meaningful as being, it is the being of nothingness (which is meaningful as nothingness). The contradiction of a *non-being-that-is* is not therefore *internal* to the meaning 'nothingness' (or to the meaning 'being' that is the being of nothingness), but it obtains between the meaning 'nothingness' and the being or positivity of this meaning. That is to say, the positivity of the signification is in contradiction with the very content of that signification, which is precisely meaningful as an absolute negativity.

6. 'Nothingness' as a self-contradictory meaning

Every meaning (every content that can be thought, i.e. every being, regardless of how it constitutes itself) is a semantic synthesis between the positivity of a signification and the determinate content of this positive signification; or, equivalently, between formal being and the determination of this formality (Chapter 2, §2) – formal being precisely consisting of the positivity of the meaningfulness of the determination. Accordingly, it is clear that the meaning 'nothingness' is a self-contradictory meaning – i.e. it is a contradiction, or a being meaningful as a contradiction: precisely, the contradiction that consists in the fact that the positivity of that signification is contradicted by the absolute negativity of the signifying content. In other words, every meaning is a synthesis of the meaning 'being' and a determination of being; that is to say, every meaning is a positivity ('being') that is determined. In the meaning 'nothingness', the determination of the positivity, *qua* absolute negativity, contradicts the positivity of the determination, i.e. its positive signification.

It is therefore clear that 'nothingness', regarded as a self-contradictory meaning, includes that semantic *moment* of 'nothingness' that, as observed in the previous section, is meaningful *as nothingness*. (Or, equivalently, 'nothingness', as a non-contradictory meaning, is a *moment* of 'nothingness' as a self-contradictory meaning).

In order to elucidate the meaning of the positive signification of nothingness, it should be observed that the positivity of this signification does not simply consist in the *being* (i.e. the formal being) of nothingness, but also in the concrete semantic content that pertains to the meaning 'nothingness' to the extent that this is distinct from the meaning of (formal) 'being'. 'Nothingness is' (in the sense indicated in §5): we are stating that the positive signification of nothingness does not simply consist in the 'is' that appears in the proposition: 'Nothingness is', but also in the concrete semantic content that is thought when, in positing nothingness, 'what is other than the totality of being' is posited. If what lies beyond the whole has no positivity or being, this absolute negativity is, however, meaningful in a way that is as complex as to even include the semantic whole in the structure of its meaning (precisely as that relative to which the meaning of that *absolute* negativity constitutes itself). What is meaningful as 'other than the whole' is nothingness, but the signification of this nothingness implies the absolute signification itself or the very semantic whole. If what is other than the whole is an absolute negativity, the presence of the latter, as such – i.e. as other than the whole – therefore even implies the presence of the whole.

If the positive signification of the nothingness that is a moment of nothingness *qua* self-contradictory meaning is constituted on the one hand by the (formal) being of 'nothingness' and on the other hand by the concrete semantic content of 'nothingness',[5] we shall nevertheless use the term *being* to indicate the entire structure of the positive signification of nothingness (i.e. to indicate the entire structure of what counts as a semantic moment of the self-contradictory meaning 'nothingness').

7. The general structure of the resolution of the aporia of nothingness

The aporia of nothingness is resolved by noting that the principle of non-contradiction *does not affirm the non-existence* of the self-contradictory meaning discussed in §6; rather, it affirms that 'nothingness' does not mean 'being' (as precisely stated in §5), i.e. it requires the non-existence of a contradiction in the meaning 'nothingness' that is a moment of the self-contradictory meaning. The non-being that appears in the formulation of the principle of non-contradiction as a negation of being is precisely a non-being that stands as a moment of non-being understood as a self-contradictory meaning.

The aporias formulated in §1 and §3 arise, on the one hand, as a result of the failure to recognize the correct meaning of the self-contradictoriness of the meaning 'nothingness', and, on the other hand, as a result of the abstract consideration of the moments of that self-contradictoriness. It should be observed that this 'self-contradictoriness' is not equivalent to a 'meaninglessness': if that were the case, the meaninglessness of nothingness would determine the meaninglessness of being – unless by meaninglessness one understands self-contradictoriness itself.

8. Solution of the aporia formulated in §1

In relation to the first aporia outlined earlier, we shall therefore respond by acknowledging that, certainly, nothingness is – but not in the sense that 'nothingness' means 'being': in this sense, nothingness is not, and being is, and it is this non-being of nothingness and this being of being that are affirmed by the principle of non-contradiction. Indeed, asserting that 'nothingness' is absolutely not meaningful as 'being' is equivalent to asserting that nothingness is not. It is therefore asserted that nothingness is in the sense that a positive signification – a *being* – is meaningful as the absolutely negative, i.e. precisely as 'nothingness': that is to say, it is meaningful as that 'nothingness' that is absolutely not meaningful as 'being'. Therefore, nothingness is in the sense that the absolutely negative is positively meaningful; or, equivalently, nothingness is in the sense that the meaning of 'nothingness' is a self-contradictory meaning. The two sides or moments of this self-contradictoriness, as already remarked, are *being* (the positive signification) and *nothingness*, as a *non-contradictory* meaning (precisely because this nothingness-moment is absolutely not meaningful as 'being').

While, therefore, the meaning 'nothingness' contradicts the positivity of its signification (or while the absolutely negative is contradicted by the positivity of its own signification), it is precisely by virtue of this contradiction – which is a self-contradiction insofar as the meaning 'nothingness' is regarded as a synthesis of that positivity and that signifying content – that the principle of non-contradiction can exist. That is to say, in order to exclude that being is not – i.e. that being is non-being – it is necessary that non-being should be: i.e. it is necessary that the self-contradictory meaning constituted by that being of non-being should exist. If the meaning 'nothingness' did not consist of this self-contradictoriness – i.e. if it were not the case that nothingness is, in the sense that must be correctly recognized – and if nothingness were therefore only that absolute negativity on account of which nothingness stands as a non-contradictory meaning ('nothingness' *qua* moment of self-contradictoriness), excluding that being is nothingness would mean not excluding anything, since there would be no term to which the exclusion would apply: nothingness would not even appear. (It is also clear, however, that the very supposition that nothingness should only be that absolute negativity on account of which nothingness stands as a non-contradictory meaning is itself a self-contradictory supposition, in that it is possible to assert that nothingness is nothing at all to the extent that nothingness is *manifest*, and it therefore *is* this being nothing at all.)

Affirming that a contradiction is the condition of the constitution of the principle of non-contradiction does not, however, mean affirming that the negation of that principle is the condition of its constitution – this being instead the sense in which, in §1, a contradiction was posited as the ground of that principle – but it rather means that the principle of non-contradiction only constitutes itself insofar as nothingness obtains as a self-contradictory meaning. This self-contradictoriness is indeed posited *as such*, and it is therefore not allowed to exist as something non-contradictory; that is to say, every positive signification is posited as something that – in order not to be realized as a self-contradictoriness – must stand as the signification of a positive determination. Or, equivalently, every *being* must stand as the being of a positive determination (or essence). Nothingness is instead posited as what cannot have any positivity: 'nothingness' means 'nothingness', and, therefore, nothingness cannot even have any semantic significance or positivity. If nothingness is nothingness, nothingness is not, and it does not mean anything: i.e. it therefore cannot even *appear*. In this respect, nothingness does not constitute itself as a self-contradictory meaning, and the principle of non-contradiction precisely affirms this being-nothing of nothingness.

The constitution of the principle of non-contradiction does not therefore require that the self-contradictoriness of the meaning 'nothingness' should not be superseded,[6] but it rather requires the semantic domain constituted by this self-contradictory meaning. In other words, that principle does not require that there should exist no self-contradictory meanings but that self-contradictoriness itself should exist as superseded, or, equivalently, that principle only realizes itself insofar as that self-contradictory meaning does so.

If it is by virtue of this self-contradictoriness that it is possible to affirm that being is not non-being – this non-being, let us repeat, consisting of the non-contradictory meaning of 'non-being' *qua* self-contradictory meaning – this means that nothingness is nothingness, as required by the principle of non-contradiction, only insofar as nothingness (which, *qua* nothingness, does not present a contradictory signification) is a semantic moment of nothingness *qua* self-contradictory meaning.

9. Clarifications of the reasons that determine the aporia

The aporia of nothingness arises insofar as the two abstract moments of the concreteness constituted by 'nothingness' *qua* self-contradictory meaning are abstractly conceived of as being unrelated to one another. Insofar as these two moments are instead concretely conceived, the nothingness-moment is not a self-contradictory meaning: precisely because that self-contradictoriness pertains to the concrete, of which that nothingness-moment is a moment.

That concreteness is such to the extent that the abstract is *superseded* as to its being abstractly conceived. If nothingness, *qua* abstract moment of that self-contradictoriness, is in turn regarded as a synthesis of the two abstract moments of being and nothingness, it is posited as *that very* concreteness of which it was a moment. This positing is simply a *repetition* of the previous positing of that concreteness. Accordingly, it will be necessary to repeat the superseding of the abstract; and if non-being, *qua* abstract moment of this repeated concreteness, is once again posited as a synthesis of being and nothingness, a second repetition will occur.

The acceptance of an *actually* infinite repetition entails that the meaning 'nothingness' is not posited, and, therefore, that being is not posited either, since the positing of being entails the positing of nothingness; furthermore, since the positing of every meaning entails the positing of being, this implies that nothing is posited.

Even leaving aside the consequences of the acceptance of an actually infinite repetition, the affirmation of that repetition is, as such, inherently contradictory. For, indeed, on the one hand, it lets what is projected to be part of an infinite repetition subsist *as something posited* – for, in order to be projected in this way, it must be somehow posited– and, on the other hand, precisely by virtue of the content of that project, what is projected *must not be posited*: for, otherwise, the infinite repetition would be limited by the superseding of that abstract moment, which is not in turn posited as a repetition of the concrete.

The exclusion of an actually infinite repetition of the semantic concreteness of nothingness therefore entails that nothingness itself must be posited – and, therefore, concretely posited as a self-contradictory meaning. As mentioned, this concrete positing furthermore entails the superseding of the abstract concept of the abstract moments of being and nothingness: this nothingness, *qua* abstract meaning, signifying – by virtue of the exclusion of that infinite repetition – *only* 'nothingness' and not, in turn, a synthesis of being and nothingness.

The aporetic argument, on the contrary, keeps the two moments of that self-contradictoriness abstractly separated, and in considering that nothingness-moment precisely finds the latter as something that can be considered, and that therefore *is*: that is to say, it precisely finds what it wished to disregard (i.e. the other moment) in abstractly considering that nothingness-moment; it finds the being of nothingness.

It is then clear that the aporia arises insofar as the nothingness-moment is *and at the same time* is not regarded as a moment. For, indeed, if one were to simply not consider that nothingness-moment as a moment so that what pertains to the concrete were to simply appear again in relation to that moment, one would be precisely and only dealing with a *repetition* of the positing of that self-contradictoriness – a repetition that, nevertheless, would be self-contradictory to the extent that it did not intend to be such. The nothingness-moment would appear again, *qua* non-contradictory meaning, as part of this self-contradictoriness. The aporetic argument, however, precludes that reappearance from taking place: that is to say, it prevents nothingness from (re)constituting itself as a non-contradictory meaning – precisely to the extent that, as mentioned, in addition to not considering that nothingness-moment as a moment, it also considers it as a moment. The fact that it does not consider it as a moment, but as the concrete itself, has just been discussed: the self-contradictoriness of the moment is identified to the extent that the moment itself is regarded as the concrete. The nothingness-moment, however, is at the same time regarded by the aporetic argument as a moment, for it is only insofar as nothingness is a moment that it stands as something that cannot be in turn regarded as the synthesis of a positive signification and of nothingness *qua* non-contradictory meaning; accordingly, if that self-contradictoriness is referred by the aporetic argument to the nothingness-moment *qua* moment, nothingness *only* appears as a self-contradictory meaning (and not as that self-contradictoriness that, in being analysed, reveals a 'nothingness' that is a non-contradictory meaning). In summary, once the moments of the concrete are abstractly considered as unrelated to one another, the nothingness-moment is regarded as that self-contradictoriness that pertains to the concrete – that is to say, the abstract is regarded as the concrete; at the same time, however, the abstract is regarded as something abstract, for the self-contradictoriness that is seen to pertain to it cannot be analysed into a 'nothingness' *qua* non-contradictory meaning, and this impossibility precisely indicates that what had been regarded as the concrete is regarded as something abstract (since something that cannot be further analysed is an abstract moment). This self-contradictoriness of nothingness is then understood by the aporetic argument in the sense excluded in §5.

The non-contradictoriness of nothingness – nothingness *qua* nothingness – therefore only manifests itself insofar as nothingness is held firm as a moment of nothingness *qua* self-contradictory meaning. For if one again argues that, therefore, nothingness *qua* nothingness 'manifests itself', and it therefore *is*, it must be *repeated* that this manifestation, this being, is precisely the other moment of the concrete self-contradictoriness. 'Nothingness is not, and it is therefore not even able to manifest itself; nothingness is the absolutely negative': all of this may be asserted only insofar as it is *held firm as a moment* of that self-contradictoriness – the other moment being the positive signification of the content of this assertion. To the extent that the two moments are distinct, the second one is not included in the first one *as distinct from the second* – whence nothingness is left in its absolute or uncorrupted negativity.

10. Solution of the aporia formulated in §3

For what concerns the second aporetic direction (§4), the abstract moments of the self-contradictoriness are once again considered abstractly. Except that, while in the first aporetic direction the abstract moment constituted by the positive signification – which is disregarded in abstractly considering the nothingness moment – once again appears as part of the nothingness-moment, as part of this second direction, disregarding that moment entails that the latter is altogether lost sight of; as a result, with the absolute negativity of nothingness in the foreground – i.e. nothingness *qua* non-contradictory meaning, whereby it cannot even stand as something present – one recognizes the impossibility of any relation (such as the one that would be realized by the principle of non-contradiction) with that absolute negativity: namely, with what, *qua* such negativity, cannot even manifest itself.

It is clear that, once again, the aporia can constitute itself insofar as the moment of the positive signification of 'nothingness' is completely lost sight of (*in actu signato*), and, at the same time, it is not (*in actu exercito*). Were this moment completely absent, or not posited, the aporetic argument would also not take place: 'nothingness' would remain ignored, for to speak of it would precisely constitute the presence of a moment that is instead absolutely disregarded. That is to say, that absolute disregarding takes place insofar as, in abstractly considering the non-contradictory moment of nothingness, one rules out the possibility of any relation with the absolutely negative – and, at the same time, that absolute disregarding does not take place, precisely insofar as that absolute negativity *is considered*, and it is therefore implicitly kept in relation to the moment of its positive signification, which is, however, supposed to be absolutely disregarded.

The aporia states: being entails and does not entail a certain horizon (the horizon of nothingness) (§3). It is now clear that the aporia arises to the extent that, in the second side of this antinomy, nothingness, which is the abstract moment of nothingness *qua* concrete meaning, is abstractly conceived of as being unrelated to the moment of its positive signification: abstract concept of the abstract moment of nothingness. In considering this moment as the horizon of being, and abstractly conceiving that moment (i.e. conceiving it as the whole of the meaning 'nothingness'), it follows that the implication of that moment results in a non-implication.

The superseding of the abstractness of the moments of nothingness *qua* self-contradictory meaning consists in the positing of that abstractness and therefore in the positing of the relation between the abstract moments. Accordingly, being, in excluding non-being (regarded as a non-contradictory meaning) in the relation of non-contradiction, excludes in fact something *distinct* from the positivity constituted by the other moment of the self-contradictoriness, but not something *unrelated* to that moment. As something distinct, that nothingness-moment is not something self-contradictory, and it can therefore be posited in a relation of contradiction with being; precisely because this nothingness-moment is something distinct and not something unrelated to that other moment, however, it does not follow that being, in referring to this nothingness moment as part of the relation of non-contradiction, does not in fact refer to it. That is to say, being, in referring to nothingness, excludes it as its contradictory only insofar as it refers to that nothingness-moment: a moment that, however, is in relation with the moment of its positive signification, and that, by virtue of this relation – which constitutes the very self-contradictoriness of 'nothingness' *qua* concrete meaning – *is capable of* or *tolerates* standing in a relation of contradiction with being.[7]

11. Notes on the concrete and abstract concepts of nothingness *qua* abstract moment

a. According to what has been said in §10, we are also able to resolve an aporia that is analogous to the one presented in §3. One may indeed state if nothingness is an absolute negativity, it cannot even stand as a *semantic moment* of nothingness *qua* concrete meaning.

It is clear that in this case, too, the aporia arises insofar as the nothingness-moment is abstractly conceived of as unrelated to its being or positive signification. Insofar as the distinction of the moments is regarded as their abstract separation, nothingness, *qua* absolute negativity, can certainly not even stand as a moment of a semantic concreteness. It must therefore be stated that this absolute negativity can distinguish itself from its positive signification and stand as a semantic moment precisely insofar as the very positivity of this counting as a moment is the other moment – i.e. is the other moment of nothingness *qua* concrete and self-contradictory meaning. That is to say, it is the same positive signification – or, more precisely, it belongs to the structure of the same positive signification – of the absolute negative: a positive signification with which the negative must be kept in relation in order for the concrete concept not to become the abstract concept of the abstract. Nothingness is a moment insofar as that distinction is not a separation; accordingly, that from which the negative is distinguished is precisely that (its) positivity, which allows it to count as a moment. At the same time, however, 'nothingness' as distinct from the positivity of its signification, to the extent that it is regarded with respect to the meaning that pertains to it insofar as it is thus distinct, does not count as a moment (as something positive): precisely because, as an absolute negativity, it does not count as anything. Nothingness is certainly meaningful as an absolute negativity insofar as it *is* a moment: this very *being*, however, belongs to the horizon that is excluded by that absolute negativity. Its *being* a moment is precisely the *other* moment; or, more precisely, its very *being* a moment belongs to the structure of its positive signification.

The absolutely other than being, *qua other than being*, is not a being; insofar as it *is meaningful* as the absolutely other than being, however, it is a being or a positivity. The positivity of this meaningfulness is not included in, or it does not determine, what this meaningfulness means. The contradiction of 'nothingness' precisely lies in the fact that a meaningfulness is the meaningfulness of the absolutely meaningless: it does not lie in the fact that the meaningless means the meaningful (i.e. has the meaning of 'meaningful') but that the meaningless *is meaningful* as the meaningless.

Nothingness, as such, is the meaningless (a non-being). The meaningless, however, is not separated from its being meaningful as the meaningless: it is only in its *being* meaningful that nothingness means 'the absolutely other than meaning' ('the absolutely other than being'). The meaning 'nothingness' is not abstractly separated but concretely distinct from the positivity of its signification. As distinct, it is able to mean the absolutely other than being and, at the same time, to stand as a moment (and, therefore, as a positivity that is a moment) of the contradiction constituted by the concrete meaning of nothingness.

In other words, nothingness is that which is affirmed to be meaningful, positive, a being. Insofar as it is the subject of this affirmation, nothingness is a moment. This being meaningful, positive, a being is the other moment of the concrete meaning of nothingness. Precisely because nothingness is that which is affirmed *to be* meaningful, positive, a being, it is correct to state that it does not include in its meaning the positive signification of its own meaning (that is to say, 'nothingness' does not mean 'being', i.e. nothingness as such is not being, but the absolutely other than being); however, it is also correct to state that this meaning of nothingness – insofar as it is *that whose* positive signification is affirmed (namely, insofar as it is that which is precisely affirmed to *be*, i.e. to be meaningful, positive, a being) – is able to count as a moment of the contradiction constituted by the concrete meaning of nothingness. Nothingness is able to count as a moment because what 'nothingness' signifies is distinct, and not separated, from the positivity of this signification.

Nothingness, in its concrete meaning, is the contradiction of a nothingness-that-is; this being of nothingness, however, which allows nothingness to be a moment, is posited in the other moment (or as the other moment) of that concrete meaning; and precisely because it is posited in or as the other moment, the nothingness-moment can be a meaning in which what is posited is only the absolutely other than every being (and, therefore, also other than that being constituted by the being of nothingness *qua* moment).

b. Furthermore, if one were to argue that: the distinct terms must be related; nothingness, however, *qua* distinct term, is an absolute negativity; therefore, it cannot *be* in any relation – one would need to respond that, in this way, the distinct terms are regarded as being presupposed to their synthesis, and, therefore, they are once again considered abstractly. If the distinct terms are at first regarded as separated, no synthesis between the positive and the negative will certainly be possible at a later point: the negative, as such, will not even have any positional significance on the basis of which a synthesis would be established. Therefore, either there is no awareness of nothingness – and the aporia does not even arise – or, if that awareness exists, the negative is thus already part of a synthesis with the positive. In order for the affirmation of that synthesis not to be a self-contradictory affirmation (i.e. in order for the positing of the self-contradictory meaning constituted by that synthesis not to be an aporetic or self-contradictory affirmation), it is sufficient to conceive that synthesis concretely: namely, as an *originary* or *immediate* synthesis, and not as a result that presupposes the unrelatedness of two distinct terms. If the synthesis is originary, whereby the distinct terms are not regarded as unrelated, the negative can be that absolute negativity that is required by the principle of non-contradiction, and, at the same time, it can be in relation with the positive: since, precisely, the negative is distinct from the positive, but not unrelated to it. Negating that unrelatedness means regarding the relation as originary.

c. It is thus also clarified that nothingness *is* nothingness (as already observed by Gorgias) insofar as the positive signification of nothingness *is* that specific signification that it is, and not insofar as the absolute negative *is* something (even if the absolute negative). Or, equivalently, nothingness *is* nothingness, not *qua* nothingness, but *qua* positive signification.

12. Corollary: Being as the absolute horizon

The character of *absolute horizon* that pertains to *being*, or to the whole, appears from the previous observations. Indeed, being – which, as we shall thoroughly elucidate, is meaningful in relation to the horizon of nothingness – includes its very other in the way that we have outlined; this inclusion is precisely that by virtue of which the whole does not leave anything beside itself.

13. Critical-historical notes on the problem of nothingness

a. The study of 'nothingness', included by Bergson in the last chapter of *L'Évolution créatrice*, is certainly among the most significant ones concerning this question. On the one hand, however, it only indicates the self-contradictoriness of the meaning 'nothingness' – whereby the value of the principle of non-contradiction is compromised – and, on the other hand, it points to the self-contradictoriness of that meaning for reasons other than the ones that must be recognized. For, indeed, according to Bergson the idea of nothingness is '*destructive d'elle-même*', since the positing of the negative entails the positing of the positive that constitutes the content that is being negated: if nothingness is a negation of the positive, the *positing* (the concept, the idea) of the negative results in a positing of the positive – in that this must be posited in order to be superseded.

The first part of the study, which proceeds by gradually eliminating the different ways in which the idea of nothingness has been introduced, ends as follows:

> The idea of absolute nothingness, understood in the sense of an abolishing of everything, is a self-destructive idea, a pseudo-idea, a mere word. If the suppression

of one thing consists in replacing it by another, if thinking the absence of one thing is only possible by the more or less explicit representation of the presence of something else, and finally, if above all else abolishing means substituting, then the idea of 'abolishing everything' is as absurd as the idea of a square circle. This absurdity is not immediately obvious because there is no single object that we cannot imagine abolished. So from the fact that there is nothing to stop the suppression in thought of each thing, one by one, we conclude that it is possible to imagine them all suppressed as a whole. We fail to see that the suppression of each thing, one by one, consists precisely in gradually replacing each one by another, and that as a result the absolute suppression of everything involves a genuine contradiction in terms since this operation would consist in the destruction of the very condition that makes it possible.[8]

As a general conclusion, it is affirmed that 'the idea of Nothing, if we claim to see here the idea of an abolition of all things, is an idea that destroys itself and ... we find in it just as much material as we find in the idea of Everything.'[9]

Bergson never refers to Hegel, but Hegel had particularly insisted precisely on the fact that the negative is richer than the negated positive, for it supersedes it and at the same time preserves it. The meaning 'nothingness' (which is, however, not to be conflated with the 'nothingness' that appears at the beginning of Hegel's *Logic*) therefore consists of a semantic domain that includes the very totality of the positive, as negated or surpassed. Positing nothingness certainly means positing what lies beyond being, and the positing of nothingness therefore includes the positing of being; is there, however, as Bergson claims, a self-contradictoriness to be recognized in this?

It is of crucial interest to observe that the reason why Bergson detects that self-contradictoriness is determined by an abstract consideration of the nothingness-moment. For, indeed, if that nothingness-moment is abstractly separated from the moment of its positive signification, it appears as that absolute negativity whose positing cannot be the positing of anything positive. If, then, one notes that the positing of 'nothingness' even entails the positing of the whole, this implication is regarded as a self-contradictoriness: i.e. as the contradiction between the intention to posit nothing positive and the actual positing of the totality of the positive. For if one wished to exonerate Bergson from that abstract consideration – thus, however, resisting the explicit meaning of Bergson's text – one would have to argue that the implication of the positing of the positive by the positing of the negative can be regarded as a self-contradiction only insofar as that implication is conflated with the situation in which the meaning 'nothingness' is meaningful as 'being' (as stated in §5); if in order to posit the negative it is necessary to posit the positive, it does not thereby follow that 'nothingness' means 'being'.

Bergson nevertheless comes implicitly close to the authentic meaning of the self-contradictoriness of nothingness, to the extent that – as we have verified – the absolutely negative is positively meaningful (and this is precisely the authentic meaning of that self-contradictoriness), and its signification is, as it were, so positive as to require the very positing of the totality of the positive.

b. One of the greatest merits of the enquiry carried out by Heidegger in *Was ist Metaphysik?* consists in having drawn attention to the fundamental opposition between being and nothingness. The psychologistic contaminations – concentrated on the concept of 'anxiety' – and the anti-intellectualistic stance lie outside that essential indication. Furthermore, those psychologism and anti-intellectualism arise from an inability to resolve the aporia of the positing of non-being – which consists, as explicitly recognized by Heidegger, in the contradictoriness of a non-being that is.

Particularly significant is the aporia – emphasized and employed by Heidegger in order to essentially determine the development of the enquiry – that consists in observing that non-being, *qua* intellectualistic negation of the totality of being, presupposes a comprehension or presence of the totality of being: a presence, Heidegger warns, which is impossible in its all-comprehensiveness or concrete determinacy, or which is only possible as something *ideal*, as the presence of the *idea* of that totality – in such a way that non-being would only stand as a *formal* negation of being. What difference is there, however, between a formal and a real nothingness? Hence the project to depart from the plane of logic in order to realize an experience of nothingness.

Except that it is clear that, in Heidegger's argument, the affirmation that the totality is only present as an idea (i.e. in a formal or non-comprehensive way) is equivalent to simply *presupposing* the fact that the totality is further determined with respect to that originary determination of the whole constituted by experience. That further determination is the *in-itself* that remains impossible to be known. (A corresponding element to this logical situation may be identified in Jaspers's concept of the *Umgreifende*, *qua* non-objectifiable horizon.)

At the same time, however, since we shall independently come to exhibit this further determination of the whole that is simply presupposed by Heidegger, it should be added that a negation of the formal whole certainly differs from a negation of the concrete whole, but this difference entails that *one must* speak of a formal nothingness and of a real one, in the sense that the distinction between formality and reality pertains to the *positive signification* of nothingness, and not to nothingness as distinct from this positivity. The absolutely negative is not or does not mean anything positive: both in case the positivity that is posited as superseded in the concept of nothingness has a formal value and in case it has a concrete value. For, indeed, the positive is superseded or surpassed in the concept of nothingness as the *whole* of the positive in such a way that any possible identification of the concrete determinations of this formal positing of the whole certainly entails a modification of the positive signification of nothingness, but it does not entail that the absolutely negative should not be truly such because the positive that is superseded is not manifest in an adequate way. Assuming that the manifestation of the positive is a process that gradually concretizes itself, this increment is certainly at the same time an increment *of the positive signification* of nothingness, but it is not an increment of nothingness regarded as distinct from its positive signification. Accordingly, in this respect, there is no difference between a formal and a real nothingness.

Heidegger, too, therefore abstractly considers the nothingness-moment as unrelated to its positive signification, and through a particular implementation of Bergson's position, he observes the inconsistency of the distinction between a formal and a real nothingness – since, due to that abstract consideration, the positive signification that is abstractly disregarded resurfaces as part of the nothingness-moment itself, thus giving rise to the aporia. Bergson therefore asserts the inconsistency of the absolute positivity of nothingness; Heidegger, complementing Bergson's position, asserts the inconsistency of the distinction between a formal and a real nothingness. According to Bergson, what determines the aporia is only that resurfacing of the positive as part of the nothingness-moment; according to Heidegger, the aporia is determined by the further observation that this resurfacing positive has a formal value, whereby this formal character and the ensuing distinction between formality and reality are attributed to nothingness as such.

c. The aporia of nothingness is not determined by a simple linguistic misconception. If instead of stating: 'Beyond or outside being there is nothing', one were to state: 'There is no positive element that lies outside the totality of the positive'; or, in symbols: '~ ($\exists$ x). x lies outside the totality of the positive' (the variable x being precisely able to take any positive value), one would still need to clarify the meaning of that 'outside the totality of the positive', which is precisely the nothingness that, with its presence, gives rise to the aporia. With good reason, Carnap asserts (*Überwindung der Metaphysik*) that in his enquiry into nothingness Heidegger is simply hypostatizing a logical form. (Furthermore, it may be added that Heidegger, as well as Schopenhauer before him and Sartre and others after him, makes an inappropriate use of the word 'nothingness' to indicate *a specific* dimension of the positive, which, certainly, *is not* another specific dimension, but it is not the *nihil absolutum*.) In the proposition: '~ ($\exists$ x). x lies outside', however, Carnap does not distinguish the following two logical situations: the one in which the variable x takes a limited number of positive values (in such a way that that relative to which x is 'outside' or 'beyond' is a limited dimension of the positive) and the one in which, as discussed earlier, x may take *all* positive values (in such a way that that relative to which x is 'outside' is the very totality of the positive). It is precisely as part of this second case that nothingness (that which lies outside the whole) *manifests itself* – precisely insofar as, in the proposition: '~ ($\exists$ x). x lies outside the totality of the positive', the meaning 'outside the totality of the positive' is manifest.

14. Nothingness and contradiction

Self-contradictoriness – every self-contradictory meaning – is nothingness itself. In order to elucidate this theorem, let us for instance consider the following meanings: 'Non-triangular triangle', 'Non-red red', 'non-here here', 'x is not x', and so on. (Let us indicate with the symbol RnR any of these meanings; R indicates any determination, and n indicates the negation of that determination.) Positing any of these self-contradictory meanings means *positing nothingness*. For, indeed, of *no* positive element can it be stated that it is a non-triangular triangle, a non-red red, a non-here here, an x that is not x, and so on. The principle of non-contradiction, in affirming that being is not non-being (this non-being counting both as an absolute negativity and as the contradictory *of a specific* positive), precisely rules out the possibility that a positive should be self-contradictory, or that self-contradictoriness itself should *be*. Being is being; accordingly, self-contradictoriness is nothingness itself: a being that is not (or a being that is its contradictory) *is not*.

However, in the same way in which *positing* nothingness is not equivalent to *not positing anything*, so positing this self-contradictoriness is not equivalent to not positing anything. Self-contradictory meanings are indeed *present*, and they therefore *are*. The aporia of the *being* of self-contradictoriness is *the same* aporia of the being of nothingness. This means that – as for the meaning 'nothingness' – the meaning 'self-contradictoriness' is a self-contradictory meaning.

Let us briefly outline the course of the solution of the aporia. Self-contradictoriness is: not in the sense, however, that a self-contradictory meaning is meaningful as a non-contradictoriness – i.e. not in the sense that, for instance, RnR is or means $RnnR$ (whereby R is equivalent to the negation of its negation) – and nor in the sense that the positive signification of that self-contradictoriness is not a positive signification. A self-contradictory meaning is *non-contradictorily* meaningful as that self-contradictoriness that it is; the nullity of self-contradictoriness is not or does not mean a non-nullity; self-contradictoriness is not or does not mean self-contradictoriness and, at the same time, non-contradictoriness. It is then precisely this self-contradictoriness, which is non-contradictorily meaningful, that *is*, i.e. that is positively meaningful. It is thus verified that this self-contradictoriness, i.e. the absolutely negative, is non-contradictorily or positively meaningful. Self-contradictoriness is non-contradictorily meaningful, or, *which is the same*, the absolutely negative is positively meaningful: this is the self-contradictoriness whose two *moments* are the self-contradictory meaning (= the self-contradictoriness-moment) and the non-contradictory or positive signification of that self-contradictory meaning. Positing, for instance, the meaning RnR means positing a self-contradictory meaning whose moments are the self-contradictory meaning RnR and the positive signification of this meaning. (These moments respectively correspond in the self-contradictory meaning 'nothingness' to the nothingness-moment and to its positive signification.) These are therefore *distinct* moments, but not *unrelated* ones. We have thus clarified the condition by virtue of which it is possible to speak of a *being* of self-contradictoriness, and the condition by virtue of which self-contradictoriness itself is on the one hand *nothingness*, and on the other hand it is *superseded*, i.e. it stands in a (positive) relation with the positive. The reader may further develop and resolve this twofold aporetic direction outlined in the previous sections.

This whole argument has nothing to do with A. Meinong's position, which simply consists in attesting that the meanings of the type RnR must have a certain mode of existence (*Sosein*) in order for their existence (*Dasein*) to be negated. That is to say, according to Meinong, self-contradictoriness, too – i.e. *the content* of the self-contradictory affirmation – *is*. What Meinong believes to be a theory is nothing but the statement of the aporia of the being of self-contradictoriness. Russel's observation, according to which that theory constitutes a violation of the principle of non-contradiction, is therefore correct. However, in the same way in which the aporia of nothingness (or self-contradictoriness) is not resolved by Frege, nor is it resolved by Russell, for his affirmation that 'the null-class is the class containing no members, not the class containing as members all unreal individuals'[10] only seemingly avoids Meinong's contradiction. For, indeed, that 'not containing any member' is, as Frege's 'meaninglessness', something positively meaningful, i.e. it is the very positive signification of nothingness. Russell's theory, too, therefore fails to move beyond the statement of the aporia.

15. Aporia and solution: The twofold sense of self-contradiction

a. What we have observed in §14 affords the formulation of the following aporia:

> The positing of the meaning *RnR* is, as discussed, the positing of a self-contradictory meaning, whose semantic moments are *RnR* and the positive signification of *RnR*. Let *r'nr'* be this new self-contradictory meaning. If *r'nr'* is self-contradictory, however, it will be necessary – according to what has been established in the previous section – to state that the self-contradictoriness *r'nr'*, too, is a nothingness; accordingly, if positing *RnR* means positing *r'nr'*, positing *r'nr'* means positing that self-contradictory meaning *r''nr''* whose semantic moments are *r'nr'* and the positive signification of *r'nr'*. The same must then be stated for what concerns the positing of the self-contradictory meaning *r''nr''*. It therefore follows that the positing of the meaning *RnR* is the positing of the infinite series of self-contradictory meanings *r'nr'*, *r''nr''*, *r'''nr'''*, … This entails that the meaning *RnR* cannot be posited, since, precisely, its positing requires an infinite development.

The aporia may be formulated by considering the meaning 'nothingness' instead of the meaning *RnR*:

> If the positing of this meaning is the positing of nothingness, regarded as a concrete self-contradictoriness (which corresponds to the *r'nr'* of the previous formulation, and which can therefore itself be indicated by the symbol *r'nr'*), the semantic moments of which are a nothingness-moment and the positive signification of this nothingness-moment, that concrete self-contradictoriness, too, will be a nothingness; accordingly, its positing will be the positing of a self-contradictory meaning whose semantic moments are that concrete self-contradictoriness and its positive signification. That is to say, the very synthesis between the absolutely negative and its positive signification is, *qua* self-contradictoriness (= *r'nr'*), something absolutely negative, whose positing is the positing of a more concrete self-contradictory meaning (*r''nr''*), which includes that synthesis and its positive signification as moments. One may then conclude as above.

b. A first type of solution of the aporia could be as follows: precisely because *every* self-contradictoriness is nothingness itself, there exists no difference between the terms of the series *RnR*, *r'nr'*, *r''nr''*, *r'''nr'''*, … and the nothingness-moment. Accordingly, in this respect not only there exists no possibility of an infinite development, but there does not even exist the possibility of any development. Before proceeding, let us briefly develop this first point.

There is only a verbal difference between the positing of the meaning 'nothingness' and the positing of any self-contradictory meaning – and, therefore, between the positing of the meaning 'nothingness' and the positing of any term of the series RnR, $r'nr'$, $r''nr''$, $r'''nr'''$, ... For, indeed, on the one hand, positing nothingness means positing the totality of the positive as surpassed (a totality that also includes the positive signification of not only nothingness but of the terms of that series); and the positing of a term of the series, e.g. RnR, is in turn the positing of something that lies beyond the totality of the positive (a totality that also includes the positive signification of not only the terms of the series but also of nothingness). If, in positing RnR, it is not posited (i.e. known) that in positing RnR one posits what lies beyond the totality of the positive, the positing of RnR results in an implicit negation of the principle of non-contradiction. (In a different respect, if self-contradictoriness itself is in its essence equivalent to nothingness, positing this self-contradictoriness while not positing it as nothingness means not positing it since that self-contradictoriness is in its essence precisely that nothingness. As a result, only the *intention* of positing it is realized: one asserts that it is being posited, while in fact it is not – and that assertion is a self-contradictory affirmation in that it is equivalent to affirming that something that is not a self-contradictoriness is one.)

At the same time, however – as already mentioned – if the manifestation of the positive consists of a development (we shall have to return with particular attention to this concept of development, as well as to the concept of the totality of the positive), one may distinguish different levels of this development. This distinction is the distinction of different levels of the positive signification of 'nothingness'. It is therefore possible to project a level of this signification in which RnR is not yet included in that horizon of the positive, which is implied by the concept of nothingness as superseded, or another level, in which RnR is included in that horizon. However, the difference that arises in this way between the positing of the meaning 'nothingness' and the positing of the meaning RnR has the same value as the difference that obtains between two acts of positing of the meaning 'nothingness' that includes the totality of the positive according to a different individuation or determination of the latter.

c. Resuming: as discussed, there exists no difference between nothingness and the terms of the series RnR, $r'nr'$, $r''nr''$, $r'''nr'''$, ... (Or, equivalently, there exists no difference between RnR and the terms of that series. The argument may be unfolded in these two ways because an infinite development arises both in considering nothingness and in considering any self-contradictory meaning RnR.)

One may, however, respond that, while that difference does not exist, there is still a difference between the positive significations of those equivalent terms: if nothingness, as much as every self-contradictoriness (and, therefore, also every self-contradictoriness constituted by each of the terms of that series) is nothingness, it is nevertheless the case that nothingness is meaningful in a different way if what is posited is 'nothingness' or if what is posited is any of the terms of that series. It is precisely due to this difference of signification that the aporia may not be avoided.

d. The aporia formulated under point a is superseded only if one distinguishes two types or senses of self-contradictoriness: the contradiction (contradicting oneself) and the content of the contradiction (the content asserted by the contradiction). If this distinction is not in place – as it precisely happens in the aporetic argument – it will be necessary to affirm that the meaning 'nothingness' cannot be posited. Consider these two self-contradictory meanings: (1) 'Non-red red' (let this be xnx); (2) 'Nothingness' (let this be εN), regarded as a self-contradictory meaning: i.e. not as nothingness-moment. What has been established in §14 concerning self-contradictory meanings is then valid for xnx but not for εN. Indeed, as already mentioned, εN is not a self-contradictory meaning to the extent that being (ε) is predicated of nothingness (N), but to the extent that what is predicated of nothingness (namely, its being other than the totality of the positive) is; that is to say, being is not here predicated (since the predicate consists in excluding that being should be predicated), but it is the being *of* the predicate. In other words, the proposition: 'Nothingness is' has a different meaning according to whether one understands that 'Nothingness, *qua nothingness*, is' or that 'Nothingness is not nothingness'. The first meaning is the one according to which that proposition precisely counts as εN, while the second one is what is excluded not only by the principle of non-contradiction but also by the contradiction: 'Nothingness, *qua* nothingness, is' (which does indeed refer being to nothingness – and, in this sense, it in turn affirms that nothingness is not nothingness – but it refers being to nothingness posited as nothingness, i.e. as the other than the totality of the positive, and not as a non-nothingness). It is therefore clear that while it is correct to state that xnx is nothingness itself (cf. §14), it is not correct (i.e. it is self-contradictory) to affirm that εN is nothingness: since being, the positive signification of nothingness, is not nothing. It is effectively the case that thinking or positing nothingness means positing something, i.e. a positivity, and, since the determinacy or the meaning of this positivity is the absolutely other than the positive, it is correct to state that what one thinks is a self-contradictory meaning; this self-contradictoriness, however, contrary to xnx, is not a nothingness but something positive: it is the positivity of contradicting oneself. What has been established for εN is then to be repeated for the self-contradictory meaning whose moments are xnx and the positive signification of xnx: this self-contradictoriness, too, is indeed not a nothingness, but something positive.

From what has been discussed, it is clear that all the self-contradictions (type 2) whose moments are either nothingness (*qua* moment) and the positive signification of nothingness or a self-contradictoriness (such as xnx or RnR) and its positive signification are not nothingness. What is a nothingness (cf. §14) are all those self-contradictions (type 1) in which the self-contradictoriness is constituted within a meaning (or, more precisely, is constituted as the meaning itself) – i.e. those self-contradictions in which the mutually contradictory terms are moments of a meaning: contrary to the self-contradictions of type 2, in which the mutually contradictory terms are a meaning (which is either a nothingness-moment or a self-contradiction of type 1) and its positive signification.

Thanks to this distinction the aporia under consideration is resolved: the series RnR, $r'nr'$, $r''nr''$, $r'''nr'''$ ... is indeed not homogeneous, since RnR is a self-contradiction of type 1, whereas all the other terms of the series are self-contradictions of type

2. Therefore, if the positing of RnR necessarily coincides with the positing of $r'nr'$ – for RnR is nothingness, and positing RnR is thus equivalent to positing the positive signification of the absolutely negative (this being precisely the positing of $r'nr'$) – the positing of $r'nr'$ does not instead coincide with the positing of a $r''nr''$, which would be in the same relation to $r'nr'$ as $r'nr'$ is to RnR: for, indeed, $r'nr'$ is a self-contradiction of type 2, i.e. it is not a nothingness whose positing must therefore coincide with the positing of $r''nr''$. The infinite development identified by the aporetic argument cannot therefore be realized; or, more precisely, the necessity of that development does not obtain.

Corollary: the self-contradiction expressed by the proposition: 'Nothingness is not nothingness' is of type 1; accordingly, the positing of this self-contradiction is the positing of a self-contradiction of type 2, whose moments are that proposition and its positive signification.

5

The structure of the totality of the Ph-immediate

1. The totality of the Ph-immediate: Scheme

The totality of the Ph-immediate[1] is posited (i.e. it appears, it is present) insofar as:

1. 'Being' (the concrete positive content that is immediately present) is *posited*. Let us call this the 'ontic positing'.
2. The immediacy (the immediate presence) of being is *posited*. Let us call this the 'exponential positing'.

The ontic positing consists, on the one hand, in the positing *of the particular determinations* $d_1, d_2, d_3, ..., d_n$ that Ph-immediately pertain to being (or whose being is Ph-immediate), and, on the other hand, it consists in the positing *of the being* of these determinations. The synthesis of these two sides constitutes the concreteness that pertains to the ontic positing as such.

The exponential positing is, on the one hand, the positing of the Ph-immediacy *of the single* determinations of the ontic positing: Ph-im. (d_1), Ph-im. (d_2), Ph-im. (d_3), ..., Ph-im. (d_n), and, on the other hand, it is the positing *of the totality* of the Ph-immediate: i.e. it is the positing of the totality of appearing. The positing of the totality of the Ph-immediate is the very positing of the Ph-immediacy of the ontic positing.

Let us refer to $d_1, ..., d_n$ as the 'ontic series', and to Ph-im. $(d_1), ...,$ Ph-im. (d_n) as the 'exponential series'.

2. Note: The form and the content of the totality of the Ph-immediate

It can be stated that the ontic positing and the exponential series constitute the positing of the *content* of the totality of the Ph-immediate, whereas the second side of the exponential positing constitutes the positing of the *form* of that totality. The latter positing is the positing of the way or mode in which the content is posited, i.e. precisely as the totality of the Ph-immediate.

The second side of the exponential positing includes, and at the same time is distinct from, the previous types of positing. To the extent that it includes them, it is the very positing of the totality of the Ph-immediate in its concreteness (*qua* unity of form and content); to the extent that it is distinct from them, it is the positing of the form as an abstract moment of the concrete.

More generally, insofar as the indicated types of positing are mutually distinct, they constitute the abstract content of the totality of the Ph-immediate. The concrete positing of this totality consists in the positing of that abstractness.

3. Exclusion of an immediate element exceeding the totality of the Ph-immediate

Precisely insofar as the concrete positing of the Ph-immediate is a synthesis of a formal positing and a material one, it must furthermore be asserted that the *totality* of the Ph-immediate is posited *as such* only insofar as one posits the exclusion of the fact that any element exceeding that totality should be immediately present – however that element may be determined. If this exclusion is not posited, even admitting that a positional horizon persists despite this positional *steresis*, this horizon cannot be posited *as* the totality of the Ph-immediate. The implication between the positing of the totality and the positing of that exclusion is analytic: that is to say, the concept of totality L-*immediately* includes the concept of that exclusion.

Positing an Ph-immediate element that is not a *moment* of the totality of the Ph-immediate is therefore inherently self-contradictory: *in one respect*, because that Ph-immediate element, insofar as it exceeds the totality of the Ph-immediate, would not be something Ph-immediate; *in a second respect*, because that totality, *qua* thus exceeded, would not be the totality of the Ph-immediate.

(What has been stated in this section in relation to the totality of the Ph-immediate may be referred with the necessary modifications to the totality *simpliciter* of the immediate.)

4. Paradigmatic note

a. The possibility of distinguishing those *two respects* of the contradiction caused by the affirmation that an immediate element exceeds the totality of the immediate[2] is grounded in the possibility – shared by all instances analogous to the present one – *of holding firm* either one or the other of the two terms that constitute the content of the contradiction in its being determined as that which it is: either the exceeding immediate element or the totality of the immediate. This is the possibility of holding firm – whenever the contradiction in question arises – that which is the exceeding immediate element *as* the exceeding immediate element or that which is the totality of the immediate *as* the totality of the immediate: i.e. the possibility of preventing the arising of the contradictory terms of (respectively) that exceeding immediate element and that totality of the immediate.

b. Let us hold firm *that which* is referred to as an 'exceeding immediate element' as something non-contradictory; that is to say, let us hold it firm *as* an exceeding immediate element. In affirming that this immediate element exceeds the totality of the immediate, the contradiction takes as its content the totality of the immediate – or, more precisely, the contradiction involves that which is affirmed to be the totality of the immediate. That which is posited as this totality is therefore affirmed and at the same time negated *qua* totality of the immediate. It is thus affirmed to the extent that one intends to posit the exceeding immediate element and, at the same time, the totality of the immediate. It is negated *qua* totality of the immediate to the extent that, precisely, that exceeding immediate element is held firm as something non-contradictory, whereby it is necessary to negate that which is thus exceeded *qua* totality of the immediate.

c. Let us now hold firm *that which* is referred to as the 'totality of the immediate' as something non-contradictory: that is to say, let us hold firm the exclusion of the fact that that which is posited as this totality is not posited as such. In affirming that an immediate element exceeds the totality of the immediate, the contradiction takes as its content this exceeding immediate element, and the latter (= that which is referred to as the 'exceeding immediate element') is affirmed and at the same time negated as such. As to its being thus affirmed, what we stated earlier applies; as to the other side, it is negated as such to the extent that, holding firm that which is predicated as the 'totality of the immediate', it is necessary to posit everything that exceeds the latter as something that is not immediate.

d. What must be remarked here is then the fact that the choice of either one or the other of the two terms in question, as well as of the one that is to be held firm as something non-contradictory, *is not equivalent*.

For, indeed, granted that this 'holding firm' means nothing but to keep referring the formal determinations ('totality of the immediate', 'exceeding immediate element') to that to which they respectively pertain, it follows that an equivalence presupposes the fact that the relation between that which is posited as the totality of the immediate and the 'totality of the immediate' (regarded as a formal determination), as well as the relation between that which is posited as the exceeding immediate element and the 'exceeding immediate element' (regarded as a formal determination), should be considered problematically or abstractly. These two types of considerations, however, have a different value.

e. As to the first type, a problematic situation is caused by the inability to determine whether, in each of the two relations indicated earlier, the formal element *must* stand in relation to the material one. Having posited this problematicity, holding firm either of the two relations – thus letting the remaining one disappear – is equivalent. (The remaining one disappears precisely because one allows the formal determination to no longer pertain to the material one – to which it is nevertheless referred.) Language then adopts the hypothetical form: '*If X* is the totality of the immediate, then that which is referred to as the exceeding immediate element is not such'; '*If y* is the exceeding immediate element, then X, which is affirmed as the totality of the immediate, is not such.'

Except that this problematicity is originarily superseded by the positing of the originary whole. In other words, the positing of the totality of the immediate is the positing of a *content* that is posited as the totality of the immediate – this positing precisely consisting in the originary surpassing of the problematic form of positing, i.e. of the problematicity of the relation between that content and the 'totality of the immediate', *qua* formal designation of that content. (The positing of this totality is therefore also the positing of a multiplicity of immediate contents that exceed those horizons of immediacy, which – precisely insofar as they are thus exceeded – are negated as totalities of the immediate.) The hypothetical form that was used in the problematic situation must then be replaced by the categorical form: '*Since X is the totality of the immediate, y, which aims to be posited as an immediate element exceeding X, does not exceed X; since z is an immediate element that exceeds k, k, which aims to be posited as the totality of the immediate, is not the totality of the immediate*'. This is the concrete way in which the existence of an immediate element that would exceed the totality of the immediate is excluded. In relation to this concreteness, it is no longer equivalent whether it pertains or it does not pertain to X and y to be, respectively, the 'totality of the immediate' and an 'exceeding immediate element'. It is precisely by virtue of this superseding of that equivalence that the term k is introduced as that relative to which y's exceeding may take place (a y that, insofar as it exceeds k, is indicated by the symbol z).

f. At the same time, it must, however, be observed that the equivalence is superseded to the extent that it entails the *problematicity* of the relation between the content and the form of the totality of the immediate and of the exceeding immediate element. At the end of point d, however, it was mentioned that these relations, in addition to being considered problematic, may also be considered to be *abstract*. In this sense, the equivalence is retained but, precisely, in the form of a reference of the abstract to the concrete, which is therefore grounded in the (originary) supersession of the problematicity of those relations.

Indeed, if the exclusion of an immediate element that would exceed the totality of the immediate is considered as to its formal value, the positing of this formal character – and, therefore, the positing of the concrete to which that formal character, posited as such, refers – *retains* that equivalence, as the formal or abstract aspect of the concrete exclusion. In other words, even if the concrete determination or content of the totality of the immediate (or of the immediate element that exceeds a specific dimension of immediacy) is posited, one may (only) consider the *indeterminate content* of this totality (or of that exceeding immediate element), i.e. the content in its being abstracted from or unrelated to its actual and concrete determination. Formal consideration of the content. This consideration leaves that content, as such, indifferent as to its being or not being posited as the content of the formal determination. One then states that 'regardless' of the way in which the content of the totality of the immediate and the content of the exceeding immediate element are determined, it is contradictory for an immediate element to exceed the totality of the immediate.

If a formal consideration of the content affords the constitution of that equivalence or indifference as to whether that formal determination should be referred to the content of the totality of the immediate or to the content of the exceeding immediate element, that consideration does not let the problematicity of the relation between the form and the concrete content of these two terms persist. It does not let it persist to the extent that the formal consideration, insofar as it disregards the concrete determination of the content of the two formal determinations, is not posited as a negation of the fact that the content that concretely pertains to these determinations should pertain to them in a categorical way. For, indeed, disregarding the concrete determination of the content, thus considering the latter as an 'indeterminate content', does not mean affirming that the configuration of that concrete determination is not known. (This lack of knowledge coincides with the very transition from the concrete concept of the abstract to the abstract concept of the abstract – the abstract precisely consisting here in that 'indeterminate content'). For, on the contrary, it is precisely insofar as that concreteness is posited that one may disregard it – the value of this disregarding depending precisely on the presupposition of that concreteness. That is to say, it is legitimate to consider the 'content' as a variable, to the extent that one nevertheless keeps in mind that this variability is actually fixed at a value whose negation is contradictory.

g. It is therefore clear that in affirming that an immediate element y exceeds X – originarily posited as the totality of the immediate – there arises a twofold order of contradictoriness: the 'material' one, whereby the synthetic judgement 'X is the totality of the immediate' is negated, and the 'formal' one, whereby it is affirmed that X is and at the same time is not the totality of the immediate (or, holding X firm as that totality, it is affirmed that y exceeds and at the same time does not exceed that totality).

h. The observations developed here concerning the exceeding immediate element are not inherent to the logical situation in question, but they are to be extended to all the analogous situations that we shall encounter (the most important of which undoubtedly consisting in the exceeding of a being beyond the totality of being).

5. Transition

In relation to the scheme outlined in §1, the following corollaries concerning the relations of inclusion between the ontic positing and the exponential one apply. These corollaries may also be regarded as the summary of a set of questions that will have to be analytically considered.

6. Relations of inclusion between the ontic and exponential modes of positing: a. The ontic series and the exponential series

While all the terms of the exponential series belong to the ontic series, not all the terms of the ontic series belong to the exponential one. Indeed, all those terms in which the immediacy (i.e. the immediate presence) is not posited are excluded – for instance, the acts of positing of the type: 'Here it is yellow', '3 + 3 = 6', and so on. It should be noted that in both cases the term *'belonging'* is regarded univocally.

In other words, the Ph-immediacy (the immediate presence), too, of the single ontic determinations belongs to the series constituted by these determinations (in that this Ph-immediacy, too, is a determination of Ph-immediately known being); on the contrary, not every ontic determination consists in the immediate presence of an ontic determination.

7. b. Ontic series and exponential positing

Insofar as what is posited in the exponential series is the totality of the Ph-immediate, this totality 'belongs' to the ontic series to the extent that it is excluded that any other term should be part of this series: i.e. to the extent that this series is superseded in its positively encompassing the totality of the Ph-immediate, and it is retained as a moment that is internal to this totality. The simple 'belonging' of the totality of the Ph-immediate to the ontic series, regarded as thus positively encompassing, would entail the contradiction of an Ph-immediate excess to the totality of the Ph-immediate. That belonging therefore requires that the ontic series should be reduced to a series of only one term. The speculative value of this expression consists in the fact that the totality of the Ph-immediate is posited by excluding to be posited as one of the similar terms of a specific series: that is to say, it is posited as the only individuation of its concept.

(It is clear that while the belonging of the totality of the Ph-immediate to the ontic series entails the reduction of this series in the indicated sense, this reduction entails in turn a reduction of the exponential series – namely, the superseding of the latter *qua* positively including the positing of the Ph-immediacy of the totality of the Ph-immediate.)

8. First note

It should be observed that the occurrence of this belonging-reduction, due to which the series value of the ontic positing comes to be lost, entails that the totality of the Ph-immediate formally takes itself as its own content: that is to say, it constitutes itself as that value of the originary judgement by virtue of which that judgement is a positing of Ph-immediacy. If, indeed, the ontic positing consists in the very positing of the totality of the Ph-immediate, the exponential positing will consist in the positing of the immediacy of the immediate.

9. Second note

While the exponential positing may not count as a term of the ontic series, it may, however, acquire this value if it is regarded as a positing of the simple *form* of the totality of the Ph-immediate, i.e. as a form that is distinct from its content. Indeed, by affirming that this form counts as *one of the terms* of the ontic series, the concrete concept of this form is not traded for its abstract concept; that is to say, it is not the case that the form is no longer regarded as the form *of* the content, whereby the content would positively encompass that particular determination constituted by the form only because the latter is abstractly considered outside of its relation with the concrete: even as concretely distinct from its content, and not abstractly separated from the latter, the form of the totality of the Ph-immediate is a particular determination of the content of that totality, and it is therefore a term of the ontic series.

10. c. The exponential and ontic series

As all the terms of the exponential series belong to the ontic series, all the terms of this second series belong to the exponential one, even if in a different sense from the one excluded in §3. The excluded sense of this belonging is the one in accordance with which all the terms of the ontic series stand *as terms* of the exponential series; the admitted sense of that belonging is the one in accordance with which all the terms of the ontic series, respectively, stand *as moments* of the terms of the exponential series. Indeed, the positing of the Ph-immediacy of a determination includes the positing of that determination that precisely constitutes the content of that Ph-immediacy.

11. Note

At the same time, however, holding firm the distinction between the positing of the Ph-immediacy of the *single* determinations and the positing of the *totality* of the Ph-immediate, it must be stated that since it is as part of this latter positing that the ontic series is posited as the horizon of everything that is known for itself, the ontic series, as such, is only something *in itself* as part of the exponential series – or, equivalently, the exponential series includes the ontic series as something in itself (whereby the including series itself, as such, is something in itself): material – i.e. non-formal – positing of the ontic series. (Naturally, what includes and what is included are posited as something 'in itself' only insofar as, following the *positing* of the ontic and exponential series – this positing taking place as part of the concrete positing of the totality of the Ph-immediate – it is verified that what is posited as part of the exponential series is the ontic series: but, precisely, as something in itself.)

12. d. Complex and hyper-complex ontic acts of positing

As discussed, that value of the originary judgement by virtue of which the latter is a positing of Ph-immediacy arises to the extent that the ontic positing consists in the positing of the totality of the Ph-immediate. If by a 'complex ontic positing' we indicate an ontic positing determined in this way, that complex ontic positing consists in turn in the concrete unity of the ontic positing and the exponential one.

One may then assume that the ontic positing, regarded as a moment of the complex ontic positing, consists in turn in the positing of the totality of the Ph-immediate – in which case, what was posited as a complex ontic positing may be said to become a 'hyper-complex ontic positing', and what was posited as an ontic positing becomes a complex ontic positing.

In this case, the originary judgement (which we are here always considering as to its reduced, i.e. phenomenological, value) has itself as its content. The originary judgement always consists in the positing of the immediacy of thinking (i.e. of immediately present being), but 'thinking' is here determined as the 'originary judgement'.

13. The bounds of the series of complex ontic acts of positing

It is clear that one may produce a *series* of complex ontic acts of positing. (The constitution of this series coincides with the very constitution of a series of complex exponential acts of positing.) That series, in its actuality, is, however, *finite*: that is to say, it consists of a finite number of terms.

Its bounds are, on the one hand, that hyper-complex positing that includes within itself all other hyper-complex acts of positing as moments – this being the upper bound; on the other hand, the 'simple positing' of the ontic horizon – this being the lower bound.

14. The simple ontic positing as the lower bound of the series

Let us indeed note that the concept of the 'totality of immediately present being', concretely conceived, refers in the last instance per its own meaning to an ontic positing – which is precisely the lower bound of the series under consideration – in which what is posited is not posited *as* the 'totality of the Ph-immediate', but *as* 'being': being, which is determined by *different* determinations from the formal determination: 'Totality of immediately present being' (different determinations that, however, belong to the content of this formal determination). For, indeed, it has been assumed that the acts of positing of the series under consideration respectively posit the *concrete* totality of the Ph-immediate: which is such – i.e. concrete – only insofar as the formal positing of this totality refers to a semantic content that is formally distinct from the semanteme constituted by the form of the totality of the Ph-immediate; this content is precisely the ontic horizon in its simplicity.

In the series under consideration, the concrete totality is therefore posited insofar as it includes *an abstract moment* – which is precisely the simple ontic positing – in which what is posited is not the totality of the Ph-immediate. It is not that totality in a twofold sense: insofar as, at that moment, the content *is not posited as* the totality of the Ph-immediate, and in the sense that, therefore, the terms of this content do not include *all* the immediately present terms. Indeed, the formal determination of the totality of the Ph-immediate, too, is an immediately present content, and this content is not included in the simple ontic horizon. (Furthermore, there is no need to emphasize that the series of complex acts of positing is the concrete content of the totality of the

Ph-immediate, in such a way that not only does the simple ontic horizon not include that formal determination, but it does not even include those determinations by virtue of which the 'complexity' of those complex acts of positing is constituted.)

15. e. Two types of simple ontic positing

It is possible to distinguish two modes of ontic simplicity.

As part of the first mode, the immediacy that is not posited is not posited insofar as it is the *totality* of immediate presence. Accordingly, as part of this first mode, it is possible for the terms of the exponential series to count as terms of the simple ontic series. As part of the second mode, the immediacy that is not posited is instead not posited not only insofar as it is the totality of immediacy but also insofar as it is a particular immediacy – i.e. insofar as it is distributed among the terms of the exponential series. A *pure* ontic simplicity is thus posited, to which *every* act of positing of Ph-immediacy refers. On the contrary, not *every* act of positing of Ph-immediacy refers to the first mode of ontic simplicity but only the positing of the totality of the Ph-immediate.

In the first case, it must be stated that while all the terms of the exponential series may belong to the ontic series, certain terms of the ontic series may belong to the exponential series. In the second case, it must be stated that, in the same way in which no term of the exponential series may belong to the ontic series, no term of this latter series may belong to the exponential one.

The simple ontic positing is the lower bound of the series of complex acts of positing, insofar as it realizes itself as the second of the two indicated types of ontic simplicity.

16. Provisional character of the established bounds

According to what we have observed, it can be stated that both the lower and upper bounds of the series of complex acts of positing are variables – and that, therefore, the values that these bounds take as a matter of fact have a provisional value.

For what concerns the lower bound, the structure in accordance with which that bound has been seen to be realized consists indeed in turn of a horizon that includes more or less extended semantic spheres – which, relative to that structure, fulfil the same bound function that this structure fulfils relative to the complex acts of positing. Furthermore, there appears to be no atomic meaning that is not in turn amenable to analysis – the terms of the analysis playing once again the role of bounds. In this respect, the lower bound thus consists in the series of values that it takes as a matter of fact (concerning this point, cf. Chapter 6).

The possible variation of the upper bound consists in the very possibility of reflecting on the very *positing* of the totality of the Ph-immediate (or, more generally, it consists in the becoming of the Ph-immediate content, cf. §26), whereby that positing comes to be included in the totality of the Ph-immediate. Accordingly, the ontic horizon that is obtained through this reflection includes what *was* the hyper-complex ontic horizon – i.e. what 'was' that horizon precisely because the *positing* of the totality of the

182 *The Originary Structure*

Ph-immediate is not (and was not) included in this horizon, which is thus reduced to a complex horizon, i.e. to a *moment* of the totality of the Ph-immediate. This makes it clear that if *the form* of the totality of the Ph-immediate is taken as the upper bound, the latter is a constant – the possible variation involving only the content of that form (i.e. the content to which that form pertains).

17. The originary judgement and the exposition of the originary judgement

As discussed, the phenomenological value of the originary judgement is realized if the ontic horizon comprises the very totality of the Ph-immediate. It has also been discussed that the originary judgement (still regarded as to its phenomenological value) has itself as content if the content of the ontic horizon is the originary judgement. Let us then note that every possible reflection on the originary judgement and on its self-inclusion – thus also and primarily the reflection or exposition that we are presently conducting – always consists (if it is posited as an immediacy) in a realization of the originary judgement. That is to say, the exposition of this judgement consists in the originary judgement itself in its taking itself, or its self-inclusion (or etc.), as the totality of the immediately present content. The exposition is indeed the immediate presence of the exposed content: that is to say, it *is* a form of keeping that content before oneself as the totality of the Ph-immediate. We are stating that it only *is* so – i.e. it is so *in actu exercito* and not in *actu signato* – as long as one does not take the very exposition of the originary judgement as an immediate content (as we are presently doing), thus realizing once again, and always, the originary judgement.

18. Concerning the determination of the relation between Ph-immediacy and L-immediacy

A determination of the relations between the horizon of being that is Ph-immediately affirmed and the horizon of being that is L-immediately affirmed must be here postponed. Let us only note – thus leaving aside the aporia to which this simple note gives rise – that the Ph-immediate totality *includes*, in a specific way, the totality of L-immediate being: that is to say, it includes it to the extent that also that being that is L-immediately affirmed is immediately present. In this respect, the totality of the Ph-immediate is not a moment but the whole of immediacy. It, however, remains a moment of the latter insofar as a domain of the immediate (precisely, L-immediate being) is not simply affirmed because it is immediately present but because what is immediately present is its being immediately affirmed according to a value of immediacy that differs from the one of Ph-immediacy: that is to say, because its L-immediacy is Ph-immediate. In a different respect, the totality of the Ph-immediate is a moment of immediacy itself because, as it will be shown, that being that is L-immediately affirmed is affirmed as being other than the totality of Ph-immediate being. (The aporia mentioned earlier thus also comes to the fore: the Ph-immediate includes and at the same time does not include that being that is L-immediately affirmed.)

Lastly, let us reiterate that if that being that is L-immediately affirmed does not belong to the totality of the Ph-immediate (or, in relation to the anticipation made earlier, it is not limited to that belonging – contrary to Ph-immediate being proper – but, while belonging in a certain respect to the totality of Ph-immediate being, in a different respect it lies beyond or it is other than this totality), the meaning of L-immediacy is, however, not limited to the L-immediate affirmation of a positive element that surpasses the totality of the Ph-immediate positive, but it also presents another value. This is the value by virtue of which the L-immediacy constitutes itself as a property of the Ph-immediate determination itself (i.e. it constitutes itself as an Ph-L-immediacy), and it is thus itself one of the Ph-immediate determinations in a strict sense (cf. Chapter 3, §§3, 17). That is to say, the L-immediacy is included in the Ph-immediacy *both* insofar as that positive element that is L-immediately affirmed and that does not belong to the totality of Ph-immediate being is itself Ph-immediate (the remainder of the exposition having to solve the aporetic character of this proposition), *and* insofar as the *non-contradictoriness* (= Ph-L-immediacy) of Ph-immediate being is itself an Ph-immediate determination. Concerning this second respect, however, it should be kept in mind that this Ph-L-immediacy is not a property that is exclusive to Ph-immediate being, but it is a property of the totality of being, or of being *qua* being: and, therefore (and in fact originarily) also of that being that is L-immediately affirmed (cf. Chapter 3, §15).

19. Transition

Independently of the aporia mentioned in the previous section, the general remarks that we have provided here give rise to a considerable aporetic development. In the remainder of this chapter, we shall only consider (and therefore eliminate) the difficulties that may hinder the exposition the most.

20. The aporia of the concept of a 'series of complex acts of positing'

The following constitutes a first aporia:

> The series of complex acts of positing, wherein the totality of the Ph-immediate may consist (§13), has totalities of the Ph-immediate as terms (elements). Since the hyper-complex positing (*qua* upper bound) includes complex acts of positing as moments, each term of the series is and at the same time is not the totality of the Ph-immediate: it is that totality by definition, and it is not that totality insofar as it is included in a larger horizon of Ph-immediacy.

This aporia may also be formulated more simply by stating that a reflection on the totality of the Ph-immediate entails a contradiction as soon as that reflection is *posited*.

Indeed, this positing determines a positional horizon that includes the totality of the Ph-immediate as a moment.

21. General solution of the aporia

The resolution of this aporia consists in general in noting that the aporia arises to the extent that the distinction between the form and the content of the totality of the Ph-immediate (§2) is not held firm. On the basis of that distinction, it must then be stated that this form is a constant while that content is a variable (§16). Accordingly, what may be included as a moment within the positional horizon determined by the arising of the positing of a reflection (immediate presence) on the totality of the Ph-immediate is not this totality in its formal value, but it is the content that constitutes its realization prior to the arising of the positing of that reflection (§9).

22. Analytic clarification of the solution

The Ph-immediacy of being is included as part of immediately present being (Chapter 2, §16). It is by virtue of this inclusion that the subject of the originary judgement (regarded as to its phenomenological value) constitutes itself as the totality of the Ph-immediate. The originary judgement thus states: the totality of the Ph-immediate is immediately present – or, equivalently (since the presence in question is the totality of presence): the totality of the Ph-immediate is *the* Ph-immediate.

The positional horizon determined by the originary judgement (let P be the positional horizon determined in this way – this horizon thus consisting in the totality of the Ph-immediate) *is* furthermore immediately present as part of this reflection on it. It only *is* so: that is to say, the Ph-immediacy of that horizon is something *in itself*, as long as this immediacy is not *posited* – as it precisely takes place in our present reflection.

Through this positing, the positional horizon *is augmented*: it now includes its own immediate presence *as posited* (let P' be the positional horizon that is thus inclusive).

The transition from P to P' constitutes, however, a *persisting* of the originary judgement – or, equivalently, of the totality of the Ph-immediate. For, indeed, the augmenting positing – i.e. the posited Ph-immediacy of P – is precisely the positing of the Ph-immediacy of the totality of the Ph-immediate: this constituting the originary judgement. Except that, now, it appears that it must be stated that the totality of the Ph-immediate, which is the subject of that judgement, is the originary judgement itself, insofar as it realizes itself as P.

Furthermore, as mentioned, the transition from P to P' equivalently consists in the persistence of the totality of the Ph-immediate, for in the same way in which in P the Ph-immediacy of being is (immediately) included in Ph-immediate being itself – whereby the originary judgement does not extend outside the totality of the Ph-immediate – so in P' the augmenting positing is (immediately) included in the totality of Ph-immediately known being; or, equivalently, the originary judgement constitutes itself anew in P' precisely to the extent that this immediate inclusion obtains.

Except that – here is the issue – due to this latter inclusion, the Ph-immediacy whose positing augments the positional horizon is not simply (as instead stated earlier) the Ph-immediacy of P, but it is the Ph-immediacy of P': precisely because P does not include its own Ph-immediacy, and, to the extent that it includes it, it is no longer P but P' (and it must include it in order for the positional increment determined by the positing of the Ph-immediacy of P to be the persistence or the renewed constitution of the originary judgement – i.e. in order for the originary judgement to persist despite that increment).

Therefore, if the transition from P to P' is the persisting of the totality of the Ph-immediate *qua* such totality, this totality does not persist as P, but as P'; or, equivalently, P is superseded as the totality of the Ph-immediate. That is to say, this superseding entails that, since P' is constituted as the positing or immediate presence of the Ph-immediacy of the totality of the Ph-immediate, this totality does not count as P – for, otherwise, the totality of the Ph-immediate would not include its own Ph-immediacy, which is, however, immediately present – but as P'. Accordingly, as a result of that increment, the totality of the Ph-immediate does not only include its own Ph-immediacy (the totality in question counting, by virtue of this inclusion, as P) but also the Ph-immediacy of its Ph-immediacy.

23. Concerning the meaning of the 'Ph-immediacy of Ph-immediacy'

It should be noted that this last expression – 'the Ph-immediacy of Ph-immediacy' – does not refer to *two* immediacies, which are two in that they have a different content: even though one must acknowledge a certain duality between the augmenting Ph-immediacy and the Ph-immediacy *qua simple* immediacy of P (i.e. the immediacy that is included in P without thus entailing that P is P'). That duality, regarded as a difference in the content of the two immediacies, is contradictory, since if the augmenting Ph-immediacy (let this be I') is included in the totality of the Ph-immediate, and if at the same time the other Ph-immediacy (let this be I) is simply the immediacy of the totality of the Ph-immediate regarded as P, it follows that the augmenting immediacy is included in P, i.e. in the positional horizon that by definition does not include that augmenting immediacy.

Further developing: if the immediate presence of the totality of the Ph-immediate ($= I'$) becomes itself immediately present, I' *does not for this reason* stop counting as the immediate presence of the totality of the Ph-immediate. Furthermore – should the value of I' change as indicated – the presence of the presence of the totality of presence would be the presence of something that is not the presence of the totality of presence. Therefore, as soon as the presence of that totality becomes present, it precisely becomes present as the presence of that totality. This, however, only takes place insofar as the content of I does not differ from the content of I'. If the content of I were to be P (which only includes I) *also* when P becomes present in I', it would follow that I' would no longer be the presence of the totality of presence, since – following the positing of I' – the totality of presence is no longer P, but $P + I'$. I' would no longer be the presence of the totality of presence in the very act in which it should become present as the presence of the totality of presence. For if one instead wishes to hold firm I' as the presence of the totality of presence – while still considering this totality as P – it follows that, to the extent that the positing of I' constitutes the realization of the originary judgement, I' must be included in P, which by definition does not include I'. (This is the difficulty that has been discussed first earlier.)

Therefore, if through the positing of I' the content of I persists as P, then either I' is no longer the presence of the totality of presence, or (if P is held firm as this totality) I' is included in something that, by definition, does not include it – or, lastly, I' is posited, but it is not included in the positional totality, in such a way that if the latter is held firm as P, it must be negated that I' is posited.

Therefore, if through the positing of I' the positing of the Ph-immediacy of the Ph-immediacy of the totality of the Ph-immediate is realized, what is realized are not *two* immediacies that have a different content, but the immediacy is an immediacy *of itself qua* immediacy of the totality of the Ph-immediate: $I = I'$. That is to say, precisely because I is the presence of that totality, it is at the same time the presence of I': in such a way that I, too – like I' – is the immediacy of immediacy itself.

It is by virtue of this sameness – or, equivalently, it is because the totality of the Ph-immediate does not only include I, but also I' (should the indicated positional increment take place) – that, in addition to the elimination of the outlined aporia, it is also possible to exclude that, if the originary judgement takes itself as its content, it should thus come to take as content something that *was* the originary judgement, or something that *was* the totality of the Ph-immediate (to the extent that P, relative to P', constitutes the *past* of that judgement or of that totality); in that way, the originary judgement would not be able to affirm itself in its being *actually and presently* the originary judgement. This impossibility depends on the assumption that the persistence of the form of the totality of the Ph-immediate – when there arises a reflection on the immediacy of that totality – consists at the same time in the persistence of the content of that totality: an assumption that is equivalent to the assumption of a *duality* between the Ph-immediacy (I) and the Ph-immediacy of the Ph-immediacy.

24. The abstract and concrete series of the complex acts of positing

At the same time, however, it is clear that the negation of that *duality* is not a negation of the *reflection* that is performed on the very presence of the totality of the immediate: i.e. it is not a negation of the possibility that the augmenting immediacy should have itself as content, *qua* immediacy of the totality of the Ph-immediate.

The abstract understanding constructs instead a reflective series whose terms (immediacy, the immediacy of immediacy, etc.) all have a different content, which is augmented in proportion to the development of that series. Indicating this series by

$$I, I', I'', I''', \ldots, I^n,$$

one thinks that the content of the terms of this series is (respectively, from the left):

$$P, (P + I') = P', (P' + I'') = P'', (P'' + I''') = P''', \ldots, (P^{n-1} + I^n) = P^n.$$

From this – as explained earlier – it follows that either the terms I', I'', I''', ..., I^n are immediately included in the very act in which they are respectively posited as part of the terms P, P', P'', ..., P^{n-1}, and a contradiction arises in that they are included in something that by definition does not include them – or they are not thus included, and each of the terms of the series I', ..., I^n then stands as the immediacy of a totality of the Ph-immediate (respectively: P, ..., P^{n-1}) that is not the totality of the Ph-immediate: precisely because it does not include its own Ph-immediacy, which is however immediately present.

The abstract series is retained as superseded as part of the concrete series. In the concrete series, the terms I, I', I'', I''', ..., I^n all have the same content: that is to say, they are all the same term that reflects on itself and at the same time augments the positional horizon of the totality of the Ph-immediate by virtue of this reflection.

25. Note on the analytic character of the originary judgement

The analytic character of the originary judgement (cf. Chapter 2, §30) is not lost due to this increment of the positional horizon. Indeed, the originary judgement (which is here always regarded as to its phenomenological value) coincides with the very structure of the Ph-immediate, in such a way that stating that the originary judgement is Ph-immediate (i.e. taking the originary judgement itself as the subject of the originary judgement) once again and always means affirming that the immediate is the immediate.

26. The becoming of the totality of the Ph-immediate

The aporia presented in §20 receives a broader formulation upon considering the *becoming* of the totality of the Ph-immediate, rather than simply that *particular* becoming constituted by the realization of the series I, ..., I^n. It is then more generally stated that the totality of the Ph-immediate becomes: i.e. that being, which is known for itself as part of the Ph-immediacy, is known for itself as something that becomes. Becoming, however, entails that, *within* the horizon opened by the totality of the Ph-immediate, this totality allows the arising – relative to *itself* – of a determination that augments the positional horizon. Due to this arising, the totality of the Ph-immediate, *qua* totality, disappears and at the same time persists; it is and at the same time it is not. It *is*, insofar as what arises is itself Ph-immediate and is as such included in the totality of the Ph-immediate – which is therefore asserted to be a form of persistence or of 'still-being'. It *is not*, insofar as that *in* which what arises is included in its being included in the totality is not that *relative to which* that element is, precisely, an arising – the latter being the very totality of the Ph-immediate, which therefore leaves beside itself an Ph-immediate element that exceeds it. As a result, a totality that tolerates this excess is something that *was* the totality of the Ph-immediate, and that, as such, is no longer that totality. At the same time, however, every form of arising of immediately present determinations must be internal to the totality of the Ph-immediate. This arising is posited as such in relation to a positional domain that already was (a domain that, in turn, is posited as something that already is relative to the positing of what arises); that arising is thus added to that domain, and it is therefore posited outside the latter. As discussed, however, that domain is the very totality of the Ph-immediate, which, through that arising, is negated *qua* totality.

27. Deduction of the distinction between the form and the content of the totality of the Ph-immediate

The becoming of the totality of the Ph-immediate therefore determines a contradiction. In order to supersede this contradiction, a distinction between the form and the content of that totality must be introduced (§§2, 16, 21).

It is then affirmed that, as to its form, the totality of the Ph-immediate does not become. (The becoming of that form is only meaningful as an annulment of the Ph-immediate – an annulment that involves the totality in question considered as to the concreteness of its form and content.) *Forma non fit nisi per accidens*: in that it is precisely to the content that becoming pertains *for itself*.

The contradiction indicated earlier is then superseded insofar as becoming is affirmed relative to the content of the totality of the Ph-immediate and negated relative to the form of that totality. As to the form, becoming is superseded or surpassed in and by that totality; as to the matter, the totality is superseded or surpassed in and by that becoming.

(For what concerns the value or the meaning of the introduction of the distinction between the form and the content of the totality of the Ph-immediate, cf. Chapter 7, §10).

28. First note: Possible and factual additional dimensions of the Ph-immediate

a. The totality of the Ph-immediate therefore includes a series of positional horizons that, after having at first been respectively posited as the totality of the Ph-immediate, are afterwards reduced to partial horizons that are included in the total horizon of the Ph-immediate, following the realization of something that, *from the standpoint of those horizons*, was at that first moment a possible Ph-immediate. Accordingly, something that was a possible Ph-immediate from the standpoint of those horizons is an effective or factual content from the standpoint of the totality of the Ph-immediate.

Let us refer to the set of Ph-immediate contents, which are included in the totality of the Ph-immediate in their arising with respect to an already given positional horizon, as the factual additional dimension of the Ph-immediate. Let us refer to the horizon of something that from the standpoint of the totality of the Ph-immediate is a possible Ph-immediacy as the possible additional dimension of the Ph-immediate.

A factual additional dimension is a past; a possible additional dimension is the present of what is additional. The first case concerns what *was* additional, the second case what *is* additional: additional dimension *secundum quid* and additional dimension *simpliciter*.

(The expression 'possible additional dimension' is not a tautology to the extent that it is correlated with that factual additional dimension. For, otherwise, to the extent that the possible is set in opposition to the actual, possibility and additional dimensions are completely equivalent.)

b. From what we have said, it appears that while the positing of the totality of the Ph-immediate L-immediately implies the exclusion of an exceeding Ph-immediate element (§3), this does not L-immediately entail the superseding – or this does not signify the immediate contradictoriness – of the *project* as part of which that excess would *become* immediately present. Or, equivalently: that excess is contradictory insofar as it is referred to the factual determination of the totality of the Ph-immediate, and it is not conceived of as belonging to the possible totality of the Ph-immediate.

c. By 'possible totality of the Ph-immediate' we understand 'possible experience' itself, i.e. the totality of those – factual or possible – determinations that enjoy the property of being non-contradictorily posited as an immediate presence. This possible totality consists in the absolute correspondence between content and form – in such a way that, if the form frees itself from this content, it constitutes itself as a contradiction.

In the expression 'possible totality' of the Ph-immediate, possibility is not set in opposition to what is factual but includes it, and it also includes possibility as set in opposition to what is factual. Possibility indicates here the non-contradictoriness of what – be it factual or possible – is posited as immediately present.

29. Second note: The totality of the Ph-immediate and time

a. The totality of the Ph-immediate is not *always* in view, but it arises *as such* (the arising *of the very* totality of the Ph-immediate being a distinctive case of arising). Furthermore, once it has arisen it again vanishes, to then arise once more. That is to say, pre-philosophical knowledge is not something merely antecedent to philosophical knowledge, i.e. something that is absolutely superseded or consummated once philosophy has appeared: pre-philosophical knowledge interrupts philosophizing, and, in addition to the form of an antecedence, it takes the form of an intermission and – in a project – that of a postponing. Even if we grant that thinking is the 'most uninterrupted of activities', as stated by Aristotle, it is in fact interrupted, and the interruption or intermission is all the more pronounced precisely because what is in question is not thinking generically considered but thinking as the originary structuring of philosophizing.

If the totality of the Ph-immediate is in view intermittently, it is *in time*: not only in the past (the past precisely appearing as that intermission), but also in the future – to the extent that it is possible to project a point in time in which something like the totality of the Ph-immediate is no longer posited or is still not posited.

b. At the same time, however, the past and the future stand as internal determinations of the totality of the Ph-immediate. Insofar as the latter has a temporal character, however, the very totality of the Ph-immediate, in belonging to the past and to the future, posits itself as an internal determination of the totality of the Ph-immediate.

This contradiction is originarily superseded to the extent that it is recognized that the past and future totalities – as well as the temporally present one, which, now that it has been fixed, is already no longer present but has become a past – are not the totality *simpliciter* of the Ph-immediate (i.e. the totality without any temporal determination). It is not thereby negated – in a contradictory way – that those totalities of the Ph-immediate are such. A contradiction would arise if the inclusion of a past totality in the Ph-immediate were a negation of its own *having been* the totality of the Ph-immediate and if the inclusion of a future totality in the Ph-immediate were a negation of its own *being about to be* the totality of the Ph-immediate. That past totality *was* and that future totality *will be* the totality of the Ph-immediate. Respectively: the former was and the latter will be a being outside of time. Precisely because the former was so and the latter will be so, however, they are not the totality *simpliciter*.

Hence, it is possible to realize that, in this case, a surpassing in time coincides with a surpassing in the logos. Or, equivalently: to the extent that the logos lets time prevail over itself, the logos is not only surpassed by time and in time, but it is also surpassed *qua* logos – what surpasses it being the authentic logos, i.e. the logos that does not let time prevail, but includes it within itself.

c. While the totality of the Ph-immediate is not in time, its content, however, *attests* that this totality is in time. That is to say, precisely because that content has been or will be something like the totality of the Ph-immediate, the very totality of the Ph-immediate, insofar as it includes that having been and that being about to be, is not a form of always being. Recollections attest the not-yet-being of what surpasses time and attest it not only to the extent that, as part of the order of recollection, a totality of the Ph-immediate that is not *the* totality of the Ph-immediate is posited, but also to the extent that certain positional horizons are posited (the intervals of pre-philosophical consciousness), in which something like the totality of the Ph-immediate is not even posited. The same is to be affirmed concerning the project that – even if in a problematic form – attests that the totality under consideration no longer is, and attests this both in case that what is projected is a totality of the Ph-immediate and in case that what is projected is any positional state.

d. The totality of the Ph-immediate surpasses and is surpassed by time. This would be contradictory only if the sense in which that totality is surpassed were to be the same sense in which it surpasses.

The totality of the Ph-immediate, instead, surpasses time in the sense that the totality of time is present, or it is the Ph-immediate: time is the Ph-immediate content of consciousness. Furthermore, time does not surpass the totality of the Ph-immediate insofar as one negates that time is a content of this totality but insofar as that content attests that this totality is not always already and forever posited. Once again, it must therefore be stated that the totality surpasses from a formal point of view, and it is surpassed from a material point of view.

For what concerns this second side, this means that the content of the totality of the Ph-immediate has not always already and forever been posited *as* such a content, but that this positing arises after the content had been posited as what it was (everyday life or pre-philosophical content), or as the content of something that was the totality of the Ph-immediate. (As posited in this way, however, it is posited according to a semantic quantity that differs from the one in accordance with which it is the content of the totality *simpliciter* of the Ph-immediate – the difference in question being precisely what determines the distinction between the totality *simpliciter* and that past totality.)

30. *Regressus in indefinitum* and the series of complex acts of positing

The second kind of aporias that we wish to keep in mind here consists of taking note of the contradiction that obtains between the exclusion of the *regressus in indefinitum*, carried out in Chapter 2 (§16), and the admission of the arising of the series $I, \ldots, I^n$ (cf. §24).

31. Solution of the aporia

In this instance, the aporia is caused by a mere misconception, even though the elimination of the latter is of significant importance.

Let us therefore recall that the exclusion of the *regressus in indefinitum* entails that the grounding of the positing of the Ph-immediacy of being is not something additional relative to the positing of that immediacy, but it is co-originary with it. For, indeed, as discussed, the ground of the positing of Ph-immediacy is the positing of the Ph-immediacy of Ph-immediacy. In the realization of the originary judgement, however, this Ph-immediacy is then immediately included in the horizon of Ph-immediate being: i.e. it is included in the very act in which it is posited. As a result, the positing of the Ph-immediacy of being coincides with the very positing of the Ph-immediacy of this Ph-immediacy (i.e. of itself). The ground of the positing of immediacy is therefore immediately given. The totality of the Ph-immediate thus constitutes itself as a self-grounding or self-foundation.

This, however, does not exclude the possibility of taking note of the immediate presence of the realization of the totality of the Ph-immediate *at an additional moment* relative to the one constituted by that realization. That is to say, the possibility of the arising of an Ph-immediate term in the positional horizon is not excluded: even if that term is the very immediate presence of the totality of the Ph-immediate. This term is therefore not necessarily required for the constitution of that self-grounding (and, in fact, in relation to the latter, it is excluded as something contradictory), and to that end nor is the realization of the series $I, \ldots, I^n$, or an indefinite extension of the latter. It is, however, not possible to rule out the possibility that there should take place ever new reflections on the horizon (of a greater or lesser reflectional order) that has already been realized.

In other words, the Ph-immediacy of Ph-immediacy, required by its self-grounding, is not the Ph-immediacy of this self-grounding – an immediacy (= an immediate presence) that can arise at a moment that is additional relative to the one constituted by that self-grounding.

Since, furthermore, what arises is the very Ph-immediacy of an already posited content – the very process of arising, in a different respect, coinciding with the persisting of the originary judgement – this Ph-immediacy is in turn grounded in the very moment or in the very act in which it is posited.

32. Aporia: The immediate inclusion of Ph-immediacy in Ph-immediate being determines a *progressus in indefinitum*

One may further respond that if the Ph-immediacy of being is immediately included in Ph-immediate being itself, that Ph-immediacy will be the immediate presence of itself. If what is present as part of this presence is that very Ph-immediacy, however, and if the latter is the immediate presence of itself, that immediacy will be the immediate presence of its being the immediate presence of itself. A *progressus in indefinitum* is thus determined; the originary judgement will therefore require an indefinite formulation – or, equivalently, it will not be possible to formulate the originary judgement.

33. Solution of the aporia

The aporia is determined by the – in itself correct – requirement that the Ph-immediacy that is included in the Ph-immediate being should be exactly the Ph-immediacy of Ph-immediate being and not another artificially constructed immediacy. Accordingly, since that Ph-immediacy is the immediate presence of itself, one concludes that the Ph-immediacy that is included in Ph-immediate being is precisely that Ph-immediacy that is regarded as the immediate presence of itself. This 'of itself', however, will have once again to be understood – for the reason indicated earlier – as the 'immediate presence of itself', and it will therefore not be possible to avoid the *progressus in indefinitum*.

The solution of the aporia must respect that requirement, for if the Ph-immediacy that is originarily included in the Ph-immediate were not the Ph-immediacy of the Ph-immediate, the originary judgement would be constituted as something groundless. Then, being is immediately present; let p be this immediacy. At the same time, however, p is originarily included in the horizon of what is immediately present. If by p' we indicate p insofar as it belongs to that horizon, it will nevertheless be necessary to hold firm the absolute identity between p and p'. The fact that the content of p is p' (which, precisely, belongs to the content of p) means that p has itself as content. Accordingly, if p' is p itself, and if p has p' as content, it is altogether correct to affirm that p', in turn, has itself as content: if this were not the case, there would be no identity between p and p'. Up to this point, the aporetic argument developed earlier is confirmed. Let then p'' indicate p' insofar as it is its own content. From what has been said, it is then clear that the propositions: 'the content of p is p'' and 'the content of p' is p''' state the same thing, or that there is no difference between them: precisely because p, p' and p'' are all the same term. This is the point of divergence from the aporetic argument. For, indeed, if it is certainly true that the content of p' is p'', *this does not assert anything different* from what is affirmed by stating that the content of p is p'. As a result, if this difference does not obtain, the first step that should lead to the *progressus in indefinitum* is not realized. The aporetic argument instead regards p'' as something different from p, and constructs the proposition: 'the content of p is p' in its including $p'' \neq p'$. The aporia is overcome by noting that p', as including p'', is not the content of p in the sense desired by the aporetic argument, but it coincides with p as including p'. The *progressus in indefinitum* then only arises insofar as the repetition of the same proposition is regarded as the positing of different propositions.

This does not rule out the *possibility* that immediacy itself, as self-including, should become the content of a *different* immediacy, which *augments* the positional content. (This is precisely the case considered in §31.) What is excluded is that this *possibility* should be a *necessity*.

Indeed, insofar as p comes to have as content p' *qua* including p'' (this p'' being p' itself and other than p), p consists in that augmenting immediacy, whereas p' (= p'') is something that *was* the immediacy of the totality of the Ph-immediate, and it is therefore presently the immediacy of a *moment* of the immediately present content. This immediate presence is precisely p, which is immediately included in what is immediately present, and if this inclusion is understood as indicated earlier, the *progressus* is already halted here. In order for the *progressus* to be resumed, it is *once again* necessary for p, as content of itself, to be posited as having a content other than that of p, *qua* containing itself.

It may further be observed that, strictly speaking, the *progressus in indefinitum* is not realized by virtue of the simple consideration of p'' as something different from p, but insofar as, *at each moment* that constitutes that *progressus*, there takes place in the same way that erroneous differentiation of the terms analogous to p and p''. The *progressus in indefinitum* is thus realized only insofar as that erroneous differentiation is indefinitely *repeated* (cf. analogously Chapter 2, §17, first corollary).

34. Note concerning an incorrect solution of the aporia

One may think to supersede the aporia solved earlier by negating that p has itself as content. That in which p must be included is a positional horizon that, prior to the inclusion of p, includes all Ph-immediate determinations except for their Ph-immediacy. What must be included is precisely this immediacy = p. However, if p, *qua* included in that horizon – and, therefore, *qua* p' – has p'' as content, what is included in this way is not what had to be included; for what had to be included was the immediate presence of that horizon, and not the immediate presence of this immediate presence. The *progressus in indefinitum* cannot therefore be constituted.

Except that, on the one hand, this argument does not counter the one that in §32 resulted in the positing of the *progressus in indefinitum*, but it simply *stands alongside* it; on the other hand, it itself rests on an erroneous premise: namely, that there exists an originary moment in which the Ph-immediacy is not yet included in the horizon of the Ph-immediate, in such a way that when that inclusion takes place at a later point what is to be included is simply the Ph-immediacy of this horizon (in its not including that Ph-immediacy), and not the Ph-immediacy of the Ph-immediacy of that horizon. It is here clear that this conclusion, too, operates as a function of that same requirement that determined the aporia: i.e. that what is included in that horizon should be precisely the Ph-immediacy of the horizon.

The horizon of the Ph-immediate, instead, originarily or immediately includes its own immediacy. Accordingly, what is originarily included is an Ph-immediacy that – precisely because it is originarily included – is an immediacy of immediacy or an immediate presence of immediate presence itself. It is then precisely in relation to this self-reflection that there arises the aporia solved in the previous section.

6

The analysis of the originary meaning: Semantic simplicities and semantic complexities

1. Does the analysis of the originary meaning give rise to a *progressus in indefinitum*?

Since the positing of the totality of the immediate is the positing of a semantic concreteness or complexity, this concreteness constitutes itself as the relation of the abstract moments of the concrete: that is to say, as the superseding of the abstract concept of those meanings that precisely count as moments of the originary meaning. The analysis of the originary meaning therefore manifests a multiplicity of meanings that count in turn as complex meanings (such as, for instance, the meanings constituted by the exponential series or the ontic horizon) – namely, meanings that are such that their analysis once again manifests a multiplicity of sets of meanings.

Since, however, it appears that *every* meaning is susceptible to analysis, it also appears that it must be concluded that the positing of the originary meaning gives rise to a *progressus in indefinitum* (namely, that the positing of the originary semantic concreteness entails that the superseding of the abstract concept of the abstract realizes itself as a *progressus in indefinitum*).

2. Formal exclusion of an infinite analysis of the originary meaning

The following is a first formal response. The totality of the immediate consists of a *finite set* of meanings: that is to say, the *number* of the immediately present determinations is *finite* (even if continuously varying). The fact that there is a finite number of immediate meanings is known for itself. This being the case, since the positing of the originary meaning (i.e. of the totality of the immediate) is a positing of the moments that constitute that meaning – the analysis of the originary constituting the very originary concrete definition of the originary – if the positing of the moments of the originary is regarded as the result of an infinite process, one will thus be affirming a semantic domain that is not immediately present. For, indeed, an infinite analysis of the originary meaning gives rise to an *infinite set* of meanings, and it is therefore not immediately present.

We have stated that this first type of response to the question formulated in the previous section has a *formal* value in that if on the one hand it is valid as an exclusion of that infinite analysis, on the other hand it does not determine the concrete content of the limit of this analysis. Strictly speaking, however, there is here, too, a certain determination of that limit, which consists in positing the contradictoriness of the *actuality* or *immediate presence* of an infinite analysis.

This contradictoriness may be here regarded as the fact that the affirmation of the presence of an infinite analysis is in contradiction *with* immediate presence itself. That is to say, we may here leave aside the question as to whether that being in contradiction *with* the immediate presence itself is also a *self-*contradiction. From the standpoint of the immediate, it must indeed be stated that excluding the immediate presence of that infinite analysis does not mean excluding the possibility of infinitely analysing the originary meaning – as a result of which an infinite semantic set would come to be immediately present; that is to say, the project of such an infinite development of the analysis of the originary meaning does not immediately appear to be self-contradictory. (In the same way, the project of an infinite development of that analysis, which would never come to the opening of an infinite semantic plane, is not immediately self-contradictory. It is clear that the infinite development of this latter project is 'infinite' in a 'syncategorematic' sense, while the infinite development of the previous project is 'infinite' in a 'categorematic' sense, i.e. the development consists in the arising of the immediate presence of a semantic infinite.)[1]

3. Transition from a formal to a concrete exclusion of the infinite analysis of the originary meaning

Stating that this first formal response (§2) determines the limit of the analysis of the originary meaning as the actual horizon itself means that the analysis is halted at a set of immediately present meanings that are not further analysed. This set precisely constitutes the limit of the analysis. This limit, however, is a *formal* one. Each of the terms of that set is not further analysed – and it is therefore present as a simple meaning – not insofar as that analysis is immediately self-contradictory but because, as a matter of fact, that analysis is not immediately present. What therefore remains undetermined, up to this point, is whether or not the terms at which the analysis of the originary meaning has been presently halted are such that they *exclude the possibility* of a further analysis of their content. In the first case, an infinite analysis is *also* excluded insofar as it belongs to the projected horizon – and any finite analysis of the final terms obtained by the actual or present analysis is excluded, too; in the second case, the possibility of a finite or indefinite extension of the analysis remains open. In this case, an infinite superseding, which is excluded as a 'categorematic' one, is possible as a 'syncategorematic' one. What is then to be established is whether the concept of an extension of the analysis of these factually simple meanings is self-contradictory (and thus not simply in contradiction with immediate presence) or whether what is self-contradictory is the very negation of the possibility of such an extension. (The problem may be specified in the sense that one may ask whether what is self-contradictory is the concept of a *finite or of an infinite* extension of the analysis and whether what is self-contradictory is the very negation of the possibility of a *finite or of an infinite* extension of the analysis.)

It should, however, be noted that even if the above alternative could not be solved, a formal response would be sufficient to ensure the positing of the concrete. This would be equivalent to the persistence of the possibility of both sides of the alternative.

4. The problem of beginning

The problem outlined in §3 is none other than the problem of *beginning*. The importance of this question in Hegel's philosophy is well known, and so is the gradual decline of this importance in post-Hegelian philosophies, as well as in Italian neo-Hegelianism. The fundamental objection that is raised against the Hegelian beginning consists in observing that the absolute emptiness constituted by pure being is a negativity that acquires a meaning only in its opposition to the negated horizon; as a result, the immediate consists of this very opposition, but not as such, but insofar as it is the originary logical whole, which may be equivalently considered (analysed) starting from any of its determinations. This equivalent or indifferent determination does indeed constitute the beginning but as a variable or something accidental.

The objection is correct, and it expresses the necessity of positing the concrete in its originarity. For what concerns a historical interpretation, it may be held that, however, that objection only makes explicit something that was already implicit in Hegel's philosophy; Hegel himself has then moved beyond that standpoint, providing a concrete analysis of the way in which the abstract (and, therefore, the abstract concept of the abstract) *structures itself* – or, equivalently, verifying the *order* and the *limit* of the de-powering of the concrete, and locating in pure being the minimum limit of that de-powering (understanding the abstract as a de-powered concrete).

We are, however, interested in establishing in what sense the concept of beginning *regains* a speculative importance as part of the present enquiry.

5. The concrete exclusion of an infinite analysis of the originary meaning

Formal *being* (Chapter 2, §2) is that meaning which belongs to the set of factually simple meanings, relative to which it is also immediately self-contradictory to project an extension of the analysis of its semantic content. As distinct from the determinations that constitute the material positing of being, it is indeed that *absolutely simple* discussed by Hegel. If 'being' were a complex meaning, the moments of this meaning would either be or not be; that is to say, being could either be predicated of them or not. In the first case, the moment would already include what should result from the synthesis with the other moments: i.e. the moment itself would be a synthesis of 'being' and of that semantic determinacy by virtue of which the moment under consideration could distinguish itself from the other moments. In the second case, there would be no synthesis – no complexity: precisely because it would be a synthesis of nothing.

We therefore obtain in this way the concrete determination of the limit of the analysis of the originary meaning, since formal being is precisely this limit. It is then affirmed that, in this respect, it is inherently contradictory for the concrete not to *begin* the superseding of the abstract concepts of the abstract by superseding the abstractness of formal being – or, equivalently, for the concrete to *arrive* at formal being as at an intermediate term in the series of superseded terms. It is clear that the beginning is not logically prior to the total process of the superseding of the abstract, but, while being co-originary with the latter, it precisely constitutes the limit beyond which every semantic-positional opening is annulled. In other words, the originary meaning constitutes the *originary surpassing* of a multiplicity of positional horizons, which therefore count as abstract moments of the originary. It must therefore be stated that it is inherently contradictory for that horizon not to *begin* as a surpassing of that positional horizon in which nothing but the meaning 'being' is posited; as a result, this horizon – in addition to being surpassed co-originarily with every other abstract horizon that counts as a moment of the originary – is at the same time *initially* surpassed, in the sense that it cannot in any way count as the *result* of a prior surpassing.

6. The persistence of the formal exclusion of an infinite analysis

While according to Hegel, however, formal being exhausts that initial level – or, equivalently, what is initial (the beginning, the limit of the analysis) consists in nothing but pure being – formal being is instead only *a moment* of that initial level: the other moment being that multiplicity of moments constituted by the set of factually simple meanings, i.e. the set of those meanings at which the analysis has actually and presently been halted.

It should be noted that this second moment of the initial level does not consist in a *synthesis* of those factually simple meanings (for a synthesis is already a semantic complexity that refers to simple meanings), but it consists in the multiplicity of those factually simple meanings in their respective existence as meanings that are *distinct* from each other, and that precisely count as simple meanings insofar as they are considered as to their being mutually distinct. Accordingly, it is not strictly speaking a question of a 'second moment' of that initial level but of a multiplicity of moments that corresponds to the number of factually simple meanings. (While the initial level is not constituted as a synthesis, but it consists of a simple multiplicity of simple meanings, it is clear that a *positing* of the initial level, as part of which this level is posited *as such*, opens a positional horizon that originarily surpasses that initial multiplicity and therefore constitutes itself as the concrete.)

The analysis of the originary meaning is therefore halted at or limited by a multiplicity of simple meanings. One of these meanings – that of formal being – appears as that relative to which it is immediately self-contradictory to project an analysis of its semantic content; the other simple meanings are present as something whose analysis is not immediately present. These meanings do not therefore count as such as limits of the analysis but only to the extent that their analysis is not present; formal being, on the contrary, counts as a limit both as such and to the extent that, as a matter of fact, its analysis is not present. As a result, while, on the one hand, that limit is a constant, on the other hand, it is a variable that takes the values given by those simple meanings at which the analysis of the originary meaning is actually halted. In this second respect, that constant has a simply formal value: precisely in the sense that it is the *actual presence* of that content (and not that content as such) that which, as the actual presence of a finite set of meanings, does not permit the actual presence of an infinite set.

7. Justification of this persistence

That twofold aspect of the limit of the analysis is affirmed because each of the factually simple meanings (as well as every other meaning) *is formally distinct* from the meaning 'being' (i.e. from formal being), and, *as distinct in this way*, it is not posited as a determination *of being* – i.e. as a semantic complexity that would include the meaning 'being' as a moment. As a result, the positing of each of those meanings is *co-initial* with the positing of formal being; whence the beginning precisely consists of this co-initiality (which, let us repeat, is not a co-initiality of two terms but of a multiplicity of terms, one of which – formal being – has a different value relative to the value of the other terms).

If one were to object that it is impossible to posit any meaning (= determinacy) without positing the meaning 'being' – or without positing that former meaning as a determination *of* being – we would need to respond that the objection is certainly valid (cf. Chapter 12), but only insofar as it is referred *to the abstract concept* of the positing of that first meaning; furthermore, insofar as that objection is referred in that way, we would need to add that it is equally impossible to posit 'being' without positing its determinations (cf. Chapter 12, §21). The *distinction* between the positing of 'being' and the positing of any of the factually simple meanings, however, is not equivalent to the abstract concept of those two acts of positing, but it is grounded in the observation that the positing of 'being' is formally distinct from the positing of its determinations. That 'co-initiality' of distinct terms would not therefore obtain if the positing of the factually simple meanings were to be absolutely identified with the positing of formal being.

8. Complex meanings and the positing of being

The factually simple meanings at which the analysis of the originary meaning is halted *are*. That is to say, 'being' (= formal being) is immediately predicated of them, in the same way in which it is predicated of every other immediately known determination. Those meanings, however, are not factually simple insofar as they are respectively considered as the synthesis between a semantic determinacy (by virtue of which each of them differs from the other ones) and the being of this determinacy, but insofar as that determinacy is regarded as distinct from its being; it is precisely insofar as it is thus distinct that it stands as a factually simple meaning – the positing of which is therefore co-initial with the positing of the meaning 'being'.

Let us then observe that complex meanings – namely, those meanings that, contrary to the factually simple ones, count as semantic complexities even when considered as distinct from their being – cannot be co-initial with the meaning 'being': not only if they are respectively considered as syntheses between their determinacy and the being of the latter (this also being the case for factually simple meanings), but also insofar as the determinacy of a complex meaning is regarded as distinct from its being. If, indeed, this determinacy is not co-initial with those factually simple meanings at which the analysis of that complex determinacy is halted, and if these meanings are co-initial with the meaning 'being', it follows that the determinacy in question cannot be co-initial with this latter meaning.

Furthermore, it should be observed that, in relation to those complex meanings as part of which the complexity is constituted by the fact that a moment of the complexity is *determined* by another moment (or other moments) of this complexity,[2] it must be stated that these complex meanings cannot be co-initial with formal being not only for the reason indicated earlier but also because the positing of this type of semantic complexity necessarily implies or includes the positing of the meaning 'being'; the latter is therefore *a moment* of that complexity, in such a way that this complexity cannot be co-initial with it. For, indeed, the positing of a meaning requires here the positing of the *determination* in which that very meaning consists, and positing this determination means positing that one of the moments of this complex meaning *is* in some way another moment (or other moments): that is to say, it means positing each of these moments as a form of *being*-other – this 'other' precisely consisting in the other moment(s). Accordingly, if the meaning 'being' is not posited as part of the semantic domain constituted by the complex meaning under consideration, nor is the determination itself, and, therefore, nor is that complex meaning. In other words, every semantic complexity of this kind is an apophantic structure, in the sense that if m' and m'' are the moments of that complexity, the set $m'm''$, concretely conceived, is equivalent to the predicative relation between m' and m'', i.e. to the affirmation: 'm' is m'''. By way of example: 'this red extension' is a complex meaning whose moments (at a cursory analysis) are this extension and the red colour of this extension. These moments constitute a synthesis such that one of the two moments – in being determined by the other one – *is* in some way the other moment. Accordingly, that synthesis may be expressed by these two judgements: 'This extension is red', 'This red is thus extended'.

At the same time, however, each of the two moments is not immediately the other one – as though the two moments were formally the same. They formally distinguish themselves in the sense that the colour of this extension is not this extension, and this being-extended is not its being-coloured. Each of the two, however, is also the other one, *through the mediation* of the superseding of its own immediate determination: whereby, on the one hand, this immediate determination is retained as something distinct from that in which that superseding results, and, on the other hand, what is superseded and this outcome of the superseding are brought to be together (§11).

9. Aporia: Semantic complexities as contradictions

Taking up the point mentioned earlier, we must now turn to an aporia of significant importance.

If a certain kind of complex meanings is an apophantic structure in which each moment of the complexity *is* in a certain way *the other* moments, every semantic complexity of this kind, the moments of which differ from one another, will be a negation of the principle of non-contradiction. Affirming that this extension is red would indeed mean affirming that this extension is not-this-extension (since the colour of this extension belongs to the horizon of the contradictory of the latter).

As it is well known, this is an age-old aporia, already discussed by Plato (*Sophist*, 251 ff.) and, however, rather avoided than solved by him. For, indeed, Plato only shows the untenable consequences that follow from the aporia without showing how the aporia itself is to be resolved. It is certainly the case that the aporia negates every κοινωνία of ideas and that therefore it will not even be possible to predicate the being of any determination – since, if a determination is formally distinct from 'being', predicating 'being' of it will entail affirming that it is 'other than itself'. What still remains to be exhibited, however, is the logical fallacy that gives rise to this aporia. More generally: if an aporetic argument *shows the necessity* of a negation of the immediate, or of one of its aspects, it is not sufficient to supersede the aporia by invoking as the reason of the superseding the very fact that the aporia is a negation of the immediate, but one must indicate how that negation of the immediate does not exist as something necessary: i.e. one must indicate the logical fallacy that makes it *appear* as something necessary. Aristotle attempts to eliminate that difficulty by introducing the distinction between substance and accidents: there is nothing that prevents something (a substance or an accident serving as the substrate of another accident) from also being something *other*, in addition to what it is; this otherness, however, is not a negation of that substance – i.e. it is not another substantial determination – but it constitutes the domain of the accidental determinations of that substance (*Metaphysics*, IV, chapter 4). This may be accepted in the sense that if one affirms that this extension is red, one does not negate that this extension is an extension, but one affirms that this extension – which is *qua* this extension – is, precisely, red; that is to say, one affirms that the identical (this extension that is this extension) is further determined relative to what constitutes the determinacy of the identity. Except that, despite this clarification, the aporia persists unchanged: precisely in that the identity *is* other than itself. What causes the aporia is precisely – to use an Aristotelian terminology – the *inherence* of the accidental determination in the substantial one: that is to say, the fact that the one is in some way the other. Every non-tautological (= non-identical) judgement thus appears to constitute a contradiction. It would therefore have to be stated that every semantic complexity that has an apophantic value is a contradiction, to the extent that it appears that this complexity cannot, as such, be equivalent to a tautological judgement.

It is clear that the aporia exists as such insofar as the kind of semantic complexity that causes the aporia belongs to the immediate content itself. The aporia may therefore be formulated in this way: on the one hand, the Ph-immediate (experience) realizes itself as a connection (of connections) of different determinations – that is to say, this connection or synthesis of different terms is immediately present; on the other hand, a connection of different terms appears to be a contradiction, for, as remarked, this connection entails that something should *be the other* with which it is connected. Experience thus contradicts the principle of non-contradiction (the logos).

This aporia must be regarded as the reappearing – in an even more radical form – of the Eleatic aporia according to which the *multiplicity* attested by experience constitutes a negation of the principle of non-contradiction. In the course of this enquiry, it will appear that the two great aporias entrusted by Parmenides to philosophical thought – the negation of multiplicity and the negation of becoming, performed in the name of the principle of non-contradiction – have an aporetic strength that extends beyond the very solution that the Platonic and Aristotelian metaphysics have given to these aporias: to such an extent that contemporary thinking itself remains immersed in them. Concerning the aporia of multiplicity, this is certainly solved by Plato; this solution, however, is limited to the explicit formulation that the aporia receives as part of the Eleatic stance: the many are not – for if they were, in being other or distinct from being, they would stand as the being of non-being. By distinguishing absolute non-being (the *opposite* of being) from relative non-being (what *differs* from being), Plato certainly solves the aporia – precisely, however, to the extent that the latter is formulated in this way. For, as already mentioned, the Platonic solution is insufficient if the aporia is formulated by stating that the predicative connection between two different meanings is a contradiction.

10. Solution of the aporia: Every non-contradictory judgement is an identical judgement

a. Hegel himself asserts that every non-tautological judgement constitutes a contradiction – which is correct, but only as long as the judgement is considered abstractly. This abstract consideration consists in regarding the subject and the predicate of the judgement as *unrelated* terms. That is to say, if it is asserted that a judgement consists of positing something (the subject) as something other than itself (the predicate) – if the subject and the predicate are simply regarded as different terms – this entails that these two terms are *presupposed* to the judgement itself: and, therefore, to their synthesis. Presupposed in this way, the subject is indeed something to which its predicate does not yet pertain (precisely because this pertaining is the very synthesis to which the subject and the predicate are presupposed). The judgement is then regarded as the establishing of that pertaining between the two terms thus presupposed; or, equivalently: the relation between the terms is considered to be logically additional relative to the positing of the terms themselves, in such a way that something that does not pertain to the subject is said to pertain to the subject or in such a way that something that *is not* the determinacy that is made to function as predicate is affirmed *to be* that determinacy. A judgement, however, is a contradiction only insofar as the subject and the predicate are presupposed in this way. (Furthermore, this contradiction does not only obtain if the subject and the predicate have a different determinacy but also if they have the same one – whereby the judgement takes the form: 'Being is being'. In this respect, cf. Chapter 3, §§9–13.)

It is only insofar as the subject and the predicate are presupposed to the judgement that they have a different determinacy and that the judgement is *therefore* a contradiction: for if that presupposition does not take place, the predicate is not affirmed of something to which, *qua* presupposed to the predication, that predicate does not pertain, but it is affirmed of that to which, precisely, that predication pertains; or, equivalently, the predicate does not pertain to the subject insofar as the latter is presupposed to its relation with the predicate, but insofar as the subject precisely is or is already part of that relation – i.e. *insofar as the subject is already itself the synthesis of subject and predicate*. In other words, the meaning *dy* may only be predicated of the meaning *dx* insofar as *dx* is posited as that to which *dy* pertains – and, therefore, insofar as the semantic domain constituted by the subject of the predication does not simply stand as *dx*, but as the very synthesis between *dx* and *dy*. Conversely, *dx* can be the subject of the predication of *dy* only insofar as *dy* is precisely predicated – and, therefore, posited – as that which pertains to *dx*, in such a way that the semantic domain constituted by the predicate does not simply stand as *dy*, but as the very synthesis between *dy* and *dx*. The concrete meaning of the proposition: '*dx* is *dy*' is therefore:

$$(dx = dy) = (dy = dx).$$

In considering, for instance, the meaning: 'This red extension' (this red extension that is part of the totality of the Ph-immediate precisely consisting of a specific meaning), it is not 'this extension' ($= dx$) that is red – understanding by 'this extension' a semantic domain that is *unrelated* to the meaning constituted by the red colour (of this extension) – but it is 'this red extension' that is red. For, otherwise – i.e. by regarding this extension as something that is not already part of a synthesis with the colour red (and thus presupposing that extension to this synthesis) – affirming that 'this extension' is red would entail affirming that something is other than itself, or, equivalently, that something is and is not something other than itself: it is that other insofar as this is explicitly affirmed in positing what is present in its Ph-immediacy; it is not that other, insofar as that something is presupposed to its synthesis with that other (in such a way that one is forced to negate the immediate). Conversely, it is also not possible to state that this extension is 'red' (*dy*) – regarding this term as a semantic domain that is not already in relation with this extension – but it must be stated that this extension is 'this red extended in that way': i.e. precisely extended in such a way as to constitute this extension.[3]

b. From what has been said, it appears that 'non-identical' judgements do not constitute a contradiction only insofar as the subject and the predicate of the judgement have themselves an apophantic value, and the apophansis constituted by the subject is the very apophansis constituted by the predicate. This means that *all* non-contradictory judgements are identical judgements, since in the case of 'non-identical' judgements, too, both the subject and the predicate of the judgement have the same apophantic value. (This verifies the first of the two points anticipated in §30 of Chapter 2.) In this respect, synthetic propositions, as ordinarily understood, are contradictory.

The aporia formulated above, relative to non-identical judgments, is not therefore solved by showing how non-identical judgements are not contradictory, but by showing that so-called 'synthetic judgements', too, are identical judgements, in such a way that it is precisely insofar as they are identical that they are not contradictory. The logos, therefore, far from standing in opposition to experience, constitutes instead the authentic comprehension of the latter – what stands opposed to experience being instead the inauthentic logos: namely, the logos that, in abstractly conceiving judgements, finds them as contradictions. If a concrete reflection shows that every non-contradictory judgement is an identical one, this is not achieved by means of a demonstration but through an analysis of the structure of judgements.

Therefore, not only is

$$(E' = E'') = (E'' = E')$$

an identical judgement – (cf. Chapter 3, §10) – but so is

$$(dx = dy) = (dy = dx).$$

In both cases, while the subject

$$E' = E'',\ dx = dy$$

is identical to the predicate

$$E'' = E',\ dy = dx,$$

the subject and the predicate are not *distinct* determinations, such that the semantic domain of the one does not include the semantic domain of the other. For, indeed, in the same way in which E' and E'' that appear in the subject are respectively *posited as the same E' and E''* that appear in the predicate (Chapter 3, §10, b), so dx and dy that appear in the subject are respectively *posited as the same dx and dy* that appear in the predicate – and this cannot be the case if $E' = E''$ and $dx = dy$ are posited as being respectively distinct, in the indicated sense, from $E'' = E'$ and $dy = dx$.

It is precisely insofar as they are regarded as distinct in this way that, analogously to what has been verified for $(E' = E'') = (E'' = E')$, it will be possible to posit the equation $(dx = dy) = (dy = dx)$ only to the extent that it is developed into

$$[(dx = dy) = (dy = dx)] = [(dy = dx) = (dx = dy)],$$

thus initiating an infinite development – if the two terms of this last equation are once again regarded as distinct determinations. It is clear that this development can also arise if $dx = dy$ is abstractly separated from $(dx = dy) = (dy = dx)$, in such a way that it in turn presents itself as something that must be developed as

$$(dx' = dy') = (dy' = dx').$$

The reader may independently apply to $(dx = dy) = (dy = dx)$ the observations developed in §10 a, b, c of Chapter 3 relative to $(E' = E'') = (E'' = E')$.

Let us add that this infinite development may *not* be avoided by positing that the subject and the predicate of the identity are *as such* – i.e. *qua* subject and predicate of the identity – *the identity itself*. If, indeed, the subject and the predicate were *as such* the identity itself, they would in turn be the identity of the identity itself, and so on, *ad infinitum*. If the subject and the predicate do not stand as such (or actually) as the identity itself, however, they become the identity itself – or the positing of that identity is repeated – as soon as they are abstractly separated from that identity: i.e as soon as they are no longer regarded as subject and predicate of that identity.

The claim that the subject and the predicate of the identity are as such the identity itself may be defended as follows:

> If the identity *between* the subject and the predicate were not the identity itself *in which* both subject and predicate *consist*, the identity (the judgement) between these two terms would be the identity between two contradictions: $dx = dy$, $dy = dx$. In each of these equations, it is indeed asserted that something (respectively: dx, dy) is other than itself (respectively: dy, dx). This is the case both if $dx = dy$ and $dy = dx$ are themselves respectively developed into
> $$(dx' = dy') = (dy' = dx') \text{ and into } (dy' = dx') = (dx' = dy'),$$
> and this development extends *ad infinitum*, as well as if the development is a finite one. In the first case, since $dx = dy$ and $dy = dx$ are respectively developed into
> $$(dx' = dy') = (dy' = dx') \text{ and into } (dy' = dx') = (dx' = dy')$$
> in order to supersede the contradiction of an identity of different terms, it follows that the infinite development – the first step of which is given by those last two equations – would count as an infinite superseding of the contradiction, which would therefore persist as something non-superseded. In the second case, the finite development leads to the two equations $(dx^n = dy^n) = (dy^n = dx^n)$, $(dy^n = dx^n) = (dx^n = dy^n)$, each of which is in turn the identity of two contradictions.

The fallacy of the argument exposed above lies in the fact that it may be argued that $dx = dy$ and $dy = dx$ must each stand as the identity itself $(dx = dy) = (dy = dx)$ – for otherwise they would be two contradictions – to the extent that the equations $dx = dy$ and $dy = dx$ are abstractly separated from the concrete identity, in such a way that, separated in this way, they each appear as a contradiction.

c. At the same time, however, negating the abstract separation of the subject and predicate of the identity and negating that the subject and the predicate of the identity are simple distinct terms *that do not mutually overlap* their positional domains does not mean negating the concrete distinction between $dx = dy$ (or $dy = dx$) and $(dx = dy) = (dy = dx)$; in the same way, dx and dy, while not to be abstractly separated from that concrete identity, distinguish themselves not only from the latter but also from that relative concreteness constituted by $dx = dy$. At this point, the reader may refer with the appropriate modifications to the observations made in §11 a, b, c, d of Chapter 3. For the differences between the two cases, cf. point e of that section.

d. The condition of an abstract consideration of two distinct terms therefore consists, in a first respect, in the presupposition of those distinct terms to their synthesis and, in a second respect (which is in fact the same one), in regarding a discursive sequence as a logical one. Indeed, discourse posits at first the subject and at a later point the predicate. If a logical value is conferred upon this sequence, the subject will appear as something to which the predicate does not pertain in such a way that the latter will be said to pertain to something to which it does not pertain. It is here clear that the predicative relation between the distinct terms, as it is realized in the linguistic or verbal formulation of the judgement, is a contradiction only as long as those distinct terms are abstractly conceived of as being unrelated to one another. That is to say, language – predominantly – realizes itself as a connection of distinct determinations; while language itself, as such, does not for the most part let the concrete meaning of a judgement become explicit as part of the linguistic structure itself, on the other hand, language is nothing more than an *occasion* for the arising of an abstract consideration of those distinct terms, and not a cause. It falls to a concrete comprehension to safeguard the untarnished nature of language and not let its ingenuousness become an error in the hands of that abstract consideration.

e. It is possible to affirm that E' is E'' (i.e. that being is being) not insofar as E' and E'' are regarded as distinct meanings, but insofar as E' is posited as that to which E'' pertains, and insofar as E'' is posited as that which pertains to E': that is to say, insofar as the concrete meaning of the proposition $E' = E''$ is regarded as $(E' = E'') = (E'' = E')$. At the same time, however, E', *qua* distinct meaning, *is* E''. Therefore, while being (E') is not *posited* as being (E'') itself insofar as being is regarded as a distinct term in the indicated sense, at the same time, however, being (E') *is*, *qua* distinct term, being (E'').

For what instead concerns the relation between dx and dy, not only is it not possible to affirm that dx is dy as long as dx and dy are considered as distinct meanings, but, to the extent that dx and dy are distinct, dx is *not* even dy.

Note: we are not stating that dx is simply not dy, but that dx is not dy *to the extent that dx and dy are considered as distinct terms*. That is to say, while it must certainly be stated that dx is dy, it must, however, be noted that it is not possible for dx to be dy *to the extent that dx and dy are distinct* but to the extent that each of them is a *concretely conceived* abstract moment of an apophansis that is constituted by the very relation between dx and dy. Accordingly, since the apophansis ($dx = dy$) of which dx is a moment is *the same* apophansis ($dy = dx$) of which dy is a moment, dx is dy insofar as the apophansis is itself: $(dx = dy) = (dy = dx)$.

It must therefore be stated that dx *is dy per accidens*: precisely to the extent that dx and dy are moments of an apophansis that counts *for itself* as an identity. (And *per accidens* is also the affirmation that posits the synthesis between dx and dy as subject, and dy as predicate, or dx as subject and the synthesis between dy and dx as predicate.)

Therefore, if on the one hand it must be asserted that one of the distinct terms that constitute a judgement or complex meaning is the other distinct term(s), on the other hand it must be excluded that one term must be the other *to the extent that the two are distinct*, for that would be equivalent to affirming that what is different is identical to the extent that it is different. What is different is identical, but in the sense indicated above, i.e. *per accidens*: that is to say, in that what is different is the abstract content of the identical. (What language primarily brings into view is precisely this identity of the different.)

We have thus clarified the meaning of what was affirmed in §8, in which we stated that a moment of a complex meaning is not immediately the other moments, but it is those other moments *through the mediation* of the superseding of its own immediate determination; this superseding precisely consists in the inclusion of that distinct term in the apophansis as an abstract moment of the latter, in such a way that it is by means of or through this inclusion that dx is dy.

If one therefore considers a distinct term dx, which stands as a moment of a semantic complexity, that distinct term certainly *is* the other distinct moments. For instance, this extension, considered as a distinct meaning, *is* red. Furthermore, as already discussed, it is not such insofar as it is a distinct meaning; *qua* distinct meaning, it (only) *is* red, but this being is not posited in the semantic domain constituted by that distinct meaning as such, since that positing constitutes the concrete – i.e. the semantic complexity – of which that distinct meaning is a moment. Or, equivalently: *dx is dy*; the semantic domain constituted by dx, however, does not include this *being-dy*; as a result, dx (as well as dy, as distinct from dx) counts as a factually simple meaning.

f. At this point, one may object that if, having acknowledged the distinction between dx and dy, it is affirmed that one is the other, what is affirmed in this way is a contradiction; in order to eliminate the latter, it will be necessary to state that, to the extent that dx and dy are considered as distinct meanings, dx is not dy.

This objection is determined by a persistence of the abstract standpoint. Indeed, it may only be affirmed that dx is not dy insofar as their distinction is abstractly regarded as a separation. If that distinction is regarded as a separation, it will certainly be necessary to state that dx is not dy. Except that, as we have clarified above, it is possible to non-contradictorily affirm that dx is dy insofar as dx as much as dy are concretely conceived of as moments of the concrete: that is to say, insofar as each of the two is concretely regarded as part of its relation with the other one. Accordingly, it is by virtue of the self-identity of that relation that each of them is, *per accidens*, the other one – and it must therefore be excluded that each of them is the other one insofar as the two terms are distinct.

11. Analytic and synthetic propositions

Affirming that every non-contradictory judgement is an identical and therefore necessary judgement is of considerable importance. In the course of this enquiry, the assertion that every judgement is necessary will be considered from different perspectives and obtained from different standpoints. Let us now remark that the distinction between analytic and synthetic propositions persists unchanged *as an internal distinction of identical propositions*. If the subject and the predicate of every non-contradictory judgement are identical, the apophansis that constitutes the subject and the predicate of a judgement can, however, have a twofold value; that is to say, it may be: (1) such that its negation does not immediately appear to be *self-contradictory*; (2) such that its negation immediately appears to be self-contradictory. In the first case, the identical judgement is said to be a synthetic judgement; in the second case, that identical judgement is said to be an analytic judgement. Concerning the first case: the proposition: 'dx is not dy' is not immediately self-contradictory, even though it is in contradiction with the immediacy (i.e. the immediate presence) of the meaning constituted by the synthesis between dx and dy. Concerning the second case: the proposition: 'E' is not E'''' ('Being is non-being') is immediately self-contradictory.

Therefore: the negation of *every* judgement is immediately self-contradictory – precisely in that every judgement is an identical judgement. However, it is not the case for every judgement – but only for analytic ones – that the negation of the apophansis that constitutes the subject (or the predicate) of the judgement is immediately self-contradictory.

12. Applications (The principle of non-contradiction and existential judgements)

a. The aporia that arises in relation to the proposition: 'dx is dy' (§9) also obtains in relation to the proposition: 'Being is not non-being' ($E = \text{nn}E$), and it must therefore be solved in the same way. Indeed, the meaning 'being' (E') distinguishes itself from the meaning 'not being non-being' ($\text{nn}E$). As a result, in predicating $\text{nn}E$ of E – i.e. in stating that being is not non-being – it is affirmed that being is other than itself. The very formulation of the principle of non-contradiction would therefore be a contradiction.

It is by now clear what produces this kind of aporia: the presupposition of E and $\text{nn}E$ to their synthesis, in such a way that it is no longer recognized that it is of being that is not non-being that one predicates not being non-being; whereby the predication is not established between E and $\text{nn}E$, as distinct meanings, but it realizes itself as

$$(E = \text{nn}E) = (\text{nn}E = E).$$

It should furthermore be noted that predicating $\text{nn}E$ of E certainly means predicating an otherness relative to E (thus regarded as a simple noetic moment); this otherness, however, is such precisely insofar as it is constituted as a negation of the otherness itself. As a result, $\text{nn}E$ is and is not other than E: it is other than E insofar as E is formally distinct from $\text{nn}E$; it is not other than E insofar as $\text{nn}E$ is precisely meaningful as 'not being other than E' (i.e. as not being non-being). It is clear that if, in spite of this note, the principle of non-contradiction is simply regarded as a predicative relation between E and $\text{nn}E$, this principle is equivalent to a contradiction: precisely because E is distinct from $\text{nn}E$. That note becomes pertinent once non-contradictoriness itself is concretely posited as $(E = \text{nn}E) = (\text{nn}E = E)$.

b. The aporia that arises in relation to the propositions '$dx = dy$' and '$E = \text{nn}E$' also obtains in relation to existential judgements. For, indeed, as part of the proposition 'dx is', the meaning 'dx' is formally distinct from the meaning 'is', in such a way that this proposition appears as a contradiction. This contradiction is superseded by noting that it is precisely of dx, which is, that being is predicated – this being (ε) precisely consisting in the being of dx:

$$(dx = \varepsilon) = (\varepsilon = dx).$$

13. The existential value of every judgement

The identical proposition $(dx = \varepsilon) = (\varepsilon = dx)$ is analytic, according to the definition given in §11. Affirming that something – a positive (dx) – is not is indeed immediately self-contradictory. In *negating that something* is – and understanding this negation to be free from contradiction – one does not therefore negate being *simpliciter*, for as already remarked this is a self-contradictory affirmation, but one negates *a certain way or mode of being* of that something. This question, which is of great importance, will be developed separately in Chapter 13.

Let us remark here that every affirmative judgement is a determination of the existential judgement. Affirming that this extension *is* red means affirming, on the one hand, that this extension *is* or *exists* in a certain way – as red – and, on the other hand, that this red *is* or *exists* in a certain way – as extended in that way. Being in a certain way is a determination of being. The semantic domain constituted by 'dx is dy' thus includes the semantic domains constituted by 'dx is' and 'dy is'.

It therefore appears that, in relation to that type of semantic complexity that realizes itself as an apophansis, it is not possible to *distinguish* – as it is instead possible for e.g. factually simple meanings – the semantic domain constituted by the *apophansis* from the semantic domain constituted by the *being* of the apophansis. For, indeed, the being *of* the apophansis (i.e. the being *of* the complex meaning in which the apophansis consists) is the very being that *constitutes* the apophansis, in such a way that making that distinction means no longer keeping the apophansis as posited in the semantic domain that is held firm as distinct from the *being* of the apophansis.

Lastly, let us observe that every negative judgement – except for the one that predicates not-being of nothingness – is not only a negation of a certain mode of being of the subject and not of the being (*simpliciter*) of the latter, but it is also a negation of a mode of being (and not of the being *simpliciter*) of the apophansis itself. Not only does stating that 'dx is not dy' not mean negating the *being* of dx (or of dy), but it also does not *simpliciter* mean negating that dx is dy; that is to say, 'dx is not dy' negates that dx is dy according to a certain mode of being – for instance, that according to which the connection between dx and dy is temporally present – for, according to that mode of being for which 'dx is dy' must be posited in order to be superseded, dx is dy (according to this mode of being).

14. Note on simple meanings

The remarks developed in relation to formal being ascribe to the latter a multiplicity of categories. (The present discussion, however, may also be referred to each of the factually simple meanings.) The discourse concerning being is indeed not exhausted by the mere utterance or verbalization of being: many things are said of being, even though being itself, *qua* pure or formal being, is not said in many ways or senses. 'Being, pure being', begins Hegel: the lack of syntax of this statement precisely expresses the identification of this positional horizon with being and with nothing other than being, i.e. it expresses the moment in which what is posited is nothing but 'being'.

The Hegelian text, however, then continues: 'Without any further determination. In its indeterminate immediacy it is equal only to itself, etc.' A semantic complexity, which is additional relative to the absolute semantic simplicity constituted by the pure utterance of being, thus qualifies and addresses being itself: an additional semantic dimension that, however, is already in place when one utters 'pure' being. We too, for our part, are affirming that formal being is a semantic simplicity, which is in relation with the originary content, and so on. It thus appears that we should conclude that formal being is in fact a semantic complexity: precisely in that it is qualified, categorized and placed in relation.

We must respond by stating that all those determinations that the enquiry is able to render explicit certainly pertain to pure being – but, at the same time, that the latter *distinguishes itself* from each of them. Given this distinction, it will also be acknowledged that positing being *as* simple, *as* related, and so on, means positing a semantic complexity. What must be negated is that, from the fact that formal being is qualified, it should follow that it is not the simple and that it is therefore simple and complex at the same time. For, indeed, the semantic complexity that is constituted by positing pure being *as an other* is not the complexity *of* pure being, as distinct from the determinations that pertain to it by virtue of that positing, but it is the complexity of the concrete itself, relative to which pure being counts as a moment. Affirming, then, that the complexity in question is not the complexity of pure being *qua* distinct meaning does not mean affirming that those determinations of being are not, precisely, determinations of being: we are only stating that being is distinct from them, and to the extent that it is thus distinct, it *is* an absolute simplicity – i.e. it *is not* the complexity constituted by that very distinction. Conversely: affirming that being is the simple does not certainly mean affirming that being is complex; that affirmation, however, is a complexity. It is therefore insofar as formal being is held firm as a distinct meaning that it stands as a semantic simplicity: the complexity consisting of the relation between being and the determinations that pertain to it.

The aporia arises to the extent that, on the one hand, formal being is held firm as a distinct term – in such a way that, as such, it is affirmed as an absolute simplicity – and, on the other hand, one confers upon this distinct term as such determinations that belong to it insofar as it is part of a relation, and not insofar as it is distinct. At the same time, however, pure being, *qua* distinct term, *is* all that pertains to it insofar as it is part of that relation – but since it only *is* those determinations, the semantic domain of pure being, *qua* distinct term, includes as what is posited simply being, without any further determination.

7

Logical immediacy and logical mediation

1. Variants and constants. Preliminary definition

The totality of the immediate is a semantic structure constituted by a multiplicity of semantic elements. Indicating the meaning: 'Totality of immediately affirmed being' (the originary meaning) by S, we state that in one respect the analysis of S exhausts or includes *all* immediate determinations, and in a different respect it only includes *a part* of these determinations.

For, indeed, every immediate determination belongs to the content of the totality of the immediate; accordingly, in this respect, the analysis of S includes every immediate determination. At the same time, however, it is possible to *project* (suppose) that the totality of the immediate – while persisting *as such*, i.e. insofar as there persists a semantic content formally posited *as S* – should no longer include specific determinations already included in its content, or should come to include other determinations that are not yet included. The 'possibility' of this project is to be regarded as the *immediate non-contradictoriness* of the project – although there exist (in relation to this project, and more generally to projecting itself) aporias of significant interest, which are in any case superseded by a correct comprehension of the very plane of immediacy. Leaving aside here every observation related to the aporias that concern projecting in general – and keeping in mind that the project under consideration, too (as well as, more generally, every form of projecting) constitutes a determination, however peculiar, of the totality of the immediate – the 'immediate non-contradictoriness' of the project in question then means that, on the one hand, the analysis of the immediate signification of this project does not attest its self-contradictoriness, and, on the other hand, it does not attest that this project is in contradiction with the Ph-immediate.[1]

This possibility of projecting does not pertain to all immediate determinations, but only to a part of these. Indicating by 'variants of S' all those immediate determinations in relation to which there exists such a possibility of projecting, we are thus affirming that not all immediate determinations are variants. This means that the analysis of S exhibits a set of determinations or meanings,[2] in relation to which it is *L-immediately known* that S *cannot* be posited as such if any of them is not posited.[3] These meanings – which can be named 'constants of S' – are not simply 'included' in S, but they constitute the meaningfulness of S (even though they are at the same time included in S: in that they are also immediate determinations that, together with the variants, belong to the totality of the immediate content). One cannot therefore state that the constants arise with respect to S, *qua* already posited *as such* – and nor can it be stated that S persists *as such* if any of its constants is no longer posited. Taking this into consideration, it is clear that the variants of S are those meanings in relation to which it is *not* L-immediately known that S cannot be posited as such if any of them is not posited.

'It is L-immediately known that S cannot be posited if any of its constants are not posited' means: 'It is immediately self-contradictory to affirm that the positing of S is not the positing of all the constants of S'. That is to say, a constant of S is a meaning such that it is immediately self-contradictory to affirm that the positing of S is not the positing of that meaning.

It must therefore be stated that while the constants L-immediately belong to the definition of S, it is instead not immediately contradictory to negate that the variants belong to that definition. (In this sense, it was stated at the beginning that the analysis of S only includes a part of the immediate determinations. For a detailed discussion of the two meanings of the term 'analysis' outlined above, cf. § 14).

While the belonging of the constants of S to the definition of S is formally distinct from the positional implication between S and its constants, this positional implication however precisely obtains insofar as those constants belong to the definition of S (and it is precisely by virtue of this belonging that a meaning is a constant of S).

2. Non-analytic positional implications: Notable cases. Extension of the concept of constant

a. From what has been said, it follows that all propositions of the type: 'The positing of S implies the positing of the constant s' are analytic propositions. Indicating the subject and the predicate of this type of propositions with the symbols 'Sj' and 'Pr', the concrete formulation of these propositions is therefore (cf. Chapter 6, § 12):

$$(Sj = Pr) = (Pr = Sj).$$

The conversion of the proposition $(Sj = Pr) = (Pr = Sj)$: 'The positing of the constant s implies the positing of S' either gives rise or does not give rise to an analytic proposition depending on the value of the constant s. There indeed exists a set σ of constants of S, whose semantic domain does not immediately or as such imply S. For instance: the analysis of meanings such as (formal) 'being', 'totality', 'immediacy', etc. – which are all constants of S – does not exhibit that immediate implication. The constants of this type constitute *a part* of the meaningfulness of S: that is to say, their signification is a part of the originary signification.

If then s belongs to the set σ, whereby the concept of Pr (as belonging to the first of the two equations formulated above) is identical *to a part* of the concept of Sj, the above conversion of the proposition $(Sj = Pr) = (Pr = Sj)$ does not give rise to an analytic proposition: in the sense that if the project of a positional horizon in which S is posited as such, but the constant s is not posited, immediately stands as something self-contradictory in that the meaningfulness of s is identical to a part of the meaningfulness of S, the project of a positional horizon in which s (which belongs to the set σ) is posited but S is not does not instead immediately count as a self-contradictory project.

For, indeed, if s is simply a component of the meaningfulness of S (or, equivalently, if Pr is a component of the meaningfulness of Sj), S cannot be a component of the meaningfulness of s; as a result, the propositions of the type: 'The positing of the constant s (which belongs to the set σ) implies the positing of S' are not analytic.

b. It should furthermore be noted that while the project of a positional horizon in which s is posited but S is not is not immediately self-contradictory, at the same time, however, insofar as that positional horizon (*qua* non-positing of S) does not constitute itself as the originary structure, this horizon is therefore not able to supersede its own negation, leaving it beside itself, and thus standing as something groundless – and, in fact, as an implicit negation of S, as something self-contradictory.

c. Let the series

$$s_1, s_2, \ldots, s_n$$

indicate the constants of S, and let the sets

$$s_1(s_1), s_2(s_1), s_3(s_1), \ldots, s_n(s_1);$$

$$s_1(s_2), s_2(s_2), s_3(s_2), \ldots, s_n(s_2);$$

$$\ldots\ldots\ldots\ldots\ldots\ldots\ldots\ldots;$$

$$s_1(s_n), s_2(s_n), s_3(s_n), \ldots, s_n(s_n)$$

respectively indicate the sets of the constants $s_1, s_2, \ldots, s_n$.

It is then certainly self-contradictory to affirm that S is posited as such if any constant of the constants of S – e.g. $s_1(s_1)$ – is not posited; accordingly, in this respect the constants of the constants of S, too, must be considered as constants of S. While this is the case, however, it must also be observed that the propositions of the type: 'The positing of S implies the positing of $s_1(s_1)$' are not analytic, since the positing of $s_1(s_1)$ is not implied by the positing of S as such, but by this positing insofar as it implies one of its constants; or, equivalently: the predicate of that proposition does not pertain to the subject as such, but insofar as it is determined in a specific way (i.e. insofar as it is determined by its implication of a constant of S). Accordingly, the pertaining of the predicate to the subject is not immediate, and the proposition is not analytic (cf. § 13).

It is furthermore clear that the propositions of the type: 'The positing of $s_1(s_1)$ implies the positing of S' are not analytic.

It therefore appears in what sense the definition of a 'constant' given in § 1 was indicated in the title of that section as being *preliminary*. That is to say, up to this point, a constant has only been a meaning with a semantic content such that the implication between the positing of S and the positing of this meaning is *L-immediately* known. This definition must now be supplemented by stating that the constants of S – the argument can however be extended to every meaning – are all those meanings whose positing is necessarily implied by the positing of S. For some of these meanings, that implication is L-immediate; for others, it is L-mediated: i.e. for the propositions of the type: 'The positing of S implies the positing of $s_1(s_1)$' ($s_1(s_1)$ being a meaning such that it is L-immediately known that the positing of s_1 implies the positing of $s_1(s_1)$), the predicate pertains to the subject *through the mediation* of the term 'positing of s_1', which is L-immediately implied by 'positing of S', and which L-immediately implies 'positing of $s_1(s_1)$'. The series $s_1, ..., s_n$ thus indicates only those constants whose positing is L-immediately implied by the positing of S.

What has been stated concerning the constants of S also holds for the constants of the constants of S; that is to say, the sets $s_1(s_1), ..., s_n(s_1); s_1(s_2), ..., s_n(s_2); ....; s_1(s_n), ..., s_n(s_n)$ do not now respectively indicate the constants *simpliciter* of $s_1, s_2, ..., s_n$, but only those constants whose positing is L-immediately implied by the positing of the constants of S.

In § 15 and § 16 we shall furthermore consider the question of whether, in relation to specific constants of a meaning that are implied by this meaning *in an L-mediated way*, it may be equally asserted – as stated in § 1 – that it is *L-immediately* known that this meaning cannot be posited as such if those constants are not posited. This is a question of significant importance, since it appears that, remaining at the level of the originary structure (i.e. of the structuring of the immediate), only those meanings whose being implied by S is *L-immediately* known may be posited as constants of S.

d. There is no need to remark that the non-analytic propositions considered in point a differ from the non-analytic propositions considered in point c: for, concerning the former ones, it does not indeed appear that their negation is a self-contradiction, while, concerning the latter ones, it is instead known (in an L-mediated way) that their negation is a self-contradiction.

3. The general classification of constants

There are two types of constants of the meaning S (the discussion may once again be extended to every meaning), depending on whether a constant is part of the meaningfulness of S as a predicate of S or whether it is part of that meaningfulness but it does not count as a predicate of S. For instance, the meanings: 'Inclusive of every part of the immediate' and 'Part of the immediate' are both constants of S; while the first one is part of the meaningfulness of S as a predicate of S (since, precisely, the totality of the immediate is inclusive of every part of the immediate), the second one is instead simply part of the meaningfulness of S in the following sense: i.e. in that since it is not possible to think the 'totality' without thinking a 'part' as that which that totality surpasses – that is to say, if thinking the totality without thinking it as including a part means not thinking the totality (in this respect, cf. Chapters 9 and 10) – something like a 'totality' can only be posited insofar as the meaning 'part' is itself posited, whereby the latter is part of the semantic domain constituted by 'totality' without however counting as a predicate of that very domain (this counting as a predicate being in fact contradictory).

It can therefore be stated: all L-immediate or L-mediated predicates of a meanings are constants of that meaning (this point will be adequately clarified in due course), but not all the constants of a meaning are predicates of the latter. Accordingly, stating that a meaning is implied by another meaning, in an L-immediate or L-mediated way, or that the positing of the former is implied by the positing of the latter – in such a way that the former is a constant of the latter – differs from stating that a meaning is predicated in an L-immediate or L-mediated way of another meaning. Or, equivalently: *for the reason* that y is predicated of x (in an L-immediate or L-mediated way), it *eo ipso* follows that the positing of x implies the positing of y, or that x implies y (this assertion, let us repeat, will be adequately clarified further ahead); *from the fact* that the positing of x implies the positing of y, however, it does not follow *for this very reason* that y is predicated of x (but nor is it excluded that it could be).

Concerning the correct meaning of this distinction between these two types of constants, cf. § 15.

4. Immediate positional implications

The totality of the immediate, as the horizon of immediacy, is therefore constituted by a system of positional implications that have an analytic value (i.e. which are L-immediate), and by a system of Ph-immediate positional implications expressed by synthetic *a posteriori* propositions (L-immediate implications being themselves Ph-immediate). Concerning this second system of implications, it should be noted that, between any two determinations (variants or constants) of the totality of the immediate, there exists in any case that type of positional relation by virtue of which they imply each other as a matter of fact: this implication precisely consisting *in the fact* (the negation of which is in contradiction with the Ph-immediate) that they are both immediately present. Every immediate determination therefore implies every other immediate determination in an Ph-immediate way, i.e. by virtue of a factual implication.

The non-analytic positional implications considered in point a of § 2 therefore only represent a part of the totality of all *a posteriori* syntheses.

The implication between the positing of S and the positing of its variants (§ 1), too, is a distinctive type of *a posteriori* synthesis.

From the standpoint of the structuring of the immediate, every true non-analytic proposition is a synthetic *a posteriori* proposition. (A true proposition is one the negation of which is either in contradiction with Ph-immediacy or with L-immediacy).

Concerning analytic implications, it must furthermore be observed that the immediate is also constituted by constants of variants, in such a way that the implication between a variant and the constants (covariants) that L-immediately pertain to it gives rise to an analytic proposition.

5. The project of synthetic *a priori* positional implications between immediate determinations

a. Consider the system of those positional implications that, from the standpoint of immediacy, count as *a posteriori* syntheses. The following proposition may be employed as a paradigm for all the terms of this system (or at least for all 'normal' terms, cf. the following footnote): 'The positing of Y implies the positing of Z'.

It must therefore be stated that the project of a positing of Y that does *not* imply the positing of Z does not immediately appear to be contradictory (i.e. it does not appear to be contradictory from the standpoint of the structuring of the immediate).[4] Therefore, also *projecting* that the positing of Y should *imply* the positing of Z does not immediately appear to be contradictory.

This implication, which appears in this second side of the project,[5] has a twofold value, depending on whether: 1) the projected implication has the same value as the implication that obtains between Y and Z insofar as these two terms are *de facto* implied (in this case, one projects the persistence of the factual implication between Y and Z); 2) the implication is projected as having a value such that it appears to be self-contradictory for Y to be posited even if Z is not. (In this case, one projects a self-contradictoriness of side 1 of the project that cannot immediately be attested).

b. Concerning this second case, it must therefore be stated that it is not immediately contradictory to project to be able to show that positing Y without positing Z implies a self-contradiction – m – whose terms (i.e. whose mutually contradictory elements or moments) are *not* the positing of Y and the lack of positing of Y (or the positing of Z and the lack of positing of Z).

In order to clarify this point, it should be noted that, in relation to those positional implications that have an analytic value – consider, for instance, an implication between the positing of S and the positing of one of its constants, s – the L-immediate pertaining of the positing of the implication of s to the positing of S entails that the terms or moments of the self-contradictoriness determined by the negation of the fact that the positing of S implies the positing of s consist in the affirmation of the positing of S and (insofar as one negates that s is posited) the negation of the positing of S; whence it must be stated that this self-contradictoriness is L-immediate, i.e. it is attested through an analysis of S (or, equivalently, through an analysis of the negation of the positional implication between S and s). Concerning instead the *projected* implication between Y and Z considered in the second of the two cases distinguished above: since the positing of the implication of Z does not L-immediately pertain to the positing of Y (i.e. it is not immediately contradictory to project – since the analysis of Y does not include Z – that Y should be posited but that Z should not), the terms or moments of the m-self-contradiction, which is projected to be realized if Y is posited without Z, must respectively consist of something *other* than the positing of Y, and by the negation of this other term. (If one of the two moments of the m-contradiction consisted of the positing of Y, then, since the two moments that constitute the content of the contradiction are one the negation of the other, the other moment of the m-contradiction would consist of the negation of the positing of Y; as a result, if one were to make the m-contradiction *thus* understood result from the negation of the positional implication between Y and Z, it would be necessary for the immediate implication between the positing of Y and the positing of Z not to be synthetic *a posteriori*, as it instead is, but analytic; this is because only in this case would the negation of the positional implication between Y and Z give rise, *as such*, to a contradiction constituted by the affirmation and negation of the positing of Y).[6]

c. Considering again side 1 of the project (cf. point a), it should be observed that, once again, the projected lack of implication between Y and Z presents a twofold value, depending on whether: 1) the positing of Y is projected as not implying the positing of Z *as a matter of fact* – in such a way that it is not possible to exclude the possibility that the positing of Y should imply the positing of Z in a later or additional moment relative to the projected one; 2) the lack of implication between Y and Z is projected to have a value such that it appears to be self-contradictory to project that Y should be posited together with Z in a later or additional moment relative to the projected one. (In this case, one projects a self-contradictoriness of side 2 of the project that cannot be immediately attested.)

Concerning this second case, it must therefore be stated that it is not immediately contradictory to project to be able to show that the project of a positing of Y that implies the positing of Z should imply a contradiction – m' – the terms or moments of which are not the positing and lack of positing of Y.[7]

It should be observed that Y and Z are implied as a matter of fact (i.e. their both being posited is Ph-immediately attested); accordingly, the self-contradictoriness that is projected to pertain to their implication may only be referred to a *projected* implication between those two terms. Instead, in relation to the second case considered with respect to side 2 of the project, since what is projected here is the self-contradictoriness of the negation of an implication that already exists as a matter of fact, it is not necessary to refer that self-contradictoriness to the negation of a projected implication.[8]

d. The result of these observation is the following: both side 2 and side 1 of the project under consideration present – in the second of the two aspects or values that pertain to them – a type of propositions that are neither analytic nor synthetic *a posteriori*, which can indeed be referred to as synthetic *a priori* propositions. The paradigm of these propositions is given by the proposition: 'The positing of Y *necessarily* implies the positing of Z', or: 'The (projected) positing of Y *necessarily* implies the lack of positing of Z' – that 'necessity' consisting, in the first proposition, in the arising of the m-self-contradiction *as* soon as the implication is negated, and in the second proposition in the arising of the m'-self-contradiction as soon as the implication is affirmed.

This means that synthetic *a posteriori* propositions are such to the extent that it is possible for them to *become* synthetic *a priori* propositions, or to the extent that the project of this becoming is not immediately contradictory.

6. Applications

Let us consider a few significant values of Y and Z:

1. $Y = S$; $Z = $ a variant v_x of S. In relation to these values of Y and Z, the result expressed above entails that it is immediately possible – i.e. it is not immediately contradictory to project – that every variant of S could become (i.e. could appear as) a constant of S. (The *lack* of positing of v_x – necessarily implied by the positing of S – too, can be considered as a constant: a negative constant). An analogous result can be obtained by positing: $Y = s$; $Z = v_x$.

2. $Y = v_x$; $Z = v_y$. Given these values of Y and Z, the result expressed above entails that it is immediately possible – i.e. it is not immediately contradictory to project – that every variant could become a covariant relative to any other variant. (The lack of positing of v_x – necessarily implied by the positing of v_y – too, can be considered as a covariant: a negative covariant.)

3. The following values of Y and Z may be grouped into a single logical situation: i) $Y = s_x$; $Z = S$; ii) $Y = s_x$; $Z = s_y$; iii) $Y = v_x$; $Z = S$; iv) $Y = v_x$; $Z = s_x$.

As in the previous two cases, one should read again the paradigmatic propositions while giving these values to the variables Y and Z. It must then be stated that it is immediately non-contradictory to project a verification of the necessary implication between, respectively, a constant s_x (belonging to the set σ) and S, between a constant s_x and another constant s_y (both having the property of not immediately implying the other one in a necessary way), between any variant v_x and S, and between any variant v_x and any constant s_x.

4. In relation to the second of the two aspects of side 1 of the project under consideration, however, it is also immediately non-contradictory to project the verification of the fact that the projected positing of each of the values of Y indicated under point 3 should necessarily imply the lack of positing of the corresponding values of Z. In relation to the cases in which the value of Z consists of S itself (first and third cases indicated under point 3), this means that it is not immediately contradictory to project a demonstration of the necessity that, were a future positional horizon to be realized (subject to specific conditions or absolutely), this horizon should be realized as something groundless, since the lack of positing of S consists in or implies a lack of positing of the originary structure. In other words, it is not immediately contradictory to project the demonstration *of the necessity* of a return – subject to specific conditions, or absolutely – of pre-philosophical knowledge.[9] Furthermore, in relation to the *recollection* of positional horizons that, as a matter of fact, do not include S (still considering the first and third cases indicated in point 3) – i.e. in relation to the recollection of pre-philosophical positional horizons – it is not immediately contradictory to project a demonstration of the necessity of the existence of these past groundless dimensions. A consideration of the cases (second and fourth) in which the value of Z is given by a constant of S (s_x, s_y) may be left aside here, since we have not yet examined the meaning of a positional horizon in which, despite the positing of S, a constant of S is not posited. Let us simply remark that a consideration of these cases would anticipate an aporia that is considered further on. This aporetic situation appears in any case already here, for after having stated that it is immediately self-contradictory to project that S should be posited as such without the positing of all its constants (§ 1), we are now stating that it is not immediately self-contradictory to project a positional horizon in which, despite the positing of S, one of the constants of S is not posited (cf. Chapter 8). Let us furthermore note that, if in those second and fourth cases one considers the lack of positing of, respectively, s_y and s_x (as values of Z), this does not mean that everything that is posited consists, respectively, of s_x and v_x (as values of Y) – in such a way that, in those second and fourth cases, too, one would be dealing with a lack of positing of S; rather, one is considering the value taken by Y in its being a moment of S, or in its being included in S: it is indeed the task of the first and

third cases (these always being regarded in relation to the second of the two aspects of side 1 of the project in question) to consider the lack of a positing of S. The second and fourth cases therefore consider the implication, or lack thereof, between s_x (included in S, in such a way that S is retained as posited) and s_y, as well as between v_x (included in S) and s_x. That is to say, it is insofar as one understands the second and fourth cases in this way that a consideration of these two cases would introduce the aporia mentioned above. At the same time, however, it is possible to understand these two cases in such a way that the value taken by Y should consist of a semantic domain that does not include S, or that even consists of s_x and v_x (respectively).

5. In the previous points, we have considered constants of S belonging to the series $s_1, ..., s_n$, i.e. such that their positing is L-immediately implied by the positing of S (cf. § 2, c). Analogous results can be obtained by considering any type of constant of S – such as, for instance, those constants whose positing is implied by the positing of S in an L-mediated way.

7. Positional and predicative implications

Understanding by a 'predicative implication' that implication between two meanings that consists in one of the two being – affirmatively or negatively – predicated of the other one, let us state that every predicative implication is *at the same time* a positional implication or co-presence of those two meanings and of their relation. Conversely, every positional implication is at the same time a predicative implication between two co-present meanings: for between any two co-present meanings there exists at least that predicative implication by virtue of which it is possible to negate that one is the other.

It should be noted that while a predicative implication is *at the same time* – i.e. it *requires* or *implies* – the positional implication between the subject and the predicate (and while, conversely, a positional implication implies the predicative implication of the co-present meanings), a predicative implication *does not however consist* in a positional implication, since the latter is nothing but the presence of the relation that obtains between multiple semantic factors, or the presence of a multiplicity of semantic factors in their being mutually part of a determinate relation. (It is clear, however, that while a positional implication between two meanings does not consist in the predicative implication between these meanings, a positional implication nevertheless consists in a predication: precisely that predication by virtue of which *it is affirmed* that the positing of a meaning implies the positing of the other meaning.)

What we wish to remark here, however, is that a positional implication is analytic, synthetic *a posteriori* or synthetic *a priori* depending on whether the predicative implication of the posited terms is, respectively, analytic, synthetic *a posteriori* or synthetic *a priori*. Concerning this third case, since an *a priori* synthesis is the result of a mediation, which – at least in relation to the *a priori* syntheses considered up to this point – is such with respect to the immediacy constituted by the factuality or aposteriority of the synthesis, it must therefore be stated that, when a synthetic predicative implication between two terms Y and Z becomes necessary after having been factual, the synthetic positional implication between Y and Z, too, becomes necessary after having itself been factual: in the sense that if, given the necessary predicative implication, one were to posit Y without positing Z, the positing of Y would realize a contradiction. For indeed, given that necessary predicative implication, being-Z belongs to the essence or meaning of Y: i.e. Y is that to which being-Z essentially pertains. Accordingly, if Y is posited but Z is not, Y is not posited as that to which being-Z essentially pertains, and, therefore, Y is not posited as such. The contradiction therefore obtains between the *intention* to posit Y as such and the *impossibility* for what is posited (i.e. for what one intends to posit) as Y to be Y, since, precisely, Z is not posited. (Suppose for instance that one should demonstrate that humans are immortal. If, after establishing this demonstration, one were to think of humans without thinking them as immortal, what would be thought in this way would not be 'humans' – and it would in fact be correct to give a different name to what would effectively be thought in this way. Further on in the enquiry, we shall return with particular attention to this series of concepts, which are of the utmost importance). Conversely, if the predicative implication between Y and Z is only a factual one, the project of a positing of Y that is not also a positing of Z does not immediately stand as the project of a contradiction: precisely because it is not immediately self-contradictory to project that Z should no longer be predicated of Y.

8. The project of the *m*-contradiction, and the modes of the Ph-immediate content

a. It should be observed that the project of the verification of the *m*-contradiction (cf. § 5, b) is not immediately contradictory to the extent that the totality of the immediate does *not* include any positing of Y that would imply the positing of a determinacy implying in turn the lack of positing of Z. Let Y be this pencil lying on my desk, and let Z be the distance between that pencil and the sheet of paper on which I am writing. In this case, Y and Z are two variants of S. Therefore: $Y = v_1$; $Z = v_2$. The positing of v_1 factually implies the positing of v_2. Except that a series of *past* acts of positing of v_1 is immediately present, each of which implies the positing of a distance between the pencil and the sheet of paper that *differs* from the distance that obtains *now* between these two objects. This means that the totality of the immediate includes a series of past acts of positing of v_1 that imply the positing of determinacies (those distances differing from v_2), which in turn imply the lack of positing of v_2. (One may also state that a series of acts of positing of v_1, such that determinacies that are contradictories of v_2 stand as predicates of v_1, is immediately present.) All the acts of positing of these determinacies imply the lack of positing of v_2; although the positing of some of these determinacies implies that v_2 is posited *in some way*. This means that every positing of those determinacies implies *a certain mode* of the lack of positing of v_2. Further developing this point: the totality of the immediate includes a series of past positional horizons, each of which includes a positing of v_1 in its implying the positing of a determinacy whose positing implies the lack of positing of v_2. *As part of some* of those horizons, v_2 is *altogether* absent; in each of the remaining horizons of the series under consideration, v_2 is posited *in some way*, and it is not posited only to the extent that it is not posited in accordance with *that mode* of positing, the realization of which would imply that those determinacies, whose positing is implied by the positing of v_1, were not posited in the way in which they are posited as a matter of fact. This is the case in which the positing of v_1, in implying the positing of a distance v_2' that differs from v_2, also implies the *positing* of v_2 *as superseded*; that is to say, this is the case in which in affirming that the distance v_2' obtains between this pencil and the sheet of paper, one negates that the distance v_2 obtains between the two objects. For, indeed, in and through this negation, v_2 is *in some way* posited – for it can be negated only insofar as it is thus posited – but the way or mode in which v_2 is posited or present is not the mode of positing that pertains to v_2', in such a way that, according to this other mode of positing, v_2 is *not* posited. (Insofar as v_2 is negated, it is posited according to a mode that, *in relation to the way* in which v_2' is posited, may be referred to as an 'ideal' mode. The mode of positing in which v_2' has been posited may therefore be referred to as a 'real positing'. What is of interest here, however, are not the terms used to indicate those two different modes of positing, but, precisely, the difference between the two modes). If, therefore, v_2 were posited in the same way in which v_2' is posited, v_2' would not be posited in the way in which it is posited as a matter of fact (i.e. as a 'real' positing). This value of the lack of positing of v_2 pertains *to all* the positional horizons belonging to the series under consideration (whereas an *absolute* lack of positing of v_2 only pertains to the first set of those horizons). It is therefore in relation to this value of the lack of positing of v_2 that we have stated that the totality of the immediate includes a series of past acts of positing of v_1, which imply the positing of determinacies (those distances differing from v_2), which in turn imply a (real) lack of positing of v_2.

The project of the verification of the contradictoriness of the concept: 'a positing of v_1 that does not imply the positing of v_2' is therefore *immediately* contradictory, in that, precisely, it is in contradiction with the immediate, as part of which, as discussed, it is possible to attest a series of past acts of positing of v_1 that imply the positing of determinacies that exclude the positing of v_2. It is thus however also established that the immediate contradictoriness of this project obtains to the extent that the positing of v_2, not implied by the positing of v_1, is not understood absolutely, but as *that mode of positing* of v_2, the realization of which would entail that v_2' (and all other distances differing from v_2) were not or had not been posited in the way in which it is or it has been posited as a matter of fact; that is to say, the immediate contradictoriness of that project obtains to the extent that the positing of v_2 has been excluded by the real positing of v_2'. (This exclusion, as we have seen, is not an absolute one, since there exists a set of acts of positing of v_2' that imply the *positing* of v_2 *as superseded*. Furthermore, that 'exclusion' is nothing but the negation of the contradiction that would obtain if v_1 were posited, at the same time and according to the same mode of positing, as v_2 and as v_2').

b. It should furthermore be noted that while the project of a verification of the contradictoriness of the concept: 'positing of v_1 that does not imply the real positing of v_2' is immediately contradictory *to the extent that* past positional implications between v_1 and v_2' (or equivalent terms) are immediately present, this immediate contradictoriness of the project no longer obtains if one does not refer to *every* positing of v_1, but only to *those* acts of positing of v_1 that are implied by the real positing of v_2 as a matter of fact, or that are projected to be thus implied by the real positing of v_2.

c. The following should however be observed – since it will play a crucial role in the resolution of the aporia considered in Chapter 8. The *Ph-immediacy* of the positional implication between v_1 and v_2' (or other terms equivalent to v_2') immediately excludes the possibility (= non-contradictoriness) of the project of a verification of the contradictoriness of a positing of v_1 that does not imply the real positing of v_2 (i.e. that does not imply that specific mode of positing of v_2 in accordance with which what is posited is instead v_2'): this project is immediately superseded by the Ph-immediacy of the positional implication between v_1 and a term (v_2') *that excludes* the real positing of v_2. In this case, it may be said that it is experience that decides about the possibility (= non-contradictoriness) of the logos – and experience decides in that it already *says* what the projected logos would come to negate. This, however, is no longer the case as soon as experience *does not say anything* concerning what the logos can say, *and it is in fact the latter that decides if that not saying anything on the side of experience is a contradiction or not*. Let v_1 still indicate this pencil that is on my desk, and let v_3 indicate the distance that separates the pencil from the left side of the desk. The positing of v_1 implies the positing of v_3 as a matter of fact. Unlike the case of the implication between v_1 and v_2, however, the Ph-immediate does *not* attest here any past positing of v_1 that would imply the positing of a distance – between the pencil and the left side of the desk – which differs from v_3. In addition, the Ph-immediate does not attest any positional implication between v_1 and v_3 prior to the one obtaining now as a matter of fact.[10] What is attested by the immediate is a series of past acts of positing of v_1, in none of which the positing of v_1 is implied by the positing of v_3 or of a distance differing from v_3. In this case, the project of a verification of the contradictoriness of the concept: 'positing of v_1 that does not imply the positing of v_3' is not immediately refuted – as in the previous case – by the presence or Ph-immediacy of the positional implication between v_1 and a determinacy that (analogously to v_2') excludes the positing of v_3. If that project is not immediately in contradiction with the Ph-immediate – precisely because, here, the Ph-immediate is not a pronouncement or a 'dictum' *contra* which the project would have something to say – this means that it is not immediately contradictory to project that all those past acts of positing of v_1 that do not imply the positing of v_3 (and that also do not imply the positing of determinacies that exclude the positing of v_3) are instances of *being in contradiction*: precisely to the extent that it is not immediately contradictory to project the contradictoriness of the concept: 'positing of v_1 that does not imply the positing of v_3', in such a way that positing v_1 without positing v_3 constitutes the realization of a contradiction. In this case, the logos has the possibility of verifying the contradictoriness of experience – which, it should be noted, is not contradictory to the extent that it *consists* in the presence of v_1, but to the extent that it does *not* consist in the presence of v_3. We shall in any case return to this question with all due attention. In particular, we shall have to clarify the following two points:

1. How one may hold firm, on the one hand, the (self-)contradictoriness of the concept 'positing of v_1 that does not imply the positing of v_3', and, on the other hand, the immediate presence of v_1 in its not implying the positing of v_3; for if that self-contradictoriness obtains, it appears to be impossible for the positing of v_1 to be

realized while not implying the positing of v_3, and while even being an Ph-immediate content. From this standpoint, contrary to what we have asserted above, it should be stated that – with respect to the relation between v_1 and v_3, too – the project of a verification of the self-contradictoriness of the concept 'positing of v_1 that does not imply the positing of v_3' is immediately superseded by the Ph-immediacy of those past acts of positing of v_1 that do not imply the positing of v_3. This aporia is solved in the following chapters.

2. A detailed illustration of the distinction, just outlined here, between that contradictoriness also mentioned above and that instance of 'being in contradiction' constituted by a positing of v_1 that does not imply the positing of v_3. We shall have to show that *it is precisely insofar as* the positing of v_1 (or of any equivalent term) – to the extent that it does not imply the posting of v_3 – realizes itself as a form of being in contradiction that it is possible to non-contradictorily hold firm both the self-contradictoriness of the concept discussed above and the Ph-immediacy of that v_1 that does not imply the positing of v_3. In this respect, cf. Chapter 8, §§ 4, ff.

d. In relation to what has been stated in point a concerning the positing of determinacies that exclude the positing of Z, it must further be observed that from the standpoint of immediacy it is possible to affirm that the positing of a determinacy implies the lack of positing of Z (or, more generally, of another determinacy) not simply for the reason that this determinacy and Z are mutually contradictory terms, but because these two contradictory terms stand as predicates of Y. In other words, what has been stated in point a is correct only if an affirmative predicative implication obtains between Y and Z, in such a way that, as part of the past acts of positing of Y, the terms in contradiction with Z are immediately present in their being affirmatively predicated of Y. This has precisely been verified with respect to the variants v_1 and v_2.

9. The base plane and the mediational plane of the originary structure

a. Synthetic *a priori* implications immediately stand as projects (cf. the first footnote in § 5). For, indeed, on the one hand their negation is not in contradiction with the Ph-immediate, and on the other hand a simple analysis of the semantic content of the negation of the pertaining of the predicate of those implications to the subject does not attest any mutually contradictory determinations. The project of those implications is the project of a *mediational plane*, in which the determinations of the immediate imply each other *in a necessary way*. It is in this sense that one can state that logical mediation belongs to the structure of the originary. The function of that mediation is to connect in a necessary way those elements of present reality that can thus be connected; or, equivalently, the function of that mediation is to manifest the necessary relation that exists (or, from the standpoint of immediacy: that is projected to exist) between the elements of the originary structure. The great 'deductions' of idealism had this type of logical mediation as their purpose; the question was precisely that of exhibiting the essential relation between the transcendental determinations of experience, i.e. the question was precisely that of positing experience as an organism of *a priori* syntheses, or as a synthesis of syntheses.

For what concerns the 'belonging' of logical mediation to the originary structure, while there is no need to repeat that this mediation is constituted by the superseding of the m(or m')-contradiction (cf. § 5, b-c), it must be emphasized that this mediation is *grounded* in immediacy itself. For, indeed, immediacy is the very totality of the immediate insofar as, on the one hand, it is the immediacy (i.e. immediate presence) of being (Chapter 2), and, on the other hand, it is the immediacy of the non-contradictoriness of being (Chapter 3). If the originary structure is the ground of every possible knowledge – and, since it is the totality of immediate knowledge, this means that it is the ground of every mediation – and if the originary structure is therefore also the ground of the mediational plane of the originary structure (this plane being considered here as something projected), it must therefore be stated that: on the one hand, this plane does not belong to the structure of the originary, and, on the other hand, it belongs to the latter precisely to the extent that it consists in the attestation of the necessary implications of the elements of the originary.

It is therefore possible to distinguish two moments of the originary structure. The first one includes the totality of immediate knowledge: the totality or structuring of the determinations that are *de facto* immediately known. It therefore also includes the project of the mediational plane (and, more generally, it can be stated that it includes a system of projects), to the extent that this project, too – like every project – is an immediate determination. This first moment may be referred to as the 'base plane' of the originary structure; that is to say, it is the originary structure, *simpliciter*. The second moment precisely consists in the mediational plane of the originary structure: as such, it is therefore no longer the originary structure, but a surpassing of the very level of originarity. (In this respect, it is not immediately contradictory to project a structuring of the determinations of the immediate, such that what in classical idealism remained a simple attempt should come to be truly realized.) The difference between these two moments of the originary is the very difference that exists between the factual level and the universal one, i.e. between a *de facto* structuring of the originary – which can therefore be projected to be constituted differently (within certain limits) – and a structure of the originary, the project of the variation of the constitution of which is either absolutely eliminated (as a limiting case) or it is restricted to a particular domain of the originary (e.g. that of 'empirical' determinations): this being a universal structure precisely to the extent that it is possible to identify that project of variation as something self-contradictory. At the same time, however, the base plane includes all those necessary implications that are L-immediately established through an analysis of S, in such a way that, already from the standpoint of the base plane, it is possible to exclude that domain of the project that projects a positing of S as such in which the constants whose positing is L-immediately implied by the positing of S are not posited.

b. While the base plane is distinct from the mediational one, the realization of any possible mediation consists however in the arising of the immediate presence of a mediation: i.e. in the immediate presence of the constitution of a contradiction of type m (or m') and of its superseding. In this respect, the mediational plane is *included* in the base plane. In other words, in the same way in which the factual implication between two determinations is immediately present, so is the logical structure that converts a factual implication into a necessary one.

c. A comprehensive exposition of the originary structure should determine all the possible ways in which the mediational plane can be projected from the standpoint of the base plane. Let us simply make a general distinction. The mediations that constitute the mediational plane can be conceived of in such a way that: (1) each of them does not presuppose anything other than the base plane, thus all belonging to the same mediational plane; (2) all of them except one (or some of them) presuppose a prior mediation in addition to the base plane, whereby a multiplicity of mediational planes is realized. If what is presupposed by each mediation differs from what is presupposed by every other mediation, one obtains a mediational process that is analogous to the deductions of idealism.

10. First note: The meaning of the introduction of the distinction between the form and the content of the totality of the Ph-immediate (Chapter 5, § 27)

As a way of applying what we have discussed above (§ 9), let us observe that the introduction of the distinction mentioned in the title of the present section must not be conceived of as the result of a mediation, but as belonging to the base plane of the originary structure. The base plane does not only include the factual existence of that distinction, but also its necessity (hence the reference in § 27 of Chapter 5 to a 'deduction' of that distinction). This distinction is indeed obtained through the analysis of the concept of the 'Totality of the immediate presence of being that becomes'; accordingly, the contradiction indicated in § 26 of Chapter 5 was caused by the simple absence of this analysis.

If that distinction were conceived of as the result of a mediation, one could legitimately ask why, instead of holding firm the *impossibility* of the arising of a determination that augments the horizon of the Ph-immediate, one introduces that distinction between form and content, which allows that arising to persist as something *possible*. The impossibility of that arising would precisely be determined by the contradiction constituted by the fact that, with the taking place of that arising, the totality of the Ph-immediate would at the same time be and not be. (Let us refer to this contradiction as: 'contradiction h'). That is to say, one might ask why, instead of superseding the h-contradiction by positing the impossibility of that arising, this contradiction is superseded by introducing that distinction, which allows the project of that arising to persist as something immediately non-contradictory. That distinction is there introduced without any mediation, i.e. immediately; since, however, as part of the hypothesis under consideration, that distinction is posited as something that is not part of the base plane of the originary structure, an immediate introduction of something that is not immediate appears to be unwarranted, thus affording the question as to why one way of superseding the h-contradiction should be chosen over the other one.

If that arising is regarded as something that stands as a 'possible additional dimension of the Ph-immediate' (Chapter 5, § 28), in such a way that the arising itself belongs to this possible additional dimension, it must be stated that the reason for that choice can only be something arbitrary – or, in relation to the possibility of justifying the positing of that distinction, there only exists the possibility of a reason. If, instead, that arising is regarded as something that stands as a 'factual additional dimension of the Ph-immediate' – whereby this arising, or more generally becoming, is something actual – the following must be stated. While the positing of the impossibility of that arising (leaving aside that it itself appears as an arbitrary choice) supersedes the h-contradiction, that positing determines however a new contradiction to the extent that the arising – which, *qua* simply possible or belonging to a possible additional dimension, did not exclude the possibility of a deduction of its impossibility – is no longer a possibility, but it is now posited as something actual, or as an Ph-immediacy, the predication of the impossibility of which is contradictory. It has thus been clarified that the positing of the non-contradictoriness of this second aspect of that arising is grounded independently of the distinction between the form and the content of the totality of the Ph-immediate.

It should however be observed that while the Ph-immediacy of that arising entails that the negation of the latter is contradictory – i.e. it entails the necessity of the fact that the h-contradiction should not be superseded by positing the impossibility of that arising – at the same time, a mere attestation of the actual or factual existence of that arising does not as such determine the way in which the h-contradiction is to be superseded. It is known *that*, given the actual existence of that arising, the h-contradiction cannot be superseded in a certain way, but it is not known how it is to be superseded.

While, therefore, the contradictoriness of the negation of that arising is verified in relation to this second value of the arising – independently of the introduction of the distinction between the form and the content of the totality of the Ph-immediate – the contradictoriness of the negation of the arising of what belongs to a possible additional dimension is however not thereby verified. That is to say, even if the actual arising cannot be negated, one can negate the arising of that possible additional dimension, thus eliminating the h-contradiction (or, more precisely: thus eliminating that quantification of the h-contradiction that refers to, or is determined by, the concept of the arising of that possible additional dimension).

Then: we state that the possibility of this way of eliminating the h-contradiction only obtains to the extent that the distinction under consideration between form and content is regarded as the result of a mediation (whereby the elimination of the h-contradiction by means of that distinction constitutes an arbitrary choice).

Except that – as already noted – that distinction belongs to the base plane of the originary structure. The verification of the contradictoriness of the arising of that possible additional dimension does not instead belong to the base plane, or it only belongs to it as something projected. The positing of the distinction between the form and the content of the totality of the Ph-immediate therefore constitutes the *originary* superseding of the h-contradiction. This originary superseding allows the project of the arising of a possible additional dimension to persist as something non-contradictory as part of the positional domain of the base plane. The 'introduction' of the distinction in question between form and content then only consists in its being originarily posited; or, equivalently: there is an 'introduction' only from the standpoint of the exposition.

The positing of the possibility of the arising of that possible additional dimension is therefore co-originary with the positing of the totality of the Ph-immediate insofar as this is posited as being originarily distinct as to its formal and material elements. This distinction, *qua* originary superseding of the h-contradiction, is the originary positing of what that contradiction precludes: i.e. the positing of the possibility of that arising.

The remarks developed in this section have a paradigmatic value. The reader may independently proceed to consider the generalizations and the single applications of this paradigm.

Let us further observe here that the abstract positing of the totality of the Ph-immediate, in which the distinction between the form and the content of this totality is not posited, while not being a negation of the concrete *in actu signato* – that is to say, while not being an explicit negation of that distinction – is nevertheless an implicit negation, or a negation *in actu exercito*. (As already observed, cf. Chapter 2, § 27, these implicit and explicit negations are the two modes in which the abstract concept of the abstract realizes itself.) The fact that the positing of the abstract (i.e. of the totality of the Ph-immediate in its not being internally distinguished) is a negation of the concrete (albeit an implicit one) follows from that consequence of this abstract positing that precisely consists in the h-contradiction, which only arises insofar as the abstract is not posited as such – whereby it is superseded in and by the concrete – but as the whole itself.

11. Second note: The extension of the mediational plane

The mediational plane that is obtained through the verification of Y's necessary positional implication or exclusion of Z does not constitute the totality of the mediational plane. In other words, the synthetic *a priori* propositions considered above are the result of a logical elaboration of synthetic *a posteriori* propositions, both in case the *a posteriori* synthesis is verified to be a necessary one (this being the superseding of the m-contradiction) and in case it comes to be necessarily negated (this being the superseding of the m'-contradiction). It must then be pointed out that there exists an immediately non-contradictory set of projects of synthetic *a priori* propositions, which are neither necessary negations nor necessary connections of *a posteriori* syntheses: for instance, the project of the necessary connections or necessary negations of the connection between terms whose factual implication is itself the content of a project.

Every implication that constitutes itself as an *a priori* synthesis thus immediately stands either as an *a posteriori* synthesis or as a projected implication.

12. Logical immediacy and logical mediation. Logical mediations *qua* implications between abstract meanings

a. If the proposition: 'A is B' is synthetic *a priori*, this means that A is that to which B *essentially* pertains (since, precisely, the negation of this pertaining is self-contradictory);

accordingly, as already discussed, thinking A without knowing that it is B means not thinking A. At the same time, however, the positing of this belonging of B to the essence of A – whereby B appears as a constant of A – is the *result* of a mediation: that is to say, a simple analysis of A cannot identify B as a constant of A. The transition from an L-immediacy, remaining at the level of which it is not possible to identify B as a constant of A, to the level of an L-mediation, in which B is precisely identified as a constant of A, is determined by the positing of a term M – the middle term – which would L-immediately appear as a constant of A, and of which B L-immediately appears as a constant. In other words, B can belong to the essence (i.e. to the definition) of A only insofar as B belongs to the essence of a meaning M that belongs to the essence of A. Therefore, B does not pertain to A insofar as A is A, but insofar as the analysis of A attests that M belongs to the essence of A. In order to clarify this last assertion, let us keep in mind the following.

b. If one negates the existence of M, while however holding firm the fact that at first the analysis of A does not identify B as a constant of A, and at a later point the negation of the pertaining of B to A appears to be self-contradictory, the transition from that first moment to the second one does not constitute a mediation, but it is a transition from a specific definitional or analytic level to another one, i.e. from a specific level of the analysis of A to a different one. Whenever we have discussed the analysis of a specific meaning in the previous sections, we have always meant the *present or actual level* of the analysis; it is however not immediately contradictory to project that what L-immediately pertains to a meaning should *not* be exhausted by the present level of the analysis of the meaning under consideration; that is to say, it is not immediately contradictory to project that the present level of the analysis is only a moment of the analysis *simpliciter*, or the totality of the analysis, of the meaning under consideration (cf. Chapter 8, § 1).

Developing this point: let

$$a_1, a_2, a_3, \ldots, a_n$$

be the determinations posited by the present level of the analysis of A as predicates of A, and let

$$a_{n+1}, a_{n+2}, a_{n+3}, \ldots, a_{n+m}$$

be the determinations that an extension of the analysis beyond its present level renders explicit as predicates of A. It is clear that, on the one hand, none of the terms of the series $a_1, \ldots, a_n$ pertains to A insofar as any other terms of this series pertains to A, or more generally insofar as A is the subject of any predication; and, on the other hand, that none of the terms of the series $a_{n+1}, \ldots, a_{n+m}$ pertains to A insofar as the terms of the series $a_1, \ldots, a_n$ pertain to A, or insofar as any other term of the series $a_{n+1}, \ldots, a_{n+m}$ pertains to A. That is to say, each of the terms of the series $a_1, \ldots, a_n, a_{n+1}, \ldots, a_{n+m}$ pertains to A *insofar as A is A*. For, indeed, if that were not the case, that pertaining would not be L-immediate (even if realizing itself beyond the present level of the analysis), but L-*mediated*: the middle term consisting of that term of which it is stated that any other considered term of the series $a_1, \ldots,$

a_n or a_{n+1}, ..., a_{n+m} may pertain to A insofar as that first term pertains to A. For instance: affirming that a_2 does not pertain to A insofar as A is A, but insofar as A is a_1, means positing a_1 as the middle term of the predication of a_2 relative to A; as a result, it means not respecting the assumption that a_1 as well as a_2 belong to the domain of the analysis of A, i.e. to the domain of the verification of the L-immediate pertaining of a meaning to A.

Since the concrete meaning of A consists in the very unity of a_1, ..., a_n and a_{n+1}, ..., a_{n+m}, it is clear that, insofar as A is kept distinct from the concreteness of its analysis, A stands as a *part* of that meaning, in the same way in which the *form* of the whole may count as a part of the whole itself. A is the formal aspect of the semantic concreteness constituted by

$$a_1, ..., a_n, a_{n+1}, ..., a_{n+m},$$

i.e. it is the whole of that meaning, but in its formal value. The 'pertaining' of each of the terms of the series a_1, ..., a_n, a_{n+1}, ..., a_{n+m} to A is therefore a 'belonging' to A: precisely in the sense in which a content belongs to or is included in a form. In the analytic proposition: 'A is a_1', a_1 is included in A, or belongs to A, precisely in the way in which any element of a content belongs to the form, which, as such, constitutes a (formal) positing of the entirety of the meaning.

The fact that each of the terms of the series a_1, ..., a_n, a_{n+1}, ..., a_{n+m} pertains to A insofar as A is a formal meaning is required by the very L-immediate pertaining of those terms to A. If none of those terms pertains to A insofar as a specific other term pertains to A, A itself, as the subject of the predication of each of the terms of that series, must exhibit that semantic value that is constituted as soon as A is precisely posited in its not being determined by any other term. At the same time, that semantic value provides the *entirety* of the meaningfulness of A, since it is to that value that *all* the terms of the series a_1, ..., a_n, a_{n+1}, ..., a_{n+m} pertain (that is to say: if that value were only a *part* of the meaningfulness of A, all the terms that L-immediately pertain to A – i.e. to the whole relative to which that part is a part – would not be able to pertain to that value or part). Insofar as the whole of the meaningfulness of A *does not include* in its semantic domain those determinations that nevertheless pertain to it, that whole is, indeed, the whole, but as the *formal whole* of the meaningfulness of A; accordingly, as stated above, it is a *part* of the concrete whole of that meaningfulness, in the way in which a form is a part.

Once again here – as in each case – it must be stated that the non-contradictoriness of the proposition 'A is a_1' obtains to the extent that this proposition is concretely conceived of as

$$(A = a_1) = (a_1 = A).$$

This point is developed in § 16.

c. As stated, a mediation obtains insofar as a determination (B) does not pertain to A insofar as A is A – i.e. insofar as A stands as a formal meaning – but insofar as a specific other determination (M) pertains to A, i.e. insofar as that formal meaningfulness is determined in some way.

Let us now specify that, on the one hand, M is one of the terms of the series $a_1, \ldots, a_n$, and, on the other hand, M is in the same relation to A as B is to M.

For what concerns the first side, there certainly exists the possibility that the structure of the middle term should itself be complex, i.e. that the middle term should itself consist of a *series* of middle terms; this series, however, is necessarily finite. For, indeed, if it is self-contradictory for B not to pertain to A, admitting an infinite series of middle terms means accepting only the *need* for that pertaining, thereby negating the latter. (In this case, the middle term is not a middle term, in that none of the terms of the infinite series may pertain to A qua A – for, otherwise, the series would no longer be infinite, but it would be delimited by that term of the series that pertains to A qua A; and if there is no term that pertains to A qua A, no term pertains to A. If, furthermore, it is asserted that M_1 pertains to A qua A, and M_2 pertains to M_1 qua M_1, but B pertains to M_2 through an infinite series of middle terms, the argument developed above in relation to A must be repeated in relation to M_2.) B may therefore only pertain to A insofar as M (or the last term – starting from B – of the finite series of middle terms) is one of the terms of the series $a_1, \ldots, a_n$. (It should be observed that A itself is one of the terms of the series $a_1, \ldots, a_n$).

For what concerns the other side or aspect above, in the same way in which M pertains to A qua A, B pertains to M qua M. It should however be noted that it can be stated that B pertains to M qua M (this being an L-immediate pertaining to M) as much as that B pertains to A as determined by M, i.e. insofar as A is determined by M (this being an L-immediate pertaining to AM). Furthermore, it can once again be stated that B pertains to M in an L-mediated way, but, in the last instance, it is necessary to state that one of the terms, through which B pertains to M, L-immediately pertains to M: for if none of the terms to which B pertains were to L-immediately pertain to M, none of these terms would pertain to M, and B, in not pertaining to M, would also not pertain to A.

d. From what has been said, it appears that *logical mediations only obtain in relation to the abstract moments of a concrete meaning, and not in relation to the semantic concreteness as such*. That is to say, the mediational implication between A and B is an implication between the two abstract moments of the concrete meaning constituted by the implication between A, M and B. This semantic concreteness consists in the very development of the analysis (in that the pertaining of M to A is posited through the analysis of A, and the pertaining of B to M is posited through the analysis of M).

More generally, it must then be stated that the totality of the mediation is the very totality of the development of the analysis; or, equivalently, that a logical mediation is an internal articulation of logical immediacy. This means that the form of necessary knowledge is analysis – the distinction between analytic and synthetic *a priori* propositions being a distinction that is *internal* to the horizon of analysis. If A is concretely conceived – i.e. if its analysis has been developed – A is AMB itself, in such a way that the proposition: 'A is B' is analytic. It is as part of this analytic character that it is possible to observe that while M L-immediately pertains to A *also to the extent that A is regarded as an abstract moment* (whereby this pertaining gives rise to an analytic proposition *stricto sensu*), B, on the contrary, immediately pertains to A only to the extent that A is regarded as a concrete meaning, i.e. in its being determined by M (that concreteness being such in relation to A as a moment that is distinct from MB). Accordingly, the pertaining of B to A, regarded as an abstract moment, is mediated by M.

e. In stating that the elements of the m-contradiction, caused by the negation of the proposition: 'A is B', do not consist of A and of the negation of A, but of something other than A and of the negation of this other term (cf. § 5, b), this other term must be precisely understood as the concrete relative to which A is an abstract moment. Negating that B pertains to A means affirming that AMB (this being the other term relative to A qua simply abstract moment) is not AMB; that is to say, it means thinking A – by means of M – as B, and, at the same time, not thinking it as B.

f. The fact that a_x (belonging to the series a_1, ..., a_n) L-immediately pertains to A means, on the one hand, that a_x pertains to A as such, and, on the other hand, that a_x as such pertains to A. That is to say, that pertaining is affirmed neither on the basis of A nor on the basis of a_x, but on the basis of the pertaining of a_x to A; that is to say, that pertaining is known for itself, or L-immediately.

However, in every synthetic *a posteriori* proposition, too, the predicate (Ph-) immediately pertains to the subject: in such a way that, also in this case, that pertaining is (Ph-)immediate. The difference between the two immediacies lies in the fact that the analytic pertaining is immediate as a superseding of its own negation such that it immediately supersedes this negation as a *self-contradictory* one, whereas the synthetic pertaining is immediate as a superseding of its own negation such that it immediately supersedes this negation as something that is *in contradiction with that pertaining*.

13. The twofold value of analysis

The analysis of a meaning has a twofold value, depending on whether it is regarded as a verification of the determinations that are L-immediately predicated of that meaning as such (which is the subject of the predication as a formal meaning) or whether it is regarded as the identification of the parts or moments of a specific semantic concreteness. In relation to the meaning 'this red extension', it is possible to establish an analysis according to the second of these two indicated values; it is indeed L-immediately and necessarily affirmed that this meaning includes the meanings 'this extension' and 'red'. The first value of analysis is instead not established, in the sense that being-red is not predicated of this extension as such, but insofar as it is immediately present (phenomenological immediacy) that this extension is red – in such a way that projecting that this extension should no longer be red is not immediately self-contradictory. (At the same time, however, this extension will no longer be red to the extent that it will consist of a specific *persistence* – essence, form – of this extension, and not to the extent that it is *this* extension, which is red. Accordingly, in relation *to this* – red – extension, i.e. considering this – red – extension insofar as it is *this* – red – extension, and not insofar as it is an extension, it is also possible to establish the first value of analysis; on the contrary, this value may not be established, this being precisely the case considered above, if this red extension is not considered insofar as it is *this* – red – extension, but insofar as it is an *extension*.)

The distinction between the two values of analysis also appears more clearly if one considers a meaning whose moments do not stand in a predicative relation with respect to one another (as it is instead the case for the meaning considered above, in which 'red' is precisely predicated of 'this extension'): in relation to the meaning 'greater than a part', it must L-immediately and necessarily be affirmed that it includes the meanings 'greater than …' and 'part', thus giving rise to the second type of analysis, but it is not possible to immediately predicate 'part' of 'greater than' as such.

At the same time, however, as part of both values of analysis, the latter consists in the attestation of an L-immediate pertaining: i.e. the attestation of the fact that a determination is L-immediately *predicated* of another one. Indeed, the proposition: 'The meaning *greater than a part* includes the meaning *part*' is analytic according to the first value of analysis, since the predicate pertains to the subject as such. More generally, it must then be stated that if x and y are terms of an analysis, y is *in any case* L-immediately predicated of x as such, but y has two values depending on whether its semantic domain counts as *the belonging of a specific meaning z to the meaning x* (this being the second value of analysis), or whether it does not count as this form of belonging, in such a way that what is predicated of x is not the belonging of a third term (z) to x, but that specific semantic content constituted by y (this being the first value of analysis).

From what has been said, it appears that simple meanings cannot be analysed only with respect to the second value of analysis, whereas they can be analysed with respect to the first value.

14. Concerning a type of mediational constants

The content of this section may be considered as a continuation and completion of the observations developed in § 3.

It is possible to distinguish three types of constants that pertain to A in an *L-mediated way* – retaining the possibility of identifying further types:

a. *Type I*. B L-immediately pertains to M – that is to say, it L-immediately counts as a predicate of M. On the one hand, however, B is not a semantic moment of M as such, i.e. B is not part of the meaningfulness of M; on the other hand, M is not part of the meaningfulness of B. It must therefore be stated that insofar as B is considered as distinct from M, in such a way that the semantic domain constituted by B is regarded as not including the domain constituted by M, and vice-versa, B persists as B and M as M; accordingly, M also (immediately) pertains to A insofar as it is considered as a meaning that is distinct from B. Insofar as B is considered in this way, B can be an L-immediate constant of M – i.e. it can 'belong' to the meaning of M – only as a predicate. This 'belonging' is not the belonging that has been excluded above in stating that B is not part of the meaning of M, but it is the belonging that consists in the very predicative pertaining of B to M.

b. *Type II*. B, which L-immediately pertains to M, is a semantic moment, i.e. it is part of the meaningfulness of M. Accordingly, if one distinguishes M from B, in such a way that the semantic domain constituted by M is regarded as not including the domain constituted by B, M no longer counts as M. It must therefore be stated that M (immediately) pertains to A only insofar as it is not thus distinct from B, or only insofar as M is posited in its including B. Furthermore, for what concerns the affirmation that B, thus understood, is a constant that pertains to A *in a mediated way*, it is indeed clear that the meanings that count as semantic moments of a predicate that L-immediately pertains to a subject – i.e. that count as semantic moments of something that L-immediately appears as a constant of that subject – are not L-immediately posited as constants of this subject, but they are thus posited in a mediated way: namely, by means of that determination that, in containing those meanings as moments, is L-immediately predicated of that subject. For instance, let 'A' = 'totality', 'M' = 'greater than a part', 'B' = 'part'. M L-immediately pertains to A, and B is a moment of the meaningfulness of M (and it L-immediately counts as a constant of M). B is a constant of A by means of M, i.e. the meaningfulness of A must include B (and the meaning 'totality' is not posited if the meaning 'part' is not posited) because B is a semantic moment of something that L-immediately pertains to A.

Furthermore, if the semantic domain constituted by M is regarded as not including B, M no longer counts as M, and it can therefore no longer pertain to A. Contrary to the first type of this kind of constants, the positing of the middle term therefore necessarily requires the positing of the mediated extreme.

In relation to the example above, it must be observed that B, while being a constant of A, is not predicated of A (cf. § 3). Not only: while B is a constant of M – in this instance, in an L-immediate way (as a clarification of this remark, cf. e) – B is also not predicated of M. All the examples available to us have this structure. It is however not immediately self-contradictory to project the arising of constants of this second type that count as predicates of A (or of M). This means that when we affirm that every semantic moment of the determinations that L-immediately pertain to a subject is a constant of that subject through those determinations, we do not mean to thereby exclude that those moments may L-immediately pertain to this subject, but we wish to affirm that if this immediate pertaining does not obtain those moments count as constants of that subject through the determination of which they are moments.

c. *Type III.* B is a semantic concreteness that L-immediately includes M as a moment. That is to say: while in the second type above the mediated extreme L-immediately stands as a moment of the middle term, in this third type the middle term L-immediately stands as a moment of the extreme. The example available to us for this type of constants has a speculative significance such that, if examined at this point, it would disturb the formal character of these remarks by drawing attention to itself. We therefore prefer to direct the reader to Chapter 13, in which that example is explicitly considered.

In this case it is B that does not persist as such if it is regarded as not including M. Once again: B is a constant of A in an L-mediated way, i.e. by means of that semantic moment of its content that L-immediately pertains to A. This means that B, as such or for itself, does not L-immediately pertain to A.

It is clear that, as part of this third type of constants, M must stand as a moment of B, but not as something superseded or negated – the relevance of this remark consisting in the fact that a meaning may also stand as negated as a moment of another meaning.

d. The distinction between these three types of constants is a distinction between three types of synthetic *a priori* propositions. In the cases in which B does not count as a predicate of A, the predicate of the *a priori* synthesis is the positing *of the implication* or *the belonging* of B to A. For instance: the synthetic *a priori* proposition established by the meanings 'totality' and 'part' is: '*Totality* is implicative of part', in which the predicate is not 'part', but, precisely, 'implicative of part'.

e. Consider again the example considered under point b. It stated: B (= 'part') pertains to A (= 'totality') as a constant in an L-mediated way because it does not pertain to A insofar as it (B) is B, but insofar as it is a moment of M (= 'greater than a part'), i.e. insofar as it is L-immediately included in M.

Except that one may object that if B is included in M, B cannot be L-immediately included in M. Consider the proposition: 'M is inclusive of B'; B does not L-immediately pertain to M (i.e. B does not L-immediately stand as a constant of M), but insofar as it is a semantic moment, i.e. insofar as it is included in the predicate ('inclusive of B') of that proposition. This entails a twofold aporia.

On the one hand, M includes B L-immediately and at the same time it does not include it L-immediately: it includes it immediately because the immediacy of this inclusion belongs to the immediate content itself (that is to say: when it is affirmed that the proposition: 'M is inclusive of B' is L-immediate, this L-immediacy is itself part of the content of which the L-immediacy is predicated); M does not include B immediately because M, as such, is not inclusive of B, but it is inclusive of B insofar as to M there pertains a predicate ('inclusive of B'), which itself, as such, is inclusive of B. This predicate is therefore the middle term of the inclusion of B in M.

On the other hand, there arises a *progressus in indefinitum*, in that, given the proposition: 'The meaning "inclusive of B" is inclusive of B' (this meaning being precisely the predicate of the proposition considered above), it must again be stated that B does not L-immediately pertain to the subject (i.e. it does not L-immediately stand as a constant of that subject), but it pertains to the subject because it (B) is included in the predicate. The *progressus in indefinitum* entails that B cannot be a constant of M, and therefore not even of A (cf. § 12, c). If, therefore, the predicate M L-immediately pertains to any meaning A, and M is a complex meaning – which therefore includes a multiplicity of semantic components – M cannot be predicated of A, since none of the components of M can be a constant of A.

The aporia is determined by the fact that the predicate of the proposition: 'M is inclusive of B' is and at the same time is not abstractly separated from the subject; or, equivalently: it is and it is not regarded as a predicate of that subject. It is abstractly separated (i.e. it is not regarded as a predicate of that subject) in that only in this way does the proposition: 'M is inclusive of B' become: 'M is an x that includes B' (in which x stands as a different meaning from M and B, i.e. as that meaning that is constituted by the predicate of the first proposition, *qua* abstractly separated). If, indeed, that predicate is concretely held firm as a predicate of M, what is predicated of M is not 'x that includes B', but, precisely, 'inclusive of B'. As part of the aporetic argument, the concrete distinction (the concrete concept of the abstract) of subject and predicate is an abstract separation, for a distinction does not alter the meaning of the concrete – and the meaning of the concrete must not be altered, for the proposition: 'M

is inclusive of B' is L-immediate. At the same time, the predicate of the proposition: 'M is inclusive of B' is not abstractly separated, but it is regarded as the predicate of the subject. Indeed, if only an abstract separation were present – i.e. if in considering the meaning 'inclusive of B' one were to only establish that this meaning is inclusive of B – then, on the one hand, it would not be possible to conclude that to M *there pertains a predicate* that is itself, as such, inclusive of B, and, on the other hand, it would not be possible to conclude that B *cannot pertain to M*. That is to say, the aporetic argument, after not having regarded the predicate as a predicate, and after having attested that the meaning that it must in this way consider is inclusive of B, *once again* refers the result of the consideration of that meaning to M, i.e. it once again considers as a predicate of M something that has been precisely constituted as a result of its not having been considered as a predicate of M. On the one hand, the aporetic argument therefore attests that B cannot be L-immediately included in M, and, on the other hand (but in fact indefinitely repeating the self-contradictory gesture described above), it identifies a *progressus in indefinitum*, and, therefore, the impossibility for B to stand as a constant of M.

15. Synthetic *a priori* propositions and the project of the non-pertaining of the predicate to the subject

The following is a significant corollary of what has been stated in the previous points, which explicitly addresses the amendment to which we referred in the first footnote of § 5. Up to this point, we have held firm the fact that, remaining at the level of logical immediacy, it is immediately non-contradictory to project that the predicate of a synthetic proposition – which, through the introduction of a middle term, is shown at a later point to be synthetic *a priori* – should not pertain to the subject. That is to say, that project is not *immediately contradictory*: i.e. it is not contradictory from the standpoint of the mediation that has not yet taken place – this being the standpoint or the level of immediacy. This affirmation must now be specified: or, more precisely, it must be restricted to the first of the three types of *a priori* syntheses distinguished above.

For, indeed, in relation to the second and third types of *a priori* syntheses, that project is immediately self-contradictory. Accordingly, these types of mediation partake of a feature that pertains to logical immediacy – since if a proposition is logically immediate it is immediately self-contradictory to project that the predicate should not pertain to the subject. In other words, the exclusion of that project is not absolutely specific to immediate logical connections.

Consider the second type of mediational constants distinguished in the previous section. Since positing M means in this case positing B, or since M is posited only insofar as B is posited, it follows that, remaining at the level of logical immediacy – i.e. at the level at which the necessary pertaining of M to A is posited – it is immediately self-contradictory to project that A should not imply B (which is L-immediately posited as a semantic moment of M). This project would be possible only if M were not regarded as to its including B, but this cannot be the case since M is what, by definition, includes B. It is clear that we are here referring to the *actual* or *present meaning* of M;

an extension of the analysis of M may show that a term C, too – like B – is part of the meaning M. If C is present, but it is not present as a part of M, the project of the non-pertaining of C to A is immediately non-contradictory.

Consider the third type of mediational constants. Since B is only posited insofar as M itself is posited, and since B L-immediately includes M, it follows that it is not possible for B to be posited and not be posited as a constant of A: precisely because if B is posited, it is posited in its L-immediately including what (M) L-immediately pertains to A. Accordingly, projecting that B is not a constant of A is immediately self-contradictory.

More generally, the following may be stated: projecting that B is not a constant of A is immediately non-contradictory if the positing of M (or B) can be kept distinct – without contradiction – from the positing of the pertaining of B to M (or of M to B). In the second and third types of mediational constants, instead, the positing of M and B – respectively – is exactly the positing of that pertaining or implication (since, respectively, B is a moment of the actual or present meaning of M, and M is a moment of the actual or present meaning of B). Accordingly, the positing of M, and B, cannot be distinguished from the positing of the implication between M and B. Hence, projecting that B should not be implied by A as a constant is immediately self-contradictory.

16. Clarifications concerning the meaning of the pertaining of a_1 to A

In order to clarify the expression: 'a_1 pertains to A *as such*' (and expanding upon a concept mentioned at the end of point b of § 12), it should be observed that A, to which – *as such* – a_1 pertains must not be regarded as a semantic domain that does not include a_1; for, otherwise, the proposition 'A is a_1' would be self-contradictory, for it would affirm that something (A) is other than itself (a_1) (cf. Chapter 6, §§ 10–11). A, to which – *as such* – a_1 pertains is precisely A to which a_1 L-immediately pertains: i.e. it is A *posited* as that to which a_1 pertains, and, therefore – according to the formula that we have repeatedly used – $A = a_1$. Accordingly, the L-immediate pertaining of a_1 to A is expressed by the equation:

$$(A = a_1) = (a_1 = A).$$

A, *as such*, is therefore the very immediate synthesis of A and a_1. Thus, stating that B does not pertain to A as such, but insofar as A is determined as a_1 (= M) – this very pertaining of B to A, independently of the justification of the pertaining itself, having to be conceived of as (A = B) = (B = A) – therefore means stating:

$$\{[(A = a_1) = (a_1 = A)] = B\} = \{B = [(A = a_1) = (a_1 = A)]\}$$

– this latter equation being itself mediated by the L-immediate equation:

$$(a_1 = B) = (B = a_1).$$

The pertaining of two determinations must therefore *in any case* be conceived of as an identity (as something analytic, as an L-immediate pertaining). It is this identity that, as already stated, distinguishes itself internally as an L-immediate or L-mediated identity. That is to say, L-immediacy itself can be L-immediate or L-mediated. Both the proposition $(A = a_1) = (a_1 = A)$ and the proposition $(A = B) = (B = A)$ are identical propositions (i.e. analytic ones, or such that the predicate L-immediately pertains to the subject); as part of the second proposition, however, the L-immediacy is L-mediated: certainly not in the sense that a middle term is required in order for the predicate $B = A$ to pertain to the subject $A = B$, but in the sense that a middle term is required for the pertaining of B to A.

In a different respect (cf. § 12, d), the distinction between L-immediacy and L-mediation is internal to logical immediacy itself, in that it indicates the nature of the relation between the abstract moments of immediacy. We have thus indicated two senses in which the distinction between logical immediacy and logical mediation is internal to the horizon of logical immediacy itself.

17. Aporia and solution. Determining the sense in which the proposition 'A is a_1' is synthetic *a priori*

a. Consider the following aporia. B pertains to A insofar as A is determined as a_1. We have however stated that a_1, too, does not pertain to A insofar as A is abstractly considered as A, but insofar as A is precisely regarded as that to which a_1 pertains: $A = a_1$. Accordingly, in this second case, too, the pertaining of a_1 to A is mediated: precisely by that a_1 that appears in $A = a_1$. As a result, no proposition can be analytic (i.e. L-immediate). Let us respond with the following observations:

Let us indicate by a_1' the a_1 that appears in $A = a_1$, and by a_1'' the a_1 that appears in $a_1 = A$, which is the predicate of the proposition $(A = a_1) = (a_1 = A)$. Then: a_1'' pertains to A insofar as A is a_1'. a_1' and a_1'', however, *are the same term*, in such a way that a_1' cannot count as a middle term relative to a_1'' (i.e. relative to itself). The appearance of a mediation may only arise if one understands that a_1' pertains to A insofar as A is abstractly regarded as a simple noesis (this pertaining thus being L-immediate), and a_1'' pertains to A insofar as it is determined as $A = a_1'$ (this being the L-mediated pertaining). In this way, however, the L-immediacy would consist in a contradiction, precisely because A would be posited as something other than itself (i.e. as a_1'), and the L-mediation would be grounded in this contradiction.

In other words, the appearance of an L-mediation may only arise insofar as, *on the one hand*, $A = a_1'$ is abstractly separated from $(A = a_1') = (a_1'' = A)$ – whereby a_1'' can no longer be posited as a_1' itself – and, *on the other hand*, $A = a_1'$, as thus abstracted, is held to retain that property that pertains to it insofar as it is a moment concretely distinct from $(A = a_1') = (a_1'' = A)$: this being the property by virtue of which A, which appears in $A = a_1'$ as thus distinct, is not in turn posited as a_1. For, without this second side, a_1' would stand in the same relation to A as a_1'' – that is to say, after having simply carried out the abstraction of $A = a_1'$ from $(A = a_1') = (a_1'' = A)$, this equation would again constitute itself as part of $A = a_1'$, and, according to the logic of the objection, a_1' would appear as something mediated. In order for a_1' to be regarded in a different respect relative to a_1'', it is therefore necessary that it should be regarded as pertaining to A insofar as the latter is a simple noesis – and, as already mentioned, this is possible only if $A = a_1'$, as abstractly separated, is held to retain that property that pertains to it insofar as it is a moment concretely distinct from $(A = a_1') = (a_1'' = A)$. (For a comprehension of this point, the reader should keep in mind the observations developed in § 10 of Chapter 3 and § 10 of Chapter 6).

b. Furthermore, it is precisely because a_1 L-immediately pertains to A, concretely considered as $A = a_1'$ – this L-immediate pertaining not only requiring that A should be concretely considered as $A = a_1'$, but also that a_1 should be concretely considered as $a_1'' = A$ – that a_1, regarded as a simple noetic moment, precisely *by virtue of that L-immediate pertaining*, can pertain to A, itself regarded as a simple noetic moment. The logic of the objection under consideration thus reverses the correct logical structure, in that it regards $A = a_1'$ – considered as distinct from $(A = a_1') = (a_1'' = A)$ – as an L-immediate proposition, and $(A = a_1') = (a_1'' = A)$ as an L-mediated one. What is authentically L-immediate is indeed $(A = a_1') = (a_1'' = A)$, whereas $A = a_1'$ is – *as such* – what is L-mediated: precisely because a_1 does not pertain to A, regarded simply as A (i.e. as a semantic domain that does not include a_1), but it pertains to A insofar as A is regarded as that to which a_1 pertains. That is to say, $A = a_1$ is affirmed *insofar as it is affirmed that* $(A = a_1') = (a_1'' = A)$.

c. More generally, it must be stated: if a determination a_1 L-immediately pertains to another specific determination A (i.e. if it L-immediately stands as a constant of the latter) – that L-immediate pertaining having to be thought as $(A = a_1') = (a_1'' = A)$ – as soon as those determinations are regarded as distinct from one another, in such a way that the semantic domain of the one does not include the semantic domain of the other, and vice-versa (or, equivalently: if one considers the pertaining $A = a_1$ as such, or if one considers the nature of the relation that obtains between the abstract terms A and a_1), it follows that each pertains to the other in an *L-mediated way*, and this pertaining is expressed by a synthetic *a priori* proposition. In considering A and a_1 as simply distinct, and positing $(A = a_1') = (a_1'' = A)$, one certainly L-immediately affirms that A is a_1, but since this is not affirmed *insofar as A* and a_1 are distinct in the sense indicated above, the relation between A and a_1, qua distinct terms, is an *L-mediated* pertaining.

In this case, too, the L-mediation consists in the relation that obtains between the abstract moments of the L-immediacy. That is to say, the L-mediation is the relation between the abstract moments of the L-immediacy not only insofar as it consists in the relation between A and B (cf. § 12, d), but also insofar as it consists in the relation between A and $M (= a_1)$ – if the pertaining of M to A is considered in its being distinct from $(A = M) = (M = A)$.

d. The mediation that we are considering here has a distinctive structure, in that the middle term between A and a_1 cannot be a determination M that would L-immediately pertain to A and to which a_1 would L-immediately pertain. At the same time, however, the pertaining of a_1 to A constitutes a mediation, for a_1 does not pertain for itself to A, but for or by virtue of something other than itself – this other being precisely the middle term. In this case, the latter is therefore the very originary synthesis between

A and a_1: a synthesis that is not expressed by the proposition $A = a_1$, but by the proposition $(A = a_1) = (a_1 = A)$. That is to say, while as part of the mediations of the type '$A = M = B$' – i.e. concretely $(A = M) = (M = A)$, $(M = B) = (B = M)$, $(A = B) = (B = A)$ – the middle term does not consist in that L-immediate pertaining, but it is that which L-immediately pertains to one extreme and to which the other extreme L-immediately pertains, as part of the mediations of the type $A = a_1$, instead, the middle term consists in the very L-immediate pertaining or originary synthesis of the extremes – which are such precisely insofar as they are regarded as simply distinct moments of that pertaining.

e. Furthermore, this mediation does not arise because A and a_1 are regarded as being abstractly separated from one another – or insofar as $A = a_1$ is abstractly separated from $(A = a_1) = (a_1 = A)$ – since in that case the pertaining of the two terms would not give rise to a mediation, but to a contradiction.

f. In §10, e of Chapter 6, we have considered an analogous logical situation. Regarding dx and dy as distinct meanings, the proposition 'dx is dy' is a *mediated* proposition. In this case, the mediation is not an *a priori* synthesis, in that the negation of that proposition is not self-contradictory, but it is nevertheless a type of logical mediation, for dy does not pertain to dx to the extent that the two terms are distinct (the pertaining being in this case L-immediate, but this L-immediacy also constituting a self-contradiction, since something would be posited as being other than itself), but to the extent that dx is conceived of as $dx = dy$, and dy is conceived of as $dy = dx$. Accordingly, the L-immediate pertaining (this L-immediacy being the L-immediacy that includes the L-immediate pertaining and the L-mediated one) is given by the proposition $(dx = dy) = (dy = dx)$.

In this case, too, the mediation is not determined by an abstract consideration of the abstract terms dx and dy, for the abstract consideration or separation of dx and dy would not give rise to a mediated proposition – as it is instead the case if these two abstract moments are regarded as being simply distinct – but to a self-contradictory proposition.

18. The principle of non-contradiction and analytic propositions. There is only one L-immediate analytic proposition

a. The principle of non-contradiction is the 'ground' (as Kant states) of analytic propositions, not in the sense that this grounding is an L-mediation, but in the sense that analytic connections are identified as individuations of the universality of non-contradictoriness, i.e. they are (immediately) traced back to the universal formulation of the principle of non-contradiction. Every analytic connection constitutes an individuation of that principle, and not one of its 'consequences'.

Indeed, it is not affirmed that A is a_1 insofar as *this* being must be thought as this being, but insofar as *being* is being, and this universal identity L-immediately includes that first identity as its individuation. (It is then stated that the proposition 'A is a_1'

is equivalent to the proposition 'This being is this being' – for excluding that 'A is a_1' is affirmed because this being is this being precisely means holding firm that equivalence – because the terms of the series $a_1, \ldots, a_n$ are constituted by A and by the negations of the different forms of the negation of A – cf. Chapter 9, § 12, e – in such a way that, in each case, predicating one of those terms of A means affirming that A is A. If, furthermore, A is itself regarded as already being a predicative synthesis, the terms of the series $a_1, \ldots, a_n$ may then also stand as a *part* of the meaningfulness of A; in this case, the proposition 'A is a_1' is equivalent to the proposition 'This being is this being' in the sense that what, in A, is identical to a_1 is precisely affirmed in its self-sameness. The same argument applies if A is identical to a part of the meaningfulness of a_1. In this case, a_1 must be understood to be the synthesis of A and of the negation of a form of the negation of A). At the same time, however, the L-immediacy of an analytic connection obtains to the extent that this connection is not regarded as another principle alongside the principle of non-contradiction, but, precisely, as an individuation of that principle. These individuations are the concrete content of the principle of non-contradiction, which cannot therefore be regarded in its formal value as a logical antecedence (as a 'ground' proper) relative to the positing of its content.

Synthetic *a priori* propositions, too, are to be traced back to the universal formulation of the principle of non-contradiction, but through a middle term; accordingly, in this case the principle stands as a ground proper.

b. Resuming. One does not affirm that A is A (i.e. that this being is this being) insofar as identity (non-contradictoriness) is a property *of this being* – in such a way that, considering another specific determination x, it would not be possible to state that x is x – but insofar as A *is identified* as a determination or individuation of that universal (*being itself*), the essence of which includes non-contradictoriness. Conversely, one does not affirm that being is being insofar as identity is a property that pertains to being, regarded as an abstract or formal universal (cf. Chapter 3, § 18), independently of the concrete content of this form, but insofar as being is the concrete universal – the concrete content of that form – i.e. insofar as that formal element is posited in its relation to a determinate content (and not in relation to a content that is indeterminately posited). Accordingly, while on the one hand it must be stated that A is A insofar as *being* is being, on the other hand it must be stated that being is being insofar as A (B, C, ...) is A (B, C, ...), i.e. insofar as every particular determination is itself.

These two aspects, which as part of their synthesis constitute the concrete, are however *distinct*. While the concrete identity – i.e. the identity in which what is identical is the concrete universal – is logically immediate, and consists in fact of logical immediacy *itself*, the identity of either side or moment of the concrete, regarded as distinct from the other one (i.e. the identity as part of which what is identical is either an abstract universal, as distinct from the determinate content, or a determinate content, as distinct from the universal) is instead *L-mediated*; that is to say, the proposition that expresses it is synthetic *a priori*.

Consider the proposition 'A is A' – or, correctly written: $(A = A) = (A = A)$ – in which A is regarded as a semantic domain that is distinct from the universal (being), of which A, *qua* specific being, is an individuation; that is to say, let us consider A as distinct from its being an individuation of the universal. (It is clear that A, as distinct from the universal of which A is an individuation, is also distinct from its being an individuation: for, indeed, the positing of an individuation as such entails the positing of the universal with respect to which that individuation constitutes itself as such). A (*qua* predicate) does not therefore pertain to A (*qua* subject) insofar as A is simply such, i.e. insofar as A is held firm as distinct in the indicated way: or, equivalently, A is A not simply because A stands as that semantic domain that is constituted in considering A as something distinct in the indicated way, but A is A *because* A stands as an individuation of the concrete universal, which is its own self L-immediately or for itself. This means that A (still regarded in the indicated way) is not A *for itself*: precisely because the identity is not specific to A, rather than to B. It is therefore affirmed that A is A *for something other*, i.e. because A is a determination or individuation of the identical universal. The pertaining of A to A is therefore L-mediated by the fact that A stands as such an individuation; or, equivalently: the middle term consists in the identical universal concretely determined as A. It is here clear that the 'other' by virtue of which A is A is not simply other than A, but it is an other *that includes A* (i.e. it is the concrete in relation to which A is a moment), and it is therefore something 'other' precisely because it does not only consist of A as a distinct term.[11]

The same argument should be repeated in considering the proposition: 'being is being', regarding the term 'being' as an abstract universal, i.e. as a determination that is distinct from the concrete content of universality. In this case, too, being does not indeed pertain as a predicate to being insofar as it is simply a form or an abstract universal, but insofar as the concrete content of this formal element – i.e. the form considered in relation to its content – is what is L-immediately or for-itself identical. The abstract universal is not identical for itself, but for something other: precisely because it is identical insofar as every determination of that form is identical. What mediates the identity of the form is the concrete, i.e. the identity of the concrete universal; once again, the 'other' by virtue of which the form coincides with itself includes this very form: in that way in which the synthesis of form and content can include the form as a moment.[12]

c. The L-immediate identity is therefore only the identity of the concrete, and this identity is expressed by the proposition: 'The whole is the whole' – the whole being precisely being *qua* concrete universal. (It is by now clear that this proposition does not simply express the L-immediate connection constituted by the identity of the whole with itself, but each – and therefore the totality – of the L-immediate connections). In this respect, this is the only analytic proposition, or, equivalently, there is no other analytic proposition apart from this one. For, indeed, positing A as an individuation of the concrete universal and positing B as an individuation of the concrete universal means positing the same content: precisely, the concrete universal. It should be noted that this does not in any sense mean that the self-identity of A does not distinguish itself in any way from the self-identity of B: the two identities are certainly distinct, but both of them, *qua* L-immediate identities, imply in an essential way a term – the universal, or the whole – which includes them both, in such a way that the concrete meaning of both is the same. For, if the identities of A and B are kept distinct from the semantic horizon that they imply, the propositions that express those distinct identities are indeed different, but, as discussed, they are no longer analytic (= L-immediate).

At the same time, however, it is possible to speak of a multiplicity of analytic propositions in a twofold sense. In a first sense, this multiplicity obtains insofar as the analytic character itself is *expressed* in many ways: namely, by expressing the identical as *A*, *B*, etc., or as the whole itself. In this respect, it is from the standpoint of the structure of language that it is possible to speak of a multiplicity of analytic propositions. In a second sense, that multiplicity obtains insofar as the *present* content of the whole (concerning the relations between presence – the totality of the immediate – and the whole, cf. Chapter 10) consists of a becoming; accordingly, the concrete content of the L-immediate identity differentiates itself, constituting itself as a multiplicity of acts of positing of that identity (and, therefore, as a multiplicity of analytic propositions). Becoming – and, therefore, the difference of the content of identity – is however included in the actual or present content; that is to say, the different contents are included in the totality *simpliciter* of the immediate, as *past totalities* of the immediate. Accordingly, the multiplicity of analytic propositions is internal to the one analytic proposition. Stating that $p, p', p'', \ldots$ are analytic propositions does not therefore mean anything but expressing the concrete content of the analytic form, or of the identical. Keeping this remark in mind, it is then possible to continue to *speak* of a multiplicity of analytic propositions.

As a corollary of what we have discussed, it must be stated that if L-immediacy is constituted by the self-identity *of the whole*, every predicative relation between terms such that the semantic domain constituted by them is a *moment* of the whole is in any case a logical mediation.

d. From what has been said, it appears that the same proposition – which is 'the same' only from the point of view of its linguistic structure – may be analytic or synthetic *a priori*, depending on whether, respectively: the subject of the proposition is regarded as a concrete meaning (i.e. either as a determination in its value of individuation of the universal or as the universal as it concretely individuates itself); the subject of the proposition is regarded as an abstract meaning (i.e. either as a determination that is distinct from its being an individuation of the universal or as a universal that is distinct from its concrete individuation). In this case, too, it must be stated that language brings to the fore the abstract, leaving the concrete as something not expressed or implicit.

e. Furthermore, it should be observed that the propositions '*A* is *A*' and 'being is being' – regarded according to the conditions indicated in point b – are not synthetic *a priori* because the abstract meaning is abstractly separated from itself, but because the subject (and, therefore, the predicate) of these propositions is precisely an abstract meaning. Insofar as *A* is a moment of the whole, and insofar as it is L-immediately or for-itself known that the whole is itself, it is certainly L-immediately known that *A* is itself (provided that this sameness should be regarded as $(A = A) = (A = A)$), but the affirmation '*A* is *A*' is not L-immediate insofar as *A* is considered as a meaning that is distinct from the whole, but insofar as *A* is posited as a moment of the whole (i.e. as an individuation of the universal), whereby the positing of *A* is at the same time a positing of the whole. Accordingly, if *A* is regarded as a distinct meaning, *A* can no longer be L-immediately predicated of itself; this predication is not L-immediate, even though it is regarded as $(A = A) = (A = A)$. The mediation does not therefore take place because

A is abstractly separated from itself, since, in this case, this would not result in an L-mediated proposition, but in a self-contradictory one (cf. Chapter 3, § 10).

Furthermore, nor does a mediation arise because the propositions 'A is A' and 'being is being', *qua* predicative connections, are abstractly separated from the concrete predication of identity: insofar as they are abstractly separated in this way, the negations: 'A is not A' and 'being is not being' are not superseded, whereas they are if those propositions are simply considered as distinct from the concrete predication of identity.

f. The proposition 'A is A' (or 'being is being') can therefore be synthetic *a priori* in two ways (in § 21, however, we indicate a third way): in the way considered in § 17 (in which strictly speaking the proposition 'A is a_1' is considered, but the same applies), and in the way considered above.[13]

It is therefore clear that, on the one hand, the proposition $(A = A) = (A = A)$ is itself synthetic *a priori* as long as A is held firm as distinct from the universal of which it is an individuation, and, on the other hand, the proposition: 'The whole (T) is the whole' is itself synthetic *a priori* as long as T is simply regarded as a noesis: i.e. as long as that proposition is conceived of as $T = T$ – this equation being regarded as a term that is distinct from $(T = T) = (T = T)$ – and not, precisely, as

$$(T = T) = (T = T).^{14}$$

The L-immediate identity – that is to say, logical immediacy itself – is expressed by this last equation. (This equation must furthermore be posited as part of its concrete relation to Ph-immediacy, cf. Chapter 3. Let us here repeat that the concrete structuring of L-immediacy is itself immediately present, i.e. it is a content of Ph-immediacy: though the latter, too, is itself in turn included in that structuring – in a sense to be determined, cf. Chapter 13).

That is to say, that equation expresses the logical value of the concrete structuring of immediacy – the latter constituting the originary judgement *qua* expression of the originary structure. Or, equivalently, in relation to the theorem formulated in § 14 of Chapter 3, that logical value is expressed by the equation:

$$(I - nC) - (nC - I),$$

understanding however – in relation to the question just discussed – by I ('identity') the very equation $(T = T) = (T = T)$, and by nC ('non-contradictoriness') the negation of the proposition: 'T is not T'.

g. In relation to the two types of synthetic *a priori* propositions discussed in point f, too (cf. § 15), it is *immediately* self-contradictory to project that the predicate should not pertain to the subject; that is to say, from the standpoint of the logical level that posits $(A = A) = (A = A)$ it is immediately self-contradictory to project that $A = A$, as distinct from $(A = A) = (A = A)$, could be negated (that is to say: the negation of that distinct term is immediately superseded). In the same way, from the standpoint of the logical level that posits $(T = T) = (T = T)$ it is immediately self-contradictory to project that the synthetic *a priori* proposition $(A = A) = (A = A)$, in which A is held firm as distinct from its being an individuation of the universal, could be negated (in such a way that the negation of this *a priori* synthesis, too, is immediately superseded).

h. Consider the synthetic *a priori* proposition 'A is B'. It is clear that the content of this proposition appears as something that, in order to be affirmed, must be *additionally mediated* (by M), both in case '$A = B$' is held firm as concretely distinct from $(A = B) = (B = A)$, and in case it is held firm as distinct from its being an *individuation* of concrete logical immediacy.

For what concerns this last expression, it should be observed that L-immediate propositions L-immediately stand as individuations of the principle of non-contradiction, whereas L-mediated propositions stand as such individuations in an L-mediated way. Furthermore, it should be noted that the principle of non-contradiction certainly consists in the system or organism of *L-immediate* predications, i.e. concrete logical immediacy consists in this system or organism; what we are stating here is that the mediations that are grounded in that system of predications come to augment this very system. It is here clear that in affirming that B pertains to A by means of M, the ground of the pertaining of B to A is not the pertaining of M to A, as distinct from that system, but the pertaining of M to A in its being posited as a moment or individuation of that system – i.e. of concrete logical immediacy.

It therefore appears that logical immediacy can only be the *ground* of a proposition insofar as the semantic domain of that immediacy includes that very proposition. If, indeed, this proposition, as 'grounded', is L-mediated, insofar as the subject or predicate of the proposition is however considered in its relation to the middle term, that proposition constitutes an individuation of logical immediacy (and, in its being posited as such, it is an L-immediate proposition). Since, however, logical immediacy itself coincides with its total or concrete individuation, it must also include in its content the individuation constituted by that proposition; as a result, the very mediational relation between the subject and the predicate of the proposition in question is *included* in the semantic domain that nevertheless stands as the ground of that relation. Logical immediacy, *insofar as it does not include* that individuation that is precisely realized through the realization of mediation, thus becomes – precisely through the realization of this mediation – something grounded (i.e. logically mediated). Authentic logical immediacy – i.e. the authentic ground – is the horizon that is constituted as a result of the very realization of mediation (precisely insofar as that horizon also includes that individuation of logical immediacy that – in the indicated sense – is determined by this mediation).

19. There is only one synthetic *a posteriori* proposition

a. In the same way in which there is only one analytic proposition, there is only one synthetic (*a posteriori*) proposition; or, equivalently: in the same way in which logical immediacy is expressed by a single proposition, so is phenomenological immediacy. In every proposition of the type: 'Y is Z' ('this extension is red'), it is affirmed that the predicate pertains to the subject on the basis of the immediate presence of this pertaining. This immediate presence, however, is not referred to that pertaining as such, but in that this pertaining is a moment or a particular content of the totality of immediately present being. What is immediately present is therefore certainly that pertaining (that particular content), but insofar as it is precisely posited as a particular content of the totality of immediate presence; or, equivalently: the pertaining of Z to Y is Ph-immediate only insofar as it is posited as a moment or individuation of that universal constituted by the very totality of the Ph-immediate. The content of every synthetic *a posteriori* proposition is therefore always the same: precisely, the totality of the Ph-immediate. (This is the case provided that, of course, those propositions are regarded as belonging to the originary structure, and not to pre- or extra-philosophical positional horizons. For, indeed, insofar as the proposition 'Y is Z' is formulated – for instance – within the domain of common or scientific consciousness, that proposition is not an *a posteriori* synthesis, but it is a groundless assertion.) There is therefore a single proposition expressing the content shared by 'every' synthetic proposition. There are not 'many' true propositions: truth is an organism – a structure, precisely. The remarks developed above concerning the only analytic proposition may be applied here with the appropriate modifications.

b. It is therefore clear that the synthetic *a posteriori* proposition 'Y is Z', too, can be the result of a *mediation*, analogously to what we have stated concerning the proposition 'A is A'. If, indeed, we regard 'Y is Z' as distinct from $(Y = Z) = (Z = Y)$, or if we regard 'Y is Z' as distinct from its being a moment of the totality of the Ph-immediate, the proposition 'Y is Z' is L-mediated. For, indeed, the fact that Y is Z is not known for itself – if Y's being-Z is regarded according to one of the two ways indicated above – but for something other: namely (with respect to the two indicated ways), it is known either for $(Y = Z) = (Z = Y)$, or for the positing of 'Y is Z' as a moment of the totality of the Ph-immediate. It should be noted that in these two cases the outcome of the mediation is not an *a priori* synthesis, in that the pertaining of Z to Y is not necessary. And yet, it is a logical mediation, for – as discussed – the predicate pertains to the subject by virtue of something other than the subject or the predicate: i.e. something that is therefore the middle term. (The immediate, to which these mediations are traced back, is Ph-immediacy itself, as it is expressed in and through the phenomenological value of the originary judgement; cf. Chapter 2.) Furthermore, affirming that the pertaining of Z to Y is not necessary – i.e. that the negation of the proposition 'Y is Z' is not immediately self-contradictory – does not entail that this pertaining of Z to Y does not follow in a necessary way from the positing of Ph-immediacy (i.e. from the phenomenological value of the originary judgement) in its including the positing of $(Y = Z) = (Z = Y)$. That is to say, having posited this Ph-immediacy in the indicated sense, it is immediately self-contradictory to negate *that this positing should imply* the proposition 'Y is Z' (having a mediational value in accordance with one of the two ways indicated above), but it is not immediately self-contradictory to negate that proposition as such: that is to say, it is not immediately self-contradictory to project that the positing of Ph-immediacy should no longer include the positing of $(Y = Z) = (Z = Y)$ (both because this positing is simply no longer included and because an opposite positing is included).

20. Clarifications concerning the meaning of logical immediacy

a. When we affirm that the negation of an L-immediate proposition is immediately self-contradictory, we do not only mean to assert that the analysis of the semantic content as such of that negation is able to *identify* the self-contradictoriness of the latter, but we also mean to assert that this self-contradictoriness is immediately *superseded*: that is to say, it is superseded on the basis of the superseding itself – a superseding that, if concretely conceived, consists in the synthesis of the L-immediate affirmation and the negation of the negation of this affirmation. As a result, to the extent that an affirmation is L-immediate, the basis or ground of that superseding is the very concrete structuring of L-immediacy.

This remark is relevant for the reason that the negation of certain synthetic *a priori* propositions (precisely those of the second, third, fourth and fifth type) is certainly immediately self-contradictory, but this self-contradictoriness is not immediately superseded (granted that it is superseded for every synthetic *a priori* proposition): in the sense that it is not superseded on the basis of this superseding itself, i.e. on the basis of the affirmation as such that is expressed by the synthetic *a priori* proposition, but it is superseded on the basis of something other – that is to say, on the basis of the concrete structure of immediacy.

This means that the negation of certain types of *a priori* syntheses is, in one respect, immediately superseded, and in a different respect (as discussed) it is not immediately superseded: it is immediately superseded in the sense that the positing of the base plane of the originary structure – i.e. the positing of the concrete structuring of immediacy – is for itself able to supersede that negation (insofar as it is self-contradictory); it is not immediately superseded in that it is not superseded by the very term that this negation negates, i.e. the content as such of the *a priori* synthesis (or, more accurately, the content of the synthesis that, precisely on the basis of the superseding of its negation, appears as an *a priori* synthesis).

b. In relation to the second, third, fourth and fifth types of synthetic *a priori* propositions, the pertaining of the predicate to the subject as such immediately counts, in one respect, as an *a posteriori* synthesis, and, in a second respect, as an *a priori* synthesis. That pertaining immediately counts as an *a posteriori* synthesis because the negation of that pertaining is not superseded as something self-contradictory *qua* negation of that pertaining, but it is superseded as something self-contradictory *qua* negation of something other, which is implied in an essential way by that pertaining. In a different respect, the pertaining of the predicate to the subject immediately counts as an *a priori* synthesis in that the project of the non-pertaining of the predicate to the subject is superseded as something self-contradictory on the basis of the simple positing of the structure of the immediate.

c. Furthermore, in relation to all those syntheses that are not immediately identified as *a priori* syntheses and that are Ph-immediate, the negation of the pertaining of the subject to the predicate is certainly immediately superseded, in that this negation negates the immediate presence of that pertaining (provided that this pertaining is posited as a moment of the totality of presence): that is to say, that negation is certainly immediately superseded *qua* negation of that pertaining, but it is not superseded as something self-contradictory, but as something in contradiction with immediate presence itself. If, furthermore, the synthetic pertaining of Y to Z is distinguished from its standing as $(Y = Z) = (Z = Y)$, or from its standing as a moment of the totality of presence, it must be stated here, too, that on the one hand the negation of that pertaining is immediately superseded, and on the other hand the negation of that pertaining is not immediately superseded (i.e. it is superseded on the basis of the simple positing of the structure of the immediate, and not on the basis of what that negation negates – namely, precisely that pertaining as thus distinct).

d. While every mediation is a relation between abstract moments of the semantic concrete (cf. § 12, d), it is however clear from what we have discussed that in certain cases the initial term of the mediation is the very formal structure of immediacy (a structure that is *formal* in that, through the mediation, it is precisely attested that this structure does not include the totality of its constants: this being the formal positing of the originary meaning; we shall however have to return to this concept with particular attention). In other cases, on the contrary – precisely the ones that we have just considered – the initial term of the mediation is an abstract moment of the structure of the immediate, in such a way that the positing of that very initial term is not something groundless only to the extent that the originary structure is posited.

21. Identity and non-contradictoriness *qua a priori* syntheses

Lastly, let us observe that both the principle of identity, as distinct from the principle of non-contradiction, and the latter as distinct from the former are synthetic *a priori* propositions. For, indeed, the concreteness of logical immediacy – as also recalled in § 18 – is the synthesis of identity ($E = E$) and non-contradiction ($E = $ nn$E$), whereby neither of the two sides of the synthesis may stand as the ground of the other.

If one turns identity into the ground of non-contradiction, it follows that while E L-immediately pertains to E (i.e. it pertains to E as such), nn$E$ does not L-immediately pertain to E, in such a way that the proposition $E = E$ is L-immediate, whereas the proposition $E = $ nn$E$ is not. At the same time, however, since the negation of $E = $ nn$E$ implies the negation of $E = E$, the proposition $E = $ nn$E$ is an *a priori* synthesis that has the ground or basis of its L-immediacy in $E = E$. Therefore: if nn$E$ does not L-immediately pertain to E, it follows that E is not, as such, the negation of the negation of the pertaining of E to E. (In the same way, as part of the pertaining of B to A through M, A – *as such* – is not the negation of the negation of the pertaining of B to A, since A can only be a negation of that negation insofar as the pertaining of M to A and the pertaining of B to M are posited. Also in the cases in which it is immediately self-contradictory to project that the mediated extreme B should not pertain to A, A does not constitute as such an exclusion of the non-pertaining of B to A). Accordingly, E stands at the same time as something to which, as such, E pertains and as something to which the negation of E can pertain (i.e. as something that, as such, does not negate this pertaining). Regarding identity, *qua* distinct from non-contradictoriness, as what is logically immediate means regarding what is logically immediate as a non-superseded contradiction. The logical situation indicated above recurs if one lets non-contradictoriness be the ground of identity.

If, however, identity, as distinct from non-contradictoriness, is not the ground of the latter – and vice-versa – both of them are instead, as distinct, the result of a mediation that has its ground in the very concrete synthesis of identity and non-contradictoriness. The negation of identity, as distinct from non-contradictoriness, is indeed not immediately superseded, i.e. it is not superseded on the basis of identity itself as thus distinct. The same is to be asserted concerning non-contradictoriness as distinct from identity. At the same time, however, these two *a priori* syntheses, too, are such that their negation is immediately superseded: that is, on the basis of the simple positing of concrete logical immediacy itself.

22. Note concerning the relation between $(D = d_x) = (d_x = D)$ and $(D = d_x)$

The observations developed in the previous sections afford a clarification of the issue left unresolved in the footnote in § 16 of Chapter 2. We stated: the Ph-immediacy of the semantic content that is precisely affirmed to be the totality of the Ph-immediate belongs to this very content; this, however, is not a simple factual belonging, for this belonging *must* obtain as soon as that content is posited as the totality of the Ph-immediate; that is to say, that belonging is necessary. Let us then indicate by D the semantic content that is affirmed to be the totality of the Ph-immediate, by $d_1, d_2, d_3, ..., d_n$ the determinations that constitute D, and by d_x the determination: 'Totality of immediately present being', which belongs to the set $d_1, d_2, d_3, ..., d_n$. The phenomenological value of the originary judgement is therefore expressed by the proposition:

$$(D = d_x) = (d_x = D).$$

Asserting that, in predicating d_x of D (cf. Chapter 2, § 16), D must include d_x itself as posited precisely means asserting that d_x is not simply predicated of D, but of $D = d_x$, since $D = d_x$ is the content of which d_x is predicated, i.e. it is precisely D in its including d_x. That predication does not therefore consist in the proposition $D = d_x$, but in the proposition $(D = d_x) = (d_x = D)$. (This also circumvents the *regressus in indefinitum* outlined in § 11 of Chapter 2). The *necessity* for D to include d_x is therefore the necessity for the predication not to be simply realized as $D = d_x$ (which would be a self-contradictory proposition), but as $(D = d_x) = (d_x = D)$.

Considering then $D = d_x$ as a content that is concretely distinct from $(D = d_x) = (d_x = D)$, the pertaining of d_x to D in that content does not constitute an L-immediate proposition; or, equivalently: the fact that the set d_1, d_2, d_3, ..., d_n should include the term d_x does not constitute an L-immediate proposition. The negation of this proposition as such is therefore not immediately self-contradictory (even though it is immediately in contradiction with the Ph-immediate). At the same time, however, having affirmed $(D = d_x) = (d_x = D)$, it is self-contradictory to negate $D = d_x$: that is to say, once d_x has been predicated of that set, it is self-contradictory to negate that this set includes d_x. The proposition $D = d_x$ is therefore L-mediated in the same sense in which the proposition 'Y is Z' is L-mediated (cf. § 19, b). This means that it is not immediately self-contradictory to project that D should no longer include d_x; in this case, if that project is at the same time the project of the persistence of the opening of the originary structure, d_x will have to be included in a semantic content that differs from D.

8

The ground *qua* contradiction

1. The project of an extension of the analysis of the originary meaning

Since $s_1, s_2, s_3, \ldots, s_n$ are all the constants of S (i.e. of the originary meaning in its concreteness, cf. Chapter 7, § 1) the positing of which is L-immediately implied by the positing of S (Chapter 7, § 2, c), it is Ph-immediately known that there are no other constants of this type. Affirming the existence of a constant s_{n+m} (the subscript m indicating from now on any constant of S that is not part of the series $s_1, \ldots, s_n$), which would be of the same type as the constants that belong to the set $s_1, \ldots, s_n$, means being *in contradiction with* the Ph-immediate. This means that $s_1, s_2, s_3, \ldots, s_n$ are all the L-immediate constants of S (i.e. constants such that their positing is L-immediately implied by the positing of S) that are Ph-immediately known. It should be noted that the set $s_1, \ldots, s_n$ also includes those *mediational* constants of S – considered in the previous chapter – which are such that the project of a positing of S that does not imply their positing is *immediately* superseded as something self-contradictory, in such a way that, in this respect, they can be regarded as L-immediate constants of S.

Developing what we have already mentioned in § 12, b of the previous chapter, we are now going to investigate the value of the project of an extension of the analysis of S that would attest one or more constants of S that are not part of the set $s_1, \ldots, s_n$; those constants therefore *supervene* or *arise* relative to this set (and, therefore, relative to the totality of the immediate).

The meaning of this investigation must be thoroughly understood. In the previous chapter, we have verified (§ 5, d) the immediate non-contradictoriness of the project of a transformation of variants into constants. It is clear that in that case, too, we projected the arising, relative to the set $s_1, \ldots, s_n$, of one or more constants of S that do not belong to this set: in the sense, however, that we projected the verification of a mediational structure on the basis of which something that immediately stands as a variant becomes a constant. The constants that arise in this way (or, from the standpoint of immediacy: whose arising is projected in this way) can be indicated with the symbol: *med.* (s_{n+m}). What we are now investigating is instead whether it is possible to project an extension, and therefore a completion, of the very analysis of S as such, which would not therefore lead to an identification of new constants of S through the introduction of a mediational structure, but which would do so simply insofar as at a later moment – which does *not* count as an additional moment from a logical point of view, but only from a temporal one – it is possible, through an analysis of S, to verify the existence of constants of S that had not been identified in a first moment of the analysis. Or, equivalently – in relation to the specific remark mentioned at the end of the first paragraph of the present section – we are asking if it is possible to verify the existence of mediational constants, *of the type indicated in that specific remark*, that are not presently attested, i.e. that do not belong to the set $s_1, ..., s_n$. Due to the particular value of this type of constants, it is possible – in this case, too – to speak of the project of an extension of the analysis of S.

Then: in order to exclude the possibility of such an extension of the analysis of S *immediately* (i.e. from the standpoint of the base plane of the originary structure), the affirmation of the positing of s_{n+m} – i.e. the affirmation of the manifestation of an L-immediate constant of S differing from the constants of the set $s_1, ..., s_n$ – must not only be (as it indeed is) in contradiction with the Ph-immediate, but it must also be self-contradictory; furthermore, this self-contradictoriness must be immediately given, i.e. it must be obtained through a simple analysis of the affirmation of the manifestation of s_{n+m}: for only in this way can the project of an extension of the analysis of S as such be immediately excluded, since it precisely projects the realization of something whose realization is impossible (in that it is self-contradictory). Except that the self-contradictoriness of the affirmation of the manifestation of s_{n+m} is *not* immediately given, in such a way that this project of an extension of the analysis of S cannot be immediately excluded – and, therefore, nor can the project of $med.(s_{n+m})$. The constants that arise (or whose arising is projected) as a result of an extension of the analysis of S – i.e. of an extension of the immediacy or present level of the analysis of S – may be indicated by the symbol: $imm.(s_{n+m})$.

At the same time, however, if the analysis of the affirmation of the manifestation of s_{n+m} does not attest the self-contradictoriness of this affirmation, it is however also not possible to immediately exclude the project of an extension of the analysis of the affirmation of the manifestation of s_{n+m} that would exhibit the self-contradictoriness of this affirmation. That is to say, it is not immediately contradictory *to project* a verification *of the immediate* self-contradictoriness of the project of the manifestation of both $imm.(s_{n+m})$ and $med.(s_{n+m})$. And, furthermore: it is not immediately contradictory to project the verification of a mediational structure on the basis of which the self-contradictoriness of the affirmation of the manifestation of s_{n+m} would be attested (cf. § 3). It is therefore also not immediately contradictory to project a (both immediate and mediational) verification of the self-contradictoriness of the negation of the arising of a constant of S.

2. Corollaries

1. A synthetic *a posteriori* proposition can not only become a synthetic *a priori* proposition, but also an analytic one – if the extension of the analysis of the subject of the proposition shows that the predicate, which at first manifests itself as a variant of the subject, is instead an L-immediate constant of the latter. Once again, however

(cf. Chapter 7, § 8, a), it is necessary to specify that if, given a synthetic *a posteriori* proposition '*Y* is *Z*', one or more past predicational implications between *Y* and a contradictory determination of *Z* are also given (= Ph-immediate), the project of the transformation of the synthetic *a posteriori* proposition under consideration into an analytic one is immediately contradictory, in that it is immediately in contradiction with those past predicational implications. Accordingly, that project must be restricted to a particular domain of the possible acts of positing of *Y* (that is to say, it must be restricted to those acts of positing of *Y* as part of which the predicate of *Y* is *Z*). Additionally, the project of a further restriction of the project under consideration is not immediately contradictory.

2. The constants of *S*, the project of the arising of which is not immediately contradictory, can both be determinations that already belong to the totality of the immediate as variants before the arising of the knowledge of their value of constants, and determinations that are not previously included in the immediate, which therefore arise the very moment they arise as constants of *S*. Respectively indicating these two types of constants with the symbols $v\ (s_{n+m})$ and non-$v\ (s_{n+m})$, we obtain the following four types of s_{n+m}:

imm.v (s_{n+m}); *imm.*non-*v* (s_{n+m}); *med.v* (s_{n+m}); *med.*non-*v* (s_{n+m}).

3. A synthetic *a priori* proposition may become an analytic proposition as a result of an extension of the analysis of the subject.

4. An analytic proposition may also acquire the value of a synthetic *a priori* proposition; that is to say, it is possible to identify a mediational structure that would exhibit how the negation of an analytic proposition *also* gives rise to one or more contradictions differing from the one that is immediately attested.

5. Every positing of the immediate non-contradictoriness of the project of a specific content leaves beside itself the immediate non-contradictoriness of the project of the verification of the self-contradictoriness of that content. Stating, for instance, that it is not immediately contradictory to project that synthetic *a priori* propositions could become analytic ones entails that it is not immediately contradictory to project the verification of the contradictoriness of that becoming.

3. Note concerning the project of the self-contradictoriness of non-contradictory meanings

From what has been established, it appears that it is not possible to immediately exclude that a further development of the analysis of *any* meaning, whose present definition does not include mutually contradictory components, may come to manifest this contradictoriness. Consider for instance the meaning: 'This red extension'. The positing of this meaning does not presently consist in the positing of a contradiction; on what basis, however, is it possible to exclude that a development of the analysis of the elements 'this', 'red', 'extension' could come to manifest mutually contradictory components? (Significant application: on what basis is it possible to exclude that a development of the analysis of S could come to manifest the self-contradictoriness of this meaning?). The aporia may also be formulated by stating that it is not possible to immediately exclude the verification of a mediational structure that would verify the self-contradictoriness of any meaning that immediately appears as something non-contradictory.

Let us respond by starting to give a determinate meaning to the aporia. If the meaning: 'This red extension' is an immediately present determinacy, in the sense that this red extension is immediately present, let us suppose that a development of the analysis of this meaning should for instance show that the element 'extension' contains a component that is contradictory in relation to a component contained in the element 'red'. Would that mean that what is referred to or meant to be indicated by the term 'extension', when this red extension is immediately present, cannot have that property to which we refer or that we wish to indicate by the term 'red'? If that were the case, the project of that development of the analysis of the meaning under consideration would be immediately contradictory (in that it would be in contradiction with the Ph-immediate). That project is not immediately contradictory only insofar as the term 'extension' is considered according to a semantic value that, while also being realized in some way as part of this red extension, is however regarded abstractly or separately from its being this red extension, i.e. disregarding its being this red extension. It is therefore clear that we are *not* stating that a development of the analysis of the term 'extension', regarded as a universal essence, may manifest a component that is contradictory in relation to a component contained in the definition of 'red' (for this is refuted by the immediate presence of the pertaining of 'red' to this individuation of that essence); we are stating that a meaning, which shares specific essential properties with the meaning to which we refer by the term 'extension' when this red extension is immediately present, may, upon further analysis, reveal to contain a contradictory component relative to 'red'. Or, equivalently: we are stating that a meaning, which shares with the meaning to which we refer by the term 'extension' when this red extension is immediately present *all* properties *except* that of being red, may, upon further analysis, reveal to contain a contradictory component relative to 'red'. This would show that there can be no other red extensions in addition to this immediately present red extension (provided that no other red extensions in addition to this one are *given*).

The same answer must be provided in relation to the project of the verification of a mediational structure on the basis of which the self-contradictoriness of an immediately present meaning should come to be manifested. The reader may further develop this point independently.

The answer to the aporia is different – and this may be considered as a corollary of what has been stated above – if the meaning is only *projected*. If, for instance, one *projects* that this red extension should be surrounded by different colours from the ones by which it is presently surrounded, it is not immediately contradictory to project that a development of the analysis of the meaning: 'This red extension surrounded by different colours from the present ones', or a mediational structure, should verify the self-contradictoriness of this meaning. Indeed, in this case, this project is not immediately refuted by the Ph-immediate. For this reason, at the end of § 1, we have stated that it is not immediately contradictory to project that a development of the analysis of the affirmation of the manifestation of s_{n+m}, or a mediational structure, should verify the self-contradictoriness of this affirmation. (It is clear that this whole argument may be applied to complex meanings as well as to those meanings that can only include the semantic multiplicity or complexity constituted by the two mutually contradictory components).

The possibility for the analysis of the sets of axioms of formal systems to exhibit, at any point of the development of that analysis, the incompatibility and therefore the contradictoriness between axioms of the same set is precisely determined by the fact that those axioms (or postulates) are *projects* – which, as such, require a demonstration of the 'self-consistency' of the set as part of which they are unified, i.e. a demonstration of the 'self-consistency' of the formal system constructed from that set. Moreover, this is a demonstration that, to the extent that it is not grounded in the originary structure – and not even suspecting the existence of the latter – not only has a simply hypothetical value, but, *qua* (at least implicit) negation of the originary structure, is a negation of the authentic meaning of non-contradictoriness (while being supposed to verify the very non-contradictoriness of that formal system).

We must now turn to consider that domain of aporias that comes closest to the central theme of this chapter.

4. The aporia of the arising of the constants of S.
a. First formulation of the aporia.

a. By affirming that it is immediately non-contradictory to project the arising of the presence of constants of S that are not part of the set $s_1, s_2, s_3, ..., s_n$ (cf. § 1), there arises an aporetic situation of significant interest, both in referring to constants of the type *imm.* (s_{n+m}) and in referring to constants of the type *med.* (s_{n+m}).

The constants of S are indeed those meanings that *constitute* the meaning S – and they are therefore the elements or components of the definition of S. Accordingly, S is posited (present, manifest) *as such* only if *all* its constants are posited. By accepting the immediate non-contradictoriness of the project of the verification of s_{n+m} – both in case s_{n+m} should count as *imm.* (s_{n+m}) and as *med.* (s_{n+m}) – one thereby admits that it is immediately non-contradictory to project that S is posited even if not all of its constants are posited, or that S is posited even if S is not posited.

b. This can easily be understood in case s_{n+m} has the value of non-v (s_{n+m}) (cf. § 2, corollary 2). In this case, it must indeed be stated that it is not immediately contradictory to project that S should be posited without the positing of the constant non-v (s_{n+m}).

In relation to this last specification, one might then suppose that the aporia does not obtain in relation to the constants of type v (s_{n+m}) – cf. § 2, *ibid.* – for, in this case, that whose arising is projected is only the knowledge of the constant-value of a determinacy that is *already present*; that is to say, what is projected is not the arising of the constant itself, which is precisely already present in its determinate content. Except that an extremely large set of variants are present as *factual additional dimensions* (cf. Chapter 5, § 28, a), and they are present as such factual additional dimensions relative to positional horizons in which S was posited as such even though all or some of these variants were not yet posited. Insofar as one projects that these variants, counting as factual additional dimensions, should become constants, one once again projects that S has been posited as such even though not all of its constants had been posited. That is to say, if one projects that this type of variants become constants, what is then immediately present is a series of acts of positing of S which count as past totalities of the immediate and in which S is posited as such even though not all its constants are posited.

c. One might therefore think that the aporia does not obtain up to this point at least in relation to those variants of S that are included as a matter of fact *in every* immediately known positing of S. As a result, that aporia might be superseded by positing that the constants, the project of the arising of which is not immediately contradictory, must respect the condition of having been variants included as a matter of fact *in every* immediately known positing of S, prior to the arising of the knowledge of their value of constants.

d. Except that, even if a determinacy that is a constant of S is present, but it is not present as a constant – i.e. it is not present in its belonging to the essence of S – S is in any case posited as a semantic horizon that does not essentially include that determinacy, in such a way that this horizon cannot count as S. For, indeed, a constant of S is not a determinacy that is simply co-present with S as a matter of fact. Accordingly, even if every positing of S includes a specific determinacy, but only as a matter of fact, if this determinacy is not identified as a constant of S, it must be stated that, in each of these acts of positing of S, what is posited is not S.

5. b. Radical formulation of the aporia

The aporia therefore appears in all its significance if we observe – thus making explicit elements already identified in the previous section – that the arising of the verification of s_{n+m} is not only the content of a project, but it is itself immediately present. That is to say, there is an experience of the arising of a certain number of constants; or, equivalently, a certain number of constants – both of type $v\ (s_{n+m})$ and of type non-$v\ (s_{n+m})$ – are themselves factual additional dimensions relative to the positing of S. Furthermore, these constants arise with respect to the positing of S both through an extension of the analysis of S and through the realization of mediational structures. (The present essay will provide a few examples of these realizations). Accordingly, if at first the aporia was determined by the concept of the *possibility* or *possibility of the project* of the arising of s_{n+m}, it is now determined by the *factual existence* of that arising. It is important to observe this since, while remaining at that first configuration of the aporia, it was possible to think of superseding the latter precisely by negating the possibility of the arising of s_{n+m} – i.e. by positing the project of the arising of s_{n+m} as something immediately contradictory – it now appears that this type of superseding of the aporia is no longer permitted, since the arising of s_{n+m}, in its being immediately present (and no longer simply projected), cannot be negated.

The aporia may then be presented according to the following general formulation: 'The positing of S implies the positing of all the constants of S; S, however, is posited even if not all the constants of S are posited'.[1]

6. c. Concerning a type of superseding of the aporia

At the same time, however, it is possible to take advantage of the type of superseding of the aporia dismissed above as follows. The acts of positing of S, relative to which specific constants count as factual additional dimensions, are not – respectively – acts of positing of the totality *simpliciter* of the immediate, but they are a positing of something that, relative to that totality *simpliciter*, counts as a *past* totality of the immediate (cf. Chapter 5, § 29): the latter being such because its content does not include at the very least that constant or constants that, in arising, are precisely posited as factual additional dimensions relative to that content. For what concerns that positing of S that counts as the totality of the immediate *simpliciter*, however, the arising of constants that do not belong to the set $s_1, \ldots, s_n$ (and, more generally the arising of any determination that does not belong to the totality of the immediate) is not something factual, but a possibility or a project: for if that arising were something factual, the totality *simpliciter* of the immediate would consist in that positing of S that includes this factual existence.

The aporia outlined above does not therefore concern the totality of the immediate, but those acts of positing of S that count as *past* totalities of the immediate. For what concerns the totality *simpliciter* of the immediate, the aporia is indeed superseded precisely by negating the possibility of the arising of constants that do not belong to the set $s_1, \ldots, s_n$. The correctness of that negation consists in the fact that what is negated is not an immediately present content, but one that appeared as something possible (i.e. as something able to be projected) only from the standpoint of an abstract consideration, and that, to the extent that it was held firm as something possible, appeared to be in contradiction with the theorem of the impossibility of a positing of S that does not imply the positing of all the constants of S; whence the arising of the aporia. The latter is therefore superseded by holding firm this theorem, and negating that possibility.

7. d. Verification of the value of this type of superseding of the aporia

a. Turning now to a determination of the value of this type of superseding of the aporia, let us refer by 'theorem N' to the proposition: 'It is a contradiction for S to be posited even if not all the constants of S are posited', and let us refer by the term 'C-contradiction' to the contradiction indicated by theorem N. *In order to supersede the C-contradiction*, we have above (§ 6) negated the possibility of the project of the arising of s_{n+m}.

At the same time, however – this being the point that we need to clarify – does theorem N state that *it is contradictory to affirm* the realization of a positing of S that does not imply the positing of all the constants of S, or does it simply state that a positing of S that does not imply the positing of all the constants of S constitutes the realization of a contradiction?

For now, it is clear that while this second interpretation of theorem N indicates *only one* contradiction (i.e. the one that arises in positing S without positing all the constants of S), that first interpretation indicates instead *a twofold* contradiction, precisely to the extent that it states that it is contradictory to affirm the realization of the contradiction indicated by the second interpretation. What therefore varies as part of these two interpretations (let these respectively be 'int. 1' and 'int. 2') is the structure of that C-contradiction, since int. 2 states that in positing S without positing all the constants of S there arises a specific contradiction, but it does not state that *it is contradictory to affirm that* this positing of S, and therefore that specific contradiction, should be realized.

It is however clear that the type of superseding of the aporia considered in § 6 requires int. 1. For, indeed, if int. 2 only states that by positing S in a certain way there arises a contradiction (which, according to int. 2 is precisely the C-contradiction indicated by theorem N), but it does not state that it is contradictory to affirm that the C-contradiction should be realized as a matter of fact, then, holding firm int. 2, it is no longer necessary to carry out the superseding of the C-contradiction through a negation of the possibility of the arising of s_{n+m}, since the C-contradiction can *also* be superseded through the *positing* of those constants of S, the lack of positing of which precisely causes the C-contradiction. If, instead, one holds firm that int. 1, according to which the C-contradiction indicated by theorem N consists in the contradictoriness of the affirmation of the realization of the contradiction indicated by int. 2 – i.e. the realization of a positing of S that does not imply the positing of all the constants of S – then the *only way* to supersede the C-contradiction consists in the negation of the possibility of the arising of s_{n+m}: precisely because if one admits that possibility, one admits at the same time the possibility that something whose realization is stated to be contradictory should be realized. This is precisely the course followed by the type of superseding of the aporia considered in § 6.

b. Which of these two interpretations of theorem N must then be accepted? Let us respond that it is necessary to retain int. 2.

For, indeed, *on the one hand*, int. 1 is in contradiction with the Ph-immediate to the extent that a set of constants of S is immediately present in their counting as factual additional dimensions relative to a series of past acts of positing of S (§ 5), each of which is therefore realized without implying the positing of one or more constants of S. Int. 1 is therefore in contradiction with the Ph-immediate insofar as a series of realizations of the contradiction indicated by the int. 2 is immediately present. *On the other hand* – i.e. in relation to that positing of S as part of which S stands as the totality *simpliciter* of the immediate – it is not immediately contradictory (as it will become completely explicit in the following pages) to *project* that this positing, too, should be affected by that very contradiction that affects that series of past acts of positing of S; that is to say, it is not immediately contradictory to project the arising of s_{n+m}; as a result, insofar as int. 1 refers to this positing of S, this interpretation is *groundless* (i.e. it is not able to exclude its contrary affirmation): precisely because it affirms without any justification that it is contradictory to affirm that the positing of S – regarded as the totality *simpliciter* of the immediate – should be realized without implying the positing of all the constants of S; that is to say, it affirms without any justification that it is contradictory for the originary structure to be free from contradiction.

c. Int. 1 would only be valid if the lack of positing of a specific constant were to necessarily imply the annulment of every positional value of S, or, even, the annulment of every positional value. It is however the immediate itself that attests that – in relation to those constants whose arising relative to specific acts of positing of S is immediately present – this annulment does not take place. Let us consider a positing of S that, for instance, does *not* imply the positing of the meaning 'relation between $s_1, \ldots, s_n$ and s_{n+m}'. As part of this positing, S is *de facto* meaningful, or, equivalently, it has *de facto* a specific positional value or positivity. Except that the meaning 'relation between $s_1, \ldots, s_n$ and s_{n+m}' is a constant of S (if anything because if the positing of S consists in the positing of $s_1, \ldots, s_n$, this positing constitutes the exclusion of the positing of s_{n+m}, and this exclusion is precisely the relation between $s_1, \ldots, s_n$ and s_{n+m}); accordingly, if that meaning is not posited, S as such is not posited either. At the same time, however, S is posited as a matter of fact even if that meaning is not posited, and it is precisely this positing of S, as part of which S is posited as a matter of fact and at the same time it cannot be posited, that constitutes the C-contradiction. This contradiction (like every other contradiction) has a positional positivity, and it is this positivity that which constitutes the contradictory *positing* of S.

8. e. Note

Leaving aside the clarifications that will have to be provided on this point by a further study of the question that we have just outlined, it appears that it must be stated that *within* the positional domain opened by the contradictory positing of S, the contradiction in question is *in itself*, i.e. it is not posited: for if it were, what would have to be posited is precisely that meaning whose lack of positing causes the contradiction. (Or, equivalently, this contradiction can only be supposed: precisely to the extent that one projects the arising of a constant of S, the semantic content of which is however not known in a determinate way.) The positional domain constituted by a positing of S that does not imply the positing of that constant of S thus appears to only include one of the two sides of the contradiction pertaining to the domain itself: namely, that side due to which S is posited as such as a matter of fact. For, indeed, insofar as at a later time it comes to be known that a specific constant of S is not posited as part of that positing of S, from the standpoint of this larger positional horizon it is then asserted that S was not posited as such as part of that *de facto* positing of S; and the contradiction that was at first 'in itself' is now 'for itself'.

The development of the exposition will however have to amend the content of this note (cf. for instance Chapter 11, § 9).

9. f. The C-contradiction

a. Stating: 'As part of a positing of S that does not imply the positing of one or more constants of S, S is posited as a matter of fact, but at the same time it cannot be posited as such' means that what one *intends* to posit as part of this positing of S is not what one *effectively* or *actually* succeeds in positing. The positional positivity of the C-contradiction does not indeed simply require that if a positing of S does not imply the positing of one or more constants of S what is realized as a matter of fact is any positional horizon; rather, it requires that this horizon *should be posited as S*. However, since – due to the lack of positing of one or more constants of S – what is posited in this horizon cannot be S, the positional positivity of the C-contradiction requires the *intention* of positing S. If the horizon under consideration were not realized as this intention, its failure to stand as S would not result in the self-contradictoriness of that horizon. (It is here clear that when we refer to the C-contradiction, we refer to a self-contradiction.)

If the C-contradiction therefore consists in the intention to posit S, thereby positing a specific content, and in the difference between the content that is effectively posited and S, this means that this contradiction does *not* consist in the positing and lack of positing of the content that is effectively posited. That, the realization of which is contradictory, is that a content should at the same time be posited and not posited; the fact that what is posited as a matter of fact should not be what one intends to posit, however, is not something the realization of which is contradictory. If the positing of a content that would *simpliciter* coincide with the lack of positing of that same content is what cannot be realized – it is what is not (cf. Chapter 4, § 14) – this nothingness consists at the same time in the positional nullity of that content. If the C-contradiction were regarded in this way – i.e. as a positing that is *simpliciter* a lack of positing – then it should certainly be stated (cf. § 7, c) that it is contradictory to affirm that S is posited even if one of its constants is not posited. As a result, the aporia under consideration would only be able to be resolved by negating the possibility of the arising of s_{n+m}.

b. Resuming: while the C-contradiction, like every other contradiction, must be superseded, this does not mean that it cannot realise itself. Or, equivalently: while thinking must not fall into contradiction, this does not mean that it cannot do so. For, indeed, contradicting oneself does not mean that a saying *is itself*, as such, a non-saying, or that an affirming *is itself*, as such, a negating. Contradicting oneself means affirming and negating the same thing: and, as part of this situation, that affirming realizes itself as an affirming and that negating as a negating. In this respect, contradicting oneself means holding together an affirming (which is an affirming) and a negating (which is a negating). Furthermore, this 'holding together' is superseded precisely because in order to hold together the affirmation and the negation of the same thing it would be necessary that the affirming *were itself*, *a*s such, a negating (or, equivalently, that the affirmed thing *were itself*, as such, the negated thing; or, more generally, that being were as such non-being). If, therefore, contradicting oneself consisted in an affirming that *is itself*, as such, a negating, falling into contradiction would mean falling into nothing (and, therefore, there would not even be something like a 'falling') – precisely because an affirming that is itself, as such, a negating *is not* – and therefore it would mean not even being in contradiction.

Contradicting oneself, however, is also *not* a saying (a positing) that is itself, as such, a not-saying (a not-positing): namely, in the same way in which on the one hand contradicting oneself does not consist in the identity between an affirmation and an explicit (= posited) negation, but it is a form of holding them together – this being the side considered above – on the other hand, nor does contradicting oneself consist in the identity between an affirmation and an *implicit* negation (= a non-posited negation: even if not posited in a specific sense, which will be determined below), but, once again, it is a form of holding these together. The C-contradiction belongs to this second structure of contradicting oneself (furthermore: a consideration of this contradiction may serve as a paradigm for at least a certain group of contradictions of this type, but not for all of them – for, indeed, it is possible to identify other modes of implicitly negating an affirmation in addition to the one for which the C-contradiction may serve as a paradigm). In this second respect, contradicting oneself therefore means saying or positing something that is not what one *intends* to say or posit – and not, as already discussed, positing and not positing what is effectively posited (and nor, let us add, intending and not intending to posit what one intends to posit). Once again: if contradicting oneself were regarded in this way, it would mean not being, and, therefore, also not being in contradiction.[2]

c. Turning then to a clarification of the meaning of the *intention* to posit S: if the positing of S does not imply the positing of one or more constants of S, we state that there exists a *difference* between the semantic content that is effectively posited and the intention to posit S; we affirm this in the sense that this semantic content that is effectively posited constitutes a *formal positing* of S, in such a way that S is effectively posited, but only in a formal way. That difference therefore obtains between the content or the concrete value of the meaning S and the form of this concreteness – a form that precisely constitutes the content that is effectively posited. Accordingly, S is posited *formally*, but not *concretely*. (Further ahead – cf. Chapter 9, § 8, d – we shall specify that the form of S that is effectively posited is not the form *simpliciter* of S, but its *abstract* form. This may already appear to be clear at this point).

In more detail: the positing of the system of the constants of S is certainly a *formal* positing with respect to the positing of the totality of the immediately present determinations. At the beginning of Chapter 7, and in § 13 of that chapter, we have indicated a sense of the analysis of S in accordance with which this analysis includes all those determinations. As part of this analysis of S, the positing of the system of the constants of S is therefore certainly a formal positing of S; this, however, is not the formality that we are discussing here, for while the concrete positing relative to which the positing of the system of the constants of S has a formal value is the positing of the totality of the immediately known determinations – variants and constants – the concrete positing relative to which we are now stating that the positing of S has a formal value is instead the *positing of the totality of the constants of S*. We are then stating that a positing of S that does not imply the positing of one or more constants of S is a formal positing in the sense that, as part of this positing, the totality of constants is not posited in a determinate way – or only its abstract form is posited – and the constants that are effectively posited fail to conform with it.

The C-contradiction therefore consists in positing S formally and in not positing it concretely; or, equivalently: in positing S in such a way that the concrete semantic value or the concrete meaningfulness of what is posited is not thereby posited. With respect to the positing of this semantic concreteness of S, the positing of S that is effectively realized when, in positing S, not all of its constants are posited therefore only consists in the *intention* to posit S: that is to say, this positing is only something *required*. It is here clear that the positing òf S that is effectively realized may only count as an 'intention' insofar as S is *in a certain way* already all posited. S is indeed already all posited as to its formal value, in such a way that what one 'intends' to think concretely is precisely this whole. The C-contradiction therefore consists in *intending* as S something that, precisely insofar as it is only the formal value of S, is not S.

S is therefore posited in a certain respect and not posited in another respect. It is precisely insofar as S is thus not posited that the C-contradiction consists in an explicit affirmation (or positing) of S and in an *implicit* negation of the latter: this negation being implicit to the extent that it is not the case that the constants that are not posited are *posited* as superseded (explicit negation), but it is rather the case that they are simply not posited.

It can therefore be stated: it is immediately self-contradictory to project that S should be posited *as such* (i.e. concretely) without the positing of all its constants; however, it *is not* immediately self-contradictory to project that S should be posited as such without the positing of all its constants if it is acknowledged that such a positing of S is a formal positing, and it is therefore a form of being in contradiction. That is to say, the project under consideration is immediately self-contradictory if it is not posited as the project of a contradiction.

10. g. Provisional conclusion

a. What must therefore be held firm up to this point is the fact that in relation to each of the (past) acts of positing of S, relative to which the positing of one or more constants of S stands as a factual additional dimension, the C-contradiction – which precisely pertains to each of these acts of positing of S – is superseded by *positing* those constants, the lack of positing of which precisely caused the C-contradiction. The process or becoming constituted by that increment of the positional horizon that is determined by the arising of the constants of S is therefore the very process or act of superseding of the C-contradiction (which – it is clear – is realized as a series of C-contradictions). Becoming, *qua* increase of the originary positional horizon, is the superseding of a contradiction.

It is thus clear that if the superseding of the C-contradiction is a process, the C-contradiction is quantified (in such a way that it is possible to speak of a *series* of C-contradictions). This quantification is determined by the varying extent or degree of the difference between the set $s_1, ..., s_n$ that is posited in each of the acts of positing of S and the totality of the constants of S.

For what concerns instead that positing of S in which S stands as the totality *simpliciter* of the immediate, it appears to be possible – given the present stage of the exposition – *both* to project that the positing *simpliciter* of S, too (like those past acts of positing of S), should be affected by a C-contradiction (in such a way that, in this respect, it is not immediately contradictory to project the arising of s_{n+m}) *and* to negate that the C-contradiction should pertain to the positing *simpliciter* of S: this being the case insofar as one negates the possibility (= non-contradictoriness) of the arising of s_{n+m}. If the project of the arising of s_{n+m} is however not immediately contradictory – i.e. if it is not immediately contradictory to suppose that the positing *simpliciter* of S should be affected by a contradiction – this means that the contradictoriness of the project of the arising of s_{n+m} is itself something projected. Therefore, also the affirmation that the positing *simpliciter* of S is not affected by a C-contradiction is a project. Accordingly, it appears that up to this point of the exposition of the originary it is as possible to project the arising of s_{n+m} as it is possible to project the arising of the verification of the self-contradictoriness of the arising of s_{n+m}.

b. At this point, it could be left undetermined whether the 'provisional' character of the conclusion indicated above is such that an extension of the analysis of S (or, simply, of the exposition of this analysis) is required for the superseding of that character, or whether a mediation is necessary. Even allowing that indeterminacy to persist, it is clear that in the first case that provisional character – and the projecting connected to it – is determined by the incompleteness of the analysis of S (or of the exposition of that analysis); in the second case, instead, that 'provisional' character has a 'strong' meaning, in that it constitutes the very character of immediacy relative to the plane of mediation.

It is however preferable to already take note of the fact that the project discussed under point a (i.e. projecting that S should or should not be affected by a C-contradiction) is superseded by a simple extension of the exposition of the analysis of the originary (as it will appear later on in the course of this enquiry; cf. Chapter 11); that is to say, that extension is sufficient in order to convert one of the two sides of that project into a categorical affirmation. As a result of this observation, it follows that the project under consideration is determined by an *abstract concept* of the horizon of the immediate, for only an abstract concept may determine a logical situation (i.e. that projecting) that is superseded by a concrete comprehension of the immediate – which is precisely obtained through a completion of the analysis of S. That concept is abstract precisely because it regards the level of the analysis of S exposed up to this point as the whole of the analysis itself, and only in this way is it able to confer upon that level a property – the opening of that projecting – that is superseded by an extension of the analysis of the originary. In other words: if an extension of the analysis supersedes a project, this means that the latter is determined by an abstract concept of the analysis (cf. § 13). As it will be shown, an aspect of this abstract concept is constituted by the concept Γ_a itself (cf. Chapter 2, § 26).

11. h. Transition

The *immediate* superseding of that projecting, determined by the abstract concept indicated above, is determined as the (immediate) verification of the self-contradictoriness of the affirmation that the set $s_1, \ldots, s_n$ constitutes the totality of the constants of S. This anticipation, too, will be adequately developed in due course.[3] In relation to the anticipation of the verification of the difference between the set $s_1, \ldots, s_n$ and the totality of the constants of S, a special consideration should be given to the concept in accordance with which the positing *simpliciter* of S – i.e. the positing of immediacy itself, or the positing of the originary structure – constitutes the realization of a contradiction. It should be noted that the following clarifications concerning the determination of the meaning of the contradictoriness of the originary are also required by the abstract concept discussed in the previous section (and therefore independently of the anticipation of that difference): to the extent that, from the standpoint of that abstract concept, projecting that the positing *simpliciter* of S should be affected by a C-contradiction is not immediately contradictory.

12. The totality of the immediate *qua* originary contradiction

a. As part of the present exposition of the originary structure, it will appear in several ways that the base plane of the originary structure consists in the originary opening of a contradiction. For now, however, the concrete meaning of the contradictoriness of the originary consists in the verification – which, up to this point, has only been anticipated – of the difference between the set $s_1, \ldots, s_n$ and the totality of the constants of S. The ground is certainly the originary opening of a contradiction, but in the very specific sense that the positing of the totality of the immediate does not consist in the positing of all those meanings whose positing is necessarily implied by the positing of that totality (i.e. the constants). This contradiction, like every other contradiction, may only be superseded by superseding what causes it: namely, by superseding the lack of positing of that system of meanings, i.e. by positing that system or *realising its manifestation*. The originary contradiction cannot therefore be superseded by negating or no longer positing the immediate, but it is in fact superseded by augmenting or enhancing the positing of the immediate and of its structure: that is to say, once again (cf. § 10), by realizing the process of an increment of the originary positional horizon.

b. Since the basis or the ground of this process nevertheless remains the totality of the immediate, *qua* base plane of the originary structure, it should also be clear that this originary contradictoriness of the base plane does not compromise in any way the validity of what is grounded in this plane.

Indeed, for what concerns the arising of constants of type $imm.(s_{n+m})$, the ground of the affirmation or positing of this arising consists in the positing of the totality of the immediate *in its including* the constant that has arisen. (Affirming that the totality of the immediate is thus inclusive means that the set of L-immediate connections that are Ph-immediately known includes the L-immediate connection constituted by S's implication of $imm.(s_{n+m})$. Accordingly, that set constitutes the ground of this connection precisely insofar as it includes it. Furthermore, it is clear that this set constitutes the ground of this connection according to the modes considered in § 18 of Chapter 7). The totality of the immediate, in its *not yet* including that constant (the argument may however be extended to every arising determination), constitutes the 'ground' of the manifestation of the arising, in the sense that it constitutes the horizon as part of which every arising can originarily take place or manifest itself; as stated, however, the affirmation of a constant that has arisen finds its ground in the positing of the totality of the immediate *qua* inclusive of that constant. That is to say, it is precisely insofar as the totality of the immediate is a contradiction in the verified sense that it may stand as the horizon as part of which the constants of S can arise; on the contrary, insofar as the totality of the immediate constitutes the ground *of the affirmation* of the arising constant, that totality – *qua* inclusive of the constant that has arisen – is no longer affected by that quantity of the C-contradiction that was precisely determined by the lack of positing of the arisen constant; accordingly, the totality of the immediate does not constitute the ground insofar as it is a contradiction, but insofar as it is the superseding of a contradiction.

Furthermore, the fact that the positing of S is affected by a certain quantity of the C-contradiction is something that is (categorically) known, and not only (indeterminately) projected, only insofar as there exists a knowledge of the concrete determinacy of the constant or group of constants of S whose lack of positing causes that specific quantification of the C-contradiction (leaving here aside the clarifications that will have to be provided concerning this point). This means that every determinate quantification of this contradiction is manifested by the very act that supersedes it – i.e. by the totality of the immediate *qua* inclusive of the arisen constant(s). (The *project* of the C-contradiction – i.e. the project as part of which the originary is affected by an additional quantity of C-contradiction relative to the one that, as anticipated, is immediately established – like the project of every other contradiction, is furthermore always *indeterminate*; or, equivalently, as part of that project the contradiction is present in its formal structure: for if the contradiction were determinately or concretely present, it would no longer only be something *projected*, but *known*).

The same should be stated in relation to the arising of the constants of type $med.(s_{n+m})$. The totality of the immediate, *qua* base plane of the originary structure, is indeed also the horizon as part of which every mediational process can appear or arise: in the sense that the mediational logical structure that leads beyond the base plane becomes itself immediately present. That is to say: it is precisely insofar as the totality of the immediate is affected by the C-contradiction that it may stand as the horizon as part of which the m-contradiction, which is realized when a constant of type $med.(s_{n+m})$ is not posited, can be manifested (cf. Chapter 7, § 5, b).[4] Relative to the positing of all the constants of type $med.(s_{n+m})$, the base plane of the originary structure constitutes in fact the maximum realization of the C-contradiction: precisely because, *qua* horizon of immediacy, it constitutes the horizon relative to which (and as part of which) every mediation may arise. This is then a first sense in which it stands as the ground. Once again, it is clear that it can stand as 'ground', *in this sense*, only insofar as it is a contradiction – and in fact, as discussed, only insofar as it constitutes the maximum realization of the C-contradiction.

Furthermore, the base plane certainly constitutes the ground *of the affirmation* of the arising of the constants of type $med.(s_{n+m})$ to the extent that it constitutes the positing of the immediacy of the non-contradictoriness of being, and it is in the immediacy of this non-contradictoriness that the superseding of the contradictions of type m is grounded; these contradictions, like every other contradiction, are superseded because non-contradictoriness itself has the value of immediacy, and the positing of the immediacy of non-contradictoriness is included in the constitution of the structure of the base plane. Once again, however, the originary structuring of logical immediacy may only serve as the ground insofar as, through the positing of a middle term, *it has come to include S's implication of* $med.(s_{n+m})$ – since (cf. Chapter 7, § 18, h), precisely, a mediation augments the content of logical immediacy. (Furthermore, it is clear that this inclusion is at the same time the inclusion of this mediational process by the totality of immediate presence, for the logical immediacy that originarily structures itself consists in the set of L-immediate connections that are Ph-immediately known). Therefore, in this case, too, the base plane does not serve as the ground to the extent that it is affected by the C-contradiction – namely, to the extent that it does not yet include those mediational processes – but to the extent that it includes them, i.e. to the extent that it is the superseding of that contradiction.

Concluding: the totality of the immediate can serve as the ground in a sense in accordance with which it *is necessary* that it should count as the realization of the C-contradiction (in this sense, it constitutes the horizon as part of which the manifestation of new constants of S can arise), and in a sense in accordance with which, insofar as it has this value of ground, it is not affected by the C-contradiction.

13. More on the extension of the analysis

Stating that there exists a necessary implication between two meanings x and y means stating that there exists a necessary implication between the present set of constants of x and the present set of constants of y. If that implication obtains between the two present sets *as such*, no extension of the analysis of x and y may be such that it entails a negation of the implication between the two present sets. Indeed, every extension of the analysis of a meaning cannot be (= it is immediately contradictory for it to be) a negation of the immediately present semantic value of that meaning, and this value includes the present set of the constants of that meaning; furthermore, the extension of the analysis could only imply the negation of the implication between the two present sets if it led to a negation of the immediate semantic value of that meaning. One speaks of a relation of *inclusion* between this value and the present set of constants – and not of an *identity* between the two – because that value can also include (and, in fact, from the standpoint of immediacy it must be stated that it also necessarily includes) the present set of variants of the meaning under consideration. (It is clear that if two meanings necessarily imply each other *insofar as* the present semantic value of one of the two, or of both, includes the present set of variants, it is not immediately contradictory to project that there should no longer obtain a necessary implication between the two meanings: precisely because it is not immediately contradictory to project that these meanings should include a set of variants that has *varied* with respect to the present one).

Instead, an extension of the analysis necessarily leads to the negation of the necessary implication between two meanings if the implication between the present sets of the constants of the two meanings does not obtain between the two sets as such, but *to the extent that they exclude* the possibility that constants that do not belong to the present sets should belong to the meanings under consideration: i.e. if the necessary implication is determined by the immediate (and, here, unwarranted) correspondence between the totality of the constants of the two meanings and the present sets of their constants. This immediate correspondence is the *abstract concept* of the present set.

All of this is particularly relevant for what has been discussed in the previous section if one considers the necessary implications that obtain between that extremely complex meaning constituted by the ground itself and other meanings. Let us introduce the concept of the *semantic levels* of the ground, in relation on the one hand to the extension of the analysis of the semantic value of the originary structure and on the other hand to the mediational plane (or the series of mediational planes). (The immediately present semantic value of the ground is the base level – or: the base plane is the base level – and every extension of the analysis and every mediation constitute a different and higher level). It must therefore be stated that the necessary implications established at a certain semantic level of the ground that is affected by a certain quantification of the C-contradiction cannot be negated by the realization of any other semantic level of the ground – while it is nevertheless the case that the realization of those necessary implications constitutes at the same time the realization of a (C-) contradiction. This means that the superseding of this contradiction constitutes the very *enhancement* of those implications: i.e. their authentic realization.

14. The totality of the immediate and the totality of mediation

The positing of S is not only affected by the C-contradiction insofar as the constants of S are not posited, but also insofar as the constants of the variants (i.e. the covariants) of S are themselves not posited. For, indeed, positing *any* meaning belonging to the totality of the immediate – and, therefore, also each of the variants of S – without positing all the constants of that meaning entails that what is effectively posited as part of the positing of that meaning is not what one intends to posit (analogously to what has been discussed concerning the positing of S). This kind of positing of that (any) meaning therefore constitutes a mode of the realization of the C-contradiction. Indeed, insofar as the positing of this meaning is a moment of the totality of the immediate, the contradictoriness of that positing consists in the contradictoriness of the positing of S.

Accordingly, we state that the positing or the manifestation of a semantic horizon that were to consist in the totality of the constants and of the covariants of S would represent the *absolute supersession* of the C-contradiction (i.e. not a supersession of this or that quantification of the C-contradiction, but of the totality of the quantifications of this contradiction). Aside from the necessary clarifications, this semantic horizon consists in the *totality of mediation*. Indeed, *every* synthetic *a priori* connection (for, as discussed, mediations are *a priori* syntheses) is *either* a synthetic *a priori* positional implication between S, or a constant of S, and a determinacy (in which case this determinacy is manifested as a constant of S), *or* it is a synthetic *a priori* positional implication between a variant or covariant of S and a determinacy (in which case this determinacy is manifested as a covariant of S). Insofar as the totality of mediation constitutes the absolute superseding of the C-contradiction, the totality of the immediate, *qua* base plane of the originary structure, constitutes the *absolute positing* of that contradiction: i.e. it constitutes its maximum realization. In other words (returning as part of this larger set of observations to what we have already discussed in the previous two sections): precisely insofar as the totality of the immediate is the ground of the totality of mediation (i.e. of every possible knowledge), the totality of the immediate is what is maximally contradictory.

In the preface to the *Phenomenology of Spirit*, Hegel states that the ground or 'principle of philosophy, if true, is also false, just because it is only a principle'. In fact, it is what above all lends itself to be refuted: 'The refutation consists in pointing out its defect; and it is defective because it is only the universal or principle, is only the beginning'. At the same time, however, 'the refutation, therefore, properly consists in the further development of the principle or ground, and in thus remedying the defectiveness': the refutation is grounded only insofar as it is 'derived and developed from the ground or principle itself'[5]; that is to say, it is the very grounding or founding act, in and through which something *other* than the ground comes to be grounded. It is well known what 'ground' indicates here: the ground is the starting point, or the *beginning* of the logic, i.e. the category of pure being. In the first lines of the first volume of the *Logic*, it is stated that 'the *progress* from that which forms the beginning is to be regarded as only a further determination of it, hence that which forms the starting point of the development remains at the base of all that follows'. Therefore, 'the progress does not consist merely in the derivation of an *other*, or in the effected transition into a genuine other', since the beginning is 'the foundation which is present and preserved throughout the entire subsequent development, remaining completely immanent in its further determinations'. 'Through this progress, then, the beginning loses the one-sidedness which attaches to it as something simply immediate and abstract; it becomes something mediated, and hence the line of the scientific advance becomes a *circle*'. It is here clear that what 'forms the beginning, because it is still undeveloped and devoid of content, is not yet truly known in the beginning, and that only science, and fully developed science, is the completed knowledge of it, with its developed content and finally truly grounded'.[6]

It is then important to note how all these remarks by Hegel are altogether valid – or, more precisely, they can be entirely referred or adapted to the relation indicated above between the totality of the immediate and the totality of mediation. (Considering the concept of 'systematic circle' as inclusive of all those remarks, it is well-known that, instead, according to Hegel the systematic circle leaves outside itself – or, more precisely, prior to itself – the phenomenological plane: i.e. that plane that, as to its most correct value, is to be regarded in its structuring itself as the totality of the immediate).[7]

We therefore state that, precisely because the totality of the immediate is the true ground, that totality is truth in the form of the absolutely false: in the sense that this totality – insofar as it is only the ground, i.e. it is only the domain of immediate knowledge – constitutes the absolute positing or full realization of the C-contradiction. That totality – still translating the Hegelian expression quoted above into our paradigm – is a form of 'defectiveness' and 'universality' in the sense that the positing of the totality of the immediate is a defectiveness or absence of the positing of the totality of the constants, in such a way that what is effectively posited is only the formal or abstractly universal meaning of S.

At the same time, however, the concrete verification of the (C-)contradictoriness of the positing of S is a mediation – insofar as it realizes itself as a verification of the constants of type *med.* (s_{n+m}), and, therefore, insofar as it consists of what Hegel refers to as the 'refutation of the ground'. That is to say, that verification coincides with the very act through which the ground realizes itself as something that lies at the basis of something else – i.e. as the ground of what is mediated. In other words: the contradictoriness of the ground is verified insofar as its constants are posited, i.e. insofar as its defectiveness is attested. Coming to posit its constants, however, means realizing a mediation – since these are constants of type *med.* (s_{n+m}). Since this mediation realizes itself as the superseding of a contradiction – and, precisely, as the superseding of a contradiction of type *m* – that superseding is grounded in the positing of the immediacy of non-contradictoriness, i.e. it is grounded in the totality of the immediate, which precisely constitutes itself as this originary positing of non-contradictoriness. It is here clear that the act that verifies the contradictoriness[8] of the ground is the very act by virtue of which the ground realizes itself as the ground of something else, or it is the very act by virtue of which the ground performs its function of grounding something else. Furthermore, the ground is not such insofar as it is a contradiction, but insofar as it is a superseding of the latter, i.e. insofar as it includes what is grounded, according to what we have discussed in the second part of § 12 (cf. also Chapter 7, § 18, h).[9]

This process of grounding something, however, does not consist of an advance from the ground to something that is *only* other than the ground: this otherness is indeed the very positing of the ground in its now being free from the (*C*-)contradiction – or from a specific quantification of that contradiction – that affected the ground before its being the ground of the mediation. The plane of the mediation, which is precisely the plane of that otherness, consists in the positing of the necessary relation between the immediate and its mediational constants – and it therefore consists in the non-contradictory positing of the immediate. Accordingly, that process of grounding something other, which is at the same time a verification of the contradictoriness of the ground of this otherness – i.e. which is at the same time a superseding of the ground *qua* contradiction – is a 'development' or 'further determination' of the ground itself. The latter, *qua* immediacy from which the development proceeds, therefore 'remains at the base of all that follows'; accordingly, the act as part of which the ground is absolutely superseded through the realization of the totality of the mediation is also the act through which the ground has absolutely realized its value of ground, i.e. it has absolutely fulfilled its task. The realization of the totality of mediation, precisely *qua* absolute negation or supersession of the ground, is therefore the complete development or realization of the ground.

The process that leads to the absolute realization of the ground is therefore the process that leads to *positing* the ground as what it is. Only at the end of this process is the ground posited as what it is. The line of the advance thus manifests itself as a circle – the beginning being the end and aim, or the beginning being the result. What one *intends* to posit in positing the totality of the immediate is what is actually posited at the end of the process of the mediation; accordingly, the ground of the mediation – the beginning of the process – is the end, aim or result of the process itself. While being immediately present as the formal positing of the immediate, this aim or end is only realized at the end. The ground, *qua* totality of the immediate, is the *primum in intentione*: it is what must be thought first, but it is the *ultimum in executione*, i.e. what is only manifested at the end.

15. Notes

a. While from the standpoint of the base plane the existence of the totality of mediation is only the content of a project, everything that we have stated concerning *the relation* between the totality of the immediate and the totality of mediation instead necessarily follows from the very immediate positing of that project.

b. From the standpoint of the base plane, there not only exists the project of the totality of mediation, but also the project of the totality of the constants of type *imm*. (s_{n+m}). Let us indicate this totality by the symbol *T.imm.* (s_{n+m}). It is clear that in the previous section we have been able to state that the positing of the totality of mediation constitutes the absolute superseding of the *C*-contradiction only insofar as the relation between the base plane and *T.imm.* (s_{n+m}) had been disregarded. Considering this relation as well, the absolute superseding of the *C*-contradiction is realized by the positing of the horizon in which *all* the constants of *S* are posited. The *C*-contradiction is therefore superseded according to two directions: the one that is bounded by the positing of the totality of mediation, and the one that is bounded by the positing of *T.imm.* (s_{n+m}).

Everything that we have discussed in § 14 concerning the mediational development is now to be referred to the development or extension of the analysis. The essential difference between the two cases lies in the fact that while in the first one the circle realizes itself through a mediation, in the second one it constitutes itself immediately. Accordingly, while in the first case the *other* of the ground, *qua* logical additional dimension, is something truly grounded, in the second case, that *other* (i.e. what is obtained through the extension of the analysis) is a specific individuation of the ground itself (i.e. of the universal of non-contradictoriness), and the extension of the analysis consists in the ground itself in its *immediate* manifestation as the concrete content (cf. Chapter 7, § 18). The latter is a concreteness that must be distinguished from the one that pertains in any case to the ground insofar as it develops as part of its mediation.

c. It is furthermore clear that precisely because the process constituted by the positing of the constants of *S*, *qua* absolute superseding of the *C*-contradiction, constitutes the absolute realization of the ground, that process constitutes for this very reason the very act of the absolute foundation of the ground. That is to say, in the same way in which the ground, precisely *qua* ground, is truth in the form of absolute contradiction, so the ground, precisely *qua* ground, is an instance of absolute groundlessness: i.e. it is what requires an absolute grounding or foundation. (Furthermore, it is not a contradiction and a form of groundlessness insofar as it is what it is, but insofar as it is not what it must be.) This should be easily understood on the basis of what has been discussed in the previous section. Accordingly, there should be no further need to note that the sense in which the ground is such is different from the sense in which what stands as the ground is an instance of absolute groundlessness. In this respect, too, it is therefore possible to identify a circular course, in that the act of grounding or foundation does not simply consist in an advance from a first term to a second one, but also, in the very act in which that second term is realized, in an advance from that second term to the first one.

It is thus also established that in the same way in which the ground, through the positing of the totality of its constants, is absolutely realized as such and at the same time it is absolutely grounded, so – through the positing of that totality – every intermediate mediational moment, and every moment obtained through an extension of the analysis of the ground, is absolutely realized as such and at the same time it is absolutely grounded.

d. The ground is an absolute groundlessness – in the indicated sense – even if it has been verified that all the constants are already posited as to their semantic content as part of the base plane of the originary structure. In other words, even if the base plane were to include the positing *of the determinacies* of all those constants, these determinacies would not for this very reason be posited as belonging to the essence of the ground – i.e. they would not be posited as constants. In this respect, the formula: 'Positing S *without positing* one of its constants' points to a limiting case – the one in which, since not even the determinacy of that constant is posited, this determinacy cannot therefore even be regarded as something that belongs to the essence of the ground. It therefore remains the case that a determinacy can be regarded as not belonging to the essence of the ground even if it is present as a matter of fact. The two cases can however be expressed through that one formula, since also in this second case that constant, as such, is not posited (i.e. only its abstract *matter* is posited).

e. In relation to the distinction established at the beginning of § 14 between the totality of the constants and the totality of the covariants of S, the following objection needs to be resolved. The project of a positing of S that does not include the positing of a variant v of S does not immediately appear as the project of a contradictory positing of S. It is therefore not immediately contradictory to project that a positing of S, which does not include the positing of all the covariants of v, should *not* be a form of contradiction. The C-contradiction that affects the positing of S insofar as the latter is not the positing of the totality of the covariants can therefore *also* be superseded *by not positing* all those variants that have covariants. That is to say, it is not necessary for that C-contradiction to be superseded through the positing of the totality of the covariants. Positing v without positing its covariants constitutes a realization of the C-contradiction; the latter can therefore be superseded *either* by positing those covariants *or* by not even positing v – since, as already mentioned, the project of a positing of S that does not include the positing of v does not immediately appear as the project of a contradiction. What we have stated in § 14 in relation to the totality of mediation would therefore only concern the positing of the constants and not the covariants of S.

This objection is made possible by the incompleteness that affects the exposition of the structure of the immediate up to this point. This incompleteness (which, were it not merely discursive, would itself constitute a realization of the C-contradiction) is what leaves unspecified the affirmation that the project of a non-contradictory positing of S that does not include the positing of v is immediately non-contradictory. A further specification – i.e. a complete or adequate exposition of the structure of the immediate – shows (cf. Chapter 10) that while the project of a non-contradictory positing of S that does not include the positing of any of the variants of S is not immediately affected *by that* contradiction that immediately affects the project of a non-contradictory positing of S that does not include the positing of any constant of S, at the same time, however, that first project is not, *simpliciter*, immediately non-contradictory, for it is immediately affected by a specific contradiction that will be determined in due course (cf. Chapter 10, § 19). *In this respect, the distinction between variants and constants of S will be shown to be a distinction that is internal to the total horizon of the constants of S*: for if the project of a non-contradictory positing of S that does not imply the positing of v is immediately contradictory – even if due to a contradiction *other* than the one that immediately affects the project of a non-contradictory positing of S that does not include the positing of a constant of S – this means that variants, too, are constants of S.

The C-contradiction, which affects a positing of S that does not include the positing of the covariants of S, cannot therefore also be superseded by not positing the variants of S, but *only by positing* the totality of the covariants. It is thus also confirmed that every mediation (in any domain it might be realized) consists in the verification of a constant $med.(s_{n+m})$ of S.

Everything that has been anticipated in this last point is however only necessary to eliminate the objection identified above, and it will be adequately clarified in due course.

f. What has been outlined in this chapter also establishes the authentic meaning in accordance with which, in Chapter 1, we have stated that the validity of the positing of every abstract moment presupposes the concrete manifestation of the originary whole (Chapter 1, §§ 10–11). This has certainly been confirmed – while noting, however, that the originary whole does not immediately exclude the possibility of verifying additional constants of the originary: i.e. it does not immediately exclude the possibility that a complete exposition of the originary – *qua* manifestation of the base plane – should only consist of an *intention* of that complete exposition. In other words, the validity of the positing of each moment of the base plane requires the concrete manifestation of the structure of immediacy; it is not however thereby immediately excluded that this concrete manifestation should constitute a realization of the C-contradiction – and, in fact, the absolute realization of that contradiction, in the clarified sense, whereby the validity of the positing of those abstract moments can only be achieved through the positing of the totality of the constants of the ground. If it were to be objected that the validity of the exposition of the originary structure is therefore not warranted, we would need to repeat that if the originary structure is something not valid this is not the case due to what it says, but due to what it does not say; accordingly, the authentic refutation of this structure consists in its absolute realization or manifestation: i.e. in bringing its exposition to completion through the positing of the totality of its constants.

g. We have anticipated (§§ 10–11) that the totality of the immediately present constants of S is *L-immediately* posited as a part of the totality *simpliciter* of the constant of S. This means that this L-immediate positing belongs to the structure of S – i.e. to the structure of the ground or immediacy; equivalently, it means that this positing is itself an immediate constant of *S*. In a different respect, we have affirmed (cf. for instance § 12, b) that the condition on the basis of which it is possible to establish that *S* is affected by a specific quantification of the *C*-contradiction – i.e. on the basis of which it is possible to establish that the totality of the immediately present constants of *S* is a part of the totality *simpliciter* of the constants of the latter – consists in the categorical positing of that set of constants whose lack of positing causes that specific quantification of the *C*-contradiction. It is clear that, in this second respect, the proposition: 'The totality of the immediately present constants of *S* is L-immediately posited as a part of the totality *simpliciter* of the constant of *S*' appears as a self-contradiction, for if the condition that is required to establish that the immediately present constants constitute a part of the totality *simpliciter* of constants is the categorical positing of those constants that exceed the immediately present ones – and given that if that establishing is L-immediate, so is this categorical positing – it follows that the structure of the immediate is and at the same time is not the positing of a specific dimension of its constants: it is not, because it is L-immediately affirmed not to be; it is, precisely because this affirmation is L-immediate.

The remainder of the exposition will show (cf. Chapter 11) that this self-contradiction does not obtain.

9

Dialectic

1. The mediated character of the immediate

We have already observed that the identity of certainty and truth that appears at the end of Hegel's *Phenomenology* may only stand as a result in the sense that the positing of this identity is such insofar as it is not an *abstract* immediacy, but it *is in relation* with the superseding of the opposition of certainty and truth. It is by virtue of this relation that one states that this identity 'results', or is 'mediated'. (In the same way, the superseding of that opposition is not an abstract immediacy only insofar as it is in relation with the positing of that identity, and therefore results from the latter.)[1] This standpoint has already been advanced in Chapter 1, granting it in fact the greatest scope that pertains to it by stating that the positing of the ground implies the superseding of the negation of the ground. *Qua* totality of the immediate, the ground is at the same time the positing of the immediacy of the presence (or thought) of being: i.e. it is the positing of the immediacy of the identity of being and thought.[2] The negation of this identity is therefore one of the modes of the negation of the ground – and, in fact, one of the modes to which historical thinking has been most committed; or, equivalently, the superseding of the opposition of thought and being is a – prominent – moment of the superseding of the negation of the ground. The latter (as already mentioned, cf. Chapter 1, §4) is not immediately superseded by the positing of the ground simply as a universal negation, but as the concrete individuation of its universality, i.e. as the system of the immediately known negations. The 'mediated' or 'resulting' character of the ground thus coincides here with the very concrete positing of the totality of the immediate, or with the very self-constitution of immediacy.

2. The system of the negations of the ground

a. As long as one only simply considers or takes into account the relation that obtains between the ground and that system of negations of the ground, all forms of negation have the same value, or they are arranged on the same level: in the sense that each of the immediately present negations is *immediately* superseded by the positing of the ground – this positing 'resulting' from or with respect to the superseding of that set of negations, and not with respect to the superseding of this or that form of negation. The negations of the ground therefore all agree in being immediately superseded for the reason that – precisely – they are negations of the ground.

The negations that are immediately superseded are all those Ph-immediate negations that appear as negations of the ground *in an L-immediate way* – i.e. through an analysis of their present meaning – and not *through* or *by means of* a term, on the basis of which specific semantic contents that do not appear for themselves or L-immediately as a negation of the ground appear, at a later time, as such negations. Verifying, on the basis of a mediation, that a semantic content constitutes a negation of the ground means surpassing the base plane – in such a way that this negation is not superseded by a simple positing of the base plane.[3] More generally, this means that the system of the immediate – and, therefore, immediately superseded – negations is the system of the negations superseded by the simple positing of the base plane: i.e. of the ground. The immediacy of these negations is therefore twofold, since on the one hand these negations are immediately present, like every other content that belongs to the totality of the immediate, and on the other hand they are present as having their value of negations *for themselves* or L-immediately.[4]

b. At the same time, however, the different forms of negation mutually distinguish themselves by virtue of their different semantic complexity. Keeping in mind that the concrete positing of the totality of the immediate is given by the positional horizon constituted by the relation between the positing of the totality of the immediate and the positing of the system of the negations of that first positing, it is clear (cf. §3) that *every* negation stands as *a moment* of that positional horizon. This horizon is the very totality of the immediate (in such a way that the system of the negations of the immediate belongs itself to the totality of the immediate), but in its including the posited distinction between itself – *qua* originary positional whole – and that part of itself that consists in the system of its negations.

Each of these negations – and their very system – is therefore a *moment* of the ground in a twofold sense: (1) in the sense that the ground, as the *totality* of the Ph-immediate, *includes* each of the Ph-immediate negations and (2) in the sense that the ground is such insofar as it consists in the superseding of its negation – whereby this negation *belongs* to the structure of the ground, or it is an essential moment of the latter.

It is in this second respect that every negation is a 'moment' in the same way as every other negation; equivalently, it is in this sense that, in point a, we stated that all the negations of the ground have the same value.

In that first respect, instead, the different forms of negation distinguish themselves from one another by virtue of their different semantic complexity; equivalently, it is by virtue of this different complexity that each of them is a moment in a different way relative to the other ones.

c. Recalling now what we stated in §11 of Chapter 1, *every* moment of the totality of the immediate, *abstractly considered* – i.e. every abstract concept of the abstract – immediately manifests itself as a negation of the ground. Since an abstract concept of the abstract is not necessarily a *positing* of the concrete (= the totality of the immediate) – or a *positing* of a moment of the concrete – *as negated*, but it can also simply be the positing of a part or moment of the concrete and the *lack of positing* of what originarily exceeds that moment (in both cases, however, the abstract not being posited as abstract, i.e. not being superseded in and by the concrete), and since the ground is a semantic complexity, the essence of the ground therefore includes the existence of *implicit* negations of the ground, as part of which the ground *is not posited* as superseded, and *explicit* negations of the ground, as part of which the ground *is posited* as superseded (cf. Chapter 2, §28).

3. Note concerning the maximum positional domain of the negation of the ground

It is possible to object in the following way to the affirmation expressed above (§2, b), according to which *every* immediately present negation of the ground is an abstract *moment* of the ground itself to the extent that the latter is the totality of the immediate (i.e. the originary positional whole).

The positional domain of that negation of the totality of the immediate, which realizes itself in such a way as to *posit* this totality as superseded, is not a *moment* of the positional domain constituted by the totality under consideration, but it is *at least* equivalent to it.

Indicating by n' the positional domain opened by that negation, let us begin to respond to that objection by specifying that n' is *at most* equivalent to the originary positional domain: for, otherwise, it would not be possible to immediately affirm the existence of n', to the extent that n' were to exceed the immediate – or, equivalently, for otherwise n' would not belong to the system of the immediately present negations under consideration. In other words: while there is certainly every reason to affirm that the positional domain opened by the *explicit* negation of a content is greater than the domain of this very content, this cannot, however, be affirmed unconditionally: precisely because if the domain of the negation is immediately present, and if the negated content is the very totality of the immediate, the domain of the negation cannot be greater than the domain of the negated content. Furthermore, in this case, the domain of this content is itself greater than the domain of the negation. For this latter domain (which is precisely n') is indeed not only immediately present, but it is immediately present *as superseded* – $n(n')$ being the positional domain opened by this superseding – because only in this way can the totality of the immediate constitute itself as such: i.e. as the ground. If n' were left to persist as something not superseded, the totality of the immediate would not be affirmed. As a result, $n(n')$ is greater than n' since it includes n' and, in addition, the negation or supersession of n'. This means that n' is a *moment* of the totality of the immediate – or, equivalently, that the latter exceeds n' at least to the extent that $n(n')$ exceeds n'.

Except that it is possible to respond that, precisely because n' posits *the totality* of the immediate as superseded, and since this totality coincides with or includes $n(n')$, n' cannot be smaller than $n(n')$. However, since it has been possible to affirm that n' is a moment of the immediate only on the basis of the affirmation that $n(n')$ is greater than n', as a result it will not be possible to affirm that n' is a moment of the immediate.

Let us indicate n', *qua* not smaller than n (n') – or *qua* negation of *also n* (n') – by n''. The counter-reply thus states: '$n' < n'''$. In positing $n' < n''$, however (i.e. insofar as the domain of the negation of the totality of the immediate is regarded as being smaller than the negation of the superseding of that negation), this new objection – as to its formal structure – is nothing but a *repetition* of the first one (and it must be therefore superseded in the same way); for n'' now has the same function that n' had as part of the first objection (a function that, holding firm the inequality $n' < n''$, n' can no longer have): namely, that of positing *the totality* of the immediate as superseded. In this respect, it is possible to project the arising of an infinite series of negations such that $n' < n'' < n''' < \ldots < n^n$ – of each of which one would need to state what has been stated concerning n'. What would vary in each of them would only be the extent of the semantic content that is negated.

It appears, from what has been stated, that if the positional domain of a negation of the ground were to succeed in coinciding with the originary positional domain itself (i.e. with the positional domain constituted by the ground), the domain of that negation would no longer be the domain of a negation: precisely because, *qua* originary positional domain, it would be the superseding of that negation.

(In a different respect, it is not immediately self-contradictory to *project* the existence of negations that are not moments of the present content of the ground, but that would themselves include that content as a moment. This project implies the project of an increment of the content of the ground; as a result, those projected negations stand as negations of this projected content, and, despite being moments of the projected ground, they are not moments relative to the present content of the ground. These negations do not therefore belong to the system of the immediate negations of the ground. That is to say, the fact that this system is a moment of the complete system of the negations of the ground is the content of a project.)

4. Corollary

It is thus verified that if every abstract concept of the abstract is an immediate negation of the ground (§2, c), every immediate negation of the ground is conversely an abstract concept of the abstract. For, indeed, since every immediate negation is an abstract moment of the immediate (§3), it consists at the same time in letting this moment stand as the originary whole: precisely to the extent that the positional domain of that negation does not include its own superseding, and it therefore constitutes itself as the whole. Precisely because every negation is an *abstract moment* of the immediate, it is therefore at the same time an *abstract concept of the abstract*.

5. The bounds of the system of the immediate negations of the ground

Since every abstract concept of the abstract is an immediate negation of the ground, and since every immediate negation of the ground is an abstract concept of the abstract, the set of the immediate negations of the ground has a *structure*, or an *order of the arrangement* of the negations, determined by the extent of the positional domain of the single negations (whereby it is truly possible to speak of a *system* of these negations). The *bounds* or the *extremes* of this structure will therefore have to consist of the negation constituted by the abstract concept of the minimum semantic content and of the negation constituted by the abstract concept of the maximum semantic content that may pertain to an abstract moment. These are, respectively, the 'lower bound' and the 'upper bound' of the system of negations.

It is clear that, on the one hand, the lower bound is an abstract concept in the sense that it consists in simply positing the minimum content without positing (as superseded) what exceeds this very content; on the other hand, this minimum content is that abstract moment that does not include as a moment any other abstract moment, and that is therefore a *simple* determination. In Chapter 6, we have, however, shown that it is not possible to speak of a single minimum content, but one must speak of a *multiplicity* of semantic minimum contents, one of which is formal being, and the others are the factually simple meanings – in such a way that the sum of the former and the latter constitutes the initial plane or 'beginning'. The initial domain is co-initial (Chapter 6, §6). This entails that the lower bound of the system of the immediate negations of the ground is not constituted by a single negation or by a single abstract concept of the abstract, but by a multiplicity of negations or abstract concepts. The 'beginning' may therefore indicate both the semantic minimum (i.e. the different minimum semantic contents) in its being concretely distinct from the concrete, and the semantic minimum in its being abstractly posited: in the first sense, the 'beginning' indicates what is initially posited (affirmed), i.e. the content at which the analysis of the concrete is halted; in the second sense, it indicates what is initially superseded.

Once the lower bound of the system of the immediate negations has been established, however, how can one concretely determine the order of progression from the lower bound to the upper one?

6. The concrete and abstract concepts of the implication between contraries

a. Hegel's philosophy represents the most significant attempt at concretely determining the structure of the negations of the ground, i.e. the order of progression from the lower bound to the upper one in the system of negations. In the following pages, we are going to indicate how the *method* of the determination of that order of progression may be positively evaluated (§§6–10), despite the fact that the concrete determination of that order proposed by Hegel may not be retained.

Let us consider this well-known passage from the *Logic* concerning the essence of the dialectical method, among the many that may be selected for our purpose:

> All that is necessary to achieve scientific progress – and it is essential to strive to gain this quite simple insight – is the recognition of the logical principle that the negative is just as much positive, or that what is self-contradictory does not

resolve itself into a nullity, into abstract nothingness, but essentially only into the negation of its particular content, in other words, that such a negation is not all and every negation but *the negation of a determinate subject matter* which resolves itself, and consequently is a determinate negation, and therefore the result essentially contains that from which it results; which strictly speaking is a tautology, for otherwise it would be an immediacy, not a result. Because the result, the negation, is a *determinate* negation it has a *content*. It is a fresh concept but higher and richer than its predecessor; for it is richer by the negation or opposite of the latter, therefore contains it, but also something more, and is the unity of itself and its opposite. It is in this way that the system of concepts as such has to be formed – and has to complete itself in a purely continuous course in which nothing extraneous is introduced. (*Science of Logic*, p. 54)

What must first of all be held firm in this respect – wishing to retrieve for ourselves the speculative meaning of the passage just quoted – is that, on the one hand, the 'determinate negation', or (in an Aristotelian way) the *contrary* of a specific determination, *necessarily belongs* to the meaning of this determination, and, on the other hand, this necessary belonging is *L-immediately* posited. This second respect, which is expressed here in general terms, will have to be specified in a crucial way, aimed precisely at determining the meaning of the immediacy of that necessary belonging (§7). In the meantime, we can however state that every contrary L-immediately stands as a constant of its contrary;[5] that is to say, it is *immediately self-contradictory* to affirm that a determination is posited as such if its contrary is not posited. The immediate superseding of this contradiction consists in the very L-immediate positing of the necessary belonging of a contrary to the meaning of its contrary determination. Let us clarify these two aspects.

b. If Z and K are regarded as paradigmatic contrary determinations, then Z, *as superseded* (negated), belongs to or is L-immediately included in K, and K, *as superseded*, is L-immediately included in Z.[6] The concrete meaning of each of the contraries is then constituted, on the one hand, by the *superseding* of the other contrary (let us indicate by nK and nZ this side of the meaning of Z and K, respectively), and on the other hand by the *determination* of this superseding, which allows the contraries to stand opposed to one another as determinate negations. (Let us indicate by z and k this determination of nK and nZ, respectively.) That is to say, the first of these two sides constitutes the opening of the 'contradictory' plane of a contrary; the second side constitutes the determination of this plane. They are, respectively, the *matter* and the *form* of the meaning of that contrary – the synthesis of this matter and this form being the concreteness of that meaning. The form then *distinguishes itself* from the matter in the sense that if z and k are, respectively, *that which*, in Z, is set in opposition to K, and *that which*, in K, is set in opposition to Z – i.e. they are the determination or form of the opposition – at the same time, however, z and k distinguish themselves as such from the opposition of which they constitute the form; or, equivalently, the semantic-positional domains constituted by z and by k are distinct as such from the semantic-positional domains, respectively, constituted by nK and nZ.

It is then precisely this *distinction* of the matter and form of a contrary – which is at the same time the distinction between the *positing* of the form and the *positing* of the matter – that must not be regarded as an abstract *separation* between these two terms, and, therefore, between the acts of positing of these terms. That distinction is indeed the very concrete concept of the abstract moments of the meaning of that contrary; this separation is instead the abstract concept of these moments – i.e. the concept of the form in its not implying the matter of the contrary, and vice versa – the taking place of which gives rise to a contradiction, as detailed in what follows.

In relation to the concept of a positing of the form that does not imply the positing of the matter, let us begin to observe that the immediacy of the necessary implication between the two contraries precisely means that the form of the contrary Z L-immediately stands as (necessarily) implying the matter of Z (which is precisely the superseding or negation of K); that is to say, it means that the proposition 'z is nK' (or 'k is nZ') is L-immediate, in such a way that the form of Z, implying the matter of Z, implies K as superseded. This is the meaning of the implication between contraries.

Referring to the observations developed in the next section for what concerns a more precise determination of the meaning of that implication, let us emphasize here that the concept of the positing of a form that does not imply the positing of the matter of a contrary is not therefore the concept of the positing of that form: i.e. it is not what it *intends* to be. For, indeed, insofar as the form and the matter of a contrary *necessarily* imply each other, the matter belongs to the essence of the form, or the form is the form *qua* form of that matter: if the determination z, which constitutes the form of the contrary Z, necessarily implies the superseding of K, positing z without positing nK means not positing Z – precisely because z is something that essentially implies nK. Accordingly, if z is not regarded – posited – as implying nK, z is not posited. It is certainly the case that, as discussed above, the semantic-positional domain of z distinguishes itself from the domain of nK, but since this distinction is internal to the essence – for z necessarily implies nK – z may be retained *as distinct* from nK, i.e. it may be retained as z, only insofar as that from which z distinguishes itself *is posited*, and it is posited in its necessarily being implied by z. The abstract understanding instead regards those distinct terms as simply juxtaposed ones, each of which must therefore remain what it is even if it is no longer part of that extrinsic relation. The abstract concept of these distinct terms is therefore self-contradictory: it is the contradiction between the intention of positing z and the impossibility of positing it – since one wishes to posit z without positing nK, or without positing nK as belonging to the essence of z. This is therefore the contradiction between the intention to posit a contrary in its abstract positivity and the impossibility for such a positing to be realized. An abstract concept of the abstract consists in an intention precisely because its content *cannot be* what one would wish it to be – this being a significant instance of the realization of the C-contradiction.

7. The mediated character of the implication between Z and K

The implication between z and nK is L-*immediate*, in that nK L-immediately pertains to z, i.e. it pertains to z as such. Let us now specify that K does not belong to the essence or meaning of z insofar as z is z – and insofar as K is K – but insofar as z is nK. That is to say, K does not L-immediately pertain to z, but it pertains to z by means of nK. In other words, it is possible to affirm that K belongs to the essence of z not insofar as z is regarded as such, or as distinct from nK, but precisely insofar as z is regarded or determined as that to which nK pertains, i.e. as that of which nK is L-immediately predicated. Furthermore, K pertains to z in an L-mediated way simply as a moment of the concrete meaning of z, and not as a predicate of z.

Since the middle term – nK – of the pertaining of K to z includes the mediated extreme – K – as a semantic moment, it is clear that K, qua constant that pertains to z in an L-mediated way, belongs to the second type of mediational constants considered in §14 of Chapter 7. It is in this sense that, in the previous section, (a), we have been able to state that the contrary (K) of a determination (z) *immediately* belongs to the meaning of that determination: not in the sense that K pertains to z as such, but in the sense that projecting that K should not be a constant of z is immediately self-contradictory – i.e. it is already self-contradictory from the standpoint of the immediate pertaining of nK to z (cf. Chapter 7, §20).

The distinction between, on the one hand, the immediate implication between z and nK, and, on the other hand, the mediated implication between z and K is not explicitly addressed by Hegel – the logical clarity of the related texts being adversely affected as a result.

8. Concerning the determination of the outcome of the abstract positing of Z and S. S as a C-contradiction

a. Positing z without positing nK means not positing z. If, in addition, this not positing z – which is the outcome of the abstract positing of z – should be the positing of something or the positing of nothing is a question that may be left aside here. It is, however, clear that if one were to successfully show that this not positing z constitutes a *positing*, it would not be possible for what is posited as part of this positing to be a semantic content that includes or implies the positing of z. Therefore – this being of interest in view of what will be discussed later on – it will also not be possible for that content to be the *contrary* of z. If, indeed, the outcome of positing z without positing nK were the positing of K, Z – which is included by K as superseded – would thus be posited, and z would no longer be abstractly posited, since Z is the concrete synthesis of z and nK. In other words: the outcome of that abstract positing of z cannot be K because K includes z as a concrete meaning; accordingly, in affirming that outcome one would not be respecting the theorem according to which positing a meaning (z) without positing one of its constants (nK) means not positing that meaning.

The possible outcomes of the abstract positing of z may be indicated as follows: (1) positing of a part (or moment) of the semantic content of z – the term 'part' being regarded as to its broadest value; (2) positing of the synthesis between a part of the semantic content of z and a determinacy that does not belong to that content; (3) positing of a determinacy that does not belong to that semantic content; (4) null positional outcome, in such a way that the lack of positing of nK results in the simple positional annulment of the synthesis z(nK).

This means that the determination of the outcome of the abstract positing of z is entrusted to an extension of the analysis (or to a mediational process), and that this determination must consist in one of the four outcomes outlined above. In other words, it is not immediately self-contradictory to project one of those four outcomes of the abstract positing of z. What must be held firm from the standpoint of immediacy is that positing z without positing nK – or, equivalently, not thinking nK as belonging to the essence of z (in such a way that, in this respect, both z and nK are posited, but precisely as not essentially implying one another) – means not positing z. What is not undertaken here is the *determination* of this contradictory of the positing of z – a determination that (it should be noted) can also be carried out through a simple phenomenological attestation, in that it is a question of *seeing* what is posited once z is posited without positing nK. That 'simple attestation', however, is extremely difficult – the reading of the phenomenological datum being often much more difficult than other complex mediational operations – in such a way that we prefer to adopt the more cautious stance of keeping to that determination of the outcome of the abstract positing of z, the negation of which is self-contradictory: this determination precisely consisting in the indeterminate positing of that outcome as the opening of the contradictory of the positing of z. It should further be observed that this difficulty in reading the phenomenological datum arises when the analysis of the latter is considerably advanced. Instead, in relation to the positing of meanings of a significant complexity – for instance, in relation to past acts of positing of S, in which S was posited but one or more of its constants were not – it is immediately present that the outcome of the abstract positing of S consists in the formal positing of S (this outcome being a subset of the second outcome that will be explicitly considered in point c). The ascertainment of the verification of this outcome cannot, however, be raised to a general rule without due justification.[7]

The outcome of the abstract positing of z therefore consists either in the positing of a contradictory term of z (in case of a positive positional outcome) or in that non-z – that contradictory term of z – constituted by the annulment of the positing of z (nK) (in case of a negative positional outcome).

It is clear that the positing of a contradictory term of z is the positing of a non-z – which, however, cannot be determined as that specific non-z constituted by K, or as any semantic content that includes z as a concrete meaning. The contradictory of z cannot therefore be posited *as* such either: i.e. as 'non-z', if z is regarded as a concrete meaning (regarding this specific clarification, cf. point c) – for in this case, too, z would be posited through the positing of non-z. What is posited as part of the positive positional outcome only *is* the contradictory of z: that is to say, it is so for the concrete – for the concrete concept of the abstract positing of z. (For the abstract concept of this positing, that contradictory of z is instead *intended* as z.) What is posited *as* such as part of this outcome is therefore that semantic content that, in this positing, (only) *is* non-z (holding firm the fact that the positing of z can only take place as the positing of the concrete meaning of z).

b. In discussing a positing of z in which nK is not posited, one does not thereby refer to a positional horizon in which nothing but z is posited, but to a positional horizon (which may also be the totality of the immediate) that includes z without including nK. The consideration of a positional horizon that is exhausted by the positing of z (i.e. that consists in the outcome to which this positing gives rise) is a particular case of the logical situation under consideration – since in this case we are not only simply dealing with the outcome of the lack of positing of nK but with the outcome of the lack of positing of the entire semantic content that immediately surpasses z.

c. While positing z without positing nK means not positing z, it is not thereby excluded that positing z without positing nK should mean positing *z in its abstractly formal value*: it is possible for z not to be posited as a concrete content (precisely because this concreteness implies the positing of nK), even though the form of this concreteness is posited (in the same way in which S is said to be posited as a formal meaning if not all of its constants are posited). As we shall clarify, this outcome of the abstract positing of z is a mode of the second of the outcomes envisaged in point a. (This outcome, to which we shall refer as 'outcome-2a', is probably – i.e. in relation to what is suggested by the appearing of the Ph-immediate content – the authentic one; in order to hold it firm as such, however, it is nevertheless necessary to show the self-contradictoriness of the other outcomes.) The outcome-2a is a realization of the C-contradiction. Precisely because only the form of z is posited, the concrete content to which the very formal meaningfulness of z points or refers is not posited; or, equivalently, what is effectively posited of that content – the form of z – is not what one intends to posit in precisely positing the form of z. Accordingly, something that is not z (the formal meaningfulness of z being precisely something that is not z *qua* concrete meaning) is posited as z.

In advancing the outcome-2a, we are certainly stating that z, as a formal meaning, can be posited without positing nK, but we are also stating that this positing of z is the realization of a contradiction. Accordingly, this presentation of the outcome-2a is not an abstract concept of the latter. The abstract concept of the outcome-2a does not indeed simply state that the form of z can be posited without positing nK, but, in addition, it conceives of that form as something non-contradictory.

All the outcomes that include z as a formal meaning – such as, for instance, the positing of 'non-z', 'kz', '$k(nz)$', 'xz' (which are modes of the third outcome) – count as variations of the outcome-2a.

d. It is important not to conflate the formal meaningfulness of z, *qua* outcome of the abstract positing of z, with the meaning z, *qua* concretely *distinct* from nK. As part of the essential implication between z and nK, z is distinct from nK – and it may also be said that z, as thus distinct, is a formal meaning. However, we are stating that this formal meaning is not to be conflated with the *abstractly* formal meaningfulness of z, *qua* content of the outcome-2a. For, otherwise – once again – one would not be respecting the theorem according to which positing a meaning (z) without positing any of its constants (nK) means not positing that meaning: in that, in affirming this, what is meant is that it is not possible to posit that meaning, *precisely considered as distinct from its constant*. Accordingly, the outcome-2a cannot consist in the positing of the meaning as thus distinct. For, indeed, that constant pertains to this distinct term, whereby it is this distinct term that can no longer be posited if it's constant is not posited. Accordingly, whereas the positing of this distinct term is not a form of being in contradiction, the positing of the formal meaning that takes place in the outcome-2a *is* a form of being contradiction; hence the semantic value of that distinct term is necessarily different from the semantic value of this formal meaning. In other words, z, as concretely distinct, is the *concrete form* of Z (i.e. the form concretely related to the content), whereas z, as content of the outcome-2a, is the *abstract form* of Z. The abstract concept, instead, conceives of that essential implication as an external relation; the difference between z posited as nK and z posited without the positing of nK would therefore only lie in the fact that in the latter case one only thinks z, whereas in the former case one thinks $z + nK$. The constant whose pertaining to a meaning is verified *would only be added* to that meaning. On the contrary, it must be stated that the constant determines or involves the meaning itself, which, as concretely distinct from that constant, is precisely distinct in its being thus determined or involved (which means that what is distinct is precisely that to which the constant pertains). The meaning is instead divested of this determination or involvement insofar as it appears as part of the outcome-2a, in such a way that one is here no longer dealing with *the same* meaning (or, as discussed: the outcome of the abstract positing of z is in any case a non-z); this is the case even if the meaning in question, as in the case of the outcome-2a, has 'the same' meaningfulness of the meaning *qua* concretely distinct from the constant. It is therefore clear that this sameness cannot obtain *simpliciter*, but *secundum quid* – in a certain respect, i.e. precisely as a sameness relative to the abstract form of the signification. (Furthermore, it is precisely the positing of this abstract form that, as part of the outcome-2a, causes the realization of the C-contradiction.)

The recollection of past acts of positing of the totality of the immediate (= S), in which not all the constants of S are posited, and which are surpassed by positional horizons that instead include those constants that were not posited, constitutes a verification of the opposite process to that which takes place when, given the essential implication between two meanings, the abstract positing of one of them results in the outcome-2a. For, indeed, the transition from those past acts of positing of S to the concrete positing of S attests that S was posited, but only as an abstractly formal meaning: this positing therefore constituting a realization of the C-contradiction. Let us therefore state in this case, too, that this abstractly formal meaningfulness of S *does not consist of S qua* concretely distinct from those constants whose arising determines the attestation of the abstractly formal value of those past acts of positing of S. That is to say: the *abstract form* of S is distinct from the *concrete form* of S. (On the one hand, S, as concretely distinct, is precisely that to which those constants pertain, whereas this cannot be held of S *qua* abstractly formal meaning. On the other hand, the positing of this formal meaning is the realization of a C-contradiction, whereas the positing of S as concretely distinct from those arisen constants – i.e. as a concretely formal meaning – does not constitute a realization *of this* contradiction, even though the latter is absent for a reason other than the fact that S is considered as thus distinct.) If that formal value of S does not consist of S as thus concretely distinct, the two however concur to the extent that, in both cases, a certain positing of S takes place.

From what has been said, it is clear that every positing of S as concretely distinct from at least one of its constants constitutes a concrete form of S (that is to say: it is sufficient for S to be distinct from one of its constants in order for the positing of S, as thus distinct, to be the positing of the concrete form of S); conversely, every positing of S as abstractly separated from at least one of its constants constitutes an abstract form of S (that is to say: it is sufficient for S to be abstractly separated from one of its constants in order for the positing of S, as thus separated, to be the positing of the abstract form of S). The same argument may be applied to every other meaning. (For a development of this point, cf. §12, b.)

e. *The fact that* the concrete form of S differs from the abstract form of S is necessarily required from what we have stated. *The fact that* the positing of the abstract form of S is in any case a certain positing of S is an Ph-immediately known fact. The abstract form and the concrete one therefore *share* a semantic component: i.e. the one by virtue of which both the positing of the concrete form and the positing of the abstract one constitute a certain positing of S. Let $\hat{S}$ be this shared component. The positing of $\hat{S}$ is necessarily realized *either* as the positing of the concrete form of S *or* as the positing of the abstract form of S; indeed, the constants of S are either posited or they are not: in the first case what is posited is the concrete form of S, in the second case its abstract form. If the concrete and abstract forms share a semantic component – and precisely for this reason they are said to have in a certain sense 'the same' meaning – they however distinguish themselves, and stand as two different meanings, to the extent that the way in which that shared component is posited as part of one meaning differs from the way in which it is posited as part of the other one.

At this point, one could object that the positing of $\hat{S}$ is therefore indifferent to the positing of the constants of $\hat{S}$; that is to say: $\hat{S}$ is a meaning that is posited *as such* whether its constants are posited or not.

Let us respond by stating that the constants of S *are not* the constants of $\hat{S}$. That is to say, the constants of S do not pertain to $\hat{S}$ as such, but to the concrete form of S (which includes $\hat{S}$), and that to which these constants do not pertain (while having to pertain) is not $\hat{S}$ as such, but the abstract form of S (which in turn includes $\hat{S}$). In other words: insofar as $\hat{S}$ is posited as that to which the constants of S pertain, it is no longer simply $\hat{S}$, but it is a concrete form; and insofar as $\hat{S}$ is posited without the positing of the constants of S, it is once again not simply $\hat{S}$, but an abstract form. Accordingly, it is not possible to state that the positing of $\hat{S}$ is indifferent to the positing of the constants of $\hat{S}$ (covertly identified with the constants of S).

It thus appears why the outcome-2a is a mode of the second outcome of abstract acts of positing (cf. §8, a). The abstract form, which is precisely the content of the outcome, is indeed constituted by a part of the concrete form (i.e. by $\hat{S}$) and by a determinacy that does not belong to the concrete form (i.e. by the way in which $\hat{S}$ is posited as part of the abstract form).

f. We have stated in §9 of Chapter 8 that the C-contradiction consists in intending or regarding as S something that, precisely because it is only the abstractly formal value of S, is not S. And yet, it is possible to object that the constitution of a contradiction requires a *difference* as part of what is posited as being the same, but this difference does not appear to obtain in the present logical situation. For, indeed, what is effectively posited is S; and the S whose positing is only an intention, or relative to which it is said that this effective positing of S is only abstractly formal, is once again the S that is effectively posited. In other words: in order to posit what is effectively posited *as S* (intending as S what is effectively posited precisely meaning to posit it *as S*) it is necessary for this S to be posited. The contradiction precisely consists in positing that effective term as S – except that the positing of that effective term precisely consists in the positing of this S. Positing something as itself does not, however, constitute an intention – i.e. it is not a contradiction – and it is in fact contradictory to affirm that there is here an intention and a contradiction.

Let us respond to this objection by first of all reiterating that a meaning is essentially related to its constants, and since a meaning, as distinct from these constants, has a formal value, the semantic form is essentially related to the semantic content. If the latter is not posited, nor is that relational value of the form, and therefore nor is the form itself. (If the content is not posited, the form – which has therefore become an abstract form – takes itself as its content: it is referred to what it should not be referred.) If, however, what is effectively posited retains in a certain sense 'the same' meaning as the form – in the sense that it is an abstract form (cf. the previous point) – it follows that something that no longer has the meaning that it had in being related to the content is said to retain that meaning (the positing of the abstract form, *qua* positing of $\hat{S}$, being indeed a certain positing of S). It is then certainly the case (as held by the objection) that the abstract form is the abstract form; accordingly, stating that the effectively posited content, i.e. S as effectively posited, is S (regarded as an abstract form), far from being a contradiction is an L-immediate proposition, the negation of which is immediately self-contradictory. In this respect, the positing of S is not an intention (in the sense that the positing of $\hat{S}$ is not an intention). There is however an intention, and therefore a contradiction, insofar as S is something that (in order not to be a contradiction) must stand in relation to the semantic content, in such a way that the effectively posited S is not S: i.e. it is not S in its being free from contradiction. In other words, what is effectively posited (the abstract form of S), insofar as it is a certain positing of S (i.e. insofar as it is $\hat{S}$), consists in an essential pointing *to something other*: i.e. to the content of S. Since this other is not posited, it follows that what is posited is not what one intends to posit in positing what is posited. That is to say, on the one hand what is effectively posited is posited as being other than itself, and on the other hand this other is only something *intended*. What is posited is not what is supposed to be posited, and, nevertheless, it is affirmed as that which is supposed to be posited, precisely because the latter is not posited. The *difference*, correctly demanded by the objection for the constitution of the contradiction, is not therefore between the abstract form and itself, but between the abstract form and that to which the very signification of the abstract form points.

9. The abstract positing of Z and the abstract concept of the abstract positing of Z

a. In affirming that the concept of a positing of z that does not imply the positing of nK is an abstract concept of the positing of z, it is clear that this concept is an abstract concept of an abstract concept – since positing z without positing nK means positing or conceiving of z abstractly. In relation to the positive positional outcomes (first, second and third outcomes), the self-contradictoriness of the abstract concept of the abstract positing of z consists in affirming that the positing of a non-z is the positing of z; in relation to the negative positional outcome (fourth outcome), that self-contradictoriness consists in affirming that a form of not-positing is the positing of z. This self-contradictoriness does not concern the abstract positing of z – leaving here aside the outcome-2a, which we shall consider further below – but, precisely, the abstract concept of this positing. This does not mean that the simple abstract positing of z is free from contradiction, but that it is free from *that* contradiction.

Indeed, the abstract positing of z, considered in itself, consists in *an immediate becoming* a positing of a non-z, or *an immediate annulment of itself qua* positional positivity (cf. point c). It is the abstract concept of the abstract positing of z that *intends* that positing of non-z, or that positional nullity, as the positing of z.[8]

However – making explicit the proviso above – in the outcome-2a, too, something that is not the positing of z is *intended* as that positing: whence this outcome is the realization of a contradiction. It must then be stated that both the abstract concept of the abstract positing of z and the outcome-2a of this abstract positing intend something that is not the positing of z as that positing; but while the abstract concept of the abstract positing *affirms* that z can (non-contradictorily) be posited even if nK is not posited (in such a way that the positional horizon of that concept necessarily includes the positing of nK), the outcome-2a of the abstract positing of z instead either consists in simply positing the form of z, without positing nK, or it indeed consists of an awareness of nK, but as not belonging to the essence of z. (In relation to this second case, the difference between an abstract positing and the abstract concept of this positing lies in the fact that the latter is a positing of what the former simply *is*: as part of the abstract positing, z and nK are co-present without a positing of their lack of implication, and they therefore simply *are* not implied; as part of the abstract concept of this positing, that lack of implication is precisely *posited*.)

The positional domain constituted by the abstract concept of the abstract positing of z is therefore greater than the positional domain that can be constituted as the outcome – whichever should be considered – of this positing. (In fact, in case the abstract positing of z should be a lack of positing, it is not even possible to speak of a 'greater' domain.)

In order for the abstract concept to be able to intend something that is not z *as z*, it is not necessary for z to be concretely posited: that is to say, it is not necessary for the concrete concept of z, in which the abstract concept would come to be grounded, to be realized. While this is not necessary, it is however possible: in this case, that self-contradictoriness of the abstract concept obtains insofar as the semantic structure of that concept implies the concrete concept itself (and, due to this implication, there appears another aspect of the self-contradictoriness of the abstract concept, for the latter precisely negates what makes it possible, i.e. it negates that essential implication between z and nK by virtue of which z can be posited as such). Let us repeat, however, that this does not mean that the abstract concept cannot break free from that implication with the concrete concept. The z that *is intended* to be the non-z that comes to be posited through the abstract positing of z (i.e. the z that is posited as part of the positional horizon of the abstract concept) can indeed also have an abstractly formal meaningfulness: that is to say, it can have the semantic value that appears as part of the outcome-2a.

b. It should furthermore be observed that, both for the abstract positing with outcome-2a and for the abstract concept of that (of every) abstract positing, the *intention* – discussed above – has a twofold value: on the one hand, as mentioned, it is the intention for that non-z, which constitutes the outcome of the abstract positing, to be z; on the other hand, it is the intention for this non-z, intended as z, not to be k – whereas it is clear that these non-z and k, *qua* both contradictories of z, are the same. (Whether they are the same not only insofar as they are both contradictories of z but also insofar as they are absolutely the same is something that at this point is left as something simply projected.)

c. If there is no intention for that non-z, which is the outcome of the abstract positing of z, to stand as z, positing z without positing nK – or not intending nK as belonging to the essence of z – does not give rise to a contradiction, but, as discussed above, to a *becoming*: i.e. to a transition from the positing of z to something that is not the positing of z. Whether the lack of positing of nK^9 should determine a contradiction for other reasons – i.e. even leaving that intention aside – is not a question that interest us at this point: we are not asserting here that the abstract positing of z is *simpliciter* free from contradiction (for, in fact, as part of the present enquiry we shall prove the contrary), but that it is free from *that* contradiction that arises if the non-z that is constituted by abstractly positing z is intended as z.

The *becoming* that instead takes place from the positing of z to the non-positing of z is at the same time an *immediate* becoming: in the sense that the abstract positing of z does not 'pass' or 'become', from a positing of z, a non-positing of z, but as soon as it is realized, it is realized as an *already passed* or *already become* positing of non-z (or, in relation to the negative positional outcome, an *already annulled* positing). In other words, in positing z without positing nK, it is not the case that something like the positing of z is realized at first, and at a later point this positing transforms itself into the positing of a non-z (or it is annulled as a positional positivity); what takes place is not that at first one succeeds in positing z without nK, and at a later point this positing of z passes into the positing of non-z (or it is annulled as a positional positivity). A positing of z without the positing of nK *is not* (= it cannot be); therefore, it also cannot *become* a positing of non-z (or a non-positing of z). If, therefore, a positing of z that does not imply the positing of nK succeeds in being, it immediately takes the form of a non-positing of z, in such a way that it must not be said to pass into its opposite but to have already passed.

As part of the abstract concept of the abstract positing of z, or as part of the outcome-2a, both the beginning (the positing of z) and the result (the non-positing of z) of that immediate becoming are instead real, whence the contradiction precisely succeeds in *being* (in accordance with the mode in which a contradiction can be – cf. Chapter 4, §14): the becoming is not attested as such, and that beginning and that result are regarded as the same. (At the same time, however, it must once again be stated that this becoming is immediate: in the sense that there is no middle term between the abstract conception of the abstract positing of z – or between only positing z as a formal meaning – and the fact that this abstract positing counts as a non-positing of z.)

10. Dialectic

a. If, therefore, the abstract positing of z is abstractly conceived, there arises a self-contradiction, the superseding of which is *immediate* precisely because the necessary implication between z and nK is L-immediately posited (provided that this implication is posited in its relation to the concrete universality of L-immediacy; cf. Chapter 7, §18). This entails – since this necessary implication between the form and the matter of a contrary is L-immediate – that this implication cannot be 'derived' or deduced from, or be mediated by, the superseding of the contradiction caused by abstractly conceiving of that form as posited without that matter. For, on the contrary, this contradiction is successfully constituted only insofar as that form and that matter necessarily imply one another: it is precisely *insofar as this implication obtains* that it is possible to affirm that the concept of a positing of z that does not imply the positing of nK entails conceiving of non-z as z. Strictly speaking, however, concrete immediacy consists in the *originary relation* between a necessary implication and the superseding of the self-contradictory negation of that implication. (More generally: the negation of an L-immediate implication is immediately or for itself self-contradictory – for, if it were so *for something other*, that implication would be L-mediated.) Accordingly, neither of these two aspects may stand as the ground of the other one.

The structure of the *immediate* superseding of that contradiction is therefore constituted by the following three moments: (1) the moment of the *abstract understanding*, i.e. of the abstract concept of a positing of z that does not imply the positing of nK; (2) the *dialectical* or negatively rational moment, in which the abstractly conceived positing of z contradicts itself and realizes itself as the positing of non-z (or as a non-positing); (3) the *speculative* or positively rational moment, in which the contradiction is superseded by positing z as the negation of *that specific* non-z constituted by K – i.e. by regarding the positing of z as necessarily implying the positing of nK. The Hegelian terminology is here appropriate in order to highlight the convergence and at the same time the divergence between the authentic concept of dialectic and the one advanced by Hegel.

Let there first of all be no more problems in understanding that which according to Hegel is 'mediation' itself as an *immediate* superseding, or as the structure of *logical immediacy*. For, indeed, the superseding of that contradiction is immediate because the necessary implication between z and nK is L-immediate, and it is on the basis of this implication that the contradiction is superseded. That is to say, strictly speaking, the immediate is a synthesis of that implication and of that superseding. Furthermore, that immediacy is a mediation to the extent that, on the one hand, z is *in relation* with nK, and in this sense it is mediated by it – and, on the other hand, this relation between z and nK is in relation with the superseding of its own negation, and in this sense it is mediated by or results from it. The negation of the relation between z and nK is precisely the abstract concept of the positing of z; accordingly, the concrete – which precisely consists in the relation between z and nK – in negating its negation, negates the contradiction that originates from this (its) negation. This point had already been addressed.

What should be noted now, however, is that while the first moment of the immediate superseding of that contradiction is precisely regarded by Hegel as that of the *understanding*, which 'stops short at the fixed determinacy and its distinctness vis-à-vis other determinacies: such a restricted abstraction counting for the understanding as one that subsists on its own account, and [simply] is',[10] the second moment is instead regarded by him as 'the self-sublation of these finite determinations on their own part, and their passing *into their opposites*'.[11] These 'opposite' determinations are the negative, i.e. precisely that 'determinate negation' discussed in the passage quoted at the beginning of §6. This means that, according to Hegel, the abstractly conceived positing of z does not only become the *positing* of a non-z (thus definitively excluding the negative positional outcome: fourth outcome, cf. §8), but it becomes the positing of that specific non-z constituted by the *contrary* of z. It is indeed of the contrary of z that it is possible to affirm that it 'contains the previous concept [i.e. the z that has been posited as part of the first moment], but also something more, and is the unity of that concept and its opposite' (cf. the passage quoted at the beginning of §6). Concerning this point, however, Hegel's text remains indeterminate, since the contrary of z may be regarded as K, as k, and as $k(nz)$ (z being regarded as a formal meaning). The first case is excluded as a result of what we have discussed at the beginning of §8; the second case (which is a mode of the second outcome – cf. §8) does not comply with the requirement demanded by Hegel: i.e. that the term into which z contradicts itself should include z as posited. This leaves the third case, which does not appear to be immediately self-contradictory to the extent that z, which appears in $k(nz)$, is regarded as a formal meaning (in such a way that this third case is a mode of the third outcome). At the same time, however, this third case persists as a project that needs to be verified (thus excluding the possibility of the other outcomes). It should furthermore be observed that Hegel's text appears to oscillate between the second and third cases: 'Accordingly, what we now have before us [when one passes from the immediate, regarded as the beginning of the dialectical process, i.e. from the moment of the abstract understanding, to the determinate negation of this moment – and this passing is precisely halted at the outcome or as the outcome of the abstract consideration of the beginning] is the mediated, which to begin with, or, if it is likewise taken immediately, is also a simple determination; for *as the first has been extinguished in it, only the second is present* [this being meaningful only if one considers that as part of the second, which is precisely the outcome of the abstract consideration of the first, or of the beginning, only k is posited; that is to say, the determinate negation of the first is not posited as the determinate negation *of* the first term, since what is posited is only that determination – k – that *is*, but that is not posited *as* the determinate negation of the first]. Now since the first *also is contained in the second*, and the latter is the truth of the former, this unity can be expressed as a proposition in which the immediate is put as subject, and the mediated as its predicate; for example, the finite is infinite, one is many, the individual is the universal [as part of which it is clear that the positional horizon of the second cannot simply be k, but it must at least be determined as $k(nz)$]."[12] From the last quoted proposition, however – let us add – there appears a fourth case, which must be added to the three cases indicated above, and which is constituted by the synthesis between z and $k(nz)$: whereby it is precisely possible to construct the proposition 'z is $k(nz)$' ('the finite is infinite'). Here, it is however clear that, as part of this outcome, there does not simply take place a 'holding fast to the positive in its negative'[13] – $k(nz)$ sufficing for this – but a synthesis between the positive and that synthesis between the negative and the positive constituted by $k(nz)$. This is most likely one of the points in which the Hegelian text suffers from the absence of a distinction between the dialectic of the abstract concept of the abstract positing of z and the dialectic of this abstract positing (cf. point b).[14]

Regardless of the meaning of the Hegelian text, the following must be held firm: the outcome adopted by Hegel constitutes an arbitrary choice. In other words: among the possible determinations of the contradictory of z – which must necessarily be held firm as the formal horizon of the outcome of the abstract positing of z – the Hegelian logic, which nevertheless constitutes the most thorough investigation into the positional outcomes of the abstract positing of a meaning, only selects one of these in an arbitrary way (without furthermore clearly defining it). We are not thereby excluding this choice as a self-contradictory one, but as a groundless one: that is to say, there is an aspect or a value of this choice by virtue of which the latter does not immediately appear to be self-contradictory (whereas, according to the other aspects – for instance, the one in accordance with which the outcome of the abstract positing of z is regarded as K – the self-contradictoriness of the choice is immediate).

What may not be said to pertain to the dialectical moment – unless by demanding the foundation whose absence has been remarked upon – pertains instead to the speculative: in the sense that the latter, *qua* concrete relation between the form and the matter of a contrary – i.e. between z and nK – is precisely that 'self-contradicting' of the form, due to which the latter results in its determinate negation. In other words, the reader is invited to re-read the passage quoted at the beginning of §6, interpreting it as no longer being referred to the dialectical moment, but to the speculative one – this interpretation thus becoming a theoretical gesture. The following observations will then result.

If the outcome of the abstractly conceived positing of z is something that is not a positing of z – and it is therefore a contradiction – it still needs to be shown that this term other than z, should a positive positional outcome take place, is determined as the contrary of z (in accordance with that meaning that does not immediately appear to be self-contradictory). The concretely conceived positing of z, instead, consists of an immediate *resulting in* or *passing into* the positing of K (which is precisely the contrary of z), *as superseded*. This passing is the *essential contradiction* of every finite determination, or the essential way in which the abstract contradicts itself in the concrete, i.e. in the whole. In the case at hand, this passing consists in that abstract z's *contradicting itself* into that concreteness constituted by the relation between z and K as superseded. It is clear that, here, this 'contradiction' has a different meaning from the one of the contradiction that pertains to the abstract concept of the positing of z. This contradiction is indeed here not a self-contradiction – the *inherent* self-contradiction of a single term – but it is the very *relation* that obtains between two 'contradictory' terms, i.e. between z and K (which are those contradictories in which the contradictoriness is determined as a relation between contraries). The essential contradiction, of which Hegel catches a glimpse time and again, therefore consists in that very essential implication that obtains between z and K (or, more generally, between a meaning and the semantic horizon that exceeds it), due to which the positing of z is an immediate passing into the positing of K, *as superseded*. And yet, this essential contradiction is precisely not a self-contradiction: in that z is not a simple passing into K, but it is a passing into K *as superseded*, i.e. a passing into nK. If this passing simply took place from z to K, z would be posited as a non-z: as that specific non-z constituted by K.[15] (The speculative – the essential contradiction – thus appears as a superseding of the contradiction, i.e. self-contradiction, in a twofold sense: insofar as it supersedes the contradiction that arises in conceiving of something that is not the positing of z as such a positing, and insofar as it supersedes the contradiction that arises in conceiving of the essential contradiction as a simple passing from z to K, or to $k(nz)$, as not superseded.) Therefore, z essentially contradicts itself into its other only insofar as the latter *is posited as* its other; and K is posited as other than z precisely insofar as z is posited as a negation of K, i.e. insofar as the positing of z essentially implies the positing of nK. That in which z contradicts itself and results is then 'richer' than z since K, *qua* synthesis of k and nZ, includes z (as superseded) and, in addition, the contrary of z.

At the same time, however, it can definitely be excluded that in the passage quoted in §6, as well as in the related passages,[16] Hegel should have meant to refer to the speculative moment rather than to the dialectical one. This is corroborated by the observation that while here Hegel always mentions that a determination contradicts itself into its contrary, he never states that this determination contradicts itself into that contrary *as superseded* – this being necessarily required by the speculative moment, as shown by Hegel himself.

From what we have said it appears in what sense the dialectical *method* uncovered by Hegel is to be regarded as something fully valid – with the caveats raised in relation to Hegel's determination of the formal horizon of the outcome of the abstract positing of z. The observations made by Hegel in this respect, appropriately understood, become an organic part of a complete exposition of the matter. (It should however also be observed that it is incorrect to think that classical logic has ignored the principle of the immediate implication of the contraries. One could refer for instance to chapter II of book IX of Aristotle's *Metaphysics*, in which it is stated that the same concept exhibits both a term and its contrary: whereby the contraries constitute a single concept. Aquinas reiterates this in his Commentary: '*Esse autem unius contrarii tollitur per esse alterius; sed cognitio unius non tollitur per cognitionem alterius; sed magius iuvatur*' (1405).[17])

b. Regardless of the outcome of the abstract positing of z (i.e. of the positing that posits z without positing nK), the abstract concept of this abstract positing always gives rise to a dialectical process that is such that the two sides of the dialectical contradiction (z and non-z) are posited within the positional domain constituted by the abstract concept. For what concerns instead the abstract positing of z, there arises a dialectical process such that the two sides of the dialectical contradiction are posited as part of the positional domain constituted by the outcome only if the outcome of this positing is the outcome-2a – or an outcome whose positional domain includes both the outcome-2a and the negation of this outcome. (Both z, as a formal meaning, and non-z are indeed posited as part of this domain: this non-z, in relation to the outcome-2a, being precisely the very formal meaning z insofar as it is simply a formal meaning whose content is only its own formal signification.) Indeed, the positional domains of the other outcomes, which do not even include the formal meaning of z, count as only one of the two sides of the dialectical contradiction: precisely the one that is constituted as a non-z (or as a not positing z) – the other side of that contradiction being thus posited outside the positional domain of the outcome and as part of the positional domain of that (abstract) concept that *intends* that non-z as z. This second domain contains that first one – or, as mentioned: this second domain includes both sides of the dialectical contradiction. It is however clear that, as part of the abstract concept, these two sides are not identified as contradictories, but as the same term – and precisely here lies the self-contradictoriness of the abstract concept.[18]

The observation above contributes to explaining why, as part of the assessment of the Hegelian concept of dialectic that we have carried out, we have considered the dialectic of the abstract concept of the abstract positing of z, rather than the dialectic of the abstract positing of z. A dialectic of this positing, which were not the dialectic of the abstract concept of this positing – in such a way that both sides of the dialectical contradiction would be included in the positional domain opened by the outcome of the abstract positing of z – would require either that the outcome of that abstract positing were the outcome-2a or that this outcome were a synthesis of z and $k(nz)$ (regarding z as a formal meaning), in which z is posited, but so is its negation, whence the constitution of the dialectical contradiction. As though one were to state: if one thinks 'finite' without thinking 'infinite' the outcome of this positing of 'finite' is: 'infinite finite [*qua* formal meaning]' – or giving a propositional form to the outcome, as done by Hegel: 'The finite is infinite'. For if the outcome is only 'infinite' – $k(nz)$ – the outcome stands as only one of the two sides of the dialectical contradiction, the other one ('finite') being thus posited within the positional domain of the (abstract) concept that intends 'infinite' as 'finite'; as a result, it would not be possible to speak of a dialectic of the abstract positing that is independent of the dialectic of the abstract concept of this positing.

A dialectic of this abstract positing, which is independent of the dialectic of the abstract concept of that abstract positing in the indicated sense, is therefore only a project (in §11, b; however, we are going to delimit this statement): precisely because the fact that the outcome of the abstract positing of z should be the outcome-2a, or an outcome that includes this outcome and its negation, is a project.

11. The limits of Hegel's contribution to a determination of the structure of the negations of the ground

a. The superseding of the contradiction produced by the abstract concept of the abstract positing of z presupposes the constitution of the contradiction itself, and the latter presupposes in turn what produces it: that is, the abstract concept of the abstract positing of z. This positing, abstractly conceived, therefore constitutes the beginning or the start of the 'process' constituted by the superseding of the contradiction, and the superseding stands as the *result* of that process – or, equivalently: this result is the very implication between z and nK. Since, however, the result is here precisely what supersedes the beginning as something contradictory – or: it is precisely that by virtue of which the beginning appears as something contradictory – that result is not something 'grounded', but it is an *immediate resulting*. As already remarked, the process constituted by the superseding of the contradictoriness of the abstract concept of the abstract positing of z therefore constitutes the internal structure of immediacy itself. Or, equivalently: the beginning is the first moment, the contradiction the second one and the implication between z and nK the third one simply in the sense that this third moment is *in relation* to the superseding of that contradictoriness – and, in this sense, it is a result. (It is furthermore clear that the implication between z and nK is precisely that by virtue of which the contradictoriness of the beginning is superseded, only insofar as this implication is concretely regarded on the one hand as $(z = nK) = (nK = z)$, and on the other hand *as* an individuation of the universal of non-contradictoriness. In a different respect, that implication stands as an *a priori* synthesis – cf. Chapter 7, §§18, ff. – i.e. as something that is not as such, or for itself, the superseding of its own negation.)

The beginning, however – regarded in this way – cannot stand as what is initially superseded (cf. §5, as well as Chapter 6, §§5–7): i.e. it cannot stand as the lower bound of the system of the negations of the ground. This is the case even if, as held by Hegel, the beginning of the dialectical process qualifies as something *simple*, i.e. as a semantically simple determination. The simple – precisely, as such – can certainly in turn be neither a synthesis of contraries nor the determinate negation of a content, whereas something complex, precisely as such, can be such a synthesis or negation. In the first place, however, what is initially superseded is not only formal being, but a multiplicity of simple meanings (cf. Chapter 6, §7), in such a way that, as already discussed (§5), the lower bound of the system of the negations of the ground is constituted by a multiplicity of negations (or abstract concepts of the abstract). Secondly, whereas the negations that constitute that lower bound must be abstract acts of positing of the simple, the beginning of the dialectical process indicated at the start of this section, insofar as it is what causes the contradiction of the dialectical moment, must be an abstract concept of the abstract positing of the simple.

b. This conclusion, however, needs to be amended, due to the possibility of regarding the Hegelian dialectic – or at least the initial part of the dialectical development described by Hegel in the *Logic* – as the dialectic of the abstract positing of z (and, therefore, not as the dialectic of the abstract concept of that abstract positing; cf. §10, b). That is to say, one may respond that the beginning consists in that abstract positing of z (this z taking the semantic value of the absolutely simple), whose positional outcome is a synthesis between the outcome-2a and the determination consisting in the determinate negation of that outcome – this synthesis being expressed by the symbol $z[k(nz)]$. The beginning is precisely that abstract positing, the dialectical moment is the contradiction constituted by the outcome ('the finite is infinite' – or, since in this case we are dealing with the *initial* dialectical contradiction: 'being is nothing'; in general: '$z[k(nz)]$'), the speculative is the concrete unity of z and nK.

We therefore respond by stating that while considering in general the values that the variable z can take, it is not possible to attest the self-contradictoriness of the affirmation that the outcome of the abstract positing of z is $z[k(nz)]$ – regarding z as an abstractly formal meaning – if z instead stands as that simple meaning constituted by formal *being*, it is possible to prove that the outcome of the abstract positing of z is *positionally null*. This assertion is justified in §21 of Chapter 10, but it may already be used here to test the assumption of considering the Hegelian beginning as the lower bound of the system of negations – aside from the critical remark, which remains valid, that this lower bound consists of a *multiplicity* of abstract acts of positing. It cannot be negated that formal or 'pure' being is a simple meaning, and that it therefore has the value of beginning (and in fact prominently so, since while for the other meanings that have this value it is not immediately self-contradictory to project an extension of the analysis, which would reveal those meanings to be semantic complexities, we have instead verified the self-contradictoriness of the concept of the analysis of formal being); that is to say, it cannot be negated that this meaning belongs to the lower bound of the system of the negations of the ground. However, while according to Hegel – continuing to consider the notion that the Hegelian dialectical development begins as the dialectic of an abstract positing and not as the dialectic of the abstract concept of this positing – the outcome of the abstract positing of the simple is the *positing* of nothingness (regarded as being), it must instead necessarily be affirmed that this outcome consists of *not positing anything*, i.e. of the *annulment* of the positional plane. It is precisely (but also only) in this sense that the Hegelian beginning – even if regarded as the abstract positing of the simple – cannot belong to the lower bound of the system of negations. For if we set aside the determination of the outcome of the abstract positing of the simple, it must then only be stated that the lower bound of that system is constituted by a multiplicity of terms, one of which is precisely Hegel's pure being.

If the abstract positing of formal being has a null positional outcome, there takes place no dialectic of this positing that would be independent of the dialectic of the abstract concept of this positing (cf. §10, b). The dialectical contradiction is indeed realized as a positional domain only to the extent that this positional nullity of the outcome is *intended* as a semantic positivity; this intention, however, cannot be part of the positional domain of the outcome of the abstract positing of pure being, since that domain is precisely null – in such a way that this intention only belongs to the positional domain of the abstract concept of that abstract positing. This means that the outcome of this positing only constitutes one of the two sides of the dialectical contradiction. Hegel may speak of a dialectic of the abstract positing of the simple, as independent of the dialectic of the abstract concept of that positing, only insofar as he erroneously conceives of the outcome of the abstract positing of pure being as the *positing* of nothingness – 'intended' as being.[19]

c. The concrete development of Hegel's *Logic* aims to exhibit the necessity for every complex logical determination to be a positional horizon constituted either by the determinate negation into which the abstractly considered determinacy contradicts itself or by the concrete synthesis of contrary determinations. In other words, every complex logical determination would consist in either a dialectical moment or a speculative one. As it is well known, this means that the very implication that results from the superseding of the contradiction caused by the abstract consideration of the simple contradicts itself into its determinate negation – provided that this implication is abstractly considered (and *having* to be in turn abstractly considered, according to Hegel); this contradiction is then superseded in and by a new implication, and so forth, until, through a necessary course, this results in that implication that, *qua* concrete totality, leaves nothing outside itself into which it may contradict itself. The *method* thus turns into the *system* of the totality (cf. *Science of Logic*, pp. 838–42). Let us take for granted that it has been established that the concrete development of the *Logic* does not correspond to the method. What remains to be seen, however – this being the most important aspect in a certain sense – is whether a logical development of this kind is possible or not. Until it has not been shown that an extension of the method into a system is inherently contradictory, from the standpoint of the structure of immediacy this remains a possibility or a project. The Hegelian dialectical development is precisely to be regarded as an attempt at a concrete determination of the structuring (or order of progression from lower to upper bound) of the system of the negations of the ground. (All the other values of Hegel's philosophy that an exegesis should be able to identify are, however, not thereby excluded.) The order of progression is precisely determined by the dialectical method; the dialectical development – the extension of the method into the system itself – constitutes a deduction of the totality of the negations of the ground. The incorrectness of this deduction is therefore also the incorrectness of the determination of the structure of the negations of the ground. It should furthermore be noted that also the abstract concepts of abstract moments that do not count as transcendental determinations, but as empirical ones, are negations of the ground (and, therefore, so are the abstract concepts of those abstract concepts); accordingly, the system of negations considered by Hegel is only a part of the totality of the negations of the ground.

At the same time, however, while the systematic development proposed by Hegel is essentially unwarranted, it is also not immediately contradictory to project – as already mentioned – that the dialectical method should realize itself in and through a correct systematic development. That is to say, it is possible to retain as something immediately non-contradictory the project as part of which it would be possible to establish that each of the negations of the ground – *in addition to being superseded by the ground*, like every other negation, precisely insofar as it is a negation of the ground – should also be superseded by something that is *its* negation (and that is therefore not the ground, since the ground is the negation *of every* negation of the ground). Negating a negation of the ground insofar as it is that specific determinacy that it is, rather than insofar as it is a negation of the ground, means opening a positional domain that – precisely insofar as it is such a negation *of that* negation – leaves all those forms of negation of the ground, whose determinacy differs from or exceeds the determinacy of the superseded negation, as something not superseded or negated; accordingly, such a positional plane is itself a form (even if a higher one) of negation of the ground.

12. The dialectical value of every implication

a. A dialectical development does not only arise in relation to the implication between z and nK, but in relation *to every* necessary implication, be it L-immediate or L-mediated. For instance, in relation to the proposition 'Being is being', understanding that being is posited even if it is not posited *as* being, i.e. as identical (this conception precisely constituting the moment of the abstract understanding), means understanding that something that is not the positing of being is this positing (dialectical moment) – precisely because being, in an essential way, is itself (speculative moment); accordingly, positing being without positing its self-sameness means not positing being.

b. In other words, and in relation to what we have established in §12, b of Chapter 7: A, *qua* abstractly posited formal meaning, is the beginning of the dialectical process; as part of L-immediate implications or predications, however, the self-contradictoriness of this positing of A is immediately superseded – i.e. A is immediately superseded as an abstractly formal meaning – precisely to the extent that the L-immediate pertaining of the single terms of the series $a_1, ..., a_n, a_{n+1}, ..., a_{n+m}$ to A is posited.

The positing of A nevertheless persists, *but in another sense*, as the positing of an abstractly formal meaning to the extent that not all – immediate or mediational – constants of A are posited; 'in another sense': for the formal value of A that is constituted to the extent that A is abstractly separated from the predicates that L-immediately pertain to it (let φ_1 be this type of formal value) is distinct from the formal value of A determined by the fact that not all the constants of A are posited (let φ_2 be this other type of formal value). The formal value φ_1, which is the beginning of the dialectical processes constituted by L-immediate predications, is superseded by the positing of *each* of the terms of the series $a_1, ..., a_n, a_{n+1}, ..., a_{n+m}$; that is to say, φ_1 is superseded as part of *each* of the predicational relations between A and one of the terms of that series. The superseding of φ_1 is not quantifiable: i.e. φ_1 is not superseded gradually. The superseding of φ_2 is instead quantifiable: in that the positing of the terms of the series $a_1, ..., a_n, a_{n+1}, ..., a_{n+m}$ (and, more generally, the positing of the – immediate or mediational – constants of A) is realized as a *development* – in such a way that at a certain level of that development only *a part* of the terms of that series (or a part of the constants of A) is posited, and at another level other terms (or constants) are added – and every level at which all the terms of that series are not posited constitutes a formal positing of A, and precisely realizes itself as φ_2. Insofar as the higher levels constitute a supersession of the formal value of the lower ones, the supersession of φ_2 is quantified, and the total supersession of φ_2 is realized when all the terms of that series – but, in fact, all the constants of A – are posited. A quantification of the superseding is instead to be excluded for φ_1, since, as mentioned, *each* of the terms of the series $a_1, ..., a_n, a_{n+1}, ..., a_{n+m}$ pertains to A insofar as A is A, and not insofar as it is determined by any other term, in such a way that the 'degree' of the formality that pertains to A insofar as it is abstractly separated from the terms of the series under consideration is identical in each of the predicational relations between A and one of the terms of the series, and this 'degree' is *entirely* superseded as part of each of those relations.

While the value φ_1 is *immediately* superseded within L-immediate predications – that is to say, while the proposition '*A* is *a*' is an immediate superseding of that formal value – the mediational connection of a term *B* to *A* constitutes a mediated superseding of that formal value, since *A*, to which *B* pertains in a mediated way, is precisely the *A* that, if abstractly posited, has the value φ_1: except for those mediational predications, the project of the negation of which is immediately posited as self-contradictory (cf. Chapter 7, §15).

In other words, if the implication is not L-immediate, the dialectical contradiction arises insofar as the abstract concept is a negation of the implication *qua* mediated implication; or, equivalently, what determines the contradictoriness of the abstract concept (what makes that concept, precisely, abstract, and therefore what supersedes this contradictoriness) is not the implication as such – since, as such (i.e. insofar as it is held distinct from the middle term), that implication is not an essential implication – but it is the implication insofar as it is mediated by a term that precisely exhibits the essentiality of the implication. It must therefore certainly be stated – in relation to the synthetic *a priori* proposition '*A* is *B*' – that the concept of a positing of *A* that is not a positing of *B* is not a concept of the positing of *A*, but this must be stated because *A* is *MB*, and not because *A* is *B*.

c. A dialectical development arises not only in relation to analytic or synthetic *a priori* implications but also in relation to synthetic *a posteriori* ones. *This* red extension is essentially or necessarily red: in the sense that while it is possible to project that this extension should no longer be red (whereby the connection between this extension and its red colour is precisely synthetic *a posteriori*), as already previously noted what is projected as no longer being red is not *this* extension (which is red), but a *persistence* of this extension – a persistence that, precisely as such, is not this extension insofar as it is *this* extension, for otherwise there would not be a persistence, but an identity. Understanding that a positing of *this* extension, as part of which it is not posited that this extension is red, is a positing of *this* extension therefore realizes an abstract concept of the abstract positing of this extension. The positing is furthermore abstract because positing this extension without positing its being red means only positing an abstract moment of the concrete, in such a way that what is posited is not *this* extension but a contradictory term of the latter. (It should be noted that the *persistence* of this extension, too, belongs to the contradictory of *this* extension.) The concept of this abstract positing is abstract precisely because it regards something that is not the positing of this extension as such a positing. It is therefore clear that a dialectical development does not concern *a posteriori* syntheses to the extent that they are such, but to the extent that these syntheses, too, present an aspect by virtue of which they count as analytic connections.

d. The implication between *z* and n*K*, on which Hegel focuses, is not only one type of implications in relation to which there arises a dialectical process, but it is also only one type of the implications that obtain between a meaning and the negation of this meaning (and, therefore, between a meaning and the negation of the contradictory of this meaning). More generally, it must be stated that the positing of a meaning L-immediately and necessarily implies the positing of the negation of everything that is not that meaning. Or, equivalently: there arises a dialectical contradiction not only insofar as a meaning is conceived of as not implying its contrary as superseded but also insofar as a meaning is conceived of as not implying the horizon of its contradictory as superseded (and, therefore, as not implying each of the terms that belongs to that superseded horizon). The propositions 'z is not non-z', 'z is not K', 'z is not a' and 'z is not b (c, d,...)' are therefore all analytic propositions. The observations made in §§6–10 have therefore a paradigmatic value also in this more specific sense.

The horizon of the contradictory of a meaning z therefore includes two types of meaning: (1) meanings that, *as such*, count as a negation of z – i.e. meanings that cannot be distinguished from their counting as a negation of z, and that, if thus distinguished, no longer persist as what they are – these meanings consisting of: 'non-z' and 'K'; (2) meanings that, while being forms of non-z, may be distinguished from their counting as a negation of z, while preserving the semantic value that pertains to them. These meanings precisely constitute the determinate content of the meaning 'non-z'. (The meaning 'non-z' belongs to that first type of meanings insofar as it is the form of that content.) The meanings that differ from z and that can non-contradictorily count as predicates of z belong to this second type of meanings. For instance: this extension *is not* its red colour, but it is nevertheless red – however, it is not red insofar as this red is a form of not being this extension (in this way, it would be impossible to solve the aporia that pertains to non-identical propositions – cf. Chapter 6, §9), but insofar as 'this red' is this red, i.e. it can exist as a meaning distinct from its not being this extension.

e. Every non-contradictory proposition is an *identical* one insofar as it is structured as $(x = y) = (y = x)$. As part of this identity, as already discussed, identical and non-identical propositions are distinguished according to whether the semantic value of the variables x and y is the same or not. Let us now observe that there can be non-identical *analytic* propositions (i.e. it is possible for difference to be part of the constitution of an analytic content) only insofar as, given a certain semantic value that pertains to x, y takes the value of the negation of the (determinate or indeterminate) negation of that semantic value. Every meaning is indeed formally distinct from the negation of its negation; and it is precisely only this distinct term – or it is only this otherness constituted by the negation of the negation – that can be immediately predicated of the meaning under consideration. The proposition 'The whole is inclusive of every term (= is greater than a part)' is analytic because – one argues – the predicate (let this be y) is contained in the subject. This means that the subject is a synthesis of y and an *other* (let this be x), which, however, is not 'the whole', precisely because 'the whole' is that synthesis that contains y and that other. We are stating that this synthesis or unity of different terms can only have an analytic value to the extent that y semantically counts as the negation of the negation of x, or x counts as the negation of the negation of y. In the example above, x may then, for instance, stand as 'that which leaves nothing outside itself'.

13. Note

A dialectical contradiction is a self-contradiction. That *being in contradiction with* the totality of the Ph-immediate, which takes place as part of the abstract positing of any moment of this totality (to the extent that this positing is the opening of a positional horizon that is prior or subsequent to the actual and present positional opening of the originary structure), must also be considered as a dialectical contradiction. This being in contradiction with phenomenological immediacy itself is precisely superseded by positing the totality of the Ph-immediate content (speculative moment), i.e. it is superseded by an increment of the appearing content.

For, indeed, every moment of the totality of the Ph-immediate essentially implies its actual and present context (cf. analogously – or, more precisely, as a specific case – §12, c); accordingly, the outcome of the abstract positing of that (any) moment is a contradictory term of the latter. If the outcome is positionally null, the dialectical contradiction of that abstract positing is not a self-contradiction, but it is only a being in contradiction with the Ph-immediate (that is to say: not positing anything is not a self-contradiction, but a being in contradiction with…). If the outcome is positionally positive, and it consists in the positing of a content that belongs to the totality of the Ph-immediate, since every moment of the latter essentially implies its present context, the content that is posited as part of that outcome can only have an abstractly formal meaning; accordingly, through a realization of the outcome-2a (which would thus become the normal outcome of abstract acts of positing), there takes place the dialectical self-contradiction that pertains to this outcome.

14. The ground *qua* beginning

The affirmation according to which the ground is the beginning is developed in this section in two ways: in point a, it is considered from the standpoint of that *abstract concept* of the ground, for which the fact that the totality of the constants of S should include the totality of the immediately present constants as a part is – from the standpoint of present immediacy – only a *project* (cf. Chapter 8, §§10–11); in point b, the affirmation in question is considered from the standpoint of the *concrete concept* of the ground – or, equivalently, from the standpoint of the concreteness of the ground – for which that inclusion of the immediately present constants by the totality *simpliciter* of constants is L-immediate, in such a way that, from the standpoint of the concrete structure of immediacy, *projecting* that inclusion is precisely a consequence of an abstract concept of the ground. It is clear that a comprehension of point b is hindered by the fact that this concrete concept of the ground has, up to now, only been generically anticipated.

a. Insofar as the project of a development of the analysis, or of a mediational development of the ground (or originary meaning, S), which would lead to the verification of new constants of S in addition to the immediately present ones, is not immediately self-contradictory, the ground realizes itself in a peculiar way as the beginning of a dialectical process. On the one hand, the ground certainly consists in the speculative (regarding this term in the sense indicated in §10) – in relation to the totality of the immediate negations of the ground. On the other hand, however, the speculative is the content of a project, in such a way that in relation to this project the ground stands as the *beginning* of a dialectical process. (That is to say: the fact that the ground is a beginning is itself something projected.) The speculative is the content of a project precisely insofar as it is projected that the present and actual positing of S is not the positing of all the constants of S: the speculative consisting in this totality, projected as exceeding the dimension of actuality. This project is itself a determination of the ground (i.e. of the beginning).

As mentioned, however, the ground is a beginning in a particular sense. First of all, if the present positing of S is not the positing of the totality of the constants of S, the present positing of S is the positing of an abstract moment of the concrete – the domain of actuality being precisely (as part of the project) an abstract moment of the whole. Since, however, nothing else is posited other than this abstract moment – since this abstract moment constitutes everything that can be immediately posited – not only is that positing of the ground an abstract moment, but it is also an abstract concept of an abstract moment of the positing *simpliciter* of the ground. As a result, the present positing of S is not the positing of S (dialectical contradiction).

In order then for the ground to be a beginning in the same sense in which the abstract concept of the abstract positing of z is a beginning, it would be necessary for the positing of something that is not S to be conceived of as the positing of S. This, however, is precisely what does not take place in relation to the ground *qua* beginning. For, indeed, while in relation to z an abstract concept is realized insofar as a contradiction is affirmed (i.e. insofar as it is affirmed that something that is not the positing of z is this positing), in relation to S the contradiction is instead not only posited as such (naturally, as *projected*, since the excess of the whole over what is present is considered here in its being projected), but it is also posited as something that must be superseded or negated.

The ground nevertheless stands as a beginning (i.e. as an abstract concept of the abstract) to the extent that, were a concretization of the ground to verify that the present positing of S is not the positing of the totality of the constants of S, it would thereby also verify that the horizon of present immediacy (i.e. precisely the horizon constituted by the ground as that which, in its structure, includes the *project* of the speculative) does indeed identify the contradiction as something that must be superseded, but leaves it nevertheless as something not superseded or is not able to supersede it; this is the case precisely to the extent that, as part of the ground, the otherness of the speculative relative to the ground, and therefore the very contradictoriness of the ground, is projected. Accordingly, while, on the one hand, the ground includes (as something projected) a recognition of the fact that what is presently posited, i.e. the ground itself, cannot stand as the positing of S, on the other hand – the ground appearing in this respect as the abstract concept of the present positing of S – this present or actual dimension is intended *as a matter of fact* as the positing of S: precisely to the extent that all that is posited is the content of that present dimension. Only a real accomplishment of the projected speculative constitutes a supersession of this factual contradicting. Let us reiterate that the fact the positional domain of the ground is such an abstract concept is affirmed from the standpoint of immediacy, i.e. of the ground regarded as that which, in its structure, includes the *project* of the speculative. Projecting that the speculative should be something other than the ground – whereby the ground realizes itself as such a project – means projecting that the ground is an abstract concept of the abstract (in the indicated sense).

b. Everything that has been affirmed in point a is then confirmed here, but in its being *categorically* affirmed, rather than as the content of a project. While in point a, the fact that the ground stands as a beginning is a project, it must now instead be asserted that the fact that the ground stands as a beginning is an L-immediate affirmation – i.e. it belongs to the structure of the ground: precisely because the fact that the totality *simpliciter* of the constants of S surpasses the totality of the immediately present constants is an L-immediate affirmation. It must therefore be stated that the ground is constituted as the L-immediate affirmation of the fact that the speculative surpasses the ground. (It is furthermore clear that, in this way, there again appears the aporia already indicated in Chapter 8, §15, g, which will have to be adequately resolved; for if the affirmation of that surpassing is L-immediate, i.e. if it belongs to the very structure of the ground, in this respect the ground is itself the speculative – and at the same time it is not, precisely to the extent that the affirmation of the difference between the speculative and the ground is L-immediate. Let us however leave this aspect of the question aside for the moment.) Due to the L-immediacy of that surpassing, the fact that the ground is a beginning is, as stated, an L-immediate affirmation. Once again, the ground is a beginning in a peculiar sense. For, indeed, insofar as it is L-immediate that the present positing of S (i.e. of the ground) is not the positing of the totality of the constants of S, it is L-immediate that the present positing of S is an abstract moment of the concrete; however, since nothing is posited other than this abstract moment – precisely to the extent that, as we shall adequately clarify, the L-immediate affirmation that the totality *simpliciter* of the constants surpasses the immediately present constants is *not* equivalent to the immediate presence of that totality of constants (even though that L-immediate affirmation is itself immediately present) – it follows that the present positing of S is an abstract moment that is abstractly conceived; as a result, it is L-immediate that the positing of S is not a positing of S. (L-immediacy of the dialectical contradictoriness of S.) At the same time, however, the abstract concept of the abstract constituted by the present positing of S differs from the abstract concept of the abstract positing of z, for while in relation to z an abstract concept is realized because it is affirmed (even if implicitly) that something that is not a positing of z is such a a positing, in relation to S the dialectical contradiction is instead not only L-immediately posited as such, but it is at the same time L-immediately posited as something that must be superseded. The ground nevertheless stands as a beginning (i.e. as an abstract concept of the abstract), for while the contradiction is immediately posited as something that must be superseded, the ground nonetheless leaves it as something not superseded: precisely because the ground L-immediately realizes itself as the positing of only a part of its constants. Or, equivalently: while on the one hand the ground consists in the recognition of the fact that the ground, as it is actually and presently posited, cannot stand as the positing of the ground, on the other hand – and it is in this respect that the ground is L-immediately posited as the abstract concept of the ground – the ground, as it is actually and presently posited, is regarded *as a matter of fact* as a positing of the ground: precisely to the extent that the L-immediate verification of the fact that the totality of the constants surpasses the immediately present constants is not equivalent to the immediate presence of that totality of the constants of S. Only the concrete presence of this totality constitutes a superseding of the factual contradiction of the ground.

From what we have stated, it appears that the concrete concept of the ground is the ground in that it constitutes itself as the very L-immediate positing of its standing as an abstract concept of the abstract (in the indicated sense).

c. The L-immediate affirmation of the difference between the totality of the constants of S and the immediately present constants of the latter does not constitute an exclusion of the *project* for the totality of the constants to be further determined relative to that determination that is L-immediately attested (cf. Chapter 8, §11, footnote); that is to say, the L-immediate affirmation of that difference affirms an excess over the present constants, but it does not exclude – i.e. it leaves as something immediately non-contradictory – the project of an excess relative to the domain constituted by that very L-immediately posited excess. In relation to *this* projecting, all that we have stated in point a is retained – no longer as an abstract concept, but as a concrete one: to the extent that the expression 'present positing of S' does not refer (as instead in point a) to that positing of S that leaves, as something projected, the fact that the totality of constants surpasses the immediately present constants; on the contrary, that expression now indicates the concrete positing of S as part of which, while that surpassing is L-immediately posited, one leaves as something immediately non-contradictory the project for the totality of the constants of S to include a domain of constants that is additional with respect to that very domain, whose excess relative to the immediately present constants of S is L-immediately established.

15. Note

Insofar as the ground immediately stands as the negation of the totality of its negations, the negation of each negation immediately stands as a constant of the ground. (Projecting that the totality of the immediate negations of the ground should not be the totality *simpliciter* of these negations therefore enhances the project for the ground to be a form of being in contradiction – C-contradiction.) The relation that obtains between the ground and each of its immediate negations consists, as already stated, in the speculative – or, equivalently, this is the sense in which the ground immediately stands as the speculative. The speculative thus stands here as the very structure of the immediate. In this respect, it is *one and the same* for all the immediate negations, and it is precisely the ground as the unity of itself and of the negation of the system of its negations. In a different respect, it is immediately possible to project a determining of the order of progression from the lower to the upper bound of the system of negations, which is such that a speculative moment *specific* to each negation is constituted. If one were able to determine the extent of the positional domains of all the immediate negations – determining that order of progression in such a way that, letting n', n'', n''', ..., n^n be the set of these negations, the concept of an intermediate positional domain between n' and n'', n'' and n''' and so on would appear to be self-contradictory – the dialectic that pertains to the immediate content would not simply consist in the superseding of each abstract concept of the abstract in and by that concrete, which, *qua* totality of the immediate, stands as the speculative *for each* abstract concept; on the contrary, it would consist in the superseding of each abstract concept in and by that positional horizon that is the concrete, or the speculative, *only* in relation to that abstract concept – and that therefore, in relation to the concrete *simpliciter*, is an abstract moment that, if abstractly conceived, is itself a negation of the concrete *simpliciter*.

At the same time, however, the positional extent of several groups of negations is immediately known; or, equivalently, certain groups of negations appear in such a way that, in each of them, it is immediately known which the minimum positional domain, which the intermediate ones and which the maximum one are. Accordingly, that structuring of immediacy, which *qua* total structuring immediately stands as a project, is immediately realized (albeit in a fragmentary way).

Since the exposition of the originary structure constitutes the very manifestation of the concrete as a superseding of every immediately known abstract concept of the abstract (cf. Chapter 1, §§9–18), if that order of the structuring of the negations were known, the ideal exposition of the originary structure would need to be realized following a course analogous to the one of the Hegelian logic: namely, starting from the abstract concept of the minimum positional domain, and ending, by way of the intermediate ones, with the concrete positing of the totality of the immediate. The discursivity or the process of the exposition as part of which the originary would thus be posited would present in this way a course or a pattern of development determined by the very content of that discursivity. Insofar as that order of structuring is instead not immediately known, that discursivity realizes itself in an arbitrary way: i.e. only with an eye towards the possibility of letting a part of the originary discourse precede another one so as to facilitate as much as possible the communication of the originary. Indeed, beginning the originary discourse with a specific part of the entire exposition – for instance, as we have done, by way of a set of general remarks concerning 'the exposition of the originary structure' – means (even if this is not explicitly noted as part of the exposition) beginning the originary discourse with the superseding of the abstract concept of that abstract moment that is precisely constituted by that part with which that discourse begins (whereby the concrete, on the basis of which that superseding takes place, is already entirely manifest from the beginning of that discourse). Proceeding then with a second part – for instance, as we have done, by way of a set of observations concerning the 'immediacy of being' – means realizing the superseding of another abstract concept, which is however considered after that first concept only for the sake of the opportunities of the exposition, and not because the positional extent of this second concept is the minimum one after the one considered in the first place. (At the same time, however, the exposition often leaves a consideration of the abstract concept implicit, addressing only the manifestation of the different abstract moments, and noting the abstract concept of the abstract moment under consideration only in significant cases.)

10

The manifestation of the whole

1. The positing of meanings and the manifestation of the whole

a. The analysis of a meaning is the positing of what this meaning is or means, and not of what is other than its being or signification; that is to say, the presence of a meaning does not consist in the presence *simpliciter* of what this meaning is not. If the analysis of a meaning were to exhibit something that is other than the analysed meaning, the latter would *simpliciter* be or mean its other: identity of contradictory terms. At the same time, however, precisely because every meaning (every being) is not its other – precisely because it L-immediately and essentially pertains to every meaning not to be its other – the analysis of every meaning attests what is other than this meaning. The aporia is immediately resolved, as already discussed in the previous chapter, insofar as the analysis of a meaning attests what is other than this meaning precisely *as something other*, i.e. as something superseded or negated – in such a way that every meaning is or means its other precisely insofar as it consists of its not being or not meaning this other. More generally, if, while considering being it is not possible to detect non-being, it must instead be necessary to discern the negation of non-being; or, equivalently, while 'being' does not mean 'non-being', it however immediately and essentially means 'negation of non-being'.

It should be observed that in the same way in which nK L-immediately stands as a constant of z, but K stands as a constant of z in an L-mediated way (cf. Chapter 9, §7), so – thus granting the discussion its due scope – not-being-its-other L-immediately stands as a constant of every meaning, but that other (i.e. the content of the horizon of the contradictory of the meaning under consideration, as well as every particular determination of that content) stands as a constant of that meaning in an L-mediated way. Accordingly, the proposition: 'The positing of every meaning necessarily implies the positing of the other of that meaning' is synthetic *a priori* (and it belongs to the second type of synthetic *a priori* propositions considered in §14 of Chapter 7); on the contrary, the proposition: 'The positing of any meaning implies the positing of the negation of the other of that meaning (or the positing of the contradictory of that meaning, as superseded)' is analytic.

b. Every meaning, however, does not simply imply (as superseded) *a part* of the horizon of the contradictory of that meaning, but the *totality* of this horizon. The meaning x must not simply be stated not to be this or that non-x, but the *totality* of non-x. The analysis of *every* meaning is therefore a *manifestation of the totality*. For, indeed, every meaning and the totality of its other make up the whole. At the same time, however, the superseded horizon varies as part of each meaning; or, equivalently, while the single outcome of the analysis of every meaning is the totality, the horizon of what is posited as superseded by the meaning under consideration varies within each analysis. (It is by virtue of this difference that every meaning differs from the other ones – and, conversely, it is because every meaning differs from the other ones that there exists that difference in the superseded horizon.) In this sense, Anaxagoras's principle is to be accepted: 'Everything is in everything.'

The positing of any meaning then implies the positing of the semantic whole in a twofold sense. In a first sense, precisely because in order to posit a specific meaning x as the negation of everything that is not this meaning it is necessary to posit, as negated, the totality of what surpasses x, and this *absolute* surpassing (as part of which both the surpassed meaning and the surpassing horizon are posited) is the semantic whole itself. (The positing of this absolute surpassing is the positing of the whole *as such*; that is to say, the whole is posited *as the whole* – precisely because the surpassing is posited as an absolute one, or because the contradictory of x is posited as the *totality* of the contradictory.) In other words, since the positing of the meaning x as the negation of everything that is not x constitutes the positing of the whole as partially negated, the positing of x implies the positing of the whole (as such). In a second sense, the meaning 'other than everything that is not x', which stands as the predicate of the proposition: 'x is other than everything that is not x' (or 'x is not everything that is not x'), is itself the whole as partially superseded, in such a way that the presence of this meaning implies the presence of the whole.

What is other than everything that is not x is certainly not the whole – but it is precisely x; at the same time, however, in order for what is other than the entirety of non-x to be present as such, it is necessary for x as much as the totality of the contradictory of x to be present (i.e. it is also necessary for the difference by virtue of which x is not the whole to be present); it is then precisely the presence of this absolute surpassing that stands as the presence of the whole. In other words, while x is not the horizon that absolutely surpasses x, the whole is precisely this absolute surpassing of x; accordingly, positing x as the negation of its surpassing horizon means positing the whole. (Conversely, if the whole is posited, and if x belongs to the concrete content of this positing, x must be posited as the negation of the horizon that absolutely surpasses it: the positing of the whole is indeed the positing of the surpassing of every particular determination, and therefore of x, too, in such a way that x is posited as other than everything that surpasses it.)[1]

c. In relation to the first of the two senses (cf. b) in accordance with which the positing of any meaning x implies the positing of the semantic whole, the semantic whole belongs – even if in a peculiar way – to the structure of the very *L-immediate implication* between the (any) meaning under consideration and the negated horizon of the totality of the contradictory of that meaning. In relation to the second of those two senses of the implication in question, the semantic whole stands as a constant of the meaning under consideration *in an L-mediated way*. What is indeed L-immediately a constant of this meaning – or what is L-immediately predicated of the latter – is the negated horizon of its contradictory, i.e. the superseded horizon that absolutely surpasses that meaning. Since this surpassing consists in the whole, however, the whole is a constant of the meaning under consideration. This constant value is *L-mediated* because the whole is not predicated as such of that meaning, but insofar as it is posited as partially superseded. The absolute surpassing of that meaning is predicated of the latter to the extent that this surpassing determines itself as the negation of a part of the whole; accordingly, that surpassing stands *as such* as a constant of the surpassed meaning in an L-mediated way. Within the surpassing as such, every part (every moment) of the whole is certainly posited as superseded in relation to its contradictory; at the same time, however, every part is posited in its being affirmed: precisely as a part or moment of the whole. It is due to this second aspect of the surpassing as such that the surpassing cannot be predicated as such of the surpassed meaning.

Insofar as the positing of the whole as partially superseded implies the positing of the whole, and insofar as that former positing is the middle term with respect to this second positing, affirming that the whole stands as a constant of the meaning x in an L-mediated way gives rise to a separate type of synthetic *a priori* propositions, which in one respect may be traced back to the second type of synthetic *a priori* propositions indicated in §14 of Chapter 7, and in another respect to the third type. For, indeed, while on the one hand it must be stated that the whole, as partially superseded, 'includes' the whole – this inclusion, however, being here strictly speaking an implication[2] – on the other hand this latter positing (this extreme) itself includes the middle term in a proper sense: to the extent that every semantic content is a moment of the semantic whole.

It is therefore *immediately* self-contradictory – in the sense indicated in §15 of Chapter 7 – to project that the positing of any meaning should not imply the positing of the whole: on the one hand, because the middle term is only posited insofar as the extreme is posited; on the other hand, because the positing of the extreme includes the positing of the middle term (and, in fact, it includes the very immediate connection between the initial extreme and the middle term; positing the whole means positing the absolute surpassing of x: namely, it means positing this horizon, which surpasses x, as negated, i.e. negated by x – the immediate connection or pertaining precisely consisting of x as a negation of that surpassing horizon).

d. It is clear that the proposition: 'The positing of any meaning x implies the positing of the semantic whole' is synthetic *a priori* only if one assigns to the variable x values constituted by meanings other than the semantic whole (i.e. other than the infinite semanteme). If x takes the value 'semantic whole', that proposition is indeed analytic.

e. The value of *a priori* synthesis enjoyed by the proposition formulated above may be attested in different ways. In the following sections, we shall consider one of these ways due to the theoretical interest of its logical structure.

f. The meaning 'x' *implies* the meaning 'other than everything that is not x', and this meaning implies the infinite semanteme. In the first case, however, the implication is also a predication (i.e. the two implied terms stand in a relation of subject-predicate), whereas in the second case the implication is a predication only if what is considered as predicate is not the infinite semanteme, regarded as a *term* of the implication, but the very *implication* of this term. (Accordingly, stating that the infinite semanteme is a constant of every meaning does not mean stating that it is *predicated* of every meaning, but that it is *implied* by every meaning – whereby the predicate is once again not the whole, but the implication of the whole.)

g. Let us conclude this first set of observations with the following corollary: since the semantic whole is a constant of every meaning, if the semantic whole is not posited as such, no meaning is posited. If, indeed, the semantic whole is not posited, the outcome of the positing of the meaning x (a positing that therefore counts as an abstract positing of x) cannot be the *positing* of a meaning, since *any* meaning y, which is posited as part of that outcome, can be posited only if the constants that L-immediately pertain to it are posited, and therefore only if the superseded horizon of the totality of the contradictory of y is posited; since, however, the positing of this immediate constant essentially implies – as we have seen – the positing of the semantic whole, if the latter is not posited it is also not possible to posit that immediate constant, and therefore it is also not possible to posit that – *any* – meaning y that should appear as part of the outcome of that abstract positing of x. The outcome of this abstract positing is therefore positionally null.

In other words: the outcome of the positing of a meaning x that is not the positing of the constants of this meaning is a contradictory term of x (cf. Chapter 9). The totality of non-x, as negated, L-immediately pertains to or is L-immediately predicated of x; that is to say, it L-immediately counts as a constant of x. Furthermore, the semantic domain constituted by that constant essentially and L-immediately implies the infinite semanteme. Accordingly, if the latter is not posited, when one intends to posit x, that L-immediate constant of x cannot be posited, and therefore x itself is not posited either. Nor is it however possible to posit *any* other meaning, since *every* meaning has the totality of its contradictory, as negated, as an L-immediate constant – that is to say: a constant that essentially implies the infinite semanteme L-immediately pertains *to every meaning*; accordingly, if that semanteme is not posited, nor is it possible to posit any meaning as the outcome of the abstract positing of x.

The same result is obtained if, in place of the positional *steresis* of the whole, one considers that simple *co-presence* of the meaning x and the infinite semanteme, as part of which the latter, despite being posited, is however not regarded as being essentially implied by the meaning x. If this failure to consider the essential implication between the meaning x and the whole also obtains in relation to every other meaning, in this case, too, the outcome of the abstract positing of x is positionally null, and it is only the abstract concept of that abstract positing that regards or intends that nullity as the positing of x; that is to say: that co-presence is not realized, but it is only something *intended* by that abstract concept.

2. Note

Verifying through a mediation that the whole is a constant of every meaning does not mean that a meaning can be immediately posited without positing the semantic whole: this is exactly what is excluded by the mediation, which precisely establishes that the positing of a meaning *cannot* be realized (i.e. it is self-contradictory to affirm that this positing should be realized) without the realization of the positing of the whole. In other words: the positing of the whole is the result of a logical mediation only insofar as it is regarded in relation to the positing of any meaning; conversely, as we shall clarify further on, the positing of the whole consists in the immediate content itself, i.e. in the very absolute horizon of immediacy.

The stance of those who are only interested in their world, and of those who are only aware of or only see a specific finite dimension of reality, cannot therefore be realized (i.e. the concept of such a stance is self-contradictory). In this respect, humans are not free to be in error – understanding that the error consists of only looking at the finite, whereby one is forced to move from finite element to finite element: to *err*, as Heidegger recalls. Or, equivalently: humans have access to the error the very moment that truth – to be precisely regarded here as the manifestation of the whole – is unconcealed to them. It is by now frequently repeated that the human, in its essence, consists of a standing before the manifested whole. 'In its essence': this means that it is not possible to project a realization of the human that would not be a manifesting opening of the whole. Kant was particularly aware of this concept when he understood metaphysics as an essential human disposition – that is to say, when he regarded the human as that originary metaphysical essence by virtue of which every finite determination is surpassed in and by the presence of the horizon of the totality. (In this sense, the negation of metaphysics in Kant represents a moment that is logically additional to the one constituted by the originary opening of the metaphysical horizon; as part of that additional moment, while the metaphysician moves towards a determination of the whole insofar as this surpasses experience itself, the enquiry of critique instead argues for the impossibility of that determination – whereby the metaphysical horizon is definitively retained as something simply ideal: as the subjective and regulative character of the horizon.) That concept of the human *qua* comprehension of the whole, however, also persists after Kant (through specific developments), gaining particular relevance to this day with existentialism. What must then be observed at this point is that, for the most part, that concept is simply asserted – and, insofar as it is asserted in this way, it is therefore also false: precisely to the extent that it is not seen in relation to its being grounded. The fact that the immediately present determinations are included in the horizon of the totality is a phenomenological truth: humans think something like a 'totality' as a matter of fact – or, equivalently, the disclosure of the meaning 'totality' is immediate, and so is the inclusion of every meaning as part of that meaning. In this way, however, the presence of the totality is only a fact – in the same way in which the presence of this red is a fact. Accordingly, in the same way in which it is possible to project the opening of positional domains that do not include the positing of this red, it is possible to project the opening of positional domains in which the meaning 'totality' is not present; that is to say, it is possible to project a type of human – or simply certain situations of the human – in which that meaning is not in view. It is then precisely the possibility of this project that is excluded when it is affirmed that the human consists *in its essence* in a comprehension of the whole. We are however stating that it is precisely this exclusion – which is no longer of a phenomenological order – that is for the most part simply asserted. The ground of this assertion instead consists in the mediational structure exposed above.

3. The totality of the immediate and the semantic whole

a. Since the meanings that are immediately known are the meanings that belong to that originary signification that precisely consists in the totality of the immediate, stating that every meaning implies the semantic whole is equivalent to stating that the originary meaning coincides with the very originary opening of the semantic whole: i.e. that *the whole is the immediate* (or that the whole is immediately present).

If the opening of the whole is not realized as the originary structure, it gives rise to a positional plane – that of pre-philosophical consciousness – that leaves beside itself its negation, and that is therefore a form of groundlessness. Insofar as the opening of the whole is instead realized as the originary structure, meaning is held firm, i.e. it is saved from its negation. Philosophizing thus consists in the authentic opening of meaning.

b. Does the Ph-immediacy of the whole, however, entail that the concept of a meaning or being that is not part of the totality of immediately present being is a self-contradictory concept, and that this self-contradictoriness is immediately attested? The answer is entrusted to the very structure of the immediate, which does not only consist in a manifestation of the immediate in its *not* including the self-contradictoriness of that concept, but, according to what we have already anticipated and according to what we shall clarify later on, it also consists in the L-immediate affirmation that the whole surpasses the totality of the Ph-immediate (cf. Chapter 13) (and therefore also surpasses the totality of the L-immediate, to the extent that the L-immediate affirmation of that surpassing, too, is Ph-immediate). Let us consider here only that first side, i.e. the non-immediacy of the self-contradictoriness of that concept (this certainly being the negative side, the positive one consisting in the positing of the immediacy of the self-contradictoriness of the negation of that concept; as long as this second side is only anticipated, however, it is appropriate to only consider that first side, which is however necessarily required by the positive one);[3] let us then state that this self-contradictoriness is not immediate because the fundamental condition of this non-immediacy is the fact that the meaning 'being' (a 'being') L-immediately distinguishes or frees itself (Chapter 3, §8) from the meaning 'Ph-immediate being' (or 'totality of Ph-immediate being', or 'possible experience'). It is precisely by virtue of this L-immediate distinction that the concept of being, as surpassing present being, is not immediately contradictory. That distinction is L-immediately manifested as something that would persist even if it were to be verified that the totality of being coincides with the totality of Ph-immediate being. As we have already noted, it is indeed possible to exclude that being surpasses Ph-immediate being only insofar as the meaning 'being' distinguishes itself from the meaning 'immediately present being'.[4]

In a different respect, it must be observed that the surpassing being, i.e. being that is not immediately present being, is itself immediately present (as part of the present discussion that takes it here as its object); being that is not immediately present being is immediately present because the L-immediate affirmation of that being – or its being L-immediately affirmed – is itself immediately present. The contradiction is immediately superseded – in such a way that in this respect, too, there is no immediacy of the self-contradictoriness of the affirmation of that surpassing – by noting that being, which is not Ph-immediate, is immediately present *as to its form*, or as to its formal meaning, but it is not immediately present as to its concrete content; and it is precisely this concreteness that is posited as something other than the totality of the Ph-immediate. In other words, (L-immediately) positing being as surpassing the Ph-immediate does not *simpliciter* consist in the presence of what lies beyond presence (and therefore it is not a positing of something that, *qua* present, cannot be other than the totality of the Ph-immediate): but it is the presence of the form of the concrete content, which is affirmed to exist beyond the present content. (This point is developed in the next section.)

If the meaning 'being' is not immediately manifested as subsumed in or exhausted by the Ph-immediate determinations of being, but it originarily frees itself for a further determination, or it is originarily available for such a determination, from the standpoint of the concrete structuring of immediacy, it is necessary to add that this originary freeing or availability is also originarily constrained or made use of: precisely to the extent that it is L-immediately affirmed that being surpasses the totality of the Ph-immediate. Notwithstanding, as we shall see, that originary availability or freeing still persists to the extent that the L-immediate affirmation of that surpassing does not constitute an originary exclusion of the project for being to surpass the very dimension of being that is Ph-L-immediately affirmed – and, in a different respect, to the extent that the L-immediate affirmation of that surpassing does not consist in the presence of the concrete content of that surpassing being, in such a way that the meaning 'being' remains available for a presentation of that concrete content. (In other words, for what concerns this second respect: that availability is originarily made use of from a formal point of view – i.e. insofar as what is other than the Ph-immediate is known as to its formal value – but not from the point of view of the concrete content of that formality.)

c. On the one hand, the semantic whole is therefore immediately present. In this respect, the originary is also what is conclusive or definitive – every human development or disclosure having to be posited as an internal determination of the originary opening of being. On the other hand, however, the fact that the whole is immediately present is L-immediately negated precisely from the standpoint of the concrete structuring of immediacy. (It should be kept in mind that the exposition has not yet come to a verification of this L-immediacy.) This contradiction is immediately superseded by positing that the semantic whole is immediately present *as a formal meaning*, i.e. *as* 'semantic whole', or 'totality of being'. Accordingly, the affirmation that the whole surpasses the totality of the Ph-immediate does not concern this formal meaning as such, but the *relation* between the originary meaning – the concrete semantic content that is immediately present – and the absolute semantic content to which that formal meaning points or refers. For, indeed, the fact that the immediately present content is not the absolute content, or that the infinite semanteme is not exhausted by the originary meaning, is the content of an L-immediate affirmation. Accordingly, the semantic whole is immediately present only as a formal meaning – despite the fact that this form is immediately determined by the originary meaning. This originary determination is indeed only a moment of the absolute determination – and it is precisely because this absolute determination is not present that it is affirmed that the whole is only present as a formal meaning. That absolute determination is not present precisely because a dimension of being surpasses the dimension of Ph-immediate being. We have already stated (cf. b) that this surpassing dimension is present as to its form, but not as to its concrete content. Accordingly, the whole is present as a formal meaning precisely insofar as that surpassing being is present as a formal meaning.

d. The distinction between the form and the content of that meaning therefore constitutes the immediate superseding of the self-contradictoriness of the affirmation that the totality of the Ph-immediate is not the whole; that self-contradictoriness is determined by the fact that this distinction is not made, in such a way that the same term is, as such, present and not present.

Concerning the meaning of the introduction of that distinction, it is possible to present observations analogous to the ones made in §10 of Chapter 7. That is to say, the distinction between the form and the content of the whole belongs to the structuring of immediacy, and it is not the result of a mediation. Accordingly, the self-contradictoriness of the affirmation that the totality of the Ph-immediate is not the whole (a self-contradictoriness that in the passage quoted above corresponds to the *h*-contradiction) cannot be superseded by negating the difference between the whole and Ph-immediacy – both because this difference is L-immediate (but, as long as one remains at this first aspect, it is precisely this L-immediacy of the difference that enters into the constitution of the structure of the aporia, due to the observation that the whole, too, is Ph-immediate) and because the distinction between the form and the content of the whole is L-immediate.

(It is furthermore clear that, insofar as the originary determination of the whole consists of a becoming, there arises in relation to the whole the same aporia considered in §27 of Chapter 5 with respect to the totality of the Ph-immediate. The resolution of this aporia will have however to be addressed separately, as it constitutes the very concrete elucidation of the L-immediacy of the affirmation of the difference between the whole and the totality of the Ph-immediate, which has only been anticipated up to this point.)

4. Aporia and solution

a. It is now possible to observe that in stating that the form, but not the content, of that surpassing being is present (indicating the meaning 'being that surpasses present being' by Q, for convenience), that content is however present: precisely to the extent that it is discussed. Accordingly, it will have once again to be concluded that this content is present and, at the same time, not present.

In this case, too, the aporia arises as a result of an operation of the abstract understanding. In stating that Q is present as to its form, but not as to its content, one posits a *relation* between Q, posited as a formal meaning, and Q, posited as a concrete one. This relation is precisely what *makes it possible to hold firm* the concrete meaning or content as something not present; it is precisely *in relation* to the positing of the presence of Q, posited as a formal meaning, that Q, posited as a concrete meaning, is held firm as something not present. If that relation is not retained, it follows that in considering the meaning 'concrete content of Q' one should acknowledge its presence. It is clear that this acknowledgement here takes place – and must take place – only insofar as one does not take into account that this acknowledgement *is already brought about* by the positing of the presence of Q as a formal meaning. For, indeed, insofar as the meaning 'concrete content of Q' is present, it is present as a formal meaning, i.e. *as that very formal meaning* that is not considered in abstractly regarding Q *qua* posited as a concrete meaning. As a result, having posited the presence of the meaning 'concrete content of Q', it will be once again necessary, by virtue of the very meaning of Q, to distinguish Q *qua* posited as a formal meaning from Q *qua* posited as a concrete one. Objecting that the very content of Q is present thus means nothing but *repeating* the distinction between Q as a formal meaning and Q as a concrete one. The contradiction of the objection consists in regarding that repetition as the introduction of a *new* element: namely, the presence of the content of Q. If the aporetic argument wishes to conclude by stating that the content of Q is present and at the same time not present, it means that Q, posited as a concrete meaning, is and is not considered in relation to Q, posited as a formal meaning: it is not considered in this relation precisely because the presence of the content is posited (but insofar as the latter is instead kept in relation to its form – as mentioned – it *only* counts as something not present, for only its form is present); and at the same time it is considered in that relation because it is retained as something not present – and, as something not present, Q is only in relation to Q *qua* posited as a formal meaning. Insofar as the content is instead retained in that relation, it *cannot* be once again split into its form and its content (whereas this can take place as part of a simple repetition of the distinction between form and content), in such a way as to allow that same term, which *qua* abstractly conceived is (= must once again be) recognized as something present, to be posited as something not present.

In other words – indicating by fQ and cQ, respectively, Q as a formal meaning and Q as a concrete meaning – affirming that the difference between the whole and Ph-immediacy is L-immediate means affirming that it is L-immediate that cQ is not present (i.e. it is L-immediate that cQ is not Ph-immediate). As we have seen, the relation and therefore the distinction between cQ and fQ is itself an L-immediately posited condition of the constitution of that L-immediate affirmation: cQ can only be posited as something non-present insofar as it is posited in relation to fQ, for – if it is not posited in this relation – cQ, too, turns into a present content. The relation between cQ and fQ, as part of which cQ is posited as something non-present and fQ is posited as something present, is therefore the concrete implication (necessarily required by the constitution of the L-immediacy), of which cQ and fQ are abstract moments. The aporetic argument arises because it regards and at the same time it does not regard cQ as an abstract moment of the semantic concreteness constituted by that implication: cQ is regarded as an abstract moment precisely insofar as it is held firm as something non-present; and, at the same time, it is not regarded as an abstract moment precisely because it is attested as a present content, and, as discussed, this may only take place insofar as cQ is no longer held firm as part of its relation with fQ, i.e. insofar as it is abstractly separated from that concrete implication.

b. The aporia resolved here should not be conflated with the one formulated in §15, g of Chapter 8. It is indeed the case that, as we shall clarify, the L-immediate affirmation according to which the totality of the constants of S surpasses the immediately present constants of the latter is at the same time an L-immediate affirmation of the fact that the whole surpasses the totality of the Ph-immediate; but while in the passage quoted above, the aporia under consideration (which is still to be resolved) is determined by the fact that the surpassing of the present constants is L-immediate, the aporia that has been solved above is instead constituted independently *of the way* in which the surpassing of the totality of the Ph-immediate is operated, and it refers to that surpassing as such. (That is to say, the aporia would obtain even if one were to posit the immediate non-contradictoriness of the *project* of the surpassing, or even if the latter were affirmed in an L-mediated way: i.e. even if the surpassing were affirmed in a different way from the one constituted by its L-immediate affirmation.) It is however the case that there exists a structural analogy between the two aporias: the latter one exhibits the self-contradictoriness determined by the fact that something that is not Ph-immediate is Ph-immediate – in such a way that the Ph-immediacy includes and does not include the whole (regardless of the way in which this lack of inclusion should be posited); the former aporia exhibits the self-contradictoriness determined by the fact that the affirmation of an excess of constants over the present ones is L-immediate – in such a way that these exceeding constants (according to what is stated in the quoted passage) must and must not belong to the structure of the immediate.

c. From the standpoint of the structure of immediacy, the positive that is not part of the totality of the Ph-immediate is precisely the L-immediately affirmed positive. (That structure therefore includes the *project* of a non-Ph-immediate positive, which is not the non-Ph-immediate positive that is L-immediately affirmed.). It therefore appears in what sense we stated (cf. Chapter 5, §18) that the non-Ph-immediate positive, which is L-immediately affirmed, belongs and does not belong to the totality of the Ph-immediate: it belongs to the latter as a formal meaning (i.e. as a determination of fQ), and it does not belong to it as a concrete meaning (i.e. as a determination of cQ). (It is clear that when we speak of a *determination* of fQ and cQ, as mentioned, it is not immediately contradictory to project a further determination.)

d. Affirming that a specific content is present as to its form but not as to its concrete semantic matter means that this concreteness is known in an Ph-mediated way, i.e. it is known *through or by means* of the form – which is itself Ph-immediately known. The positive whose non-belonging to the totality of the Ph-immediate is L-immediately affirmed, is therefore known in an Ph-mediated way: the L-immediate positive is Ph-mediated. (As already stated, instead, the Ph-L-immediacy – i.e. the non-contradictoriness of the Ph-immediate content – is at the same time Ph-immediate.)

5. The matter and the form of the semantic whole

The semantic whole is the synthesis of the form and the absolute matter of meaning. It should however be observed that this absolute matter cannot stand as something *distinct* from that form: for, in that case, the semanteme 'semantic whole' (which precisely constitutes the formal value of the infinite semanteme) would not be included in the absolute matter, in such a way that the latter would not be the absolute matter of meaning. If the set $\sigma_1, \sigma_2, \sigma_3, ..., \sigma_n$ indicates *all* meanings, and it therefore constitutes the absolute semantic matter, by regarding this matter as distinct from its form the proposition: '$\sigma_1, \sigma_2, \sigma_3, ..., \sigma_n$ is the semantic whole' would be self-contradictory: precisely because the predicate – which is the form of the whole, or the whole as a formal meaning – as distinct from the subject, could neither be included in the subject nor be identical to it; as a result, the subject would not be able to be the semantic whole (or the predicate would not be able to be referred to the subject).

That proposition is therefore not self-contradictory only to the extent that the subject is the absolute matter, *qua* synthesis of matter and form, and the predicate is the form, *qua* synthesis of form and matter, in such a way that matter and form are the same, and they are only distinct as *abstract moments* of this sameness – and, as thus abstracted, neither of them is the whole.

6. Note

The positing of the semantic whole as such L-immediately implies the positing of the exclusion of the fact that the whole is surpassed by a larger horizon. If the positing of the whole did not imply the positing of the exclusion of the surpassing of the whole, the latter would not be posited *as such*. Once again, however, the whole must not be regarded as simply being the sum of the whole, in its not including that exclusion, and this very exclusion: if this were the case, the exclusion of the surpassing of the whole would exclude that the whole as not inclusive – and therefore surpassed by the exclusion – should be surpassed by a horizon. What is not surpassed by any horizon, as mentioned, is instead the whole as inclusive of the very exclusion of its being surpassed.

If the semanteme 'semantic whole' excludes for itself to be surpassed by any semantic horizon, it does not operate this exclusion on the basis of its originary matter – i.e. on the basis of the content that determines the whole, or as part of which the whole originarily determines itself – but on the basis of its form, by virtue of which it precisely realizes and manifests itself *as* 'semantic whole'. The originary determination or matter of the whole – i.e. the totality of the Ph-immediate – is indeed L-immediately negated *qua* absolute matter, and it therefore cannot stand as that by virtue of which the whole excludes its being surpassed.

Beyond the whole, nothing. The whole is only posited insofar as it is posited that beyond the whole there is nothing, i.e. insofar as the horizon that surpasses the whole is posited as superseded. This horizon therefore itself belongs, as superseded, to the whole. (The aporias caused by the positing of nothingness have been discussed and resolved in Chapter 4.)

Corollary: if the positing of the whole as such implies the positing of nothingness, it follows that, if nothingness is not posited, nothing is posited (since if the whole is not posited nothing is). The meaning and value of this type of corollary will be adequately determined further on.

7. The absolute semantic matter must be posited

The L-immediate affirmation of the difference between the absolute semantic matter and the originary meaning entails that the originary structure is the originary contradiction *in an enhanced sense* with respect to the one established in Chapter 8.

In order to clarify this statement, it is in particular necessary to keep in mind the following theorem:

'Every meaning L-immediately stands as a constant of the infinite semanteme'; or, equivalently: 'No meaning can be a variant of the infinite semanteme.'

Every meaning is indeed part of the essence of the meaning 'Totality of meaning', or 'Totality of being'. That is to say, the totality of meanings (= of beings) is included in the meaning 'being' – which, once again, is not to be regarded as formal being, but as that semantic horizon that, precisely, *continet omnia*; that is to say, each of those meanings or beings belongs, in the way that pertains to it, to the essence of being (or of the whole). The fact that every meaning is a constant of the infinite semanteme is L-immediately affirmed; that is to say, every meaning is L-immediately known in its belonging to the essence of the meaning 'being'. Or, equivalently: by 'being' we refer to the concrete totality of beings; accordingly, every being is L-immediately known in its belonging to the essence of being – precisely to the extent that every meaning is L-immediately affirmed to be a being.

Precisely by virtue of this all-encompassing character of the infinite semanteme, it is necessary to affirm that *if any meaning is not posited, the semantic whole is not posited either*: precisely because a meaning is only posited if *all* the constants of that meaning are posited, and *every* meaning is a constant of the semantic whole. The L-immediate affirmation of the difference between the originary meaning and the absolute semantic matter therefore entails that the originary opening of the whole is not the positing of the whole, i.e. that it only counts as an *intention* to realize that positing; accordingly, the positing of the whole that is effectively realized is only an *abstractly* formal positing, and what is effectively posited is not what one intends to posit. If the absolute semantic matter is not originarily posited, the originary meaning, *qua* positing of the whole as such – i.e. insofar as it constitutes as a matter of fact the positing of the semantic whole as such (*qua* 'semantic whole') – posits as the whole something that is not the whole, precisely because it only consists in the abstractly formal meaningfulness of that whole. The meaning 'semantic whole' certainly distinguishes itself from any other meaning that is a determination of the whole; but insofar as it is held firm as distinct in this way, it counts as a formal meaningfulness of the whole. (This formal meaningfulness varies, or presents a different value of formality, depending on the extent of the semantic domain from which it is distinct – or, equivalently, depending on the semantic quantity that concretely determines the formal meaning as thus distinct.) The whole, as a formal meaning, therefore means something other than itself, or it is a reference to something other – namely, to the concrete content of the whole (or, more precisely, to the concrete content from which the form distinguishes itself); it consists of this reference to something other, precisely because the simple formal meaningfulness of the semantic whole is not, as such, the semantic whole. If that 'other', however, which is the term of the reference of the formal meaning, is not present – and if, at the same time, something like the 'semantic whole' is nevertheless posited (while standing however as a formal meaningfulness to be distinguished from the formal meaningfulness that pertains to the form insofar as it is concretely distinct from the content: cf. Chapter 9, §8, d) – that reference to something other collapses upon itself: that is to say, the reference realizes itself without the realization of the term of the reference. As a result, as mentioned, something that is not the whole – precisely because it is only an abstractly formal signification of the whole – is posited as the whole.[5]

It is clear that we are speaking here from that broader standpoint from which it is possible to consider the C-contradiction (cf. Chapter 8, §9). With the appropriate amendments, the reader may unfold the analytic observations developed in Chapter 8 in relation to this logical situation. For our part, we shall only consider the following remarks.

a. The positing of any meaning, as we have said, essentially implies the positing of the semantic whole; accordingly, if the whole is not posited, nor is any meaning (§1, g). At the same time, however (cf. Chapter 13), the difference between the originary meaning and the absolute semantic matter is L-immediately affirmed, in such a way that it is L-immediately affirmed that the originary meaning is posited without the positing of the semantic whole.

Furthermore, the totality of the immediate is the horizon of a semantic *development*: that is to say, what is immediately present is a series of positional horizons – in which a certain quantity of meanings is not posited – which are therefore realized without the positing of the semantic whole.

The contradiction that arises in this twofold way is superseded as follows. No meaning is posited if the semantic whole, *as a formal meaning*, is not posited. If the whole is not posited *as* the whole, nothing is posited: annulment of every positional horizon. If, instead, a specific semantic dimension is posited without the positing of another specific dimension, and therefore without the positing of the absolute semantic matter, the outcome is not the annulment of every positional horizon; on the contrary – according to what we have stated above – the posited semantic dimension realizes itself as the opening of a contradiction. This contradiction, let us repeat, consists in positing the infinite semanteme only as a formal meaning, in such a way that this abstract form is regarded as something other than itself (i.e. as the concrete, to which it nevertheless refers).

In other words, every meaning is posited only if the semantic whole is posited; if the latter is then not concretely posited as to its absolute matter, and it therefore counts as a formal meaning, any meaning that is posited, too, will be posited as a formal meaning, and the semantic horizon that is constituted in this way will be the opening of a contradiction.[6]

Categorically positing (rather than simply projecting) the difference between the absolute semantic matter and the originary therefore means categorically positing (rather than simply projecting) that the originary consists in the originary opening of a contradiction. At the same time, however, that categorical positing determines the *task* of the originary: namely, the superseding of the contradiction that has been deduced.

The task of the originary is thus to be the whole. It is clear that, here, that task precisely consists in the necessity of freeing the originary from that contradiction.

b. Instead, from the standpoint of that mode of the structuring of immediacy, in accordance with which that difference immediately stands only as something projected, the fact that the originary has a task is only a project (this being the standpoint that pertains to the concept Γ_a: holding firm that the totality of the Ph-immediate is the entire positive that can be immediately affirmed, the fact that there should obtain a difference between the absolute semantic matter and the originary is only a project, which the plane of immediacy is not able to verify). (It will however be possible to partially amend this affirmation, by showing how there also exists an originary task for Γ_a, in its concrete constitution – cf. Chapter 11, §13.)

That the absolute is the *idea*, to which reality must conform, is only an arbitrary presupposition as long as it is not known whether the absolute surpasses the originary reality: until then, this reality originarily conforms to the idea, or the task is originarily fulfilled; there only exists the project of a task to be fulfilled (and for this task to be definitively fulfilled). One thing, however, is to remain with that presupposition, and another is to exhibit the concrete structure of the L-immediate affirmation of the difference between the whole and the originary (a verification that the present exposition will carry out in the next chapters). From the standpoint of Γ_a, the originary situation appears in any case as one in which tasks are *chosen*; precisely because they are chosen, however, there exists the possibility for what is chosen to be something that cannot be fulfilled. The originary situation is here the one as part of which it is not possible to exclude that beyond this very situation there should be nothing; choosing a task means deciding to surpass or go beyond a situation, i.e. deciding to supersede a *possible* contradiction – in such a way that there exists the possibility that this decision should have decided for the unfulfillable. If 'living' means choosing tasks, i.e. deciding to surpass the originary situation in some way (and one decides to surpass it even when deciding to remain in it), life is in this respect a surveying.

c. The originary *must* in any case be the whole. This does not mean that it is self-contradictory for it not be the whole, but that, to the extent that it is L-immediately known that it is not, it is also known that the originary is a form of being in contradiction – whereby it only frees itself from that contradiction through that *increment* that identifies it with the whole. It is indeed not immediately contradictory for the originary to be a form of being in contradiction (cf. Chapter 8). This being in contradiction, on the side of the originary – let us reiterate once again – is not determined by what the originary is, but by its not being something (precisely: its not being the manifestation of the absolute semantic matter); accordingly, the contradiction constituted by the originary is not superseded by negating the originary, but by absolutely realizing it: by realizing it as the opening of the concrete totality.

d. Lastly, let us observe that the originary contradiction cannot be superseded by no longer positing anything (annulment of every positional opening); for, on the contrary, in this way one renounces to supersede it: the contradiction is eternally left to itself – i.e. the contradiction does go in the past (and in this sense it no longer is), but as something not superseded.

8. Scheme

The following scheme should be kept in mind for the sake of the clarity of the exposition:

[1] The proposition: 'The positing of any meaning (not including the semantic whole itself) necessarily implies the positing of the semantic whole' (cf. §1) is L-mediated. Let p_1 be this proposition:.

[1'] The equivalent proposition: 'The semantic whole is a constant of every meaning', too, is L-mediated.

[1"] The same is to be affirmed of the proposition: 'If the semantic whole is not posited, no meaning is posited' (cf. §1, g).

[2] If p_1 is L-mediated, projecting that the predicate of this proposition should not pertain to the subject is however immediately self-contradictory (cf. §1, c).

[3] The proposition: 'The positing of the totality of the immediate necessarily implies the positing of the whole' (let P be this proposition), too, is L-mediated;

[3'] and it enjoys the property indicated in [2].

[4] The proposition: 'The semantic whole is' is Ph-immediate.

[5] The proposition: 'Every meaning is a constant of the semantic whole' (cf. §7) is L-immediate.

[5'] The proposition, equivalent to the one in [5], 'The positing of the whole necessarily implies the positing of every meaning', too, is L-immediate.

[5"] The same is to be affirmed of the proposition: 'If any meaning is not posited, the semantic whole is not posited'.

[6] The proposition: 'Positing the semantic whole without positing any meaning is the opening of the C-contradiction' is L-immediate.

[7] The proposition: 'The originary semantic matter, constituted by the totality of the immediate, is not the absolute semantic matter' ('There exists a difference between the originary and the whole', 'The positive surpasses the originary') – let Q be this proposition – is L-immediate (cf. Chapter 13).

[8] The proposition: 'The originary is the opening of the C-contradiction' – let R be this proposition – is L-immediate.

Indeed, if the originary is concretely regarded as the structure having as components, on the one hand, the very implication between the totality of the immediate and the whole and, on the other hand, the positing of the difference between the immediate (i.e. between that very concrete structure) and the whole – i.e. if the subject of the proposition R is regarded as the structuring of the proposition P and of the proposition Q – the proposition R is L-immediate: if the originary consists in positing the whole (= P) without positing the totality of the determinations of the whole (= Q), the fact that the originary is the opening of the C-contradiction is L-immediately affirmed. (It is thus clear that, from the standpoint of the concept Γ_a, the proposition R may only stand as the result of a mediation: to the extent that, from the standpoint of Γ_a, the proposition Q is not posited as L-immediate – in such a way that from the standpoint of Γ_a the structure of immediacy is constituted as the project for the predicate of the proposition R to pertain to the subject.)[7]

The implication between the originary and the whole is a mediation only insofar as this implication is regarded as a necessary one. Conversely, the originary consists in the Ph-immediate positing of the whole, i.e. the whole – even if in its formal value – is the Ph-immediately known content. (In this case, too, the affirmation of a content that is not part of the totality of the Ph-immediate does not however affirm, as already stated, a surpassing of the form of the Ph-immediate content – i.e. a surpassing of this content considered as to its formal value – precisely because the formal value of that content is the whole; that surpassing is only affirmed in relation to the *determination* of that formal value: a determination that is precisely constituted by the totality of the Ph-immediate content.) In this respect, it is clear that the proposition R is L-mediated only if the originary is not regarded as including the proposition Q.

[9] If every meaning is a constant of the whole, and if the whole is a constant of every meaning, 'every meaning is a constant of every other meaning'. This proposition is L-mediated.

The proposition Q therefore implies that the totality of the immediately present constants of S is not the totality *simpliciter* of the constants of S. It is thus certainly established that affirming the proposition Q entails affirming the excess of the constants of S over the present ones; and yet, the proposition: 'The immediately present constants of S are not the totality of the constants of S', in the way in which it has been presented, is *L-mediated*. This means that when we affirmed (cf. Chapter 8, §11) that this latter proposition is L-immediate, we did not consider the way in which this proposition has been deduced here, but a different mode of positing of that proposition, which will be considered in the next chapter. In the present chapter, we are therefore also going to show a different value of the L-immediacy of the proposition R. (In a different respect, it is clear that if the proposition R is considered – as it is indeed possible to do – as a consequence of the proposition: 'The immediately presents constants are not the totality of the constants of S', then, insofar as this proposition is L-mediated, the proposition R, too, is constituted as an L-mediated proposition.)

9. 'Constant'-constants and 'variant'-constants

If the originary structure is the originary opening of the whole, and if every determination is a constant of the whole, every determination is a constant of the originary meaning. *In this respect*, the distinction between the variants and the constants of S, made at the beginning of Chapter 7, does not obtain: the originary structure is only posited if *every* determination is posited. In a different respect, the originary opening of meaning is not what it *intends* to be, and it stands as an abstractly formal opening (and, therefore, as the originary contradiction).

At the same time, however, the distinction between the variants and the constants of S is retained (with all the ensuing corollaries, as indicated in Chapters 7 and 8) as a distinction that is internal to the totality of the constants of S. This means that the lack of positing of a 'constant' of S (regarded either as a specific determination of that totality or as a proper constant) implies an *additional* contradiction relative to the one determined by the lack of positing of a 'variant'; or, equivalently, this means that a determination pertains to *S* as a 'constant'-constant for a reason additional to that for which another specific determination pertains to *S* as a 'variant'-constant. In other words: not positing a 'constant' gives rise to a (dialectical) C-contradiction *not only* insofar as that constant, like every variant, is a determination of the whole, but also insofar as that determination is *that specific* determination that it is. It is then precisely this possibility to attest this C-contradiction *independently* of the fact that the determination that is not posited is a constant of the whole that which makes it possible to distinguish this determination from the variants. Therefore: not positing a variant of *S* – or, equivalently, positing it as not belonging to the essence of *S* – gives rise to a contradiction *C* insofar as that variant is a constant of the whole; not positing a constant of *S* (or positing it as not belonging to the essence of *S*) *also* gives rise to a C-contradiction insofar as that constant is *that specific* determination that it is. These constants, the lack of positing of which gives rise to a twofold attestation of the C-contradiction, may be referred to as *syntactic constants* (or transcendental constants). It is clear that the discussion must also be – analogously – extended to the variants and constants of all meanings other than *S*.

10. Another sense in which every true proposition is a necessary one

Analogously, in relation to the distinction between analytic, synthetic *a posteriori* and synthetic *a priori* propositions (cf. Chapter 7), it must be stated that *all* true propositions (i.e. all non-problematic propositions that are free from contradiction) are either analytic or synthetic *a priori*. If, indeed, every meaning is a constant of the semanteme 'semantic whole', and if the latter, insofar as it is necessarily implied by every meaning, is a constant of every meaning, it follows – as already stated – that every meaning is a constant of every other meaning; accordingly, the predicative implication between any two meanings is always necessary: i.e. such that its negation is self-contradictory. In this sense, merely synthetic propositions (i.e. such that their negation is not necessarily excluded) only comprise false propositions (= self-contradictory propositions, i.e. such that their negation is necessarily affirmed). For instance: given the immediate presence of this *red* extension, in the proposition: 'This extension is *not* red (= is non-red)' the determination that constitutes the predicate *is not*, simply, a constant of the whole – precisely because this predicate is such a constant *insofar as it is superseded*, i.e. in its being superseded. That is to say, the fact that this extension (which is Ph-immediately known as red) is not red is certainly, as such, a constant of the whole: precisely insofar as it has a specific semantic value. But since it is Ph-immediate that this extension is red, its not being red is superseded, in such a way that the latter is, *qua superseded*, a constant of the whole. The pertaining of this superseded determination to the subject of that proposition gives rise to the synthetic *a priori* proposition: 'This extension is red'. That first proposition is therefore (simply) synthetic insofar as it is self-contradictory (and it is self-contradictory insofar as it is synthetic). (It should be observed that while every meaning is a constant of every other meaning, this does not mean that every meaning is affirmatively predicated of every other meaning: among the constants of a meaning, certain ones count as such as predicates, while the other ones are constants precisely to the extent that their determinacy is negated by the meaning under consideration.)

At the same time, however, the distinction between analytic, synthetic *a posteriori* and synthetic *a priori* propositions is retained as a distinction that is internal to the totality of necessary propositions. It must therefore be stated that synthetic *a posteriori* propositions are those necessary propositions (i.e. those synthetic *a priori* propositions) in which the predicate pertains to the subject, or is a constant of the subject, not insofar as the subject and the predicate have *that specific* semantic content by virtue of which they distinguish themselves from the other meanings, but insofar as the subject as much as the predicate are constants of the semantic whole (in such a way that, as stated above, the predicate is a constant of the subject because the infinite semanteme is a constant of every meaning). Conversely, synthetic *a priori* propositions (as opposed to synthetic *a posteriori* ones) are those propositions that, *in addition* to being *a priori* for the same reason for which synthetic *a posteriori* propositions are *a priori*, are also *a priori* for another reason: namely, insofar as the predicate is a constant of the subject *also* to the extent that the subject and the predicate have that specific semantic content that pertains to them and by virtue of which they distinguish themselves from the other meanings. The same should be asserted concerning analytic propositions. In this sense, also the dynamic relations among the different types of propositions, as indicated in §2 of Chapter 9, are therefore retained.

At this point, however, there arises a series of aporias of significant importance, the formulation and solution of which will be presented further on (cf. Chapter 13).[8]

11. The positing of the whole and dialectic

a. Taking up here the point indicated in the footnote of Chapter 9, §10, b, the dialectical process is regarded as to its broadest realization to the extent that it is understood as the dialectic that pertains to the abstract positing *of any* finite determination. Positing any finite semantic domain (i.e. a domain such that it does not consist of the absolute semantic matter) without positing the semantic context of that domain means understanding – should the outcome of such an abstract positing of the finite be positive – that a term coincides with its contradictory. For, indeed, in relation to the theorem according to which every meaning is a constant of every other meaning (a theorem that is grounded in the theorems by virtue of which the infinite semanteme is a constant of every meaning and every meaning is a constant of the infinite semanteme), the abstract positing of any finite content – i.e. the positing of a finite element that is not the positing of its context – consists in positing a semantic plane without positing all the constants of that plane. If the outcome of this abstract positing is positive – and it should be noted that in order for that outcome to be positive it is necessary for the whole to be posited as a formal meaning – that (any) meaning that is effectively posited as part of the outcome of that abstract positing will be a finite meaning (since we are precisely considering the semantic situation that arises if the absolute semantic matter is not posited). As a finite meaning, the content of the outcome of that abstract positing will itself be a meaning that is posited without the positing of all its constants, and it will therefore be a formal meaning in the sense in which the content of the outcome-2a is a formal meaning (cf. Chapter 9, §8, c, d, e). In this way, the content that is effectively posited will be *intended* as that concrete to which the formal meaning of the outcome points or refers – that concrete precisely consisting in the positing of all the constants of the content that is effectively posited, i.e. consisting in the positing of the absolute semantic matter. Since the content that is effectively posited as part of the outcome is something other, i.e. a contradictory of the concrete referred to by that formal meaning precisely constituted by the content of the outcome of that abstract positing, positing only this content means intending or regarding something that is other than the concrete as the concrete itself: i.e. as discussed, it means intending or regarding a term as its contradictory.

It is precisely by keeping in mind the set of theorems outlined above that it is possible to affirm that the abstract positing of *any* finite meaning is dialectical: in a different respect – the dialectical process having been considered from this more restricted standpoint in Chapter 9 – the abstract positing of a finite content is dialectical only if the semantic plane that is not posited is affirmed as a constant of the posited content for a reason additional to the one for which it is stated that every meaning is a constant of every other meaning.

In relation to the maximum application of the dialectical process, it thus appears why, if the outcome of the abstract positing is positive, both sides of the dialectical contradiction are included in the positional domain constituted by the outcome of the abstract positing, as asserted in the footnote of §10 of Chapter 9 mentioned above; whence it must be stated that the abstract positing of any finite content – should the outcome of that positing be positive – is characterized by a dialectic that is independent of the dialectic of the abstract concept of that abstract positing (cf. Chapter 9, §10, b).

The positional *steresis* of any meaning therefore causes a dialectical contradiction. If the meaning that is not posited is the very formal value of the infinite semanteme, the dialectical contradiction is only constituted as the *abstract concept* of the (abstract) positing that only posits that finite semantic content that does not include the form of the infinite semanteme: that is to say, the dialectical contradiction is only constituted as the abstract concept of that abstract positing, and not as that abstract positing, because the outcome of the latter is a positional annulment (cf. §1, e); accordingly, the contradiction only arises in *intending* (= abstract concept) this positional nullity as the positing of that finite semantic content. If the meaning that is not posited is instead not the form of the infinite semanteme – whereby there exists the possibility that the outcome of the abstract positing should be positionally positive – the dialectical contradiction is constituted both as an abstract positing and as the abstract concept of an abstract positing.

b. At the same time, however, the fact that the positional *steresis* of any meaning should imply a dialectical contradiction can also be demonstrated in the following additional way. If a specific set of meanings is not posited, in such a way however that a finite semantic domain x is posited (whereby the positing of the form of the infinite semanteme is required), the horizon of the contradictory of that domain, i.e. non-x, is necessarily posited, as superseded (§1). The meanings that are not posited, however, are *all* constants of the contradictory of x – i.e. the concrete meaning of 'non-x' is constituted by the entirety of the concrete content that is not x (and that also includes the constants of x) – and, therefore, since that horizon of the contradictory of x is a constant of x, they are constants of x itself. It follows from this that the positing of x, as it is realized as a matter of fact, only consists in the *intention* to posit x; or, equivalently, what is effectively posited is x as an abstractly formal meaning – i.e. it is not that to which the very abstract meaningfulness of x refers.

It thus appears that the theorem 'Every meaning is a constant of every other meaning' has at least a twofold foundation: in that every meaning is a constant of the infinite semanteme, which is a constant of every meaning; and in that every meaning is a constant of the contradictory of any other meaning (a contradictory that, as superseded, is a constant of this other meaning).

12. The outcome of the abstract positing of formal being

As a corollary of what we have stated so far, it must be affirmed that the outcome of the abstract positing of formal being – i.e. the outcome of that positing that posits nothing but that absolutely simple semantic content constituted by pure being – is positionally null. (This affirmation may be extended to the abstract positing of every simple meaning.) Only positing the simple means not positing anything. For, indeed, if nothing but the simple is posited, it follows that, insofar as the infinite semanteme distinguishes itself from formal being also to the extent that this semanteme is regarded as to its formal value, the infinite semanteme cannot even be posited as a formal meaning – and it has already been demonstrated that the lack of positing of this formal value implies that nothing is posited. The outcome of the abstract positing of pure being does not therefore consist, as Hegel claims, in the *positing* of nothingness, but in not positing anything. We have thus demonstrated what we anticipated in Chapter 9, §11, b.[9]

13. Aporia and solution. a. Aporia: 'If any meaning is not posited, nothing can be posited'

Let us consider the positing of a specific semantic domain x that does not include the positing of another specific meaning y (for instance, this shade of green that I see in my garden), and that therefore counts as a finite domain. X's not being y is a constant of x, or, equivalently, the positing of x is essentially (and L-immediately) a positing of x as non-y. It follows that y is a constant of x; as a result, if y is not posited, neither that not-being-y nor x *as such* can be posited. If x' is the positive outcome of the abstract positing of x (x' indicating that contradictory of x that must be posited as part of the outcome), it must however be noted that not-being-y is also a constant of x'; accordingly, if y is not posited, x' cannot be posited either. It is clear that since the semantic situation under consideration is defined by the lack of positing of y, it will not only be necessary to state that the outcome of the abstract positing of x' is x'', but it will also be necessary to conclude that the outcome of the positing of x cannot consist in the positing of any meaning, since y is a constant of *every* meaning, and if y is not posited no meaning can be posited.

One will have to conclude that if any meaning is not posited it is not possible to posit anything. This is a doubly aporetic conclusion, because on the one hand a multiplicity of past positional horizons that do not include a specific semantic quantity is immediately present – that is to say: immediately present being is present as a development or increment – and on the other hand one comes to rule out the difference between the originary meaning and the absolute semantic matter (for if the latter were not posited the originary would not be able to be posited either), whereas this difference had been presented above as something L-immediately affirmed. In other words, there arises an aporetic situation because an opposition between logos and experience is attested: on the one hand the logos, represented here by the dialectical principle of the positional implication between a meaning and its constants, and on the other hand experience, which, *qua* experience of becoming – i.e. of semantic domains that are finite as to their content – appears to attest to the very negation of that dialectical principle. (The experience of becoming is the experience of the variation of the content: past positional domains that do not include a specific semantic quantity are immediately present, and they are past precisely due to the arising of this quantity.)

14. b. The solution of the aporia

In order to solve the aporia outlined above, let us first of all observe that x's not being y is a constant of x – i.e. x is essentially and L-immediately non-y – not insofar as y is simply y, but insofar as y is *a specific non-x*: x is not a negation of y insofar as y is simply y, but insofar as y is a specific non-x.[10] Accordingly, if the lack of positing of y consists in the lack of positing of that formal property of y constituted by the meaning 'non-x', x cannot be posited as such (cf. §1). The same should be asserted concerning the meanings x', x'', x''', ..., x^n if their positing is regarded as the lack of positing of, respectively, 'non-x'', 'non-x''', 'non-x'''', ..., 'non-x^n'; it will not be possible to posit any meaning if the horizon of the contradictory of that meaning, which aims to stand as the outcome of the abstract positing of x, is not posited.

The discussion must therefore be restricted to the case in which a specific determination or individuation (precisely, y) of the horizon of the contradictory of x is not posited, while holding firm the positing of this horizon as such. It must therefore be asserted that x is only posited if the totality of non-x is posited. This totality is posited precisely with the positing of the contradictory of x: insofar as x is posited as the negation of *everything* that is not x, the totality of non-x is precisely posited; the totality of non-x is present precisely insofar as something like 'totality of non-x' is present. Except that the positing of this totality is formal (at least) because y is not posited; the totality of that contradictory is not posited, but it is not posited as to its concrete content, not as to its form. There is nothing of non-x that is not posited, precisely in that something like 'totality of non-x' is posited, in such a way that x can be posited; at the same time, however, a specific quantity of non-x ($= y$) is not posited, in such a way that the positing of the totality of non-x, and therefore the positing of x, is only a formal (i.e. abstractly formal) positing.[11]

If the semantic value of y therefore consists in a meaning that stands as an *individuation* of the meaning 'non-x', the lack of positing of y does not imply the lack of positing of x in the sense that x can no longer even be posited *as such* (i.e. as an abstractly formal meaning), but it implies that lack of positing of x that precisely affords that *positing of x* as an abstractly formal meaning – x being able to be posited *as* such, let us repeat, to the extent that the totality of non-x is posited as superseded precisely through the positing of something like 'superseded totality of non-x'.[12]

15. c. A self-contradictory aspect of the aporetic argument under consideration

The aporetic argument developed in §13, however, also succeeds in constituting itself thanks to this other logical fallacy. Let us recall the aporetic reasoning: 'The outcome of positing x without positing y is the positing of x'; but since y is also a constant of x' – for x' is essentially a negation of this non-x' constituted precisely by y – the outcome of the abstract positing of x cannot be x' either, but it must be a term x''; since this must be stated of every meaning that one intends to posit as part of that outcome, it must be concluded that the lack of positing of any meaning implies that nothing is posited.'

Here is the error hidden in the reasoning: in asserting that, since y is not posited, x' cannot be posited either because y is also a constant of x', one asserts for this very reason that if y were posited then x' could indeed be posited, since it could be posited as the negation of this non-x' constituted by y. Except that – and this is the point that, if not held firm, affords the opening of the aporetic argument – if x' *is posited* as a negation of y, x' no longer differs from x: precisely because this difference only obtains if x is posited without the positing of y (x' precisely constituting the outcome of this abstract positing of x). Therefore: the positing of x' as the negation of this non-x', constituted by y, is *the same* positing of x as the negation of this non-x, constituted by y.[13] This sameness is instead not recognized by the aporetic argument, which regards the positing of x' qua negation of y *as something other* than the positing of x qua negation of y; as a result, the aporetic argument is compelled to apply once again to this other term the same observations presented in relation to the positing of x qua negation of y: i.e. it states that, since y is not posited, x' cannot be posited *either*, but it is necessary to posit a term x''. That is to say, the aporetic argument regards the relation between the implication of x' and y and the implication of x'' and y analogously to the way in which it has regarded the relation between the implication of x and y and the implication of x' and y – in such a way that it believes to be entitled to conclude that the lack of positing of y implies an absolute positional nullity. Instead, in recognizing that the implication between x' and y is, in the sense indicated above, *the same* implication between x and y, it appears that, affirming that the lack of positing of y requires that x' should not be posited either, one is merely *repeating* what has already been affirmed (i.e. that the lack of positing of y requires the lack of positing of x); this repetition is a contradiction if, as in the aporetic argument, it is regarded as the positing of a new content. It is thus explained why, once it has been affirmed that the lack of positing of y implies the lack of positing of x (granting y that semantic value that has been established in the previous section), it is not possible to once again apply this theorem to the content (x') that is posited as part of the outcome of the abstract positing of x. As a result, this eliminates the reason why the aporetic argument would conclude by affirming that if the meaning y is not posited nothing can be posited.

In other words: x' is posited precisely insofar as y is not posited as a constant of x; accordingly, it is not possible to assert that x' is only posited if y is posited as a constant of x': this cannot be asserted precisely to the extent that x' is held firm as being other than x. Stating that x' – held firm as other than x – is only posited if y is posited as a constant of x' means renouncing to hold firm x' as other than x, i.e. it means *repeating* what has already been established, and therefore regarding x' as x. For if this otherness is not renounced, it is in fact necessary to state that x' – the formal meaning – can only be posited insofar as y is not posited: if y is posited, that formal meaning is indeed still posited, but as an abstract moment that is superseded in and by the concrete positing of x; that is to say, that meaning is superseded as an *abstractly* formal meaning.

16. d. Note

It should be noted that the verification, carried out in the previous section, of the logical fallacy at play in the aporetic argument is only valid in relation to the logical situation that arises if y takes *a specific* semantic value – that is to say, that fallacy of the aporetic argument does *not* obtain in relation to *any* semantic value taken by y, but, as stated, only if y takes a specific semantic value: namely, that by virtue of which y is an *individuation* of non-x (or, more generally, an individuation of a constant of x).

The importance of this remark – and its precise meaning – becomes clear if we now consider the aporetic structure (of significant interest) that precisely arises in case this remark is not taken into account.

17. New aporia and solution. a. Formulation of the aporia: The positional *steresis* of S does not imply a positional annulment

The new aporia can be formulated in general as follows: 'The same logical structure has been at the same time affirmed and negated: it has been affirmed in § 1, g, and negated in § 15.' That is to say, that very logical structure that had been used to demonstrate that the lack of positing of the infinite semanteme implies that nothing is posited (§1, g) is now (§15) no longer considered suitable to fulfil that demonstrative task. Indeed, briefly recalling what was stated in §1, g, it is clear that the reason why we have affirmed that if the infinite semanteme is not posited no semantic domain can be posited consists in the principle that the infinite semanteme (S) is a constant of every meaning – in such a way that, if the meaning x is posited without the positing of S, x will fail to be posited, and the outcome of the abstract positing of x will be the positing of x'; since S is also a constant of x' and of every meaning (x'', x''', ...) that one should intend to posit as the outcome of the abstract positing of x, it follows that the lack of positing of S implies an absolute positional nullity. It is clear that this reasoning has the same structure of the aporetic argument presented in §13; accordingly, if we apply to that reasoning the observations that we used in §15 to exhibit the logical fallacy of the aporetic argument, we shall have to assert:

'In affirming that, if S is not posited, x' cannot be posited either because S is also a constant of x', one affirms for this very reason that x' could only be posited if S were posited. If S is posited as a constant of x', however, x' is no longer a meaning that differs from x, but it is precisely x: whereby it follows that it is possible to exclude that the outcome of the abstract positing of x should be x', x'', x''', ..., or any other meaning only to the extent that one does not realise that, precisely, positing S as a constant of x' is *the same* thing as positing S as a constant of x – in such a way that affirming that x' cannot be posited either if S is not posited means *repeating* that x cannot be posited if S is not posited – or, equivalently, only to the extent that the repetition of the same logical operation is regarded as the positing of all the different semantic contents that purport to stand as the outcome of the abstract positing of x. Becoming aware of this repetition entails that one should realise that the outcome of positing x without positing S is not an absolute positional annulment (as instead held in §1, g), in the same way in which it was realised (§15) that the lack of positing of y does not imply a positional annulment; as a result, the outcome of that abstract positing of x consists in the *positing* of x'.

18. b. Solution of the aporia: Syntactic and non-syntactic constants

a. The aporetic situation outlined above is solved precisely by the remark mentioned in §16, i.e. through the introduction of the distinction between the *syntactic* and *non-syntactic constants* of a meaning. The aporia in question precisely arises to the extent that this distinction is not taken into account. If we indicate the constants of a specific meaning x by the variable y, it must be stated that, on the basis of that distinction, the verification carried out in §15 of the logical fallacy of the aporia formulated in §13 is *not* valid in relation *to all* values that y can take, but only in relation to those values of y that precisely consist in the non-syntactic constants of x. That is to say, that verification is *not* valid in relation to those other values of y that – as it is precisely the case when y takes the value S – consist in the syntactic constants of x. Accordingly, it will be possible to hold firm without contradiction what is stated in §1, g and, at the same time, what is stated in §15.

Insofar as y takes the semantic value assigned to it in §§13–15, y is certainly a constant of x – but, as stated, not insofar as y is simply y, but insofar as y is a specific non-x: as such, y is a constant of the meaning 'totality of non-x'. This meaning is 'non-x' as a universal (an essence, or form) posited as to the totality of its individuations. (That is to say, the totality of non-x is the essence – 'non-x' – in its absolute or total individuation; in the same way, the totality of being is the essence – 'being', *qua* abstract universal, cf. Chapter 3, §18 – in its absolute or total individuation and determination.) An individuation is, however, a constant of a universal:[14] in the sense that the proposition: 'The totality of non-x includes this non-x' expresses a necessary and L-immediate connection.[15]

Accordingly, the positing of the meaning 'totality of non-x' – precisely insofar as this meaning is meaningful in this way – is the positing of the totality of the individuations of non-x. Therefore, if that specific non-x constituted by y is not posited – when the meaning 'totality of non-x' is posited – the totality of non-x is nevertheless posited. The contradiction is superseded by asserting that the totality in question is posited – if y is not posited – as to its form, and not as to its concrete content (or, equivalently, by asserting that the totality is posited in a formal way and not in a concrete one). The positing of that specific non-x constituted by y does not therefore add anything to the formal meaning as such, but only to its content (and, therefore, to the relation between form and content). That is to say, the positing of the semantic content constituted by that individuation of 'non-x' that is y does not add anything, in terms of form, to the meaning 'totality of non-x'. Since y is a constant of x insofar as it is a constant of 'totality of non-x' (since this latter meaning is a moment of the concrete meaning of x), it must then be stated, on the one hand, that positing x without positing y means positing a formal (i.e. abstractly formal) meaning – for, indeed, if a part of the definition of x is formal, x is a formal meaning – and, on the other hand, that the positing of y does not add anything, in terms of form, to the positing of x. (That a meaning has a formal value is said in many ways. A value φ_1 and a value φ_2 have been distinguished in Chapter 9, §12, b. Another value appears through the last observations: a meaning x is formal to the extent that, whether it realizes itself as φ_1 or φ_2, it is considered as being distinct from the individuations of its constants. It can certainly be asserted that x is also a formal meaning insofar as it is considered as distinct *from a part* of those individuations; but it is clear that, precisely as we affirmed above, y does not add anything in terms of form to x only if one considers that the formal value of x is determined by the fact that x is regarded as distinct, *simpliciter*, from the individuations of its constants – i.e. if one considers that this formal value is the semantic domain that is constituted when x is held distinct from the totality of the individuations of its constants. For if x is posited as a formal meaning insofar as it is distinct *from a part* of those individuations, then y adds something in terms of form: that is to say, the gradual positing of those individuations is the process of the elimination of that formal value. Furthermore, each of these formal values becomes an abstract form if – as it happens for instance in the case of the lack of positing of y – it is abstractly separated from the terms from which it is distinct. The formal meaning that is posited if x is posited without positing y is then an *abstractly* formal meaning. More generally, it is possible to assert that there are as many types of formal values of a meaning as there are types of constants of a meaning; accordingly, the definition of a specific type of formal value is determined by the definition of the type of constant from which the semantic content of that value distinguishes itself – for every meaning from which x distinguishes itself is a constant of x, and x has a formal value precisely insofar as it is distinct in this way. This is therefore the general condition for the constitution of a formal value.)

The *non-syntactic constants*[16] of x (or, more generally, of a meaning) are precisely those constants of x that, as it is precisely the case for y, do not determine the semantic domain constituted by the formal meaningfulness of x in terms of form, but in terms of the individuation of that form; as a result, the outcome of a positing of x that does not imply the positing of a non-syntactic constant of x is a positing of x *qua* abstractly formal meaning: x'.

The *syntactic constants* of x are instead those constants that determine the formal meaning of x: i.e. that determine x as to its very semantic form, in such a way that if one of those constants is not posited, nor is something like x; that is to say, x is not even posited as an abstractly formal meaning.

This may also be stated as follows: the syntactic constants are all those constants that do not stand as simple individuations of other constants. It should, however, be noted that since all the syntactic constants of x, *qua* meanings that are distinct from x, are instances of non-x – i.e. individuations of the syntactic constant 'non-x' – it must be stated that the syntactic constants of x are those individuations of the syntactic constant 'non-x' that stand as determinations of the semantic form of x; on the contrary, non-syntactic constants are those individuations, of 'non-x' and of the other syntactic constants, that are not able to perform that formal determination of x. (In other words: a constant is not non-syntactic because it is an individuation of another constant, but because it does not determine the form of x – and, therefore, it only stands as the individuation of another constant. Conversely, a constant of x is not an individuation of another constant of x for the reason that it does not determine the form of x.) Or, equivalently: the non-syntactic constants of a meaning x are all those meanings that, *in addition* to being individuations of the constant non-x (of x), are also individuations of another constant (or other constants) of x; the syntactic constants of x are instead all those meanings that, in determining the form of x, are only individuations of the constant non-x (this also being the case for the meaning 'non-x', which is itself a non-x).

b. It is now possible to solve the aporia outlined in §17. The outcome of positing x without positing a non-syntactic constant of x ($= y$) is the positing of x', which is the abstractly formal meaning of x. Affirming then that if y is not posited x' cannot be posited either means not realising that, were y posited as a constant of x', x' would no longer be x *qua* formal meaning, but x itself as a concrete meaning; that is to say – and more precisely – it would no longer be x *qua abstractly* formal meaning, but x *qua concretely* formal meaning.[17] If one therefore affirms that the outcome of positing x without positing y is x', it is not once again possible to regard x' as something that cannot be posited if y is not posited; as a result, the outcome of this abstract positing of x is not positionally null (cf. §15). The argument in §13 is therefore logically flawed (cf. §15) – and it causes an aporetic situation – insofar as y is regarded as a non-syntactic constant of x.

In instead considering that abstract positing of x, the abstractness of which is given by the lack of positing of the infinite semanteme (S) – this being precisely the case considered in §1, g – one is dealing with the lack of positing of a syntactic constant of x, i.e. with the lack of positing of a meaning that determines the form of x. This entails that the outcome of this abstract positing of x can no longer be x as a formal (i.e. abstractly formal) meaning (as in the previous case) – since, precisely, if the syntactic constant constituted by the infinite semanteme is not posited, the form of x is for this very reason not posited. The outcome of such an abstract positing of x can only consist of a meaning w that is *formally different* from x. Due to this necessary difference between the form of x and the form of w, it follows that if one affirms that if S is not posited w cannot be posited *either*, one no longer incurs in the logical fallacy that instead pertains to the affirmation that, if x is posited without the positing of the non-syntactic constant y, x' cannot be posited either. Positing y as a constant of x' is equivalent to positing y as a constant of x; or, more precisely, positing x' as something to which y pertains as a constant means positing x itself as a concrete meaning (whence there takes place the *repetition* and the logical fallacy described in §15). Instead, positing S as a constant of w *is not* the same as positing S as a constant of x; or: positing w as something to which S pertains as a constant does not mean positing x itself as a concrete meaning (since, precisely, w is a meaning that formally differs from x). Accordingly, as discussed, if one remarks in relation to w, which is purported to stand as the outcome of the abstract positing of x, that w cannot be posited either if S is not posited, one is not thereby considering something that is x itself as something other than x (i.e. the self-contradictory repetition of the previous case is not realized), but one considers something other than x precisely as something other: as that other of which it must be stated that, if S is not posited, it cannot itself be posited either. Furthermore, since any meaning that is posited as part of the outcome of this abstract positing of x formally differs from x, it must be concluded that the outcome of positing x without positing that syntactic constant of x (S), which is a syntactic constant of every meaning, is the positional annulment of every semantic horizon.

19. The persyntactic field

The theorem that affirms 'Every meaning is a constant of every other meaning' must therefore be understood in the sense that every meaning can be at least said to be a non-syntactic constant of every other meaning. The infinite semanteme is instead a constant of every meaning as a syntactic constant.

The meanings that count as syntactic constants of every meaning may be referred to as 'unlimited syntactic constants', or '*persyntactic constants*'; on the contrary, the meanings that count as syntactic constants of certain meanings, or only one, may be referred to as 'limited syntactic constants', or simply as syntactic constants.

From what we have said, it follows that all those meanings that count as syntactic constants of every meaning are such that the lack of their positing implies the positional annulment of every semantic horizon.[18]

Already from the standpoint reached at present by the exposition, it is indeed possible to observe that the infinite semanteme is not the only persyntactic constant: on the one hand, all the meanings that stand as syntactic constants of the infinite semanteme are persyntactic constants;[19] on the other hand, there are meanings – such as, for instance, 'being' (i.e. formal being) – that can be affirmed for themselves (or *also* for themselves) as persyntactic constants. For instance: every meaning or determination (including the meaning 'nothingness', cf. Chapter 4) *is*. That is to say, being is necessarily predicated of every positive element; it is immediately self-contradictory for any semantic positivity not to be. Furthermore, 'being' determines the form of every meaning in a distinctive way: in the sense that every semantic form is realized as a specific determination of being. (Strictly speaking, however, being determines – i.e. is a condition of the constitution of – *every* semantic aspect, and, therefore, it also determines the semantic form; it therefore stands as a constant to the utmost degree.) Accordingly, if the meaning 'being' is not posited, nothing can be posited; for if x is posited and being is not (in such a way that the being of x is therefore not posited either), x cannot be posited, and nor can any other meaning w, since being is a constant of every semantic content.[20] (Stating then that the term 'being' is meaningless can only have the following meaning: that if 'being' is abstractly separated from its determination, it no longer means anything – or, in thinking it, one does not think anything: cf. §12. Conversely, i.e. if that term is concretely in relation with its determination, if one does not think it one does not think anything, as mentioned.)

Referring to the semantic organism constituted by all the persyntactic constants as the '*persyntactic field*', we shall therefore assert that the opening – positing, presence – *of any* semantic horizon is essentially the opening of the persyntactic field. However, the present content may vary, whichever the *metabasis* upon which humans may embark or whatever destiny may be in store for them, if something is manifest, there is always the same content that manifests itself, as the immutable spectacle that accompanies the unsteady manifestations of being.

20. The presence and the awareness of the presence of the persyntactic field

What must first of all be clarified at this point is that while on the one hand it must be stated that no semantic horizon is present if the persyntactic field is not present, on the other hand we are not presently able to determine what all the persyntactic constants that belong to the persyntactic field are – or equivalently, in a different respect, past openings of the originary structure, which do not include the positing of one or more persyntactic constants, are immediately present. If one then keeps in mind the semantic nature of the constants in question, it is immediately present that pre-philosophical consciousness[21] is never able to rise to the positing of these constants, so that it appears that this positing is the task of philosophical knowledge.

Recalling here a distinction that we have already made, let us therefore state that the *presence* of a meaning is formally distinct from the *presence of the presence* of that meaning; therefore, the presence of the persyntactic field is formally distinct from the presence of the presence of that field. As a result of this formal distinction, it follows that everything that is known (everything that is present or posited) does not necessarily coincide with what is known to be known; that is to say, it is not self-contradictory to affirm that what is known to be known should constitute a more restricted horizon than what is known. Then: while *every* positional horizon necessarily constitutes the positing of the persyntactic field, not every positional horizon constitutes the positing of the positing of that field. The latter always stands before us – and it is therefore the immutable destiny of humans – as the essential content of presence, the essential clearing or epiphany; it only remains concealed to the extent that one does not realize that it is always before us, in the same way in which light only remains concealed to the extent that the eye loses itself in the colours – and while seeing that light in every colour, it does not even spare a glance for it. This is precisely the situation in which common or pre-philosophical consciousness finds itself: in that it is never aware of or it never posits the presence of the persyntactic field. What draws all the attention is the novelty of the content: the change, the surprise, the unexpected all have such a hold that does not grant any respite for a tranquil gaze upon the permanent persyntactic field. The novelty is responsible for the conspicuousness – what is conspicuous being precisely what common consciousness knows that it knows: what is permanent, despite being the very condition of the manifestation of what is conspicuous, does not instead arouse any interest, and while being constantly known, it is not known to be known. From Plato to Heidegger, philosophical knowledge has always spoken of a kind of distraction of the human from the essential content: what has instead been lacking, or altogether absent, is a demonstrative process on the basis of which it could be verified that *every* positional horizon is the positing of the same essential content, which therefore remains concealed as long as one does not come to the awareness of this essential presence. (It will therefore be possible to speak of a forgetting – and, therefore, of a recollection – in relation to the possibility of verifying the project of an Edenic human state, but, in the meantime, we must only speak of a distraction of humans from what is essential, and of their losing themselves in what is conspicuous. Common language, i.e. every type of non-philosophical language, is one of the principal forms of that distraction, because what is addressed by common language, or what is commonly spoken about, is always only an aspect – precisely, the most conspicuous one – of what also manifests itself in common consciousness.)

It therefore appears how, on the one hand, it must be stated that every positional horizon constitutes the positing of the persyntactic field, and how, on the other hand, the latter manifests itself as part of a process. As it is by now clear, this process or development does not pertain to the positing of the persyntactic field, but to the positing of the positing of the latter.

The originary structure – the originary opening of philosophizing – is precisely the site in which the presence of the persyntactic field comes to presence, or the site in which that essential content is testified to. This testimony, however, is such that while every positional horizon that is not the originary structure leaves beside itself its own negation as something not superseded – i.e. it is not able to ground itself, and realizes itself as an arbitrary form of assertion (in such a way that the persyntactic field itself is arbitrarily asserted) – the originary structure is instead the opening of the ground, in such a way that the semantic horizon, and therefore the persyntactic field, that is manifested here is necessarily held firm in opposition to its negation. The testimony of the persyntactic field is at the same time its safeguard. For instance, every positional horizon is a positing of the infinite semanteme, but the negation of the whole is only superseded as part of the originary structure: on the one hand, insofar as the immediate presence of the whole is posited, on the other hand, insofar as it is shown that the whole belongs to the essence of every meaning.

At the same time, however – as already mentioned – the originary structure is not presently able to determine what all the persyntactic constants that constitute the persyntactic field are. That is to say, it is not immediately contradictory to project, on the one hand, an extension of the analysis, and, on the other hand, a mediational process, which would lead to the verification of new persyntactic constants. This means that it is not immediately self-contradictory to project that the set of meanings, which are presently known to be persyntactic constants, should not be all the persyntactic constants. That is to say, it is not immediately self-contradictory to project that, in relation to a specific domain of the persyntactic field, the originary structure should find itself in the same situation in which common consciousness finds itself in relation to the whole field: i.e. that it knows without knowing that it knows, or that it is aware of certain meanings without knowing that it is aware of them, whereby there exists the possibility of projecting a logical development that would lead to a verification of all the persyntactic constants. (That development is however something immediately present to the extent that a multiplicity of past acts of positing of the originary structure is immediately present, in which one or more persyntactic constants were not verified.) This verification, let us reiterate, does not consist in the positing of a meaning that the positional horizon *simpliciter* did not include, but one that is a verification of the inclusion of that meaning in every positional horizon. It is clear that this property of the persyntactic constants is not enjoyed by the non-syntactic constants and by the limited syntactic ones, which can not only arise as part of the positional horizon as to the verification of their being already included in it (as it is also the case for the persyntactic constants) but also as to their positing or presence *simpliciter* (something that – let us repeat – cannot be the case for the persyntactic constants).

21. Clarification

In every pre-philosophical positional horizon, the presence of the persyntactic field consists in the presence of a system of essential implications. For instance, every meaning, which is posited as part of that horizon, is posited as part of its essential implication of the meaning 'being'; that is to say, the positing of every meaning is the positing of a positivity ('being') that is determined, i.e. it is the positing of the essential implication that obtains between a determinacy and the positivity of that determinacy. If that essential implication were not posited, but there only existed a simple co-presence of the meanings that constitute the pre-philosophical positional horizon under consideration and of that persyntactic constant, there would be no opening of that horizon: for, as already repeatedly stated, it is not enough to posit the constant of a meaning for the latter to be posited, but it is necessary for this meaning to be posited in its essentially implying its constants.

It is thus clear that the (any) pre-philosophical positional horizon under consideration, *qua* positing of the persyntactic field, consists in the positing of a system of essential implications: not only to the extent that the present content includes the implications between the meanings of that horizon and those terms of the persyntactic field that *L-immediately* stand as constants of those meanings, but also to the extent that the present content includes the implications to those terms of the persyntactic field (such as, for instance, the infinite sememe) that stand as constants of the meanings under consideration *in an L-mediated way*. In both cases, however, the presence of the essential implication is not the presence of the latter *qua essential implication*; or, equivalently: the persyntactic field is present, but it is not present *qua persyntactic field*. In order for that essential implication to be present *as such* – i.e. in order for the essential character of that implication to be seen as such – the opening of the originary structure is indeed necessarily required. Insofar as the latter constitutes the very structuring of immediacy, it is only as part of this structuring that every immediate implication – thus including those immediate implications to the persyntactic constants – can be posited *as such*: in the same way in which it is while being grounded in that structuring that it is possible to validate every mediation, thus including those mediational implications to the persyntactic constants.

22. Aporia: There can be no opening of any non-philosophical positional horizon

Except that the positing of the persyntactic field, which is realized with the opening of the originary structure, consists in the verification of a structure of constants of that very persyntactic field: the originary opening of philosophizing, precisely to the extent that it posits the persyntactic field *as such* determines it according to a structure of constants; the philosophical discourse concerning the essential content, precisely to the extent that it attests it as such, endows it with a set of determinations that essentially pertain to that essential content, and that therefore stand as constants of the latter. These are furthermore constants that, precisely by virtue of their meaning, cannot be classified as non-syntactic – or *hyposyntactic* – constants, i.e. they cannot be regarded as simple individuations of persyntactic constants (cf. footnote 3 in §18, a), for, as stated, they count as a determining of the persyntactic field carried out by that philosophizing. Hence there arises an aporia of significant interest, which may be presented as follows.

While a hyposyntactic constant of a persyntactic constant is not in turn a persyntactic constant, on the basis of what has been stated in §§13–18, every non-hyposyntactic constant of any persyntactic constant is instead in turn a persyntactic constant. The originary opening of philosophizing, *qua* essential determination of the persyntactic field (i.e. *qua* structure of non-hyposyntactic constants of the persyntactic field), therefore, itself belongs to the persyntactic field. This entails that if a semantic horizon is posited, the originary structure is *eo ipso* posited; that is to say, there can be no opening of a positional horizon other than the one constituted by the originary structure. Furthermore, affirming that the possibility of verifying new persyntactic constants (in the sense indicated in §20) pertains to the development of philosophizing entails that the originary is posited without the positing of certain persyntactic constants (precisely, those constituted by the development of the essential determining of the persyntactic field carried out by that philosophizing); as a result, it will have to be concluded that such a development of the originary is impossible. If a semantic horizon is posited, the originary structure is necessarily posited, and so is the verification of all the persyntactic constants. There exists no pre-philosophical positional horizon; or, equivalently, if a consciousness exists, it exists as an absolute awareness of the essential content. It is clear that the aporetic character of this conclusion consists in the fact that, on the contrary, the totality of the immediate attests, on the one hand, to the opening of pre-philosophical positional horizons and, on the other hand, to the processual character of the verification of the persyntactic constants. Once again, the aporia is constituted as a contradiction between logos and experience.

Let us illustrate by way of example the general formulation of the aporia presented above. *First example*. In the (synthetic *a priori*) proposition: 'The infinite semanteme is a persyntactic constant', the predicate necessarily pertains to the subject (as previously demonstrated), i.e. it counts as a constant of the subject (in a mediated way). Since this constant is – manifestly – not hyposyntactic, it follows that the meaning constituted by this constant is itself such that, were it not posited, nothing would be posited; that is to say, the meaning 'persyntactic constant' is itself a persyntactic constant. It is clear that also – and, if one may say, all the more so – the mediational process that leads to the proposition: 'The infinite semanteme is a persyntactic constant' belongs to the persyntactic field, and, therefore, so does the originary structure, as the ground of that mediation. *Second example*. Given that the meaning 'being' belongs to the persyntactic field, this field does not only include the *identity* (or non-contradictoriness) of being, but also the *L-immediacy* of that identity. In other words, it is not only the being of being – the self-identity of being – that is a persyntactic constant, but also the L-immediacy of that identity, or its being known for itself; in the proposition: 'The identity is L-immediately known', the predicate, *qua* (non-hyposyntactic) constant of a (non-hyposyntactic) constant of a persyntactic constant, is itself a persyntactic constant.

Returning to the general formulation of the aporia: the philosophical discourse concerning the persyntactic field consists in the attestation of non-hyposyntactic constants of that field, and, therefore, it itself belongs to the persyntactic field.

23. Solution of the aporia: Metasyntactic constants

The aporia is superseded by introducing a second type of non-syntactic constants, in addition to the hyposyntactic ones: i.e. by introducing that type of constants that, in accordance with their semantic function, may be referred to as '*metasyntactic constants*'. (We do not however intend to thereby exhaust the typology of non-syntactic constants.) In general: in the same way in which the hyposyntactic constants of a meaning do not add anything to the form (or syntax) of that meaning, but they are individuations of the syntactic form, i.e. they constitute its concrete content, so the metasyntactic constants of a meaning do not add anything to the syntactic form of that meaning, but they take the syntactic form itself (and the related hyposyntactic content) as content, thus constituting themselves as the form of the syntactic form, i.e. as a metasyntactic form. In the specific case in question: the philosophical comprehension of the persyntactic field certainly does not consist in the attestation of the hyposyntactic constants of that field, but nor does it consist in a syntactic extension of the latter – indeed, the constants of the field, attested by that philosophical comprehension (or in the attestation of which that comprehension consists), take that field as content, thus constituting themselves as the metasyntactic form of that field. This clearly appears in comparing propositions of the type: 'The whole is surpassed by nothing', 'Being is not non-being' with propositions of the type: 'The whole is a persyntactic constant', 'The non-contradictoriness of being is immediately known'. In the propositions of the first type, the predicate enters into the constitution of the meaning of the subject, whereas in the propositions of the second type the predicate is a property that pertains to the meaning (in which the subject consists) as already constituted. In the first case, the predication is the constitution of the meaning, in the second case it is a determination of an already constituted meaning. While this determination does not add anything to the syntax of that meaning, it should be noted that it is, however, necessarily predicated of the latter, in such a way that, although it is not a syntactic constant of that meaning, it has, however, a constant value – and since it cannot be regarded as a hyposyntactic constant, it must be a different type of non-syntactic constant.

It appears, from what we have said, that if a metasyntactic constant of a persyntactic constant (or, more generally, of the persyntactic field) is not posited, the outcome of the ensuing abstract positing of that persyntactic constant will be the positing of that contradictory of that persyntactic constant that consists in the very *abstract matter* of that constant: an abstract matter that is the very syntax or the very abstractly posited formal meaningfulness of that persyntactic constant. In more detail: let x be a meaning that counts as a persyntactic constant, y a hyposyntactic constant of x, and k a metasyntactic constant of x. As already established, if x is posited without the positing of y, the outcome of this abstract positing of x is a positing of x as an abstractly formal meaning. If x is posited without the positing of k, the syntax of x is likewise posited, i.e. the outcome of the abstract positing of x consists in the positing of the syntax of x, which, however, once again counts as an abstract syntax. While, however, in the case of the positional *steresis* of y, the syntax of x stands as an abstract formal element, in the case of the positional *steresis* of k the syntax of x stands instead as an abstract material element – the formal character consisting here in the metasyntactic dimension of x (that is to say: the form of x itself stands as an abstract matter in relation to the metasyntactic form of x). In both cases, the outcome of the abstract positing of x is the positing of the formal meaningfulness (or syntax) of x – a meaningfulness, however, which is no longer a formal meaningfulness *qua* concretely distinct from the hyposyntax and from the metasyntax of x (i.e. *qua* posited as part of its concrete implication of these two semantic dimensions), and a meaningfulness that therefore counts as an *abstract* formal meaningfulness. It is in any case the persistence of the form of x that prevents the outcome of the positional *steresis* of y or k from being an absolute annulment of the positional horizon.

If, therefore, a metasyntactic constant of the persyntactic field is not posited, the outcome of the abstract positing of that field is not an absolute positional annulment but the opening of a contradiction. This is the contradiction that consists in positing the formal meaningfulness or syntax of the persyntactic field without positing that to which that formal meaningfulness refers: precisely, the persyntactic field, but in its concrete implication of the domain of its metasyntactic constants – an implication as part of which the formal meaningfulness of that field is no longer an abstract matter, but the concrete matter of the metasyntactic dimension.

What constitutes a persyntactic constant is therefore neither x, as a concretely formal meaning (i.e. as concretely distinct from the hyposyntax and from the metasyntax), nor x, as an abstractly formal meaning, but x, as what is shared by both the concrete form and the abstract one: i.e. $\hat{x}$ (in the same way in which $\hat{S}$ is what is shared by the concrete form of S and by the abstract one; cf. Chapter 9, §8, e). It is indeed $\hat{x}$ – namely, *the formal meaning as such* (i.e. as distinct from its concreteness and from its abstractness) – what is posited both in case a hyposyntactic or metasyntactic constant is not posited (in which case $\hat{x}$ is realized as an abstract form – or, in relation to the lack of positing of a metasyntactic constant, as an abstract matter) and in case those constants are posited (in which case $\hat{x}$ is realized as a concrete form or matter). (That is to say, a persyntactic constant is only real insofar as it constitutes itself either as an abstract form or as a concrete one.)

It should furthermore be noted that (1) while the positional *steresis* of hyposyntactic and metasyntactic constants is the opening of an abstract syntax (and, therefore, of a contradiction), the abstract character of that syntax is in any case different according to whether it is determined by a positional *steresis* of the hyposyntax or a positional *steresis* of the metasyntax – a syntactic identity nevertheless underlying that difference in the abstract character; (2) the positional *steresis* of any metasyntactic element entails that not only the syntactic level but also the hyposyntactic one should stand as an abstract semantic matter – and, conversely, the positional *steresis* of any hyposyntactic element entails that not only the syntactic level, but also the metasyntactic one should stand as an abstract semantic form.

24. Determination of the meaning of the solution of the aporia carried out in the last section

The aporia presented in §22 is therefore solved through the verification of the conditions of possibility of the opening of non-philosophical positional horizons. It should therefore be observed, for what concerns the meaning and therefore the value of the superseding of that aporia, that this superseding did not consist in showing that the proposition: 'The outcome of the positional *steresis* of a metasyntactic constant of the persyntactic field is an absolute positional annulment' is self-contradictory, but it consisted in showing that the proposition: 'The outcome of the positional *steresis* of a metasyntactic constant of the persyntactic field is not an absolute positional annulment' is not self-contradictory. The verification of this non-contradictoriness has been achieved through the positing of the distinction between syntactic and metasyntactic constants. As a result of this distinction, that absolute positional annulment is not necessary (i.e. its negation is not self-contradictory), in such a way that the *immediate presence* (or experience) of both pre-philosophical positional horizons and of a processual character in the verification of the metasyntactic constants of the persyntactic field – an immediate presence that attests that the positional *steresis* of the metasyntactic elements has not entailed an absolute positional annulment – is not in contradiction with a logical structure that must necessarily be held firm. The aporia is thus superseded. At the same time, however, while the possibility of verifying the self-contradictoriness of the first of the two propositions formulated above is not immediately excluded, it is also not immediately self-contradictory – as long as that verification is not realized – to *project* that the positional *steresis* of any metasyntactic constant of the persyntactic field should imply an absolute positional annulment.

This determination of the meaning of the superseding of the aporia under consideration here is also valid in relation to the superseding of the aporia that has been superseded through the introduction of the hyposyntactic constants (cf. §§13–18). We have indeed certainly shown that it is self-contradictory to affirm: '*If* the outcome of the abstract positing of x, in which the hyposyntactic constant y is not posited, is x', x' cannot stand as that outcome either, because y is also a constant of x''' (cf. §15); however, we have not thereby shown that it is self-contradictory to suppose *that* the outcome of the abstract positing of x should be positionally null (i.e. we have not shown that the proposition: 'The positional *steresis* of a hyposyntactic constant of the persyntactic field implies an absolute positional annulment' is self-contradictory). Insofar as experience attests that the outcome of that abstract positing is x', it is certainly possible to show that it is self-contradictory to claim that the outcome cannot be x' either, but it is nevertheless immediately non-contradictory to *project* that a positional *steresis* of y should imply an absolute positional annulment.

25. Prospective reference

We have not thereby determined in any way *which* the metasyntactic constants of the persyntactic field are; accordingly, the task that is incumbent upon philosophical knowledge ('incumbent' because by not fulfilling it one remains in a contradiction) is to concretely determine on the one hand the elements of the persyntactic field, and on the other hand the metasyntactic constants of that field.

26. Notes

a. In affirming that every positional horizon constitutes an opening of the persyntactic field, one supports what is probably the only correct form of 'innatism' or 'apriorism'. The 'a priori' may be defined here as that semantic element that is necessarily posited with the positing of any semantic content – what is new here consisting, however, in the way in which this definition has been obtained, and not in the definition as such.

b. Insofar as the infinite semanteme is an element of the persyntactic field (and it is in fact the all-encompassing element or the very form of that field), and insofar as every meaning is a constant of the infinite semanteme, every meaning must be said to be either a hyposyntactic, a syntactic or a metasyntactic constant of the persyntactic field.

11

The abstract (Γ_a) (and concrete) concept of the originary as the originary problem and contradiction

1. General overview of the chapter

a. In the first part of this chapter (§§2–14), we are going to present the fundamental propositions that express the structuring of the originary from the standpoint of the concept Γ_a (cf. Chapter 2, §26), i.e. the propositions that express that structuring *qua* structuring of Γ_a. In this first part of the chapter, the exposition is therefore an exposition *of the abstract concept* of that abstract constituted by the originary structure insofar as this is *not* structured as an L-immediate affirmation (cf. Chapter 13) of a positive that does not belong to the totality of the Ph-immediate (i.e. insofar as that structure does not include this affirmation). An ideal exposition of the originary should certainly consist in the exposition of all the abstract concepts of the abstract (i.e. – cf. Chapter 9, §4 –all the negations of the originary): in this case, however, we are considering a distinctive type of abstract concept of the abstract. This distinctive character is indeed due to the fact that the difference between the concrete (the originary structure) and this abstract concept is as *reduced* as only having to posit the L-immediacy of the surpassing of the totality of the Ph-immediate in its concrete semantic value in order for that abstract concept to be realized as the concrete itself (in such a way that the exposition of Γ_a takes advantage of all the elements that the exposition of the concrete has secured up to this point, except for the positing of that L-immediacy, which has so far only been anticipated); at the same time, however, since the L-immediacy of the surpassing of the totality of the Ph-immediate constitutes the aspect of the originary that *most eludes* the reflection of philosophy – and, therefore, in this respect that 'reduced' difference that we have just mentioned is reduced to the distance that is hardest for that reflection to surmount – the distinctive character of Γ_a is due to the distinctive character of that aspect of the originary (i.e. the L-immediacy of the affirmation of a non-Ph-immediate positive) that from the standpoint of the present structure of the originary is the only one missing from Γ_a.

Another reason for a schematic exposition of the concept Γ_a, however, is the wish to present its authentic configuration: the historical realization of that concept, which can be found in contemporary thinking (cf. Chapter 1, §3), leaving some fundamental elements of that concept implicit. We indeed assert that the authentic structuring of the concept Γ_a – namely, of that opening of the originary in accordance with which the metaphysical *categorem* is a *project*, or a possibility, i.e. in accordance with which the surpassing of the Ph-immediate by a positive is a project – includes, or is structured as, a (categorical) L-immediate affirmation of the fact that a positive surpasses the totality of the Ph-immediate (cf. §9). This is an assertion that is not self-contradictory to the extent that we are going to show that the sense in which the concept Γ_a is a (categorical) *L-immediate affirmation* of the fact that a positive surpasses the totality of the Ph-immediate is not the same sense in which this surpassing is only a *project*; in fact, we are going to show how, precisely because the originary is constituted as such a projecting, the originary must realize itself as that L-immediate affirmation. (It is therefore clear that, with respect to that structuring of the originary that does not even include that L-immediate affirmation, regarded as to the value that pertains to it *qua* element of the concept Γ_a, the concept Γ_a already stands as the concrete.)

b. In the second part of the chapter (§15), the exposition of Γ_a is completed by a group of observations that may be regarded as an appendix of Chapter 10, developed from the standpoint of Γ_a.

c. In the third part of the chapter (§§16–18), in one respect we are going to carry out the superseding of Γ_a in and through the concrete concept of the originary – even if by means of an anticipation – and in a different respect we are going to posit in a determinate way the L-immediacy of the proposition: 'The immediately present constants of S are not the totality of the constants of S'; that is to say, we are going to exhibit the persistence in the concrete structuring of the originary of a logical configuration that, as we shall verify (§7), already pertains to the structuring of the originary constituted by Γ_a (we are indeed going to show that the way in which that L-immediacy is posited is, formally, the same in which that L-immediacy is posited in Γ_a). This verification constitutes the very superseding of the abstract concept Γ_a, in and through the concrete concept of the originary, as the originary problem and contradiction.

From §2 to §15, the discussion is carried out from the standpoint of the concept Γ_a, and the standpoint of the concrete is always expressed by (sets of) propositions in square brackets. This does not mean that all other propositions can *only* be affirmed from the standpoint of Γ_a – for, in fact, it must be stated that, except for the propositional structure that posits as a *project* the affirmation of a positive element that does not belong to the totality of the Ph-immediate, all the other propositions of Γ_a are also retained as part of the concrete structuring of the originary, even though they realize themselves according to a different form (precisely, the one determined by the superseding of Γ_a); rather it means that the propositions in square brackets can *only* be formulated from the standpoint of the concrete.[1]

2. Overview of §§3–14

In the following, we are going to verify that the originary structure *L-immediately* manifests itself as a *C*-contradiction. This is the case even if, in a different respect – but the two respects cannot be separated – the originary structure presents itself as a *possible* contradiction, i.e. as a contradiction that is not immediately attested, or that immediately [i.e. from the standpoint of the abstract structuring of the originary constituted by Γ_a) manifests itself as something only projected. If, indeed, the difference between the whole and the totality of the immediate is a project, it must be stated that the fact that the positing of the whole is a formal positing is only a project (since, precisely, it is not immediately contradictory to affirm that the absolute semantic matter is the totality of the immediate), and therefore so is the fact that the positing of the whole, in accordance with which the originary is structured, only consists of an *intention* to posit the whole – due to the theorem that affirms that every meaning is a constant of every other meaning – and therefore so is the fact that the originary constitutes a realization of the C-contradiction. At the same time, however – let us reiterate – it is precisely because the C-contradiction is thus *projected* (i.e. it is a possible contradiction) that, as we shall see, the originary L-immediately manifests itself as a C-contradiction (more precisely: as a C-contradiction that differs from the projected one).

In order to clarify what we have stated above, let us repeat that, in affirming that the originary is a possible contradiction and an immediate one, we do not here intend to say, respectively, that the originary can become a contradiction after having been non-contradictory (in such a way that the contradiction is 'possible' because at first *it does not obtain*), and that the originary is a contradiction from that first moment (in such a way that an 'immediate' contradiction would only mean that there exists no such first moment in which the originary is not a contradiction). The originary is instead a possible contradiction in the sense that the contradiction of the originary is not L-immediately attested, i.e. it is not immediately known that the realization of the originary as such is the opening of a contradiction; what is not immediately known here is not a contradiction that is supposed to arise or that would have not yet determined the originary, but one that determines the originary as such, or as soon as the latter is such – i.e. it is a contradiction that, if attested, is attested as something that *was* before having been *known*. 'Possible contradiction' does not therefore mean that what is possible is the contradiction, but that what is possible (what can be projected, what is not L-immediate) is the recognition of the contradiction. 'Immediate contradiction' means that it is L-immediately known that the originary is a contradiction.[2]

3. The project of being and the project of immediate being

In the same way in which the meaning 'being' is not immediately present in its being exhausted by the totality of immediate being, so the meaning 'totality of immediate being' is not immediately present in its being exhausted by all those determinations that, taken as a whole, are said to constitute the totality of the immediate. That is to say, in the same way in which it is not immediately contradictory to *project* that being should surpass the totality of immediate being (i.e. in the same way in which the contradictoriness of this project cannot be attested as part of the present structuring of the originary), so it is not immediately contradictory to *project* that the totality of the immediate should be determined in a different way from the one that pertains to it as a matter of fact: namely, that this totality should come to include different determinations from the ones that it includes as a matter of fact.

This twofold form of projecting coincides with the very originary availability of the meanings 'being' and 'totality of the immediate' for a further determination – or, equivalently, it constitutes their originary *freeing* from their factual determination. (This opening of the projected horizons may be regarded as the originary manifestation of 'freedom'.) This availability and freeing – let us repeat – are afforded by the *absence* from the originary plane of the self-contradictoriness of both the concept of a being that does not belong to the totality of the immediate and of the concept of a different determination of this totality. [In Chapter 10, §4, we have established the non-contradictoriness of that first concept independently *of the way* in which this is posited, and therefore also to the extent that it is the content of a *project*. Analogous observations may also be made in relation to that other concept.]

The project of the horizon constituted by the totality of that different or additional determination of the totality of the immediate, in its unity with the factual determination of this totality, constitutes 'possible experience' itself. The other projected horizon is projected as something additional to that possible experience. Being, therefore, originarily frees itself from possible experience, in the indicated sense.

It should furthermore be observed that the distinction between a being that would lie beyond possible experience and a being that would not yet belong to the factual determination of the immediate (and that would therefore belong to possible experience) is itself something projected or problematic: precisely because from the standpoint of present immediacy it is not possible to exclude that the factual determination of the immediate should constitute the whole. (We shall soon see, however, in what sense this latter affirmation is to be amended.)

The originary structure, therefore, consists of an originary problematicity.

4. The structure of the project

a. Something that does not belong to the totality of the immediate – namely, the content of those projected horizons – cannot be affirmed for the reason that it is immediately present; as a result, its negation is not immediately excluded. At the same time, however, this negation in turn leaves beside itself that affirmation – this distinctive relation of negation and affirmation precisely constituting the project – to the extent that the concept of a positive that is not immediately present is not immediately contradictory.

Kant's Transcendental Dialectic has certainly the greatest merits in relation to the verification of the speculative structure of the project of a horizon that surpasses possible experience. The problematicity of the project is, however, here compromised by the results of the Analytic. Indeed, the meta-empirical horizon (i.e. that which, as projected, lies beyond possible experience), of which the transcendental ideas constitute a determination, is not something whose nullity or positivity *can* be verified, since this verification is made *impossible* by the doctrine of the empirical use of the categories – whence the problematicity of what is projected acquires a different meaning in Kant's text. Concerning the empirical use of the categories, it should suffice here to observe, on the one hand, that this concept is determined by the epistemological framework of Kant's *Critique*, and, on the other hand, that a verification of that use represents in any case – from a logical point of view – an additional moment to the one of the positing of the immediate and of the co-implied positing of what is other than the immediate: this otherness being precisely problematic in an altogether undetermined sense.

b. In this sense, the alternative that constitutes the originary problematicity may be regarded as a twofold one: namely, on the one hand, as the possibility of determining what is other than the immediate – as being or as nothing – and, on the other hand, as the possibility (of a Kantian type) of the verification of the impossibility of any determination of that otherness.

c. It should, however, be observed that even if one were to establish the impossibility of determining that otherness, the validity of the alternative that constitutes this determination would in any case be held firm: namely, the fact that the otherness is either being or nothing. That is to say, either it is possible to determine this otherness or it is not; if one were to verify that the determination itself is impossible, the content of the determination would in any case be either being or nothing.

d. *Contra* this latter affirmation, it is possible to object that, as also observed by Kant, two contradictory propositions can both be false if the subject of these propositions is a self-contradictory concept. Accordingly, it is possible to verify the impossibility of resolving the alternative discussed above precisely by showing that the subject of the two contradictory propositions that constitute that alternative is a self-contradictory concept. In this way, the verification of the impossibility of resolving the alternative would not allow the latter to be retained; that is to say, it is not possible to state that, even if one were to verify that it is impossible to determine whether what is other than the totality of the immediate is being or nothing, it would nevertheless remain true that this other is either being or nothing.

Let us respond in the following way.

The verification of the self-contradictoriness of the subject, or predicate, of a proposition may be of two types:

1. The subject (or the predicate, or both) is self-contradictory because it constitutes a realization of the C-(self-)contradiction; that is to say, the positing of the subject is not the positing of all its constants;
2. The subject (or the predicate, or both) is self-contradictory because it consists in an explicit affirmation of the identity of two mutually contradictory terms – this explicit affirmation being absent in the first case, as part of which the self-contradictoriness is *undergone* due to the inability to concretely posit what is posited as a matter of fact.

The superseding of the first type of self-contradictoriness consists in the very concrete positing of the subject of the proposition; the superseding of the second type of self-contradictoriness consists in the superseding of the subject of the proposition. In the first case, that superseding consists in the concrete positing of the proposition; in the second case, that superseding consists in the superseding of the proposition.

Therefore, in relation to the two mutually contradictory propositions that constitute the alternative discussed above, in the first of the two indicated cases the superseding of the self-contradictoriness of the terms of those propositions consists (at least) in the authentic positing of the alternative ('at least': for the positing of the constants of the subject may constitute the very resolution of the alternative, should it be verified that the predicate of one of the two propositions has precisely the value of being a constant of the subject); in the second case, the superseding of the self-contradictoriness of the terms of those propositions consists in a positing of the impossibility of resolving the alternative that is such that it precisely realizes itself by superseding the alternative. The objection formulated at the beginning of this point d refers to this second case.[3]

Holding firm the clarification indicated above, let us then assert that the articulation of that alternative can be of two types, depending on whether the relation of the totality of the immediate to its other is included, i.e. it constitutes the subject of each of the two propositions that constitute the alternative, or whether this relation is given by the synthesis between the subject and the predicate of each of those propositions. In the first case, one obtains propositions of the type: 'The other than the totality of the immediate is', 'The other than the totality of the immediate is not'; in the second case, one obtains propositions of the type: 'The totality of the immediate is not the whole', 'The totality of the immediate is the whole'.

Verifying the self-contradictoriness of the subject of the propositions of the first type, far from verifying the impossibility of the resolution of the alternative, precisely means resolving the aporia: i.e. resolving it through the categorical positing of the identity between the whole and the totality of the immediate, since it would precisely be verified that the concept of an 'other than the totality of the immediate' is self-contradictory. Concerning the propositions of the second type, the very project of a verification of the self-contradictoriness of the subject is instead immediately self-contradictory,[4] for this subject is the originary structure itself.

Furthermore, the project of the verification of the self-contradictoriness of the predicates ('is', 'is not') of the first type of propositions is immediately self-contradictory. For, indeed, on the one hand, insofar as the propositions 'Being *is* being' and 'Being *is not* non-being' are L-immediate, projecting the self-contradictoriness of the meanings 'is' and 'is not' is equivalent to projecting the self-contradictoriness of the principle of identity and non-contradiction.[5] In a different respect, 'being' – the positivity of the immediately present content – is itself an immediately present content, and, like every other content of this type, it is immediately present as something non-contradictory; accordingly, projecting that, at a later time, 'being' should be attested as something self-contradictory is in contradiction with the immediately present content. It is effectively the case that 'being', which is immediately present in its non-contradictoriness, is the being of the present content (i.e. the being of the experienced reality), in such a way that it is possible to project that 'the being of a content that is not present' should be a self-contradictory meaning; in this case, however, what is projected is not the self-contradictoriness of the meaning 'being' *as such* – it should be noted that here 'being' is formal being, whereas, in the proposition: 'being is being', 'being' is the concrete universal – for otherwise the 'being' of the experienced reality, too, would have to be self-contradictory, but what is projected is the self-contradictoriness *of the reference* of that (non-contradictory) 'being' to a content that is not present; that is to say, what is projected is the resolution of the alternative discussed above. (The same should be stated in relation to the meaning 'is not': if this red extension is immediately present, it is immediately present that 'this white extension' *is not*,[6] and this nullity is immediately present as something non-contradictory, in such a way that the project for the meaning 'nothingness' to be verified as something self-contradictory is also in contradiction with the Ph-immediate content. It is effectively the case that the meaning 'nothingness' is self-contradictory in the sense established in Chapter 4, but it is not self-contradictory if it is regarded as a *moment* – the 'nothingness-moment' – of that self-contradictoriness. If nothingness is predicated of a term – 'this white extension', 'other than the totality of the immediate' – this nothingness is precisely predicated as that nothingness-moment. It is here clear that if nothingness is predicated of that other than the totality of the immediate for the reason that this 'other than the immediate' is a self-contradictory concept, the latter, too, would be a mode of the positive signification of nothingness.)

Lastly, the project of a verification of the self-contradictoriness of the predicate ('whole') of the second type of propositions indicated above is self-contradictory, insofar as the whole essentially belongs to the originary meaning of the non-contradictoriness of being (since being that is not non-being is not this or that being, but *every* being, the *whole* of being), and it is therefore immediately self-contradictory to project the verification of the self-contradictoriness of this originary non-contradictoriness. While the originary structure constitutes the originary opening of the (*C*-)contradiction, it constitutes at the same time the originary structuring of the non-contradictoriness of being (and it is precisely due to the way in which that structuring is constituted that it is the originary opening of the *C*-contradiction). It is therefore immediately self-contradictory to project a verification of the self-contradictoriness of that structuring and of the semantic moments that are structured as part of it.

5. The originary structure *qua* originary contradiction

a. The horizon as part of which *being* originarily frees itself from possible experience (cf. §3) is something that can be verified – in an additional moment relative to the one constituted by present immediacy – both as a *positive* horizon and as the horizon of *nothingness*. It originarily consists of this ambivalence or alternative, and it is therefore a projected horizon. A project is something twofold in an essential way, for the thesis is *possible* (= immediately non-contradictory) only to the extent that the antithesis, too, is *possible*.

It is then precisely this holding before oneself the thesis as much as the antithesis as something possible that constitutes a being in contradiction: precisely because *both* sides of the alternative are posited as possible, while only *one of the two* is 'truly' possible, and the other one is impossible – since the two sides stand as mutually contradictory terms.

The contradiction of projecting may also be expressed in this other way: insofar as the *other* than possible experience is either being or nothing – i.e. insofar as it cannot be both being and nothing – that projecting either entails that being is posited as nothing or that nothingness is posited as being: precisely because that projecting allows both the side as part of which that *other* is posited as being, and the side as part of which that *other* is posited as nothing, to stand as something possible. The moment of projecting is that in which one is not able to determine *which of these two sides* is the one *simpliciter* possible. Due to the inability to carry out this determination, both sides are regarded as something possible (= non-contradictory): namely, both the one that is impossible and the one that is necessary.

b. At the same time, however, the moment in which one is able to establish which of the two sides is the 'truly' or '*simpliciter*' possible one is the very moment in which the moment of projecting is already *surpassed*. One is indeed able to establish that one of the two sides – and not the other one – is the 'truly' possible side only insofar as one shows that the other side constitutes an inherent contradiction: whence the remaining side is the one that must *necessarily* be accepted in order not to fall into contradiction. The moment in which one is able to establish which of the two sides is the 'truly' possible one is therefore the moment in which it is verified which of the two sides *was* 'truly' possible: this side *was* 'truly' possible precisely as part of that moment in which it was not known which of the two sides was the truly possible one; for, presently – i.e. as part of this new moment – it is no longer a simple possibility, but, as discussed, a *necessity*. In the meantime, however, as long as one remains as part of the moment of projecting, both sides are and must be considered in the same way – whereby something that is an impossibility is instead considered as something possible (or something that is an inherent contradiction is considered as something that is instead non-contradictory).

c. This contradiction is originary, or immediately attested, because it is attested on the basis of the analysis of the immediate semantic structure of the originary projecting.

6. Note

a. The originary is also a contradiction insofar as it realizes itself as the project of a possible experience or immediacy: i.e. as the project for the totality of the immediate to be determined or individuated in a different way from the one that pertains to it as a matter of fact. For, indeed, the factual determinations of the totality of the immediate count *either* as exhaustive determinations of the meaning 'totality of the immediate' *or* as determinations that afford a further determination or individuation of that meaning. That projecting instead regards both of those sides as being immediately non-contradictory, and it therefore posits the one of the two that is a self-contradictoriness as a non-contradictoriness – and, conversely, the one of the two that is a non-contradictoriness as a (projected) self-contradictoriness.

In general, however, *every* projecting – every positing of a problem, every question – is a form of being in contradiction: precisely because one confers the same value on the two sides of the project.

b. The positing *of any* immediately present meaning is a form of projecting. For instance, the positing or the presence of this red is at the same the *project* for the meaning 'red', of which this red is a factual determination, to be further determined with respect to this factual existence. Projecting, therefore, belongs to the structure of the *universality* of meaning, since this universality precisely consists in the freeing of a meaning from its factual determination, thus becoming available for a further determination (= individuation) – and, in the last instance, for the totality of determinations. Attesting that a meaning is not absolutely exhausted or contained by its individuation – i.e. that a negation of that exhausting is not immediately contradictory – means projecting the horizon of the totality of the further individuations of this meaning: this horizon precisely consisting in the repose or domain in which thinking expands, insofar as it negates that absolute exhausting.[7] Insofar as projecting belongs to the structure of universality, universality is therefore itself a form of being in contradiction, in the indicated sense.

c. It is therefore clear that a project is immediately non-contradictory in the sense that, from the standpoint of immediacy, one is not able to establish the self-contradictoriness of either side of the project – although it is precisely this inability to carry out that determination that entails that a project consists in a form of being in contradiction. The originary is therefore in contradiction precisely because its projecting is not immediately or originarily contradictory: were the contradictoriness of that projecting immediately posited – i.e. were it immediately posited which of the two sides of the project is self-contradictory – the problematic element would originarily be superseded in and by the categorical one, and, in this respect, the originary would not be in contradiction.

7. The meaning of the originary contradiction

As we have verified, projecting that being surpasses possible experience constitutes a form of being in contradiction. May the contradiction of projecting be superseded by superseding that very projecting? We shall answer: *no*, if this superseding simply means positing the totality of the immediate (or of possible experience) *without positing* what is other than the latter; *yes*, if that superseding means the *surpassing* of the moment of projecting in and through the moment in which one is able to establish which of the two sides of the alternative is inherently contradictory, whereby the other one turns out to be necessarily posited. That is to say, the contradiction of projecting is superseded through the *resolution* of the problematic positing, and not through a *forgetting* of the latter. The exclusion of the possibility that the contradictoriness of projecting could be superseded by forgetting the project is based on the essential belonging of the project to the originary structure. (Concerning this essential belonging, cf. §8.)

It should furthermore be observed that the originary contradiction – which has been verified in the previous sections – constitutes a particular type of the C-contradiction (dialectical contradiction). For, indeed, since every meaning necessarily includes its other, as superseded – whence this other is a constant of that meaning (cf. Chapter 10, §1) – for what concerns the originary meaning its *other* is posited as a problem (i.e. it is posited both as being and as nothing), in such a way that this constant is not posited, and the originary meaning is not what it nevertheless intends to be. (If it were to be objected that, to the extent that as part of that projecting the being as much as the nullity of the other than the originary are posited, what counts as a constant of the originary is in any case posited, we would need to reply that a constant is posited only to the extent that it is seen in relation to its essential belonging to the originary – something that precisely cannot take place as long as one does not rise above that projecting.)

In addition, it should be noted that the *other* than the originary is not posited as a problem insofar as it is a formal meaning, but in relation to the determination of this formality – a determination that is a hyposyntactic constant of that formal meaning (and that, since we are dealing with the very positivity and nullity of that other than the originary, constitutes the horizon of every hyposyntactic determination of the formal meaning under consideration). The originary is therefore a realization of the C-contradiction because a part of the hyposyntax of the originary is not posited – i.e. because the totality of the constants of the originary is not posited. (We shall return to this point later.)

Therefore, to the extent that, from the standpoint of present immediacy, one is not able to establish whether the other than the originary (i.e. the other than present immediacy) is being or nothing, there exists the *project* for the originary to be a contradiction, in that, should that other be something positive, the originary would be posited without the positing of one of its constants – due to the theorem according to which every meaning is a constant of every other meaning. Together with this *projected* contradiction, however, there is an *immediately attested* one: precisely because the other than the originary is necessarily either being or nothing, in such a way that one of these two sides of the alternative is a constant of the originary (or, more precisely: both sides have the value of constants, but one is a constant in its being affirmed, the other one in its being negated, and the alternative obtains to the extent that it is not known which of the two is the affirmed one and which the negated one); accordingly, as long as the alternative is not resolved, thus leaving the dimension of that projecting behind, the originary is posited without the positing of one of its constants – precisely, the one that is determined by the resolution of the alternative. If the originary consists of a possible contradiction in relation to the inability to determine its other, then – precisely as a result of this inability –the originary L-immediately manifests itself as a contradiction. This L-immediately attested contradiction – let us reiterate – is the very originary contradiction verified in §5.

From what we have discussed, it also appears that the proposition: 'The immediately present constants of S are not the totality of the constants of S' is L-immediate: precisely to the extent that S is regarded as an originary problematicity, the semantic horizon of which is L-immediately posited as not including a part of the hyposyntax (of that horizon). [In §8 of Chapter 10, proposition [9], on the one hand we have presented the exposition of the *mediational* process that leads to the proposition: 'The immediately present constants of S are not the totality of the constants of S', but, on the other hand, we have anticipated the positing of the L-immediacy of this proposition. It is clear that the authentic structuring of Γ_a already itself includes the positing of the L-immediacy of the proposition in question; that is to say, the anticipation of this positing is already accomplished with the exposition of Γ_a.]

The originary moment of philosophizing (the originary structure), therefore, appears – at this point of the exposition of the originary – as the originary synthesis of the categorical element (the positing of the totality of the immediate) and the problematic one (the project of being – indicating here the most relevant aspect of the problematic): an originary synthesis that, in the verified sense, is an originary contradiction. This contradiction is of a particular type, because in its structural concreteness it is the originary result of the originary superseding of the contradictoriness that derives from the negation of the originary structure; or, at least, that contradiction is such a result in relation to the present structuring of the originary. (This last remark concerns the project for what, at this point, appears as the originary projecting *to be originarily resolved* [as we shall precisely verify] on the basis of an extension of the analysis of the originary, i.e. on the basis of a more adequate comprehension of the structure of the originary. If this were to be the case, the authentic originary result of the originary superseding of the contradictions caused by a negation of the originary structure would not be the originary contradiction insofar as this is realized as an originary projecting, but it would precisely be the superseding of this contradiction realized by the *immediate resolution* of that originary projecting.) The nature of the contradictoriness of the originary structure is therefore altogether different from the one of the contradictoriness of which the originary structure constitutes an originary superseding. That contradictoriness is indeed only superseded through a surpassing of the originarity in its present realization, i.e. only through a resolution of the originary problematicity.

(It should be observed that this problematicity is in itself only something abstract, and, therefore, a contradiction: a contradiction that belongs to that total complex of contradictoriness, which is superseded by the originary structure *qua* concrete synthesis of the categorical and the problematic. As already mentioned, the originarity of the problematic further consists in its own standing as a moment of the categorical, i.e. in its own standing as a content of the totality of the immediate – a content that, in a different respect, is posited as to its meaning precisely as what is *other* than the horizon that in turn includes it as a moment.)[8]

8. The essential belonging of the project to the originary structure

Given that the positing of the originary semantic plane is the originary opening of the whole, that plane, *qua* present immediacy, essentially or necessarily consists of a problematic relation with the whole. Even admitting that an extension of the analysis or a deeper understanding of the immediate should be able to supersede – and therefore immediately supersede – that problematicity, from the standpoint of the present structuring of the immediate, such an extension of the analysis nevertheless remains itself a project.' Accordingly, the semantic plane of immediacy is related to the whole as something that may constitute either its absolute or its partial determination. This problematic relation with the whole precisely consists in the project for being to surpass the immediate. That is to say, it is precisely insofar as being surpasses the immediate determination of being in a problematic way that there originarily exists the possibility of an inequality between the whole and the immediate.

If the immediate *essentially* consists of a problematic relation to the whole, the concept of a positing of the immediate that is not the positing of this problematic relation to the whole delineates the immediate as a form of being in contradiction (or, equivalently, it conceives of something that is not the immediate as the immediate): precisely because the immediate is something that is essentially a problematic relation to the whole. Projecting, therefore, belongs to the essence of the originary structure. In other words: if from the standpoint of present immediacy it is not possible to affirm the equality or inequality between immediacy and the whole, this problematicity comes to belong to or define the essence of present immediacy, in such a way that if the latter is posited without the positing of that problematicity, immediacy is posited without the positing of one of its constants, and the positing of immediacy is therefore the opening of a contradiction. It must in any case be observed that this problematicity does not belong to the essence of the immediate in the sense that it is self-contradictory for this problematicity to be resolved, but in the sense that, should this resolution take place, the immediate can no longer be said to *simpliciter* be the immediate to which that problematicity pertained. This is precisely what takes place in the case of *this* red extension, in relation to which it is stated that the colour red belongs to its essence: *this* extension, *hic et nunc*, is essentially red; accordingly, if 'this' extension is no longer red, it will no longer *simpliciter* be *this* extension *hic et nunc* that is no longer red, but a persistence (form, essence, etc.) of *this* extension. Analogously: if that problematicity is resolved, it will not *simpliciter* be the present immediacy that comes to be posited in a categorical relation to the whole, but it will be a form of 'persistence' of this present immediacy. Accordingly, it is a specific moment of the individuation of the immediate – i.e. it is the immediate insofar as it realizes itself in and through a specific individuation – that is posited as part of that problematic relation, and it is another moment of that individuation that is posited as part of the categorical relation: whereby that problematicity does not belong to the essence of the immediate as such, but to the extent that the immediate realizes itself in and through that first moment of its individuation.

It is thereby confirmed that if the problematic relation of the immediate to the whole consists in the immediate's being in contradiction, this contradiction cannot be superseded by not positing the problematic relation itself – for, as we have seen, this positional *steresis* would equally leave the immediate in a contradiction (in such a way that the contradiction of the projecting would be superseded through the realization of another contradiction) – but by resolving the problematic situation in and through the categorical.[9]

9. The L-immediate difference between the whole and the originary structure

a. Insofar as this dimension of projecting belongs to the structure of the originary – i.e. insofar as this structure is an originary contradiction – the proposition: 'The originary is the whole' is *immediately self-contradictory*. This means that the originary

L-immediately stands as a moment of the whole. Simply asserted in this way, this appears to be a contradiction, for if the originary is the very structure of the (logical and phenomenological) immediate, and if the difference between the originary and the whole is L-immediate, it must be stated on the one hand that this difference belongs to the structure of the immediate – in such a way that in this respect there is nothing that surpasses the immediate – and at the same time it must be stated, by virtue of the very positing of that difference, that the whole surpasses the immediate. This apparent contradiction is superseded by making explicit the sense in which it is affirmed that the proposition: 'The originary is the whole' is immediately self-contradictory.

It should first of all be noted that, in affirming that proposition, we do *not* thereby mean to negate what we have held up to this point: namely, that from the standpoint of present immediacy the equality and inequality between the originary and the whole are only a project. For, indeed, it is precisely insofar as the originary (the structure of the immediate) is a form of projecting that it leaves as something undetermined whether its *other* is being or nothing, and – as a limiting case – it leaves as something undetermined whether it is non-contradictory or not to determine if the other than the originary is being or nothing. If the originary, *qua* project or problematicity, consists of this indeterminacy – i.e. if it is not able to resolve the problematicity that constitutes it – that resolution is in any case necessarily either non-contradictory or self-contradictory: and if it is non-contradictory, it is necessary for what is other than the originary to be either being or nothing. The originary is therefore not the whole precisely to the extent that, *qua* problematicity, it does not include the resolution of this problematicity: i.e. it does not include the semantic structure constituted by that resolution. (As a limiting case, the latter can consist in the very attestation of the self-contradictoriness of a resolution *of that aspect* of the problem, in which it is asked whether the other than the originary is being or nothing. It is thereby clear that an aspect of the problem – or, more precisely, a domain of the problematicity – must in any case be able to be resolved: the resolution of this limited domain of the problematic consisting in determining whether the residual domain of the problematic can be resolved or not.) The resolution of the originary problematicity is therefore something *other* than the originary: being, or the positive, surpasses the originary for the very reason or to the very extent that the originary is not able to establish whether being surpasses it or not. That surpassing of the originary is posited as part of the very structure of the originary, since in the proposition: 'The originary problematicity is surpassed by a positive dimension (= is surpassed by that positive element constituted by the resolution of the originary problem)' the predicate L-immediately pertains to the subject. It is L-immediately known that the immediate is not the whole. Or, equivalently, it is L-immediately known that a property that is not immediately known pertains to the immediate (i.e. its being or not being surpassed by the whole, or, as a limiting case, its being or not being that whose problematicity – indicated in its foremost aspect precisely by the alternative formulated first – can non-contradictorily be resolved). It should, however, be noted that while being originarily surpasses the originary in a categorical way, precisely to the extent that the surpassing of the originary originarily stands as a problem, this does not constitute a contradiction, because the positive, which is categorically and originarily affirmed to surpass the originary, is not the positive whose surpassing of the originary originarily stands as a problem. That former positive is the positivity constituted by the resolution of the originary problematicity (regardless of how this resolution should be determined); that latter positive is instead that additional positivity referred to by the resolution of the problematicity (i.e. referred to by that first positivity) in case that resolution is determined as the affirmation that a positive surpasses the originary – in such a way that what is surpassed here is not simply the originary, regarded as an originary problematicity, but it is also the semantic plane that includes the semantic structure constituted by the resolution of that originary problematicity. In this second respect, affirming that being surpasses the originary – this precisely constituting the affirmation that from the standpoint of the present originarity appears as a problem – means affirming that being surpasses that very surpassing of the originary that consists in the resolution of the originary problematicity.

A surpassing of the originary therefore obtains both in case it is verified that being lies beyond the originary and in case it is verified that nothing surpasses the originary (as well as in the – limiting – case in which it is verified that a resolution of this problematicity is self-contradictory). In both cases (as well as in the limiting case), there takes place a surpassing of the originary: precisely because, as discussed, this surpassing consists in the resolution (either way) of the dimension of projecting. It is thereby clear that the originary, which is in any case surpassed, is not the originary regarded as possible experience, but the originary *qua* factual determination of the totality of the immediate – since the verification of the fact that what is other than (possible or actual) experience is nothing does indeed lie beyond the factual determination of the immediate, but it does not lie beyond the experience of the problem.[10]

The immediate therefore immediately only stands as a project, in the sense that – leaving aside the limiting case here – it is not immediately possible to establish if what surpasses the immediate only consists in the verification of the fact that nothing surpasses the immediate (this second immediate being regarded as a simple synthesis of the verification and of the factual determinations surpassed by that verification) or if it consists in an additional positive dimension, constituted by the verification of the fact that a positive surpasses factual immediacy and by this very positive, in the case of the project of immediate being (cf. §3), and constituted by the verification of the fact that a positive surpasses possible experience and by this very positive, in the case of the project of being (cf. §3).

b. Stating that the originary problematicity is not the whole means affirming that the contradiction – which, as we have seen, belongs to the essence of the problematic – is not the whole. This affirmation follows on the one hand from what we have discussed above, and on the other hand it asserts itself by itself, for if the contradiction is the whole, or what is definitive, that contradiction is allowed to persist as something not superseded: that is to say, being is regarded as something self-contradictory. In other words, claiming that being in contradiction (as it pertains to the originary problematicity) is what is definitive, i.e. that the contradiction cannot be superseded – since surpassing that being in contradiction is equivalent to falling into nothing – means claiming that being is self-contradictory, for only if being is self-contradictory is it *impossible* to surpass that positing of the self-contradictoriness constituted by the problematic situation.

Through this last remark we are therefore in a position to determine the value of that 'limiting case' (repeatedly mentioned above) of the originary problematicity (consisting in the problem as to whether the resolution of the problem is non-contradictory or not), which up to this point has been allowed to persist as a non-contradictory structure. For a development of this concept, cf. §14.

It is therefore contradictory to affirm that the being in contradiction constituted by the originary is the semantic whole. Therefore, on the one hand, if it is verified that the whole surpasses the originary, it is at the same time verified that the originary consists of a being in contradiction – precisely insofar as, *qua* originary opening of the whole, it is not the positing of the totality of the constants of the latter; on the other hand, if the originary consists of a being in contradiction, it cannot stand as the whole, for (as discussed) that contradiction cannot be allowed to persist.

The originary projecting is therefore immediately posited in its differing from the whole for a twofold reason: insofar as the solution of that projecting is not known, and insofar as the contradiction constituted by that projecting *must* be superseded – in such a way that the superseding of this contradiction is that positive by virtue of which the whole surpasses in any case the originary projecting.

c. Affirming that the proposition: 'The originary problematicity is the whole' is immediately self-contradictory does not therefore mean affirming a contradiction, as it instead appeared at the beginning of point a; for if the difference between the originary and the whole is L-immediate, it cannot for this reason be affirmed that nothing surpasses the originary. While the resolution of the problem is indeed immediately posited as something that surpasses the domain of the originary problematicity – i.e. while the being of that resolution must immediately be affirmed, in addition to its problem – the originary does not, however, include *the way in which* that resolution is realized, and it is precisely the *steresis* of this concrete modality of the resolution that makes it possible to hold firm, as something immediate, the surpassing of the immediate. What is L-immediately known is *that* the solution surpasses the problem, in such a way that in this respect the immediate is not surpassed: that is to say, *whether* the solution surpasses the problem is not an originary problem; or, in this respect, the originary does not realize itself as a problem. What is not L-immediately known is *how* the originary problem is resolved – whence it is in this respect that the surpassing of the immediate is verified, i.e. it is possible to *L-immediately* affirm that a positive surpasses the immediate.

10. Note

We have stated in point a of the previous section that affirming that the proposition: 'The originary problem is the whole' is immediately self-contradictory does not mean negating what we have held up to this point: namely, that from the standpoint of immediacy the equality and inequality between the originary and the whole are only a project. It should be observed that we thereby mean to refer to the *fact* that the present structuring of the immediate is not able to resolve that project – that is to say, we do not mean to exclude the possibility that a development of the analysis of the structure of the immediate could realize itself as an immediate resolution of that projecting. This can be affirmed without any immediate contradiction: for in the same way in which above we have established the non-contradictoriness of the affirmation of the immediacy of the surpassing of the originary problematicity, so it is not immediately contradictory to project a logical structure by virtue of which one would show the self-contradictoriness of the negation of the fact that the whole immediately surpasses the immediate – provided that the immediate resolution of the projecting should consist in the immediate positing of the difference between the immediate and the whole (for it is precisely in this respect that it would be possible to suppose a contradiction within the project of that logical structure). It is clear that the whole does not immediately surpass the immediate simply in the sense that the solution surpasses the originary problem (this being what has already been established – a surpassing that may be referred to as a surpassing in the weak sense), but as the surpassing of this very surpassing – which may be referred to as a surpassing in the strong sense.

It is clear that in case the structure of the immediate is an opening that consists in an immediate resolution of that projecting (i.e. of the problem of whether being surpasses the immediate in a strong sense or not), the standpoint retained here would prove to be an abstract concept. Considering that moment of the structure of the immediate (this structure being regarded in its realizing itself as the immediate resolution of that projecting), which is constituted by what in the originary structure is distinct from the domain constituted by that immediate resolution, then: it is only insofar as this moment is abstractly conceived that it can realize itself as a *project* for that other than the structure of the immediate to be either being or nothing. Once that abstract concept is superseded, that project is immediately resolved.

11. The originary structure *qua* formal superseding of the originary contradiction

The originary, *qua* projecting structure, is a contradiction. This contradiction (which may still be considered here as to its most significant aspect, namely as the contradiction of the project of a positive element that surpasses possible experience) is originarily (= L-immediately) *for itself*, or posited. This means that the totality of the immediate is immediately known *qua* this contradiction – or, equivalently, that the positing of this contradiction belongs to the structuring of the immediate. Precisely because the contradiction in question is originarily manifest, however, the fact that it must be superseded is itself originarily affirmed. *The contradiction is, however, thereby originarily superseded*: that is to say, the contradiction is originarily superseded precisely because the fact that it must be superseded is originarily (= L-immediately) posited. Or, equivalently: in stating that it is *necessary* to move beyond the project, i.e. that the latter must necessarily be resolved, one has thereby already moved beyond it and resolved it.

It should, however, be noted that the superseding of the contradiction precisely consists in recognizing that the originary contradiction must be superseded. It is precisely because such a superseding of the contradiction includes nothing but that recognition that it must be stated that this originary superseding of the originary contradiction has a simply *formal* value. A formal superseding entails knowing *that* the contradiction must be superseded (= that the problem has a solution), without however knowing *how* it must be superseded. Or, equivalently, that 'how' is itself formally known: in the sense that – while it is originarily known that the superseding cannot consists of a *forgetting* of the projecting (for otherwise the contradiction would be superseded through the affirmation of another contradiction), but it must consist in the *resolution* of the projecting, or in the surpassing of the moment of problematicity – the determination of that surpassing is, however, not originarily known: i.e. it is now known whether that determination consists in positing the nullity or the positivity of the horizon in which being originarily frees itself.

(The formal superseding of the originary contradiction consists in the very categorical positing – which is also itself formal – of the logical whole, i.e. of the definitive dimension that surpasses the originary problematicity.)

12. The originary structure *qua* formal originarity of metaphysics

Insofar as the originary realizes itself as that formal surpassing of the problematic moment, the originary structure stands as the *originary* opening of metaphysical knowledge.

It should be noted that the metaphysical horizon is already opened by the dimension of projecting. That is to say, that projecting is already a surpassing of possible experience. This surpassing, however, is something problematic: in the sense that the horizon in which being originarily frees itself is opened as an alternative between its positivity and its nullity. (Heidegger's 'ontological horizon' and Jaspers' '*Umgreifende*' may be considered as the most self-aware conceptions of the originary opening of the problematic metaphysical horizon to have been carried out by contemporary philosophy.)

That problematic opening, however, is only an aspect – or, more precisely, a moment – of the originary opening of the metaphysical horizon. For, indeed, the formal superseding of the originary contradiction consists in the *categorical* opening of this horizon. The categoricity of the metaphysical horizon is precisely given by the necessary positing of the moment in which the project is resolved – and this positing is necessary because the negation of that moment implies the persistence of the contradiction, which pertains to the originary, as an *affirmed* contradiction.

It is, however, also clear that such an originary categoricity pertains to the metaphysical horizon to the extent that the latter is a formal or indeterminate horizon. The metaphysical content, which constitutes itself as such an originary possession, has indeed no other determination than the one of being the resolution of that projecting – i.e. of being the superseding of the contradictoriness of the project. The resolution, and superseding, in question is indeed achieved – whence the fact that its positing is categorical – but its concrete determination is not (originarily) accomplished: that is to say, it is not possible to establish which among the projected determinations (i.e.

among the determinations that constitute the alternative) is the one that stands as the metaphysical content, in its excluding its negation. If this originary metaphysical knowledge consists in positing the formal solution of the originary problem, it is clear that this originary metaphysics – precisely to the extent that it is formal – is no more 'transcendentist' than 'immanentist'. Immanentism and transcendentism belong to the projected metaphysical horizon.

In affirming the formal originarity of metaphysical knowledge, one does not exclude the possibility of (= it is not immediately contradictory to project) a verification of the concrete originarity of that knowledge. It is clear that, should that verification be realized, the affirmation of the formal originarity of metaphysical knowledge would come to be identified as an abstract concept, in the sense already indicated in §10. [This is precisely the case (cf. Chapter 13). In relation to the anticipation made in §3 of Chapter 1 of this enquiry concerning the originarity of metaphysical knowledge, it is therefore clear that the originarity of that knowledge anticipated there[11] is not the formal originarity discussed in the present section; this formal originarity is in fact the form or the authentic mode of opening of the concept Γ_a, i.e. of that concept that is abstract precisely to the extent that it is not able to discern the concrete originarity of metaphysical knowledge – in such a way that, from the standpoint of that abstract concept, that concrete originarity must stand as the content of a project.]

13. Note. (Problematicity and categoricity of the originary metaphysical horizon)

On the one hand, the originary superseding of the contradictoriness of the project (formally) supersedes the project itself, but, on the other hand, it allows it to persist as a content of the categorical horizon itself. The project is resolved in the sense that the fact that it must be resolved is posited; as discussed, however, since this necessity of the resolution leaves the very mode of the resolution undetermined, this mode remains something projected, and the contradiction of the project persists as something not superseded: formally superseded, but materially not superseded.

In relation to the originary contradiction, there thus exists an originary task (namely, the necessity of superseding the contradiction), and this task is originarily fulfilled to the extent that the contradiction is formally superseded. The task is instead retained as such insofar as the contradiction is not materially superseded. [It is thus clarified why, in §7, b of Chapter 10, it has been affirmed that already from the standpoint of Γ_a it is possible to exclude that only the project of a task is originarily given: that is to say, the task is already originarily posited from the standpoint of Γ_a. At the same time, however, the task originarily stands as a project to the extent that, from the standpoint of the originarity that is structured as Γ_a, whether being surpasses the immediate or not, in a strong sense, remains something projected; accordingly, in relation to the theorem according to which every meaning is a constant of every other meaning, the fact that the originary, as surpassed in a strong sense by a positive, constitutes a realization of the C-contradiction is a project, and so is therefore the task that consists in the superseding of this contradiction.]

14. The concept of the 'impossibility of metaphysics' is immediately contradictory

a. It is thus verified, on the basis of the above considerations, that the broader alternative mentioned in §4, b (i.e. that 'limiting case' of the project, discussed in the previous sections) is originarily self-contradictory. It should be noted, however, that it is not originarily self-contradictory in the sense that the contradictoriness is due to the absence of the resolution of the project constituted by that alternative, but in the sense that one of the two modes of the resolution of the project is originarily manifest as a self-contradiction; as a result, the alternative under consideration is immediately (and concretely) superseded. Let us clarify.

As already mentioned, the two sides of this broader alternative – the 'encompassing alternative' – consist in the possibility of the resolution of the alternative-moment (i.e. of the resolution of the project of the positivity-negativity of the horizon in which being frees itself) and in the impossibility (self-contradictoriness) of that resolution. We are therefore stating that projecting the impossibility of the resolution of the alternative-moment – i.e. projecting that it is possible to verify that the concept of a 'resolution of the alternative-moment' is inherently contradictory – originarily appears as a self-contradictory outcome of the encompassing alternative.

The alternative-moment is indeed what determines the originary contradiction, which is formally superseded in the domain of originarity. We have stated that this formal superseding consists in the very positing of the necessity of the superseding of the originary contradiction: this is equivalent to stating that the formal superseding of this contradiction consists in the very positing of the necessity of the resolution of the alternative-moment. If the originary contradiction is therefore only superseded by resolving the alternative-moment, it is inherently contradictory to suppose that the resolution of the alternative-moment should be an inherent contradiction. The 'limiting case' of the originary project is therefore immediately self-contradictory, in that one of the two sides of the alternative that constitutes that limiting case precisely consists in the affirmation that the superseding of the contradiction is itself a contradiction. If this side of the limiting case of the originary project – i.e. if this side of the encompassing alternative – is an inherent contradiction, that alternative does not originarily exist as a problematic opening, but as a contradiction that belongs to the total complex of the contradictions that are originarily superseded by the originary structure. This contradiction is not therefore superseded by surpassing the project (precisely because the project does not obtain), but by not allowing this project to be constituted as such. In other words, the two sides of the alternative-moment are both immediately non-contradictory; the second side of the encompassing alternative, on the contrary, is immediately self-contradictory; therefore, the first side is necessary, i.e. it does not realize itself in a problematic form, but in a categorical one. In this second case, therefore, the alternative does not obtain, i.e. it is immediately superseded *qua* alternative. The alternative-moment is instead an authentic alternative, and, in the verified sense, it therefore realizes itself as a contradiction whose superseding consists in the surpassing of the problematicity of the alternative.

The limiting case is retained as something non-contradictory only to the extent that one does not realize that it consists in affirming that the negation of a contradiction is a contradiction. This failure to realize this fact constitutes the abstract concept of a moment of the structure of the immediate (namely, of that moment constituted by the limiting case). It is clear that in case an extension of the analysis of the immediate should come to an immediate resolution of the alternative-moment itself [and this is precisely what takes place as part of the concrete structuring of the originary], we would need to state in relation to the alternative-moment what we have stated concerning the encompassing alternative: namely, that one of its two sides immediately appears as something self-contradictory, in such a way that the concrete concept of immediacy does not allow the constitution of the alternative-moment as an alternative, or as a project, but it immediately supersedes it through the categorical positing of one of its two sides. The alternative in question would therefore only obtain as the content of the abstract concept of a moment of the structure of the immediate. [It is thereby clear that the concrete structuring of Γ_a includes the project for this structuring to be the abstract concept of the originary.]

b. The corollary that is obtained based on the previous observations is of a significant importance. It can be formulated as follows:

'The concept of a deduction of the impossibility of metaphysics immediately stands as a self-contradiction'. That deduction should indeed consist in a verification of the inherent contradictoriness of the concept: 'resolution of the alternative-moment'. As we have seen, however, it is immediately contradictory to project the contradictoriness of this concept. This means that every possible deduction or foundation of the impossibility of metaphysics is a priori self-contradictory (this apriority precisely consisting here in originarity itself, i.e. in the structuring of immediacy).

c. As stated, it is immediately self-contradictory to affirm that the superseding of the contradiction constituted by the alternative-moment is a self-contradiction; the concept of the impossibility of metaphysics is therefore immediately self-contradictory. At the same time, however, it appears that, while still holding firm the self-contradictoriness of the affirmation that the superseding of the contradiction is a self-contradiction, it is not immediately self-contradictory to project a verification of the fact that the originary structure *should not be able* to constitute itself (= that it should be self-contradictory for the originary structure to constitute itself) as a superseding of that contradiction; namely, we are stating that this project may appear not to be immediately self-contradictory in case one affirms the existence of a positional horizon other than the originary structure: a horizon that would itself be realized as a superseding of that contradiction that affects the originary, and that would therefore itself be realized as the metaphysical categorem. In other words, while it is immediately self-contradictory for the superseding of the contradiction (which is here considered as the contradictoriness of the project constituted by the alternative-moment) to be a self-contradiction – in such a way that the concept of the impossibility of metaphysics is therefore immediately self-contradictory – it appears that the superseding of that contradiction should be able to be realized either in the very domain of the originary structure (or also as part of a mediational development of the latter) through an extension of the analysis of the originary, or in a positional domain that differs from the originary structure (and from every possible positional domain constituted by any mediational development of the originary). That is to say, it does not appear to be immediately self-contradictory to project that it should be impossible to realize the metaphysical discourse in the domain of the originary or as a development of the latter (= impossibility of the metaphysical discourse as a human discourse, or, more precisely, as *my* discourse), should however a different positional horizon (or a different horizon of consciousness) be posited, in which that discourse would be realized; for if this different horizon were not affirmed – i.e. if that project of the impossibility of the metaphysical discourse were not at the same time the project of the existence of this horizon – one would once again be affirming that the superseding of the contradiction is, *simpliciter*, self-contradictory. (It is here clear that the superseding of the contradiction can be self-contradictory *secundum quid*: i.e. *to the extent that* it pertains to the originary structure.) In this different positional horizon, everything that is posited as part of the originary structure must, however, be posited, for only under this condition can it be established in that horizon if a positive surpasses the originary positional horizon or not, in a strong sense (this precisely constituting the resolution of the alternative-moment).

Affirming a positional horizon, however, which differs from the originary horizon and from its development, and in which the metaphysical discourse realizes itself, means – even if in a limiting case – realizing the metaphysical discourse as part of the domain of the originary horizon, in such a way that what was stated in point b is thereby confirmed. For, indeed, affirming the existence of that positional horizon, differing from the originary one, means affirming that the horizon in which being frees itself is a positive – i.e. that the positive surpasses the originary in a strong sense – and it therefore means resolving the alternative-moment. Therefore, if projecting the verification of a demonstration (from the standpoint of the originary or of a mediational development of the latter) of the impossibility of the resolution of the alternative-moment *necessarily* implies the affirmation of the resolution of the alternative-moment, it follows that this project can be retained as something non-contradictory to the extent that the impossibility of solving the alternative-moment is not regarded *absolute*, but as to a specific quantification. Leaving aside the fact that (should one come to project the verification of the impossibility of resolving the alternative-moment) the originary must immediately be regarded as being surpassed by that different positional horizon, that specific quantification consists in the impossibility of determining whether the positive surpasses or does not surpass the originary to a further extent relative to the one that must immediately be affirmed when one precisely affirms the existence of that different positional horizon in which the contradiction is superseded. Therefore, that horizon must not be projected as something as part of which it is *simply* established whether the positive surpasses or does not surpass the originary positional horizon in a strong sense (for this surpassing must already be affirmed from the standpoint of the originary, in order for the project of the verification of the impossibility of the metaphysical discourse not to be self-contradictory), but it must be projected as something as part of which it is established whether the positive surpasses the originary in a strong sense, to a further extent relative to the one constituted by this very surpassing horizon – i.e. to a further extent relative to the one immediately required by the non-contradictoriness of the project of the impossibility of the metaphysical discourse.

Demonstrating the impossibility of a metaphysical knowledge therefore means demonstrating that the part of the whole constituted by the originary structure and by its development consists of a necessarily being in contradiction (in which this 'contradiction' must not be understood indeterminately, but as *that specific* self-contradictoriness constituted by the alternative-moment insofar as it realizes itself according to the quantification indicated above).

[It is clear that from the standpoint of the concrete structuring of the originary, as part of which the affirmation that the positive surpasses the originary is L-immediate – i.e. as part of which the originary constitutes itself as the concrete and categorical metaphysical knowledge – projecting that the originary should be essentially unable, in the indicated sense, to realize a metaphysical knowledge is immediately superseded: since, precisely – as we shall verify – the alternative-moment is immediately or originarily superseded, in such a way that the metaphysical theorem, *qua* determinate and not simply formal affirmation, is originarily realized.]

15. Corollary concerning the contradiction of the opening of a totality of the immediate that does not include a specific quantity of variants

a. The results that we have achieved allow us to verify – in a different way from the one already considered in Chapter 10 – that a positing of the originary structure that is affected by a positional *steresis* relative to one or more of its variants constitutes the opening of a contradiction. This theorem has already been proved on the basis of the theorem that the positing of every meaning implies the positing of the infinite semanteme and the theorem that *every* meaning (thus including those meanings that are constants of the originary structure) is a constant of the infinite semanteme – in such a way that the variants of a meaning, too, are constants of the latter. We are therefore stating that it is possible to identify another way of proving that theorem, independently of the use made in Chapter 10 of the two theorems formulated above.[12]

From the standpoint of the present structuring of the immediate, a positional opening of the totality of the immediate can *immediately* be posited as being affected by a positional *steresis* relative to a determinate quantity of variants only insofar as that opening is something projected or recollected, i.e. insofar as the totality *simpliciter* of the immediate includes, as posited, those determinations that the positional opening in question lacks. For, otherwise, the *steresis* is only something projected. Indeed, if the originary, *qua* originary problematicity, is immediately posited as a positional *steresis* relative to the solution of the problem, this solution is not, however, a variant, but a constant (i.e. a syntactic constant) of the originary. (Projecting a positional domain that is affected by a *steresis* is something different from projecting the *steresis* itself. In the first case, one projects the being of a positional domain that does not include specific determinations that are, however, included in the totality *simpliciter* of the immediate. In this case, since those determinations are included in this totality, what is projected is not the fact that this domain – regarded in the indicated way – is affected by a positional *steresis*, but, let us reiterate, what is projected is the being of such a domain. In the second case, instead, the *steresis* itself is projected: that is to say, one projects that the positional *steresis* pertains to the very totality *simpliciter* of the immediate).

b. The distinction between the projected horizon of being and the projected horizon of immediate being (cf. §3) is internal to the projected horizon of being. That is to say, the freeing of the meaning 'being' from possible experience is all the more so a freeing of 'being' from the factual determination of the immediate. The horizon in which being frees itself does not therefore lie beside the horizon in which immediate being frees itself, but it includes the latter. That is to say, the projected horizon of being includes everything that is other than the totality of immediately present being. Even if the project of immediate being (the project that does not surpass possible experience) were not posited, the positing of the projected horizon of being would still include the projected horizon of the immediate – even if in an implicit way. The deduction of the contradictoriness of an opening of the originary structure that is affected by the positional *steresis* of any of its variants precisely relies on this observation, as we shall clarify further below.

c. While the positing of the totality of the immediate necessarily implies the positing of the projected horizon of being (cf. §8) – whereby this horizon is a syntactic constant of the totality of the immediate – the recollection or the project of a totality of the immediate that non-contradictorily realizes itself as the totality of the immediate is a recollection or a project of the implication between this totality and the projected horizon of being (i.e. the horizon that is a syntactic constant of the recollected or projected totality of the immediate). If a recollection were to attest the positing of that totality as something that does not imply the positing of that projected horizon, what would be recollected is only the intention or the attempt to posit the totality of the immediate, and, therefore, what would be recollected is a being in contradiction. Furthermore, projecting a totality of the immediate whose positing does not imply the positing of that projected horizon is immediately self-contradictory, should one suppose to be projecting something non-contradictory; on the contrary, it is non-contradictory as the project of the intention to posit the totality of the immediate, i.e. in case this projecting is aware of the contradictoriness of the projected content – the intention to posit the totality of the immediate being in contradiction with what would effectively be posited. (In the first case, the projecting itself constitutes an intention, and, therefore, a contradiction; in the second case, it consists in the non-contradictory project of the existence of an intention, and, therefore, of a contradiction.)

In what follows, care should be taken not to conflate the projected totality, i.e. the totality *qua content* of the project, with the project that pertains to the projected totality itself, i.e. the project that this totality must in turn open in order not to realize itself as a contradiction.

d. Let us therefore consider the project whose content is a totality of the immediate that is affected by a positional *steresis* relative to a specific quantity Q of variants. This *steresis* is first of all posited within the totality *simpliciter* of the immediate. Furthermore, insofar as the *steresis* is posited in a determinate way – i.e. insofar as the determination with respect to which the *steresis* is such is posited – the positing of the *steresis only* belongs to the totality *simpliciter* of the immediate.

Then: insofar as the projected totality of the immediate, in order not to realize itself as a contradiction, must imply the positing of the projected horizon of being – i.e. the positing of something that is other than itself – that totality *implicitly includes as part of what is projected*, i.e. as part of the horizon that is projected *for that totality*, that quantity Q of determinations (variants) that it itself does not posit (relative to which the totality *simpliciter* posits the projected totality of the immediate as something that is affected by a positional *steresis*). For, indeed, insofar as the projected totality projects something that is other than itself, it problematically includes in a horizon everything that is not included in its positional opening; therefore, it also includes in that horizon that quantity Q of determinations that – while being originarily posited in the totality *simpliciter* of the immediate – it does not itself posit.

Indicating by $p(P)$ the projected horizon of the projected totality of the immediate, it must be noted that the mode of inclusion of that non-posited quantity Q of determinations in $p(P)$ is a particular one, since, in relation to the projected totality, the inclusion in question is only something *in itself*, i.e. it is not *for* that totality, in such a way that $p(P)$ (only) *is* inclusive of Q. Furthermore, it is clear that $p(P)$ includes everything that is not posited in the projected totality of the immediate, and it therefore includes Q, too, but it does not include it as something posited: i.e. Q is not posited in $p(P)$ – precisely because one is projecting a totality of the immediate that is affected by the positional *steresis* of Q. The fact that Q belongs to $p(P)$ is only posited in the totality *simpliciter* of the immediate, which includes Q in its being posited, and which is therefore able to attest that the projected totality does not posit Q, and that Q is therefore found to *be* included in $p(P)$. This is therefore an implicit inclusion, precisely in the sense that Q is not *posited* in $p(P)$, while still *being* included in it.

e. It follows that, insofar as that non-posited quantity Q of determinations is included in $p(P)$, that quantity stands as a possibility (i.e., precisely, as something projected), and, therefore, as something that may be regarded as much as being as nothing.

However, if Q is implicitly included in $p(P)$, it then follows that the projected totality of the immediate, insofar as it is affected by the positional *steresis* of Q, is in contradiction. For, indeed, projecting that something that is – i.e. the quantity Q – is nothing at all means realizing a contradiction. The quantity Q indeed belongs to the totality of immediately present being; insofar as it is implicitly included in $p(P)$, however, it is implicitly considered as a possible nullity, to the extent that the opening of $p(P)$ precisely allows the nullity of its content to persist as something possible. One thereby precisely supposes that being is not (a supposition that is not to be conflated with the supposition that something that is may become a nullity at a later time. That is to say, that former supposition is a supposition of the immediate nullity of a certain dimension of being).

(To the extent that Q is implicitly included in $p(P)$, i.e. to the extent that the supposition that Q is nothing is only implicit, the contradiction that we are discussing here, too, is only an implicit one, or something 'in itself', as part of the positional domain opened by the projected totality of the immediate. That contradiction is only posited as part of the present reflection, which precisely consists in the positing of the totality *simpliciter* of the immediate.)

f. It should be observed that the quantity Q that is not posited in the projected totality (only) *is* something projected relative to this totality, and precisely because it only *is* so, it can be regarded as being or as nothing (absolute nothing). For, indeed, in projecting a determinate content, i.e. when a determination is *posited* as part of the projected horizon, that determination is already included within being itself, even though its being is only the being of a possibility. Relative to this determination, it is therefore not possible to suppose that it is – absolutely – nothing, but only that it does not have that mode of being that pertains to that with respect to which it is posited as a possibility. Since here we are instead considering the case in which the projected horizon $p(P)$ (only) *is* an inclusion of the non-posited quantity Q, the latter shares the same outcome of the whole content of $p(P)$: namely, that it is as possible for this content to be as it is possible for it not to be in any way. (It is here clear that, in affirming that Q – *qua* included in $p(P)$ – is a *possibility*, we do not mean to say that Q has a 'possible being', but that its being, whether it is a being *qua* possibility or *qua* factual existence, is regarded as nothing and as being).

It should, however, be noted that *insofar as* the meaning '$p(P)$' *must in any case be present* within the domain of the projected totality of the immediate (as well as, of course, within the domain of the totality *simpliciter*), it cannot be stated of that meaning – *as present in this way* – that it is possible that it could be absolutely nothing: this cannot be stated precisely to the extent that it is a specific present meaning. (That is to say, Q may be implicitly regarded as being absolutely nothing because Q is not *posited* as belonging to $p(P)$.) However, since here it is the meaning itself that refers to something that, *qua* other than the totality of the immediate, is not present, it is this term of the reference of the meaning that, together with its being, can be supposed to be an *absolute* nothingness. (This 'other' than the totality of the immediate belongs on the one hand, i.e. as a present meaning, to the totality of the immediate, but, on the other hand, i.e. insofar as it is what the meaning itself expresses, it precisely lies beyond the totality of the immediate. If, once again, one observes that this 'lying beyond' is itself present, it must be *repeated* that this presence, *per* its own meaning, refers to something that is not present. Repeating this repetition *ad infinitum* means not thinking or not holding firm the very content of presence, which in this case is precisely determined as a form of lying beyond presence.)[13]

g. It is clear that there is an analogy between the observations developed above and the ones developed in §5, through which it was shown that, insofar as the totality *simpliciter* of the immediate implies the dimension of projecting, this totality posits being as nothing, or nothingness as being – or, equivalently, self-contradictoriness as non-contradictoriness, and vice versa. In relation to the totality *simpliciter* of the immediate, as long as one does not surpass the moment of the originary projecting (i.e. the originary in its present structuring), one is, however, not able to indicate which of the two sides of the alternative that constitutes the project is the self-contradictoriness that is regarded as a non-contradictoriness (i.e. whether it is the positivity of the other than the totality of the immediate that is regarded as a nullity, or whether it is the nullity of that other that is regarded as a positivity). Instead, in relation to the projected totality of the immediate, remaining within the domain of the originary problematicity, it is possible to attest that a part of the otherness projected by that projected totality – which is precisely a part of $p(P)$ – is regarded as a possible nullity, whereas this part is a positivity: namely, that positivity precisely constituted by the quantity Q that is not posited as part of the projected totality.[14]

From what we have discussed, it appears that this new type of foundation of the statement 'A positional opening of the originary structure that is affected by a positional *steresis* relative to a specific quantity of variants constitutes a being in contradiction' consists in the attestation of an *enhancement* of the contradictoriness determined by the projecting. In other words: the totality of the immediate is already a being in contradiction for the very reason that it consists of a projecting; if such a totality is projected (or recollected) in its being affected by a positional *steresis* relative to a specific quantity of variants, the contradictoriness determined by the projecting is enhanced for the reason that, in addition to the fact that being is regarded as nothing or nothing as being, Q is regarded as nothing. Or, equivalently: that contradictoriness is enhanced for the reason that, in addition to the fact that what in $p(P)$ exceeds Q – as something projected – is regarded both as being and as nothing (whereas it is only one of the two), Q is regarded both as a being and as nothing (whereas it is a being, and it is immediately attested as such).

That new type of foundation of the statement formulated above, however, may be simplified. That is to say, up to now we have considered the positional *steresis* of a *determinate* quantity of variants (i.e. a quantity known as to its concrete content), which must therefore be posited as part of the totality *simpliciter* of the immediate (cf. §15). Indeterminately, however – i.e. in not considering the positional *steresis* of a *determinate* quantity of variants (which precisely requires that this quantity should be *categorically* posited) – the following can also be stated: if the totality of the immediate were posited without the positing of any one of its variants, the projecting essentially implied by the positing of the totality in question (cf. §8) would implicitly include in the projected content that non-posited variant, which would therefore be regarded as a possible nullity (that is to say: the possibility that a positive should be nothing would be implicitly allowed to persist). In other words – for the sake of that new type of foundation – it is not necessary to consider a positing of the totality of the immediate, whose positional *steresis* of a specific quantity of variants is *categorically* posited (in which case that totality can only be recollected or projected, since the totality *simpliciter* of the immediate must include those variants), but it is sufficient to consider a positing of that totality which is *supposed* (i.e. projected) to be affected by the positional *steresis* of one or more variants (in which case the discussion may also be referred to the totality *simpliciter* of the immediate). These specifications also apply to what is stated in the following points.

h. In the same way in which a future totality of the immediate, projected as being affected by the positional *steresis* of the quantity Q, is in contradiction insofar as $p(P)$ implicitly includes Q, so a past totality of the immediate, recollected as being affected by the positional *steresis* of a quantity Q' of variants belonging to the totality *simpliciter* of the immediate, is in contradiction insofar as the projected horizon $r(P)$, opened by that past totality, implicitly incudes the quantity Q'.

That is to say, if a recollection attests the positing of a totality of the immediate affected by the positional *steresis* of Q', then to the extent that the positing of this totality necessarily implies the positing of $r(P)$ in order not to be realized as a contradiction, Q' is implicitly included in $r(P)$, and the already identified contradiction therefore ensues.

i. Concerning the way in which the contradictoriness determined by the positional *steresis* of Q and Q' has been affirmed above, the following objection may be raised.

Let the symbols T, $p(T)$ and $r(T)$, respectively, indicate the totality *simpliciter* of the immediate, the projected totality of the immediate and the recollected totality of the immediate.

For what concerns the positional *steresis* of Q, which affects $p(T)$, it is objected that an *ontological* annulment of Q may correspond to the *positional* annulment of Q in $p(T)$. In this case, it is no longer possible to affirm that Q is implicitly included in $p(P)$, and that $p(T)$ therefore realizes itself as a contradiction. For, indeed, the contradictoriness of $p(T)$ consisted in the fact that the *being* of Q determined the implicit inclusion of Q in $p(P)$, in such a way that through this inclusion the being of Q was posited as a possible nullity.

For what concerns the positional *steresis* of Q', which affects $r(T)$, it is objected that (Q')'s *not-having-yet-been-realized*, i.e. once again the ontological nullity of Q', may correspond to the *positional* nullity of Q' in $r(T)$, in such a way that $r(P)$ does not implicitly include Q', and $r(T)$ is therefore not realized as a contradiction.

We respond to the first objection by stating that – even admitting the possibility of the annulment of a being – the possible ontological annulment of Q, which corresponds to the positional *steresis* of Q in $p(T)$, is not an absolute annulment, but the annulment *of a specific mode of being* of Q. That is to say, it is inherently contradictory for Q's *having-been* to be annulled, even if Q 'no longer is' – whence that mode of being that consists in its having been *always* or essentially belongs to Q. This means that T includes $p(T)$ as something to which there always corresponds an ontological persistence of Q; accordingly, to the extent that $p(T)$ is affected by the positional *steresis* of Q, and to the extent that the positing of $p(T)$ implies the positing of $p(P)$, the ontological persistence of Q is implicitly included in $p(P)$. It is thereby confirmed that the positional plane constituted by the implication between $p(T)$ and $p(P)$ constitutes a being in contradiction.

We analogously respond to the second objection by stating that – still supposing the possibility of the annulment of a being – the possible ontological nullity of Q', which corresponds to the positional *steresis* of Q' in $r(T)$, is not an absolute nullity but the nullity of a specific mode of being of Q'. That is to say, it is contradictory that the nullity of the *possible being* of Q', or of its *being about to be*, should correspond to the positing of $r(T)$, even if Q' 'is not yet' as part of $r(T)$. Hence, that mode of being that consists of its being about to be already belongs or has always belonged to Q'. This means that T includes $r(T)$ as something to which there already corresponds an ontological substantiality of Q'. If, then, $r(T)$ is affected by the positional *steresis* of Q', as a result of the positional implication between $r(T)$ and $r(P)$ it follows that $r(P)$ implicitly includes that ontological substantiality of Q' determined by the possible being of Q'. Accordingly, the positional plane constituted by the implication between $r(T)$ and $r(P)$ constitutes a being in contradiction.

l. Insofar as the totality of the immediate includes the recollection of totalities of the immediate that are affected by a positional *steresis* relative to a specific quantity of determinations belonging to the immediate, it is therefore confirmed that this totality includes positional domains in which the originary opening of philosophizing consisted of a being in contradiction. Analogously, when that totality includes the project of totalities of the immediate that are affected by a positional *steresis* relative to a specific quantity of determinations belonging to the immediate, that totality projects that the originary opening of philosophizing will consist of a contradiction. That is to say, it has already occurred, and it may occur, that – respectively – the originary structure has been and will be in contradiction.

For what concerns its having been in contradiction, the originary structure has already freed itself from the contradiction precisely by positing that quantity of determinations that had not been posited as part of those past individuations of the originary. For what concerns the possibility of its being in contradiction, the originary structure, in order to avoid the contradiction, *must* not allow anything of its present content to be lost, i.e. it must prevent the positional annulment of *any* part or moment of its content.

This does not mean that it is not possible for the originary structure to be found in a contradiction: the possibility of being in contradiction belongs to that structure as a matter of fact – in the same way as it does its having been in contradiction. We are instead stating that the *task* of safeguarding the manifestation of being, or the *obligation* to prevent its annulment, essentially belongs to the originary structure. Since the originary consists in the very manifestation of being, this means that the *task* of saving the content of the originary from being annulled essentially pertains to the originary itself. The fact that the originary is entrusted with the safeguard of the appearing of being means that its task is to take care that nothing of itself is lost. This task is essential because what it has to fulfil is the freeing from and the protection against the contradiction. The essentiality of the task, however, bears no guarantee of its realization, for the contradiction impends on the originary as a possibility. That is to say, it is the originary itself that, in projecting a realization of the originary in which it is affected by a positional *steresis*, is aware of the impending contradiction. (Furthermore, it is clear that the contradiction is a possibility not only insofar as such a realization of the originary is projected, but also insofar as it is projected that the originary, in its present reality, consists of a positional *steresis*.)

m. To the extent that becoming consists of an increment of the content of the totality of the immediate, the latter realizes itself as a process of the superseding of a contradiction. If S indicates the totality of present determinations at a moment m, and if S' indicates a determination that arises at a moment m', the positional plane $S + S'$ that is realized at m' stands, with respect to the positional plane S that is realized at m, in the same way in which T stands with respect to $r(T)$, which is affected by the positional *steresis* of S'. If the equation $S = r(T)$ is therefore valid in relation to the positional plane $S + S'$, it follows that to the extent that $r(T)$ realizes itself as implying $r(P)$, S' is *implicitly* included in $r(P)$ as a possible nullity. Since, however, the *real possibility* of S' corresponds to m, which is precisely realized as the implication between $r(T)$ and $r(P)$ – i.e. since S' counts at m as a *real possibility*, and it therefore enjoys an ontological substantiality – it follows that $r(P)$ implicitly posits the positive S' as a possible nullity, in such a way that m is realized as a being in contradiction. The arising of S', or the transition from m to m', *qua* superseding of a positional *steresis*, is therefore the superseding of the contradiction caused by the latter.

16. The superseding of the abstractness of the concept Γ_a

The concrete structuring of the originary constitutes the originary superseding of the problematicity of Γ_a: indeed, the affirmation that being surpasses the totality of immediately present being (regarded as possible experience) is L-immediate (cf. Chapter 13). It is clear that this L-immediacy pertains to the affirmation that this surpassing obtains *in a strong sense* (cf. §10), since the affirmation that this surpassing obtains in a weak sense is already L-immediate from the standpoint of Γ_a (and, to the extent that it is implied by the problematic situation in accordance with which Γ_a is realized, it is originarily superseded: precisely insofar as the concrete structuring of the originary consists in that very surpassing in a weak sense – that is to say, the L-immediate affirmation that the positive surpasses the originary in a strong sense constitutes the very surpassing, in a weak sense, of the originary regarded as Γ_a).

In this respect, the originary is not simply the originary opening of metaphysics as a formal knowledge, but it is the originary opening of metaphysics as concrete knowledge.

Furthermore, in relation to this first respect, the proposition: 'The immediately present constants of S are not the totality of the constants of S' is L-mediated (as already discussed, cf. Chapter 10, §8, [9]).

17. The originary structure *qua* originary problematicity

While the concrete structuring of the originary constitutes the originary superseding of the problematicity of Γ_a, *it does not, however, constitute a superseding of the totality of the problematic.*

Indeed, on the one hand, while it is L-immediate that being surpasses possible experience in a strong sense (cf. Chapter 13), it is not L-immediate that Ph-immediate being surpasses the factual determination of experience in a strong sense, i.e. that the totality of the Ph-immediate may realize itself in a different way from the factual one (different in a strong sense). The surpassing of factual experience by possible experience in a weak sense is instead L-immediate: to the extent that the very solution of the problem, as to whether Ph-immediate being surpasses the factual determination of experience in a strong sense, surpasses the situation constituted by this problem – and, more generally, the situation constituted by the problematicity that pertains to the originary. That is to say, the first of the two projects indicated in §3 is originarily superseded, whereas the second one is not – even though it is not immediately contradictory to project an extension of the analysis of the originary that would also exhibit the L-immediacy of the superseding of that second project.

On the other hand, as already mentioned, positing the L-immediacy of the surpassing of possible experience by being does not thereby mean excluding the being of a positive that does not belong to possible experience, and that would differ from that positive that, while itself not belonging to possible experience, is L-immediately affirmed. That is to say, in this second respect, too, the concrete structuring of the originary is realized as an originary problematicity. As such, it is an originary contradiction: i.e. precisely insofar as every problematic situation constitutes a being in contradiction. The fact that the concrete structuring of the originary is the opening of a contradiction is an L-immediate affirmation, in that it is L-immediately affirmed that the problem (or the project) confers the same value on the contradictory propositions that constitute it. Another meaning (cf. Chapter 10, §8, [8]) of the L-immediacy of the proposition: 'The originary is the opening of a contradiction' is thereby established.

The two aspects of projecting, which have been identified above as belonging to the concrete structuring of the originary, are the moments of the project as part of which being surpasses the totality of Ph-L-immediately affirmed being (i.e. the project of the existence of a surpassing of the originary that is additional relative to the originarily affirmed one).

18. Determination of the meaning of a retrieval of the first part of the present chapter as part of the concrete structuring of the originary

Accordingly, if by 'totality of the immediate' (= 'originary' = 'originary structure', etc.) one does not simply refer to the totality of the Ph-immediate – as it is instead the case if the originary is structured as Γ_a – but to the concrete totality of the immediate, i.e. to the horizon that includes both the totality of Ph-immediate being and the totality of that being that does not belong to possible experience and that is L-immediately affirmed, then *all* that has been affirmed in the first and second parts of this chapter is to be repeated as referring to the problematicity that, following what has been discussed above, comes to define the concrete horizon of immediacy. Sections 2–15 of the present chapter can therefore be translated into the standpoint of the concrete by taking as subject matter the concrete horizon or structuring of immediacy. It is clear that as part of this logical operation one should not take into account the propositions in square brackets, since the actual and concrete structuring of the concrete, precisely as such, cannot actually or presently be diminished to an abstract concept, in the way in which Γ_a is precisely diminished to an abstract concept in relation to that actual and concrete structuring.

In order to ease the adaptation to the concrete, let us only add the following notes.

a. The way in which §3 is to be adapted has already been indicated above (§17). The adaptation of §4, according to the established criteria, does not present any difficulties either.

b. It should instead be emphasized that an adaptation of §5 and §7 shows what has been anticipated in §8 [9] of Chapter 10 – namely, the L-immediacy of the proposition: 'The immediately present constants of S are not the totality of the constants of S'.

c. §6 is instead retained as part of the adaptation, since, as verified in §17, the concrete structuring of the originary is not an L-immediate affirmation of the fact that the totality of the Ph-immediate may realize itself in a different way (in a strong sense) from the one realized by the factual determination of the immediate.

d. While the adaptation of §8 does not present any difficulties, the adaptation of §§9–12 must be carried out in the following way (already addressed in §17). The concrete structuring of the originary consists in the L-immediate difference between the whole and the originary structure, according to the sense that follows from the logical adaptation of §9, to the extent that, *in addition* to the L-immediate difference (which is not at issue) determined by the positing of the L-immediacy of the affirmation that the positive surpasses the originary in a strong sense, there *also* obtains – precisely insofar as the originary nevertheless persists as an originary problematicity, as seen in §17 – the difference or inequality determined by the fact that the solution of this originary problematicity surpasses the originary: in such a way that, also in this sense, it is necessary to L-immediately affirm the difference or inequality between the whole and the originary. The concrete structuring of the originary, in addition to being the opening of concrete metaphysical knowledge, is therefore the opening of a formal metaphysical knowledge.

e. The concept of the immediate self-contradictoriness of the concept of the impossibility of metaphysics, too, must therefore be held firm (thus carrying out the logical adaptation of §14). By 'metaphysics' we do not refer to the originary and concrete opening of metaphysical knowledge, as it is precisely realized *qua* originary structure (for, indeed, in this respect, it is not only immediately self-contradictory to suppose that it should be possible to verify the self-contradictoriness of the metaphysical solution, but metaphysical knowledge, or the metaphysical solution, is originarily realized), but we refer to the horizon constituted by the resolution of the problematicity that pertains in any case to the concrete structuring of the originary.

f. The adaptation of §15 will have to meet the condition of verifying – *in a different way* from the one already established in Chapter 10 – that a positing of the originary structure that is affected by a positional *steresis* relative to a specific quantity of variants constitutes the opening of a contradiction.

12

The inherent contradictoriness of the negation of the presence of being

1. The inherent contradictoriness of the negation of Ph-immediate being

As already observed (cf. Chapter 10, § 19), 'being' (regarded as formal being) L-immediately stands as a syntactic constant of *every* determination or semantic content. (Common language is a form of *implicitness*, which, for the most part, leaves unexpressed what confers meaning upon what is given prominence by the word; this implicitness, however, then consists in such a preoccupation with the determination, which tends to lapse into a *distraction* from being).

This means that being is L-immediately predicated of *every* semantic content: namely, it is immediately self-contradictory for any determination – any *positivity* or any *being* – not to be. The propositions of the type: 'This red is', as much as the proposition: 'The semantic whole is' – and therefore, more generally, all the propositions that affirm the being of any determination (all these propositions being expressed by the proposition: 'Being is') – are therefore analytic propositions, in accordance with the definition of the term 'analytic proposition' given in § 11 of Chapter 6.

The proposition: 'The totality of Ph-immediate being is', too, is therefore analytic. That is to say, it is inherently contradictory to negate that being, which is Ph-immediately known, Is. What has been anticipated in §§ 26, 28 of Chapter 2 is thereby confirmed: namely, that the superseding of the negation of Ph-immediate being – which does not supersede that negation insofar as this is an inherent contradiction, but insofar as it is simply *in contradiction with* the Ph-immediacy of being – is only a *moment* of the concrete superseding of the negation of Ph-immediate being.

2. Analyses must be regarded in the form of Ph-immediacy

If $d_1, d_2, d_3, \ldots d_n$ are all the Ph-immediately known determinations, let us indicate by D the semantic domain constituted by all these determinations; that is to say, let us indicate by D the subject of the analytic proposition: 'The totality of Ph-immediate being is'. Then: what is the ground of the knowledge of D? On what basis are exactly these determinations of being, and not other ones, affirmed? Or: on what basis are these determinations, and not other ones, attributed to being? This is equivalent to asking on what basis it is affirmed that D is. It should be noted that here it is not possible to reply that it is affirmed that D is because the being of D L-immediately pertains to D: it is not possible to reply in this way because what is being sought here is precisely the ground of the *disclosure* or *knowledge* of the meaning D, to which its being L-immediately pertains. The fact that being is – i.e. that the being constituted by D is – is an analytic affirmation; but what is the ground of the disclosure of being, and of that being that is precisely determined as D? That is to say: on what basis is the subject of the analytic proposition: 'D is' held firm? Or: what allows us to *speak* of being, or to *name* it? And lastly: what is the ground of the fact that *there is* being, or what is the ground of the being-there of being?

It is clear that the positing of the Ph-immediacy of being (cf. Chapter 2) constitutes the *originary supersession* of these questions: there is being, or being is known, for itself; the knowledge, disclosure or being-there of being is Ph-immediate, i.e. it is the ground itself in its phenomenological value. The disclosure of being precisely realizes itself in the proposition: 'Being (i.e. being which is determined as D) is'; and the Ph-immediacy of this proposition is expressed by the proposition: 'The fact that being is known for itself' = 'Being that is known for itself is'. The first of these last two formulations makes it explicit that the analysis (the being of being) is precisely what is Ph-immediately known; the second formulation makes it explicit that the Ph-immediacy of being *determines* the subject (the term, or content) of the analysis, in such a way that the analytic proposition: 'Being is' must be determined as 'D is' (leaving aside that determination – considered in the next chapter – which is obtained through an L-immediate affirmation).

3. The mutual implication of Ph-immediacy and L-immediacy

a. From what we have said in the previous two sections, it appears that, on the one hand, the analysis – i.e. the L-immediacy – takes as its content the totality of Ph-immediate being, in the sense that this totality is the subject of the analytic proposition: 'D is'; and, on the other hand, the Ph-immediacy takes as its content the analysis, in the sense that it is Ph-immediately known that being is, i.e. in the sense that the being of the Ph-immediate determinations – namely, the being of being – is Ph-immediately known.

b. Furthermore, to the extent that the Ph-immediate content is the opening of the semantic whole itself, or, equivalently, of the very totality of being (cf. Chapter 10) – i.e. to the extent that the *being*, of which being is L-immediately predicated (or to which being L-immediately pertains) and which in its standing as the subject of that predication is the Ph-immediate content, is meaningful as the *whole* itself – it must be stated that the content of the analysis is not, precisely, a finite determination, but the whole itself. Accordingly, the proposition: 'Being is', which is the content of the Ph-immediacy, means: 'The whole (the totality of being) is'.

At the same time, however, the term 'being' that appears in the proposition: 'Being is' means *D*, i.e. a (finite) *determination* of the whole, to the extent that the originary structures itself as a project (cf. Chapter 11, §17) as part of which the absolute semantic matter surpasses the totality of originarily – i.e. Ph-L-immediately – affirmed being in a strong sense: *D* being able to be considered here as a designation of both Ph-immediate being and of that non-Ph-immediate being that is L-immediately affirmed (cf. Chapter 13). It is here clear that it is only a project that *D*, with this new definition, should stand as a finite determination of the whole, and not as the absolute semantic matter.[1]

In other words, the term 'being' that appears in the proposition: 'Being is' is in any case meaningful as the whole, even if it is a project that originary being (= *D*) should be the absolute semantic matter.

Lastly, insofar as it is L-immediately known (cf. Chapter 13) that being surpasses the totality of Ph-immediate being in a strong sense, a domain of the originary content of the whole (precisely, the domain constituted by that surpassing being) has a formal value, and the residual domain (the totality of the Ph-immediate) has a concrete value.

4. Summary and transition

The concrete supersession of the negation of Ph-immediate being consists in the relation between the supersession of that negation insofar as the latter is in contradiction *with* the Ph-immediacy of being (cf. Chapter 2) and the supersession of that negation insofar as the latter is inherently contradictory (and can in fact be considered as the very definition of contradiction). It should therefore be noted that this result cannot simply be indicated by stating that the negation of Ph-immediate being is inherently contradictory. That result must instead be expressed as follows: since the negation of Ph-immediate being is in contradiction with the Ph-immediacy of being, the positing of the Ph-immediacy of being – i.e. the affirmation according to which it is known for itself that being is – is *at the same time* the positing of the inherent contradictoriness of the negation of Ph-immediate being. That is to say, as already mentioned, the Ph-immediacy of being is the very Ph-immediacy of the inherent contradictoriness of the negation of the Ph-immediate. Therefore, if one negates Ph-immediate being, thus coming to be in contradiction *with* the Ph-immediacy, one incurs for this very reason in an *inherent* contradiction. In this sense, it must precisely be stated that the negation of the Ph-immediate is inherently contradictory.

More generally, an analysis presupposes what is analysed: in the sense that the positing of the L-immediacy of the pertaining of *y* to *x* is only realized if the being of *x* is known (posited, affirmed). And the positing of the being of *x* enjoys a value of immediacy that – assuming that the positing of the L-immediacy of the pertaining of *y* to *x* expresses the totality of the analysis – cannot be the one that gives rise to the L-immediacy, but it is the one that gives rise to the Ph-immediacy. Indeed, claiming that the positing of *every* semantic content takes place by virtue of an analytic connection means affirming a *regressus in indefinitum* in the foundation of the being of every semantic content: i.e. it means negating that the affirmation of being is grounded, and this negation is a negation of the horizon of Ph-immediate being.

Furthermore, if one wished to avoid the inherent contradiction indicated here by arguing that what is being negated is not the fact that being is, but that being *is present*, one falls into *another type of self-contradiction*. The following section addresses precisely this different type of self-contradiction.

5. The inherent contradictoriness of the negation of the presence of being

a. Let us negate that being is present. Then, this negation is either present or it is not.

In the second case, it does not set itself in opposition to the affirmation of the presence of being; that is to say, this case consists in its own not obtaining.

If the negation of presence is instead present, the presence of the negation *contradicts* the content of the latter. The inherent contradictoriness of the negation of presence is 'in itself' or implicit: in the sense that presence is negated *in actu signato* and it is affirmed *in actu exercito*, in such a way that the positional domain constituted by the negation only includes one of the two sides of the contradiction that affects it.

b. This argument does not however succeed in preventing the *inherent* contradictoriness of the negation of presence from no longer obtaining if the negation is regarded as the negation *of a specific dimension* of total presence: a dimension that does not include the negation of the dimension itself. That is to say, if in negating the presence of being one admits the presence of a dimension that includes the negation of the residual dimension of total presence, that negation – based on the argument developed above – will certainly be in contradiction *with* the Ph-immediacy of that residual dimension, but it will not be *inherently* contradictory. For, indeed, that negation, thus restricted, is not posited as a negation and affirmation *simpliciter* of presence, but as the negation of a specific presence and as the affirmation of another specific presence.

c. The inherent contradictoriness of the negation *of a finite region* of the totality of immediate presence can however be attested in many ways. In general, let us here state that insofar as this negation is equivalent to the positing of a finite dimension of the semantic whole (precisely because, at least, it does not consist in the positing of that finite region of Ph-immediate being), the positional horizon of that negation constitutes the opening of a C-contradiction, i.e. it entails finding oneself in an inherent contradiction; the latter is precisely superseded by positing or affirming the totality of immediately present being.

The argument, however, takes a different course depending on the type of meanings that the positional domain of the negation in question does not include as posited. (For instance, if $\delta_1, \delta_2, \delta_3, \ldots, \delta_n$ is the protocol that indicates all those determinations that, in the positional domain of the negation, are recognized as being present, and if that protocol does not include a specific persyntactic constant, the argument dismissed above will once again be valid, insofar as that specific persyntactic constant will be present *in actu exercito* in the positional domain of the negation, and it will be negated *qua* present to the extent that one of the terms of that protocol consists in the affirmation that the terms of the protocol constitute all that is present: this being an implicit negation of that persyntactic constant, for the latter is implicitly included in the horizon that surpasses the terms of the protocol.)

The inherent contradictoriness identified above obtains both in case the negation of a finite region of presence is explicit – i.e. in case that negation *posits as something superseded* the affirmation that the totality of presence surpasses the quantity of presence recognized by the negation – and in case that negation is implicit, i.e. in case that negation only affirms a part of the totality of presence without explicitly negating the residual part, and in any case leaving the semantic plane that constitutes this residual part as something non-posited.

d. It is still possible to advance the following remark, which may be considered as a specification of what has been discussed in the previous point. The *affirmation* of the totality of immediate presence, which posits being according to all the determinations that pertain to it insofar as it is known for itself, is, as superseded (but in fact, in a mediated way, also as such), a constant of the negation of a finite region of presence (this argument being however valid for every type of negation of presence). Positing a negation of presence without positing this (its) constant is therefore an inherent self-contradiction; this self-contradiction is precisely superseded by positing the constant in question. This positing, however, is itself a self-contradiction, as we shall clarify below, in such a way that a (partial or total) negation of presence counts in any case as a self-contradiction.[2]

For, indeed, precisely because that affirmation is negated, that affirmation is *posited* (known, disclosed, manifest), and what is negated is precisely this, which is posited. (What is negated, and therefore posited, is not a *formal* affirmation – i.e. such that the totality of presence is only posited in a formal way, and not according to all the determinations that pertain to it – for the constant constituted by the affirmation in question would have a formal value, and the positional domain of the negation of presence would persists as a self-contradictoriness). And yet, that, which in order to be superseded (negated) must be posited, is superseded *in the same sense* in which it is posited. That is to say, the affirmation of presence, which the negation of presence must posit in order to be able to negate, is negated in the same sense in which it must be affirmed (posited) in order to be able to be negated. Let us elaborate on this point.

This red surface belongs to that being that is Ph-immediately known. If one states: 'This surface is not present as a white surface', this negation is a superseding of the presence of this surface as a white surface. What is negated – that whose presence is negated – is 'this surface as a white surface'. At the same time, however, this surface as a white surface is not *absolutely* absent, or absolutely external to presence, for otherwise that negation would not negate anything: that is to say, in order to affirm that this surface as a white surface is not present, it is necessary for this surface as a white surface to be present. The contradiction is superseded by stating that this white surface is present *in some way*. That is to say, there arises no contradiction precisely because the mode (or the sense) according to which this surface is present as a white surface is not the mode (or sense) according to which it is negated that it is present as a white surface. Equivalently, the contradiction does not obtain to the extent that, as part of presence itself, it is possible to distinguish certain *modes* of presence (thus stating, for instance, that this surface as a white surface is not present in a 'real' way, but in an 'ideal' one).

If we now consider the negation of the affirmation of the present totality, it is then to be attested that this distinction of the modes of presence is not possible here. For, indeed, now the negation does not simply negate that a term has a specific mode of presence (thus letting that term have that mode of presence that is necessarily required by the negation of the presence of that term): here, the negation aims to negate, *simpliciter*, presence itself. (Furthermore, that negation negates presence itself, *simpliciter*, both in case it negates a finite dimension of the totality of the Ph-immediate and in case it negates this very totality). The positional domain opened by the negation of presence therefore implies the positing of the totality of presence, and, at the same time, it is a negation of this very domain of presence that it implies. In other words, the necessary condition for the constitution of the negation of presence is the very affirmation of presence; or, equivalently, the negation can realize itself only by implying what it negates. It is here clear that an inherent contradiction is realized to the extent that the negation of presence does not negate a mode of presence, but it *simpliciter* negates the presence of the totality (or a part) of Ph-immediate being.

e. Furthermore however, making use of elements upon which we have already elaborated: insofar as *every* proposition is *identical*, in the sense indicated in § 10 of Chapter 6, the proposition: 'Being is immediately present', too, is identical; accordingly, its negation is self-contradictory. Since every meaning is a constant of every other meaning, insofar as every true proposition is a necessary proposition (cf. Chapter 10, § 10), the proposition: 'Being is immediately present', too, is necessary: that is to say, its negation is self-contradictory.

6. In what sense the negation of the presence of being is immediately self-contradictory

a. If the negation of the proposition: 'Being (= $d_1, d_2, d_3, \ldots, d_n$ = D) is immediately present' is self-contradictory, at the same time, however, the predicate: 'immediately present' L-immediately pertains neither to the single meanings $d_1, d_2, d_3, \ldots, d_n$ as such, nor to the meaning D as such, which is precisely the set of these meanings. (The primary condition of this lack of pertaining consists in the fact that the concept of each of the terms of the series $d_1, d_2, d_3, \ldots, d_n$ is respectively distinct from the concept of its immediate presence; and the same holds for D. For instance, 'd_2' does not mean: 'immediate presence of d_2'. And if one posits 'd_3' = 'immediate presence of d_2', 'd_3' does not mean: 'immediate presence of d_3'.) (It is indeed the case that the ground of the positing of $d_1, d_2, d_3, \ldots, d_n$ consists in the positing of the Ph-immediacy of this positing, but it is also the case that the content of that first positing does not have the same meaning as the content of this second positing.)

If the positing of the Ph-immediacy of any determination does not L-immediately pertain to that determination as such, the predicational connection between that determinacy and its Ph-immediacy has a *synthetic* value. This synthetic character originarily means that it is affirmed that being is immediately present because this immediacy is included in the horizon of what is immediately present.

b. Before proceeding in this direction, however, it is necessary to consider the following objection. If D indicates the *totality* of the immediately present determinations, D also includes that determination constituted by the very immediate presence of the totality of present determinations: it *must* originarily include it in order for the proposition: 'Being (= D) is immediately present' not to be a groundless – and in the last instance self-contradictory – affirmation (cf. Chapter 2, § 16). Due to this inclusion, the affirmation of the immediate presence of being is analytic: precisely because it takes place on the basis of the analysis of the meaning D.

The resolution of this objection leads to an actual specification of what we have affirmed above. The proposition: 'Being, which is immediately present, is immediately present' is certainly an analytic proposition; if 'D' indicates the immediate presence of a content, nothing but the analysis of D is required in order to affirm that this content is immediately present. Furthermore, not only is that proposition analytic, but it is an identical proposition: the analytic character indeed consisting in the fact that the proposition in question is considered in its concrete structure (cf. Chapter 6, § 10): (D = π) = (π = D), in which 'π' means 'immediately present'; that is to say, it is considered according to that value for which every proposition is identical, and, therefore, analytic.

Now, however, what is at issue is not the pertaining of π (= D) to D (= π), but the pertaining of π to D, in which D is held distinct from π, and vice-versa (in the sense that the semantic domain of each of the two terms does not include the other one); accordingly, in the present section, the term 'D' indicates the totality of the immediately present determinations, *except for* π, i.e. *except for* that determination that consists in the immediate presence of the totality in question (and the term π indicates the meaning 'immediate presence' in its being formally distinct from that of which that presence is precisely an immediate presence). It is precisely relative to the relation that obtains between D and π, regarded in this way, that in point a) we referred to a *synthetic* value of that relation. Let us here add the following: while the negation of (D = π) = (π = D) is immediately self-contradictory, negating that π pertains to D (these two terms being regarded in the sense established above) is not immediately self-contradictory, even though that negation is immediately *in contradiction with* the Ph-immediacy of the pertaining of π to D, and, therefore – *qua negation of* (D = π) = (π = D) (this equation precisely expressing the Ph-immediacy of the pertaining of π to D) – it is a self-contradictory negation. The proposition: 'D is π' is therefore synthetic in the sense indicated in § 11 of Chapter 6. It is furthermore clear that this proposition is synthetic and not self-contradictory to the extent that D = π is not abstractly separated from (D = π) = (π = D).

c. From what we have stated, it therefore appears that D, as distinct from π in the sense indicated above, *cannot* stand as or *cannot* indicate *all* the determinations that are immediately present, because the totality of presence precisely consists in the synthesis of D and π. This means that the proposition: 'Being is immediately present' can only be analytic (and, in fact, identical) if the term 'being' indicates the *totality* of immediately present being: for if the predicate is not included in the subject in the very act in which the predicate is referred to the subject (i.e. if D is not posited as

$D = \pi$), the subject is negated as to its semantic value, i.e. it is no longer the *totality* of the Ph-immediate. Affirming that the pertaining of π to D has a synthetic value therefore means attesting the connection that obtains *between two moments* of the totality of the Ph-immediate.

d. This does not mean that the very totality of the Ph-immediate cannot *come* to be posited as something immediately present. This side of the matter has already been addressed in § 22 of Chapter 5, in which P indicated the positing of that totality, and P' the positing of the immediate presence of P. In relation to the symbols used here, P' corresponds to π' and P corresponds to $(D = \pi) = (\pi = D)$. Accordingly, if $(D = \pi) = (\pi = D)$ does not include π', the pertaining of π' to $(D = \pi) = (\pi = D)$ has a synthetic value, and $(D = \pi) = (\pi = D)$ no longer expresses the *totality* of immediately present being. The situation that takes place with the pertaining of π to D thus occurs again.

The exclusion of a *regressus in indefinitum* in the positing of the immediate presence of being (cf. Chapter 3, § 16) should indeed not be conflated with the exclusion of the *possibility* of constructing a series of multiply reflectional terms: the presence of presence, the presence of the presence of presence, etc. In order to posit the immediate presence of being, it is not necessary to realize an infinite series of acts of positing; hence, in order to avoid the realization of this series, it is necessary for the positing of the immediate presence of being to be constituted as an *identical* proposition, in which the immediate presence is immediately included in the horizon of what is immediately present; that is to say, it is necessary for that positing to be constituted as $(D = \pi) = (\pi = D)$. That second exclusion, however, is not necessary; that is to say, once the Ph-immediacy of being has been posited, it is possible to start the construction of that series of multiply reflectional terms, and carry it forward. In relation to the possibility of this construction, there exists the possibility of constructing a series of *synthetic propositions* whose subject is that which, in a prior moment, counted as the totality of the Ph-immediate, and whose predicate is, respectively, a multiply reflectional term of that first series. The pertaining of π' to $(D = \pi) = (\pi = D)$ considered above may be regarded as the first term of the series of these synthetic propositions. Once again, let us reiterate here that these propositions are synthetic and not self-contradictory to the extent that they are not abstractly separated from the concrete equation that expresses the totality of the Ph-immediate, which must constitute itself again (or must persist) throughout the construction of that series in order for the propositions of the series not to be groundless, and, in the last instance, self-contradictory. For instance: the pertaining of π' to $(D = \pi) = (\pi = D)$ is synthetic and not self-contradictory to the extent that

$$[(D = \pi) = (\pi = D)] = \pi'$$

is not abstractly separated from

$$\{[(D = \pi) = (\pi = D)] = \pi'\} = \{\pi' = [(D = \pi) = (\pi = D)]\}.[3]$$

This last equation is the originary judgement itself, i.e. it is the very positing of the totality of the Ph-immediate (insofar as this totality must precisely include π).

e. The affirmation according to which negating that π pertains to D is not immediately self-contradictory (whereby it is not immediately self-contradictory to *project* that π should not pertain to D) is also not in contradiction with the verification of the inherent contradictoriness of the negation of the presence of being (carried out in § 5 a, d). Negating, *simpliciter*, that being – or a region of present being – is present is a self-contradiction, but it is not immediately self-contradictory to *project* that being, or a region of present being, should no longer be present (even though projecting that a region of being is no longer present means projecting a positional domain that is realized as a self-contradiction, due to the theorem according to which every meaning is a constant of every other meaning).

f. However, let us specify: the project that 'this' extension, which is Ph-immediately known as a red extension, should no longer be red is only non-contradictory to the extent that it is the project for a *persistence* of this extension (i.e. the essence in a *different* individuation) to no longer be red – for, indeed, *this* extension is *necessarily* red, i.e. this property L-immediately pertains to it (even though the fact that there is something like this red extension is known through an Ph-immediate affirmation), in such a way that the project of the non-pertaining of that property is immediately self-contradictory; *in the same way*, the project for π to no longer pertain to D is only non-contradictory to the extent that it projects that π should not pertain to a *persistence* of D, i.e. to a different individuation of the essence of D. For projecting that π should not pertain to D, insofar as the latter is *hic et nunc* in its concrete specificity, is immediately self-contradictory. If Ph-immediate being will no longer be present, or if it had not been present, what will no longer be or what would not have been present is not, *simpliciter*, that being that is present, but the essence of this being, in a different individuation.

In other words: even if $D = \pi$ is considered as concretely distinct from $(D = \pi) = (\pi = D)$, if D is held firm in its being *hic et nunc*, the negation of the proposition $D = \pi$ is self-contradictory. That proposition is however *synthetic a priori* (cf. Chapter 7, § 20), in that its negation is not superseded as something self-contradictory insofar as it is a negation of $D = \pi$, but insofar as it is a negation of $(D = \pi) = (\pi = D)$ – since, if $D = \pi$ is concretely distinct from $(D = \pi) = (\pi = D)$, the negation of $D = \pi$ implies the negation of $(D = \pi) = (\pi = D)$, and that negation is immediately self-contradictory. The proposition $D = \pi$, however, *immediately stands as a synthetic a posteriori proposition* precisely insofar as its negation is not superseded as something self-contradictory insofar as it is a negation of $D = \pi$; and, at the same time, it *immediately stands as a synthetic a priori proposition* because its negation is superseded by the very concrete structuring of immediacy (cf. Chapter 7).[4]

7. Aporia and prospective reference

The affirmation according to which negating that π pertains to D is not immediately self-contradictory – and, more generally, the affirmation that there exist synthetic propositions of the type: 'D is π' (synthetic *a posteriori* propositions) – gives instead rise to an aporetic situation of a primary importance, in relation to the way in which the inherent contradictoriness of the negation of Ph-immediate being has been verified in § 1. The present chapter ends with a general formulation of this aporia: the concrete formulation of the aporia, outlined in its broadest scope, and its resolution are the task of the next chapter. The (*originary*) resolution of this aporia consists in the very concrete positing of the L-immediacy of the affirmation that being surpasses the totality of Ph-immediate being in a strong sense – a concrete positing that up to now has only been anticipated.

It must therefore be stated that insofar as the synthesis of D and π (letting $D\pi$ be this synthesis) is a specific semantic positivity, or a specific being – and the same should be stated of every *a posteriori* synthesis – whereby the proposition: '$D\pi$ is' is analytic (cf. § 1), it follows that projecting that π should not pertain to D is equivalent to projecting a no longer being, i.e. an *annulment*, of $D\pi$: that is to say, it is equivalent to projecting *that being is not*. Accordingly, if on the one hand the proposition: 'Being is not' is posited as being immediately self-contradictory, on the other hand it is argued – in contradiction with the immediacy of this self-contradictoriness – that the project for being not to be is not immediately self-contradictory.

13

Originary metaphysics

1. The meaning of the analytic character of existential propositions

If *being* is L-immediately predicated of any determination or semantic content x (cf. Chapter 12, §1), that meaning x is however distinct, as such, from the 'being' that pertains to it. For instance, in the proposition: 'This red is', the meaning 'this red' is distinct from the meaning 'is'. That proposition is therefore analytic (in the sense conferred upon this expression in §11 of Chapter 6), but it is not identical. This is the case for all the values that x can take, except for one: namely, that for which x counts as formal being itself. Insofar as the meaning 'semantic whole' = 'totality of being' = 'being' (the latter term, however, being regarded as the concrete universal) is one of those values of x, the proposition: 'Being is' (in which the subject counts as the concrete universal) is analytic, but not identical.

It should be noted that what has been affirmed above must be understood in the sense that while *every* non-contradictory judgement is *identical* (cf. Chapter 6, §10) – in such a way that, indicating the 'being' (formal being) that is L-immediately predicated of every semantic content by ε, this predication must be conceived of as $(x = ε) = (ε = x)$ – at the same time, however, considering the proposition $x = ε$ as concretely distinct from $(x = ε) = (ε = x)$, x, in the proposition $x = ε$, distinguishes itself from ε for all its values except one (precisely that for which x stands as ε), and, in this sense, we are stating that the obtained propositions are not identical.

2. Note

The Parmenidean position may be deduced here as follows: if $x = ε$ is abstractly separated from $(x = ε) = (ε = x)$ – or, equivalently, if x and ε are presupposed to their synthesis – one will be compelled to recognize that it is self-contradictory for ε to pertain to x for all those values of x that differ from ε; the only non-contradictory predication will therefore be the identical proposition: 'Being is', in which the subject of the predication is not the concrete universal, but that absolute semantic simplicity constituted by the predicate: $ε = ε$.

However – leaving aside the original fault consisting in the abstract separation of $x = \varepsilon$ from $(x = \varepsilon) = (\varepsilon = x)$ – on the one hand, the very proposition $\varepsilon = \varepsilon$ is self-contradictory if it is not conceived of as $(\varepsilon = \varepsilon) = (\varepsilon = \varepsilon)$, and, on the other hand, to the extent that 'not being non-being' is formally distinct (cf. Chapter 6, §12) from 'being', it will also not be possible to affirm that 'Being is not non-being': that is to say, this will not be possible for the same reason for which ε cannot be predicated of any of the values of x that are distinct from ε (that 'not being non-being' constituting one of these values).

As already clarified, it is only the originarity of the synthesis of subject and predicate – an originarity that must be conceived of as $(subject = predicate) = (predicate = subject)$ – that affords the constitution of identity and non-contradiction (as well as their realizations as the identity and non-contradiction of the concrete universal). *Differentiae entis sunt formaliter ens*: with this principle, traditional ontology precisely recognizes the substantiality or originarity of the synthesis between being and the determination (i.e. of existence and essence).

3. Determination of the meaning of the existential judgement

Affirming that being is L-immediately predicated of any semantic content means affirming that every semantic content – and, therefore, the semantic whole – is not non-being, and this not being non-being L-immediately pertains to it. The whole is; or, equivalently: being (which, *qua* propositional subject must now always be regarded as the concrete universal) is; in no way is it possible to think that it is not; 'in no way is it possible to think that...' means: affirming that being is not is immediately self-contradictory.

4. In what sense the proposition 'Being is' is the principle of non-contradiction itself

Insofar as the proposition 'Being is' (or, equivalently: 'Beings are' – in which 'beings' indicate the semantic whole, or any of its determinations) is L-immediate, or analytic, its relation with the principle of non-contradiction has already been implicitly investigated in §18 of Chapter 7, in which L-immediate propositions have been identified as *individuations* of the principle of non-contradiction: namely, propositions such that their L-immediacy precisely obtains insofar as they are *posited* as such individuations, i.e. insofar as logical immediacy itself is posited in its concrete value (cf. Chapter 7, §18, c, f). In relation to the proposition under consideration now, however, the following clarifications are necessary.

The proposition: 'Being is' may be considered, on the one hand, as a specific individuation of concrete L-immediacy (i.e. of the concrete value of the principle of non-contradiction); this is not the case, however, because the term 'being' is a moment of the semantic whole – for, in fact, 'being' counts here as the concrete universal (i.e. as the semantic whole itself) – but because *the relation* between the predicate and the subject of the proposition under consideration stands as an individuation (moment, aspect, part) of that relation between predicate and subject according to which the L-immediacy is realized in its concreteness. Indeed, this immediacy, in its concrete value, consists in the positing of the totality of L-immediate connections (even though this totality is posited in a formal way to the extent that the totality of the determinations of the positive is known in a formal way – this latter affirmation being justified, on the one hand, by what we have discussed in Chapter 11 and, on the other hand, by what we shall establish in the present chapter). In the proposition: 'Being is', instead, only the L-immediate connection that obtains between being (each being) and its being is posited, and, in this sense, it must be stated that the positing of this connection is a moment or individuation of the totality or the universal of the L-immediate connections.[1]

In a different respect, however, the proposition: 'Being is' is not an individuation of concrete logical immediacy, but it is this very immediacy in its concreteness. For, indeed, insofar as 'being' stands as the semantic whole itself, or as the very totality of the positive, it includes the totality of L-immediate connections (and, therefore, also that connection that consists in the proposition: 'Being is'), in such a way that the proposition in question consists in predicating being of L-immediacy itself (i.e. being of the L-immediacy that has the value of a concrete universal). That is to say, concrete L-immediacy, insofar as it includes the L-immediate connection: 'Being is', is this very L-immediate connection insofar as it includes that concrete L-immediacy. Equivalently, stating that the system of L-immediate connections includes the connection: 'Being is' means stating that this latter connection includes the system of L-immediate connections, i.e. it means stating that this system is. Accordingly, it is only possible to affirm that this system 'includes' that connection by disregarding the fact that the subject of the connection: 'Being is' is the very totality of L-immediate connections; and it is possible to state that being 'includes' that system only by disregarding the fact that *every* determination of the whole is part of that system at least to the extent that it is a self-identity and a negation of what is other than itself. The difference between the proposition: 'Being is' and the proposition: 'The whole is the whole' (which, as discussed in §18 of Chapter 7, precisely expresses concrete logical immediacy), therefore, has a simply linguistic character, in the sense that it is only at the level of language that, in that first proposition, the emphasis is placed on 'only' one connection of the totality of L-immediate connections.

5. Corollaries

a. It is clear that only the proposition: 'Being is' is able to stand as concrete L-immediacy itself. On the contrary, propositions of the type: 'This red is' – i.e. propositions such that their subject is not the semantic whole – while being L-immediate, only count as an individuation of L-immediacy; what has been verified in §18 of Chapter 7 must be stated of their relation with L-immediacy.

b. All L-immediate propositions whose subject is the semantic whole are each a concrete realization of logical immediacy: what varies in each of them is only the linguistic expression of that immediacy. In other words, in L-immediate propositions in which the subject is the whole, the specific L-immediate predication that is brought to the fore by the linguistic expression in each of those propositions *is necessarily posited* as a moment of the totality of the L-immediate predications, i.e. as an individuation of the universality of logical immediacy: precisely because the subject of the proposition is the whole. Accordingly, each of those propositions must stand as a formulation of the principle of non-contradiction.

6. The ontological value of the principle of non-contradiction

As a result of what we have established in §4, the principle of non-contradiction does not therefore have a simply *logical* value – i.e. it does not simply affirm that, *in case* being is, being is being (or being is not non-being), and, *in case* being is not, non-being is not or it is not being – but it also has an *ontological* value: namely, it is precisely an exclusion of the *supposition* that being is and of the *supposition* that being is not (since also *supposing* that being is corresponds to an affirmation of the possibility that being is not); that is to say, the principle of non-contradiction is the affirmation that *being is*.

In other words, even when realizing that the principle of non-contradiction is not only a rule of thought, but it concerns being itself, if one then regards being (what is non-contradictory) as in itself indifferent as to its own being or non-being – in such a way that through the principle of non-contradiction one states nothing but that being is, when it is, and that being is not, when it is not – one still regards non-contradictoriness itself in a formal way, and, exactly for this reason, one negates it: precisely because the supposition of a moment in which being is not is allowed to persist.

It is part of the very meaning of being that being must be – accordingly, the principle of non-contradiction does not simply express the self-identity of an essence (or its difference from the other essences), but the identity of essence and existence (or the otherness of essence from non-existence). Every existential affirmation is the positing of this identity of essence and existence: not in the sense that every existential proposition is identical (for, on the contrary, we have verified that no existential proposition but one is identical, cf. §1), but in the sense that the being (the positivity, the existence) of a determination is originarily included in the meaning of the determination (the essence) of which that being (that existence) is predicated.

7. The meaning of the relation between $(E = \varepsilon) = (\varepsilon = E)$ and $E = \varepsilon$

While the proposition '$A = A$' may count as synthetic *a priori* for a twofold reason (cf. Chapter 7, §18, f), the proposition 'Being is' – precisely because it is equivalent to the concrete formulation of the principle of non-contradiction – cannot instead count in any way as an *a priori* synthesis. Let us briefly develop this point.

Insofar as the proposition 'Being (E) is' must be concretely conceived of as ($E = \varepsilon$) = ($\varepsilon = E$), if ($E = \varepsilon$) is concretely distinguished from ($E = \varepsilon$) = ($\varepsilon = E$) – in the sense that the positional domain of $E = \varepsilon$ is not inclusive of the positional domain constituted by ($E = \varepsilon$) = ($\varepsilon = E$) – E can no longer stand as the semantic whole: i.e. it is the whole in a formal value. If this formal value pertains to E, the proposition: 'Being is' – '$E = \varepsilon$' – is certainly synthetic *a priori*, because it is thus *mediated* by the concrete logical immediacy, but, precisely, 'being' means here something other than 'being' *qua* semantic whole. (Accordingly, that proposition, contrary to the proposition '$A = A$', is mediated in a single sense: it is indeed not possible to state that '$E = \varepsilon$' can be affirmed *on the one hand* only insofar as ($E = \varepsilon$) = ($\varepsilon = E$) is posited, and *on the other hand* only insofar as the non-contradictoriness of the absolute content is posited; this cannot be affirmed because that second positing – i.e. the positing of the non-contradictoriness of the absolute content, or of the whole – is precisely the positing of ($E = \varepsilon$) = ($\varepsilon = E$).)

In other words: if the proposition $A' = A''$ (in which A indicates a finite determination of the whole) is held firm as concretely distinct from ($A' = A''$) = ($A'' = A'$), in such a way that the positional domain of $A' = A''$ does not include the domain of ($A' = A''$) = ($A'' = A'$), the proposition $A' = A''$ is synthetic *a priori* (cf. Chapter 7, §17), but the A' that appears in $A' = A''$ is *the same* A' that appears in ($A' = A''$) = ($A'' = A'$). When $E = \varepsilon$ is instead held firm as concretely distinct from ($E = \varepsilon$) = ($\varepsilon = E$), in such a way that the domain of $E = \varepsilon$ does not include the domain of ($E = \varepsilon$) = ($\varepsilon = E$), the proposition $E = \varepsilon$ is indeed synthetic *a priori*, but the E that appears in $E = \varepsilon$ is *not* the same E that appears in ($E = \varepsilon$) = ($\varepsilon = E$), since in this latter equation E counts as the whole, whereas, in $E = \varepsilon$, E only counts as a formal realization of the whole. Therefore, according to what we have already implicitly remarked,[2] the term E that appears in ($E = \varepsilon$) = ($\varepsilon = E$), precisely insofar as it is the whole, is itself realized or structured as the equation of which it is a term. At the same time, however, the analysis of ($E = \varepsilon$) = ($\varepsilon = E$) certainly leads to a positing of ($E = \varepsilon$) in which E does *not* count as the whole – and it is in fact precisely for this reason that an infinite development in the positing of ($E = \varepsilon$) = ($\varepsilon = E$) is avoided – in such a way that the proposition $E = \varepsilon$, in which E has that reduced value, is synthetic *a priori*.

Nor is it possible to state that the proposition ($E = \varepsilon$) = ($\varepsilon = E$) is synthetic *a priori* insofar as the L-immediate connection between E and ε is held distinct from all other L-immediate connections, i.e. it is considered as a positional domain that does not include all other L-immediate connections; for if that distinction were made, it would once again no longer be possible to regard E as the whole: i.e. as that horizon that is structured as the totality of L-immediate connections.[3] If E counts as the whole, the positing of the L-immediate connection between E and ε cannot open a positional domain that does not include the totality of L-immediate connections.

It is clear that the proposition 'x is' may instead count as an *a priori* synthesis according to both modes excluded above in relation to the proposition 'Being is', if x takes the value of a finite determination of the whole.

8. The immutability of being

Let us now take into consideration the following propositions:

'Being (the whole) does not become' ('Being is immutable');

'Being (the whole) is not annulled and does not issue from an initial nullity'.

These propositions are mutually equivalent, and, strictly speaking, they are only two different formulations of a single theorem. In any case – i.e. aside from this substantial semantic identity – what must now be observed is that a negation of these propositions is inherently contradictory.

By the term 'becoming', we indeed indicate a 'transition from non-being to being, or from being to non-being' ('transition from the lack or non-being of a positivity to the realization or being of that positivity, or vice-versa'). Accordingly, affirming that being becomes means affirming that being is not: it is not either in the initial or in the final moment of becoming. This is the case both if the becoming of the whole is the becoming (the coming into being, or the going into non-being) of the whole as such, and if the becoming of the whole is the becoming of a moment or domain of the whole: in the first case, in affirming the becoming of being, the being of the totality of being is negated; in the second case, what is negated is the being of a specific being.

The same should be stated – and in fact from a linguistic point of view the matter appears even more clearly – for the annulment of being, or for the issuing of being out of nothingness: in both cases it is required for being not to be, i.e. for being to be nothing. This is the case both if the annulment or the issuing from nothingness pertains to the whole as such, and if it pertains to the whole with respect to one of its moments or parts.

All of this may be *expressed* by stating that being is eternal, or, equivalently, that being is pure act: what is important being the fact that these terms should be understood as we have determined above.

9. The L-mediational value of the affirmation of the immutability of being

a. What must, however, be examined with particular attention now is the logical structure of the propositions formulated at the beginning of the previous section. Let us therefore observe that, in both propositions, the predicate pertains (as negated) to the subject *ratione suae partis*, and not *ratione sui ipsius*. That is to say, one does not negate that becoming pertains to being insofar as becoming is such, but insofar as becoming implies as such the non-being of what becomes – and therefore, if it is predicated of being, it implies as such the non-being of being. This non-being – which, as such, is negated *qua* pertaining to being – is a *moment* or a semantic part of the meaning 'becoming'. This means that, in the proposition 'Being does not become', the predicate does not pertain (as negated) to the subject in an L-immediate way (i.e. it does not pertain as such, or *ratione sui ipsius*), but *by means* of a term: this term precisely consisting in the 'non-being' implied by the transition from non-being to being, or vice versa (a 'non-being' that, as negated, L-immediately pertains to the subject) – a term that, however, counts as a semantic *moment* of the actual meaning of the predicate, i.e. of the actual meaning of the mediated extreme. For this reason, we have stated that the predicate pertains (as negated) to the subject *ratione suae partis*.

The same argument must be repeated in relation to the proposition: 'Being is not annulled (and does not issue from an initial nothingness)': the annulment *includes* in its semantic value the non-being of what is annulled (while not being exhausted by this inclusion, since it, too – like becoming – includes in addition the concept of a transition from or to non-being), and it is predicated (as negated) of being insofar as it is inclusive in this way, and not *qua* annulment as such; accordingly, that term that is included in the annulment, which L-immediately pertains (as negated) to the subject of the proposition under consideration, is the middle term of the predication.

b. In the meantime, from what we have said it is possible to conclude that the propositions 'Being is immutable' and 'Being is not annulled (or does not issue from nothingness)' belong to the third type of *a priori syntheses* defined in §14, c of Chapter 7.

The corollary indicated in §15 of that chapter therefore holds in relation to these propositions: that is to say, the project of the non-pertaining of the predicate to the subject is *immediately* superseded, i.e. it is superseded on the basis of the very concrete structuring of logical immediacy. Accordingly, those propositions already belong in this respect to the structure of the ground, even if in a distinctive way.

c. A separate discussion is needed in relation to the proposition: 'Being (the whole) is not incomplete' – οὐκ ἀτελεύτητον, says Parmenides. This proposition is indeed L-immediate, in that it is equivalent to negating that something – a being – would not be, i.e. that it would not belong to the domain of being.

It is clear that this proposition is L-immediate insofar as it is posited as an individuation of concrete logical immediacy; conversely, if that proposition is held firm in its being distinct from its standing as such an individuation, it is synthetic *a priori*, for excluding that being is incomplete means excluding the *steresis of a part* of the positive, and the affirmation that a part of the positive is not non-being is only L-immediate insofar as it is precisely posited as an individuation of the universality of logical immediacy, which excludes the non-being of the positive as such: i.e. *of every* positive, or *of the totality* of the positive.

10. Concerning the logical value of propositions in which the subject is the whole: The necessity of their L-immediacy

The result expressed in §9, b must, however, be further specified.

The subject of the synthetic *a priori* propositions considered above is the whole, or the totality of beings; the following discussion may however be referred to every type of synthetic *a priori* (L-mediated) predication, whose subject is the whole. Affirming that a determination x pertains to the whole in an L-mediated way means that x does not pertain as such to the whole, or that the whole is not something to which, as such, x pertains. (In stating that x does not pertain to y for itself, but for something other – i.e. it pertains to y in an L-mediated way – this other is not only something other than x, but also other than *y* as such, for otherwise the pertaining of *x* to *y* would be L-immediate, i.e. *x* would pertain for itself to *y*.) However, if the whole is not something to which, as such, *x* pertains, it follows that the whole – i.e. that to which *x* pertains in an L-mediated way – is not the whole: precisely insofar as there exists that *otherness* relative to the whole as such, which itself, as such, makes it possible to predicate *x* of the whole.

This otherness consists in the (L-immediate) pertaining of *x* to *m* – *m* being the middle term of the pertaining of *x* to the whole. (That is to say, that otherness is not constituted by *m*, for insofar as *m* is L-immediately predicated of the whole, *m* is L-immediately included in the whole. We shall however return to this point further ahead.)

Accordingly, if one holds firm that the subject of the paradigmatic proposition: 'The whole is *x*' is the whole, every predication whose subject is the whole and that is not L-immediate is self-contradictory; if, instead, one holds firm that this predication is not L-immediate, but it is synthetic *a priori*, the subject of that proposition cannot be the whole as such: i.e. the subject is the whole, but insofar as it is realized according to a simply formal value.

In relation to the proposition: 'Being (the whole) is immutable', it is possible to adapt what we have verified above by stating that if the semantic horizon opened by the meaning 'whole' does not include its immutability (as well as, more generally, all the predicates that pertain to the whole), that horizon is not the horizon of the whole; for if that horizon is held firm as the horizon of the whole – and, therefore, as inclusive of the immutability of the whole – the proposition: 'The whole is immutable' is not synthetic *a priori*, but L-immediate. The same should be stated concerning the proposition: 'Being (the whole) is not annulled and does not issue from nothingness'.

It is indeed the case that, in the proposition: 'The whole (which is immutable – i.e. which includes its immutability in its meaning) is immutable', the predicate pertains to the whole insofar as the whole includes that specific determination that consists in its immutability, and it does not pertain to the whole as such (i.e. *qua* inclusive of all determinations). The fact that the predicate does not pertain to the whole as such does not now mean that there exists an otherness that is not included in the whole and that functions as a middle term, but that the term to which, as such, the predicate pertains is not the totality as such of determinations, but the totality of determinations insofar as it is inclusive of that determination that is the immutability of all determinations. The proposition: 'The (immutable) whole is immutable' is therefore not 'identical' (in the specific sense in which 'identical' propositions are distinct from 'non-identical' ones as part of identical propositions). In this sense, the whole is that to which, *as such*, its immutability pertains L-immediately (this as-such-ness being determined by the whole's inclusion of its own immutability).

11. Determination of the meaning of logical mediation in propositions in which the subject is the whole

Every non-contradictory proposition in which the subject is the whole is therefore *necessarily* L-immediate, since every determinacy that counts as a predicate of the whole must be posited with the very positing of the meaning: 'whole', i.e. it must belong to the semantic domain opened by this latter positing; at the same time, however, that the whole should have these predicates rather than other ones – i.e. that this semantic domain should include (as affirmed) these predicational determinations rather than the opposite ones – is known, in certain cases, because the predicate is recognized (= posited) as L-immediately pertaining to the subject, but in certain other cases this is not known because that L-immediate pertaining is recognized, but because it is posited that the predicate pertains to the subject *by means* of a certain other term (which, as such, is L-immediately connected both with the subject and with the predicate).

The arising of a logical mediation precisely consists in the verification of the fact that the positing of the subject (the initial extreme of the mediation) is a formal positing of the whole: i.e. it is not a positing of the concrete content of the whole, but of a formal value of the latter. This means that the positing of the whole, insofar as the latter stands as the initial extreme of the mediation, is the positing of a self-contradictory meaning, i.e. it is a realization of the C-self-contradiction, since what one intends to posit is not what is effectively posited. The formal positing of the whole under discussion here also obtains if x, which pertains to the whole in an L-mediated way, is already posited as to its semantic content prior to the positing of its (L-immediate) pertaining to the whole. That is to say, the whole is not simply formal in the sense that it does not include x (even though a formal positing of the whole also takes place as a result of this lack of inclusion), but in the sense that it does not include (or it only includes as something projected) that determinate content that consists in the L-mediated pertaining of x to the whole.

12. Note

a. Let us consider any L-mediated proposition 'A is B'. Here, too – i.e. in relation to *every* mediational connection, too – the realization of the mediation consists in the verification of the fact that the positing of A is the positing of a formal meaning: in the sense that, as a result of the arising of the positing of B, the pre-existing positing of A *qua* subject of a specific set of predications (regardless of whether these are L-immediate or L-mediated; let us however consider here the limiting case in which that set is constituted by L-immediate predications) is attested as the positing of a formal meaning, and, therefore, a self-contradictory one (in relation to what we stated in §12, b of Chapter 9, the formal value that is discussed here is φ_2). In other words, the arising of B finds A as such a formal meaning. For, indeed, B is a constant of A (in the specific sense in which, as part of general constants, constants are distinct from variants; cf. Chapter 7, §12, a).

However, as mentioned, while for any mediational predication 'A is B' the realization of the mediation consists in the verification of the self-contradictoriness of A insofar as B is a constant of A, and not insofar as A is posited as the initial extreme of a mediation, instead in relation to the mediational predications of the type: 'The whole is x', the realization of the mediation consists in the verification of the self-contradictoriness of the meaning 'whole' not only because x is a constant of this meaning (this being the case for every other mediation), but also because x pertains to the whole in a mediated way – whence the constitution of that *otherness* relative to the whole, discussed in §10. The existence of such an otherness relative to A does not instead necessarily imply that A is a self-contradictory meaning (in such a way that the self-contradictoriness of A is simply determined by the fact that B, verified through the mediation, is a constant of A).

b. Insofar as A is the subject of the L-immediate predication of the terms of the series $a_1, \ldots, a_n, a_{n+1}, \ldots, a_{n+m}$ (cf. Chapter 7, §12, b), A is a formal and therefore self-contradictory meaning (this self-contradictoriness being however immediately superseded). For, indeed, each of those terms is a constant of A. The self-contradictoriness of A is therefore determined by the fact that, as discussed, those terms are constants of A, and not by the fact that the semantic domain of A – to the extent that A has a formal value (φ_1) – does not include any of those terms. In this case, the formal value under consideration is φ_1 (cf. Chapter 9, §12, b). As part of L-immediate predications, φ_1 is immediately superseded; as part of L-mediated ones, it is superseded in a mediated way. Insofar as the mediation does not simply consist in the verification of the formal value φ_2 of A, but it also constitutes a superseding of this formal value – precisely because the mediation posits that whose lack causes φ_2 – the mediation constitutes a superseding of both φ_1 and φ_2 (in this second case, both if it is a quantification and if it is the entire supersession of φ_2 – for the meaning of this statement, cf. the passage referenced above). At the same time, however, φ_2 is not simply superseded by the mediation, but also by the development or extension of the analysis (since this extension, too, identifies the pre-existing level of the analysis as a formal meaning or self-contradictoriness).

In relation instead to L-immediate predications in which the subject is the whole, the whole is a formal and therefore self-contradictory meaning not only insofar as the predicate is a constant of the whole, but also insofar as none of the predicates that L-immediately pertain to the whole (nor any other predicate) can be included in the semantic domain of the subject insofar as this is the subject of an L-immediate predication. Towards the end of point (b) of §12 of Chapter 7, we have indicated the reason why A, *qua* subject of an L-immediate predication, must have a formal value (determined as φ_1 in Chapter 9, §12, b). The same must be repeated in relation to the L-immediate predications in which the subject is the whole: in this case, however, there is an additional reason for the constitution of that formal value – and, therefore, of that self-contradictoriness. For if the whole is held firm (insofar as it is the subject of an L-immediate predication) as a semantic domain that cannot be determined by any predication (for, otherwise, that L-immediate predication would not be L-immediate), and as a domain that therefore leaves outside itself all those determinations whose inclusion in that domain would entail that that L-immediate predication were not L-immediate (since the predicate would not pertain to the whole as such, but to the whole as thus inclusive), the whole is not the whole.

c. Lastly: the development of the analysis of a meaning A consists in the verification of the fact that the pre-existing level of the analysis of A has a formal value φ_2 (and is therefore the opening of a self-contradictory meaning) precisely insofar as that level does not include that constant (or constants) of A attested by that development.

The development of the analysis of the meaning 'whole' consists instead in the verification of the fact that the pre-existing level of the analysis has a formal value φ_2

(and it is therefore a self-contradictory meaning) not only because the pre-existing value of the analysis does not include a constant of the analysed meaning, but also because it *does not include* a specific determination.

13. Continuation of §11

The realization of the mediation, however, does not only consist in the verification of the fact that the whole, *qua* subject or initial extreme of the mediation, is a self-contradictory meaning, but it also consists in the superseding of this self-contradictoriness: to the extent that, precisely through that mediation, the whole is posited as something to which the mediated predicate pertains – and insofar as the whole is posited in this way it is no longer posited in a formal way, and it no longer stands as a self-contradictory meaning (since, as already observed, the formal positing that is at issue here, and the ensuing self-contradictoriness, was precisely determined by the fact that the whole was not conceived of as including in its semantic horizon that predicate *as such*).

In other words, insofar as the whole is simply the subject of a mediational predication, it stands as a self-contradictory meaning; since, however, the whole can only be attested as such a self-contradictoriness insofar as the mediation is carried out, and since through this mediation the whole is posited as something to which the mediated predicate pertains, it follows that in the very act in which the self-contradictoriness of the whole is attested, it is superseded: the whole is posited as a self-contradictoriness insofar as it is the *beginning* of the dialectical process constituted by the mediational predication; the self-contradictoriness of the whole is superseded insofar as the latter realizes itself as the *speculative moment* of the dialectical process (cf. Chapter 9, §10).

It should be observed that, as part of the L-immediate predications in which the subject is the whole (cf. §12, b), the self-contradictoriness of the whole is immediately superseded both in the sense that the formal value φ_1 is superseded on the basis of the positing of the constant represented by the predicate, and in the sense that the determinacy of the predicate, precisely by virtue of the L-immediate predication, is immediately included as affirmed in the whole (that is to say, by virtue of the L-immediate predication, the whole is immediately posited as including the L-immediate predicate); that second aspect of the self-contradictoriness, indicated in §12, b, is thus superseded. If m is a determination that is L-immediately predicated of the whole, the proposition: 'The whole includes the meaning m as one of its predicates' is indeed L-immediate. The same holds if a mediational predication whose subject is the whole is realized: with the difference that the twofold aspect of the self-contradictoriness is superseded in a mediated way.

14. In the propositions in which the subject is the whole, the mediation becomes a logical immediacy

Since the whole must include every determination, and since through a mediation a predicate of the whole comes to be posited, in such a way that the whole is posited as including that predicate and not the opposite one – the latter being, however, included as negated in the whole[4] – the mediational predication *becomes* an L-immediate predication, since the positing of the predicate is the positing of a determination that must belong to the meaning of the subject. That is to say, insofar as the realization of the mediation constitutes the superseding of the self-contradictoriness of the whole, the realization of the mediation also constitutes a superseding of the very mediational value of the predication.

This is not irrespectively the case for every mediational predication in which the subject is a finite determination, for in this case it is not necessary that this determination should contain every semantic content – thus also including the L-mediated predicate. It is effectively the case that, in relation to the proposition: 'A is B (by means of M)', this proposition can be regarded as being L-immediate if B is made to pertain to AM; here, however, it is not necessary for B – by virtue of the meaning of A – to be included in the semantic domain of A; accordingly, the relation between A, as such, and B can retain a mediational value. (This does not thereby exclude the possibility of verifying mediational predications whose subject is a finite determination, which are however such that the predicate must necessarily be included in the concept of the subject.)

15. Logical immediacy *qua* originary superseding of mediation

In relation to the propositions formulated at the beginning of §8, the observations developed in the previous section give rise to a logical situation of the utmost interest. As we have already recalled (cf. §9, b), to the proposition: 'Being is immutable' (or to the other equivalent proposition) there pertains the property that the project of the non-pertaining of the predicate to the subject is immediately superseded (even though that proposition has a mediational value): precisely insofar as the positing of the predicate necessarily includes the positing of the middle term (cf. §9, a). *Projecting* that immutability itself does not pertain to being means projecting that being, insofar as it becomes, is not before arising, or it is not after having been; accordingly, if one remains at the level of logical immediacy, which excludes that being may not be, it would not be excluded that being is not. That project is therefore immediately superseded. This entails that the logical situation, as part of which the whole is not something to which, as such, its immutability pertains – in such a way that the positing of this pertaining requires the realization of a mediation – is *originarily* or *immediately* superseded: the concrete opening of logical immediacy (and, therefore, the opening of the originary structure) is, *as such*, a superseding or negation of the non-pertaining of the predicate of the proposition: 'Being is immutable' to the subject. Accordingly, the formal positing of the whole – precisely determined by a positing of the whole as something to which, as such, that predicate does not pertain – and, therefore, the positing of the whole *qua* self-contradictory meaning is *originarily* superseded. What is therefore *originarily superseded* (according to what we have stated in §14) is the mediational value of the affirmation of the immutability of the whole; that is to say, the mediational predication constituted by that affirmation *originarily becomes* an L-immediate predication – or, equivalently, the L-immediacy of that predication consists in an *originary resulting*.

It should be observed that the 'originary superseding of the mediation' does not here mean that the mediation does not exist or is not constituted, but it means that the mediation – which is therefore realized as a mediation – is such that the project of its negation is immediately self-contradictory; and since the subject of the mediation is the whole, the originary positing of the whole as something to which its immutability pertains entails (since the whole must include every determination) that the proposition: 'Being (the whole) is immutable' is L-immediate. What stands as the originary superseding of the L-mediated character of that proposition is then precisely the originarity of this L-immediacy. That proposition is not therefore *simpliciter* L-immediate and L-mediated, but it is only L-mediated insofar as it is regarded as to that abstract value that disregards the fact that, since the positing of the predicate necessarily includes the positing of the middle term, the negation of the pertaining of the predicate to the subject is originarily superseded, and the predicate is originarily included in the concept of the subject.

16. Corollaries

If the proposition: 'Being (the whole) is immutable' has the value of an L-immediacy that is realized as an originary superseding of the L-mediated character of the predication that constitutes that proposition, this may not be stated in relation to propositions of the type: 'd is immutable', in which d stands as a *finite determination* of the whole. It is effectively the case that the propositions of this type, too, are such that their negation is immediately superseded (insofar as they, too, belong to the third type of *a priori* syntheses defined in §14, c of Chapter 7);[5] but insofar as d is a finite determination (which is, however, distinct from the determinacy constituted by the predicate of the proposition 'd is immutable', in such a way that the semantic domain of d does not include this predicate), the originary superseding of the negation of the pertaining of that immutability to d lets the proposition 'd is immutable' persist as a mediational predication. That is to say, while the semantic whole must include every meaning – in such a way that the originary superseding of the negation of the proposition 'The whole is immutable' entails that the whole can originarily be regarded as being immutable, and this proposition originarily becomes L-immediate – the same cannot be stated of d; hence, the proposition 'd is immutable', while being such that its negation is originarily superseded, is originarily retained as an *a priori* synthesis.

The way in which the proposition 'The whole is immutable' is L-immediate is therefore *specific* to this proposition, or to any other predication in which the subject is the whole and in which the predicate pertains to the subject through a term that is either part of the present meaning of the predicate or includes the predicate as a part of its own present meaning (respectively, third and second types of *a priori* syntheses considered in §14 of Chapter 7). More generally, however, it can be stated that the L-immediacy of that proposition is specific to every other predication, whose subject is the whole and which is such that, while the predicate pertains to the subject through a certain other term, the project of the non-pertaining of the predicate to the subject is originarily posited as self-contradictory. In relation to those other mediational propositions, whose subject is the whole, but that do not enjoy the property indicated above, the L-mediated proposition therefore becomes L-immediate in a moment that is additional relative to the one constituted by the concrete opening of immediacy.

17. The immutability of being *qua* concrete positing of the principle of non-contradiction

Insofar as the propositions 'Being is immutable' and 'Being is not annulled and does not arise from an initial nullity' are L-immediate, in the way we have seen, and insofar as the L-immediate propositions in which the subject is the whole consist in the very principle of non-contradiction in its different formulations (cf. §5, b), it follows that also those first two propositions that affirm the absolute immutability or persistence of being stand as formulations of the principle of non-contradiction.[6]

In this respect – thus entering, however, a new order of observations – the principle of non-contradiction constitutes the very essential meaning of the ontological argument: indeed, the immutability or absolute persistence of the whole – i.e. the whole, *qua* absolute persistence – coincides with absolute Being itself; equivalently, the positing of the immutability of the whole, i.e. the opening of concrete logical immediacy, is the very presence of absolute Being. This affirmation is not to be regarded as a conclusion of what has been established above, but as an anticipation of what we shall state. What, indeed, needs to be clarified is the meaning of the 'absoluteness' of being, *qua* absoluteness that differs from the whole insofar as this leaves nothing beyond itself.

18. The aporia of becoming

The new order of observations, mentioned above, is introduced by the aporia – anticipated at the end of the previous chapter – caused by the affirmation that the whole, i.e. *each* of the determinations of being, in their systematic unity, is immutable: while this affirmation is L-immediate – whereby its negation is originarily self-contradictory – the affirmation that being *becomes* is however Ph-immediate. The horizon opened by the totality of Ph-immediate being is precisely the realm of being's arising and taking leave; furthermore, not only is that totality the site that receives the particular determinations of Ph-immediate being and the site from which they take leave, but the arising of the very totality of Ph-immediate being is itself Ph-immediate. (Cf. Chapter 5, §29. It should be noted that this arising is however internal to the totality of the Ph-immediate, which includes the plane relative to which it, itself, arises; accordingly, insofar as that totality is inclusive in this way, its arising is *not* Ph-immediate.)

Therefore, while the originary logos affirms the immutability of being, experience attests its becoming: contradiction between logical immediacy and phenomenological immediacy.

A most familiar aporia, which, even if in an implicit form, appears for the first time to human awareness with Parmenides's philosophy. Not only: it is precisely Parmenides who affirms the immutability of the whole exactly in the way in which this affirmation has been achieved above. Accordingly, before developing this theoretical discussion, it will be appropriate to dwell on this decisive historical situation, and on the way in which historical thinking, embodied by Plato's and Aristotle's metaphysics, has proceeded to overcome Parmenides's grand aporia.

19. Historical notes concerning the aporia of becoming and its resolution

'Of the first philosophers, most thought that the principles of all things were only the ones of the nature of matter': thus Aristotle begins his seminal historical enquiry in the first book of his *Metaphysics*. In the general context of Aristotle's thought, the conclusion of this enquiry is that the ancients had not truly been able to rise to a comprehension of the *totality of things*, for the horizon that their investigations never surpassed is the one of the physical world, and, as a result, they were only 'physicists', or cosmologists. This critical remark can be retained in its validity to the extent that the Aristotelian metaphysics, proceeding in the direction indicated by Plato, succeeds in demonstrating that the physical (becoming) world does not exhaust the totality, since beyond the reality that becomes there is an immutable one. Accordingly, from the standpoint of those who know that the world is not the whole, it is altogether warranted to regard the interest of the pre-Socratics as being directed to a limited dimension of the whole. If 'physics' indicates that interest, constituted as a knowledge of reality *qua* cosmic reality, and 'metaphysics' indicates an interest in the whole, i.e. in reality *qua* reality, it is altogether warranted to affirm that the first philosophers only engaged in physics, and not in metaphysics. Except that, from the standpoint of those 'physicists', who did not suspect any reality other than the world, making the world the object of their interest did not mean limiting their enquiries to the consideration of a particular dimension of the whole, but it meant exhibiting the concrete content itself, or the very all-encompassing determination of the whole. Hence, the ancients set out to enquire into the principles of *all things*. This means that they held before themselves the totality *qua* totality (even though they thought that the world was that totality); in this respect, they were not physicists, but metaphysicians.[7]

In their search for the *principle*, the first metaphysicians searched for the unifying principle of the manifold; equivalently, the search for that unifying principle took the form of a determination of the primordial matter. It is precisely as a result of the opening of the horizon of the totality that there arises the problem of determining what makes it so that all things, while mutually differentiating themselves, agree in their belonging to the same horizon, thus coming to constitute something like a 'totality'. The fact that things each belong to the whole, and that they all agree in this belonging, means that the manifold is constituted as a unity; accordingly, enquiring into that by virtue of which the many things belong to the same horizon means enquiring into that by virtue of which they realize themselves in a unity – and, therefore, enquiring into their unifying principle. The type of metaphysics that the pre-Socratics began to advance lets us know the sense in which they regarded that unifying principle. Stating that the principle of every thing is water, or air, or something similar, is meaningful or can claim to be meaningful only if the principle is regarded as a form of *matter* – and it is precisely in this sense that Aristotle interprets these early qualifications of the principle – in such a way that the unity of the manifold is regarded as a material principle. The unity that is achieved is therefore a unity *secundum quid*: it is the unity *of an aspect* of the whole (granting that the determination of the unity *qua* water or air may be held firm): it is not the unity of the whole.

Anaximander anticipates Parmenides: the unifying principle cannot be a particular determination. Parmenides's *being* is precisely the positive qualification of Anaximander's indeterminate. Parmenides provides the desired solution: the horizon of the whole can only be realized insofar as it is opened as the horizon of being; that is to say, being is that by virtue of which the whole is constituted, and, therefore, it is that by virtue of which the manifold is a unity.

Plato and Aristotle's ontologies constitute a stabilization of this intuition. The stabilization imposes itself: for the discovery is too far-reaching for the discoverer not to be blinded by it. The world disappears in the pure light of being: it disappears *qua* value (ἀλήθεια), and this value is being, *qua* immutability and absolute simplicity. In this way, the unification of the manifold, which is achieved by positing being as the unifying principle, comes to be equivalent to the very negation of the manifold: pure being is the all-encompassing determination of the whole. (With Parmenides, a type of humanity certainly – and forcefully – gains prominence: namely, one that does not give any importance to the world, or does not hear its voice; ultimately, however, the priority that Parmenides reserves for being rather than for the world is due to the appeal that the new type of self-evidence – i.e. that of logos – holds for those accustomed to the self-evidence of the world, in such a way that the latter is sacrificed for the former.)

In the meantime, it is being that captures all the attention; but this capture also acquires an ultimately radical form: *being is*. This, and nothing else, is Parmenides's principle – or, in its negative formulation: being is not non-being: ὅπως ἔστιν τε καὶ οὐκ ἔστι μὴ εἶναι. The principle of the *ex nihilo nihil* is inherited by Parmenides from the philosophical tradition, and plays in any case a secondary role in Parmenides's metaphysics. Aristotle himself recalls time and again that all the ancients concurred in affirming that nothing originates from nothing, whence Parmenides, strictly speaking, 'aggravated the consequences' (*Physics*, I) of that principle, by negating the very being of every becoming. For, indeed, the negation of becoming directly originates from the principle: 'Being is'. If being becomes – if the positive arises or is annulled – before arising, or in being annulled, being is not: and this is precisely the absurd, or the very definition of the absurd – that being is not, i.e. that it is nothing. It is sufficient to read fragment 8 in order to verify that the affirmation of the immutability of being is simply or directly based on the affirmation that being is and cannot not be. The reason why being is not generated (οὔτε γενέσθαι) and does not arise is *simply* that 'it is not possible to say or think that it is not' (vv. 12–13). Further ahead, it is once again stated: 'For if it has come to be, it is not, and similarly if it is ever about to be' – εἰ γὰρ ἔγεντ᾽, οὐκ ἔστι, οὐδ᾽ εἴ ποτε μέλλει ἔσεσθαι (cf. v. 24). This demonstration also holds for the exclusion of the annulment of being: οὔτ᾽ ὄλλυσθαι (vv. 16–17) – for being is not (οὐκ ἔστι) if it is annulled, too.

It can be argued that it is precisely the tradition inaugurated by Melissus that fails to comprehend the formidable power of Parmenides's principle, thus feeling the need to refer back to the principle of the 'physicists', according to which nothing is generated out of nothing. The most unambiguous example consists in fragment 1, in which Melissus affirms: 'Whatever was always was and always will be. For if it came to be, it must have been nothing before it came to be. Now if it was nothing, in no way would anything come from nothing.' If one has understood the meaning of Parmenides's principle, it is clear that the last proposition of the quoted passage is altogether superfluous, or that it can only be held firm by not realizing that it is precisely the supposition that 'being was nothing' that constitutes the absurd. Accordingly, the principle of the *ex nihilo nihil* is introduced here to the extent that one is not able to rise to a comprehension of Parmenides's principle.

Everything is then *necessary*. However, how can this affirmation be reconciled with the becoming of the world? This is precisely the seminal problem that Parmenides has entrusted to philosophical thought. Plato and Aristotle went to great lengths to find a solution, but the complexity of the problem is such that contemporary thinking itself is still dealing with it. This, how Plato regarded Parmenides: 'venerable and terrifying' (*Theaetetus*, 183e).

Being is immutable: in a certain sense, it may be held that metaphysics begins and ends here. In this respect, the aberration, the deviation from the logos, consists in the world: i.e. the presence of becoming and history. From the standpoint of the logos, the unexpected, the unsuspected, is the world, not God – if this latter term precisely indicates the whole in its immutability. But if the logos lets the world take it by surprise, in such a way that it is only able to overcome that surprise by negating the world – i.e. precisely by negating that the world is surprising – that logos becomes an abstract logos; and Parmenides goes as far as this logos. What surprises must be held firm: precisely because it has a 'hold' [*presa*] – a value of self-evidence or immediacy – from which one cannot break free. In the *De generatione et corruptione*, Aristotle states that the Eleatics 'were led to transcend sense-perception and disregard it, and asserted that the whole is one and unmovable. Following the reasonings, it seems that these must be the consequences, yet, following the facts, thinking in this way almost seems madness.' Especially Aristotle's philosophy is fully aware of this need to 'follow the facts', whence the reconciliation between experience and logos can rightly be asserted to constitute the fundamental question of the Aristotelian enquiry.

The solution provided by Aristotle to Parmenides's aporia unfolds in two principal moments: the verification of the inherent structure of becoming, and the verification of the complete conditions of the possibility of thinking becoming (i.e. the conditions of its non-contradictoriness). The first moment hinges on the deduction of the *elements* of becoming. It involves introducing, in place of the indeterminate and in the last instance contradictory concept of becoming, the concept of a 'becoming content': a well-known concept, even though quite rarely seen as a function of the rationale that pertains to it in Aristotle's philosophy. Becoming consists in a transition from non-being to being. This concept may be further analysed: Aristotle himself provides a series of studies of this type of analysis, establishing for instance that becoming does not take place between being and non-being *qua* indeterminately regarded, but insofar as they are determined as contraries (whereby becoming consists in a transition from a specific non-being to a specific being). What should be remarked, however, is that if the structure of becoming only consisted in that transition, becoming would be an identification of non-being and being: nothingness would become being. This point had already been raised by Plato in a seminal moment of the *Phaedo* (103d–104d). The contradiction determined by that identification of non-being and being is superseded by introducing a *third* term – referred to by Aristotle as 'substance' – which at first lacks a determination that it receives at a later moment (or vice versa); what *becomes* is then precisely this third term. The becoming content is therefore such insofar as it is the persisting term that exists both in the moment of the *stéresis* and in that of the *ktêsis*. '*Calidum enim non facit esse calidam ipsam frigiditatem, sed subiectum frigiditatis, nec e converso. Videtur ergo quod oporteat poni aliquod tertium quod sit subiectum contrariorum.*'[8] That is to say, while it is contradictory for non-being to become being, *this* contradiction no longer obtains in positing that it is *something* – which differs from that non-being and from that being – that is at first affected by that non-being and later by that being. In relation to the way in which the concept of substance is introduced, it is possible to affirm that, in the last instance, this substance is experience itself, i.e. the totality of immediately present being, *qua* persisting horizon that gradually realizes itself in and through determinations that it did not at first possess – without thereby wishing to negate that multiplicity of instances of persistence internal to experience, which precisely count as that multiplicity of substances to which the technical details of Aristotle's philosophy refer. (The fact that the totality of the Ph-immediate is the *horizon* as part of which the different Ph-immediate determinations arise and from which they take leave – and, therefore, the fact that this totality, as such horizon, precisely functions as a substratum or substance – is itself Ph-immediate: the Aristotelian deduction of the concept of substance exhibits the *necessity* for the becoming of the Ph-immediate determinations to take place as part of a horizon that underlies as much the moment of the presence as the one of the absence of those determinations; that deduction therefore excludes the project for the becoming of presence to be able to be realized without that substratum – a project that is not excluded by the simple Ph-immediacy of the totality of the Ph-immediate in its function of substratum.) Chapter five of book eight of the *Metaphysics* and book one of the *Physics* are the most relevant passages for the identification of that mode of introduction of the concept of substance.

This introduction realizes the originary meaning of the principle of the *ex nihilo nihil*. As already mentioned, Aristotle repeatedly notes that the logical structure of the early philosophies is determined by this principle. The latter initially indicates that things are generated from a pre-existing matter, in such a way that, since only the material aspect of things is known, it follows that 'nothing absolutely comes or ceases to be' (*Metaphysics*, 983b). Parmenides's principle is already somehow implicitly at work, but since no conscious reflection yet addresses being and non-being as such, the immutability of being is expressed by stating that everything that is generated was already in the originary substance. While the principle of the *ex nihilo nihil* constitutes, on the one hand, an anticipation of Parmenides's pure metaphysical principle – playing precisely the role of absolute metaphysical principle as part of pre-Parmenidean philosophies – on the other hand, it is reduced to the role of a particular principle with the arising of the knowledge of the many meanings of ground (especially in Aristotle's philosophy), whereby the originary substance of the pre-Socratics is precisely seen in its value of a material principle. Abstracted – necessarily abstracted – from its outcome in the pure metaphysical element, the principle of the *ex nihilo nihil* appears as a simply presupposed assertion. The presupposition is superseded by Aristotle precisely with the introduction of the concept of substance: if becoming only consisted in the substitution of non-being by being (first non-being, then being), this substitution, as discussed, would be an identification of the two terms; the substrate that must therefore be introduced, *qua* persisting term, is the *ex quo* of becoming. Becoming is not *ex nihilo*, but *ex ente*, i.e. precisely from the substrate insofar as it lacks what arises, or insofar as it is what arises 'potentially'.

In this way, however – or, more precisely, up to this point – all we have done is to grant Parmenides's aporia the greatest degree of accuracy that pertains to it. For, indeed, the way in which the aporia is presented in Parmenides's text (in which, of course, it is not regarded as an aporia) suffers from the lack of a verification of the inherent structure of becoming: that is to say, the negation of becoming comes to take place as part of an inadequate logical context. Once that structure has been established, however, the Parmenidean objection appears once again, taking advantage this time of the soundness of the logical structure elucidated by Aristotle's analysis. That is to say, even if regarded in this way – i.e. even if regarded as the transition of a substratum from a lack to a form (or vice versa) – becoming entails either that being (what has become) is not (was not), precisely because it is something that has become, or that being is not, insofar as becoming consists in the substratum's loss of a determination (i.e. in the annulment of that determination).

The Aristotelian solution is well-known: what has become *already is* (being is, and therefore it 'already' is with respect to its own arising), but not simply in the sense that the substratum is already, potentially, what will arise at a later time: this constituting the aspect of that 'already-being' thanks to which the Parmenidean aporia finds the most suitable conditions for its taking place. What has become already is *qua* actual reality; therefore, it cannot already be as part of the very reality that becomes – this being the type of solution provided by Anaxagoras, who in this way, however, let opposite determinations pertain *simpliciter* to the same term – but it already is in a reality that *differs* from the one that becomes: and therefore, in the last instance, in (or as) the immutable reality.[9]

This resolution of Parmenides's aporia is made possible by the realization of the analogical value of being: it is only possible to state that the positive that arises already is as part of something *other* than what becomes insofar as it is possible to speak of something that becomes and of something other than this. This is something that Parmenides had excluded, to the extent that, according to him, the distinction between the meaning 'being' and the other meanings entails the nullity of the latter – and, therefore, the negation of multiplicity. This may also be stated as follows: Parmenides abstractly conceives of essence (the system of essences) and existence as unrelated to one another, in such a way that insofar as essence is regarded independently of its relation with being, it falls into nothingness – pure being, as the absolutely simple, thus remaining to fill the horizon of positivity. Abstractly considered in this way, 'being' takes the form of an *individuum*, to the extent that the logos is held separate from sensory consciousness, whereby it is then no longer possible to establish an agreement with the latter. The agreement is achieved by superseding that abstract separation, and by letting things *speak* – and letting them precisely say that being is in many ways. The analogical character of being requires no demonstration, but it is in itself self-evident. Accordingly, it is sufficient to attest this self-evidence in order to solve this other aspect of Parmenides's aporia. The phenomenological self-evidence of the reality of the manifold is indeed the self-evidence of the multiple modes of being. This theorem had already been achieved by Plato: insofar as the meaning 'being' is distinguished from the other meanings, it must be stated that 'as many times those others are, as many times being is not' (*Sophist*, 257a) – or, as many times an other than being is distinguished, as many times non-being is. This non-being that is, however, is not absolute non-being, but a specific non-being, i.e. a specific being: a specific determination of being that, precisely as such, *is not* the other determinations (and, therefore, nor is it 'being', regarded as a meaning distinct from the other ones) (*Sophist*, 259a).

The Aristotelian theorem of the primacy of actuality over potentiality, in implying the distinction between a pure act and one mixed with a potentiality as a distinction between two realities – even if each one being real in its own way – therefore constitutes the very resolution of Parmenides's aporia. In this respect, the complex mediational process that in the Aristotelian texts leads to the affirmation of a pure act is not essential: the existence of the pure act, i.e. of the whole *qua* absolute immutability, is indeed directly achieved on the basis of Parmenides's principle – as seen above. What the Aristotelian and Platonic philosophies come to secure is the existence of the world: this being secured in the sense that the world must not simply be affirmed, but it must be affirmed while holding firm that pure act that, from Parmenides's standpoint, required the nullity or illusory character of the world. The world is secured in the sense that the conditions of its coexistence with God are exhibited (or, in any case, one goes a long way in this direction). The Aristotelian theorem of the primacy of the act is therefore the very Platonic theorem of the implication of the *idea* by the sensible (that is to say, both theorems fulfil the same task in relation to the Parmenidean problem). In relation to Plato: every determination of the world is something positive, a *being*; the arising and the vanishing of every worldly positivity is, however, manifest; as long as one remains at the presence of the world, being is therefore manifest as something that is not – this presence being that of the *doxa*; the affirmation that being is not is circumvented by positing that every determination that appears over here, *simpliciter*, is; and therefore it is in another world, i.e. as a divine existence – provided that the divine is the horizon of absolute self-possession.

It must, however, be noted that this essential relation between the grand Platonic and Aristotelian metaphysics, on the one hand, and the Parmenidean one, on the other, is only something *for us*: as part of the historical element that pertained to them, they *are* in that relation – they are not fully aware of it (also to the extent that the pure metaphysical essence of the Eleatic standpoint was obscured by the materialistic perspective in which it had developed). Parmenides's being, in its historical concreteness, consists of that contiguity in which 'being touches being', 'akin to the mass of a well-rounded sphere'. For someone dealing with the historical Parmenidism, the affirmation of a pure act is therefore something to be achieved, or a task to be fulfilled. It is then no surprise that Plato as much as Aristotle have pursued their own peculiar paths, which departed from that essential metaphysical core concealed in the historical concreteness of the Eleatic standpoint. As part of the Platonic metaphysics, the relation between the sensible and the idea therefore becomes more complex as a result of the involvement of the epistemological problem of Socratic origin, and the idea – the pure act, the immutable – is affirmed on the basis of the purported necessity of giving the concept a content other than the one of sensory consciousness. Aristotle, in turn, presents the affirmation of that pure act as the result of that exacting demonstrative process based on the principle of the *omne quod movetur ab alio movetur*. The grounding of that principle (*Physics*, 1, VII, VIII) is analysed by Aquinas in chapter XIII of the *Summa contra gentes*. Strictly speaking, multiple ways of grounding that principle may be identified within the Aristotelian text. In the first of these a proof is established *ad absurdum*, by showing the contradiction that arises in negating the principle in question. Except that the proof undoubtedly presupposes (*Physics*, 241b) that if the being in motion is not moved by something else it is moved by itself, whereas this is precisely what is to be proved: namely, that what is in motion is *moved* – whether by itself or by something else is a secondary question at this point. The second proof, *per inductionem*, is the weakest, and every comment is superfluous (*Physics*, 254b). The third proof is the most challenging one, and it turned into the core of Aquinas's 'first way'. The text appears in book eight of the *Physics* (257a). Aquinas presents it as follows: '*Nihil idem est simul actu et potentia respectu eiusdem. Sed omne quod movetur, in quantum huiusmodi est in potentia …. Omne autem quod movet est in actu, in quantum huiusmodi: quia nihil agit nisi secundum quod est in actu. Ergo nihil est respectu eiusdem motus movens et motum. Et sic nihil movet se ipsum.*'[10] However, it is once again clear that what is to be demonstrated is in fact presupposed: namely, that what is in motion is *moved*. And nor is it possible to leave this presupposition behind by affirming that the transition from potentiality to actuality is determined or conditioned by the actual reality, for that transition – in which becoming consists – indicates a *limit* of what becomes, and what limits cannot be nothing, for otherwise nothingness would be regarded as a positive. For, indeed, it is once again presupposed that a being is limited as an *effect* of a limiting act.[11]

The Aristotelian standpoint therefore attempts to once again achieve the Parmenidean theorem of the immutability of being. It does so, however, by introducing a *new* logical structure relative to the one in accordance with which that theorem is realized in the Parmenidean text. What is new consists in the fact that the Aristotelian approach is not directly based on the principle that being is not non-being, but it is achieved through the mediation of the concept of a limitation of being (or equivalent concepts); accordingly, Parmenides's metaphysics enjoys an ultimate simplicity or radical character, whereas the Aristotelian standpoint – echoing Melissus's position, and becoming in fact its main proponent – extends a discussion that that has already found its completion.[12]

Furthermore, if we keep in mind the way in which, taking advantage of that Parmenidean core, the proposition 'The whole is immutable' has been manifested as to its value of logical immediacy (cf. §15), the difference between the Parmenidean and Aristotelian stances – which are thus no longer considered as to their simple historical effective existence, but in their theoretical living value – may be traced to the difference between the concept of metaphysical knowledge *qua* belonging to the structure of the ground and the concept according to which metaphysical knowledge constitutes an additional dimension relative to that structure, a dimension that needs to be achieved through a mediational process. This second concept finds its most rigorous configuration in the concept Γ_a, since – as already discussed, and as we shall clarify in more detail – the positing of immutable being, i.e. of the whole *qua* absolute immutability, precisely consists in the L-immediate positing of the positive that surpasses the totality of Ph-immediate being.

However, let us now consider again – from a more strictly theoretical point of view – the formulation and the solution of the aporia in question, both of which, to a certain extent, have been anticipated as part of the historical observations developed above.

20. The modes of formulation of the aporia of becoming. Clarifications

a. The L-immediacy of the immutability of the whole and the Ph-immediacy of the becoming of being thus cause an aporetic situation.

b. This aporia can also be expressed (cf. Chapter 12, §7) by stating that the L-immediacy of the immutability of the whole is in contradiction with the affirmation of the existence of *a posteriori* syntheses, i.e. of positive contents (precisely constituted by those syntheses) whose arising or annulment is not posited as something self-contradictory (even though it must be recognized that synthetic *a posteriori* propositions are types of necessary propositions; cf. Chapter 10, §10).

c. It should furthermore be observed that the presence of becoming already causes an aporetic situation in relation to the concept of the *totality* of Ph-immediate being (cf. Chapter 5, §26). This type of aporia also obtains in considering becoming in relation to the whole, i.e. in considering that the content of the whole, *qua* totality of the Ph-immediate, becomes. The reader may apply the remarks made in §§26–27 of Chapter 5 to the present case. The resolution of this aporia, however – which, analogously to the case considered in Chapter 5, consists in the originary distinction between the *form* and the *matter* of the whole – lets the aporia now under consideration (i.e. the one formulated in points a, b) persist as something unresolved. That is to say, while it is indeed the case that the becoming of the content of the whole entails that the whole is and is not such (cf. analogously Chapter 5, §26, in which this latter assertion is justified), it is however also the case that, in distinguishing the form of the whole from its content – whereby the whole persists, or it is immutable, as to its formal meaning, and it becomes as to its concrete content – it is nevertheless affirmed that the positivity constituted by this content, insofar as it becomes, is not. Furthermore, that first type of aporia, whose paradigm is found in Chapter 5, no longer obtains in relation to the project of the *annulment* of the very totality of the Ph-immediate – or, in the case at hand, in relation to the project of the annulment of the whole. (Indeed, the aporia only arises if becoming pertains to particular determinations of the totality of the Ph-immediate, or of the whole, in such a way that, if the horizon in which those determinations arise or from which they take leave *persists* – to the extent that the distinction between form and content does not obtain – that horizon is and is not, *qua* totality of the Ph-immediate, or, in the present case, *qua* whole; it is clear that *this* contradiction does not arise in relation to the project of the annulment of the horizon itself.) In relation to the aporia that is being considered in this chapter, it is instead precisely the affirmation of the annulment of being – and therefore, if one may say, even more so the affirmation of the annulment of the totality of being – that is manifested in its being self-contradictory.

21. The L-immediacy of the affirmation that the positive surpasses the totality of the Ph-immediate

a. The aporia (formulated in §20, a, b) is superseded by affirming that the whole, *qua* absolute immutability, *is not* the totality of Ph-immediate being, to the extent that the latter constitutes the horizon of becoming. This affirmation is L-immediate – that is to say, the aporia is originarily superseded: the originary structure realizes itself as the originary supersession of this aporia. The latter therefore only persists to the extent that the distinction between the whole, *qua* absolute immutability, and the totality of Ph-immediate being is not posited. The meaning of this distinction must be determined in the following way.

Insofar as the totality of Ph-immediate being is not nothing, the distinction between the whole, *qua* absolute immutability, and that totality is a distinction *between two positivities*, i.e. it consists in the affirmation that the totality of the Ph-immediate belongs to, is included in or is a moment of the whole, but (due to that distinction) not of the whole *qua* immutability. Affirming that the whole, *qua* absolute immutability, is not the totality of Ph-immediate being therefore means affirming that the whole surpasses this totality, i.e. that a positive surpasses the totality of the Ph-immediate, in such a way that the meaning 'whole' appears according to two different meanings: as an absolute immutability – and therefore in its being opposed to the totality of the Ph-immediate – and as including this totality. That positive that surpasses Ph-immediate being has, however, a distinctive value, in that it is not simply a *part* of the whole, but it is the whole itself *qua* absolute immutability.

b. Before proceeding in this direction – i.e. before determining the nature of the relation between the whole, *qua* immutability, and the totality of the Ph-immediate – let us observe that in the same way in which the proposition 'The whole, *qua* immutability, is not Ph-immediate being' is L-immediate, so too is the proposition 'A positive surpasses the totality of Ph-immediate being' (or, as an equivalent proposition, 'The totality of the Ph-immediate is a moment of the whole').

Concerning the L-immediacy of that first proposition: once the L-immediacy of the immutability of the whole is posited, there is no need for a middle term in order to affirm that the whole, *qua* absolute immutability, *is not* the dimension of becoming constituted by the totality of the Ph-immediate. A middle term is required only if the whole is not posited in its immutability, i.e. if it is posited as a formal or self-contradictory meaning: the middle term being in this case that immutability. Insofar as that formal or self-contradictory meaning is originarily superseded, however (namely, insofar as that immutability is originarily posited as an internal determination of the meaning: 'whole'), the distinction between the immutable whole and the horizon of becoming is originarily posited.

Concerning the L-immediacy of that second proposition: if the affirmation of the immutability of the whole is L-immediate, the affirmation of the *positivity* of the Ph-immediate content is Ph-immediate; accordingly, the L-immediate positing of the distinction between the immutable whole and the totality of the Ph-immediate is an L-immediate positing of the distinction between two positivities: that is to say, it is an L-immediate positing of the fact that the immutable whole is *other* than, or lies *beyond*, the totality of the Ph-immediate; equivalently, it is an L-immediate positing of the fact that the whole of the positive includes the totality of the Ph-immediate as a moment (precisely to the extent that the surpassing is realized). Once again: there is a mediation – in affirming that the whole includes the totality of the Ph-immediate as a moment – only insofar as the whole is regarded as a formal or self-contradictory meaning: i.e. one that does not include the immutability of the whole and the distinction between the whole, *qua* immutability, and the horizon of becoming. That is to say, the mediation obtains between that *finite determination* (or abstract moment) precisely constituted by the whole *qua* formal meaning and the property of being *inclusive* of the totality of Ph-immediate being. Analogously, in relation to that other formulation: 'A positive surpasses the totality of Ph-immediate being', the L-immediacy of this proposition does not obtain insofar as the property of surpassing the totality of the Ph-immediate L-immediately pertains to the concept of a certain positive indeterminately considered, but insofar as that positive is regarded as the immutable whole.

c. This realizes the concrete positing of the L-immediacy of the proposition: 'A positive surpasses the totality of the Ph-immediate' – a positing that up to this point had only been indeterminately anticipated. It must therefore be stated: the originary structure realizes itself as an affirmation of the fact that the immutable whole surpasses the totality of the Ph-immediate, i.e. it surpasses the originary structure itself (insofar as every element of the originary is a moment of the totality of the Ph-immediate; cf. §23). In this sense, the originary structure constitutes the concrete originary opening of metaphysical knowledge.

d. Insofar as the proposition: 'The immutable whole surpasses the totality of the Ph-immediate' is L-immediate, and insofar as its subject is the whole, that proposition constitutes a formulation of the principle of non-contradiction (cf. §5, b). The sense in which it is stated that the immutable whole is the whole – while holding firm that the totality of the Ph-immediate is a positivity, and that this positivity *is not* the immutable whole – is clarified in §29. In the meantime, it is worth reading once again point c of §16 of Chapter 3.

22. First note

From what we have stated, it appears that that the L-immediate proposition: 'Being is' (cf. §1), also as distinct from the positing of the immutability of the whole and from the positing of the distinction between the immutable whole and the horizon of becoming, constitutes, as such, a positing of the positivity that surpasses the totality of the Ph-immediate – although, as part of the positional domain of that proposition as thus distinct, that positivity *is not posited as* something that surpasses the totality of the Ph-immediate.

23. Second note

The aporia caused by the affirmation that the positive surpasses the totality of immediately present being has already been considered and resolved in §4 of Chapter 10. See also §31 of Chapter 5.

24. The meaning of synthetic *a posteriori* propositions

If a 'synthetic *a posteriori* predication' indicates the possibility for the predicate to no longer (or not yet) pertain to the subject, i.e. if it indicates the possibility of the annulment or initial nullity of a synthesis – namely, the annulment or initial nullity of the positive constituted by that synthesis – it is then confirmed, also in this respect, that there can exist no synthetic *a posteriori* propositions. It must then be stated that there only exist analytic and synthetic *a priori* propositions. It is this latter type of propositions that can be divided into two sub-types of *a priori* syntheses, depending on whether the subject *cannot in any way* realize itself without the predicate or whether, *within the domain of the totality of Ph-immediate being*, the subject can realize itself without the predicate. (In this second case, it is clear that, strictly speaking, what realizes itself without the predicate is a *persistence* of the subject – or, more generally, it is the essence of the subject in an individuation other than that to which the predicate pertains). The first of these two sub-types is the one commonly referred to when speaking of synthetic *a priori* propositions; the second sub-type is the one referred to when speaking of synthetic *a posteriori* propositions. It thus appears, from what we have stated, that every '*a posteriori* synthesis' *is* absolutely or 'eternally' – but as something whose subject, *within the domain* of the totality of Ph-immediate being, may realize itself without the predicate. Insofar as the positive constituted by an *a posteriori* synthesis *is* (i.e. it is absolutely or immutably), the predicate *necessarily* pertains to the subject: but, precisely, as something that, *within that specific sphere of being* constituted by the totality of the Ph-immediate, is able to not pertain to the subject.

25. The immutable and becoming

Let us resume the discussion interrupted in §21, a. The distinction between the whole, *qua* absolute immutability, and the totality of the Ph-immediate is, as stated, the distinction between *two* positivities. Let us, however, now specify that the totality of the Ph-immediate is a positive that cannot include any value, quantity, aspect or mode of positivity that is not included in the immutable whole: otherwise, the latter would not be the whole of positivity – for that immutability does not pertain to this or that being, but to *every* being. The development and the increment – or the vanishing and disappearing – i.e. the becoming of the content of the totality of the Ph-immediate neither adds any positivity to the immutable whole nor takes it away from it, for, otherwise, the positive that arises or that vanishes would not be (before its arising or after its taking leave from the horizon of presence). Accordingly, the positive that is added or that vanishes already or still is in the circle of the immutable whole, always already seized from the future and forever retained in the circle of being.

The immutable whole, instead, includes within itself the totality of the positive. That is to say, the *entirety* of the positivity of the positive that becomes, which the immutable whole leaves 'beyond' itself (precisely insofar as the immutable is not the becoming content) – the immutable leaving beyond itself precisely and only the totality of that positive that becomes – is immutably included in the immutable whole. The circle of the immutable is thus the abode or the dwelling place of being, and it also preserves that which, in the world, does not escape the plunder of nothingness.

This may also be stated as: the whole, in its including that reality that becomes as well as the immutable whole, does not contain any positivity that is not contained in the immutable whole – in such a way that the latter, while being *other* than the reality that becomes, is not a 'part' of the whole.

26. Becoming as the appearing of the immutable

a. The totality of Ph-immediate being, as the horizon in which the birth and the annulment of being come to be manifested, must therefore be determined as the horizon in which the appearing and disappearing of being is manifest; that is to say, that which, from a standpoint that remains at a simple consideration of the totality of Ph-immediate being (or, equivalently: that which from the standpoint of the concept Γ_a), manifests itself as an *arising* and an *annulment* is revealed, as part of the concrete structuring of the originary, as an *appearing* and a *disappearing*. Care should be taken to understand this point correctly.

There is a becoming (= a becoming is Ph-immediate), which pertains to that being that is Ph-immediately known (consider, for instance, the body x that moves from the place l_1 to the place l_2 – what becomes precisely consisting of x), and there is a becoming, which pertains to the knowledge or presence of being, i.e. which pertains to the appearing of being, and not to the being that appears. This second type of becoming does not necessarily imply the first one; and therefore, in relation to the realization of this second type of becoming, it is not immediately contradictory to *suppose* (project) that there should be no arising or annulment of present being, but only its appearing or disappearing. (At the same time, however, it is also not immediately contradictory to project that every appearing should be an arising of immediately present being, and every disappearing an annulment of the latter. This affirmation will be clarified further below.)

What we are then stating is that, *in relation to the horizon of the immutable whole*, that *first* type of becoming, *too* – i.e. the becoming of immediately present being – consists of an appearing and a disappearing (in such a way that the presence whose content is Ph-immediate being is a presence whose content is this appearing and disappearing). In fact – given the present level of the exposition – the becoming *of presence* is only something *supposed* or *projected* as an appearing and a disappearing, for while it is not immediately contradictory for the becoming of presence *not to imply* in itself the becoming of the present content – in such a way that, relative to the becoming of presence, that being that becomes present is, as such, a form of persistence (a *relative persistence*: precisely, relative to the becoming of presence) – it is however also not immediately contradictory to project that this implication should necessarily obtain. (That is to say, it is not immediately contradictory to project that – even though every time a content *becomes present* it does not present itself as something that becomes – the present content should change or be produced every time it becomes present, and should change or be annulled every time it takes leave from presence.) Therefore, while the becoming *of presence* is only *projected* as an appearing and a disappearing (whence there exists the possibility of demonstrating the *negation* of the content of this project), the becoming *of the content* of presence, in relation to the horizon of the immutable whole, is instead *categorically* and originarily posited as an appearing and a disappearing. Indeed, what is originarily posited is the *absolute persistence* of being (in such a way that, in relation to this absolute persistence, every becoming of Ph-immediate being consists in an appearing and disappearing): in this sense, the originary structure is an originary or immediate realism. What is instead only projected at the level of originarity is the *relative persistence* of Ph-immediate being (or, more precisely, of an aspect or part of Ph-immediate being): that persistence that, for the most part, has been presupposed by the different forms of naturalistic realism or phenomenalism – the persistence of the 'world' or 'nature', the 'independence' of natural being (which is precisely a particular dimension of the Ph-immediate content) with respect to thought.

b. It should furthermore be observed that, while *in relation to the immutable whole* the becoming of the Ph-immediate content consists in an appearing and a disappearing, that becoming, *qua* generation and annulment, is not for this very reason something not real – for, on the contrary, it is precisely the Ph-immediately known being. That is to say, while *absolute* or *simpliciter* there is no birth or annulment of being – in such a way that, *in relation to the immutable whole*, that birth and that annulment consist in an appearing and a disappearing – *as part of the domain of the totality of the Ph-immediate*, becoming, *qua* birth and annulment of Ph-immediate being, is instead fully real, precisely insofar as it belongs to or constitutes the structure of the Ph-immediately known content. *Relative* to the Ph-immediate content, i.e. to the extent that being is regarded as the totality of Ph-immediate being, the birth and death of being are real: *absolute*, instead, i.e. *qua* properties of being as such, they are not real, or they are self-contradictory (in such a way that the reality of the birth and death of Ph-immediate being, considered in relation to the absolute persistence of being, is the reality of an appearing and disappearing of being). What is born and dies is therefore being *qua* totality of Ph-immediate being; what appears and disappears is being *qua* absolute persistence.

27. The originary determination of the meaning of the otherness between the immutable and what becomes

The totality of Ph-immediate being lies 'beyond' the immutable whole, as a positive that does not add anything to the eternal circle of being: this is the way in which the originary distinction between that totality and the immutable whole must (originarily) be understood; that is to say, that originary distinction is not a contradiction only insofar as it is understood in this way. If this way of understanding that distinction is such that the negation of the proposition that expresses it is immediately self-contradictory, the affirmation that the horizon of the Ph-immediate does not add anything to the immutable whole appears itself as something self-contradictory only to the extent that one wishes to apply to being as such certain categories that pertain to the level of 'quantity'. It is at this level – but here, too, with significant restrictions, according to what has been clarified by the developments of mathematics – that it is possible to carry out this type of reasoning: 'If x is a number such that, if added to or subtracted from a number y, it does not cause y to increase or decrease, x is equal to zero'. Accordingly, applying this type of affirmation to the present logical situation, it would follow that the totality of the Ph-immediate is nothing.

What should be noted here is that the concept of the otherness (difference, contradictoriness) between any two terms a and b *does not imply as such*, or L-immediately, that there exists a positivity in a that does not exist in b, *and vice versa*. If that concept, *as such*, were to imply this property, it would be impossible to speak of an otherness between being and nothingness, or between the whole and a part – the otherness being realized in this case, but, precisely, not according to that property. It is effectively the case that the immutable whole is not other than the totality of the Ph-immediate in the same way in which being is other than nothing, and nor in the same way in which the whole is other than a part, since in the first case the positivity of the totality of the Ph-immediate is Ph-immediate, and in the second case the horizon of becoming cannot *as such* be a part of the whole of immutability. Here, however, it is sufficient to note that if there are precisely types of otherness as part of which it is *not* the case that the two terms that stand in a relation of otherness are such that *each of them* includes a positivity that the other one does not include, it follows that it is not immediately self-contradictory to project an additional type, mode or value of otherness, by virtue of which the totality of the Ph-immediate, while differing from the immutable whole, does not include any positivity that is not included in the latter. However, insofar as the negation of that difference is furthermore immediately self-contradictory, and insofar as it is immediately self-contradictory for the totality of Ph-immediate being to include a positive that is not included in the immutable whole, that additional type or value of otherness is projected only as to its concrete meaning, for the fact *that* this additional type must exist is *necessarily* required by that twofold immediate self-contradictoriness. Accordingly, what is projected is only the '*how*' of that '*that*'.

28. The nature of the belonging of becoming to the whole

The totality of Ph-immediate being, and more generally the totality of becoming, does not therefore necessarily belong to the whole (the latter being regarded as something that, as a matter of fact, includes becoming – and the immutable). Precisely because the dimension of becoming does not include any positivity that is not included in the immutable whole, it is not self-contradictory to suppose or project the annulment or initial nullity of that dimension of becoming; that is to say, it is not self-contradictory to affirm that this dimension or reality exists as something that might not have been and something that might not be.

However, not only is it not self-contradictory to affirm that this becoming reality does not necessarily belong to the whole, but it is self-contradictory to affirm the necessity of that belonging. For, indeed, stating that it is necessary for what becomes to belong to the whole means that the negation of that belonging is self-contradictory, i.e. that the non-being of what becomes, as such, is self-contradictory; if this self-contradictoriness were to obtain, however, the horizon of becoming would have to include a positivity that is not included in the immutable whole: for if the non-existence of becoming causes a self-contradiction, the horizon of becoming includes something that the immutable does not include. Since this latter assertion is self-contradictory, however, it follows that it is self-contradictory to affirm the necessary belonging of becoming to the whole.

29. Aporia and solution

The affirmation according to which the totality of Ph-immediate being, and more generally the totality of the dimension of becoming, does not necessarily belong to the whole – and it is in fact self-contradictory that it should necessarily belong to it – may itself appear as a negation of the principle of non-contradiction. It is indeed possible to object that, precisely to the extent that this affirmation asserts that the dimension of becoming might not have been and might no longer be, this affirmation comes to thereby assert the possibility for being (i.e. precisely for the being of that becoming dimension) not to be. The superseding of this contradiction therefore consists in the affirmation of the necessary existence – i.e. the immutability – of the dimension of becoming *as such*. This once again gives rise to a contradiction, in that this becoming dimension is Ph-immediately known as something that becomes (i.e. as a being that, at some time or another, is not), in such a way that this dimension or reality, as such, cannot be immutable.

This aporetic situation is resolved in the following way. In general, the aporia only arises insofar as, on the one hand, the semantic relation between the immutable whole and the dimension of becoming is considered abstractly, and the concept of that becoming dimension is abstractly separated from the concept of the immutable whole, while, on the other hand, that relation is at the same time held firm. That is to say, the aporia arises insofar as one wishes to hold firm two logical operations that are mutually contradictory (according to what we have already seen in other contexts, cf. e.g. Chapter 10, §§4, 15). For, indeed, it is certainly the case that *every* positive, or *every* being, is, and is immutably (and it necessarily belongs to the whole), in such a way that also the *entirety* of the positivity or the *entirety* of the being of the totality of Ph-immediate being – or, more generally, of the dimension of becoming – is immutably.

Insofar as being is immutably, however, it stands as the horizon of the immutable whole, and, therefore, as something *other* than that being that becomes (which, at the same time, must be affirmed by virtue of its Ph-immediacy). If, at this point, the concept of what becomes is abstractly separated from the concept of the immutable – i.e. it is considered in its standing outside that semantic relation with the immutable constituted by the allocation of the entirety of the positivity of what becomes in the circle of the immutable – it follows that the dimension of becoming *once again* appears as a positivity of which non-being cannot be predicated, a positivity that therefore is immutably. (This is the result of that abstract separation, which is precisely the first of those two mutually contradictory logical operations: namely, the *repetition* of that positing of the horizon of the immutable – a repetition that is a self-contradiction if it is regarded as a logical act that differs from the one of which it constitutes a repetition.) Furthermore, insofar as, after having abstractly separated the concept of what becomes from the concept of the immutable, one once again considers or wishes to hold firm what becomes as part of that semantic relation that had, however, been disregarded (this being the logical operation that is contradictory to the one constituted by that disregarding), it follows that one attests that the immutability, whose pertaining to the being of the dimension of becoming has been verified as part of the first operation, cannot give rise to a horizon that differs from the one constituted by the dimension of becoming, since the horizon as part of which the totality of the positive is immutably has already been posited (this being what is taken into account by the second of those two mutually contradictory operations). Accordingly, it must be concluded that the immutability (verified by the first of those two operations) must pertain to what becomes, as such.

The aporia is therefore superseded insofar as, firstly, one no longer holds firm both of those mutually contradictory operations, and, secondly, insofar as the concept of what becomes is not abstractly separated from the concept of the immutable. In relation to this second aspect, it must be stated that the dimension of becoming, *as posited in its distinction from the horizon of the immutable*, consists as such, or as thus distinct, in the dimension of what might not have been and what might not be. In other words, what has been stated in this section shows that what obtains is not a structure that is in contradiction with what has been verified in §28 – or that such a structure only obtains to the extent that, as discussed, one wishes to hold firm two mutually contradictory logical operations (the first of which is, however, an abstract separation that, as such, must be superseded).

This means that the affirmation of the very being of the domain of the dimension of becoming gives rise to an *a posteriori* synthesis (in the sense indicated in §24): what becomes is eternally or immutably as part of the circle of the immutable, as something that, outside that circle, might not have been, and might not be.

30. The nature of the relation between the immutable and what becomes

The totality of the Ph-immediate – and, more generally, the totality of that being that becomes – only is to the extent that the immutable whole is; affirming that only the horizon of becoming is, i.e. that the totality of becoming coincides with the totality of being, means affirming that being is not: the horizon of becoming, regarded in this way (i.e. as a positivity that is even if the immutable is not), is a self-contradiction, and it is therefore nothing. Therefore, the horizon of becoming – i.e. of everything that presently and actually becomes, or can become, or has been able to become – can only be insofar as the immutable whole is.

31. Note

Since it is self-contradictory that there should be something beyond the immutable whole and the totality of becoming[13] – that is to say, since every positive that is not immutably, i.e. which does not dwell in the circle of the immutable, is something that becomes, at least in the sense that its belonging to the whole is not necessary – there is nothing beyond the immutable without which the totality of becoming would not be. That is to say, this latter totality does not require anything other than the immutable whole in order to be. Accordingly, the immutable is not simply *that without which* the dimension or reality of becoming is not, but it is *that by virtue of which* that reality is.

32. Continuation of §30

Conversely, the immutable whole *is*, even if the totality of becoming is not. This follows, on the one hand, from the verified self-contradictoriness of the necessary belonging of becoming to the whole and, on the other hand, it is obtained in a direct way, for if the immutable whole were to be only insofar as the horizon of becoming is, this latter horizon would include a positivity that is not included in the immutable.

33. The decision

Since the totality of becoming does not necessarily belong to the whole, and since the immutable whole is that by virtue of which that totality is, the fact that the totality of becoming is is a *decision* of the immutable.

34. The immutable is a persyntactic constant

Since the whole is a persyntactic constant (cf. Chapter 10, §19), and since the immutability of the whole is a syntactic constant of the whole, it follows that the immutable whole is a persyntactic constant. This means that any meaning can only be posited insofar as the circle of the immutable is present in its manifestness; accordingly, the immutable is not simply that by virtue of which every being is, but it is also that by virtue of which every knowledge opens up: the source and light of every being (as already observed by Plato).[14]

35. Determination of the originary task

Insofar as the originary is structured as the affirmation that the immutable surpasses the originary, the originary opening of the whole is a *formal* one: that is to say, the immutable is manifest in its formal value (and, as thus manifests, it is itself part of the domain of originarity); the concrete content of that form is what lies beyond the originary. The authentic *task* of the originary is thereby posited: to the extent that this formal manifestation is the opening of a contradiction (Chapter 10), the task consists in the necessity of the superseding of this contradiction. The task – that which is to be fulfilled – is the manifestation of the immutable. Are we not perhaps to say that this is an infinite task, and that, precisely, herein lies 'the sign that we are destined for eternity' (as Fichte stated in relation to a logical situation that bears a significant analogy with the one appearing here)?

Notes

Foreword

1. *The Originary Structure*, Chapter 1, §20.
2. Ibid., §22. Cf. ibid., §25.
3. For a partial introduction to the principal elements of Severino's theoretical apparatus, cf. D. Sacco, 'Emanuele Severino: A Testimony of the Language That Testifies to Destiny', *Journal of Italian Philosophy* 6, 2023, 95–116; D. Sacco, 'The Translation of Destiny, and the Destiny of Translation' in Emanuele Severino, *Law and Chance*, trans. D. Sacco, ed. G. Goggi, D. Sacco and I. Testoni (London: Bloomsbury, 2023); D. Sacco, 'Beyond Translation' in Emanuele Severino, in *Beyond Language*, trans. D. Sacco, ed. G. Goggi, D. Sacco and I. Testoni (London: Bloomsbury, 2024).
4. *The Originary Structure*, Chapter 2, §1.
5. *The Essence of Nihilism*, trans. G. Donis, ed. A. Carrera and I. Testoni (London: Verso, 2016), p. 77.
6. *The Originary Structure*, Chapter 2, §20.
7. Ibid., §19.
8. Ibid., Introduction, §2.
9. *The Essence of Nihilism*, pp. 64–5.
10. Ibid., pp. 62–3.
11. Emanuele Severino, *La Gloria* (Milan: Adelphi, 2001), p. 434. Equivalently, insofar as everything that is and is posited is something 'positive', the analysis in *The Essence of Nihilism* shows the self-refuting character of every refutation of the opposition between the positive and the negative (*The Essence of Nihilism* reads: 'The aim of the entirety of the enquiry contained in *The Originary Structure* is to rigorously determine the meaning of the opposition between the positive and the negative'. *Essenza del nichilismo* [Milan: Adelphi, 1982] pp. 116–17; this section is not included in the English translation of this text). Once again, it must be stated that 'the apophantic organism in which the ἔλεγχος consists is an individuation of the universal opposition; and such opposition'can constitute itself as the originary truth only insofar as it is posited *as actually and presently inclusive* of that individuation. If the universal and its individuation are abstractly separated, then the universal is left lacking this individuation, which thus supervenes as something other than the universal posited in this way; and therefore that inconceivable situation occurs, whereby the originary (the universal in its presently not including that individuation) finds in something other (that supervening individuation) the reason for its being held firm, and it is thus posited as something derived. The originary consists in the co-originarity of the universal opposition and this, its individuation. This individuation – in turn – like every other individuation of the universal opposition, has value only insofar as it is regarded in relation to the universal of the opposition'. *The Essence of Nihilism*, p. 74.

12. Cf. *The Originary Structure*, Introduction; Emanuele Severino, *Tautótes* (Milan: Adelphi, 1995), Chapter XXIII.
13. *La Gloria*, pp. 431–2.
14. Cf. Emanuele Severino, *Oltrepassare* (Milan: Adelphi, 2007), Chapter VII, §V; *The Originary Structure*, Chapter 4.
15. G. W. F. Hegel, *Science of Logic*, trans. A. V. Miller (Abingdon: Routledge, 1969), p. 25.
16. G. W. F. Hegel, *The Encyclopaedia Logic*, trans. T. F. Geraets, W. A. Suchting and H. S. Harris (Indianapolis: Hackett, 1991), p. 130.
17. Emanuele Severino, *Gli abitatori del tempo* (Roma: Armando, 1978), p. 108.
18. *Essenza del nichilismo*, pp. 321, 325. Cf. Emanuele Severino, *War* (London: Bloomsbury, 2025).
19. Emanuele Severino, *Il parricidio mancato* (Milan: Adelphi, 1985), pp. 119–21. Cf. *Law and Chance*.
20. Concerning the translation of the term '*originario*', cf. the translator's preface of *Law and Chance*, referenced above.
21. *The Encyclopaedia Logic*, p. 6.
22. *The Originary Structure*, Introduction, §1.
23. Ibid., §9.
24. Ibid., §11.
25. *The Essence of Nihilism*, p. 110 (footnote).
26. Ibid., p. 207.
27. *Gli abitatori del tempo*, p. 7.
28. Emanuele Severino, *Destino della necessità* (Milan: Adelphi, 1980), pp. 425–6. However: '[Metaphysics] thinks nothingness – precisely, we are saying that it thinks nothingness, not that it does not think anything'. *Tautótes*, p. 156.
29. First appearing, respectively, in *Destino della necessità* and in *La Gloria*.
30. *The Originary Structure*, Introduction, §1.
31. See references above.
32. *Destino della necessità*, p. 556.
33. *The Encyclopaedia Logic*, p. 289.
34. *Destino della necessità*, p. 549.

Introduction

1. Emanuele Severino, *Essenza del nichilismo* (Milan: Adelphi, 1982), p. 287. [Translator's Note: The essay 'Risposta ai critici', quoted here, is not included in the English translation of *Essenza del nichilismo*].
2. Emanuele Severino, *Gli abitatori del tempo* (Rome: Armando, 1978).
3. Emanuele Severino, *The Essence of Nihilism* (London: Verso, 2016), 'The Earth and the Essence of Man'.
4. [Translator's Note: The latter term is meant to be read as 'F-immediacy', in order to mirror the Italian ('*L-immediatezza*' and '*F-immediatezza*'), while retaining the connection to 'phenomenology'].
5. Emanuele Severino, *The Essence of Nihilism*, 'Returning to Parmenides (Postscript)'.
6. Cf. *Gli abitatori del tempo* ('Tramonto del marxismo'; 'Götterdämmerung'). For the general meaning of this claim, cf. also Emanuele Severino, *Law and Chance* (London: Bloomsbury, 2023).

7. The universality of logical immediacy is not only individuated in the identity-non-contradictoriness of the *parts* of the totality of beings but also in the *modes* of that identity; as a result, the form by virtue of which *A* is a positive that is opposed to that negative of *A* constituted by the positive *B* is an individuation of a universality that differs from the individuation constituted by the mode of that identity-non-contradictoriness of beings, by virtue of which *A* is opposed to that negative of *A* constituted by nothingness itself. In this regard, *Essenza del nichilismo* states:

> The aim of the entirety of the enquiry contained in *The Originary Structure* is to determine in a rigorous way the meaning of the opposition between the positive and the negative. Referring to the most general aspect of this opposition, 'Returning to Parmenides' (from now on: R.P.) recalls that, as part of the opposition between the positive and the negative, 'the negative is not only pure nothingness (Parmenides), but also the *other* positive (Plato)'. That is to say, the opposition between being and nothingness is one of the modes in which the positive is opposed to the negative; the truth of being, in its concreteness, consists of this opposition *in its universality*, and not according to this or that mode or individuation – even if this appears as the individuation constituted by the impossibility for being not to be. R.P. indeed states that 'negating that being is not is an individuation of the universal opposition between the positive and the negative', for 'as part of the originary opposition [and the opposition may be originary only insofar as it is regarded in its universality], every being (and the totality of being) turns in a number of directions – that is, it enters into a plurality of relations'. This plurality of directions or relations is precisely the plurality of ways in which each positive is opposed to its negative. This plurality is even spelled out in *R.P.*: *a)* a tree is not a mountain, *b)* a tree is not a mountain, a house and everything that is other than the tree, *c)* a tree is not a nothingness, i.e. *d)* a tree is never non-existent, etc. The originary opposition consists neither in this nor in that mode of the opposition, but in their being co-originary, i.e. in the opposition in its concrete universality, precisely expressed by the proposition: 'Being is not non-being' – this proposition, let us repeat once more, referring not only to the opposition between being and nothingness, but to the opposition between being and every form of the negative (thus including the opposition to nothingness itself). If each of the modes of the individuation is regarded in its standing as something distinct from the universality of the opposition (or if that universality is regarded as to its standing as distinct from those modes), each of those modes is not posited as the originarity of the logos, but as something that is derived from or founded upon the originary itself. This is a principle that is thoroughly presented in Chapter 7 of *The Originary Structure*, particularly in §18. In that section it is stated, for instance, that it is not insofar as this tree is this tree that this tree is not this house (almost as if, were this tree another determination instead of being this tree – for instance this pen – then it would be possible to say that this pen is this house), but insofar as this tree is a being and being is not non-being (given that it is posited that being is not non-being insofar as it is posited that every concrete determination of being is not its negative). As a result, the opposition between this tree and this house, if regarded in its being distinct from the universal opposition, is grounded in that very universality (and it is thus not something originary), whereas if it is regarded *in its being related* to the universal opposition, then, as part of this relation, it

coincides with that very universal opposition, i.e. with the very originarity of logos. The originarity of the universal opposition, in turn, coincides with the originarity of the single individuations, but not – let us repeat – as long or insofar as they are held firm in their being distinct from the universal opposition (since, thus distinct, they are not originary, but something derived), but rather insofar as they are posited in their being mutually related. The universal opposition is the originary insofar as it is the concrete universal: i.e. it is neither a mere individuation nor a mere universality, but the relation between the universal and the individual – which can only take place insofar as what is regarded as the 'concrete universal' is the *being* that appears in the proposition: 'being is not non-being' (cf. *The Originary Structure*, Chapter 3, in particular §18). These concepts were recalled in *R.P.*, noting that if the individuation of the universal opposition that consists in the negation that being is not 'is held firm in its concrete relation to the universal, it participates in the originarity of logos' (*Essenza del nichilismo*, pp. 116–18). [Translator's Note: This Note to the Postscript to 'Returning to Parmenides' is not included in the English translation of *Essenza del nichilismo*].

8. [Translator's Note: the essay 'Risposta alla Chiesa', quoted here, is not included in the English translation of *Essenza del nichilismo*].
9. Emanuele Severino, *Studi di filosofia della prassi* (Milan: Adelphi, 1984).
10. It is in this sense that one should understand the remarks of §2, a of Chapter 7 (which, moreover, already anticipate the standpoint of Chapter 10), such as the assertion that the project of the appearing of a specific type of constants of the originary structure that do not imply the appearing of that structure is not immediately self-contradictory. While it is effectively the case that – letting x be a constant of this type, and letting y take the value that it takes in the text – the reference of y to x as to a distinct meaning is not L-immediate, however, asserting that the supposition that the positing of x does not entail the positing of y is not immediately self-contradictory means regarding x not as being concretely distinct from y (and, therefore, concretely connected to it), but as being *isolated* from y, i.e. from its predicate – as explicitly stated in part b of the section (§) mentioned above. In the latter, the appearing of a constant that does not entail the appearing of the originary structure, of which that constant is a constant, is regarded as an appearing of untruth. In other words: on the one hand, it is effectively the case that a constant (x) of S (i.e. of the originary structure), which is a semantic part of S, is such that, *qua meaning that is distinct* from the predicate (y): 'that whose necessary predicates constitute themselves as part of S', it is something to which this predicate does not pertain L-immediately, but in an L-mediated way, i.e. by way of the equation $(x = y) = (y = x)$, cf. Chapter 7, §17, and the affirmation that its appearing entails the appearing of y is thus not L-immediate, but L-mediated; on the other hand, however, y L-immediately pertains to x-that-is-in-a-synthesis-with-y, and projecting that the appearing of x should not entail the appearing of y is L-immediately self-contradictory. If a particular constant of S is regarded as to its concrete relation with S, projecting that the appearing of that constant should not entail the appearing of S is L-immediately self-contradictory. It is not L-immediately self-contradictory – as, precisely, asserted in §2, a of Chapter 7 – only if that constant is regarded as being isolated from S, in accordance with what is indeed explicitly stated in part b of that section (§).
11. [Translator's Note: The introduction ends with a comparative table of the sections of the first and second Italian editions; this table has been omitted in the present translation].

1

1. It should be noted that, in the present volume, the exposition of the originary achieves a positing of the originarity of metaphysical knowledge only in the last chapter – which, furthermore, opens a set of investigations that, in a second volume, will need to complete the exposition of the originary structure (in accordance with the way in which that completion is possible). The reader should therefore bear in mind from the outset that a perspective that fails to locate the constitution of metaphysical knowledge at the level of originarity consists in the opening of an *abstract concept* of the originary content. However, insofar as the concrete opening of the originary consists in a superseding of that abstract concept – in such a way that this also needs to be posited, and exposed, precisely in order to be superseded – the present exposition of the originary will also be an exposition of the fundamental elements, developments and implications of that abstract concept (cf. in particular Chapter 11). The meaning of these latter expressions, as well as the appropriateness of this mode of exposition of the originary content, will be clarified in the course of this work.
2. The distinction that has been made between the two kinds of negation does not aim to rule out the possibility that the negations that have not occurred may be projected as being themselves the content of a certainty (this being the project of the occurrence of new certainties); rather, it aims to rule out the possibility that while the negations that have occurred are, as a matter of fact, the content of a certainty – in that the bearer of those negations appears at least to be certain of them – the negations that have not occurred do not immediately take the form of a certainty, even though it is possible to consider or project that they will be. Outside of this project, they are a content of that different certainty that considers them as what has been originarily *superseded* by the by the ground.

    Leaving then aside aside the realization of that interest, mentioned in the main text, the 'occurrence' of a negation is not only a moment of the system of the negations of the ground, since the explicit unfolding and manifestation of that system consists in its occurring; that is to say, this occurring coincides here with the very self-positing of the system *qua* horizon that is originarily superseded by the positing of the ground.
3. *Encyclopaedia Logic*, §1.
4. Concerning this last point, cf. §6.
5. This fundamental lesson of Hegel's philosophy is already implicitly present in classical metaphysics. The most remarkable exceptions are rather to be found in the metaphysics of rationalism. By way of example, the seminal Thomistic 'ways' precisely constitute the signification of the term 'God', which only becomes meaningful as a *result* of those reasonings. Concerning the Thomistic 'ways', an interesting oscillation takes place in them in this respect, which is made explicit in the twofold type of conclusion of the reasonings: the oscillation between the '*quod omnes dicunt* Deum' and the '*hoc dicimus* Deum' (the 'quod' and the 'hoc' indicating the result of the discussion or reasoning). The 'omnes dicunt' indicates the pre-philosophical consciousness, or, more precisely, the conflation between the latter and the philosophical one; the '[nos] dicimus' indicates the philosophical consciousness. This second expression correctly makes explicit the fact that what is referred to as 'God' is precisely what results from the reasoning itself. That first expression, on the other hand, mixes this resulting – and, therefore, the semantic plane that corresponds to it – with the representation that common consciousness has of God. For, indeed, it

is clear that what 'everyone' refers to as 'God' is not the immutable being that results from the superseding of the contradictory absolutization of becoming. That 'quod omnes etc.' must therefore have this meaning: 'What everyone refers to as God must be understood as etc.'

6. There are two ways of asking for the ground, which differ from one another in an essential way: (1) the problematization of the ground; (2) the request for the ground. In the first case, the ground is the object of a negativity; in the second case, the object of the negativity is that of which the ground is requested (the ground itself thus counting as a positivity). A problematization consists in general in not settling with what is present as something whose ground cannot be identified. It is therefore always a request for a ground. It thus follows that the problematization of the ground is self-contradictory: it is a mode of the negation of the ground. Conversely, the request for the ground is always a problematization of that whose ground is requested.

The request for the ground, in turn, consists of two sides, the first of which is the one that (to a certain extent) has already been indicated above, and the other one consists in requesting the ground itself. That is to say, while in the first case a ground is requested of something whose immediate coincidence with the ground itself is not manifest, in the second case, the ground is requested *simpliciter*.

This second meaning of requesting a ground is to be regarded, together with the problematization of the ground, as a specific form of the negativity that refers to the ground. Indeed, asking for the ground in this way means placing oneself outside the ground – and, therefore, negating it precisely to the extent that one requests it.

The ground of the request for the ground, *simpliciter*, or the meaning of the question into meaning, *simpliciter*, is the originary structure. The ground grounds the request for the ground – or, the originary meaning makes the question into meaning meaningful: in that it posits it as being part of the horizon of what is originarily meaningful. Precisely for this reason, however, this requesting is immediately or originarily superseded as such the very moment it is grounded – the ground or meaning of that requesting being its very originary answer. It is possible to ask for the ground – and, more generally, every specific form of negativity, which has the ground as content, is possible – insofar as one is already within the ground. The ground thus grounds that asking in that the latter, too, is posited as being part of the horizon of the immediate; in grounding it, however, it supersedes it as an asking: that is to say, *qua* asking, it is immediately posited as being self-contradictory.

The other side of the request – that as part of which what is asked for is not the ground itself, but the ground *of something* – is instead not immediately superseded in and by its being grounded, i.e. in and by its being posited as belonging to the plane of immediacy. Once again, the ground of the request for the ground is the ground itself (or: the meaning of the request for the meaning of something is the originary meaning). Asking for the ground of something without originarily placing oneself within the ground means making that request groundless. That asking is here grounded in that it is the ground itself that stands in relation with an *other*, and, by virtue of this relation, it is not simply the ground, but a request for the ground. This 'other' is precisely that whose coincidence with the ground is not immediately manifest.

Insofar as this non-coincidence – and, therefore, that which does not coincide – is itself immediately posited (insofar as it appears), that other of the ground is not simply something other, but it belongs to the ground itself (which is precisely the horizon of the immediate). At the same time, however, that other is something other precisely in that it does not coincide with the ground. The contradiction is originarily superseded by distinguishing between the material aspect – i.e. the aspect of the content – and the formal aspect of the otherness in question. The other is such with respect to the material aspect, i.e. with respect to its logical content; with respect to the formal aspect, instead (i.e. to the extent that the other of the ground is immediately posited), the other belongs to the ground, and this belonging is what makes the relation between the ground and its other possible. As part of this relation, the ground does not therefore immediately find itself – or, precisely, it posits that in which it does not find itself as an 'other': that is to say, it immediately casts it away, and expels it outside itself, whence that 'other' falls outside the ground, into groundlessness.

That as part of which the ground does not immediately find itself may be of two different types, according to whether it is immediately present as a negation of the ground or whether the negation that it entails is not something immediate, but only exists as a project or a possible negation. The originary superseding of that other has a different value in these two cases. With respect to the first type of otherness, affirming that the other is 'that whose coincidence with the ground is not immediately manifest' is erroneous, in that in this case the relation of mutual exclusion between the other and the ground is immediately manifest. That affirmation is instead correct insofar as it is referred to that second type of otherness. Concerning the latter, it will be necessary to elucidate, more precisely than we have done above, what it means to be an other relative to the ground without immediately standing as the otherness of an excluding element. This otherness – which is therefore still to be specifically determined – may be defined here in a generic way by stating that it must be constituted by a propositional structure akin to the one in relation to which alone it is possible to make a distinction between the form and the matter of meaning (in the sense indicated above). That distinction does not obtain for non-propositional structures – such as, for instance, this colour as distinct from the judgement that recognizes it as such – which all stand as particular contents of the originary, and which therefore cannot include in their meaning the concept of an otherness relative to the originary meaning itself.

2

1. Concerning the meaning of this negation – and, therefore, of the corresponding affirmation – cf. §4, b.
2. This expression may appear ambiguous. However, its meaning has been indicated: the semantic horizon of which the immediacy is predicated includes this very predication; since there may not be a moment in which – as soon as that prediction is realized – that horizon would be posited without being posited as thus inclusive, this inclusion is said to be 'immediate'. 'Immediate' inclusion therefore means that if that horizon is the subject of that predication, it is inclusive in the indicated way. In this respect, it would be more appropriate not to speak of an *immediate* inclusion, since the term 'immediate' and derived terms are used in the text in another sense. On the other hand, however, that inclusion is immediate in the sense that it is immediately present: precisely insofar as that immediate presence belongs to the content that is immediately present (in such a way that this 'belonging' is immediately present). That this is not simply a *de facto* belonging follows from the fact that this belonging (i.e. this inclusion) *must* obtain as soon as the semantic horizon relative to which that belonging is established is posited as what is immediately present. Given this positing, that belonging is thus necessary. For the development of this point, cf. Chapter 7, §22.

3. Edmund Husserl, *Ideas Pertaining to a Pure Phenomenology* (The Hague: Nijhoff, 1983), §24, p. 45.
4. John Dewey, *Logic: The Theory of Enquiry* (Carbondale: Southern Illinois University, 1986), p. 143. This remark already appears in Hegel – naturally in a different logical context, cf. e.g. *Encyclopaedia*, §66.
5. Dewey, *Logic*, p. 146.
6. Ibid., p. 144.
7. Cf. Gentile, *Sistema di logica come teoria del conoscere*, vol. I, part II, Chap. I.
8. The historical basis of the notion of intentionality is found, above all, in Aristotle's *De anima*, which constitutes the starting point of the further investigations of both those who explicitly have this concept in view (Scholastics, neo-Scholastics, Husserl, Heidegger, etc.) and of those who only deal with it implicitly (idealists, neo-positivists, etc.); we therefore refer the reader to that series of investigations. In order to give substance to this generic citation, we refer to what is said in this regard in Chapters III and IV of G. Bontadini's *Saggio di una metafisica dell'esperienza* (Milan: Vita e Pensiero, 1938).

3

1. [Translator's note: 'What is proper to them is that it is necessary not only that they *be* true of themselves, but that they *be seen* to be such'].
2. Or, equivalently: if a noesis is abstractly separated from its dianoesis, what is posited is not being – precisely because being, *in its essence*, is that which is its own self. Positing being without positing its self-identity means not positing being – precisely because being is a self-identity. The contradiction consists here in the fact that what one aims to posit as being is not being. This set of observations – which in our view is of significant importance – will be developed in due course.
3. Or, equivalently: $E' (= E'') = E'' (= E')$
4. *Sistema di logica,* Vol. I, Part II, Chap. III, §9.
5. Ibid., §2.
6. Ibid., §5.
7. Ibid.
8. The expression 'L-immediacy' (or 'L-immediate'), however, is *not* thus left to only indicate that aspect of logical immediacy by virtue of which that immediacy is an immediate affirmation of a positive element that exceeds the Ph-immediate. (This aspect may be referred to as the *metaphysical* aspect or value of L-immediacy.) Rather, that expression indicates every aspect of logical immediacy, in such a way that it will each time fall to the context to establish the meaning of that expression.

4

1. It may be argued that Aristotle formulates this aporia, without, however, recognizing it as such, in observing that of non-being, too, we state that it 'is' non-being: διὸ καὶ τὸ μὴ ὂν εἶναι μὴ ὂν φαμέν (*Metaphysics*, IV, 2, 1003 b10).
2. [Translator's note: 'The question is then as follows: whether nothing is something or not. If someone answered: "It seems to me to be nothing", his very negation, as he

supposes it, compels him to admit that something is nothing, since he says: "*It seems to me to be nothing*" – which is as though he were to say: "It seems to me that nothing is something."']
3. 'Nec aliquid potest mente concipi nisi intelligatur ens' (Aquinas, *In duodecim libros metaphysicorum Aristotelis expositio*, p. 605).
4. It is clear that non-being is not *other* than or *different* from being *by virtue of something* that it is and that being is not, but precisely because it is not something. Accordingly, if one were to state that – insofar as non-being is different from being, but it is not different *by virtue of something* – non-being is not different from being, it would be necessary to reply that, certainly, in this sense it is not different (this being the sense in which two beings are different), but it is different in the sense that it is an absolute lack of being. The aporia in question involves instead this absolute lack, which, in the present discussion, appears as a *being*.
5. One might think that the positivity of nothingness coincides with formal being only if nothingness is not regarded as the negation of the whole, but, as for instance in Hegel, as an *indeterminate nothingness*, in which what is negated is not the semantic maximum, but the semantic minimum (pure being). This is in any case the difference between Hegel's nothingness and nothingness *qua absolute* negativity: the former is a negation of the minimum positive, and the latter is the negation of the maximum one.
6. Let us reiterate that this superseded self-contradictoriness is the one by virtue of which the absolutely negative is positively meaningful; the two sides or moments of this self-contradictoriness (the negative and the positive) are non-contradictory: nothingness is nothing, and the positive is positive.
7. To avoid any misunderstanding, let us add the following clarifications, which to a careful reader might rather appear like repetitions. (1) *Being, qua* synthesis of formal being and a determination or essence (Chapter 2, §2), is not to be conflated with *being*, which is posited as a moment of nothingness *qua* concrete (self-contradictory) meaning. The former is the whole relative to which the latter is a moment; to the extent that nothingness succeeds in being, nothingness is akin to a determinate being – i.e. to that being whose determinacy is the absolute negation of the positive. (2) Nothingness, *qua* concrete self-contradictoriness, constitutes the superseding of the abstract that it includes: in the sense that it retains the two mutually contradictory moments as posited together, i.e. it supersedes their mutual separation. That unity of being and non-being that is the very concrete meaningfulness of being (and of non-being) – which consists in the very relation of exclusion of non-being by being – is not to be conflated with the unity of being and non-being constituted by nothingness *qua* self-contradictory meaning. In the former case, that unity is a superseding of the contradiction, a superseding that posits the two contradictory terms in a negative relation; in the latter case, that unity is the very constitution of the self-contradictory meaning. In the former case, the superseded abstract is being, which, conceived of as unrelated to non-being, fails to stand in opposition to the latter (and vice-versa); in the latter case, the superseded abstract is non-being, which, conceived as unrelated to being, on the one hand, it is constituted as a concrete meaning (§1), and, on the other hand, it intends to persist as a pure negativity (§3). As a result, on the one hand, distorting the meaning of being and non-being, one supposes that the principle of non-contradiction is in this way negated; and, on the other hand, the implication of nothingness by being results in a non-implication.

8. Henri Bergson, *Creative Evolution*, trans. Donald A. Landes (Abingdon: Routledge, 2023), pp. 247–8. [Translator's Note: All quotations from *L'Évolution créatrice* are in French in the original].
9. Ibid., p. 259. The following passage should also be kept in mind:

> There is *more*, and not *less*, in the idea of an object conceived of as 'not existing' than in the idea of this same object conceived of as 'existing,' since the idea of the object as 'not existing' is necessarily the idea of the object as 'existing' with, in addition, the representation of an exclusion of this object by the current or actual state of reality taken as a whole. Ibid., p. 250.

Bergson does not distinguish nothingness, regarded as the absolutely other than being (absolutely other than the totality of being), from nothingness regarded as the annihilation of the totality of being. Bergson's text always presents this second connotation. It is clear, however, that nothingness is not an annihilation, even though the outcome of an annihilation is nothingness. At the same time, however, in both connotations of the term 'nothingness', the positing of nothingness entails the positing of the totality of the positive, in such a way that, on the one hand, Bergson's observations may also be extended to that value of nothingness that is not taken into consideration by Bergson, and it is in this sense that they are considered in the present text; on the other hand, what is stated in the text may also be referred to that value of nothingness that is considered by Bergson. In this second respect, it must be stated that the concept of an 'annihilation of the whole' does not present the self-contradictoriness that Bergson believes to identify. This does in no way exclude – and this is a crucial remark – that this concept should be self-contradictory, for, on the contrary, as we shall see, the verification of the self-contradictoriness of that concept belongs to the originary structure itself, and it arguably constitutes its most determining aspect.
10. [Translator's Note: Bertrand Russell, 'On Denoting', *Mind*, vol. 14, no. 56 (1905), 479–93, p. 491].

5

1. Cf. Chapter 3, §15, b.
2. While the following observations are to be primarily referred to the relation between the Ph-immediate and the totality of the Ph-immediate (because the subject of the present chapter is Ph-immediacy), these observations may, however, be extended – and, therefore, they must necessarily be extended – to the relation between the immediate, *simpliciter*, and the totality, *simpliciter*, of the immediate.

6

1. It may be objected that since the contradiction of an infinite analysis consists in the fact that one wishes to posit something that, *qua* infinite, transcends the positional horizon – and since, however, that infinite analysis is actual or present, and therefore posited, as part of the very argument that we are conducting here – it follows that the exclusion of that infinite analysis from the domain of actuality is carried out on the grounds of its inclusion in what is actual.

It is clear that this difficulty is a specification of that broader difficulty as part of which one asks how it should be possible to exclude what is not present from what is present without, however, including it (cf. Chapter 10, §14). Let us briefly indicate the solution to that specific difficulty by stating that an infinite analysis is posited or actual simply as a formal determinacy. At the same time, however, the very meaning of that determinacy points to a semantic content that, as such, is not actual. What is not actual or present is the *determination* of this content in a way that is analogous to the one in which the actual quantity of that meaning is determined. Accordingly, that infinite analysis is actual as a formal determinacy, and it is not actual as to its concrete content. What is included in the domain of the actual therefore differentiates itself from what is excluded from that domain.
2. Not every complex meaning is a meaning of this kind. In the complex meanings: 'Dark place', 'Rational number', and so on, the first term constitutes a determination or qualifier of the second one (and vice-versa). This is not the case for other types of complex meanings, such as: 'Greater than x', 'This red and this green', and so on. In this second case, there is indeed no *determination* in the sense occurring in the first case. We may, however, leave the question open as to whether what is stated in the text concerning *a certain type* of complex meanings can be extended, upon further analysis, to other types of complex meanings – and, in case, to every type of complex meaning.
3. The colour red does not therefore pertain to this extension, regarded as a term that has all the properties that pertain to it except for the one of being red (i.e. conceived of with all its properties except this last one): precisely because being red cannot pertain to that term conceived in that way. And the colour red, which is predicated of this extension, cannot be predicated in its being considered according to all the properties that pertain to it, except for the one that consists of being the red of this extension: precisely because the colour red, thus regarded, is not a predicate of this extension. Conceiving the subject and the predicate in this way precisely means presupposing them to their synthesis; or, equivalently: if the subject and the predicate are presupposed, they are conceived in that way. It must therefore be stated: dy can only be predicated of dx insofar as, on the one hand, dx is known as something to which dy pertains (i.e. as $dx = dy$), and, on the other hand, dy is known as something that pertains to dx (i.e. as $dy = dx$). This *condition* of the predication is not to be conflated with the *ground* of the latter: a ground that, in this case, consists in the Ph-immediacy of the predication.

7

1. It should be observed that projecting itself is not in contradiction with the Ph-immediate precisely insofar as it is a projecting, i.e. insofar as it consists in the problematic opening of a horizon that is additional relative to the one of Ph-immediacy. For, if one disregards the form of this projecting, the content of a project is always in contradiction with the Ph-immediate – this contradiction being precisely superseded by concretely considering that content in its problematic form.
2. Unless explicitly stated, the term 'meaning' is never used in a restrictive sense in this essay – for instance, limited to the logico-linguistic apparatus to the exclusion of 'objects' or 'things' – but in its most comprehensive value: i.e. that by virtue of which the totality of meaning coincides with the totality of being: *ens et verum convertuntur*.

3. This affirmation must be specified in the sense indicated in § 2, c. Concerning the concrete meaning of the relation between L-immediate propositions and the principle of non-contradiction – concerning the concrete meaning of Ph-L-immediacy – cf. § 19.
4. It should be noted that this assertion will have to be amended, or, more precisely, restricted: in the sense that there are certain – so to speak, anomalous – types of *a posteriori* syntheses, in relation to which the project of a non-pertaining of the predicate to the subject is immediately contradictory (cf. § 15). The observations developed in §§ 5–10 concerning the paradigm formulated in the main text do not therefore refer to all values of that paradigm, but to that specific series of values that may be considered to be normal – this 'normality' being regarded here as the property, enjoyed by *a posteriori* syntheses, in accordance with which the project of the non-pertaining of the predicate to the subject does not immediately appear to be contradictory.
5. Let us respectively refer to these two sides of the project – i.e. projecting that the positing of Y does not imply the positing of Z, and projecting that the positing of Y *does* imply the positing of Z – as 'side 1' and 'side 2' of the project under consideration.
6. In more detail, it should be noted that the L-immediate self-contradictoriness of the negation of those implications that have an analytic value can be attested in two ways. Retaining the implication between the positing of S and the positing of s as a paradigm of these implications, the self-contradictoriness of the negation of this implication consists indeed on the one hand in the positing and lack of positing of S, and on the other hand in the positing and lack of positing of s as a constant of S. If, indeed, one holds firm that s is a constant of S, the affirmation that S is posited even if s is not entails that S is posited and is not posited (it is not posited precisely in that, *since s is a constant of S*, not positing s means not positing S); if instead one holds firm that S is posited, the affirmation that S is posited even if s is not entails that s is posited and is not posited as a constant of S (it is not posited as a constant of S precisely in that, *since S is posited but s is not*, s must not count as a constant of S). Concerning this clarification, it must be stated that the moments of the m-contradiction can be neither the positing and lack of positing of Y – this having been discussed in the main text – nor the positing and lack of positing of Z as a constant of Y (since it is precisely as a result of the superseding of the m-contradiction that Z appears as a constant of Y, in such a way that this value of constant cannot constitute itself as a moment of the m-contradiction); in this second case, the moments of the m-contradiction must then consist in something *other* than the positing of Z as a constant of Y and in the negation of that other term.
7. Or, in relation to the clarification made in the previous footnote: the terms of which are not the positing and lack of positing of Z in its immediately excluding the positing of Y.
8. By way of example: this red (= Y) and this green (= Z) are two variants of S. They are co-present: that is to say, the positing of one is implied by the positing of the other as a matter of fact. Due to this factual implication, it is immediately contradictory to project a verification of the contradictoriness of the implication *simpliciter* between this red and this green, since in this way one would be projecting a negation of the Ph-immediate; that project, however, is not immediately contradictory to the extent that the implication between this red and this green is not considered as such, or *simpliciter*, but *secundum quid*: i.e. as projected, or as itself a project relative to the

factual implication between this red and this green. Furthermore, insofar as the totality of the immediate includes the recollection of a positing (or a series of acts of positing) of this red as part of which this green was not posited – i.e. the recollection of a lack of factual implication between this red and this green – it is also not immediately contradictory to project a verification of the self-contradictoriness of the implication between this red and this green, to the extent that this red is regarded as that red of which one recalls the lack of factual implication with this green. (Insofar as this lack of implication is a factual one, affirming that implication means already being in contradiction *with* the Ph-immediate; we are now stating that it is possible to suppose a verification of the *self*-contradictoriness of that affirmation).

9. It is clear that the pre-philosophical level whose return is projected also counts as something projected with respect to that positional level that is projected to include the demonstration of the necessity of the return of pre-philosophical knowledge.

10. The form of the *supposition* is normally used in these 'examples'. One states: '*Suppose* that a series of acts of positing of a specific meaning implies the positing of determinacies that exclude the positing of another specific meaning'. In relation to the case at hand: '*Suppose* that no positional implication obtains between two meanings prior to the one obtaining as a matter of fact'. The form of the supposition, however, is only correct in relation to the *communication* of the originary structure *to another* thinking individual; that is to say, it is only correct in relation to the project of the existence of other instances of consciousness in addition to the one (mine) that is included in the totality of the immediate. Taking into account these other instances of consciousness and the communication with them, it certainly cannot be taken for granted that, if the immediate does not attest any positional implications between two meanings prior to the factual one, this must also be the case for those other instances of consciousness. In relation to the possibility that things could be different, one precisely uses the form of the supposition.

Insofar as one remains within the scope of the exposition *simpliciter* of the originary, however, that supposition is incorrect. For, indeed, a series of past implications between the positing of this pencil and the positing of the distance between the pencil and the sheet of paper on which I write is immediately present – rather than a simple supposition – and so is the fact that no positional implication between this pencil and its distance from the left side of my desk is prior to the factual one.

11. It should be observed that the proposition: 'A is A' is synthetic *a priori* both in case what is posited as part of the distinct term A is nothing but that determinacy (i.e. essence) by virtue of which A distinguishes itself from the other determinacies – i.e. in case the *being* of this determinacy is not posited – and in case the semantic domain constituted by the distinct term A includes the being of this determinacy. For, indeed, A, posited as this *being*, is nevertheless distinct from being itself, regarded as a concrete universal; accordingly, even if A is considered as thus distinct, the proposition: 'A is A' is synthetic *a priori*.

12. It should be observed that the proposition: 'being is being' is synthetic *a priori* not only if 'being' is regarded as an abstract universal – as a form in which the content is indeterminately posited – but also if the form is considered in its being in relation to a part of the concrete content. It is clear that this second case is equivalent to the second of the two cases distinguished in the previous footnote.

13. Let these two types respectively be the fourth and fifth ones after the three types considered in § 15. While it is effectively the case that the last two types that we have identified may be traced back to the first three (the fifth type, for instance, manifestly

being a subset of the second one), since they have certain particular properties with respect to the first three, they may as such be considered separately.

14. Concerning this equation, it should be observed that, by virtue of the very meaning of T, each of the terms of the equation cannot be an *abstract moment* of the positional domain constituted by the equation itself, for otherwise the whole (T) would no longer be such. Each of the terms of the equation therefore includes – or, more precisely, it realizes itself as – the equation of which it is a term. This does not mean that T cannot be kept distinct from $T = T$ and from $(T = T) = (T = T)$; rather, it means that, as thus distinct, the positional domain of T is not the semantic whole, and it precisely constitutes only a *formal* positing of the whole.

8

1. It is clear that the present observations may be extended to every meaning. The reader may independently do so by substituting (with the appropriate modifications) the concept of the 'Project of the arising of the constants of any meaning' to the concept of the 'Project of the arising of the constants of S'. This latter concept is addressed in the main text because of the particular significance of S in relation to other meanings, as well as because – as we shall clarify – this second aspect of the matter in question includes the first one.
2. The most significant aporia that arises in relation to this question consists in the fact that this annulment, too – i.e. this identity between affirming and negating, positing and not positing – is in some way real: at least to the extent that one reasons about it. Accordingly, what cannot be – in some way – is. As the reader may recall, this aporia can be considered as an aspect of the general aporia determined by the existence of a reasoning concerning nothingness: cf. Chapter 4, §14.
3. Here let us only observe that an immediate verification of the self-contradictoriness of the affirmation of the identity between the present set of the constants of S and the totality of these constants does not exclude the *project* of the existence of a certain quantity of constants of S in addition to the set of constants that is L-immediately attested. The aporias to which that anticipation gives rise as such, as well as in relation to certain elements of the exposition that will be considered in the meantime, will also be considered in due course. (For a preliminary clarification, cf. § 15, g).
4. It is once again clear that while the m(or m')-contradiction is *already* immediately present, as something projected, as part of the base plane of the originary structure, that contradiction is however only present there in an indeterminate or formal way. That is to say, the formal structure of the projected m-contradiction is known as part of the base plane, but the concrete semantic elements that stand as the matter of the contradiction are not known: for if those elements were known, the contradiction would no longer be only something projected, but known – and this knowledge would have led beyond the base plane.
5. [Translator's Note: G.W.F. Hegel, *Phenomenology of Spirit*], trans. A.V. Miller (Oxford: Oxford University Press, 1977), p. 13.
6. [Translator's Note: G.W.F. Hegel, *Science of Logic*], trans. A.V. Miller (Abingdon: Routledge, 1969), pp. 71–2].
7. There are at least two meanings of 'immediacy' in Hegel's philosophy. The first, more specific meaning is the one by virtue of which 'immediacy' is opposed to 'relation'. It is clear that the totality of the immediate is not an immediacy in this

sense, since it consists in the immediate presence of a complex system of relations. Relative to this first meaning of 'immediacy', a 'mediation' does not consist in that specific type of relation or implication constituted by an *a priori* synthesis, but in *every* type of relation. In this sense, only pure being, which opens the deductive process of the *Logic*, is absolutely immediate – equivalently, however: every determination, insofar as it is not regarded in relation to its opposite, is immediate. The second meaning of 'immediacy' – which in the text has been equated with the concept of the totality of the immediate – consists in that identity of certainty and truth, or of thought and reality, which on the one hand appears at the end of the *Phenomenology* and on the other hand constitutes the 'third position of thought with respect to objectivity' discussed in the 'Preliminary Conception' of the *Encyclopaedia*. ('What the principle of immediate knowing rightly insists on is not an indeterminate, empty immediacy, abstract being, or pure unity on its own account [1st meaning of immediacy], but the unity of the Idea with being', in such a way that what is affirmed is that 'neither the Idea, as a merely subjective thought, nor a mere being on its own account, is what is true [...] What is immediately asserted by this is that the Idea is what is true only as mediated by being, and, conversely, that being is what is true only as mediated by the Idea.' *Encyclopaedia*, § 70). Here, it is not necessary to ascertain the nature of the relation between this latter form of the phenomenological process and the previous ones. Suffice it to say that if the identity of certainty and truth is a *result* of those previous forms, this cannot be the case in the sense that these forms constitute its ground (i.e. that whose validity grounds the validity of that identity), but in the sense that the positing of that identity is such only *qua* superseding of the opposition – and not *qua* superseding of the abstract opposition, but of all its concrete forms (which, for Hegel, are given as part of the historical consciousness); accordingly, that identity is not abstractly immediate (first meaning of immediacy), but it is mediated, placed in relation and resulting through the superseding of the opposition (cf. Chapter 1, § 16, and Chapter 9).

It should furthermore be observed that, through the use of the Hegelian concept of 'systematic circle' that we intend to make in the main text, we do *not* thereby mean to claim that the 'mediation', which is included in the definition of that concept, counts in Hegel's text as an *a priori* synthesis – even though it is regarded as an *a priori* synthesis to the extent that it belongs to the structure of the systematic circle that we have put forth. At the same time, however, the observations developed concerning the systematic circle understood as an *a priori* synthesis may also be referred, with the appropriate modifications, to that circularity that, as we shall clarify, constitutes itself through an extension of the analysis of S. In other words, the systematic circle has a mediational development (the one considered now in the main text) and an analytic one (the extension of the analysis): the two developments have an analogous structure, in such a way that Hegel's propositions, quoted in the main text, are to be referred to both of them. Lastly, the validity of the concept of systematic circle *as part of the explicit meaning that it takes in Hegel's texts* constitutes a question that will be addressed in the next chapter.

8. C-contradiction: verifying and therefore superseding an m-contradiction means verifying that the ground consists in a form of having been a C-contradiction; superseding the contradiction that arises from negating that a determinacy belongs to the essence of S means verifying that S has been a form of contradiction precisely because it has not included that determinacy as posited, or also because

this determinacy was only included as a matter of fact, without being regarded as belonging to the essence of S.
9. The fact that S cannot be the ground if it does not include in its semantic opening the very dimension of what is grounded may be explained, on the one hand, by the reason indicated in Chapter 7, § 18, h, and on the other hand by the fact that the ground, *qua* not inclusive of what is grounded, does not consist in the positing of all its constants; therefore, insofar as it is a realization of the C-contradiction, it cannot stand – precisely *qua* contradiction – as the ground. (A contradiction, as such, cannot be that *on the basis of which* something is affirmed). Furthermore, these two reasons may be reduced to simply one, since logical immediacy, *qua* not inclusive of that individuation constituted by mediation itself (cf. Chapter 9, § 19, h), is only an *intention* of logical immediacy (i.e. it is not what it intends to be), and it therefore stands as a realization of the C-contradiction. The C-contradiction determined by the ground's lack of inclusion of what is grounded coincides with logical immediacy in its not including that individuation.

9

1. Abstract immediacy is therefore to be understood according to the first of the two meanings of immediacy that have been distinguished in the footnote of §14 of the previous chapter.
2. This identity means that being, which is present, is not something 'phenomenal' or simply subjective relative to a reality in itself, but it is that very reality in itself in its manifestation. It is furthermore clear that this identity of being and presence is at the same time a *difference* of the two terms – to the extent that being *does not consist* of its presence, and the latter is the presence *of* being: *fieri aliud*.
3. Strictly speaking, this is only correct in relation to those negations that negate the first type of *a priori* syntheses considered in §14 of Chapter 7. (Verifying, by means of M, that B is predicated of A – conferring upon B and M the semantic value that pertains to them insofar as the proposition 'A is B' belongs to that first type of *a priori* syntheses – means precisely verifying, on the basis of a mediation, that the semantic content 'A is not B' is a negation of the ground; accordingly, this verification entails a surpassing of the base plane.) In relation to the second and third types of *a priori* syntheses identified in the passage quoted above, however – as well as in relation to the fourth and fifth types (cf. Chapter 7, §18) – there exist negations of the ground that, while being identified as such on the basis of a mediation, do not require a surpassing of the base plane. For instance, the proposition: 'The meaning *whole* does not imply the meaning *part*' is identified as being self-contradictory – and, therefore, a negation of the ground – only insofar as a mediation takes place: i.e. insofar as the immediate pertaining of 'greater than a part' (= M) to 'whole' is posited; that identification, however, does not entail a surpassing of the level of logical immediacy – or, concretely, of the base plane. Accordingly, these types of negations, too, can be considered as belonging to the system of the immediate negations of the ground. (Furthermore, the negations of the synthetic *a priori* propositions of the type $A = A$ – according to the two aspects of this type considered in §18 of Chapter 7 – or the negations of mediations that do not count as *a priori* syntheses – cf. Chapter 7, §19, b – immediately appear as negations of the ground: the former as a negation of

logical immediacy, and the latter as a negation of phenomenological immediacy. This is the case even though, as previously seen, their superseding does not take place on the basis of the very content that these negations negate.)

4. In relation to the previous footnote, let us specify that the proposition 'A is not A' has *for itself* a value of negation of the ground, and it is therefore an immediate negation; the proposition 'The meaning *whole* does not imply the meaning *part*', however, does not have the value of negation of the ground *for itself*, but it can be considered to be immediate to the extent that the simple positing of the structure of the immediate identifies it as a negation of the ground (i.e. as a negation of this very structure).

5. Let us reiterate (cf. Chapter 7, §2) that a determination is a constant of another determination not only insofar as it stands as a predicate of the latter, but also insofar as it stands as a semantic *moment* of that predicate: a moment for which – as in the case at hand – it may be contradictory to stand as a predicate of that subject-determination. More on this further on.

6. That is to say, the propositions 'Z is included, as superseded, in K' and 'K is included, as superseded, in Z' are L-immediate.

7. This clarification manifestly points to an extension of the discussion that we are conducting here – an extension that is also implied by the observation that the relation between z and nK is the relation between a meaning and one of its constants, in such a way that everything that is attested concerning this relation has a paradigmatic value with respect to the relation between any meaning and one of its constants. At the same time, however, the project as part of which the outcomes of the abstract acts of positing of meanings are differentiated in relation to the different semantic values of the implied constants may be retained as something immediately non-contradictory.

8. It should be noted that when, in these pages, we speak of the abstract concept of z, we refer to *that* abstract concept that consists in positing z without positing nK, and when we speak of an abstract concept of that abstract concept, we refer to *that* abstract concept that intends something that is not the positing of z as the positing of z.

9. Both if nK is absolutely not posited and if nK is not posited as a constant of z, this is a lack of positing of nK.

10. *Encyclopaedia*, §80.
11. *Encyclopaedia*, §81.
12. *Science of Logic*, p. 834.
13. Ibid.
14. In addition, a presentation of this fourth case is made more complex by the observation advanced by Hegel after the passage quoted above: 'However, the inadequate form of such propositions is at once obvious. In treating of the judgement it has been shown that its form in general, and most of all the immediate form of the positive judgement, is incapable of holding within its grasp speculative determinations and truth. The direct supplement to it, the negative judgement, would at least have to be added as well' (ibid.). We speak of a more complex situation because the negation of the negative constitutes the essence of the speculative, and it cannot belong to the dialectical moment, as it would instead be the case if the latter were to be expressed through a negative proposition, in addition to the affirmative one. This imbalance is probably remedied by giving a paradigmatic value to to what Hegel states concerning the difference between being and nothing: this difference is only *intended*, in such a way that the proposition: 'Being is not nothing' is the expression of an intention (i.e. the intention, which pertains to the abstract concept of that abstract positing, for – abstractly posited – being to be being and not nothing). That difference is no

longer just intended, but real, only if one leaves behind the abstract positing of being and nothing, thus opening that first concreteness constituted by becoming (the first concrete concept), as part of which being and nothing exist as different terms (cf. ibid., p. 82 ff.).

15. It should be noted that the dialectical contradiction intended by Hegel precisely consists in this (self-contradictory) passing from z to K; alternatively, conferring a greater correctness upon the Hegelian text, the dialectical contradiction consists in a passing from z to $k(nz)$ (understanding z as a formal meaning), in such a way that the outcome of the abstract consideration of z is the synthesis or 'unity' of z and $k(nz)$; in the passage quoted above, Hegel states: 'This unity can be expressed as a proposition in which the immediate is put as subject, and the mediated as its predicate.' The fact that this passing from z to K, or to $k(nz)$, in the indicated sense, should be the realization of a self-contradiction – which is superseded by the positing of the negative of the negative – is not only not disputed here, but it is precisely what is being affirmed. What is being disputed – or, more precisely, what does not appear to be warranted – is that this self-contradiction should constitute the positional outcome of a positing of z that does not imply the positing of nK. A disputing nevertheless takes place if that self-contradictory passing is regarded as a passing from z to K, since, as already mentioned, K cannot belong to the positional domain constituted by the outcome of the abstract positing of z.
16. Cf. for instance: *Science of Logic*, p. 834; *Encyclopaedia*, §82, *Zus.*
17. [Translator's Note: While the being of one contrary is eliminated by the being of the other contrary, the knowledge of one contrary is not eliminated by the knowledge of the other one, but is rather supported by it].
18. All of this is correct in relation to the positing of a term (z), which is an abstract positing insofar as it does not posit a determination (nK) that is a constant of that term, but not of other ones. But in relation to the broader application of the dialectical process (cf. §12, e; Chapter 10, §11), by virtue of which the abstract positing *of every* finite determination is dialectical, it must be stated that if the outcome of that abstract positing is positive, the two sides of the dialectical contradiction are both included in the positional domain constituted by that outcome.
19. It is indeed the case that, according to Hegel, the nothingness that is posited in the outcome of the abstract positing of formal being is not nothingness *qua* determinate negation of the concrete positivity (in such a way that the positing of this negation would imply the positing of the concrete that is negated), but an indeterminate nothingness: 'the abstract, immediate negation: nothing, purely on its own account, negation devoid of any relations – what could also be expressed if one so wished merely by "not"' (*Science of Logic*, p. 83). At the same time, however, it is clear that the positing of this indeterminate nothing is nevertheless *a positing*, even if of a minimum logical content; that is to say, it is not the annulment of the positional plane.

10

1. The positing of the meaning 'everything that is not x', too, constitutes a positing of the whole as partially superseded (in this case, however, the superseded part is not the totality of non-x, but, precisely, x). This meaning, however – contrary to the meaning 'other than everything that is not x' – is not predicated of x.

2. The meaning 'whole' is a *part* of the meaning 'whole as partially superseded' (or 'other than everything that is not *x*'), but not in the sense that the *remainder* that lies beyond that part includes the whole as a moment of a larger semantic horizon – since that remainder consists in negating a part of the whole, or in considering a part of the whole as negated. This is a negation or consideration that is itself an internal determination of the whole: for the latter, in including every part, includes it as something superseded or negated by every *other* part or determination. That is to say, the remainder that in the meaning 'whole as partially superseded' lies beyond the whole consists in the very internal limit of the whole (and it is one limit in the totality of these internal limits of the whole).
3. The verification of the L-immediacy of the affirmation that being surpasses the totality of the Ph-immediate implies the verification – precisely operated now in the main text – that the affirmation that being surpasses the totality of the Ph-immediate is not immediately manifested as a self-contradiction. It is clear that if, at this point, one were to claim that this second verification does not exclude the *project* of a verification of the self-contradictoriness of that affirmation (on the basis of an extension of the analysis or through a mediational development), this condition would proceed from the standpoint of the concept Γ_a (cf. Chapter 3, §22), since the L-immediacy of that affirmation constitutes an immediate supersession of that projecting, i.e. it constitutes an immediate identification of that project as a self-contradiction.
4. Concerning the concept of the existence of an object of thought independently of the mind, Berkley observes that in order for this concept to be realizable it would be necessary for that object to be thought as not-thought – 'which is a downright contradiction' (Berkeley, *Treatise*, §22). This observation finds its greatest significance as part of actualism. It is an altogether correct observation, except that, observing this, one states nothing but that the independence of being from its actual or immediate manifestation is not Ph-immediately manifest, and to the extent that one Ph-immediately affirms it, one incurs in a 'a downright contradiction'. There is, however, no downright or immediate contradiction in the *project* of an annulment of the actual presence of being, to which there would correspond no annulment of being. It is certainly the case that this annulment and that persistence are present, but they are contents of that presence whose annulment is precisely projected – in such a way that the contradiction identified above does not pertain to the project. The set of issues to which we refer in the main text is analogous to the one considered here (aside from the fact that while here we speak of a 'project', in the context of the observations addressed in the main text it is instead not possible to speak of a project, as we have already mentioned). That is to say, it is affirmed that it is not immediately contradictory to affirm that being surpasses the order of presence: an immediate self-contradictoriness would obtain if the surpassing were the content of an Ph-immediate affirmation (and not of an L-immediate one). Indeed, Ph-immediately affirming that surpassing means stating that what is not immediately present is *simpliciter* immediately present: precisely insofar as it is the content of an Ph-immediate affirmation.
5. Let us reiterate that – as we shall concretely present in Chapter 13 – this contradiction exists in its being categorically affirmed precisely insofar as the difference between the originary meaning and the absolute semantic matter is categorically (and L-immediately) affirmed; the content of the whole is certainly categorically posited through this affirmation (and not only problematically, as it is the case if that difference is projected), but it is nevertheless a formal content – and, in fact, that affirmation categorically exhibits precisely the formal character of that content – in such a way

that the whole is in any case formally posited, and something that is not the whole is posited as the whole. This is the case even if one recognizes that the categorical content is only formal, and that the contradiction that arises from positing this formal element as the whole must be superseded: the superseding of this contradiction, together with that recognition, is indeed itself formal, and the contradiction is retained as not superseded to the extent that the absolute semantic matter is not effectively posited.

6. We shall return further ahead, and in more detail, to this aporia solved here (cf. §§13–16).

7. If the originary were instead regarded as that abstract moment of originarity that consists in the positing of the totality of the immediate in its being distinct from its implying the positing of the semantic whole – i.e. if the structure of the originary were regarded as not including P – then the predicate of the proposition R would only pertain to that distinct term *through* the term that in the proposition P functions as middle term: this middle term, as verified in §1, being the negated totality of the contradictory of the totality of the immediate, which L-immediately pertains to this totality as its predicate. The proposition R would appear as something L-mediated even if the originary were regarded as a structure that does not include Q (and, therefore, all the more so if it is regarded as that abstract structuring that includes neither P nor Q). It should furthermore be observed that the proposition Q does not affirm the difference between the whole and the originary insofar as the latter is regarded as a moment or abstract structuring, but insofar as the originary is regarded as to the concreteness of its structure.

8. Here let us only observe that a synthetic *a posteriori* proposition distinguishes itself from the other types of propositions because it is not immediately contradictory to project – in accordance with what we have already previously stated – that the predicate that presently pertains *to the essence*, or more generally *to a persistence*, of the meaning that constitutes the subject of the proposition (and therefore not to that meaning as such) should no longer pertain to it. If being-red is a constant of *this* extension, it is certainly immediately self-contradictory to project that *this* extension should not be red, but it is not immediately self-contradictory to project that a persistence of this extension (and, therefore, not this extension a such) should not be red. Being-red is a constant of this extension, but if *this* extension no longer is, it is not immediately self-contradictory to project that a persistence of this extension should no longer be red. To the extent that this persistence implies a 'no longer being' relative to this extension, we still need to establish the meaning of a 'no longer being' relative to a determination of being. A development of this remark leads to the formulation of the aporias anticipated in the main text.

9. Formal being is not to be conflated with the infinite semanteme regarded as a formal meaning (and it is precisely for this reason that the abstract positing of formal being results in a positional nullity). The infinite semanteme, regarded as a formal meaning, is indeed the *synthesis* of formal being and the indeterminately posited determinate, i.e. it is 'being', but regarded as the positivity of the determination, or as the determining of the positivity. The formal value of the infinite semanteme only results from the fact that this determining is formal, or indeterminate, i.e. it is not the absolute semantic matter. Formal being is instead only the positivity of the determinate, i.e. it is the simple signification of this positivity – in such a way that it stands as a limited meaning: it is a formally limited meaning because it is a part or moment of what is formally unlimited.

10. *Corollary*: If y is regarded as a meaning that is distinct from its not being x, the proposition: 'x is non-y' is L-mediated (precisely because it is affirmed that x is non-y

on the basis of something other than this proposition, i.e. on the basis of that not being x – which, however, pertains to the distinct term y – insofar as it is negated by x); on the contrary, that proposition is L-immediate if y is regarded as the synthesis between its semantic content (i.e. between what was posited as a distinct term) and this content's not being x.
11. For the meaning of this formal value, cf. Chapter 9, §8, c, d, e.
12. More generally, the aporia can be formulated by stating that if every meaning is a constant of any other meaning, the lack of positing of y implies a positional annulment, since every meaning that is posited as part of the outcome of the positing of a semantic domain that does not include y is a constant of y and therefore it cannot be posited if y is not posited. This general formulation of the aporia suffers from the shortcoming of not taking into account the concrete way in which the theorem that every meaning is a constant of every other meaning is established. That concrete way is instead taken into account by the formulation of the aporia presented above, which considers that mode of foundation of the theorem in which it is verified that every meaning (e.g. y) is a constant of the contradictory of any meaning (x); cf. §1, a, b. The aporia can then also be formulated in relation to that other mode of foundation of the theorem in which it is verified that every meaning is a constant of the infinite semanteme (which is a constant of every meaning). This second formulation of the aporia has already been considered (§7, a). It must in any case be asserted that if the positing of a meaning x requires the positing of the semantic totality, the latter is precisely posited insofar as something like 'semantic totality' is present; due to this presence, there is no meaning that is not present, and x can therefore be posited. Accordingly, the lack of presence of y does not entail that the semantic whole is not present, but that it is present in a formal or indeterminate way, whereby the presence of x is itself formal or indeterminate. Concerning the meaning of the solution we have provided – regardless of how the aporia should be formulated – cf. §24.
13. For instance: if this red were present without the presence of this green, this red would not be present (since this green is a constant of this red), but what would be present is only this red as a formal meaning – as long as, of course, the totality of what is not this red is present, as negated. It is clear, however, that if this red that is posited as a formal meaning is then posited as the negation of this *not-this-red*, constituted by this green, then this red is no longer a formal meaning, but it is precisely that concrete meaning that only becomes a formal one as a result of the lack of positing of this green.
14. This affirmation must be extended to every meaning (regarded *here* as an essence or universal), with significant corollaries, the formulation of which can however be left aside here.
15. The meaning 'this non-x', which is a part of the predicate, therefore stands as a constant of the subject in a mediated way.
16. In relation to the clarifications made in §23, the non-syntactic constants under consideration now may be referred to as '*hyposyntactic constants*'.
17. In stating that if y were posited as a constant of x', x' would no longer be an abstractly formal meaning, but a concretely formal one, we do not intend to say that y can be posited as a constant of x' *insofar as the latter is an abstractly formal meaning* – i.e. insofar as x' is something to which y does not pertain as a constant – but insofar as both the abstract form of x and the concrete one share the form, *simpliciter*, of x (in the same way in which $\hat{S}$ is what is shared by both the abstract and the concrete forms of S; cf. Chapter 9, §8, e); accordingly, stating that y is posited as a constant of x' means that y is posited as a constant of that shared element that is found in x'; hence, there

is no longer an implication between y and x' (the abstract form), but an implication between y and x (the concrete form), i.e. – as stated in the main text – the purported implication between y and x' is nothing but *the same* implication between y and x. For if one instead holds firm that y pertains to x' as a constant insofar as the latter is an abstract form, i.e. insofar as it is something to which y does not pertain as a constant, it is then clear that this self-contradictory pertaining *is not* the same pertaining of y to x (the concrete form).
18. Let us reiterate here that x is not posited insofar as its constants are simply posited, but insofar as they are posited as belonging to the essence or form of x: if a meaning that counts as a constant of x were posited, but it were not posited as belonging to the essence of x, x would not be posited. For the sake of brevity, however, the main text states that x cannot be posited if one of its constants is not posited.
19. What mediates – or, in any case, what belongs to the structure of what mediates – their standing as persyntactic constants is the infinite sememe: in as much as the latter is itself posited as a persyntactic constant in a mediated way. In §6, we have implicitly anticipated the present set of observations in stating that if 'nothingness' (which is a syntactic constant of the infinite sememe) is not posited, nothing can be posited.
20. Kant's discussion of the theorem according to which being does not add anything to the concept of a thing is entirely developed on a subordinate level: namely, the one of the distinction between 'possibility' and 'reality' (i.e. the belonging of the object to the unity of experience). Possibility and reality are indeed nothing but two modalities of being; accordingly, also what is 'possible', as such, *is*. From this higher standpoint, stating that being does not add anything to a semantic content only means that being adds something in a different way compared to how a syntactic moment of that content adds to the other moments: x, simply considered as such, and x, considered in its *being*, are not identical, in such a way that being does add something; at the same time, however, being is here precisely the being of x, and, therefore, what is added does not require x to become something other than itself as a result of its being. (In other words: 'x', as concretely distinct from 'x is', is, precisely, *other* than 'x is', but x, which is, is precisely x, which is concretely distinct from 'x is'.) The meaning 'being' does not therefore determine the semantic form of x in the same way in which a syntactic moment of x can determine that form, but, as already stated, it does so in the sense that x is necessarily a specific determination of being (i.e. it is a specific being, or it is being as determined in a specific way). Furthermore, the meaning 'being' is not an individuation of a constant of the (any) meaning x that is not the constant 'non-x'.

Insofar as the implication between x and its being is a necessary one, positing x without positing being, and therefore without positing the being of x, means not positing x. If the outcome of this abstract positing of x is the positing of a meaning w (which must differ from x), it is not possible to affirm – as instead it must be affirmed if x is posited without the positing of the non-syntactic constant y – that, if the being of w is posited, w is x itself: if w differs from x (regardless of the difference), being is predicated both of x and of w; that is to say, it is also predicated of w to the extent that w differs from x (and, in fact, w can exist as something different from x only insofar as being can also be predicated of w), and this predication is not a repetition of the positing of the being of x. Insofar as x' is instead posited as non-y, x' no longer differs from x; that is to say, non-y cannot be predicated of x', *qua* different from x (precisely because x' exists as something different from x only insofar as y is not posited, and, therefore, only insofar as non-y is not predicated of anything). If, therefore, x's not being y is not posited, x is posited as an abstractly formal meaning, whereas if *being* is not posited when x is posited (and, therefore, if the being of x is not posited), nothing is posited: precisely because being is necessarily predicated of that (any) meaning w that is posited as part of the outcome of the abstract positing of x, without this predication constituting a repetition of the predication in which being is predicated of x.

21. Pre-philosophical consciousness, i.e. the different forms of pre-philosophical knowledge of which it is possible to speak at present, precisely consists in those immediately present forms, i.e. those positional horizons, that – as already observed – constitute *my* pre-philosophical past; from the standpoint of present immediacy, the fact that pre-philosophical knowledge should extend beyond my past (i.e. that there should exist other instances of consciousness, in addition to mine) is only a project that must be verified.

11

1. An example of the type of analysis carried out in this chapter is already given in §14, a, b of Chapter 9.
2. With the specification that we have made in the main text, we do not, however, mean to exclude that it should *also* be possible for the originary to *become* a contradiction. More generally: if the lack of positing of any determinacy of the semantic whole entails that the positional horizon that is affected by that positional *steresis* should be the opening of a contradiction, it follows that, to the extent that it is not immediately contradictory to project that the originary should no longer posit determinations that are presently posited, it is not immediately contradictory to project that the originary could *become* a contradiction: i.e. that there could arise a contradictoriness of the originary that does not presently pertain to it. As already mentioned, however, in the following we are going to exhibit another sense of the contradictoriness of the originary, and we are going to show that this contradictoriness is immediately known. In relation to this new sense of the originary contradiction, too, however, it must be added that, at the same time, it is also not immediately contradictory to project that the originary should *become* a contradiction also according to this new sense. This last observation may, however, only be understood as part of the context of what we shall present. In this regard, cf. the footnote at the end of §7.
3. Let us add that if the propositions that constitute the alternative are understood in such a way that the pertaining of the predicate (p) to the subject (s) is not concretely posited as ($s = p$) = ($p = s$), the superseding of the self-contradictoriness that originates from that abstract understanding does not consist in a superseding of those propositions, but in their concrete positing (i.e. it consists in the superseding of their abstract positing). Accordingly, the objection under consideration does also not refer to this type of superseding of the self-contradictoriness of the propositions of the alternative, since it is precisely that superseding that affords the positing of the alternative (which, as in the case considered in the main text, fails to be realized to the extent that the propositions that constitute it fail to be realized).
4. [From the standpoint of the concrete, also the *project* of the verification of the self-contradictoriness of the subject of the first type of propositions is immediately

contradictory, due to the L-immediacy of the affirmation of the existence of an other than the totality of the Ph-immediate.]
5. If one objects that in the propositions 'x is' and 'x is x' the term 'is' has a different meaning (in such a way that the solution provided in the main text is merely apparent, for what is in question is the non-contradictoriness of the meaning 'is' having an existential function, and not of the meaning 'is' having a copula function), we must respond that the meaning 'is', having a copula function, *includes* the *existential* value (cf. Chapter 6, §13), whereby this meaning is considered in the main text precisely to the extent that it is thus inclusive.
6. The positing of 'this white extension' is the positing of a self-contradictoriness, since *this* extension is red. The proposition: 'This white extension is not' is therefore analytic, in that every self-contradictoriness is nothing (cf. Chapter 4, §14). The presence of the nullity of 'this white extension' is furthermore the presence of one of the many modes of the positive signification of nothingness. In this case, the presence of the nullity of 'this white extension' implies the presence of the positivity of this red extension, since that nullity can be posited by virtue of the Ph-immediate presence of this positivity. (Furthermore, the presence of the fact that this white extension is not is the very presence of the fact that this red extension is not white.)
7. It is effectively the case that insofar as experience includes sets of individual elements that belong to the same class (i.e. that have the same meaning), a meaning frees itself from its individuations without entailing that this freeing should be a form of projecting. If $a_1, a_2, a_3, ..., a_n$ indicate a set of individuations of the meaning a, which belongs to experience, the meaning a frees itself *from each* of these individuations, and this freeing is not a form of projecting (i.e. it does not constitute a surpassing of experience). However, to the extent that one is not able to verify that the term a_{n+1} indicates a self-contradiction, the totality of the individuations of a is projected as surpassing the set $a_1, ..., a_n$. Furthermore, the universality of a meaning does not consist in its freeing itself *from some* of its individuations, but from all of these: precisely because, in freeing itself from all of them, it can realize itself in and through each of them. Accordingly, the horizon of the totality of the individuations is necessarily posited as soon as the universality of a meaning is posited; and it is precisely in relation to the positing of that horizon that the present individuations are projected as being moments of the totality of individuations.
8. In relation to the point left unresolved at the end of the footnote in §2, it should be observed that to the extent that it is not immediately contradictory to project an increment of the originary projecting (i.e. an opening of problems that are presently not posited), and since every projecting is a being in contradiction, it is not immediately contradictory to project that the originary could *become* a contradiction to a further extent relative to the one that presently pertains to it.
9. What has been stated concerning the project of a being surpassing possible experience should be repeated concerning the project for the totality of the immediate to be determined in a different way from the one that pertains to it as a matter of fact. (More generally, the discussion should be repeated for every project.) The factual determinations of the immediate are indeed essentially in a problematic relation with the meaning 'totality of the immediate', in that, from the standpoint of immediacy, those factual determinations may stand either as the absolute determination of that meaning or as a partial determination. (For what concerns this second side: not in the sense that it is immediately non-contradictory to suppose that something else is immediately present in addition to or beyond the factual determinations that are

affirmed to constitute the totality of the immediate – for something is posited as the totality of the immediate only insofar as an immediate element exceeding what is posited as such a totality is excluded – but in the sense that it is not immediately contradictory to project the *arising* of different determinations from the factual ones.) If this factual immediacy is in that essential problematic relation with the meaning 'totality of the immediate', the concept of a positing of the factual dimension, which is not at the same time the positing of the problematic relation between this factual dimension and that meaning, conceives of something that is not the set of the factual determinations of the immediate as this set: precisely because this set is something that essentially consists in a problematic relation to the meaning 'totality of the immediate'.

10. In other words: even if one were to establish that the totality of the immediate constitutes the absolute matter of the semantic whole, this absolute matter would not be able to constitute the present and actual determination of the immediate: for, indeed, this determination does not include that logical-semantic process on the basis of which it would be verified that the totality of the immediate constitutes the absolute matter of the whole. From the standpoint of the present originarity, this process is indeed a possibility, and it is therefore not posited according to those concrete determinations that constitute it in case of its existence. The factual determination of the immediate precisely consists in this originarity, which allows that process to be retained as something possible. It is therefore originarily non-contradictory for possible experience to constitute the absolute semantic matter, but not for this matter to be constituted by the factual determination of experience.

11. Cf. also Chapter 10, §8, proposition [7].

12. This new type of foundation of that theorem has, however, a more limited domain of applicability, for while the foundation already identified is able to show that *any* positional domain that is affected by a positional *steresis* relative to *any* determination constitutes a being in contradiction, through the new foundation we instead only show the being in contradiction of those positional domains that count as a positional opening of the originary structure and that are affected by a positional *steresis* relative to one or more of their variants. Furthermore, the new foundation holds firm an already established principle: namely, that a positing of the totality of the immediate that is not the positing of those determinations that count as syntactic constants of the meaning 'totality of the immediate' constitutes a being in contradiction. It should be noted that since the new foundation is independent of the two theorems formulated above – i.e. it is independent of the concept that every determination is a constant of the infinite semanteme, and, as such, it is a constant of the meaning 'totality of the immediate' – the already established principle that is held firm by the new foundation is the following: a positing of the totality of the immediate constitutes a being in contradiction, in case it is affected by a positional *steresis* relative to those determinations that are not affirmed as constants of the meaning 'totality of the immediate' insofar as they are simply determinations, but insofar as they are *those specific* determinations (which are therefore identified as constants independently of the observation that every determination is a constant of the meaning 'totality of the immediate' because it is a constant of the infinite semanteme).

13. The observations developed in the main text in relation to $p(P)$ may be extended with the appropriate modifications to the dimension of projecting that pertains to the totality *simpliciter* of the immediate. Let us furthermore observe here that the meaning that stands as the content of the project is able to stand as a reference to something that lies beyond the totality of the immediate not only in case this meaning

is formally meaningful as 'other than the totality of the immediate', but also if that meaning is simply meaningful as that specific semantic content that it is, and that is, however, not immediately present. (This is not the case with $p(P)$, since, on the one hand, $p(P)$ is determined according to that formal reference to something other, and, on the other hand, $p(P)$ has been defined as the simple positing of an otherness, i.e. as a positing that does not include any other determination than 'other than the totality of the immediate' and the determinations formally implied by the latter.) In the first case, the problematic surpassing of the immediate is posited as such, whereas in the second case that surpassing is realized, but it is not posited. Let us consider this immediately present red, located at the place L1. The project for this red to be found at a place L2 has a semantic content ('this red at L2') that is as such able to refer to something that lies beyond the immediate – even though that reference is not posited as such as part of the project under consideration. Therefore, both this red at L1 and this red at L2 are immediately present (and insofar as that second content is present, it is not projected as such, but it is the very condition of projecting); the two contents, however, are present – i.e. are real – in different ways: the project is constituted when one projects for this red at L2 to have the same mode of presence and reality as this red at L1, and what is not immediately present is precisely the identity of these modes. Observing that this identity, too, is present, precisely to the extent that one speaks of it, means abstractly conceiving the terms of the relation between the projected content, *qua* present, and that to which that content refers: it is only insofar as this second term is abstractly conceived, i.e. it is abstractly separated from that first term, that its immediate presence can *once again* be posited, thus initiating in this way a *progressus in indefinitum*. This aspect of the matter at hand will be considered – even if in a different context – in §14 of Chapter 12.

14. The main text refers to 'a part of the otherness' in that we are not able to exclude that the content of $p(P)$ may not be exhausted by Q. If one were to affirm the identity between the quantity Q and the content of $p(P)$ it would follow that, since the difference between the projected totality and the totality *simpliciter* is constituted by Q, and since Q is a moment of the totality *simpliciter*, the other than this totality would be categorically posited as a nothingness, for if everything that is other than the projected totality consists of Q, the totality *simpliciter* would simply be the whole. To the extent that we are not able to originarily posit this totality as the whole, however, we state that Q constitutes a 'part' of $p(P)$. In another respect, however, i.e. to the extent that we are also not able to originarily exclude that the totality *simpliciter* of the immediate is the whole, the fact that Q is only a part of $p(P)$ is itself, too, only something possible (and it is therefore possible that Q should constitute the exhaustive determination of what is not the projected totality of the immediate). At the same time, it is clear that in relation to the question developed in the first part of this chapter – as part of which the totality of the immediate is immediately posited, *qua* projecting structure, as a moment of the whole – the formulation of this note will have to be amended by taking into account that positivity X that is not part of the structure of the immediate while nevertheless being L-immediately affirmed, which constitutes the concrete mode of resolution of the originary projecting, and by virtue of which the totality *simpliciter* of the immediate (which precisely consists in the structuring of the originary projecting) is reduced to a moment of the whole. It must then be stated – holding firm the fact that the projected totality is itself projected as an originary problematicity – that $Q + X$ necessarily belongs to the content of $p(P)$ (since the being of Q and X is immediately affirmed) and that, from the standpoint of the

present structuring of the immediate, whether the content of $p(P)$ is exhausted by $Q + X$ remains a project: that is to say, the fact that $Q + X$ stands as a 'part' of $p(P)$ remains a project. Or, equivalently: the fact that X is the only positive element surpassing the present structuring of the immediate is a project.

12

1. Naturally, leaving aside the fact that D stands as a finite determination of the whole to the extent that the originary realises itself as an originary problematicity (cf. Chapter 11, § 17).
2. In point c, the self-contradictoriness of the negation of presence is attested in general making use of the fact that the positional domain of the negation cannot be the positing of the semantic whole: indeed, we have proved (cf. Chapter 9, § 3) that the positional domain of every negation is a moment of the positional domain of the ground. Then, as a consequence of the theorem according to which every meaning is a constant of every other meaning, it follows that the domain of the negation is the opening of the C-self-contradiction. As part of the remarks being addressed in the main text, we instead attest the self-contradictoriness of the domain of that negation independently of that theorem: i.e. insofar as that negation includes, as a constant, the affirmation described in the main text. Moreover, as already mentioned in the main text, we attest that despite the positing of that constant – and, in fact, precisely by virtue of this positing – the domain of the negation of presence is realised as a self-contradiction.
3. Concerning the nature of the relation between π and π', cf. Chapter 5, §§ 23–24.
4. It should furthermore be observed that while, on the one hand, D may be held firm in its being *hic et nunc* even if $D = \pi$ is concretely distinct from $(D = \pi) = (\pi = D)$, on the other hand, if D is considered in its structuring itself as part of this latter equation, D is for this very reason considered in its being *hic et nunc*: stating that being, *which is present*, is present (and that this presence is of that being that is present) precisely means considering being as *hic et nunc*.

13

1. The *individuation* obtains in relation to the L-immediate connection regarded as an abstract universal; its *being a moment* (or part) obtains instead in relation to the connection in question regarded as a concrete universal. It should be observed that every determination (thus including the determination 'L-immediate connection') presents a value according to which it is an abstract universal – i.e. it is an essence or meaning insofar as this has the possibility of realizing itself in a multiplicity of individuations – and a value (which however includes that former one) according to which the determination is a concrete universal: namely, it consists in the totality of its individuations, i.e. the totality of the realization of the essence or meaning of the determination according to the different modes of realization that pertain to that essence. In relation to this second value, it is not possible to speak of an *individuation*, i.e. there is no individuation of the concrete universal as such: precisely because the whole, and every relative totality, is the only individuation of its meaning.

2. Cf. the footnote in Chapter 7, §18, f.
3. The whole is not structured in this way because the L-mediated connections, and more generally every determination, do not belong to the whole, but because, as already mentioned, *every* determination is part of the system of L-immediate connections, at least to the extent that every determination is realized as a self-identity (i.e. as a non-contradictoriness).
4. The whole, *qua* beginning of the dialectical process constituted by the mediation, is a self-contradictory meaning, but not because it cannot include the determinacy of the predicate additionally verified by the mediation: this determinacy, as well as the determinacy of the opposite predicate, can indeed be included in the semantic domain of the whole. And yet, insofar as that domain counts as a beginning, in the indicated sense, that domain counts all the same – i.e. despite that inclusion – as a self-contradictoriness. Indeed, this self-contradictoriness is determined by the fact that the whole, as such, is not (*qua* beginning) that by virtue of which it is possible to establish *which* [*quale*] of those two opposite determinacies is the actual predicate of the whole, in such a way that the term by virtue of which that *qualification* is carried out must be something other than the whole – whence the latter is precisely realized as a self-contradictoriness.
5. d does not become in that, if it did, d – i.e. this specific being – would not be. It is clear that the proposition: 'd is not non-being' is not in turn mediated to the extent that it is posited as an individuation of concrete logical immediacy.
6. The L-mediated propositions whose subject is the whole and that are such that the project of the non-pertaining of the predicate to the subject is not immediately superseded, *become* formulations of the principle of non-contradiction *in a moment that is additional* relative to the one constituted by the originary positing of that principle. Let 'The whole is δ' be one of these propositions; at the level of the structuring of the immediate, the fact that the whole is δ is the content of a project. It is effectively the case that the subject of this proposition includes logical immediacy itself in its concrete structuring, but this structuring does not include the connection between the whole and δ. If this connection is instead mediated – i.e. it is no longer the content of a project but of a categorical affirmation – it becomes L-immediate, and it therefore becomes a formulation of the principle of non-contradiction: but, as discussed, it becomes such a formulation in a moment that is additional relative to the one constituted by the originary formulation of that principle. The L-immediate propositions discussed in the main text, instead, *originarily become* formulations of that principle: that is to say, the originary opening of the latter includes those propositions in its structure.
7. It is no coincidence that, at the beginning of his *Physics*, Aristotle examines those same thinkers that he examines as part of his metaphysical enquiry in the first book of the *Metaphysics*. It is once again Aristotle the one who notes (*Metaphysics*, VI, 1) that if there were no other reality beyond the cosmic one, the science of physics – whose object of enquiry is precisely this reality – would be the most universal of all sciences. That is to say, it would no longer simply be a 'physics'. And therefore, once again, it would and it would not simply be a 'physics': it would not, insofar as its object would be the totality itself; it would, insofar as the cosmic reality would constitute the concrete and all-encompassing content of that totality. The first thinkers precisely realize this situation, in which the cosmic reality is known as the totality.
8. Aquinas, *In octo l. phys. Arist. commentaria*, 63. [Translator's note: 'For heat does not make coldness itself to be hot, but makes the subject of coldness to be hot: nor

vice-versa. Therefore, it seems that it is necessary to posit some third thing which will be the subject of the contraries'].
9. The Aristotelian text appears instead to lack the resolution of that other aspect of the aporia by virtue of which becoming consists in a vanishing or annulment of the positive. The reasoning however is the same: what is annulled – i.e. what is annulled at a phenomenological level – *still is*; therefore, it cannot still be as part of the very reality that becomes (i.e. as part of the reality defined by the annulment), but it still is in a reality that differs from the one that becomes: and therefore – once again – in the last instance, in (or as) the immutable reality.
10. [Translator's Note: 'The same thing cannot be at once in act and in potentiality with respect to the same thing. But everything that is moved is, as such, in potentiality… That which moves, however, is as such in act, for nothing acts except according as it is in act. Therefore, with respect to the same motion, nothing is both mover and moved. Thus, nothing moves itself'].
11. The value of limitedness that is to be attributed to that reality that becomes is however explicitly in view in Aquinas's text, when he affirms that a potential being is something imperfect, i.e. limited: '*Si igitur alicuius esse sit finitum oportet quot limitetur esse illud per aliquid aliud quod sit aliqualiter causa illius esse*' (Aquinas, ibid., chapter XLIII). This logical structure also appears with the great metaphysicians of classical idealism. Schelling, for instance, states that 'a becoming is unthinkable save under a condition of limitation. If we fancy an infinitely producing activity as expanding without resistance, it will produce with infinite speed; its product is a being, not a becoming. So the condition of all becoming is limitation or restraint'; F. W. J. Schelling, *System of Transcendental Idealism (1800)*, trans. P. Heath (Charlottesville: University of Virginia Press, 1978), p. 38.
12. The unmoved is in any case the mover of everything that moves in the sense that becoming implies the unmoved as that without which becoming itself would be a contradiction: i.e. it would consist – in an Eleatic way – in the non-being of being, or – in an Aristotelian way – in a non-being that limits being (and therefore a being of non-being). Book XII of the *Metaphysics* presents the corollaries that follow from the affirmation of a pure act: eternity, immateriality, absolute self-consciousness. The metaphysical dualism of pure act and eternal matter does not constitute the result of a logical structure that implies, as such, a negation of the concept of 'creation', but it simply results from an absence of this concept. In understanding becoming as the transition of a substratum from potentiality to actuality, i.e. as the arising of a positive as part of a pre-existing dimension, it is not possible to exclude that this possibility of arising could also pertain to the substratum, thus implying in turn a more originary substratum (precisely because, otherwise, that arising would imply that non-being becomes being); but it must be excluded that *every* substratum should be able to arise – and, therefore, that an infinite regress should take place – for, otherwise, without a primary non-arising substratum, the system of substrata would once again be affected by the contradiction of a non-being that becomes being. It is therefore necessary to recognize a primary substratum, which is correctly affirmed to be 'unbegotten', 'incorruptible', and therefore 'eternal': precisely in the sense that if becoming is defined as something that implies a substratum, the primary substratum cannot become. In his commentary to one of the most important passages in which Aristotle discusses the eternity of matter (*Physics*, I, 192a), Aquinas does not deny that matter is eternal, in the sense determined by the Aristotelian text, but he only notes that thereby '*non excluditur quin per creationem*

in esse procedat'. That is to say, what is understood by the term 'creation' should not be conceived of as a 'becoming'.
13. It is, however, not immediately self-contradictory for the totality of the Ph-immediate not to be the totality of becoming.
14. Furthermore, however, the immutable is not simply this light *for us*, but *in itself*; that is to say, the immutable is the consciousness or presence of the concrete totality of being. For, indeed, the very presence of the whole, too – as it is realized in the originary structure – immutably dwells as part of the circle of the immutable, like every other determination. However, it cannot dwell there as a formal and, therefore, self-contradictory presence, for, otherwise – i.e. in affirming such a formal presence of the immutable – this self-contradiction would be allowed to persist as what is definitive, and therefore as something not superseded. One would thus come to assert that being is a self-contradiction; that is to say, this self-contradiction would not be negated (cf. Chapter 11, §9, b). And nor is it possible to state that, as part of the domain of the immutable, the concrete presence of the whole is something that arises, for, in that way, one would be affirming that the being constituted by that concrete presence is not (before arising).

Index

absolute
  matter 316–19
  negativity 91, 156–67
abstract understanding 28, 105, 107–11, 128–32, 186, 281, 290–1, 298, 314
accident 24, 59, 77, 82, 201
act of positing
  complex 179–86, 191
  hyper-complex 179–83
actual presence 58, 60–2, 76, 86, 199
actuality 29, 99, 180, 196, 302, 404–5
alienation
  of nihilism 2, 60
  of truth 2, 5, 14–16, 60
  of the West 1, 4, 23, 57, 59
analogical character of being 145, 403–4
Anaxagoras 308, 403
Anaximander 400
annihilation 22, 165n9
annulment
  of being 6–7, 22, 369, 384, 390, 400, 406, 410–13
  positional 57–8, 258–9, 283, 288, 296, 319, 320, 325, 329, 330, 333, 339–41, 369, 370
anxiety 166
apodeixis 71, 99
apophantic
  saying 12, 129–30, 137, 200–9
  structure 130, 200–1
aporia
  of the arising of the constants of S 255
  of becoming 44–6, 398–406
  of multiplicity 202
  of non-contradictoriness 146
  of nothingness 153–72
  of predication 41
  of a 'series of complex acts of positing' 182
  of the *Tractatus* 89
appearing
  of beings 5–6, 20, 41, 43–4, 47, 56, 58
  content of 6–7, 13, 21, 51, 53
  and disappearing 5–8, 46, 58, 410–11
Aquinas, Thomas 123, 293, 405
Aristotle 12, 16, 38, 71–2, 96, 128, 140, 189, 201, 293, 399–405
atomic meaning 117, 181
authentic
  concept of dialectic 290
  content 7, 57
  determination 45
  ground 244
  immediacy 244
  logos 190, 204
  meaning 1, 6, 23, 47, 62–3, 70, 72, 83, 117, 165, 255, 272
  refutation 43, 272
  saying 13
  structuring 344, 352
  task 416
axiom 89, 255

becoming
  of beings 4–7, 9, 31–2, 36, 45, 68, 406, 411
  of the totality of the Ph-Immediate 181, 187–8, 410, 411
  of the whole 390, 401
Bergson, Henri-Louis 164–7
Berkeley, George 312n4
Bontadini, Gustavo 122n8
Boole, George 13
bound
  lower 180–1, 279, 295–6
  upper 180–3, 279, 297, 304

Carnap, Rudolf 90, 167
certainty 73, 74, 122, 275
Christianity 92

circle
  of appearing 64
  of the immutable 410, 414–16
co-initiality 199–200, 279
communication 77, 81–2, 89, 95, 103, 305
Concept, the 28–38
concept Γ_a 6, 119, 141, 263, 320, 343–4, 360, 371, 406, 410
consciousness
  of becoming 32–3, 36
  common 4, 93–5, 120, 245, 335–6
  of the Concept 32
  of the originary structure 88
  other instances of 86–7, 96, 363
  of self-consciousness 63–6
  sensory 403–5
  of the West 3, 60
constant
  'constant'- 322–3
  hyposyntactic 54–5, 337–41, 352
  mediational 232, 235, 251–2, 269, 282
  metasyntactic 53–8, 338–41
  non-syntactic 330–9
  persyntactic 51–5, 333–40, 378–9, 415
  syntactic 51–7, 89, 323–3, 339, 364–5, 375, 415
  'variant'- 322–3
contradicting oneself 10, 171, 260–1
contradiction
  C- 47, 257–73, 281–6, 304, 319–23, 345, 349–52, 360, 378
  h- 225–7, 314
  m- 216, 220, 227, 231, 265
  originary 49, 264, 318–22, 351–61, 372
  possible 320, 345, 352
contradictory 27, 35, 38–40, 47, 162, 168, 220, 289, 293–4, 300, 309–10, 324–5
contrary 35, 38, 279–81, 290, 292–3, 295, 402
co-originarity 51, 94, 112–14, 132, 149–50, 191, 198, 227
covariant 215, 218, 267, 271–2

decision 8, 56, 59, 93, 320, 415
De generatione et corruptione (Aristotle) 401
De interpretatione (Aristotle) 12
Descartes, René 122

Destino della necessità (Severino) 69
destiny 2, 44, 63, 66, 108, 334
Dewey, John 116–17
dialogue 78, 82, 95–6
dianoesis 129–30, 134, 136
disclosure 4, 50, 82, 92, 100–6, 126, 153, 311, 313, 376
discursivity 80–8, 108, 111–13, 148–9, 206, 305

earth 2–12, 15, 23, 52–69
Encyclopaedia of the Philosophical Sciences (Hegel) 30–7, 275–306
epistemological presupposition 72, 122
Epistola de nihilo et de tenebris (Fridugisus) 154
erring 23, 66
error 56, 76, 80, 95, 311
eternal being 5, 7, 8, 22–3, 47–8, 56, 61–6, 390, 409, 412, 414
ex nihilo nihil 400–3
existentialism 311
experience 8, 76, 166, 202–4, 222–4, 256, 311, 327, 341, 398, 401–2
exponential positing 173–4, 178

factual additional dimension 188–9, 226, 255–8, 262
factually simple meanings 196–200, 209, 279
faith 8, 23, 28, 31, 34, 36–8, 60–2, 68, 92
Fichte, Johann Gottlieb 82, 142, 416
forgetting 84, 335, 351, 359
formal system 255
foundation
  of knowledge 72, 90, 142
  self- 66, 106, 191
Frege, Gottlob 13, 154, 168–9
Fridugisus of Tours 154

Gentile, Giovanni 76, 132–4, 138
Gli abitatori del tempo 1, 28, 34
Gorgias 142, 164
groundlessness 82, 91–4, 149, 270–1, 312

Hegel, G. W. F. 2, 11–12, 17, 23, 27–38, 54–5, 82, 85, 92, 127, 165, 197–202, 209–10, 268–9, 274–305, 326

Heidegger, Martin 2, 73, 76, 166–7, 311, 335, 359
hermeneutics 2, 8
history
  of the ground 71, 73–5
  of philosophy 71, 84–5, 87
  of the West 2, 8–10, 12, 27, 56, 62–3, 67–9
Husserl, Edmund 4, 41, 52, 59, 92

idealism 28–9, 62–3, 73, 142, 223–5
immanentism 73, 360
immutability of being 45–6, 390, 398, 400, 402, 405
immutable
  appearing and disappearing of the 6–8, 46, 410–16
  whole 8, 45, 405, 408, 409–16
immutables, the 67–8
infinite
  development 131–3, 139–40, 169–70, 172, 196, 204, 205, 389
  semanteme 48, 309–41, 364
intention 9, 93, 102, 126, 130, 134, 165, 170, 220, 260–1, 272, 281, 287–9, 296, 318, 326, 345, 365
isolation of the earth 3, 5, 7–8, 10, 12, 15, 23, 52, 55–7, 61, 66–9

Jaspers, Karl 166, 359

Kant, Immanuel 143, 239, 311, 346–7
knowledge
  common 93, 96
  ground of every possible 88, 93, 224
  immediate 71, 105, 115–16, 224, 268
  metaphysical 72, 359–60, 364, 373, 406, 408
  originary 72, 86–8
  philosophical 75, 92–6, 189, 334–5
  pre-philosophical 56, 60, 90–95, 189–91, 218, 312, 335–40

L'Évolution créatrice (Bergson) 164
language 1–11, 14–5, 18, 21–8, 32, 40, 44, 51–69, 78, 80, 82, 89–90, 94, 175, 206, 242, 335, 375, 387

Lévi-Strauss, Claude 63
logos 4, 18, 96, 190, 202, 204, 222, 327, 338, 398, 400–4

manifestation of the whole 48, 80, 308–41
Marx, Karl 2, 28, 34
mathematics 42–4, 57, 89, 117, 412
mediational structure 251–6, 311
Meinong, Alexius 168–9
Melissus 401, 405
metaphysics
  anti- 9–10
  impossibility of 361–2, 373
  originary 8, 311, 360, 385–415
Metaphysics (Aristotle) 128, 140, 201, 293, 399, 402
multiplicity of subjects 84, 86–7

naturalistic realism 73, 82, 411
Necessity 1–10, 12–13, 15–18, 20–7, 29, 32, 34, 36, 41–5, 47–57, 59–69
negation
  of the ground 71, 74, 76, 79, 119, 275–8, 297
  of identity 133, 248
  of the immediate 89, 120, 125–6, 133, 201
  of the originary structure 20–4, 45–50, 71, 86–8, 96, 255, 353
  of present being 105, 375–84
  of truth 58–60
neo-positivism 43, 89–91
never-setting, the 51–2, 57, 64
Nietzsche, Friedrich 2, 68
nihil absolutum 153, 167
noesis 129–31, 134–8, 153, 208, 237–8, 243
nothingness
  absolute 164, 367
  positive signification of 156–7, 161, 163–4, 166, 168–72, 349

ontic
  horizon 76–7, 180–2, 195
  positing 173, 177–81
  series 173, 177–81
ontological horizon 76, 77, 359

originary
    judgement 65, 76–83, 89, 99–100, 121–5, 178–92, 243–8, 382
    meaning 1, 35, 51, 61, 89, 96, 195–211, 247, 251, 301, 312–13, 318–21, 327, 349–51, 402
    problem 343–7, 352–60, 364, 367, 371–3

paradox of classes 42, 43
Parmenides 1, 17, 21, 46, 67, 73, 153, 202, 391, 398–406
parricide 17
Path
    of Day 48, 62, 67, 69
    of Night 62, 67
persistence 22–3, 65, 106, 125, 184–7, 231, 299, 354, 369, 383, 398, 409, 411
persyntactic field 51–8, 333–41
Phaedo (Plato) 402
phenomenalism 6, 411
phenomenology 4–6, 41, 51–2, 56, 59, 76, 116
Phenomenology of Spirit (Hegel) 268
physics 117, 399, 401
Physics (Aristotle) 402, 405
plane
    base 223, 226, 246, 252, 264–72, 276
    mediational 223–7, 267
Plato 11–13, 17, 153–4, 201–2, 335, 399–405, 415
positive surpassing the originary 321, 344, 356–7, 363–4, 371, 373, 407–9
possible
    additional dimension 189, 225–7
    experience 189, 312, 346, 349–51, 356, 358–9, 365, 371–2
potentiality 29, 404–5
pre-Socratics 399, 403
presupposition 32, 34, 42–3, 72, 92, 111, 122, 129, 132, 134, 177, 203, 205, 208, 320, 403, 405
principle
    of identity 127–9, 131, 138, 247, 348
    of non-contradiction 4–5, 12, 71, 123–8, 139–61, 164, 167–71, 202, 208, 239–40, 244, 247, 386–9, 398, 408, 413
progressus in indefinitum 192–5, 234–5

recollection 87, 190, 218, 285, 335, 368–9
regressus in indefinitum 66, 90, 105–10, 146, 191, 248, 377, 382
Russell, Bertrand 13, 43, 168–9

Sartre, Jean-Paul 167
Scholastics 127–8, 154
Schopenhauer, Arthur 167
science 9–10, 33, 51, 63, 68, 76, 90, 92, 120, 245, 268, 279
Science of Logic (Hegel) 11, 29, 31, 280, 297
self-contradictory meaning 156–64, 167–171, 348, 393–6, 408
    evidence 22, 29, 31–2, 36–8, 68, 400–4
    grounding 115–16, 191–2
Sistema di logica (Gentile) 76
Sophist (Plato) 11–12, 17, 153, 201, 404
speculative moment 290, 292–3, 296–8, 301–5, 395
structuralism 2, 63
Studi di filosofia della prassi (Severino) 46
superseding of the aporia 107, 111, 256–8, 341

task 74, 92, 96, 319–20, 334, 341, 360, 370, 405, 416
tautology 11, 189, 201–2, 280
testimony 1–3, 5, 7–8, 10, 12, 18, 22–3, 39, 44, 51–2, 58, 66–9, 335
The Essence of Nihilism 1, 9, 21, 46, 48, 52–67
Theaetetus (Plato) 401
Tractatus Logico-Philosophicus (Wittgenstein) 89–90
truth
    appearing of 51, 55–6, 60–1
    of being 1, 5, 7–8, 10, 52–5

Überwindung der Metaphysik (Carnap) 167
Umgreifende 166, 359
unconscious 2–6
untruth 34, 36, 52, 55–61, 68

Was ist Metaphysik? (Heidegger) 166
will to power 8–9, 23, 67–8
Wissenschaftslehre (Fichte) 82
Wittgenstein, Ludwig 89–90